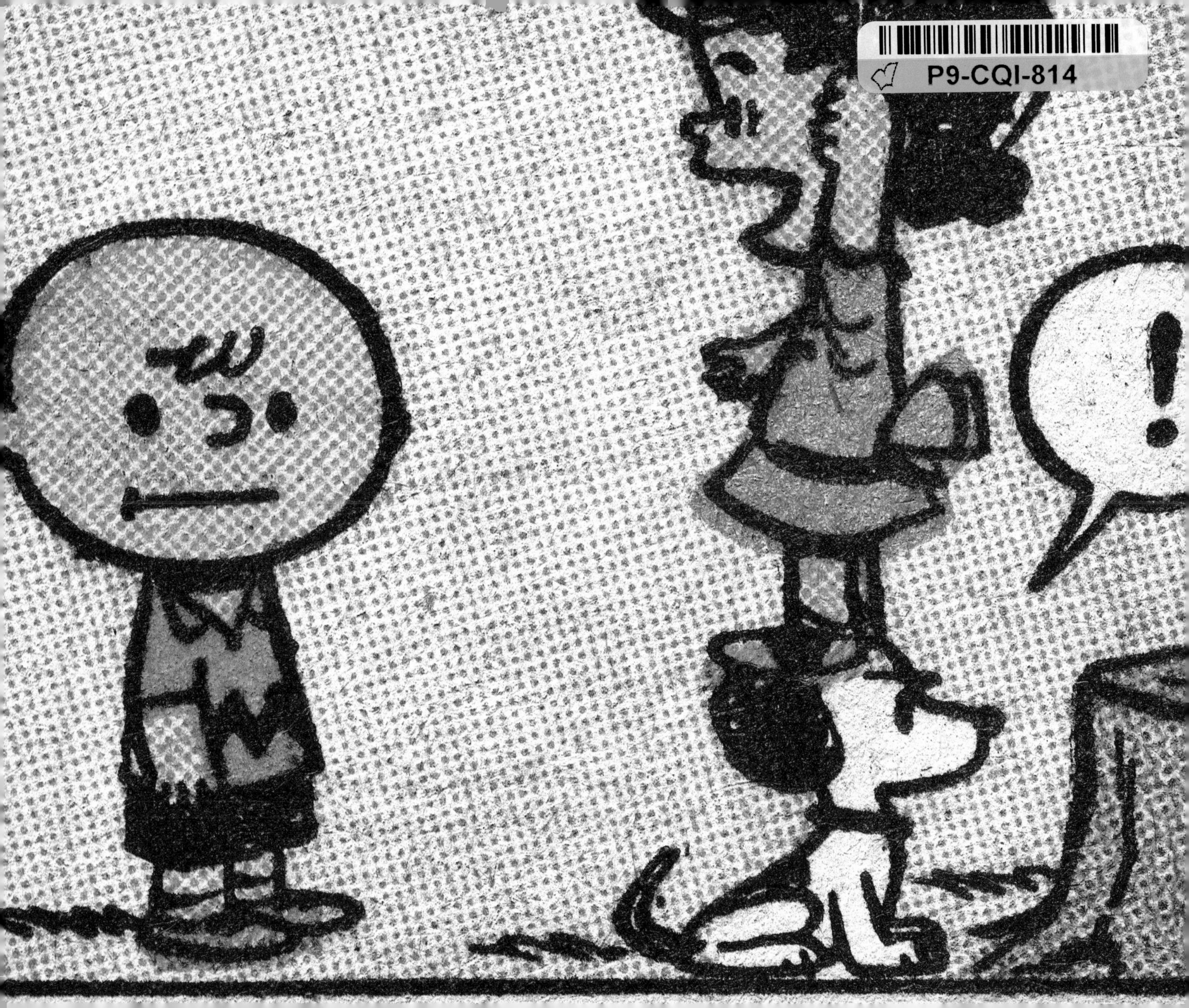
!

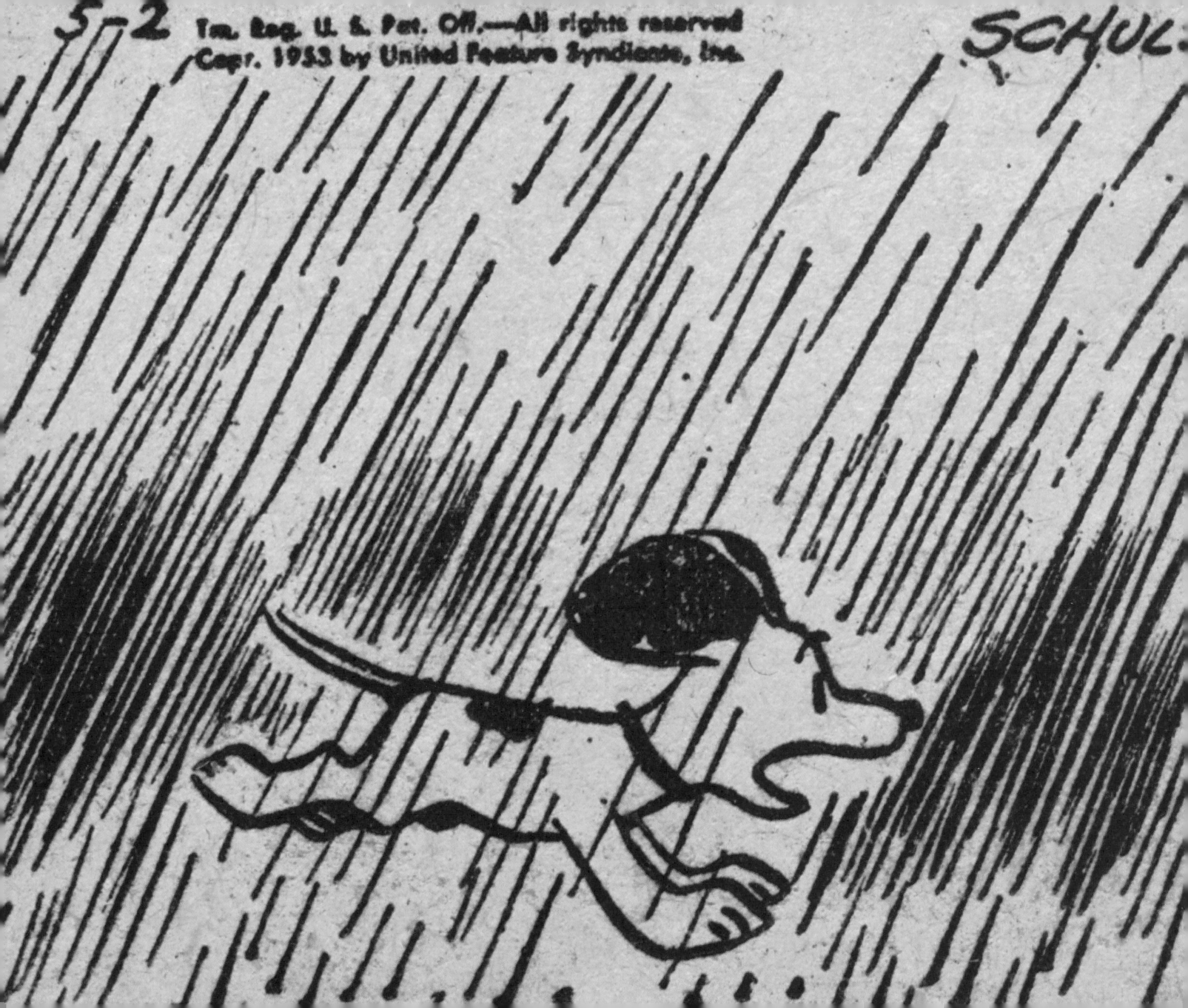
5-2
Tm. Reg. U. S. Pat. Off.—All rights reserved
Copr. 1953 by United Feature Syndicate, Inc.
SCHUL.

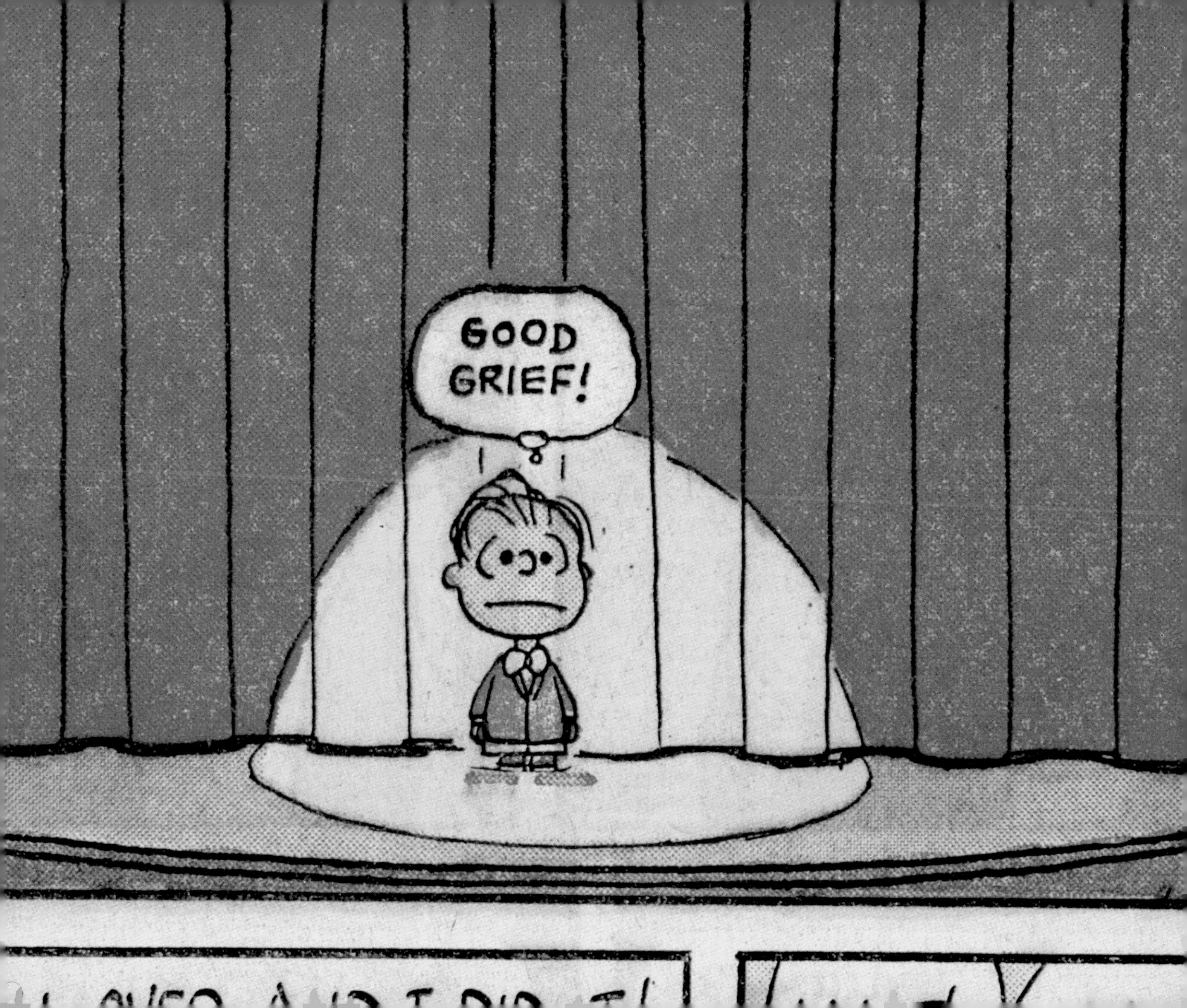
GOOD GRIEF!

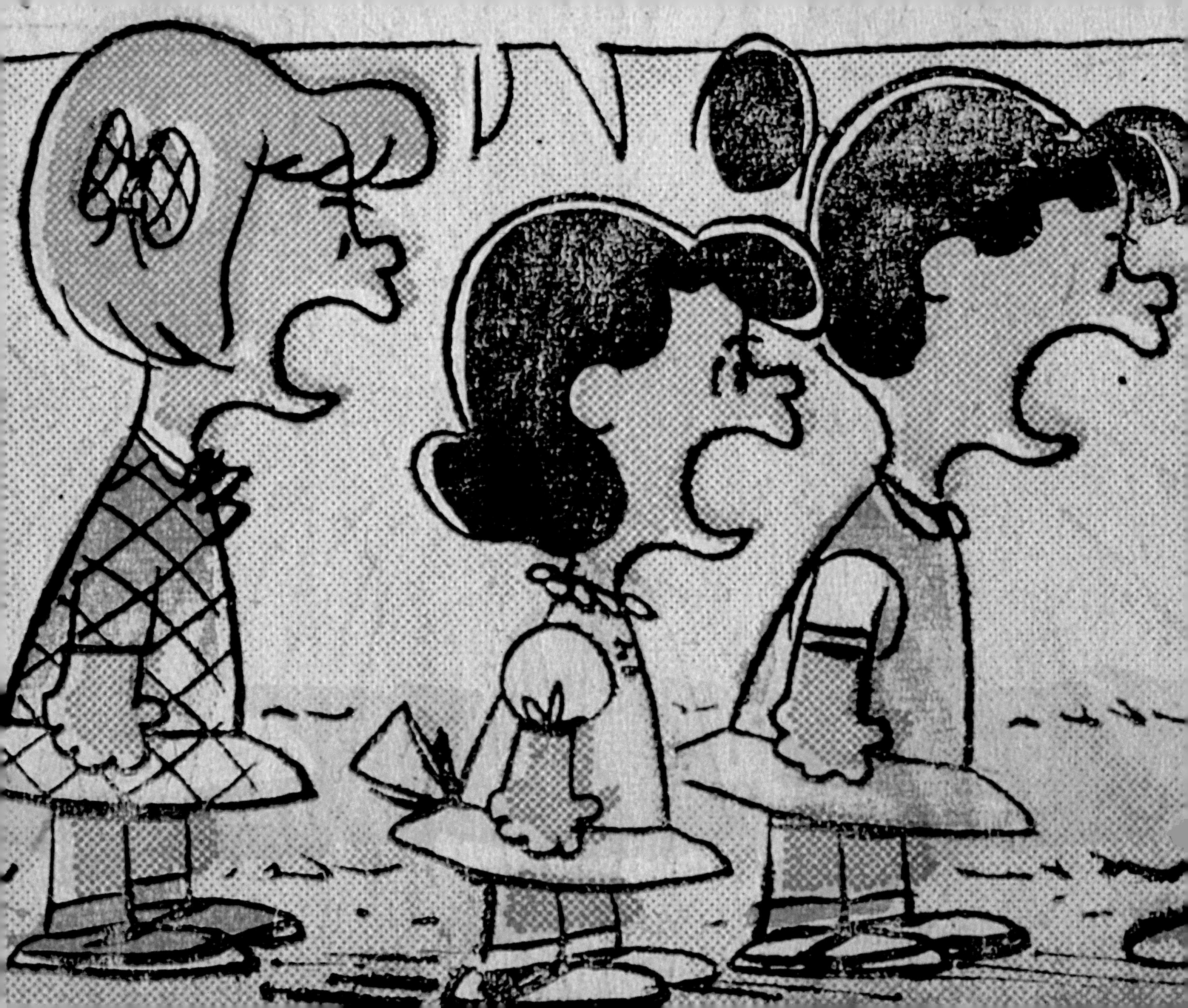

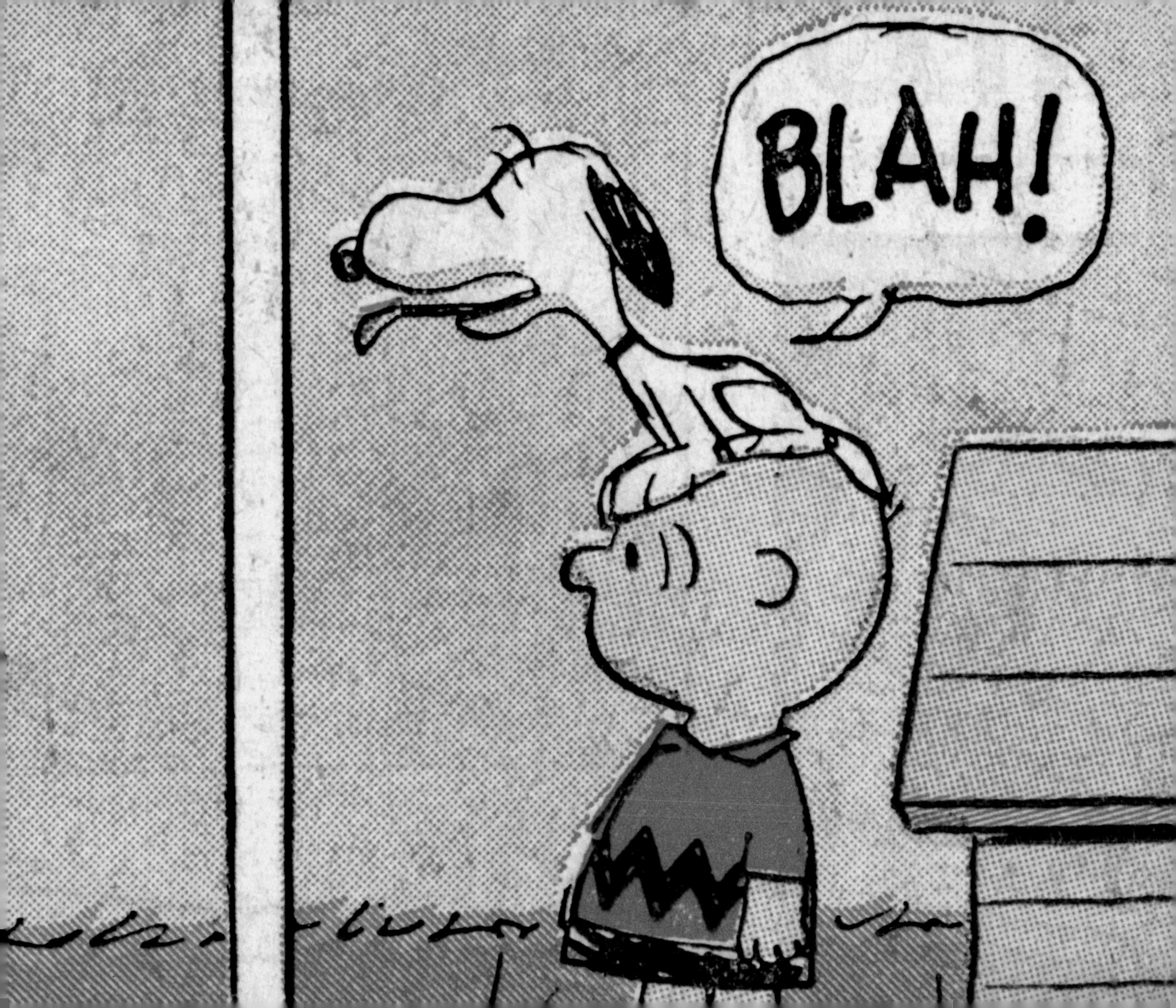
BLAH!

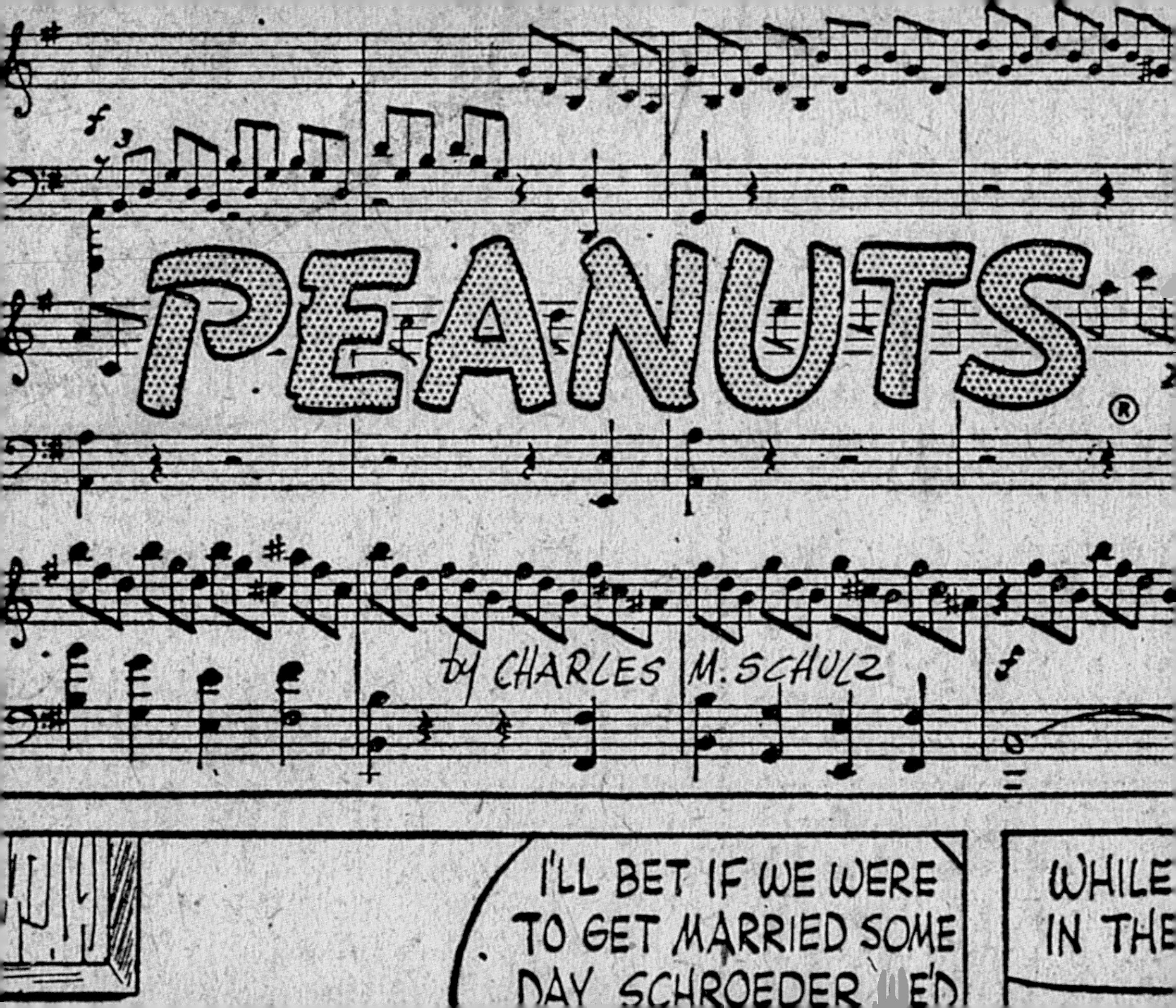
PEANUTS
by CHARLES M. SCHULZ
I'LL BET IF WE WERE TO GET MARRIED SOME DAY SCHROEDER
WHILE IN THE

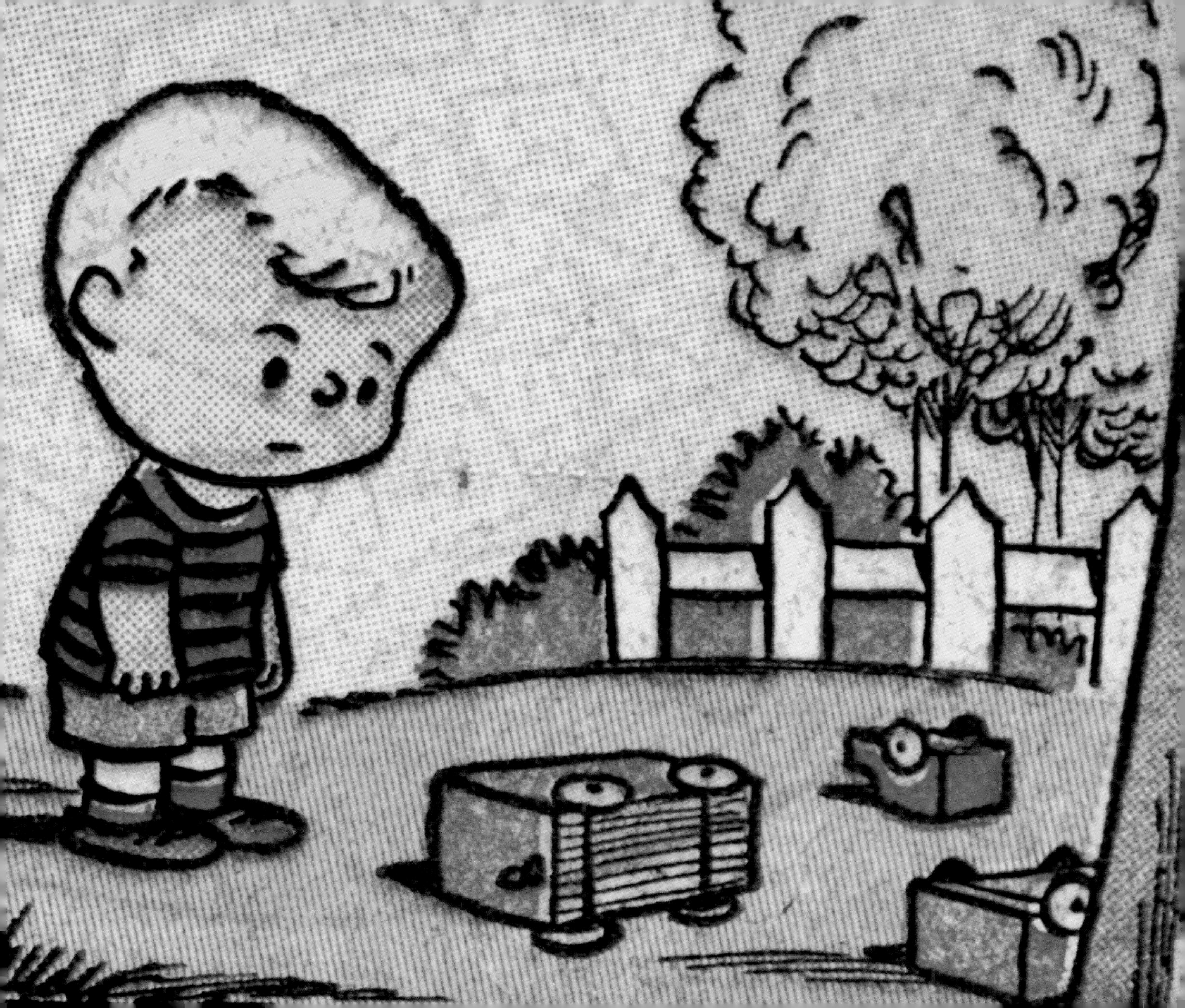

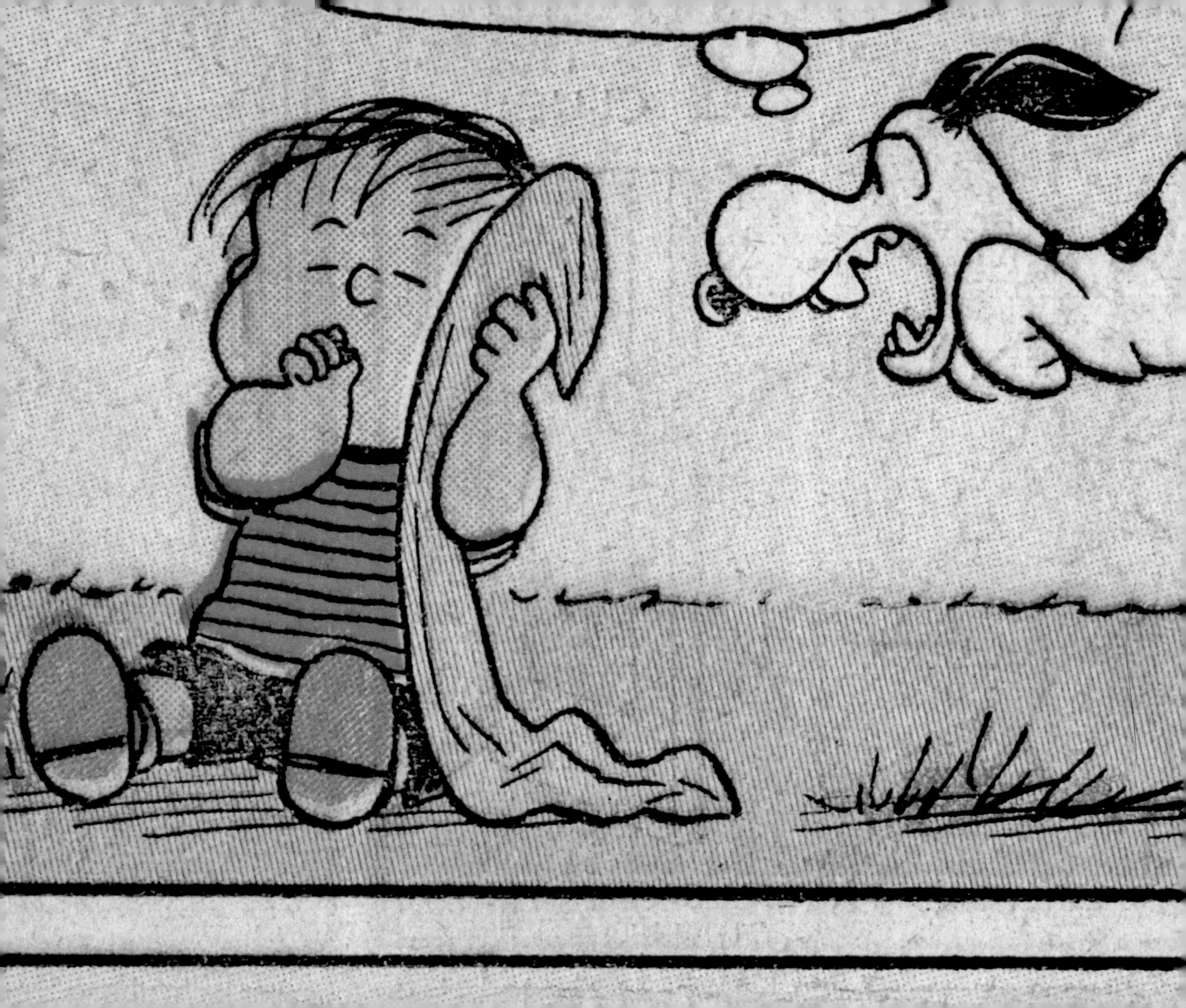

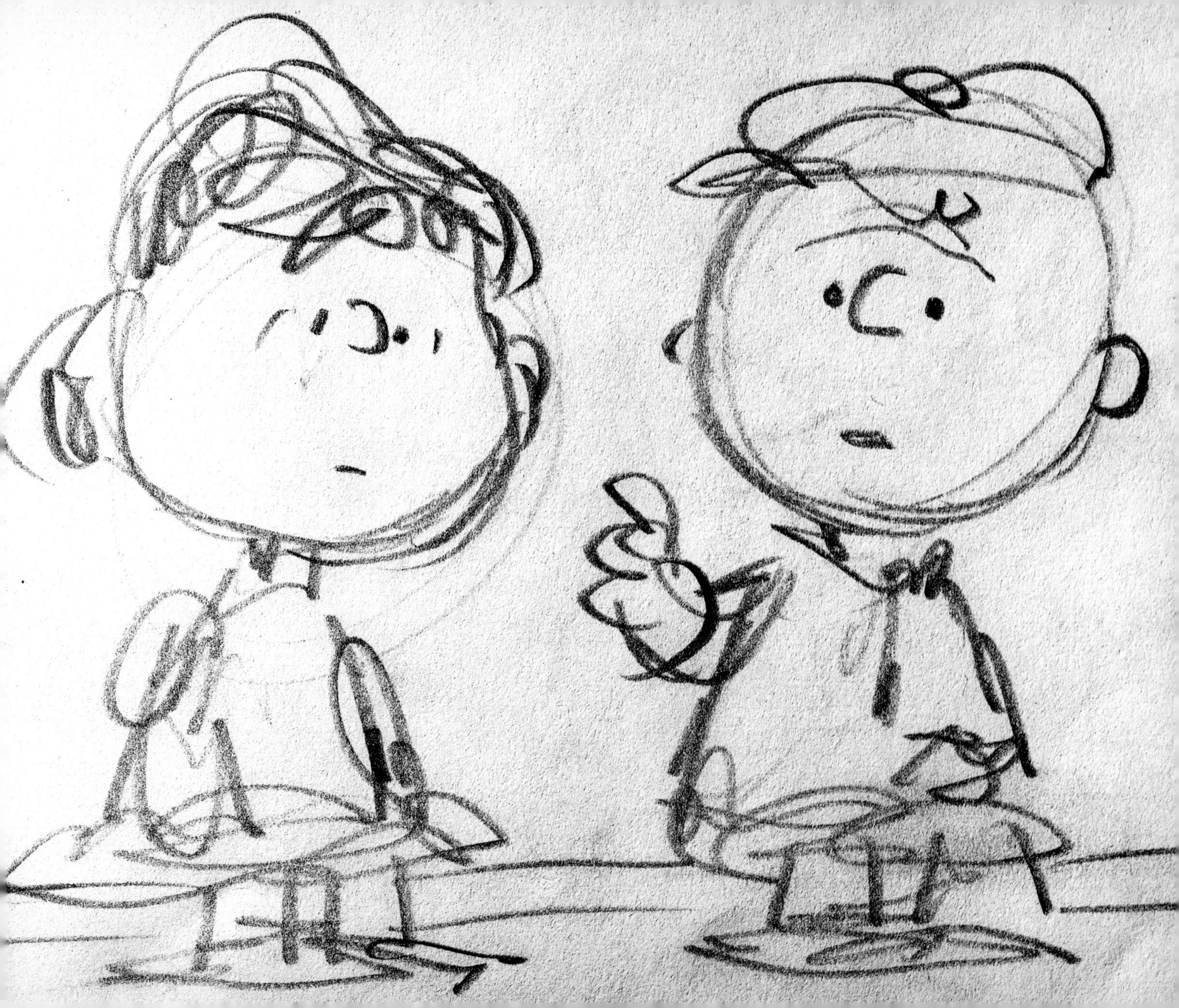

PEAN

THE ART OF

b

CHARLES

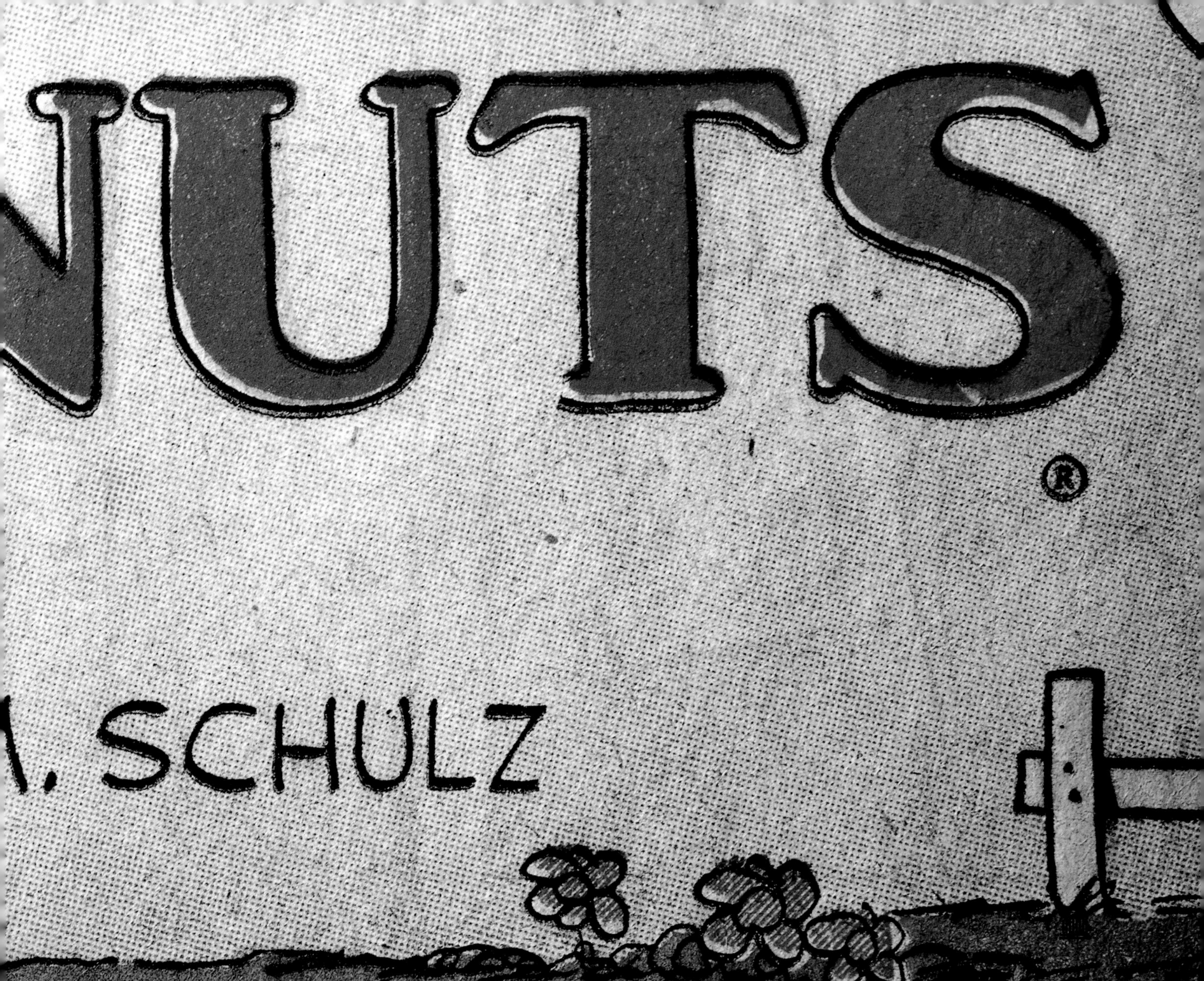
UTS®
A. SCHULZ

Edited and designed by Chip Kidd

PANTHEON BOOKS NEW YORK 2001

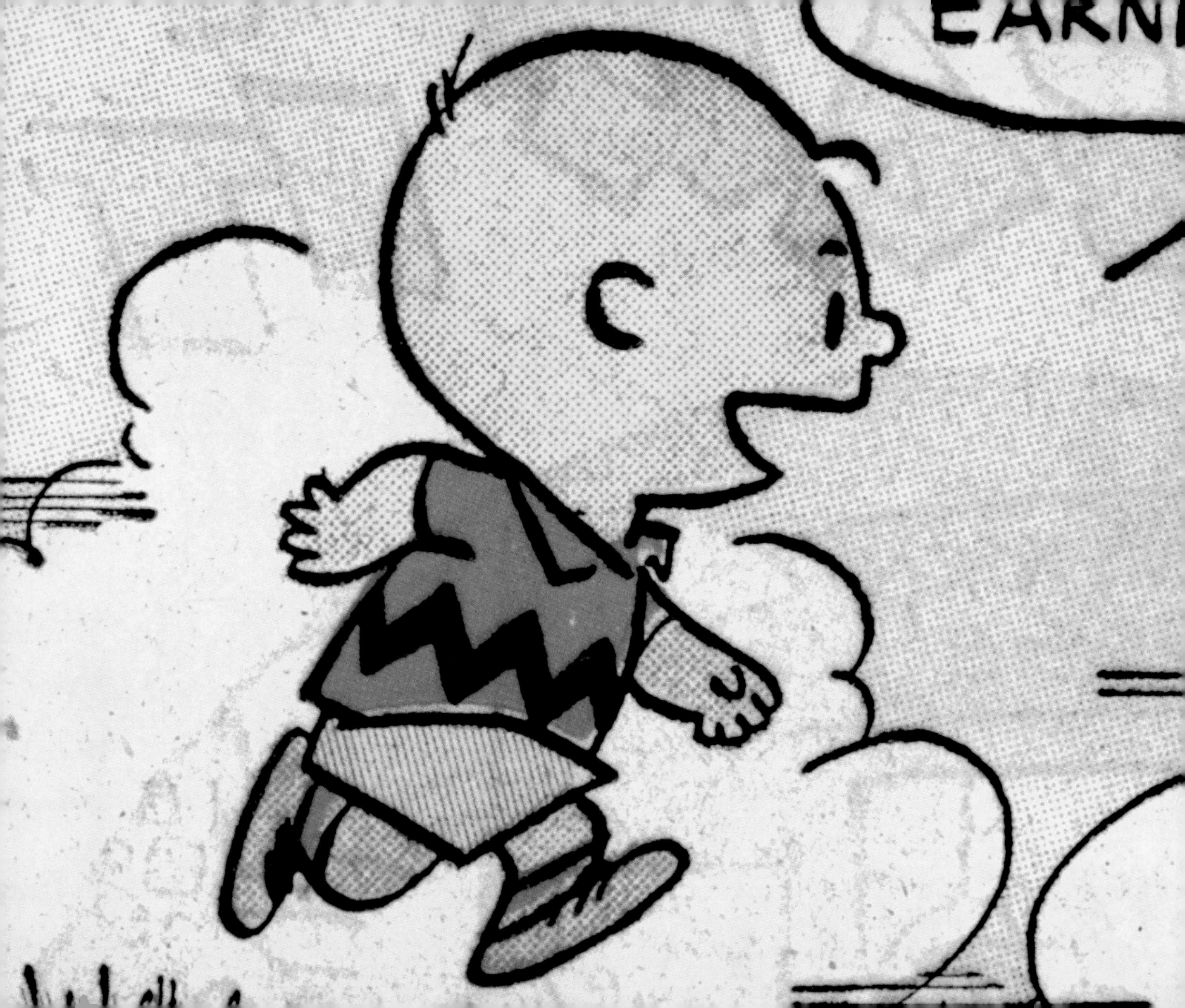
EARN

With an introduction by Jean Schulz

and commentary by Chip Kidd

"PEANUTS"
Copr. 1951 by United Feature Syndicate, Inc.

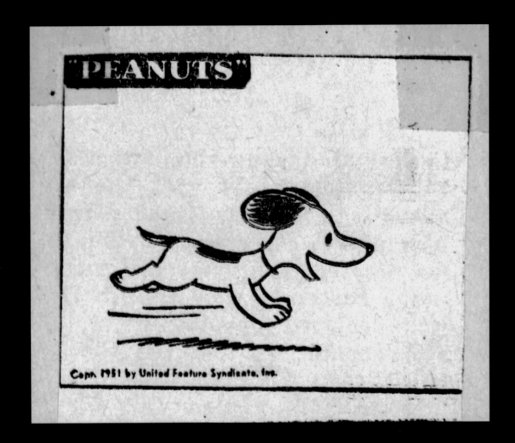

Photographs by Geoff Spear

Original art from the collections of Jean, Craig, and Monte Schulz
Archival *Peanuts* strips from the collections of Chris Ware and Chip Kidd

Production assistance by John Kuramoto

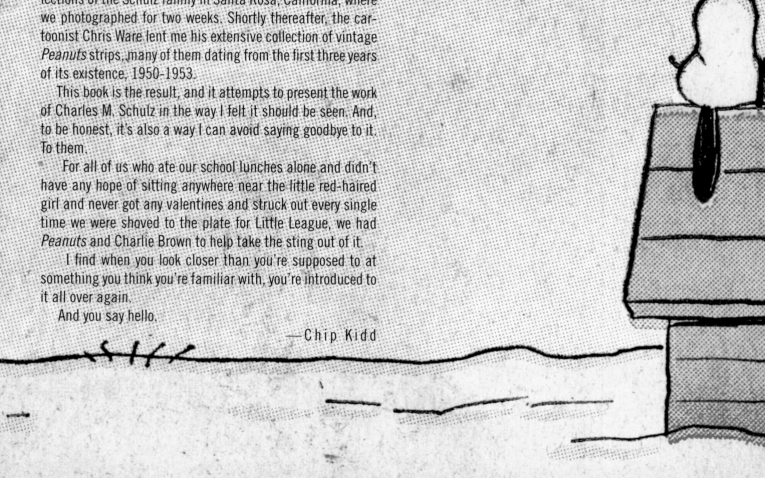

"Goodbys always make my throat hurt . . . I need more hellos . . ."
— *Charlie Brown, 1967*

In July of 2000, at the invitation of the executors of Charles Schulz's estate, the photographer Geoff Spear and I were granted unlimited access to the *Peanuts* archive and the collections of the Schulz family in Santa Rosa, California, where we photographed for two weeks. Shortly thereafter, the cartoonist Chris Ware lent me his extensive collection of vintage *Peanuts* strips, many of them dating from the first three years of its existence, 1950-1953.

This book is the result, and it attempts to present the work of Charles M. Schulz in the way I felt it should be seen. And, to be honest, it's also a way I can avoid saying goodbye to it. To them.

For all of us who ate our school lunches alone and didn't have any hope of sitting anywhere near the little red-haired girl and never got any valentines and struck out every single time we were shoved to the plate for Little League, we had *Peanuts* and Charlie Brown to help take the sting out of it.

I find when you look closer than you're supposed to at something you think you're familiar with, you're introduced to it all over again.

And you say hello.

— Chip Kidd

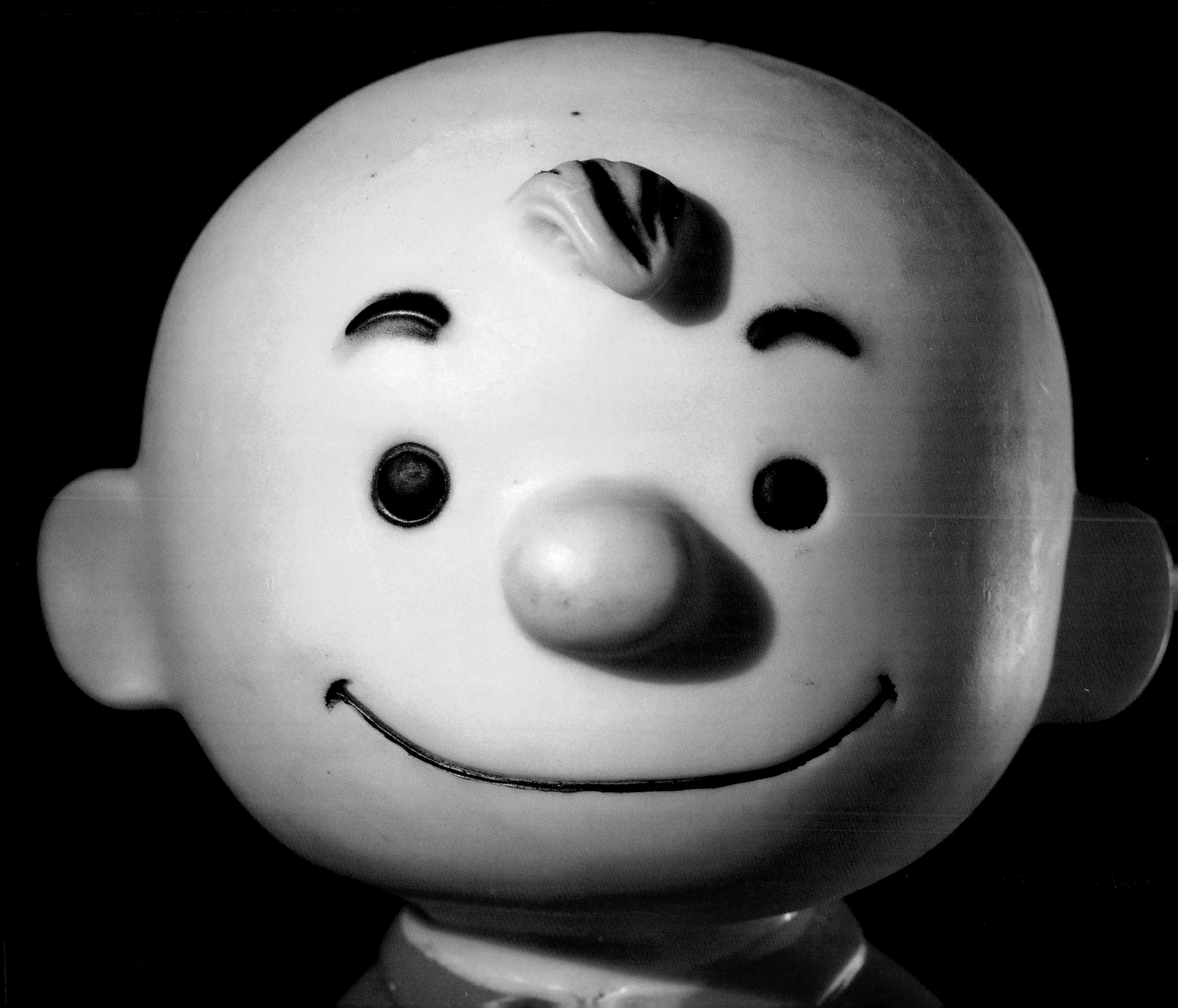

INTRODUCTION

Sparky was a genius.

That is the answer to the unanswerable questions of "why" and "how." I recognized it when I first knew him, I spent the next 25 years asking the same things others ask, and always came back to the same answer. The essence of his genius is: We can't know it, quantify it, explain it; we can, simply, enjoy it. If those of us who are part of his circle puzzle over the questions and struggle for answers, no one struggled more than Sparky himself.

He understood intuitively things he couldn't explain. Things he couldn't even put into words. He could go only so far as to answer the perennial question "Where do your ideas come from?"

The ideas Sparky used are out there in the world. We all know them and that is why we relate to them. It is the particular twist Sparky put to the ideas that described his genius, and that draws us, enchanted, into his frame.

I believe there are people of genius around us, but few are fortunate enough to have their genius match the moment. A thousand years ago, Sparky would have been a storyteller, the person in the tribe or the clan who collected the tribal lore and repeated it for each generation. He understood instinctively the value of the story which illustrates a human truth, and which allows his listeners to take from it what they need at the time. The best stories can be told over and over again—forever new—because the listener changes.

Sparky loved his *Big-Little Books* when he was small, when he was in high school he escaped into the world of Sherlock Holmes, and always he loved adventure comics. He actually wanted to draw an adventure strip, but it was the wistful, innocent way he illustrated an emotion, expressed through the eyes of a small person, that caught the attention of the comics editors. And so it was children he drew on for his cartoons.

Children, he would have told you, are simply adults "with the lids still on." He believed firmly that we are the product of our genes and that all of the characteristics are there within us as children, simmering, waiting to emerge. So the envy and anger expressed in "Good Ol' Charlie Brown. How I hate him" in the first strip, shocks us, but Sparky knew, whether or not we want to admit it, children feel that emotion. When Sparky saw a child with a very strong personality, he observed how difficult that person would be "when the lid comes off."

Sparky loved to sit in his ice arena over lunch and have an interesting and varied group around, and he was very good in front of an audience. He knew how to draw his story out to hold people's attention. His directness enlivened any conversation and he probed others with questions. In these situations he was like the storyteller of old—interacting with his audience in a very intimate way.

But the comic strip is a long way from the storyteller of a thousand years ago. The cartoonist puts his drawings and words on paper and it is weeks before his audience sees them. Immediacy and personality must be elucidated in a different way. The comic strip storyteller of 20th century America has to tell a story that stretches across 3000 miles, and draw scenes of snow pranks that make people laugh in Hawaii as well as in Vermont or Michigan.

Like the novelist, the cartoonist must go into himself or herself, and draw upon what is there. It is a solitary craft.

Sparky frequently wasn't sure if something he'd drawn was funny. Certainly he'd receive feedback, but it would be months later. The spontaneity was missing. Often I'd stop at his studio and look over a stack of dailies on his desk. When I laughed out loud, or told him how funny I thought they were, he was truly grateful. "Oh, I'm so glad you think it's funny. I'm never sure," he'd say. He loved people's positive responses, and at the same time, he had to shut out the voices. He had to draw what *he* thought was funny and *hope* that his audience liked it too. He was always glad to know people liked his characters or a particular storyline, but he knew he couldn't write to that audience; he always wrote for himself.

He began quite early in his career to use biblical references. Occasionally, someone would write to say, "How dare you use religious material in a comic strip?" His response was that as long as he had used the reference with integrity, he was satisfied that he was on firm ground. On the other hand, once in the 70s, he used a take-off on the title *I Heard the Owl Call My Name*. He got a letter saying this was a sacred phrase in a Native American tribe. Sparky wrote an apology. He admitted he hadn't realized that he was overstepping propriety.

Sparky sometimes tried out an idea on me or others. For example he'd say, "How would it be if Charlie Brown goes to camp and meets this other kid who won't say anything except 'Shut up and leave me alone.'?" Well, it's difficult to imagine that as a funny storyline, but I knew better than to say no, and of course, because of the funny drawing and the particular way he paced the strip and the story, it became a funny sequence. If this or any new character made for a good storyline, Sparky might go back and resurrect the character a year later for a second camp episode, but more often than not, that first appearance would be the last. He explained that the character was too one-dimensional to create opportunities for humor.

In order to produce a strip every day, he had to rely on characters whose personalities themselves engendered ideas. Sparky always had a pen handy to write down any notions that came to him, or if we were in the car he'd ask me to write for him. Frequently, at the symphony, I'd see him reach into his pocket for his pad and pencil. On the way home he'd tell me the idea he had—but what he related to me at the time was only the germ of what would become a fully realized daily or Sunday page. He could come up with ideas from almost any situation because his characters had such distinct personalitites and idiosyncrasies.

As much as most of us are drawn to the personalities and the situations and the lines the characters deliver, Sparky was always quick to point out that the appeal of *Peanuts* is still funny drawing. He would use a yellow lined pad to "doodle," drawing the characters in antic poses, rolling over, flying upside down, etc. These provided him with ideas.

When the strip ended, the response was overwhelming. Sparky touched people deeply and often changed their lives, as the thousands of letters attested:

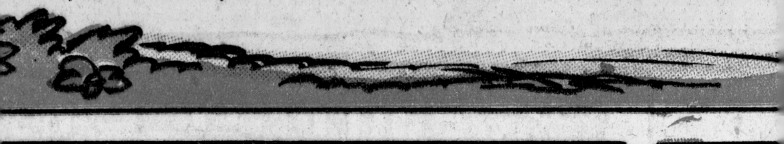

"I remember [as a child] often being consumed by feelings of profound anxiety and unrest, and yet as soon as I could come home to read my Peanuts *books, I was peaceful, even happy."*

"When I was about 11 years old I had to go into the hospital and I was very scared. My mother had to leave me after visiting hours, but my stuffed Snoopy didn't. I held it all night long."

"I often identified with Charlie Brown's feelings of inadequacy, of not fitting in anywhere. And my favorite character was always Linus, who was sensible but had an almost magical sense of the power of his innocence and imagination."

"Charlie Brown and the gang were a solace and a balm to my soul. I always wanted to tell this to Mr. Schulz. So now I tell you."

Sparky once said, "I would be satisfied if they wrote on my tombstone 'He made people happy.'"

He did that, and so much more.

— Jean Schulz

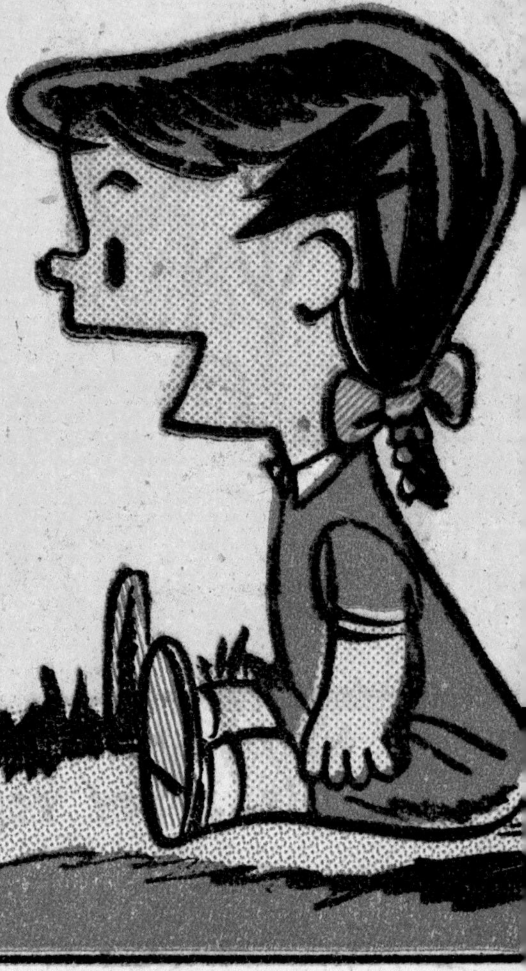

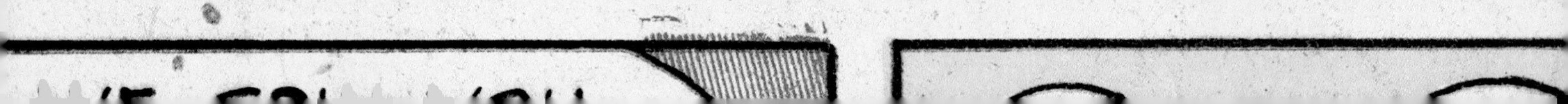

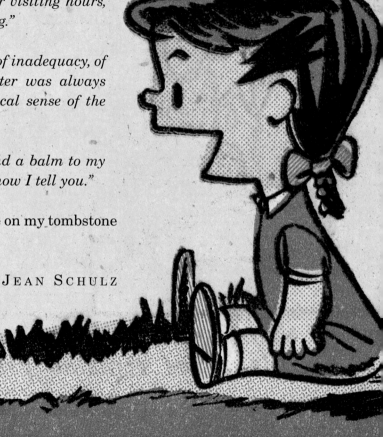

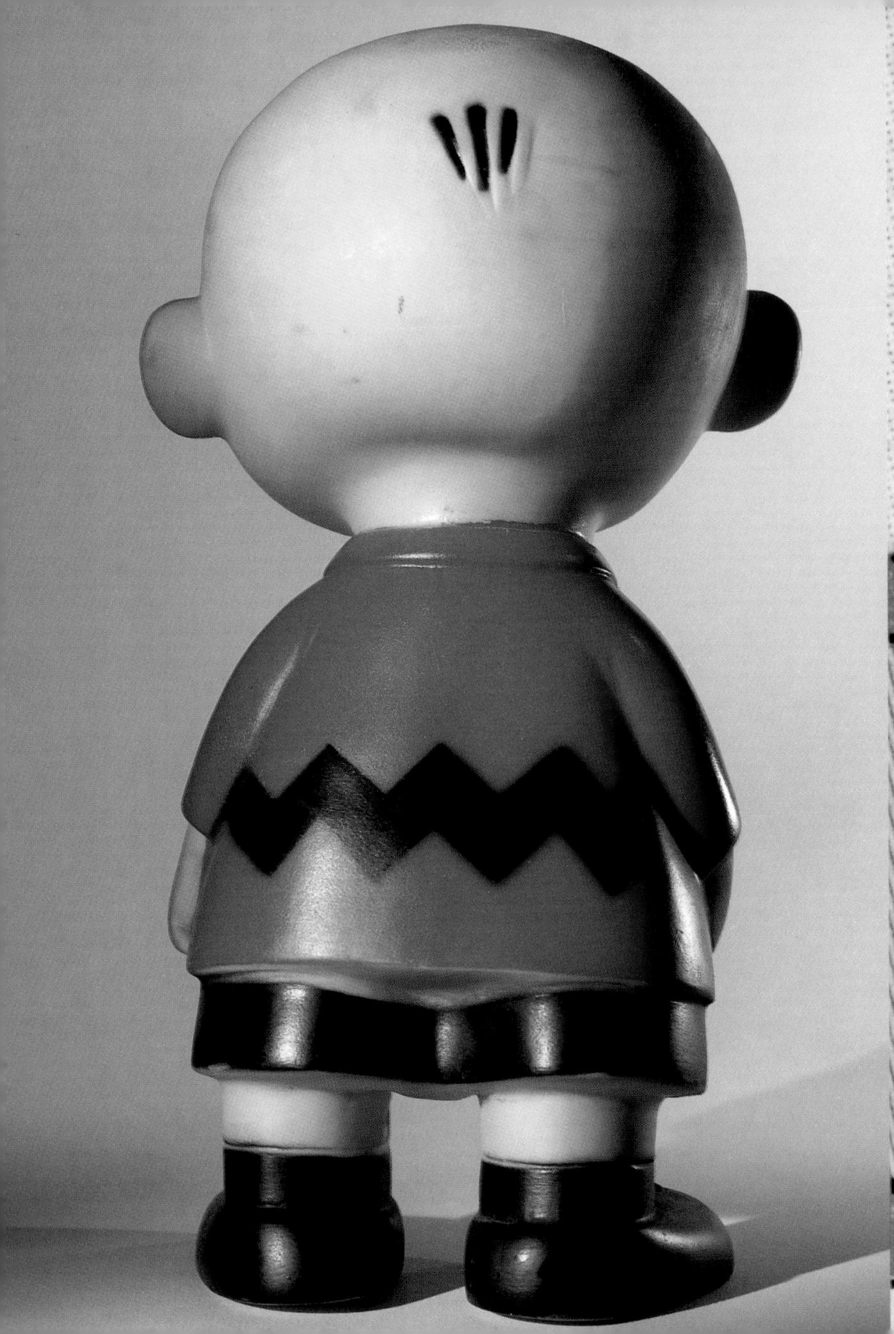

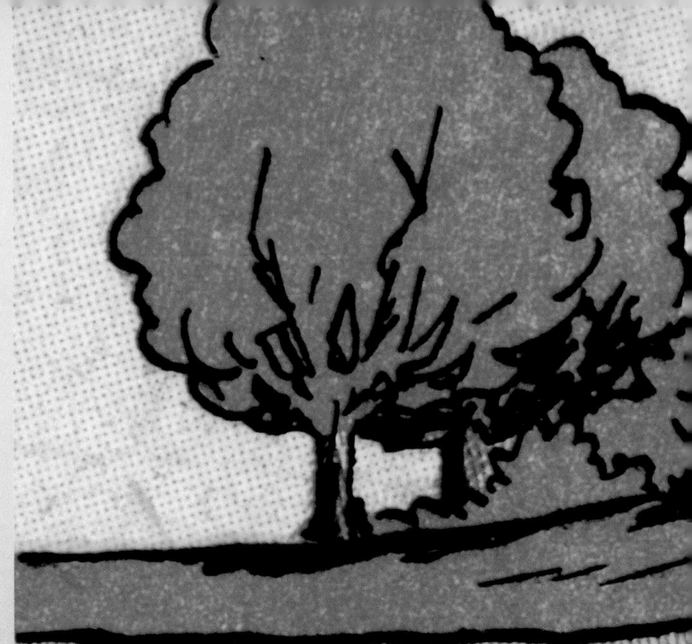

Library of Congress Cataloging-in-Publication Data: Schulz, Charles M.
Peanuts : the art of Charles M. Schulz.
p. cm. • ISBN 0-375-42097-5
1. Schulz, Charles M.--Peanuts. I. Title.
PN6728.P4 S3262 2001 741.5'973--dc21 2001021577

www.pantheonbooks.com • BOOK DESIGN BY CHIP KIDD
Printed in China • First Edition
2 4 6 8 9 7 5 3 1

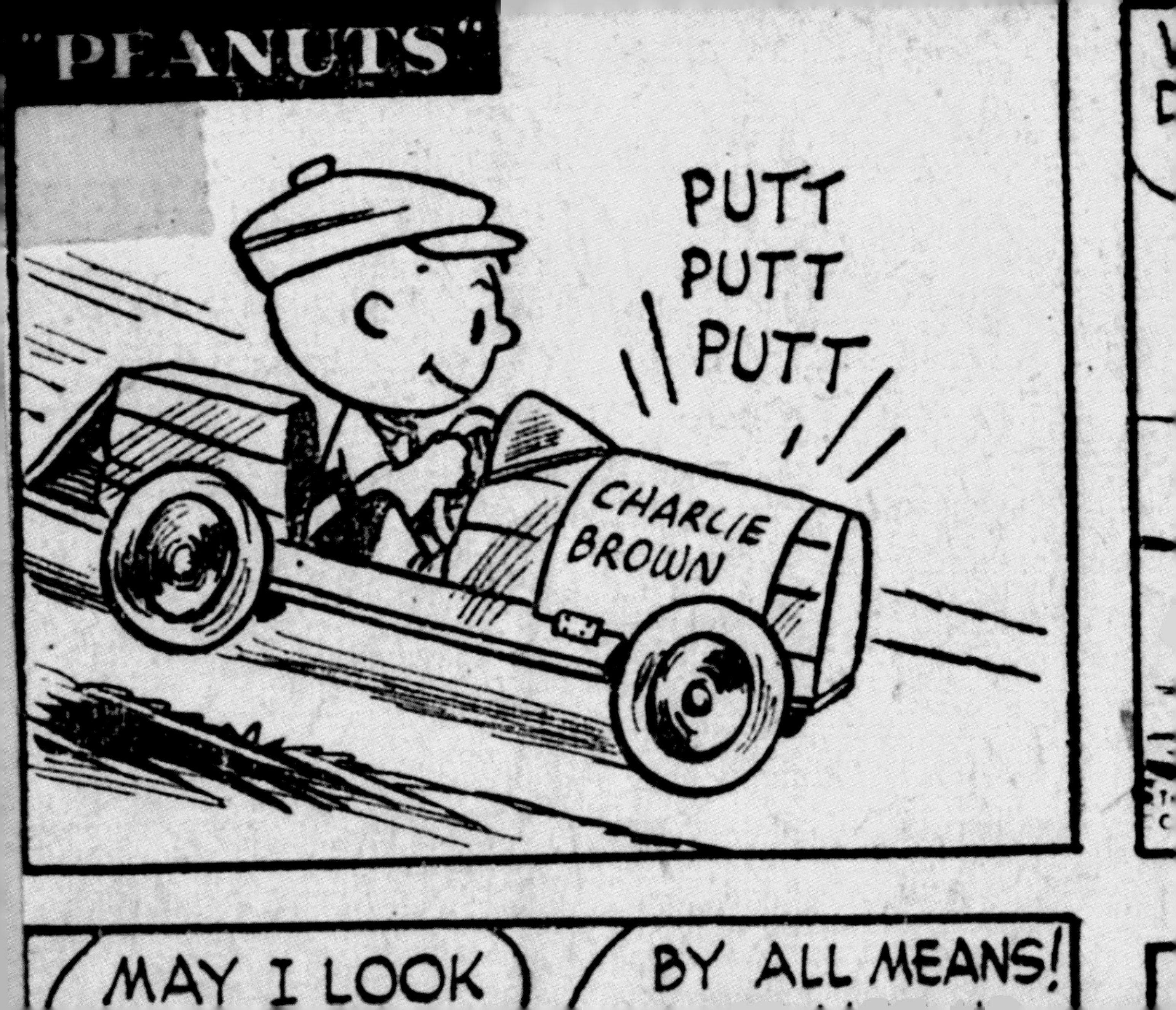
"PEANUTS"
PUTT
PUTT
PUTT
CHARLIE BROWN
MAY I LOOK
BY ALL MEANS!

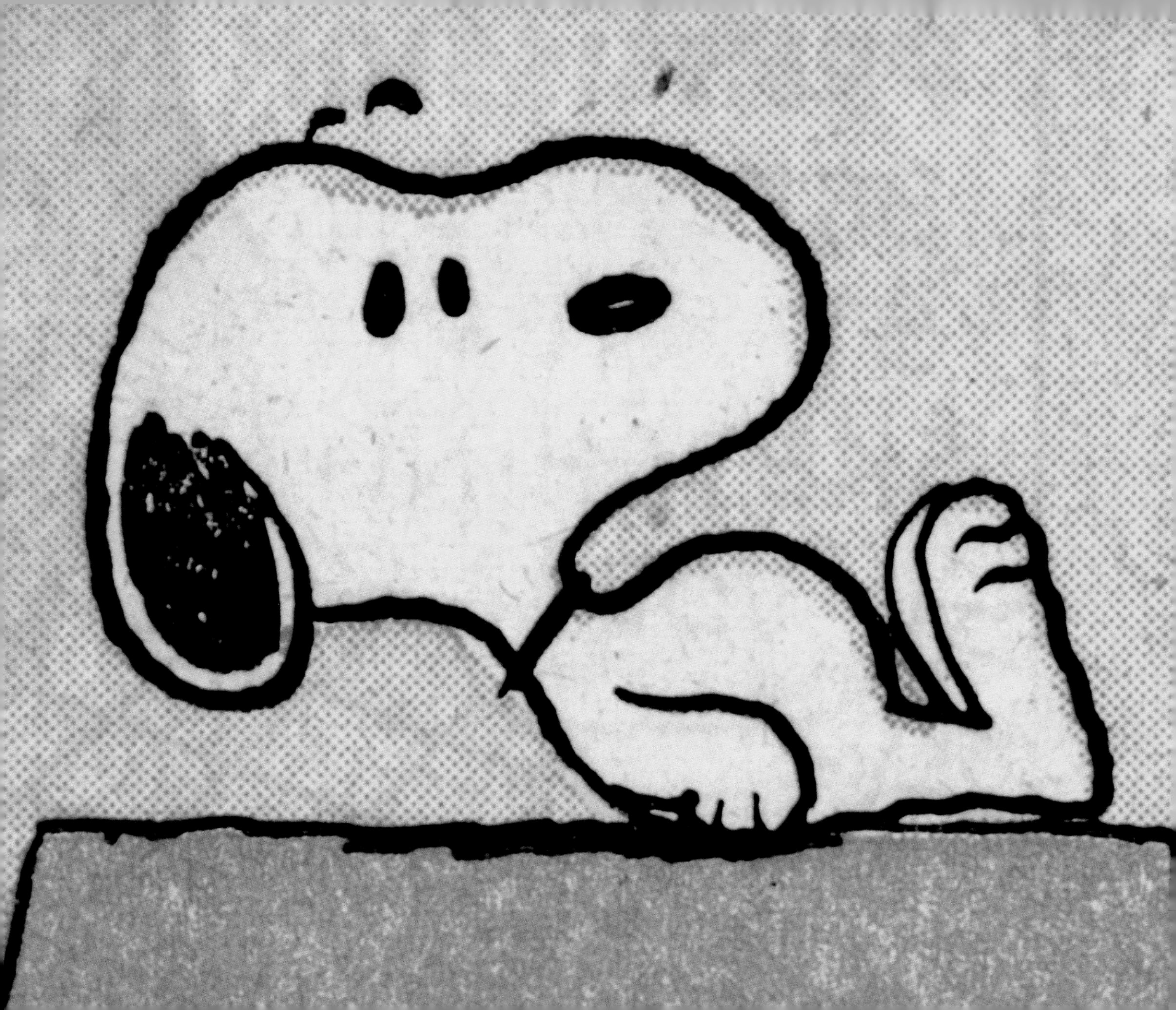

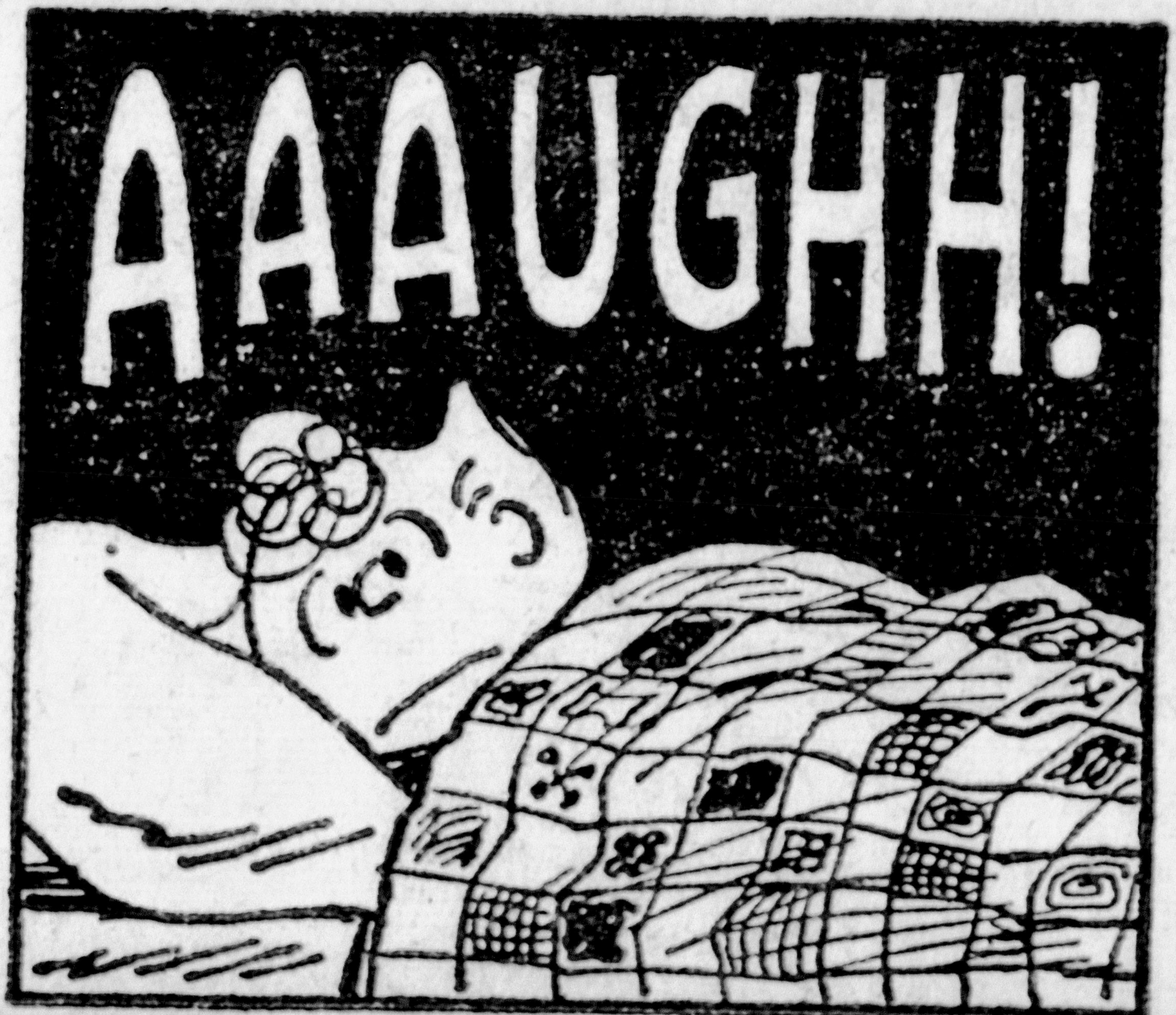
AAAUGHH!

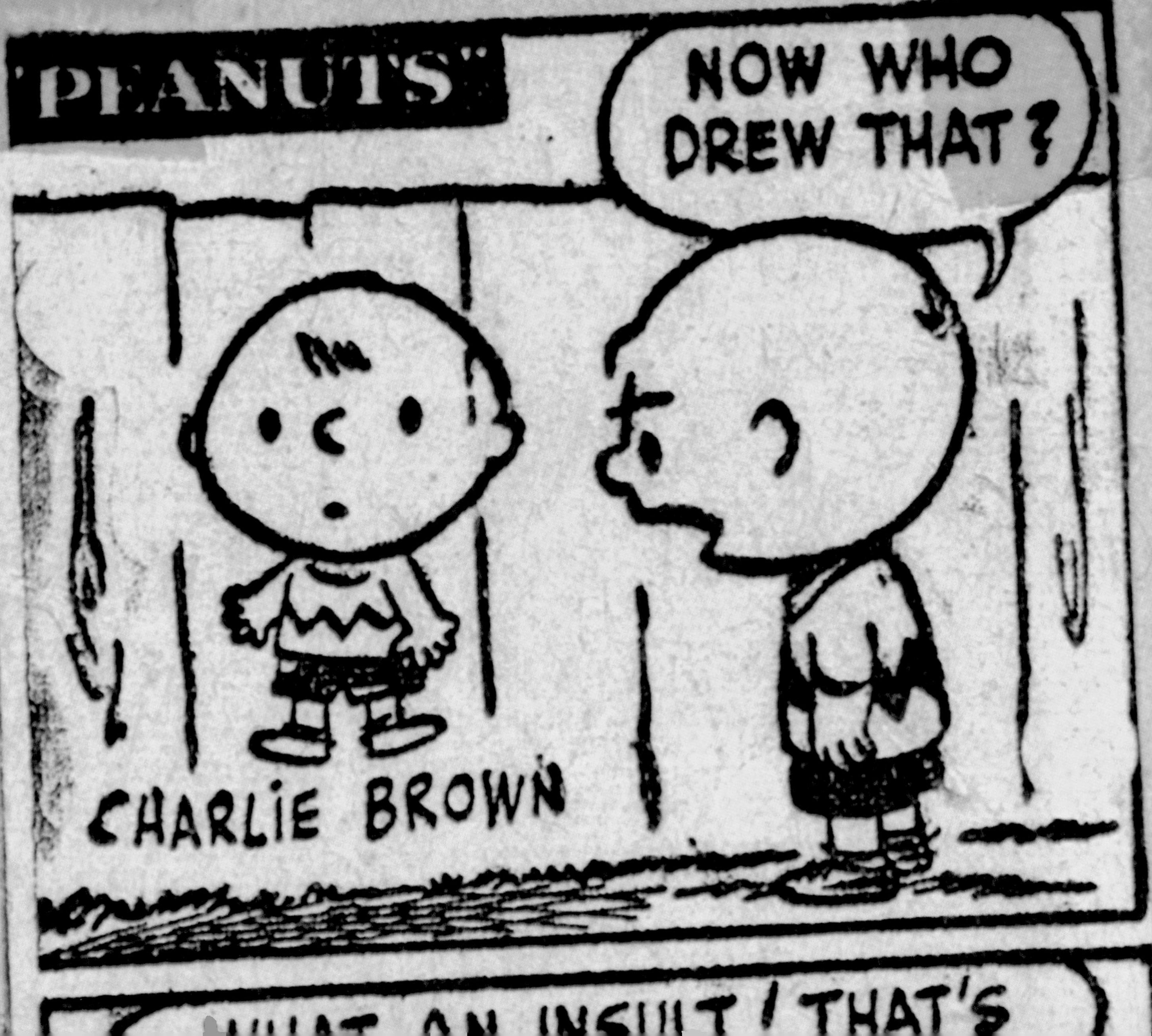
PEANUTS
NOW WHO DREW THAT?
CHARLIE BROWN

chulz's drawing tools, photographed July 2000. The tray is as it was left the previous December, when he had finished s last strip. It sat vertically along the right side of his drawing table. Note the Snoopy bandage.

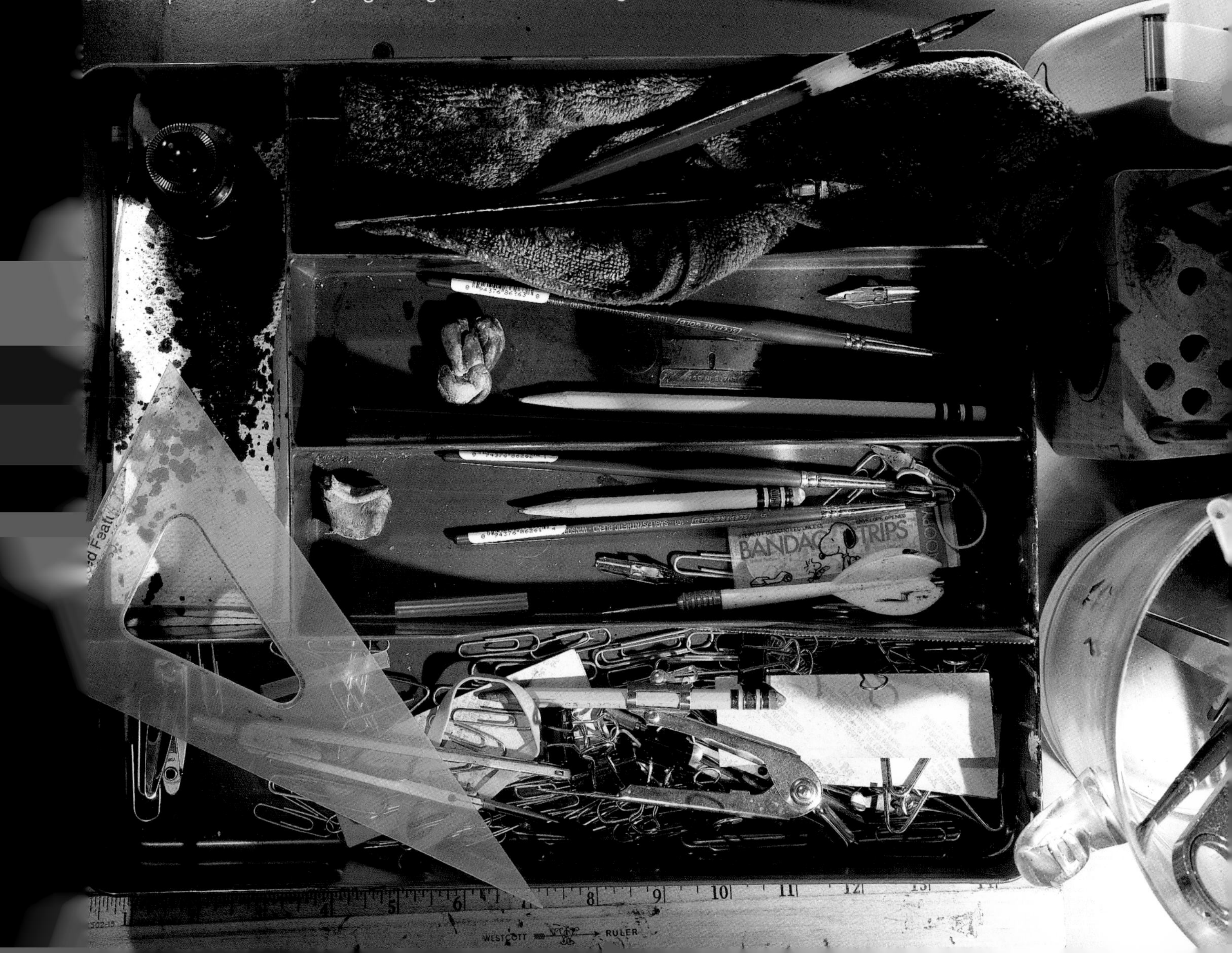
BANDAGE STRIPS
WESTCOTT
RULER

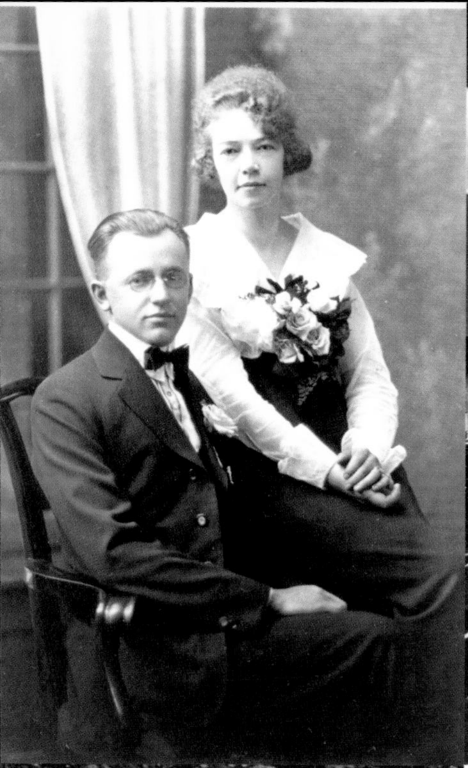

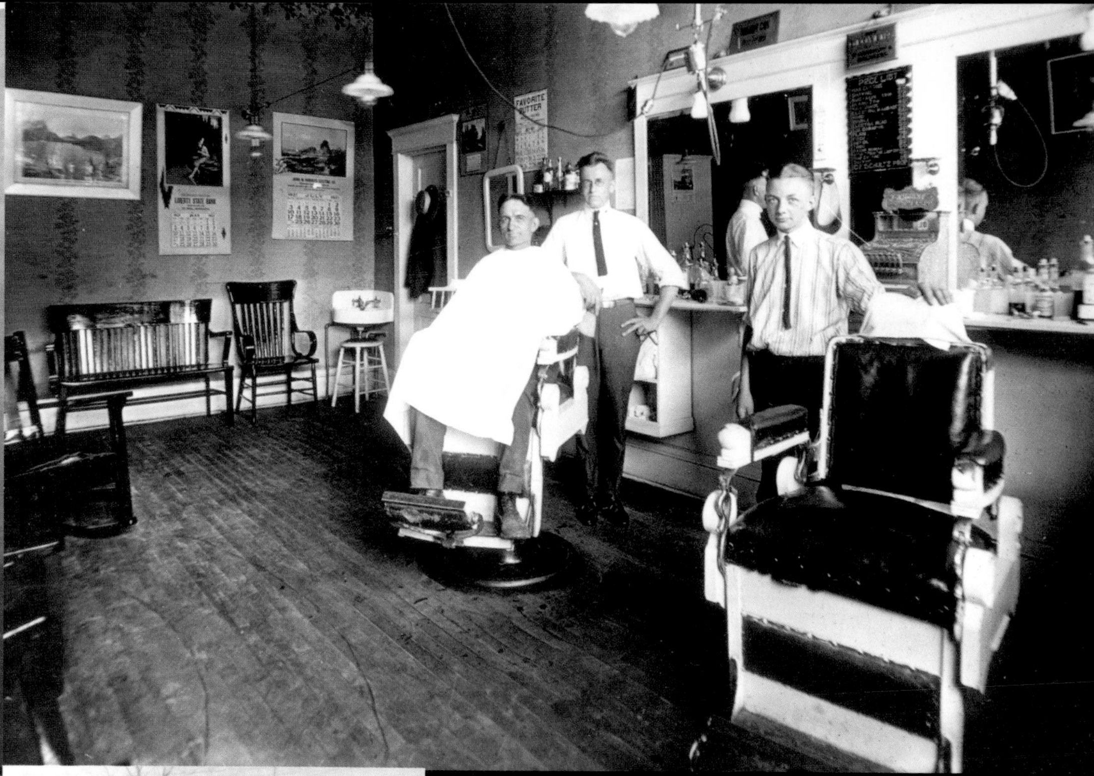

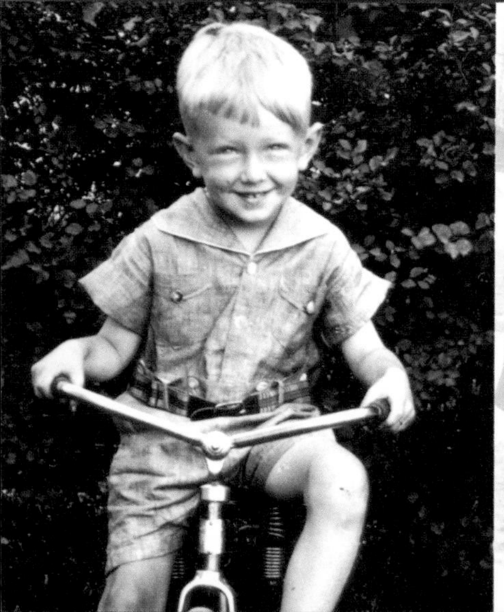

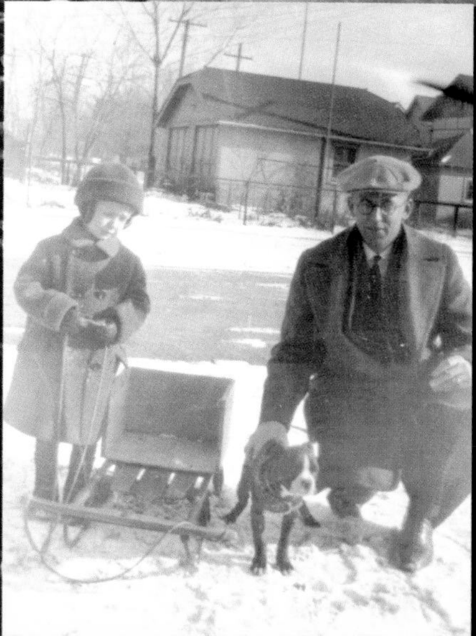

Upper left: Dena and Carl Schulz, 1920

Above: Carl (at left) in his barbershop with Monroe Halverson

Far left: Sparky as a young boy, 1927

Left: A boy, his dad, his dog and his sled. Winter in Minnesota, 1926

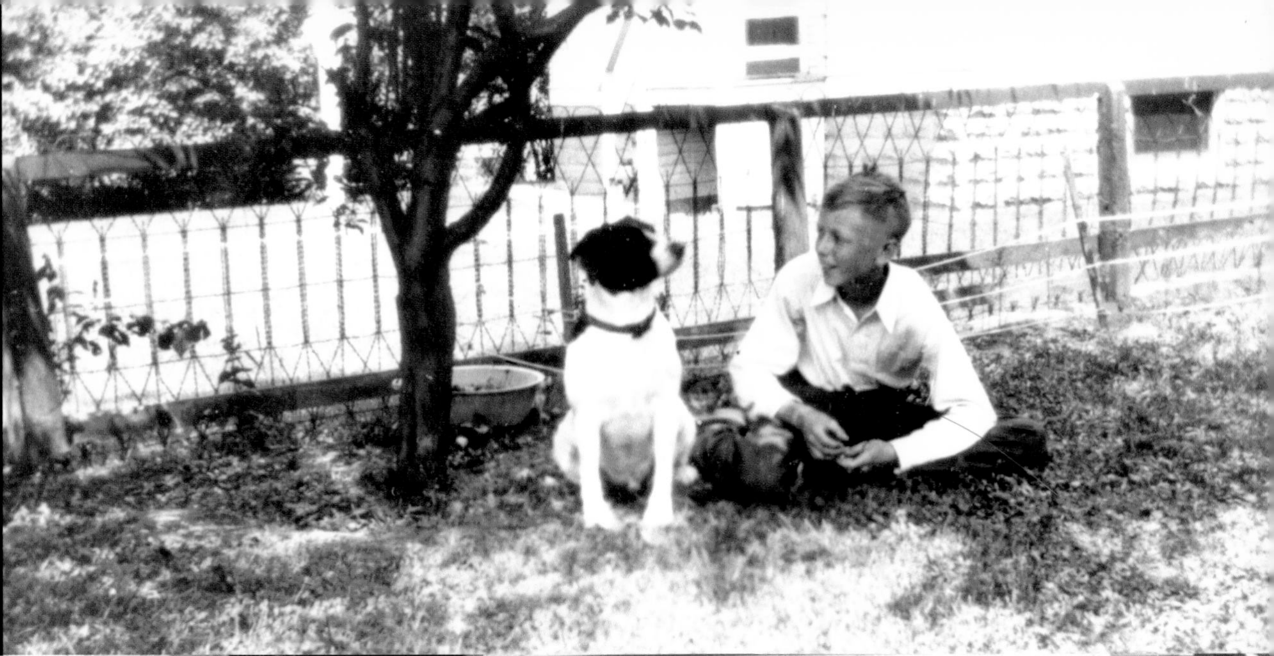

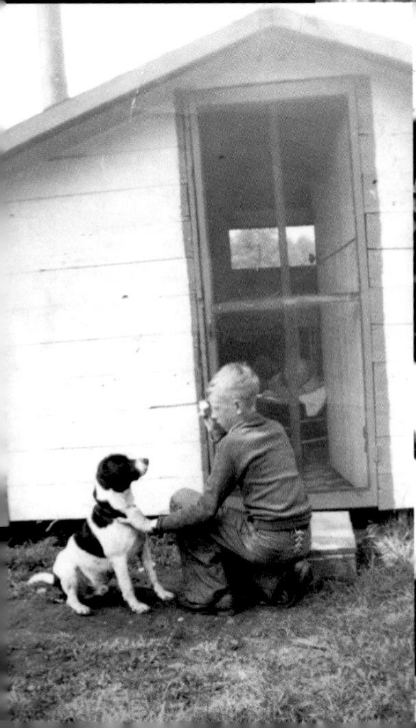

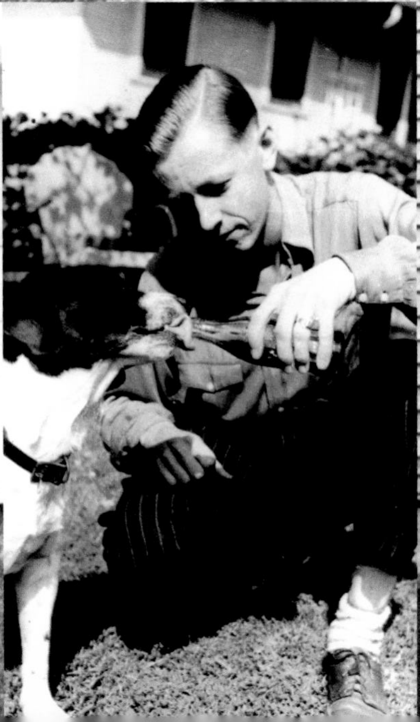

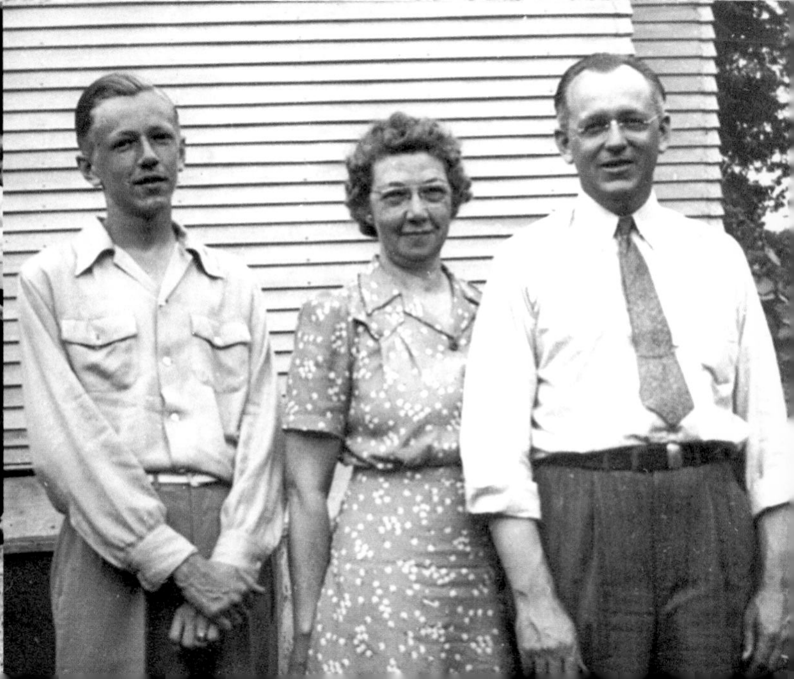

Right and lower left: Sparky and Spike—a pointer, not a beagle, 1935

Below, center: Sparky offers Spike a drink, early 1940s

Lower right: Sparky, Dena and Carl, taken shortly before Sparky's February 1943 departure for Fort Snelling, in Minneapolis

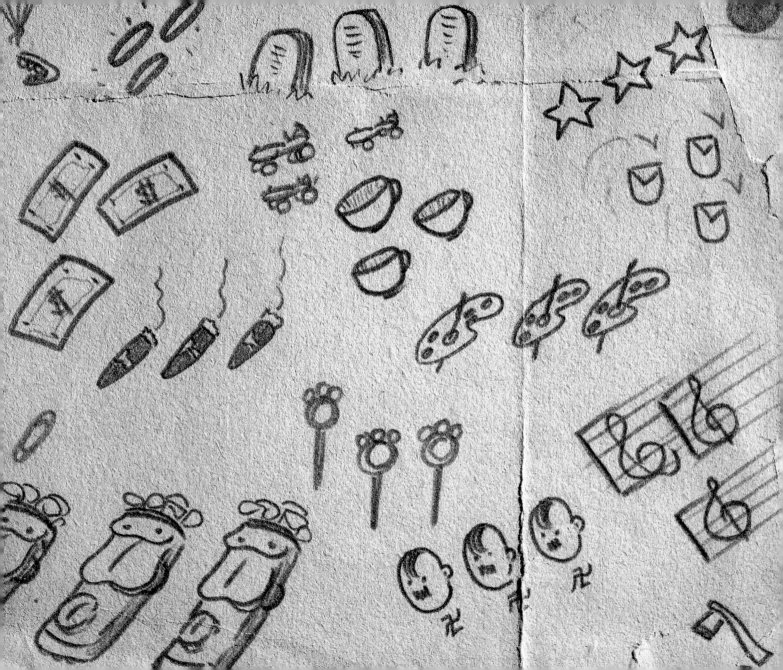

tral Hi-Y; Wrestling; Football; Basketball; Assemblies; Stage Force; J. S. Com.; "Times Revue."

Edward Schmidt—Thumb Tacks; German Club; Treas., Vice-Pres. International Club; Class Com.; "Cehisean"; Commence. Com.

If Sparky (nicknamed for the horse "Sparkplug" from the comic strip *Barney Google*) doesn't look too happy in his high school yearbook photo, that's because he wasn't. And if he looks a little young to be graduating, that's because he is—after first grade he was "promoted" two grades ahead and Charlie Brown was effectively born. "I was the smallest, the youngest, the shyest. I managed to flunk at least one subject a year."

Idelle Schnitzer—Girls' League; G. A. A.

Dorothy Schroeder—Girls' League; Girl Reserve; Treas. Triads; Vice-Pres. Masque and Foil; Ex. Bd. G. A. A.; "C" Club; All-City Letter; Referee; Commence. Com.; Honor Roll.

Charles Schulz—"Cehisean." But he did love to draw. On the opposite page is an exercise from his high school art class. The teacher, Minette Paro, asked the students to draw small objects in groups of threes. "They were spectacular because they were things you wouldn't even think of," Miss Paro recalled. "That means that his mind was working every minute. He isn't worried about what's going on the paper, it's in his mind, it's got to come out."

Howard Schultz—Dramatic Club; Bowling Club; Pres., Sec. Mid. Hi-Y; Assemblies; Student Council; Baseball; Capt. Basketball; "C" Club; National Honor Society.

Beverlie Schuneman.

Marjorie Searing—Ski Club; Table Tennis Club; Girls' League; "Times"; Honor Roll; Quill and Scroll.

Note: Little could Schulz have known that in less than ten years he'd be in Hitler's Germany while Dachau was being liberated.

Hyam Segell—Stamp Club; International Club; Pres. Latin Club; Vice-Pres. Chess Club; Pres. Debating Club; Chr. Class Com.; Assemblies; "Cehisean"; Commence. Com.; Honor Roll; National Honor Society.

Don Shannon—Aeronautics Club; Pres. Ski Club; Orchestra; Chr. Class Com.; "Cehisean."

Lois Shirley—Girls' League; Girl Reserve; Masque and Foil; Ski Club; Gym Demonstration; "Cehisean."

In an unfortunately symbolic turn of events, his drawings for this yearbook were accepted by the editors, and then, unbeknownst to him, unceremoniously dropped. He found out only when the book was released.

Stanley Simon—Table Tennis Club; Chess Club; Stamp Club; "C" Club; International Club; Class Com.; "Cehisean"; Tennis; I. M. Basketball; Commence. Com.; Honor Roll.

Mavajean Simpson—Girl Reserve; Dramatic Club; Treas. Literary Club; Girls' League; J. S. Com.; Class Com.; Band Concert; Gym Demonstra-

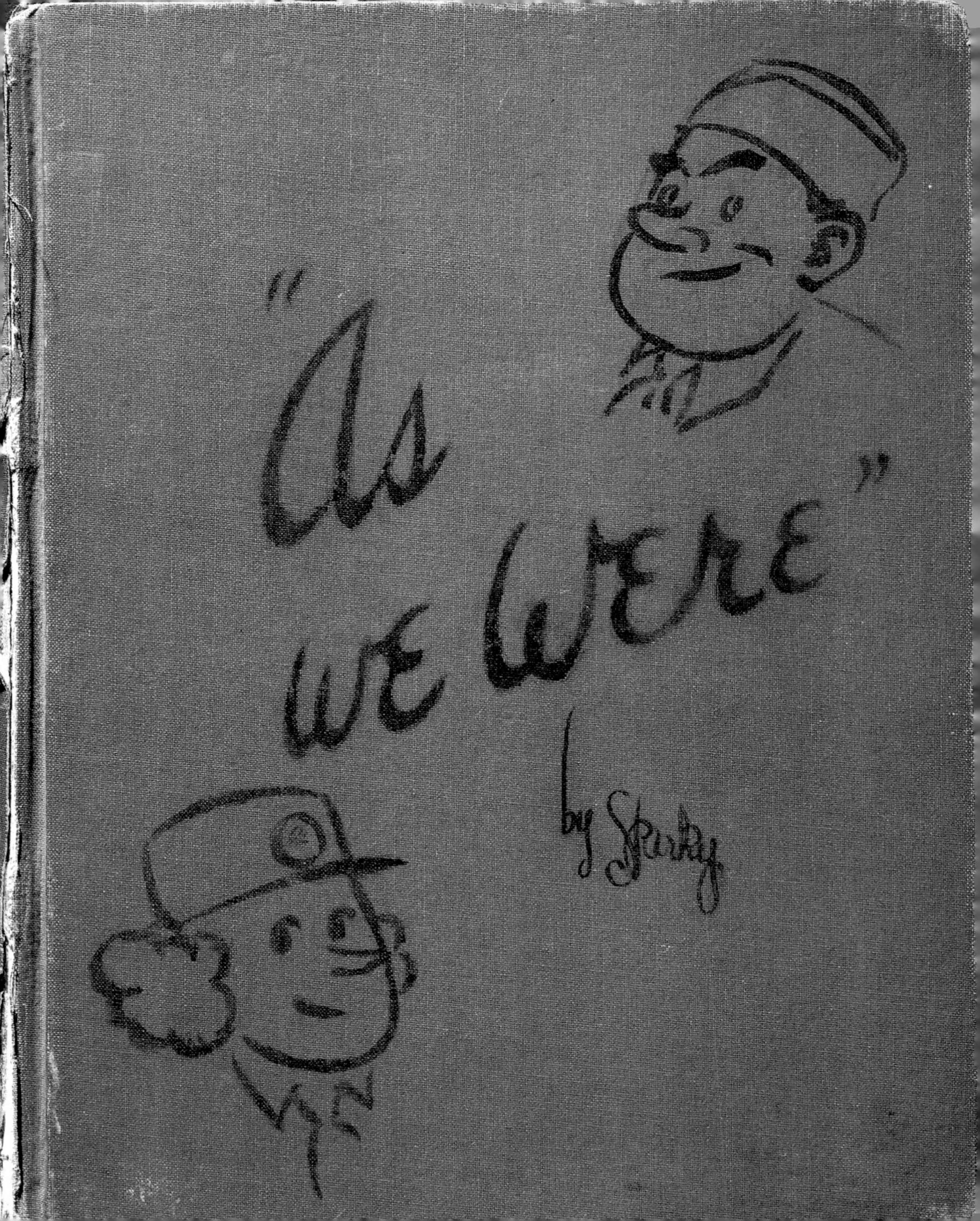
"As We Were"
by Sparky

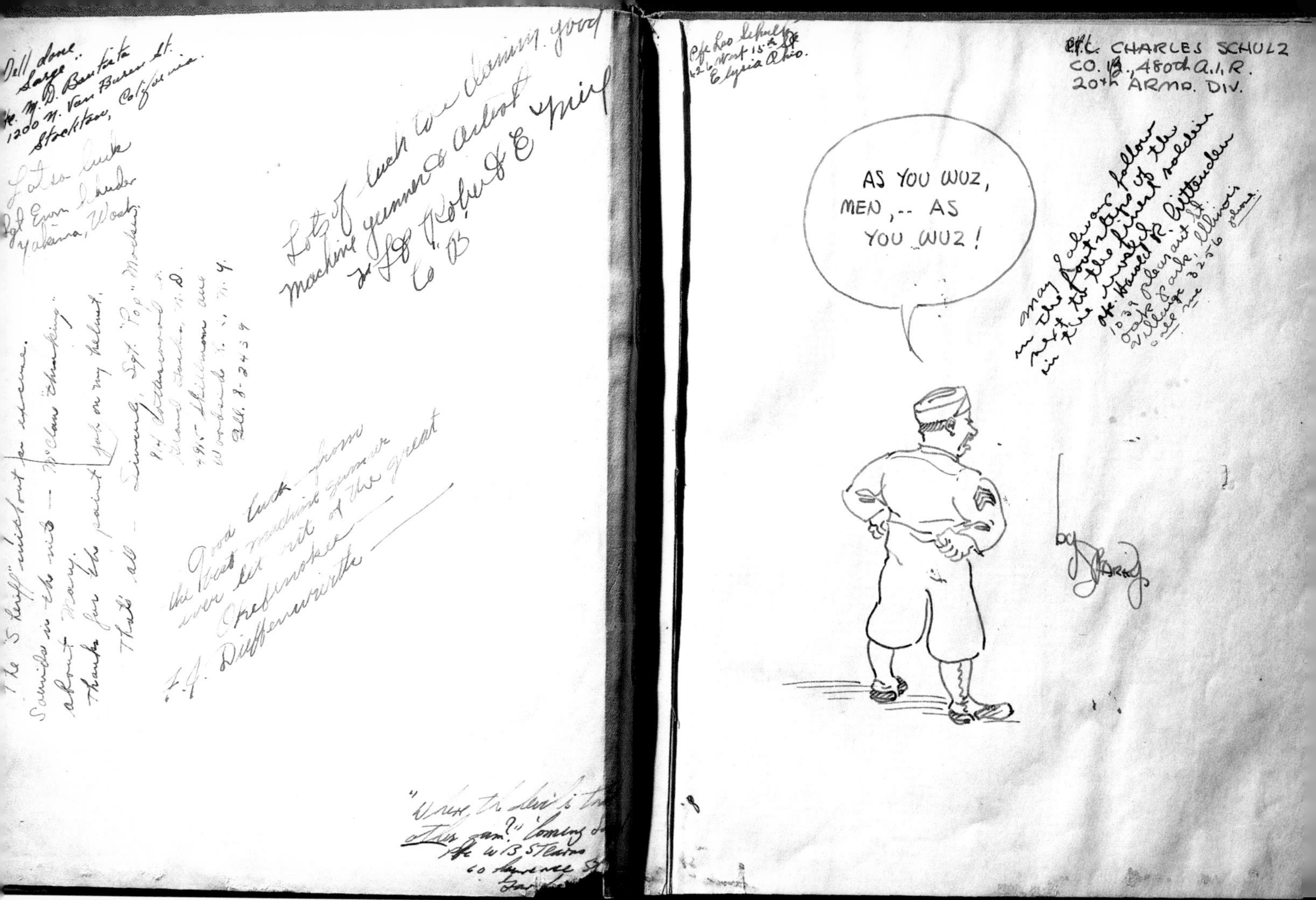
PFC. CHARLES SCHULZ
CO. B., 480th A.I.R.
20th ARMD. DIV.
AS YOU WUZ, MEN,-- AS YOU WUZ!

In 1943 Schulz was drafted and sent to Camp Campbell, Kentucky, where he spent the next two years, eventually shipping out to Germany. Though a true patriot, he hated the realities of military life and kept a sketchbook, called "As We Were," in order help pass the time. The drawings vary between being realistic and "cartoony."

"Sparky always told me that if you wanted to cartoon well, you first had to be able to draw things in a realistic manner," said Paige Braddock, a senior vice president at Schulz's Creative Associates and a cartoonist in her own right. "He didn't feel realism and cartooning were mutually exclusive, but rather integrated in the final caricature."

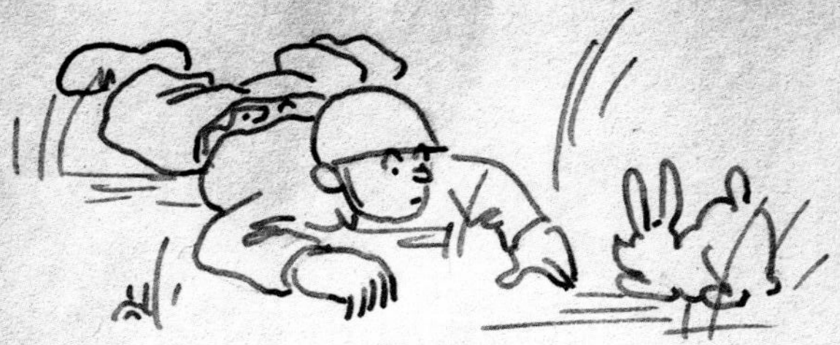

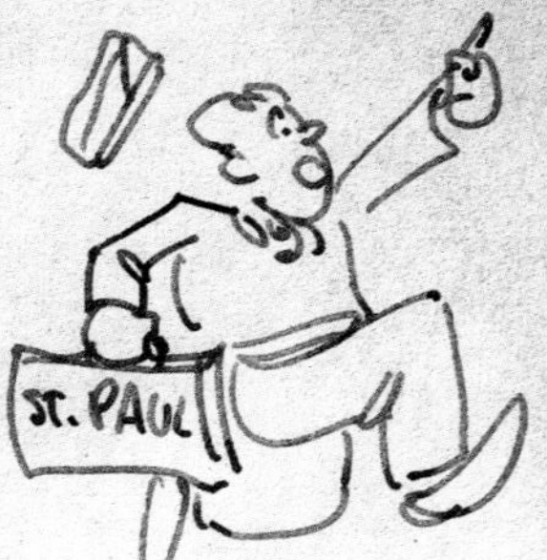
ST. PAUL

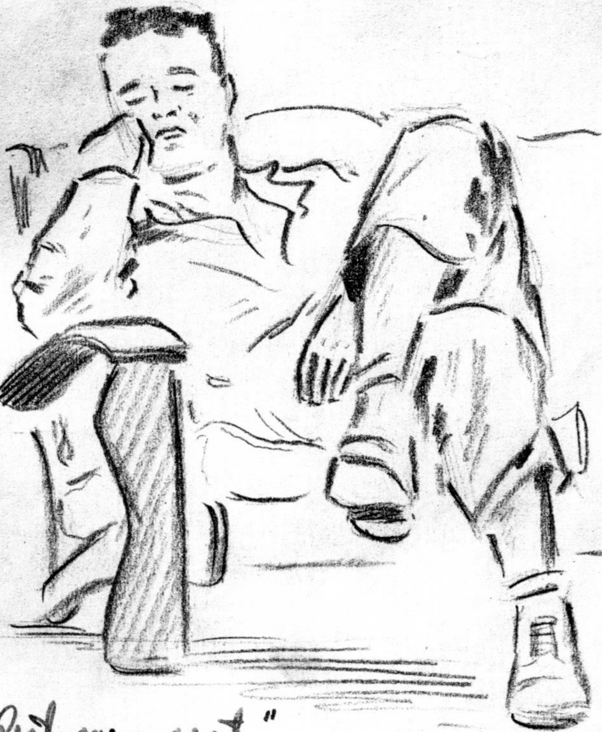

"Rest, men, rest"

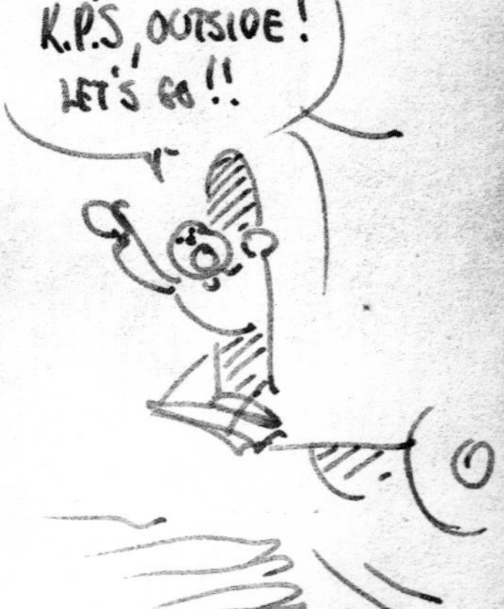
K.P.'S, OUTSIDE!
LET'S GO!!

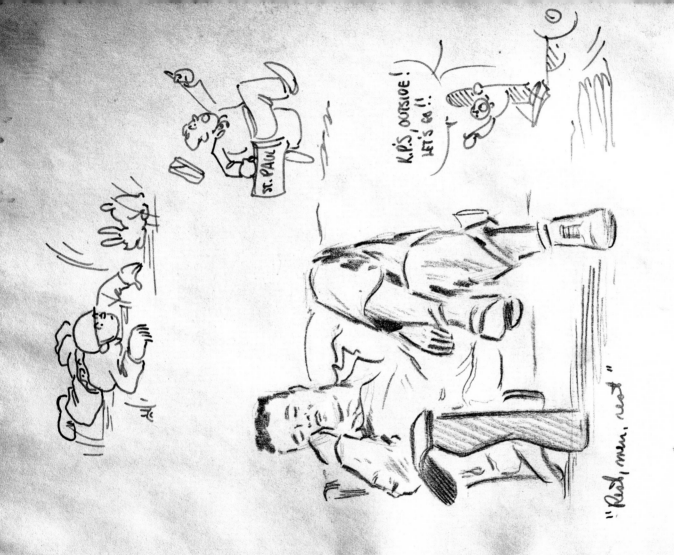

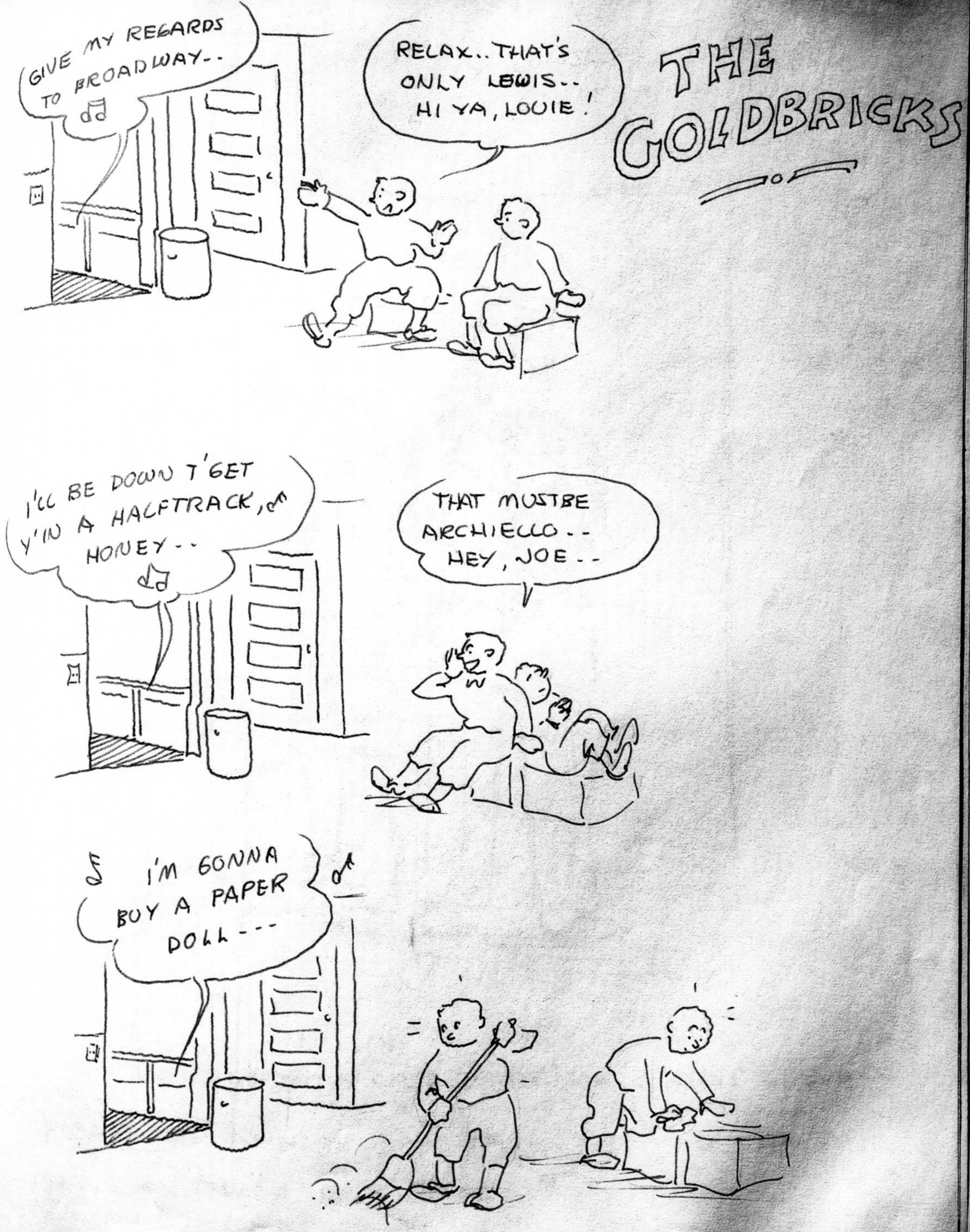
THE GOLDBRICKS
GIVE MY REGARDS TO BROADWAY..
RELAX.. THAT'S ONLY LEWIS.. HI YA, LOUIE!
I'LL BE DOWN T'GET Y'IN A HALFTRACK, HONEY..
THAT MUSTBE ARCHIELLO.. HEY, JOE..
I'M GONNA BUY A PAPER DOLL---

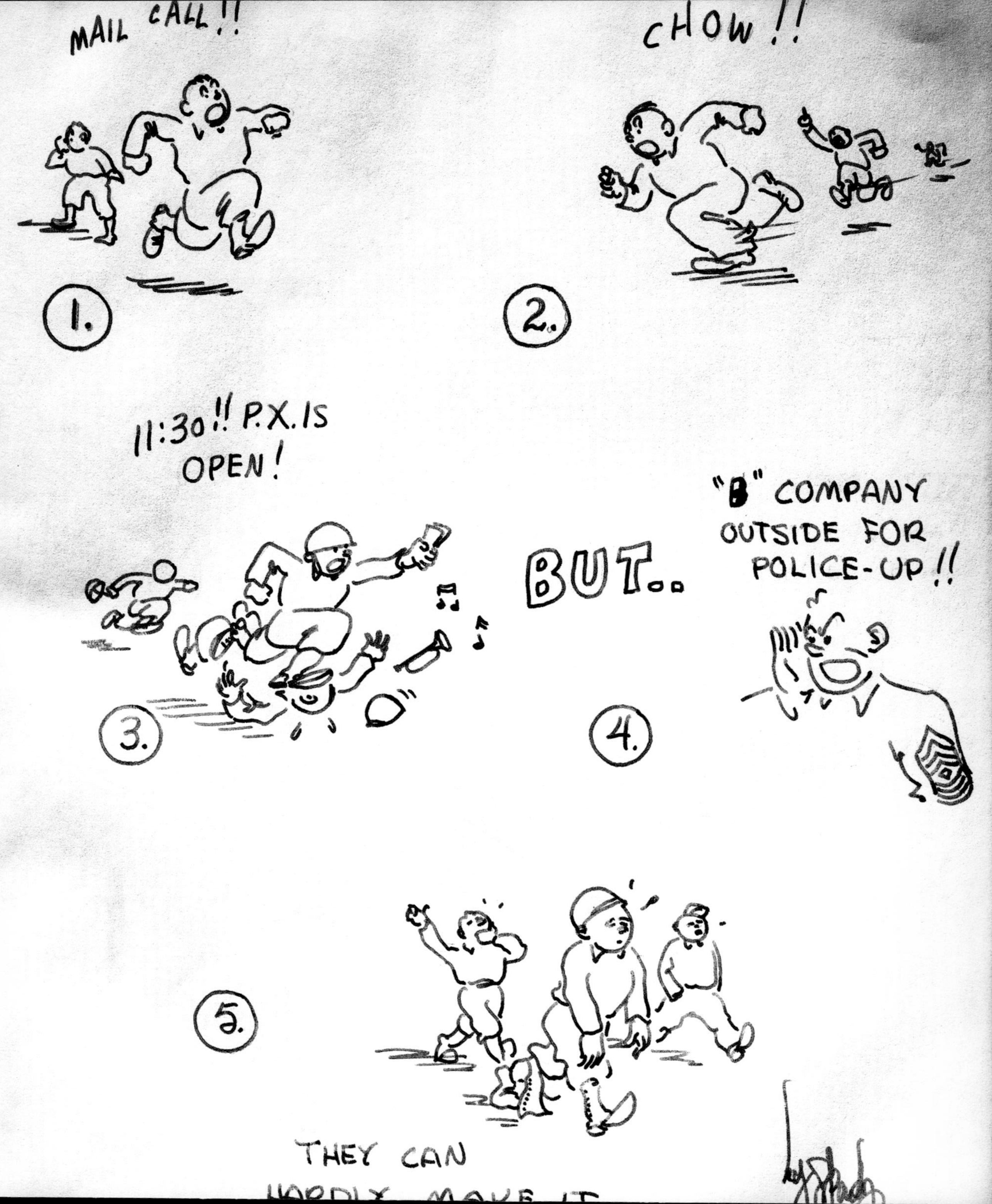
MAIL CALL!!
1.
CHOW!!
2.
11:30!! P.X. IS OPEN!
3.
BUT..
"B" COMPANY OUTSIDE FOR POLICE-UP!!
4.
5.
THEY CAN

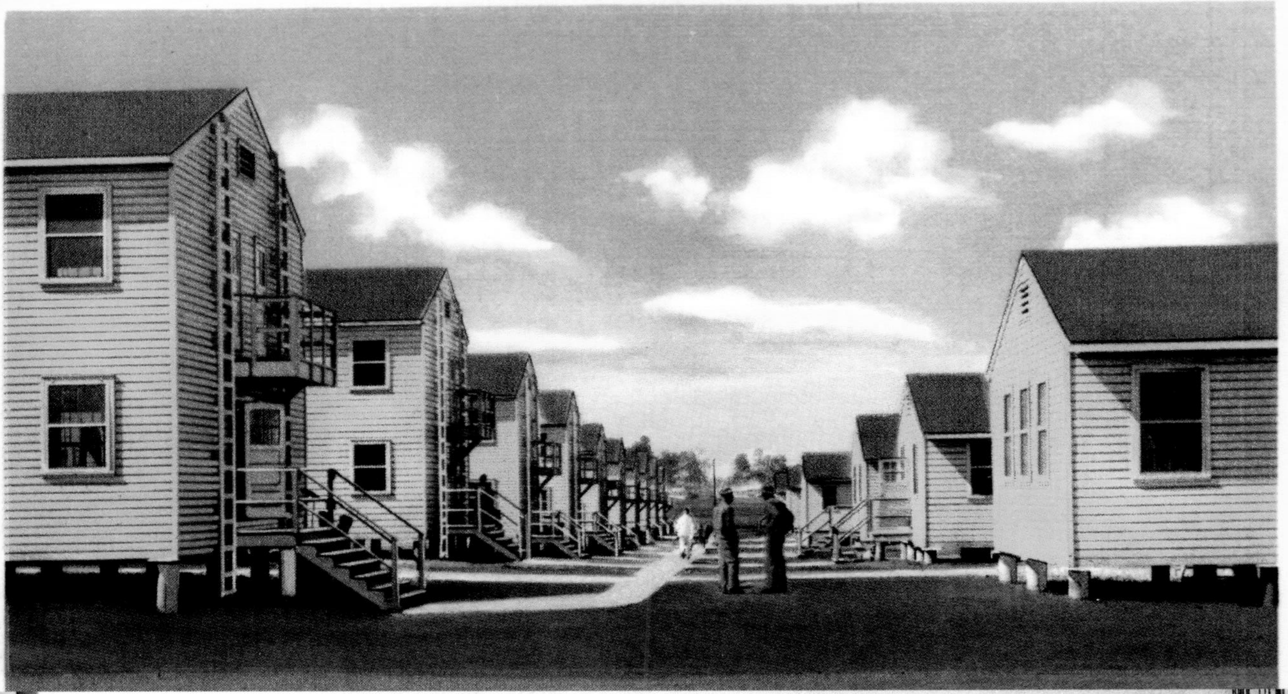

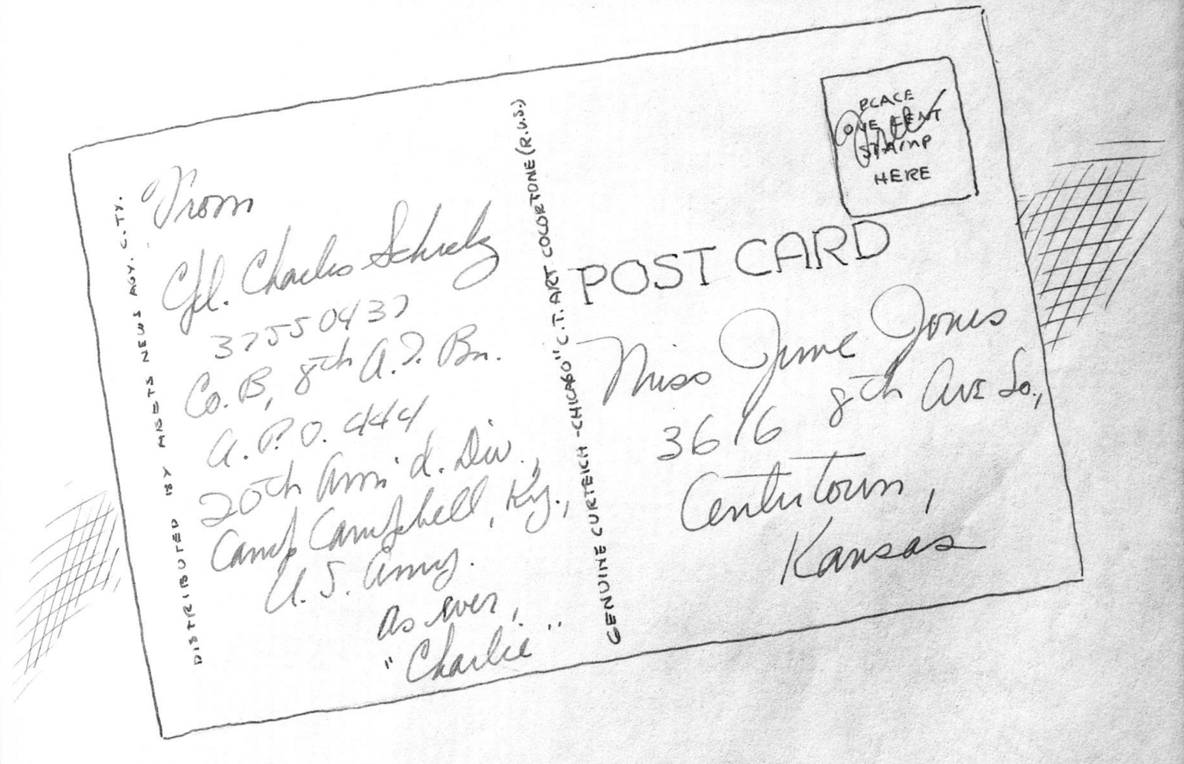
PLACE ONE CENT STAMP HERE
POST CARD
DISTRIBUTED BY MEETS NEWS AGY. C.T.Y.
GENUINE CURTEICH-CHICAGO "C.T. ART COLORTONE" (R.U.S.)
From
Cpl. Charles Schulz
37550437
Co. B, 8th A.I. Bn.
A.P.O. 444
20th Arm'd. Div.
Camp Campbell, Ky.
U.S. Army.
As ever,
"Charlie"
Miss June Jones
3616 8th Ave So.,
Centertown,
Kansas

"ARMY ADDRESSES"

Art Instruction Inc.

Back from the war in 1945, Schulz took a job as instructor at his alma mater in St. Paul, Art Instruction Inc. Here he met the man who would become his mentor, Frank Wing, creator of the depression-era strip *Yesterdays.*

Wing and Sparky forged a lifelong friendship, though the older cartoonist was wary of the young upstart's "modernist" style of draftsmanship.

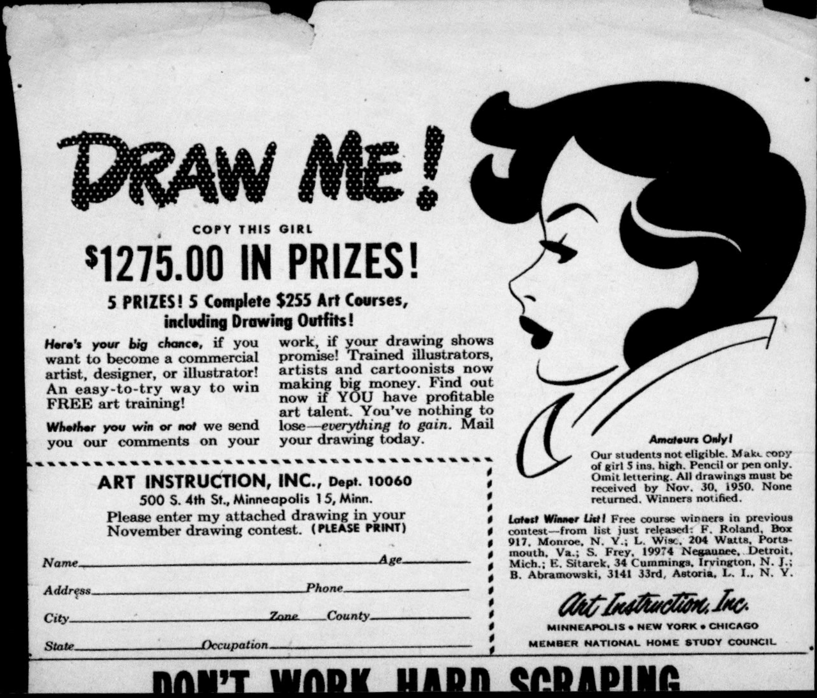

DRAW ME!
COPY THIS GIRL
$1275.00 IN PRIZES!
5 PRIZES! 5 Complete $255 Art Courses, including Drawing Outfits!
Here's your big chance, if you want to become a commercial artist, designer, or illustrator! An easy-to-try way to win FREE art training!
Whether you win or not we send you our comments on your work, if your drawing shows promise! Trained illustrators, artists and cartoonists now making big money. Find out now if YOU have profitable art talent. You've nothing to lose—everything to gain. Mail your drawing today.
ART INSTRUCTION, INC., Dept. 10060
500 S. 4th St., Minneapolis 15, Minn.
Please enter my attached drawing in your November drawing contest. (PLEASE PRINT)
Name Age
Address Phone
City Zone County
State Occupation
Amateurs Only!
Our students not eligible. Make copy of girl 5 ins. high. Pencil or pen only. Omit lettering. All drawings must be received by Nov. 30, 1950. None returned. Winners notified.
Latest Winner List! Free course winners in previous contest—from list just released: F. Roland, Box 917, Monroe, N. Y.; L. Wise, 204 Watts, Portsmouth, Va.; S. Frey, 19974 Negaunee, Detroit, Mich.; E. Sitarek, 34 Cummings, Irvington, N. J.; B. Abramowski, 3141 33rd, Astoria, L. I., N. Y.
Art Instruction, Inc.
MINNEAPOLIS • NEW YORK • CHICAGO
MEMBER NATIONAL HOME STUDY COUNCIL
DON'T WORK HARD SCRAPING

HERE ARE THE **ARTISTS** WHO WILL INSTRUCT YOU:

This drawing, from 1950, looks worthy of *The New Yorker*, but Schulz didn't think so—he never submitted any of his work to the venerable weekly, "because it was hopeless."

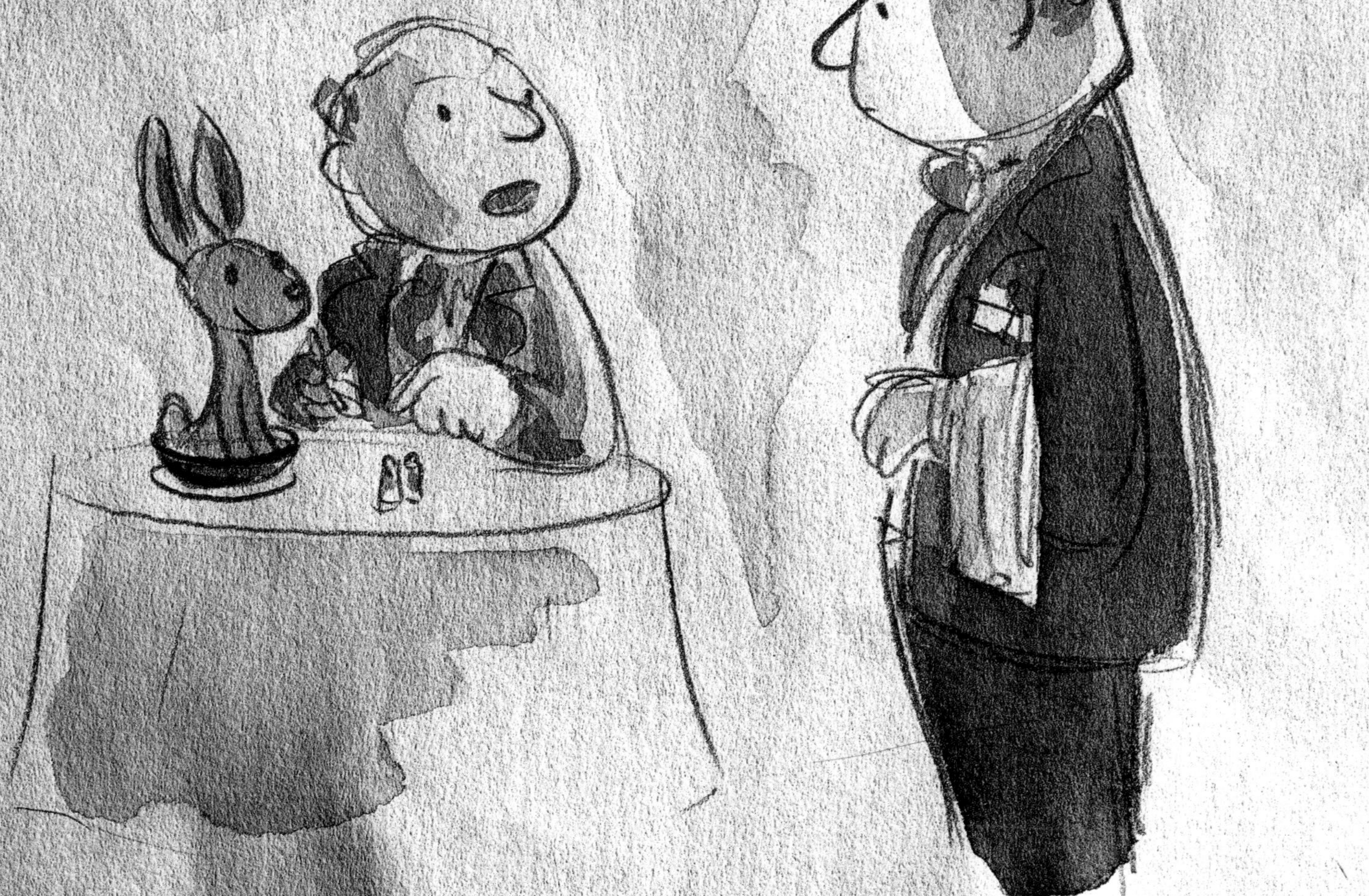

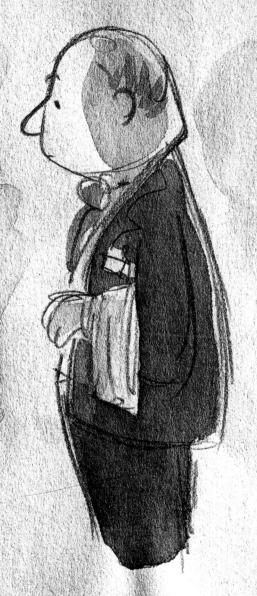

" Waiter, there's a hare in this soup ! "

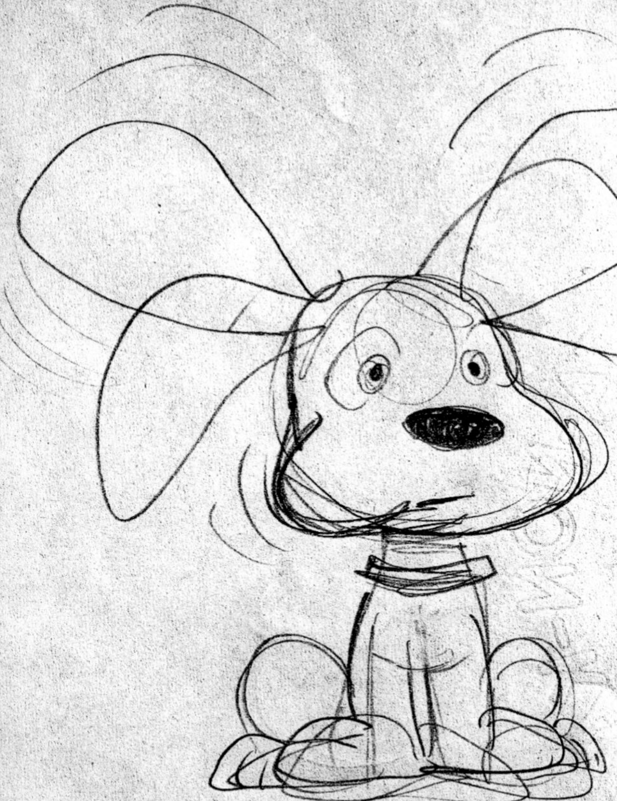

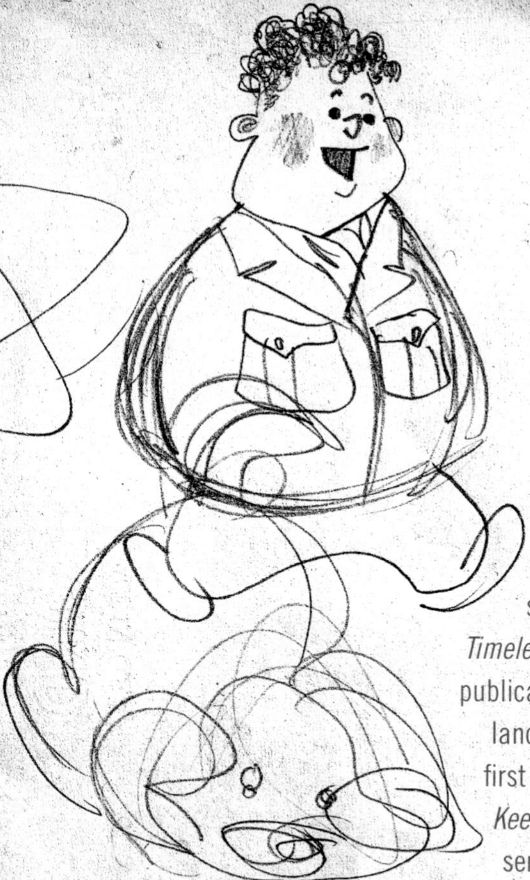

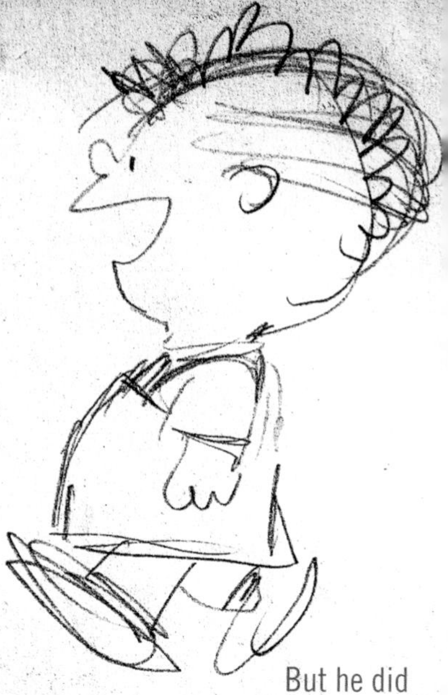

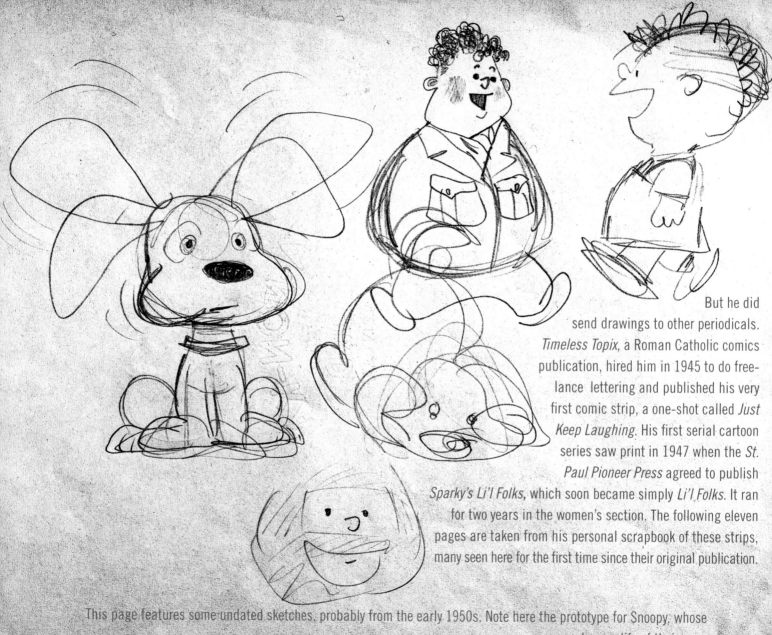

But he did send drawings to other periodicals. *Timeless Topix*, a Roman Catholic comics publication, hired him in 1945 to do free-lance lettering and published his very first comic strip, a one-shot called *Just Keep Laughing*. His first serial cartoon series saw print in 1947 when the *St. Paul Pioneer Press* agreed to publish *Sparky's Li'l Folks*, which soon became simply *Li'l Folks*. It ran for two years in the women's section. The following eleven pages are taken from his personal scrapbook of these strips, many seen here for the first time since their original publication.

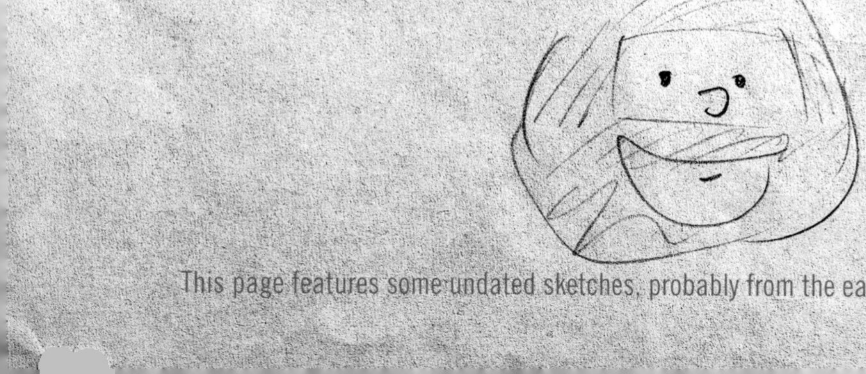

This page features some undated sketches, probably from the early 1950s. Note here the prototype for Snoopy, whose ears have a life of their own.

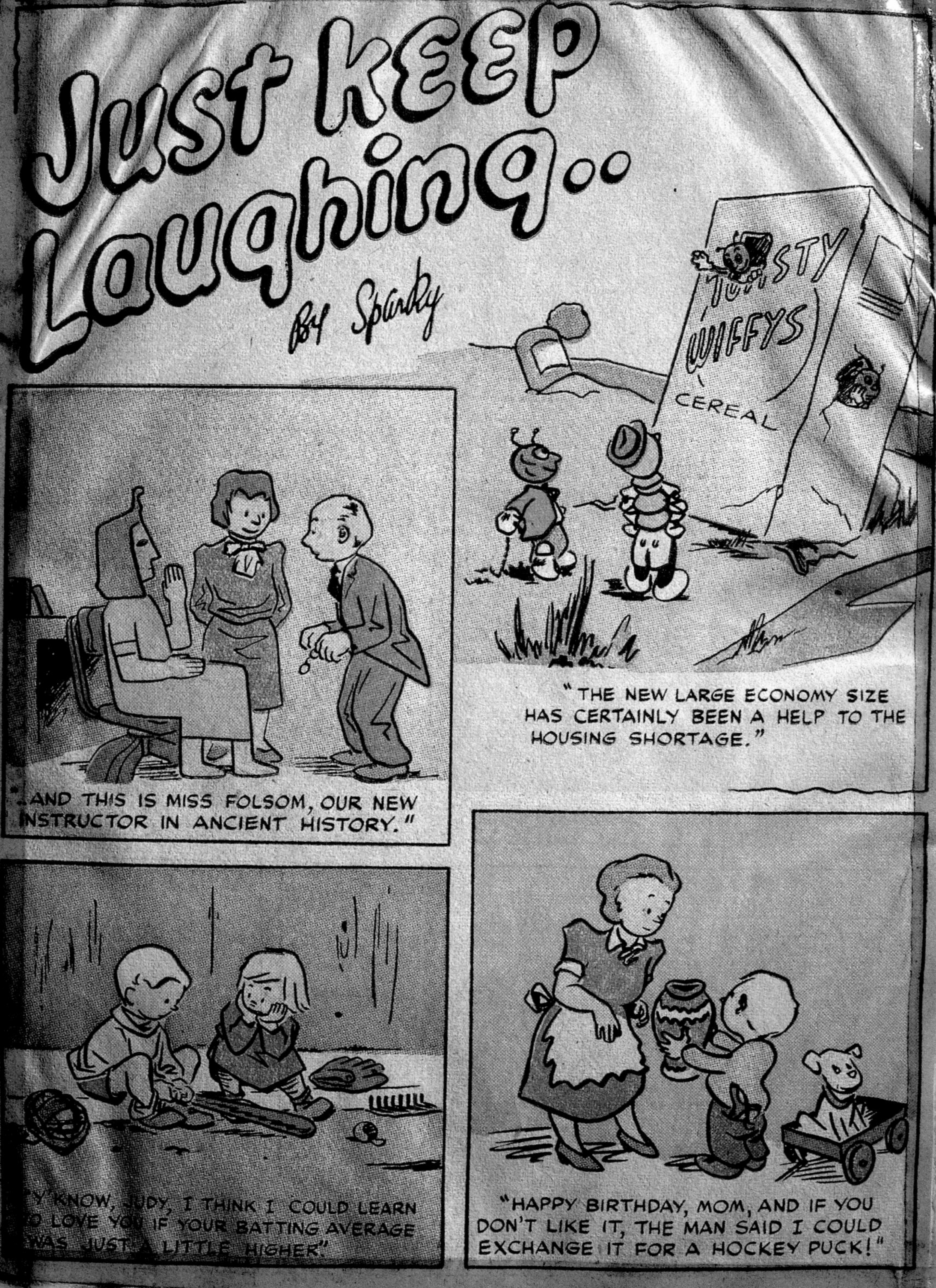
Just KEEP Laughing..
By Sparky
TOASTY WIFFYS CEREAL
"THE NEW LARGE ECONOMY SIZE HAS CERTAINLY BEEN A HELP TO THE HOUSING SHORTAGE."
"...AND THIS IS MISS FOLSOM, OUR NEW INSTRUCTOR IN ANCIENT HISTORY."
"Y'KNOW, JUDY, I THINK I COULD LEARN TO LOVE YOU IF YOUR BATTING AVERAGE WAS JUST A LITTLE HIGHER."
"HAPPY BIRTHDAY, MOM, AND IF YOU DON'T LIKE IT, THE MAN SAID I COULD EXCHANGE IT FOR A HOCKEY PUCK!"

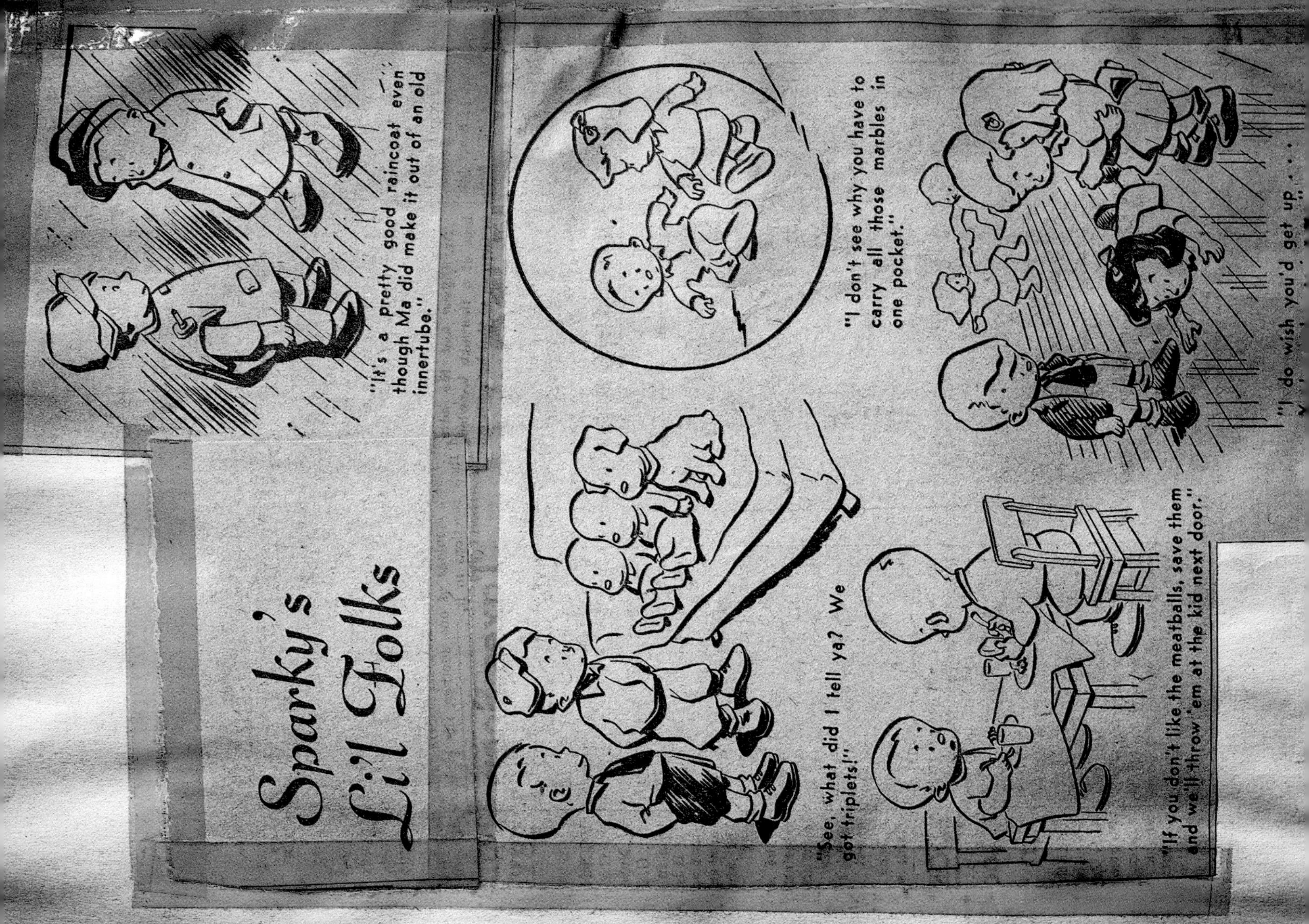

Sparky's Li'l Folks
"It's a pretty good raincoat even though Ma did make it out of an old innertube."
"See, what did I tell ya? We got triplets!"
"I don't see why you have to carry all those marbles in one pocket."
"I do wish you'd get up . . ."
"If you don't like the meatballs, save them and we'll throw 'em at the kid next door."

Top right: Children feeling the emotions normally attributed to adults started in *Li'l Folks* and became a staple of Schulz's work throughout his career.

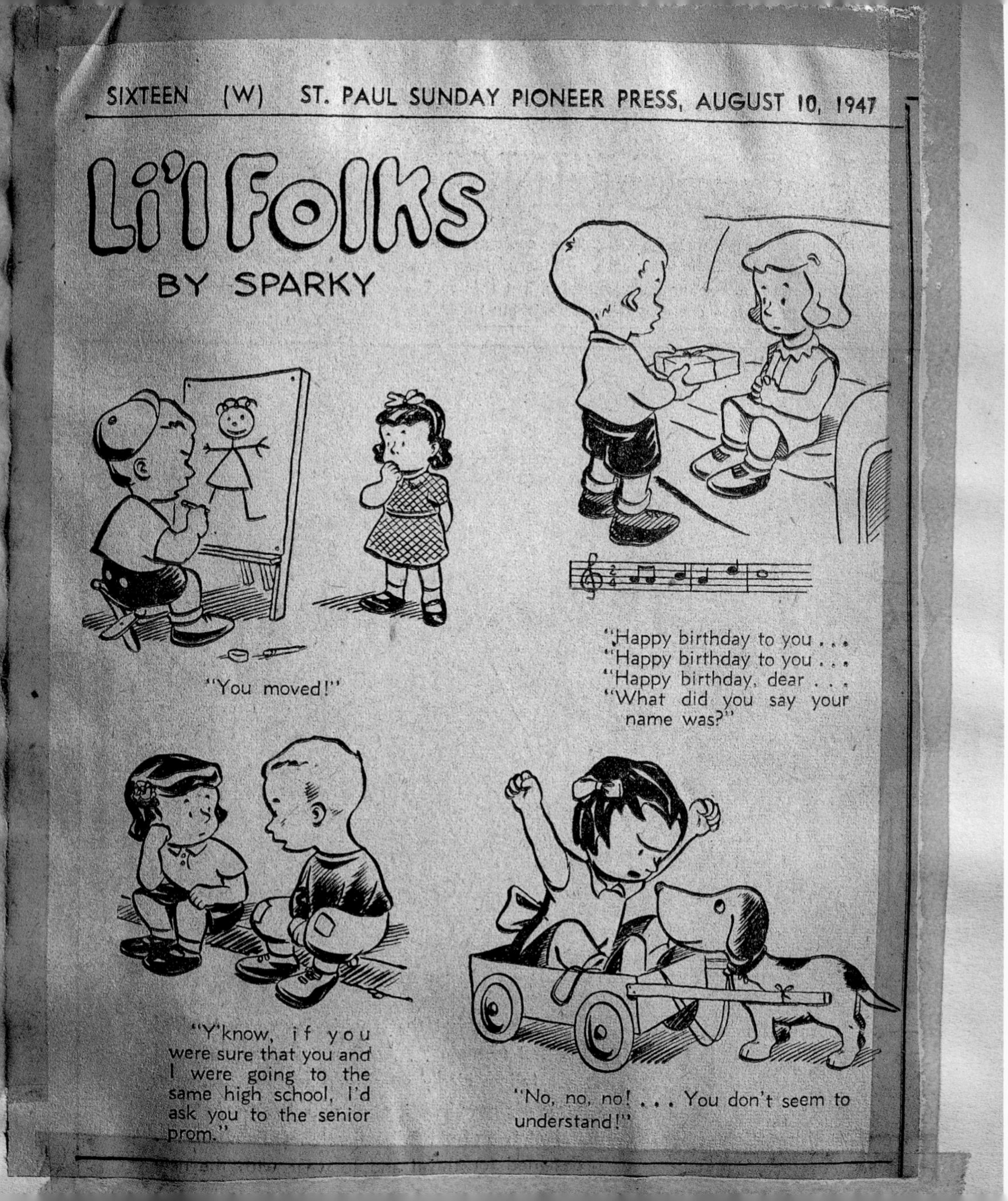
SIXTEEN (W) ST. PAUL SUNDAY PIONEER PRESS, AUGUST 10, 1947
Li'l Folks
BY SPARKY
"You moved!"
"Happy birthday to you . . .
"Happy birthday to you . . .
"Happy birthday, dear . . .
"What did you say your name was?"
"Y'know, if you were sure that you and I were going to the same high school, I'd ask you to the senior prom."
"No, no, no! . . . You don't seem to understand!"

It's not Beethoven, but it was a sign of things to come.

The "dog as rebel" theme appeared as early as 1947.

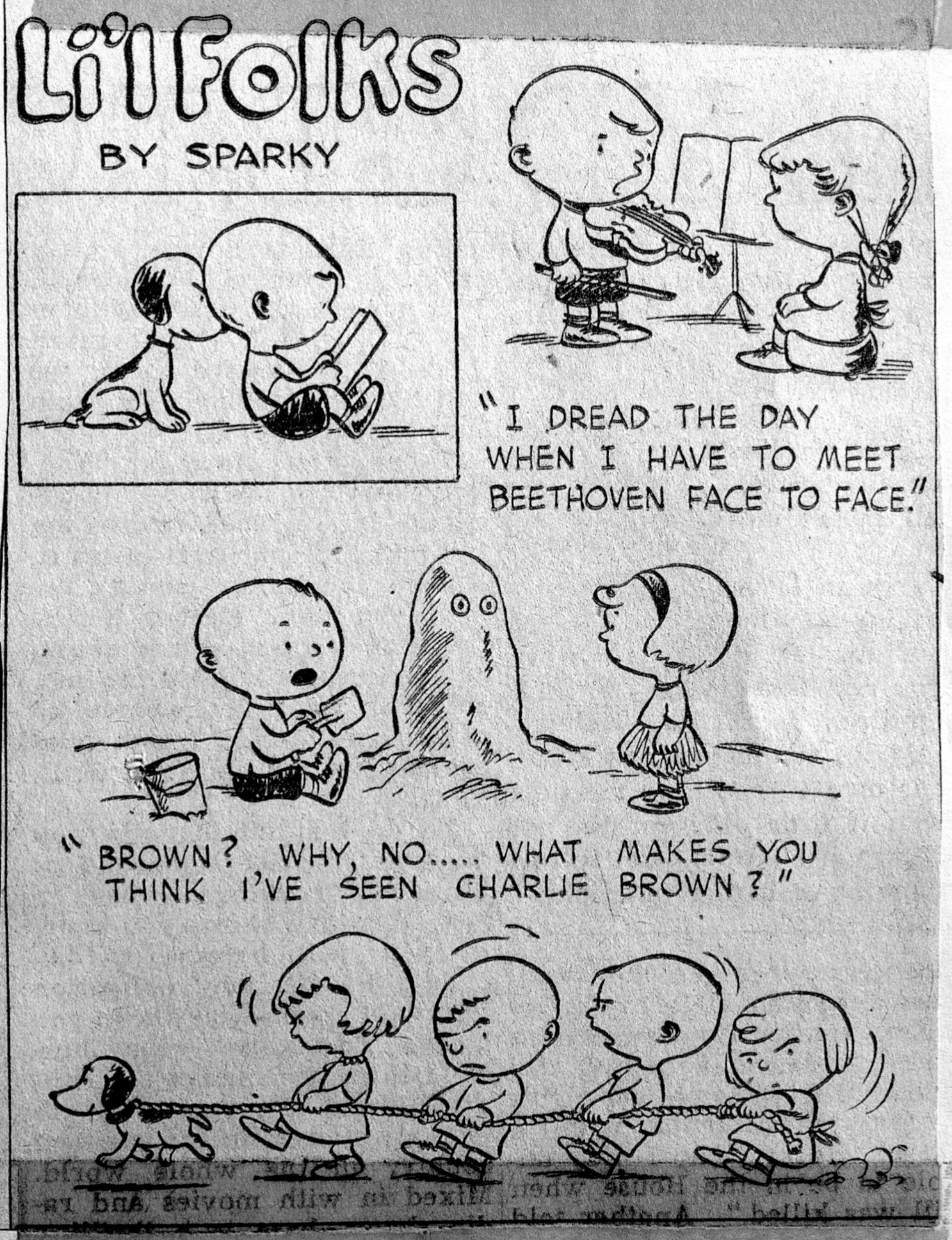
Li'l Folks
BY SPARKY
"I DREAD THE DAY WHEN I HAVE TO MEET BEETHOVEN FACE TO FACE."
"BROWN? WHY, NO..... WHAT MAKES YOU THINK I'VE SEEN CHARLIE BROWN?"

The seeds of *Peanuts* are planted all over this cartoon from 1948, as Charlie Brown sees print for the first time (buried in sand), a very Snoopy-like pup is a head-rest and head-starter, and Beethoven makes a cameo during Schroeder's pre-piano phase.

Our cap-clutching li'l friend uses a line that Schroeder will paraphrase more than a decade later (note the typo), when he describes his feelings about Lucy.

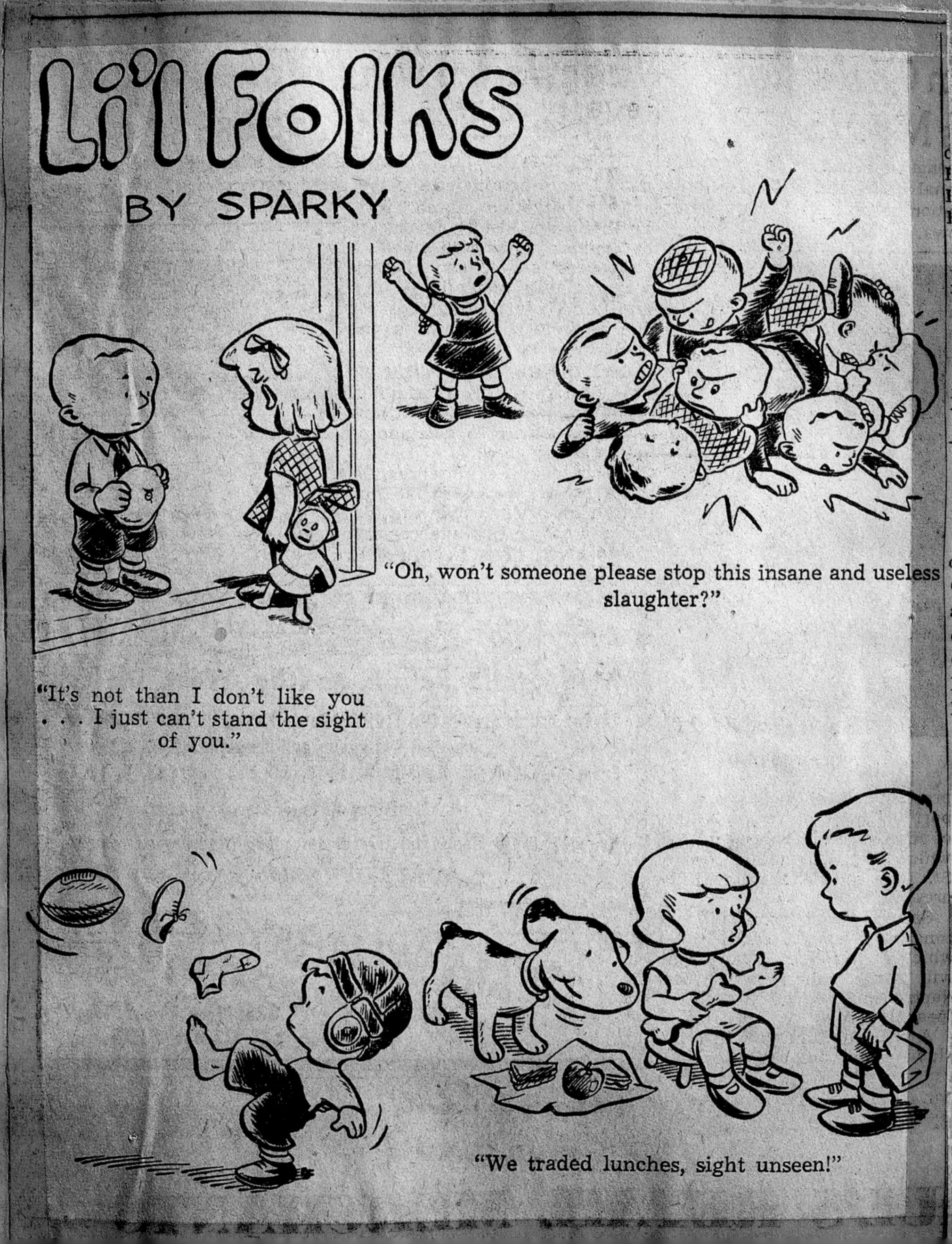
Li'l Folks
BY SPARKY
"It's not than I don't like you . . . I just can't stand the sight of you."
"Oh, won't someone please stop this insane and useless slaughter?"
"We traded lunches, sight unseen!"

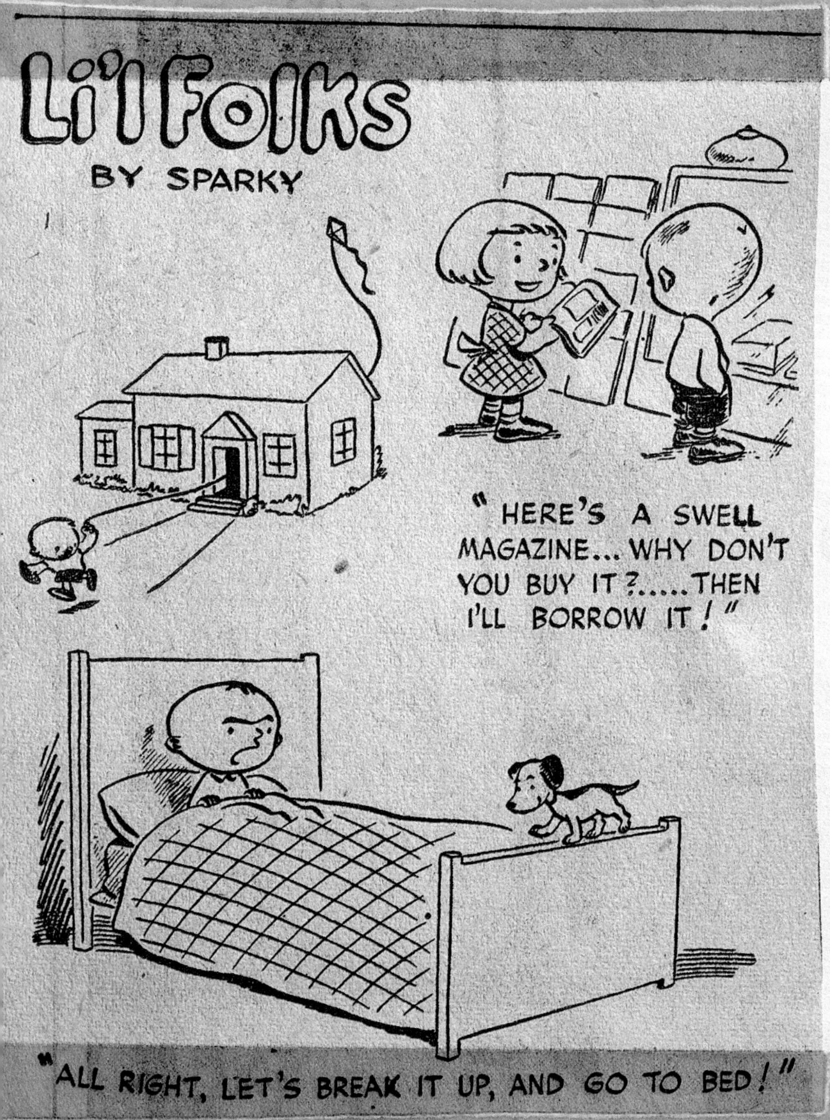
Li'l Folks
BY SPARKY
" HERE'S A SWELL MAGAZINE... WHY DON'T YOU BUY IT?.....THEN I'LL BORROW IT!"
"ALL RIGHT, LET'S BREAK IT UP, AND GO TO BED!"

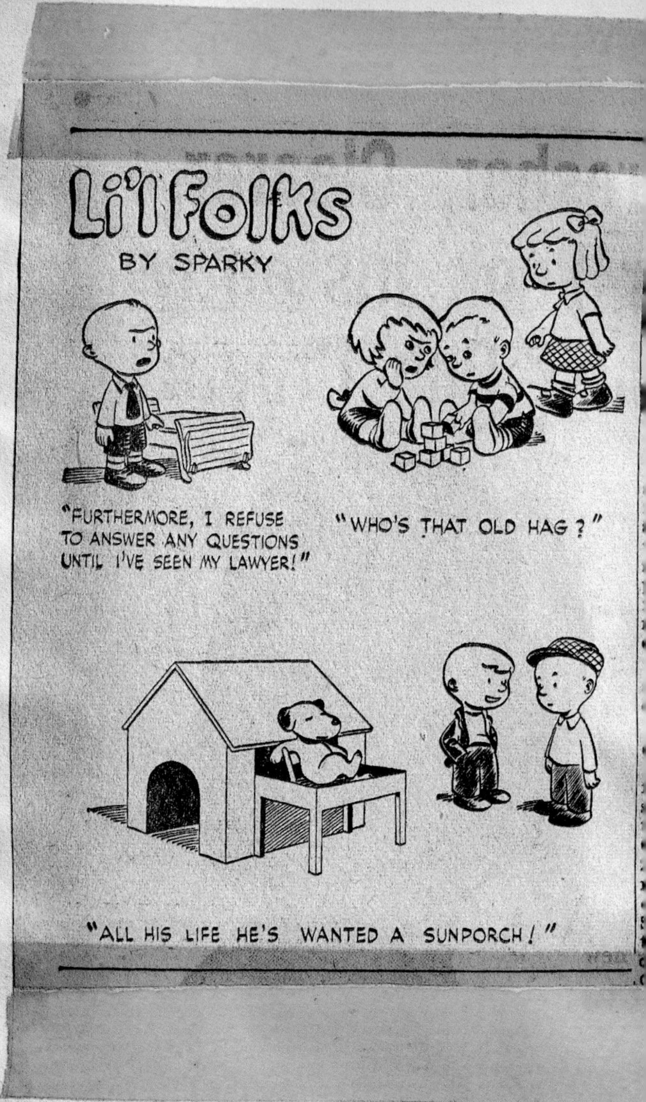
Li'l Folks
BY SPARKY
"FURTHERMORE, I REFUSE TO ANSWER ANY QUESTIONS UNTIL I'VE SEEN MY LAWYER!"
"WHO'S THAT OLD HAG?"
"ALL HIS LIFE HE'S WANTED A SUNPORCH!"

The playful use of scale in *Li'l Folks* puts small children into a world that's often too big or too small for them, an idea that would be continued in *Peanuts*—first physically and then emotionally.

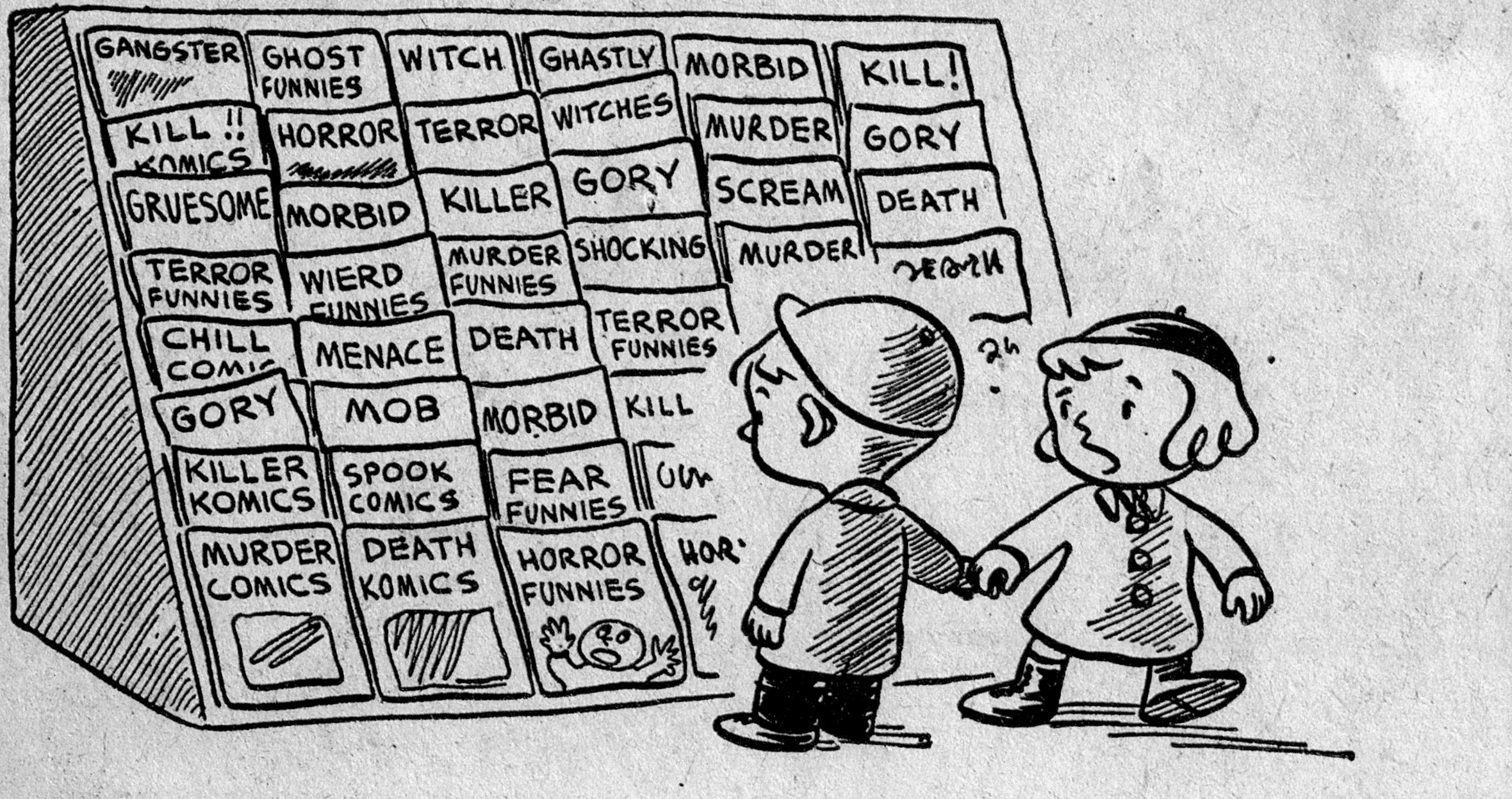
GANGSTER
GHOST FUNNIES
WITCH
GHASTLY
MORBID
KILL!
KILL !! KOMICS
HORROR
TERROR
WITCHES
MURDER
GORY
GRUESOME
MORBID
KILLER
GORY
SCREAM
DEATH
TERROR FUNNIES
WIERD FUNNIES
MURDER FUNNIES
SHOCKING
MURDER
CHILL
MENACE
DEATH
TERROR FUNNIES
GORY
MOB
MORBID
KILL
KILLER KOMICS
SPOOK COMICS
FEAR FUNNIES
MURDER COMICS
DEATH KOMICS
HORROR FUNNIES

"LET'S GET OUT OF HERE...THIS GIVES ME THE CHILLS!"

This gag, from the late 1940s, seems eerily to predict the government's impending crackdown in the mid-1950s on comic books deemed "too intense" for young children. Though the titles Schulz chose seem gratuitous, they're remarkably similar to what was being published at the time.

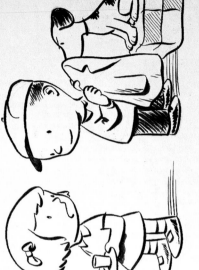

Li'l Folks
BY SPARKY

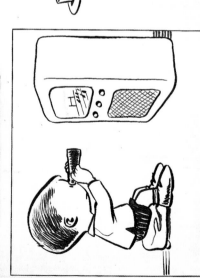

"JUST HANG YOUR COAT ANYWHERE, AND MAKE YOURSELF TO HOME."

"TRY TO BE MORE PATIENT...WEINERS DON'T ROAST IN A SECOND, YOU KNOW!"

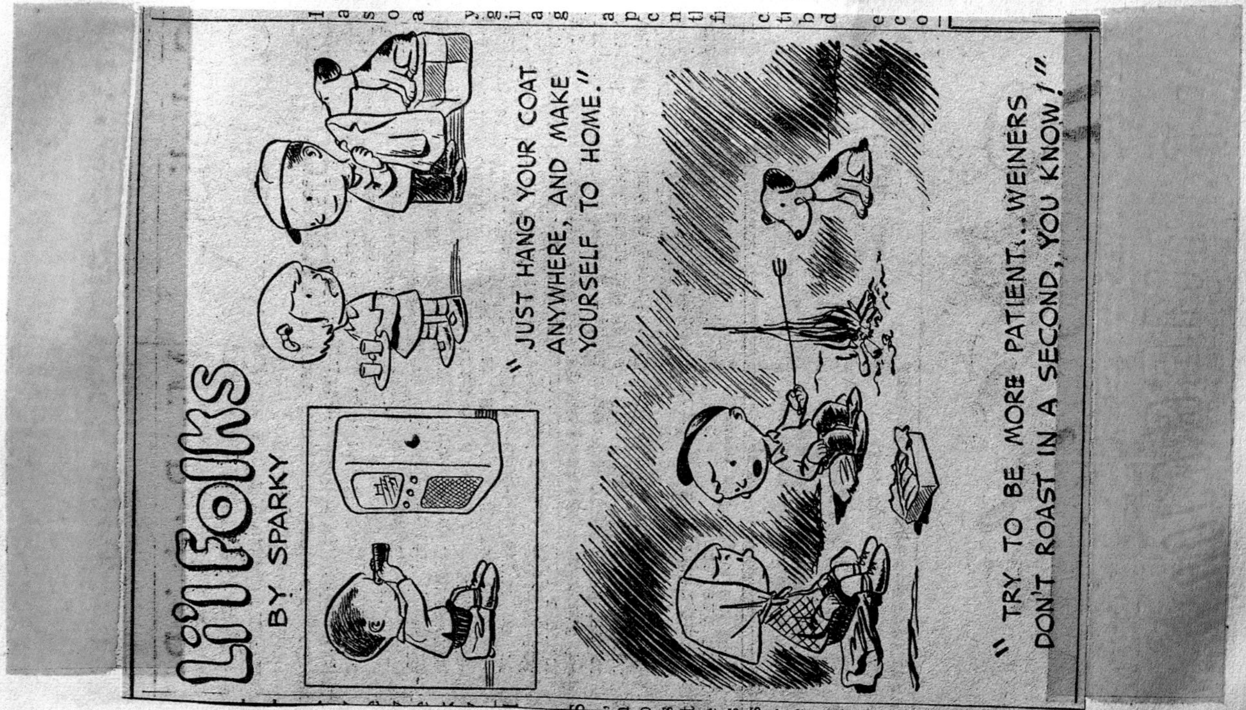
Li'l Folks
BY SPARKY
"JUST HANG YOUR COAT ANYWHERE, AND MAKE YOURSELF TO HOME."
"TRY TO BE MORE PATIENT... WEINERS DON'T ROAST IN A SECOND, YOU KNOW!"

At left is the original art for the strip above, from the late 1940s. Schulz was ever mindful of the loss of line quality that a drawing suffered on its way to newsprint, and his minimal, simplified style was easily able to withstand a possible increase in line thickness in the final printed version.

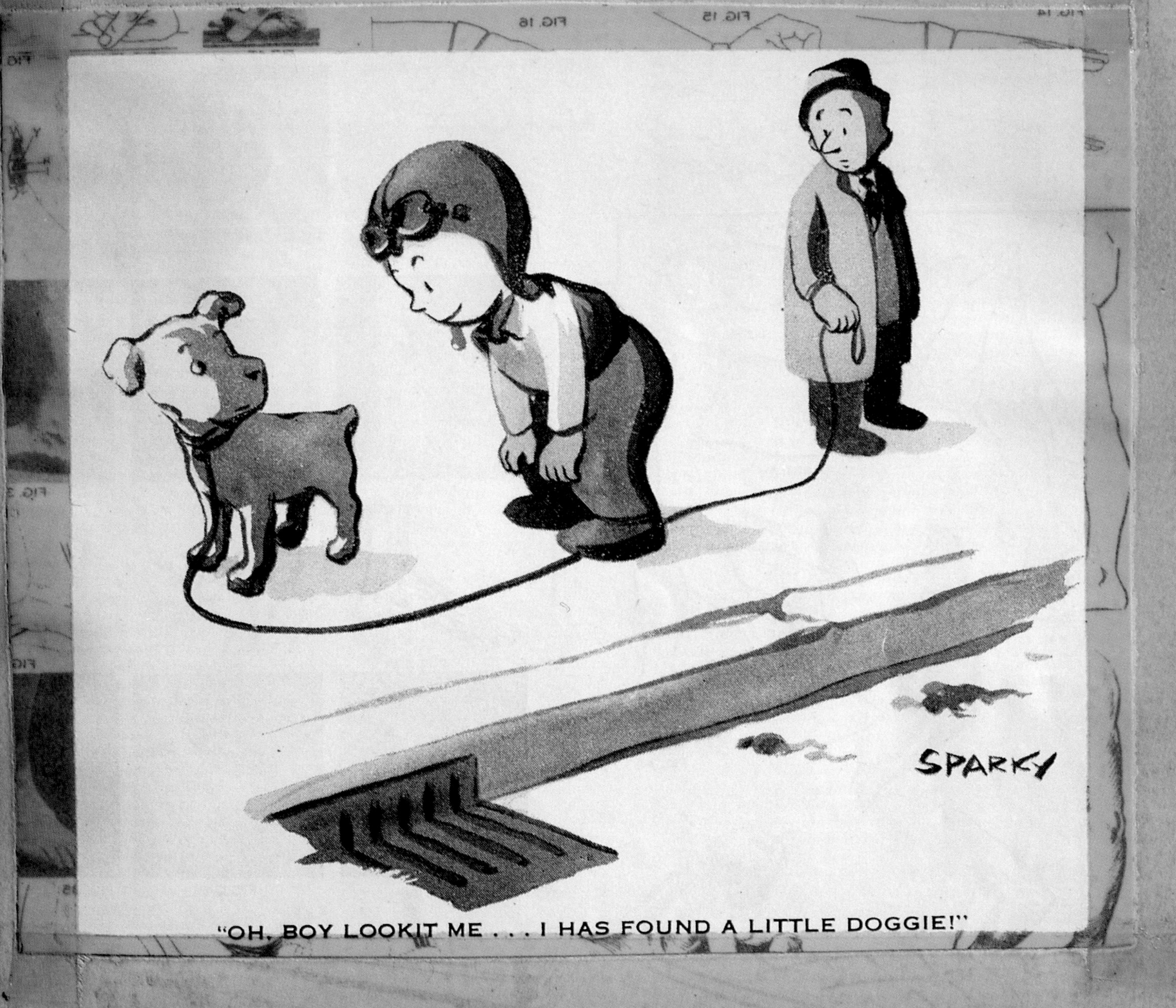
SPARKY

"OH, BOY LOOKIT ME . . . I HAS FOUND A LITTLE DOGGIE!"

In May of 1948, Schulz got his first big break.

"Although I realized it was against all rules of professionalism, I sent a finished drawing to *The Saturday Evening Post.* [Submissions to such magazines were usually done in rough form and sent in batches of ten to fifteen.] Several days later I received a note in the mail that said 'Check Tuesday for spot drawing of boy on lounge.' I was so used to having my work rejected I thought the note meant that I should check my mailbox on Tuesday, that they were going to send the drawing back. A couple of hours later I figured it out and, of course, was ecstatic. This was my first sale to a major market."

Between 1948 and 1950, he eventually sold seventeen cartoons to editor John Bailey. He was paid forty dollars apiece.

"I tried all sorts of different things, and could never sell anything, and it was the breakthrough to *The Saturday Evening Post* with the style, then, that I was working on . . . Little kids with great big heads saying things that were a little bit out of context."

At right is an idea that would eventually be "recycled" into a future *Peanuts* strip.

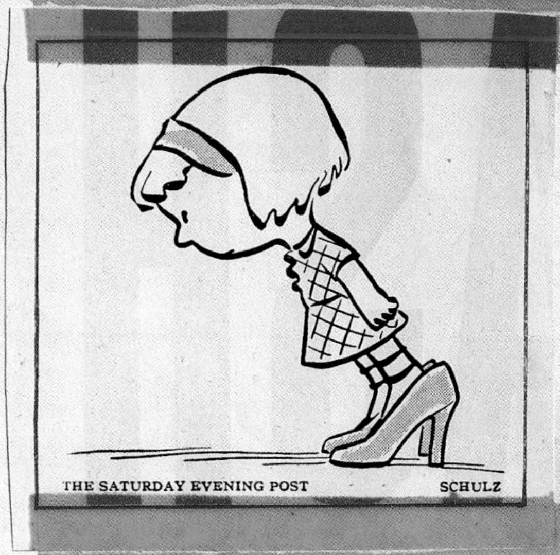
THE SATURDAY EVENING POST
SCHULZ

GUIDE TO STRIPS IN
THE SATURDAY EVENING POST
BY CHARLES SCHULZ

MAY 29, 1948—PAGE 116
JULY 17, 1948—PAGE 42
SEPTEMBER 25, 1948—PAGE 152
NOVEMBER 6, 1948—PAGE 91
NOVEMBER 13, 1948— PAGE 179
JANUARY 1, 1949—PAGE 60
FEBRUARY 19, 1949—PAGE 119
MAY 21, 1949—PAGE 72
MAY 21, 1949—PAGE 166
JULY 16, 1949—PAGE 114
NOVEMBER 19, 1949—PAGE 132
FEBRUARY 11, 1950—PAGE 45
FEBRUARY 18, 1950—PAGE 129
APRIL 19, 1950—PAGE 140
APRIL 29, 1950—PAGE 87
MAY 6, 1950—PAGE 79
JULY 8, 1950—PAGE 54

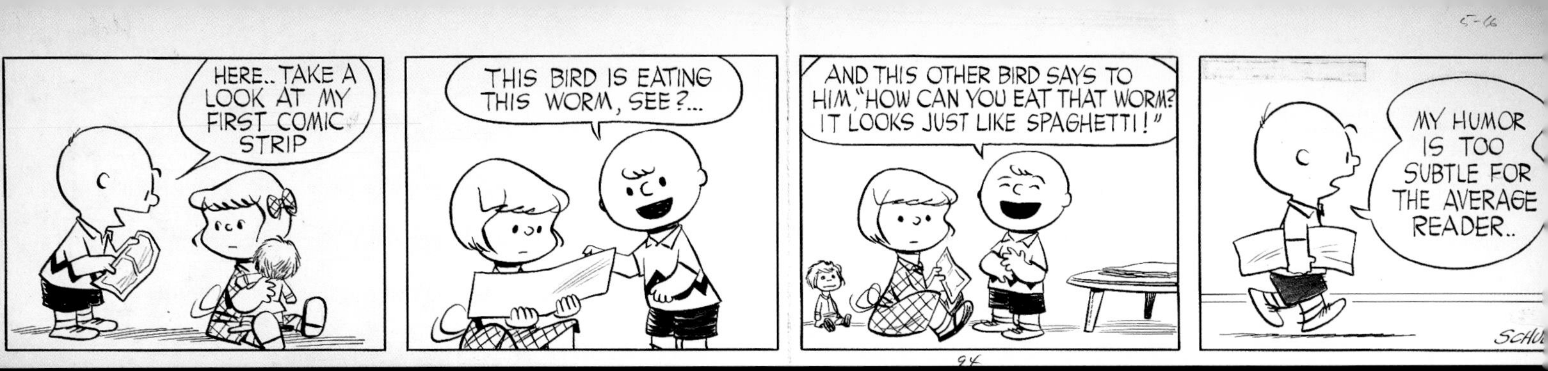
HERE.. TAKE A LOOK AT MY FIRST COMIC STRIP
THIS BIRD IS EATING THIS WORM, SEE?...
AND THIS OTHER BIRD SAYS TO HIM, "HOW CAN YOU EAT THAT WORM? IT LOOKS JUST LIKE SPAGHETTI!"
MY HUMOR IS TOO SUBTLE FOR THE AVERAGE READER..

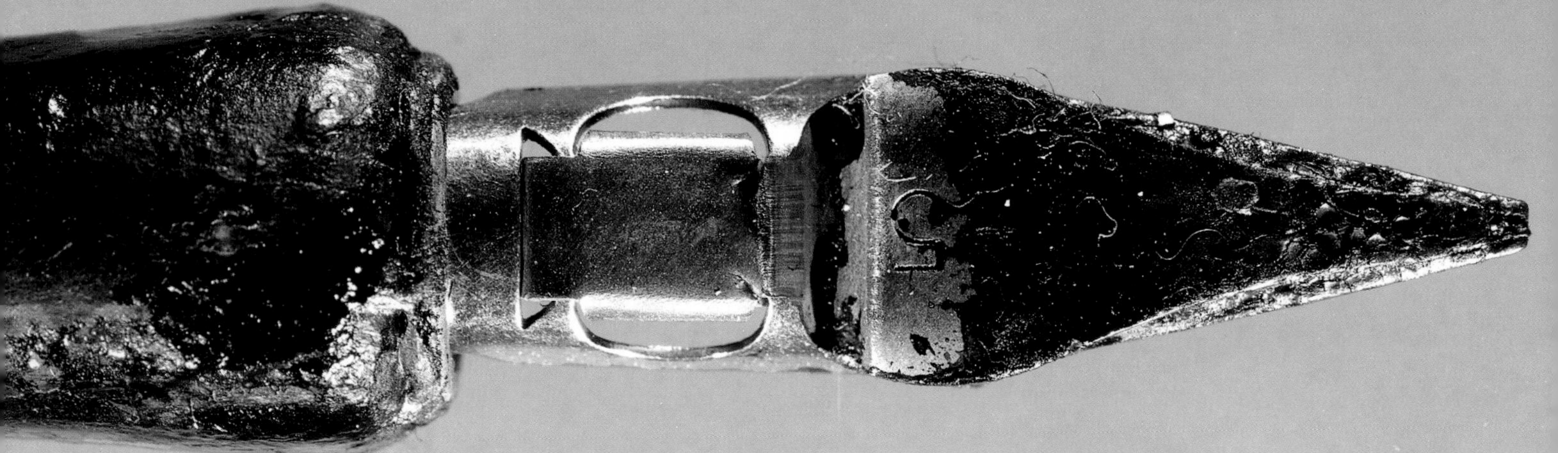

Schulz would use a yellow legal pad to script and rough the strip. He'd then do the lettering first, before the art, inking it in with this C-5 pen tip. Once he was satisfied with the text, then he'd draw the finished art.

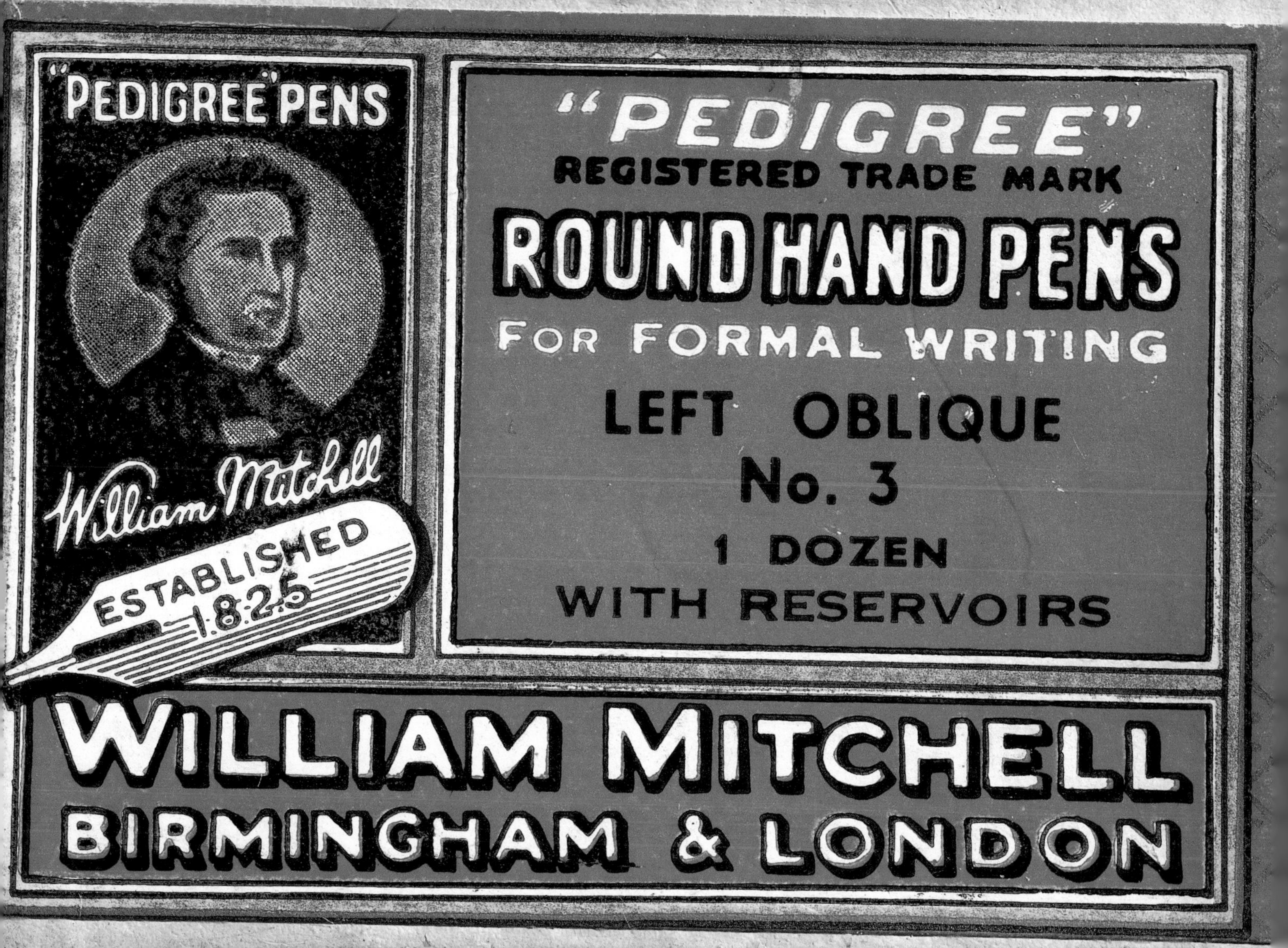
"PEDIGREE" PENS
William Mitchell
ESTABLISHED 1825
"PEDIGREE"
REGISTERED TRADE MARK
ROUND HAND PENS
FOR FORMAL WRITING
LEFT OBLIQUE
No. 3
1 DOZEN
WITH RESERVOIRS
WILLIAM MITCHELL
BIRMINGHAM & LONDON

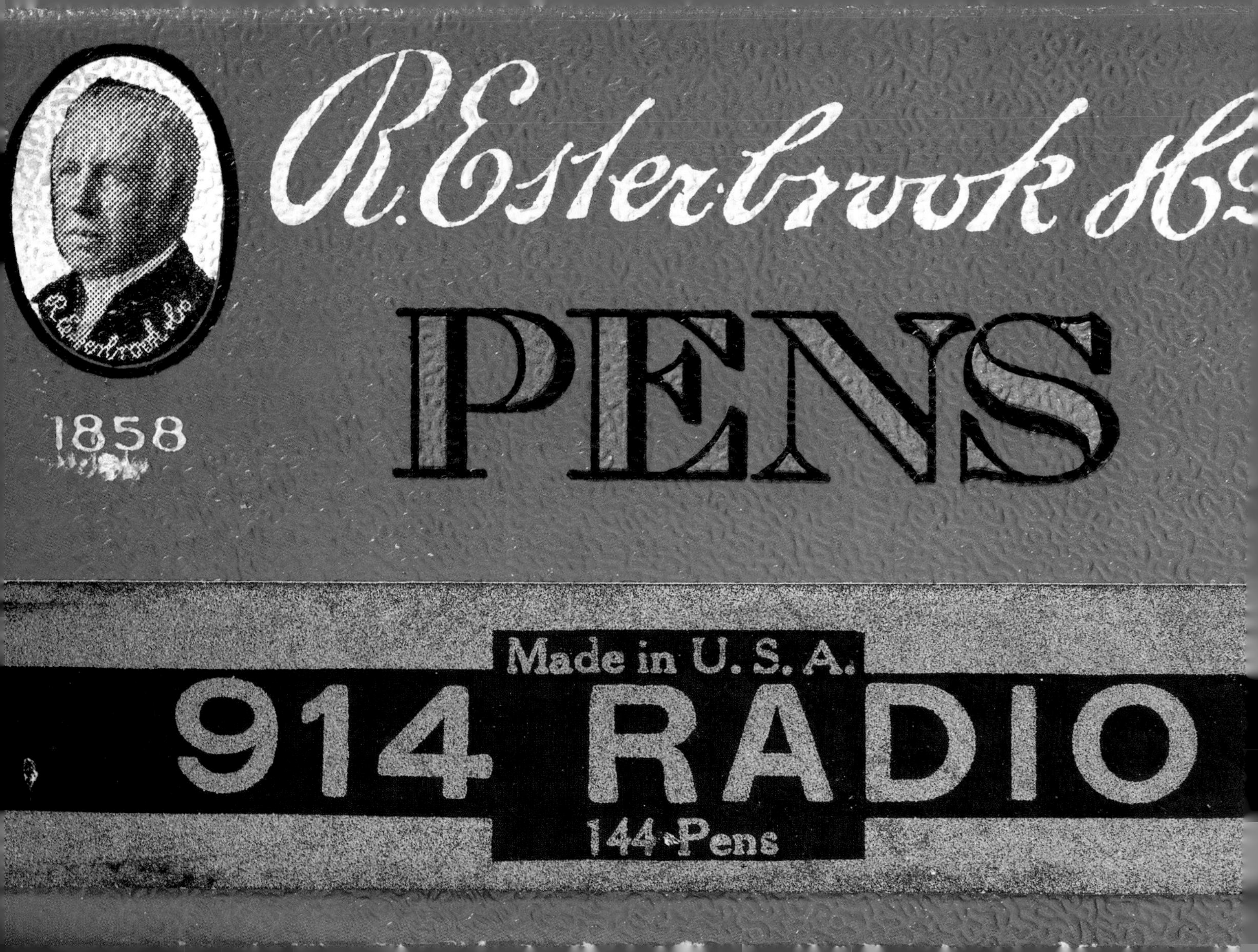

R. Esterbrook & Co
1858
PENS
Made in U.S.A.
914 RADIO
144 Pens

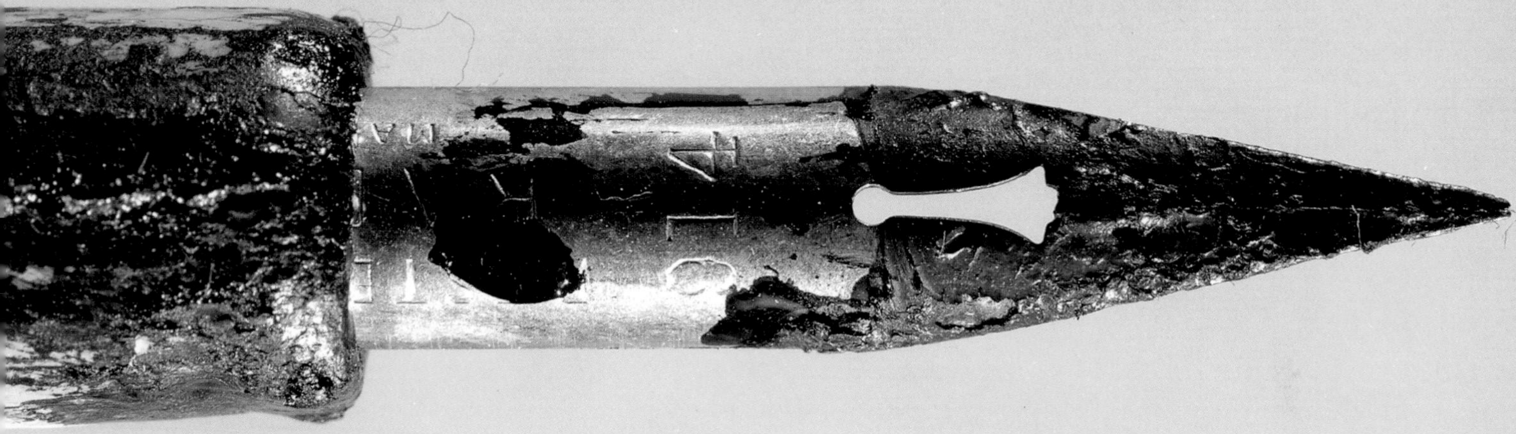

He didn't pencil everything in first, as most cartoonists do. "I pencil as little as possible," Schulz said in 1997. "Just enough to get the heights and the space right. But I draw the faces with the pen when I'm doing it. Because you want that spontaneity, you don't want to be just following the pencil line."

He used a 914 Radio, and relied on these pen nibs so much that when the company announced it was going out of business, he bought the entire remaining stock. The hundreds of boxes saw him through the rest of his career.

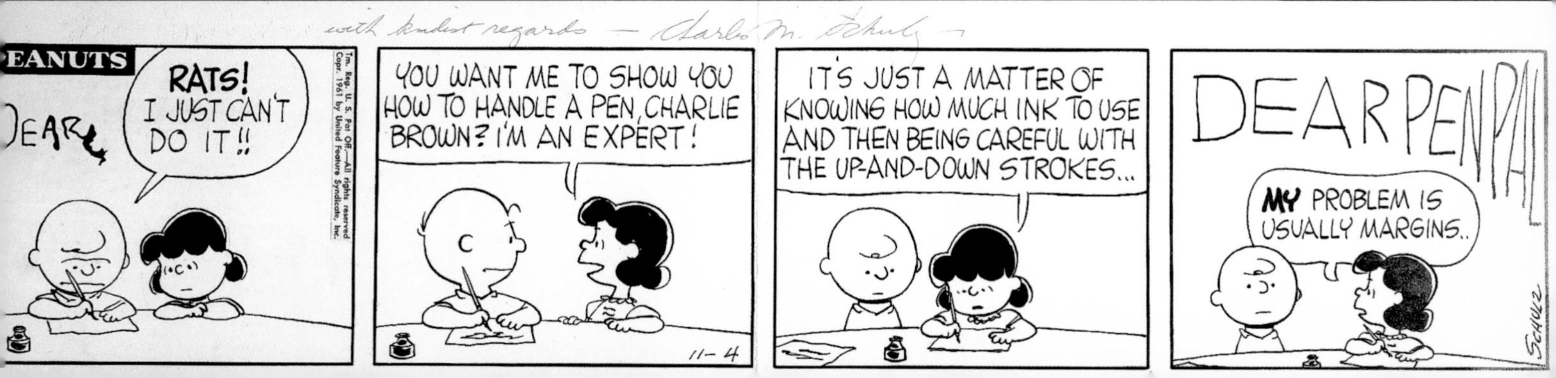
with kindest regards — Charles M. Schulz
PEANUTS
DEAR
RATS! I JUST CAN'T DO IT!!
Tm. Reg. U. S. Pat. Off.—All rights reserved
Copr. 1961 by United Feature Syndicate, Inc.
YOU WANT ME TO SHOW YOU HOW TO HANDLE A PEN, CHARLIE BROWN? I'M AN EXPERT!
11-4
IT'S JUST A MATTER OF KNOWING HOW MUCH INK TO USE AND THEN BEING CAREFUL WITH THE UP-AND-DOWN STROKES...
DEAR PEN PAL
MY PROBLEM IS USUALLY MARGINS..
SCHULZ

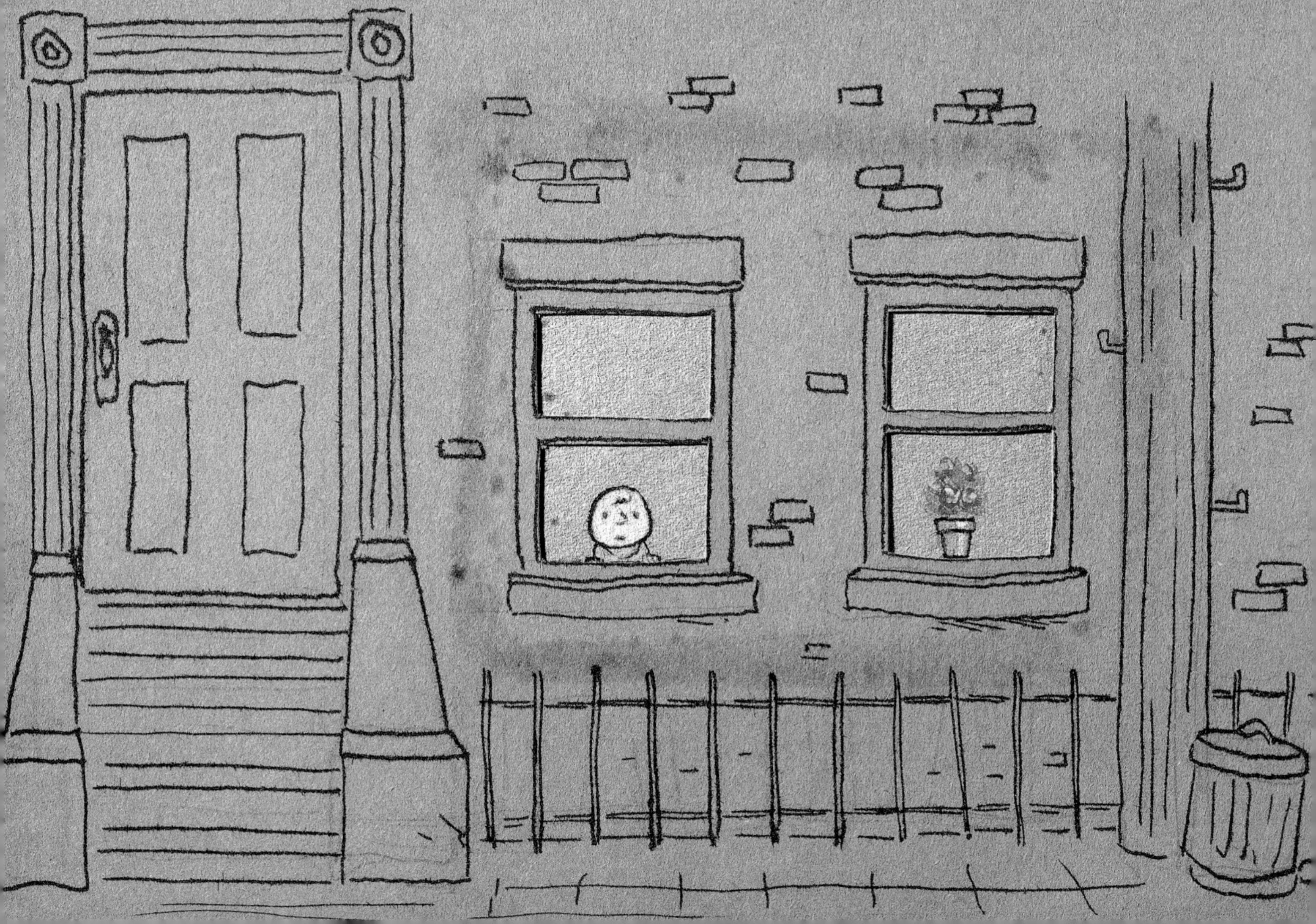

This two-layer drawing, on construction paper, was done in 1950 as part of a proposal for a magazine to be called *Divertimento*, organized by Schulz's friend from Art Instruction Bill Ryan. The project never left this developmental stage.

The top orange layer has die-cut windows, behind which sits a pre-Charlie Brown round-headed figure. When the page was turned, it revealed the image below with its visual "trick" of the flowers as paintings.

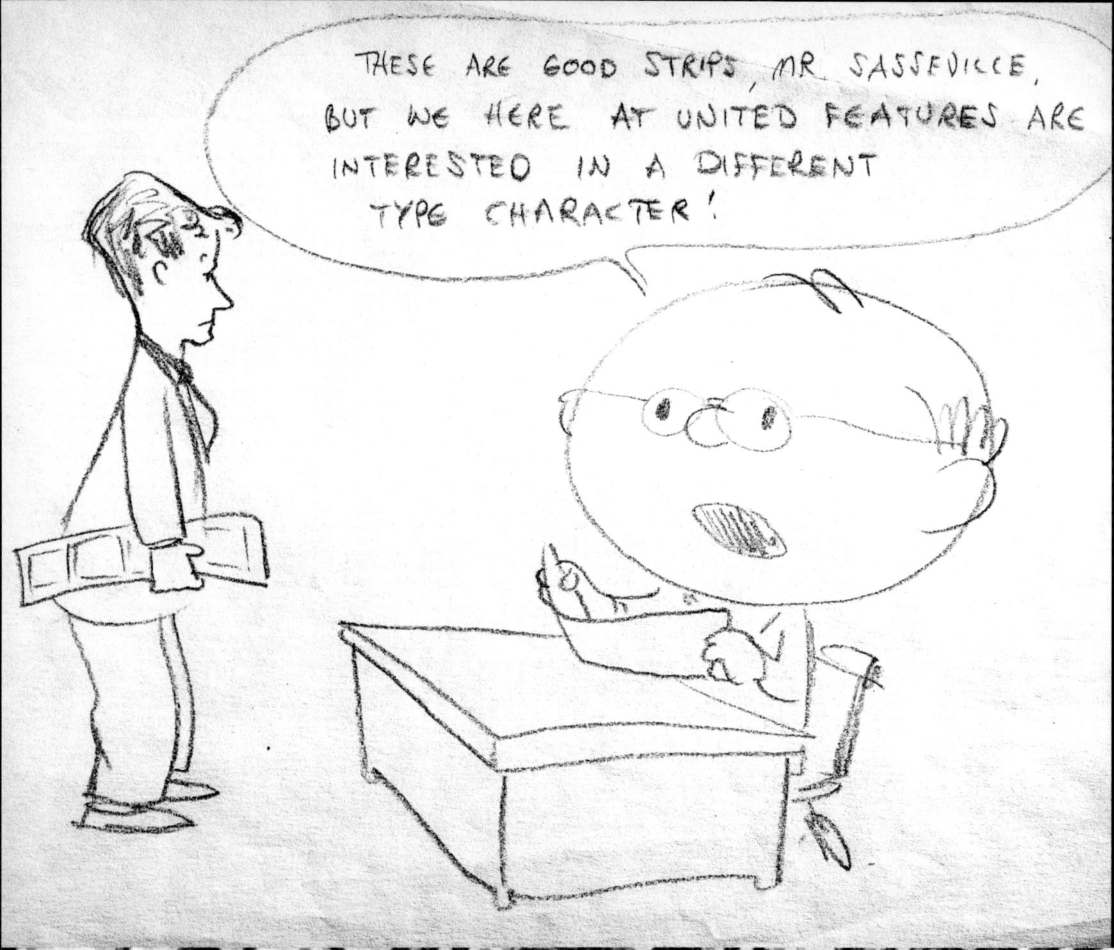
THESE ARE GOOD STRIPS, MR. SASSEVILLE, BUT WE HERE AT UNITED FEATURES ARE INTERESTED IN A DIFFERENT TYPE CHARACTER!

In the spring of 1950, Schulz collected his best strips from *The Saturday Evening Post* and *The St. Paul Pioneer Press* and sent them to United Feature Syndicate in New York City. After more than six weeks with no response, he wrote them asking if his package had been lost.

Soon after, he received a letter saying not only had they gotten the package, but they wanted him to come to Manhattan and meet about publication. He did, and on October 2, 1950 ***Peanuts*** was born.

It's no secret he wasn't fond of the name, thrust upon him by United Feature. He wanted to call it 'Good Ol' Charlie Brown,' but the syndicate was wary of focusing attention on just one character and wanted something that suggested a whole 'cast.' Sparky was so thrilled to be syndicated he accepted their mandate.

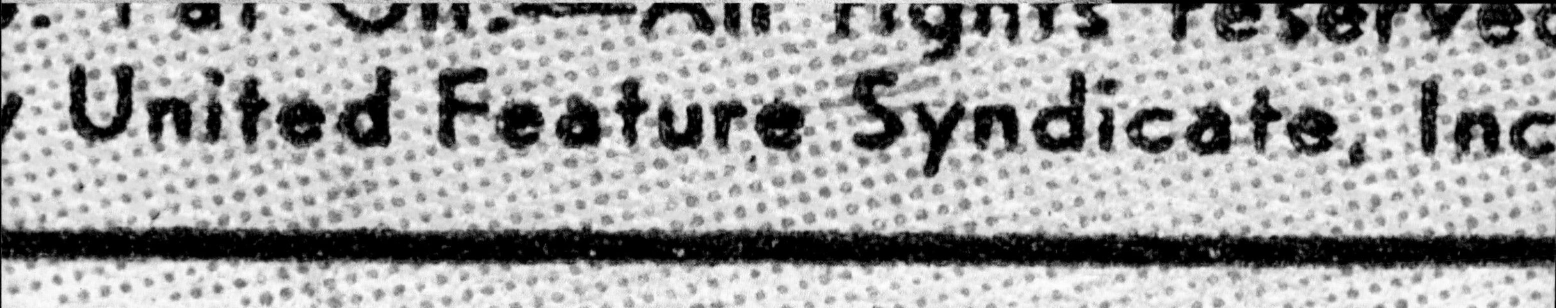
United Feature Syndicate, Inc

Above: This gag (probably from 1950) refers to Sparky's friend from Art Instruction Jim Sasseville, and is a goof on the shape of Charlie Brown's head. Sasseville's style was more representational.

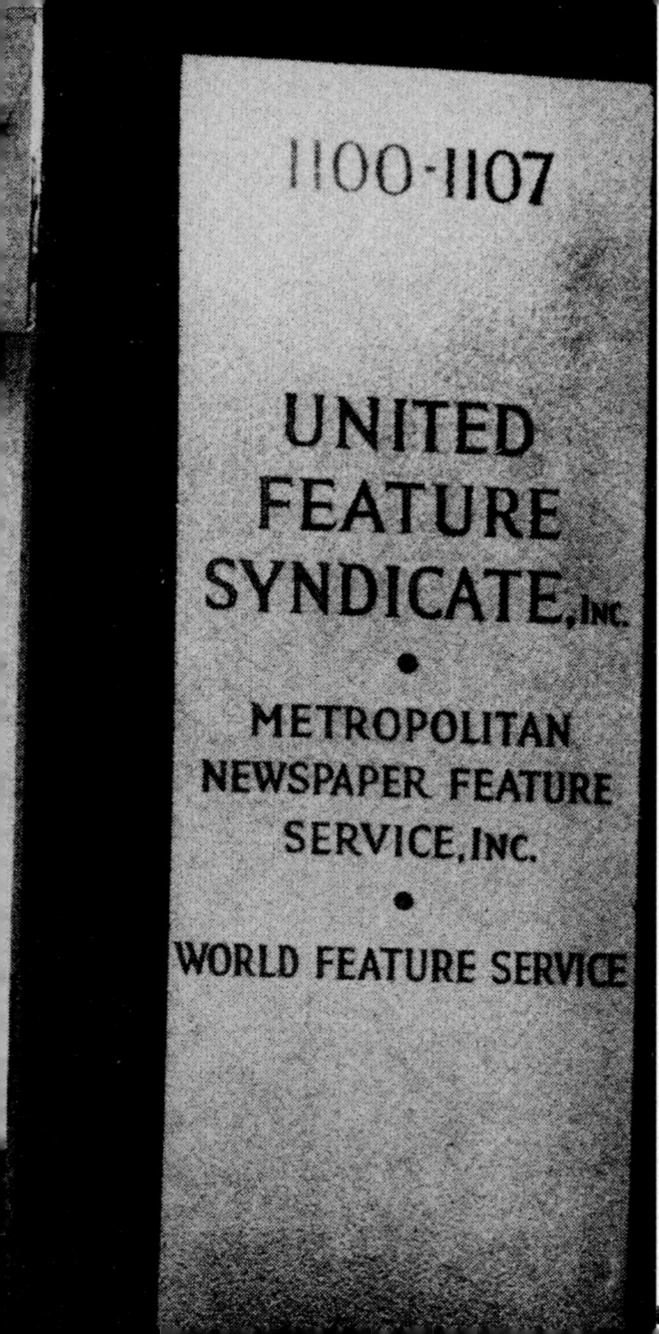
1100-1107
UNITED
FEATURE
SYNDICATE, INC.
METROPOLITAN
NEWSPAPER FEATURE
SERVICE, INC.
WORLD FEATURE SERVICE

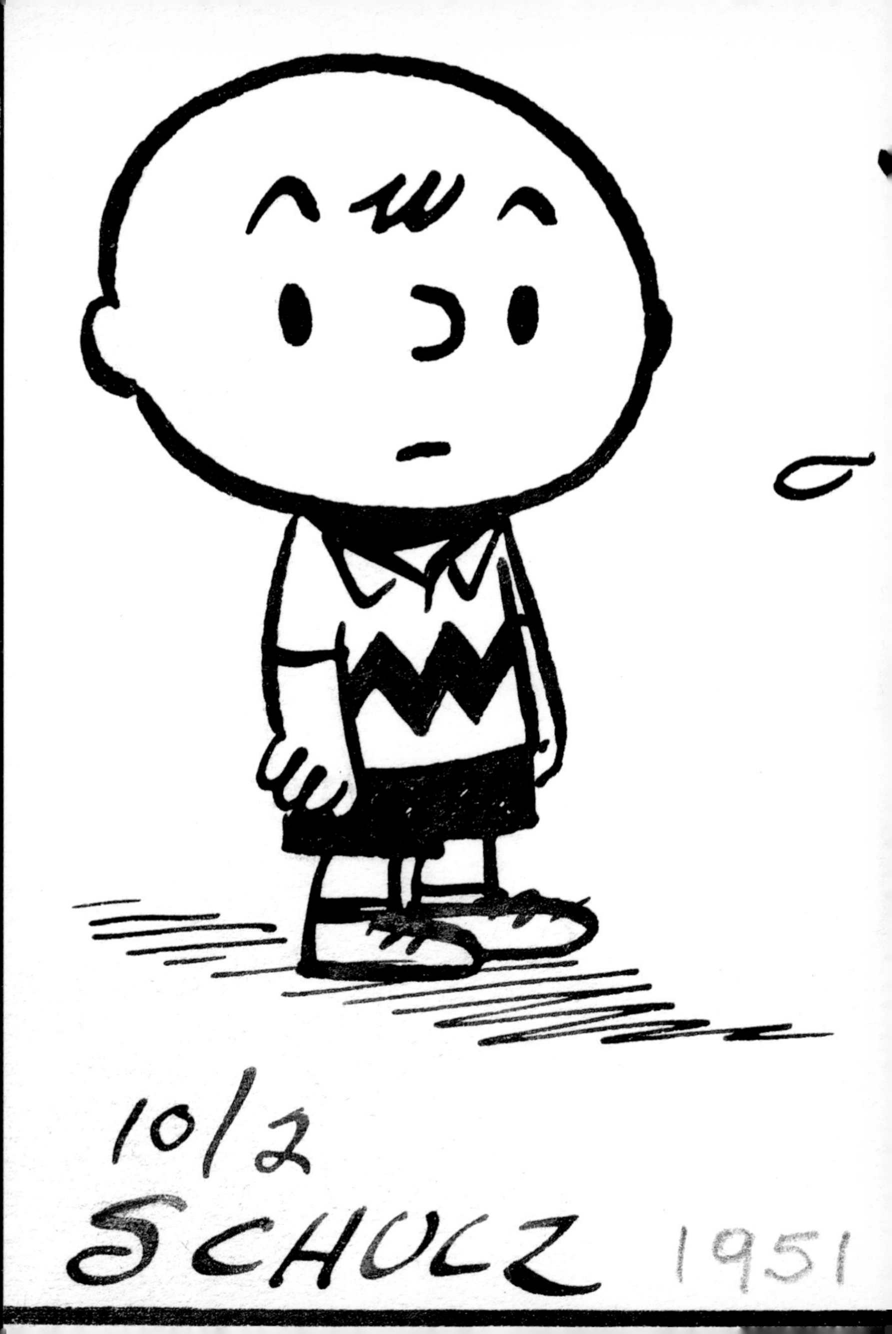
10/2
SCHULZ
1951

Schulz pays homage to one of his heroes, George Herriman (creator of *Krazy Kat*), in this witty drawing of Ignatz beaning Charlie Brown, from 1952. He couldn't have known how prophetic this image is: the passing of the torch from one genius of the the form to the next.

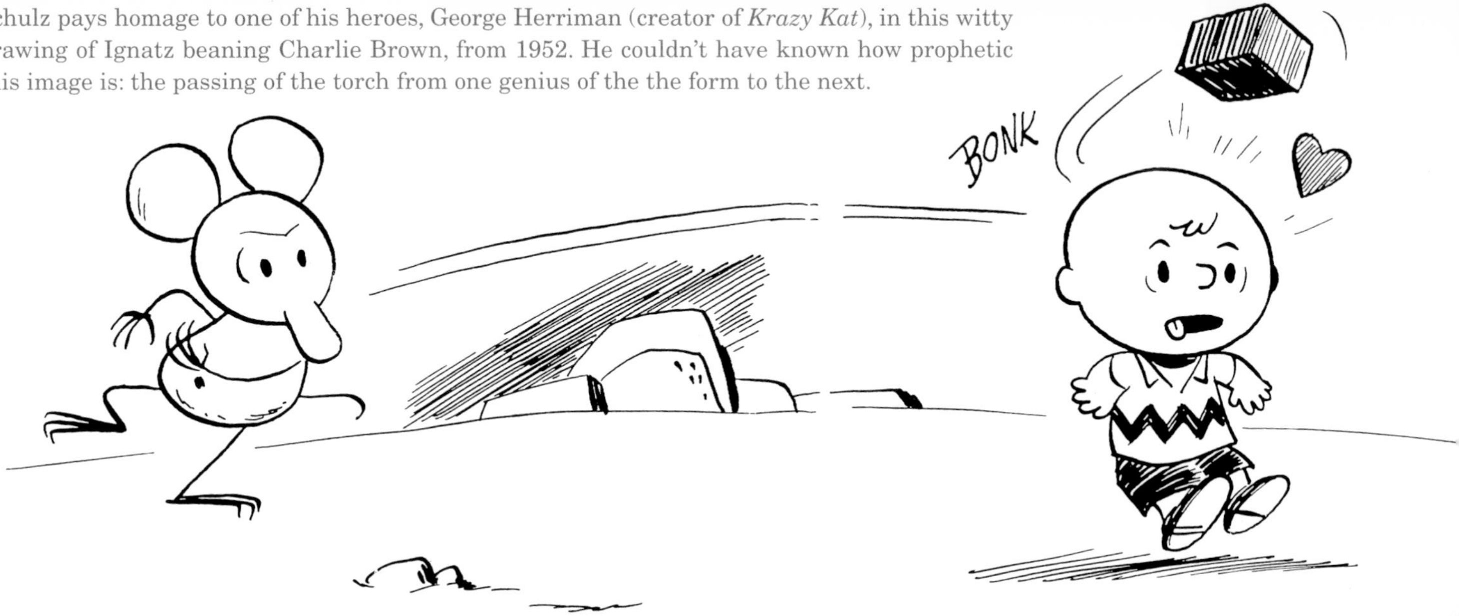
BONK

PEANUTS BEGINS

The four-panel nature of *Peanuts* freed Schulz from the group-montage format of *Li'l Folks*, a change that allowed him to grow as a draftsman and storyteller. Instead of one-liner, single-panel gags, he could now develop situations for the characters that went from point a to b, then c, and d. But this could prove restrictive as well—the syndicate limited the format to *exactly* four panels of equal size , so it could be run vertically, horizontally, or in stacked blocks of two. Decades passed before Schulz was able to pull rank and construct the panels as he saw fit, even occasionally going back to a single panel.

It's hard to imagine how different *Peanuts* was from its contemporaries when it started, because so much of what made it unique—its graphic simplicity, its poetic yet embittered and alienated sense of humor—has been so widely copied since. Schulz maintained that the strip was anything but an instant hit and took years to develop an audience.

Seeing *Peanuts* from the very beginning is fascinating in light of what it would become. The roots of the iconic characters are there, but they have a long way to go. Knowing how they will evolve makes their debuts all the more intriguing, like seeing baby pictures of celebrities.

"PEANUTS"

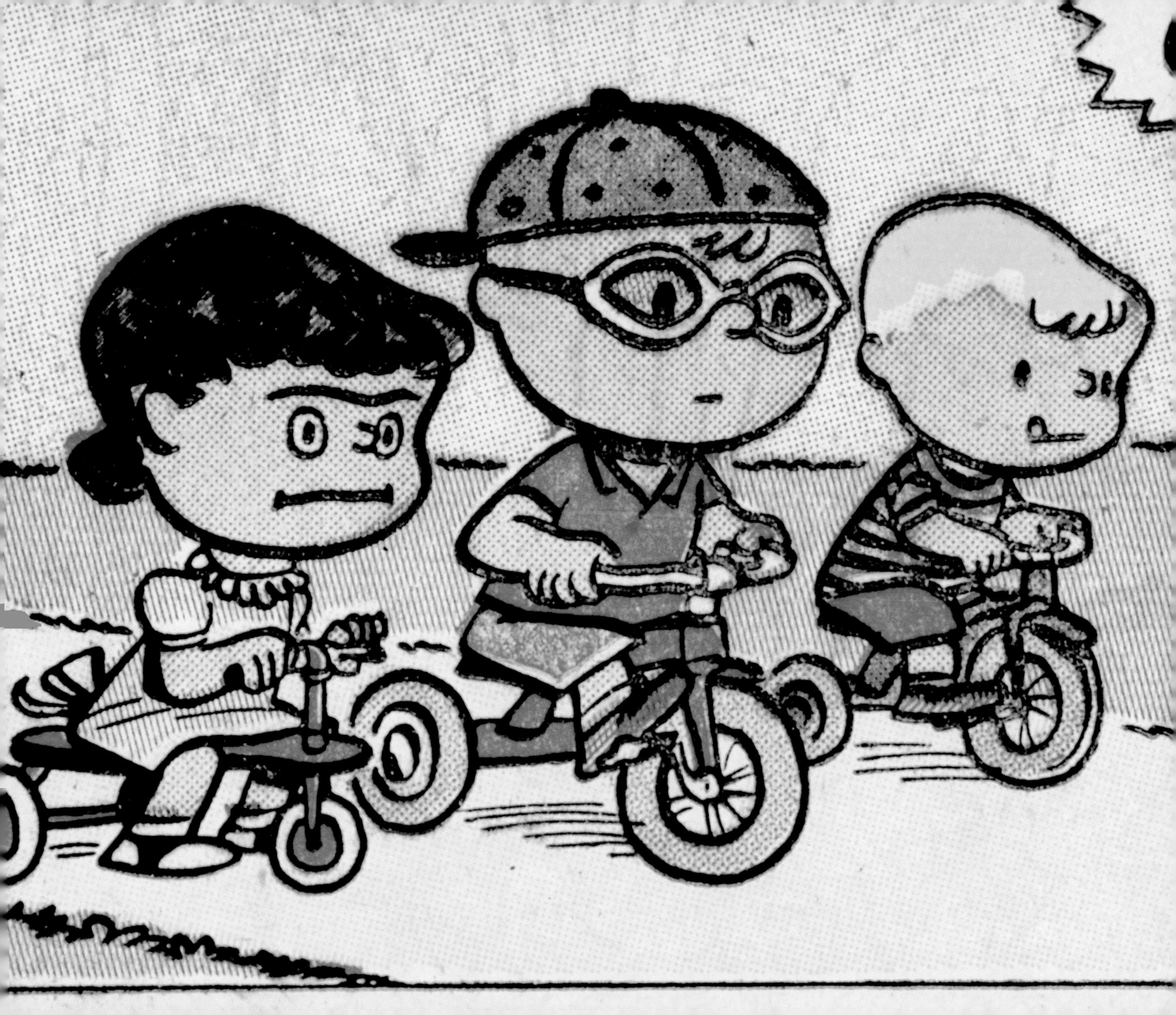

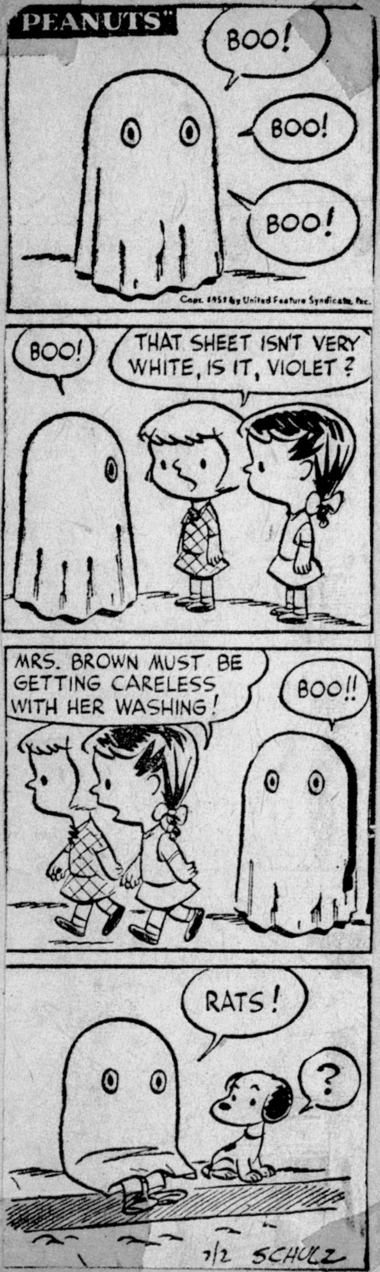
"PEANUTS"
BOO!
BOO!
BOO!
Copr. 1951 by United Feature Syndicate, Inc.
BOO!
THAT SHEET ISN'T VERY WHITE, IS IT, VIOLET ?
MRS. BROWN MUST BE GETTING CARELESS WITH HER WASHING !
BOO!!
RATS !
?
7/2 SCHULZ

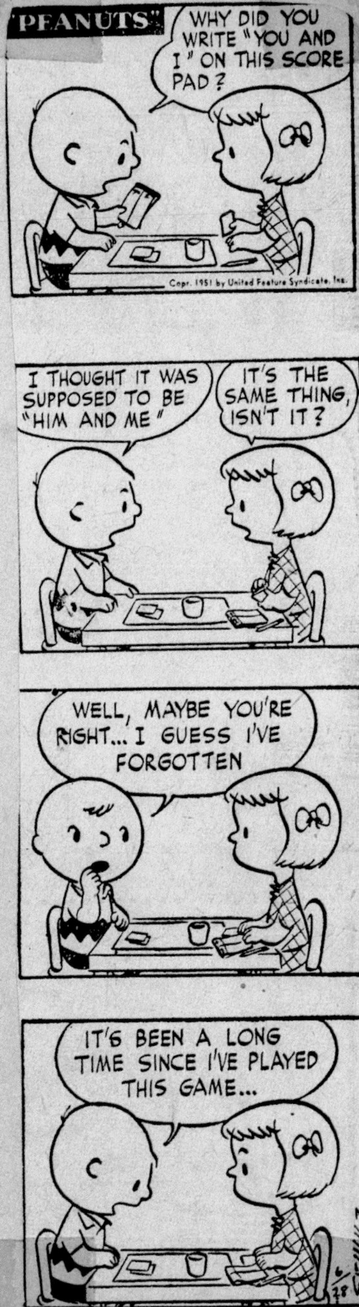
"PEANUTS"
WHY DID YOU WRITE "YOU AND I" ON THIS SCORE PAD ?
Copr. 1951 by United Feature Syndicate, Inc.
I THOUGHT IT WAS SUPPOSED TO BE "HIM AND ME"
IT'S THE SAME THING, ISN'T IT ?
WELL, MAYBE YOU'RE RIGHT... I GUESS I'VE FORGOTTEN
IT'S BEEN A LONG TIME SINCE I'VE PLAYED THIS GAME...
6/28 SCHULZ

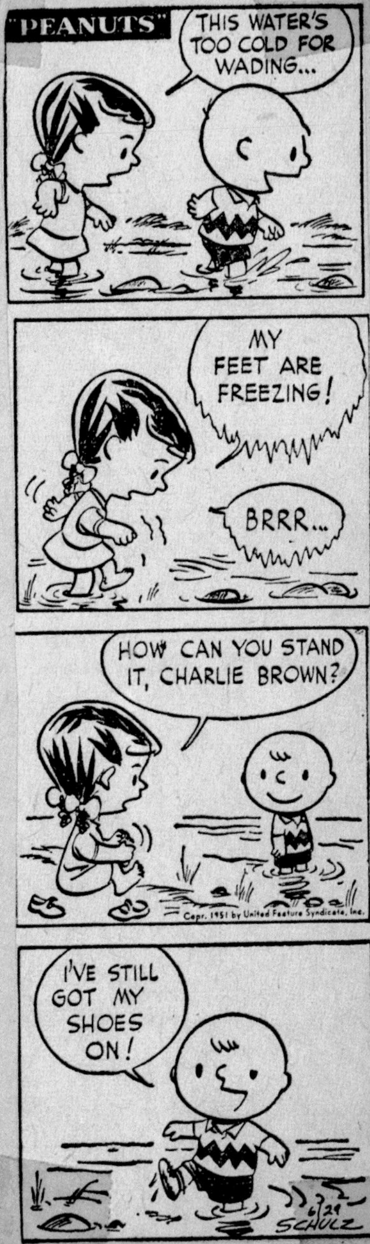
"PEANUTS"
THIS WATER'S TOO COLD FOR WADING...
MY FEET ARE FREEZING !
BRRR...
HOW CAN YOU STAND IT, CHARLIE BROWN ?
Copr. 1951 by United Feature Syndicate, Inc.
I'VE STILL GOT MY SHOES ON !
6/29 SCHULZ

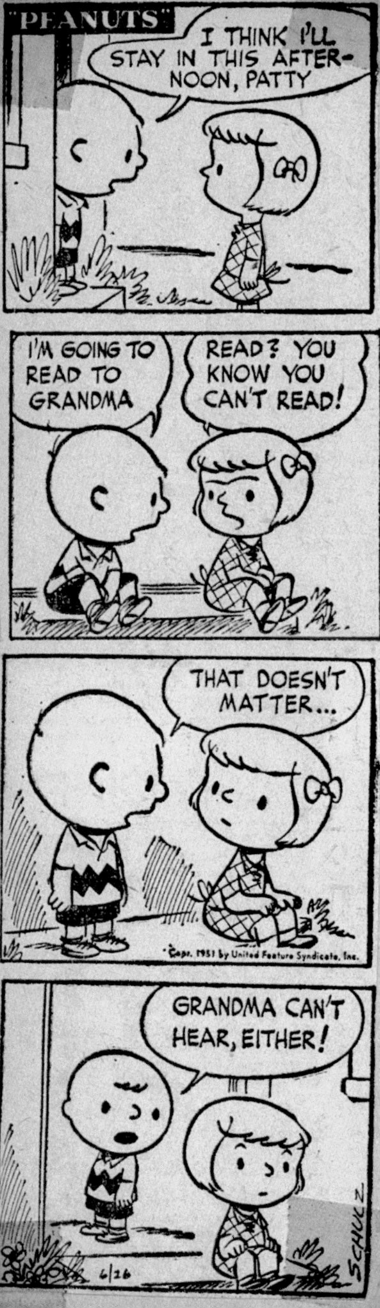
"PEANUTS"
I THINK I'LL STAY IN THIS AFTERNOON, PATTY
I'M GOING TO READ TO GRANDMA
READ? YOU KNOW YOU CAN'T READ!
THAT DOESN'T MATTER...
Copr. 1951 by United Feature Syndicate, Inc.
GRANDMA CAN'T HEAR, EITHER!
SCHULZ
6/26

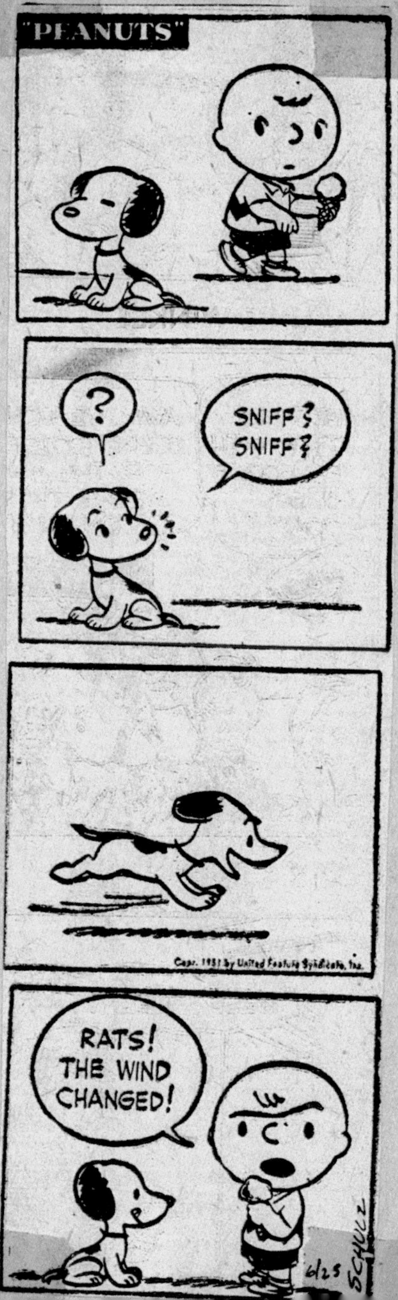
"PEANUTS"
?
SNIFF? SNIFF?
Copr. 1951 by United Feature Syndicate, Inc.
RATS! THE WIND CHANGED!
6/25
SCHULZ

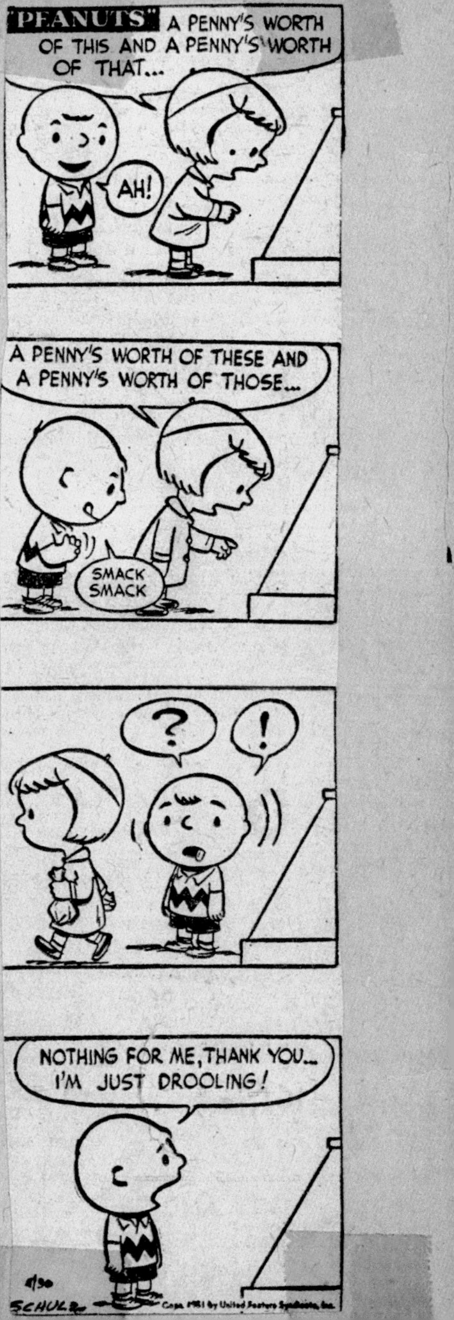
"PEANUTS"
A PENNY'S WORTH OF THIS AND A PENNY'S WORTH OF THAT...
AH!
A PENNY'S WORTH OF THESE AND A PENNY'S WORTH OF THOSE...
SMACK SMACK
?
!
NOTHING FOR ME, THANK YOU... I'M JUST DROOLING!
6/30
SCHULZ
Copr. 1951 by United Feature Syndicate, Inc.

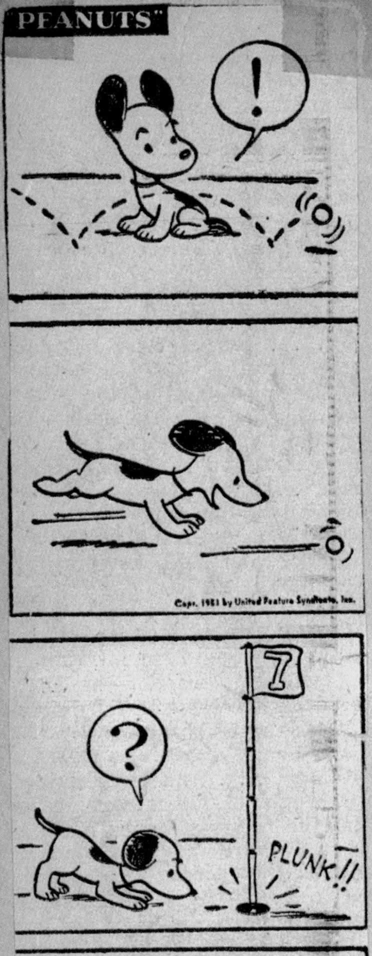
PEANUTS
!
Copr. 1951 by United Feature Syndicate, Inc.
7
?
PLUNK!!
5/8
SCHULZ

Snoopy did not "think," at first, at least not in words.

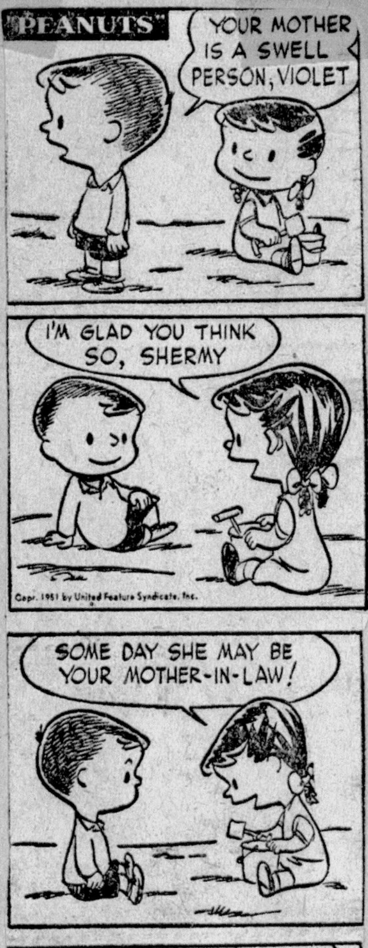
PEANUTS
YOUR MOTHER IS A SWELL PERSON, VIOLET
I'M GLAD YOU THINK SO, SHERMY
Copr. 1951 by United Feature Syndicate, Inc.
SOME DAY SHE MAY BE YOUR MOTHER-IN-LAW!
I CAN'T STAND THAT WOMAN!
8/14
SCHULZ

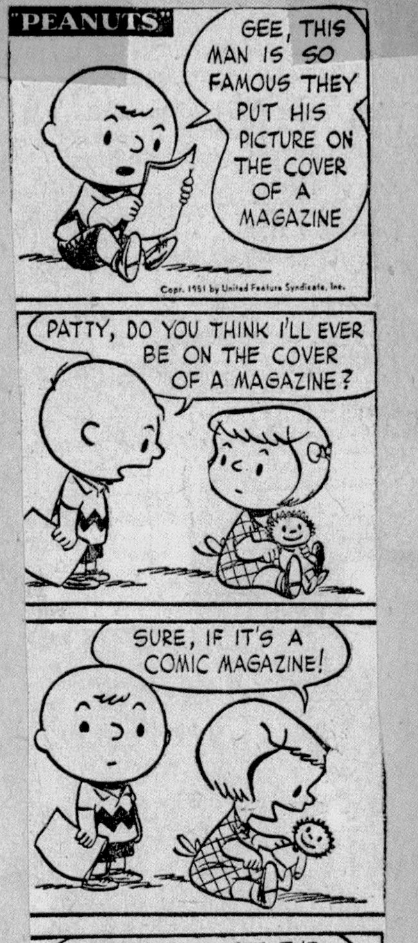
PEANUTS
GEE, THIS MAN IS SO FAMOUS THEY PUT HIS PICTURE ON THE COVER OF A MAGAZINE
Copr. 1951 by United Feature Syndicate, Inc.
PATTY, DO YOU THINK I'LL EVER BE ON THE COVER OF A MAGAZINE?
SURE, IF IT'S A COMIC MAGAZINE!
SOMETIMES I GET THE BEST OF THAT OL' CHARLIE BROWN!
8/13
SCHULZ

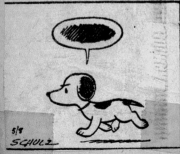

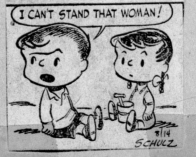

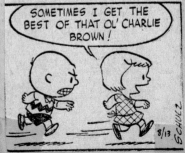

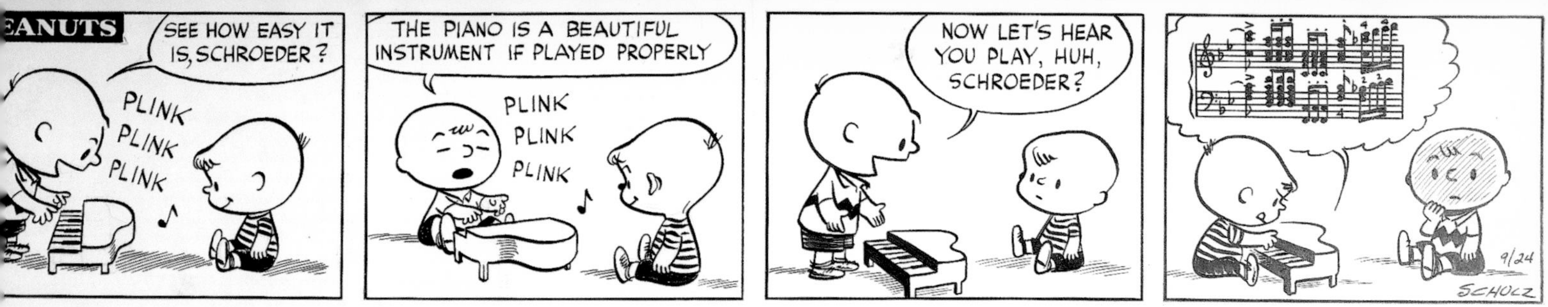
PEANUTS
SEE HOW EASY IT IS, SCHROEDER?
PLINK PLINK PLINK
THE PIANO IS A BEAUTIFUL INSTRUMENT IF PLAYED PROPERLY
PLINK PLINK PLINK
NOW LET'S HEAR YOU PLAY, HUH, SCHROEDER?
9/24
SCHULZ

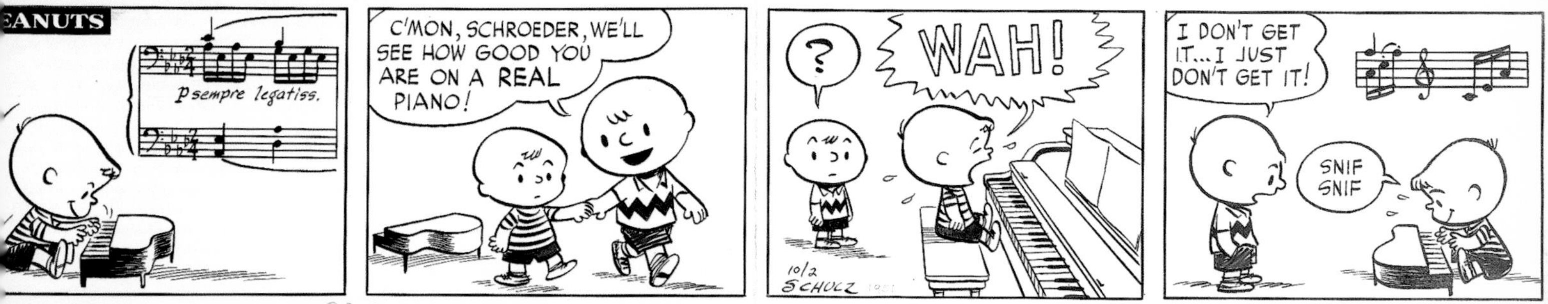
PEANUTS
p sempre legatiss.
C'MON, SCHROEDER, WE'LL SEE HOW GOOD YOU ARE ON A REAL PIANO!
?
WAH!
10/2
SCHULZ
I DON'T GET IT... I JUST DON'T GET IT!
SNIF SNIF

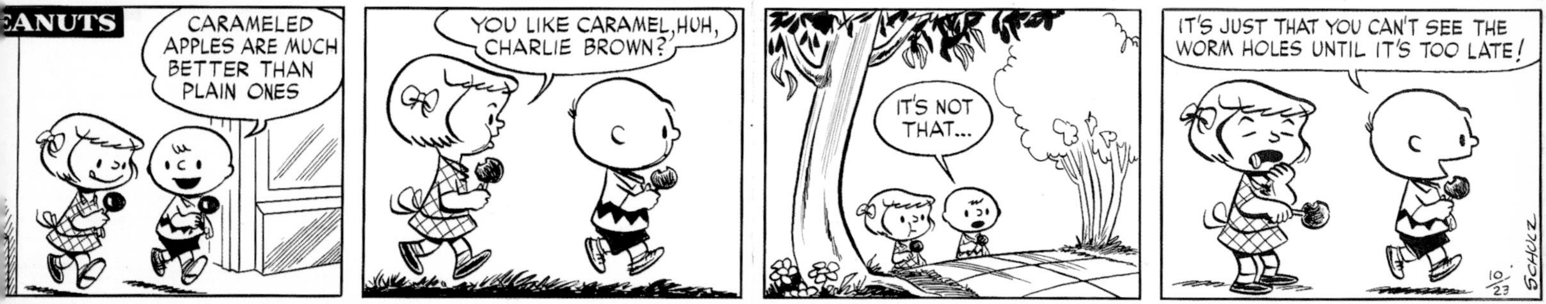
PEANUTS
CARAMELED APPLES ARE MUCH BETTER THAN PLAIN ONES
YOU LIKE CARAMEL, HUH, CHARLIE BROWN?
IT'S NOT THAT...
IT'S JUST THAT YOU CAN'T SEE THE WORM HOLES UNTIL IT'S TOO LATE!
10/23
SCHULZ

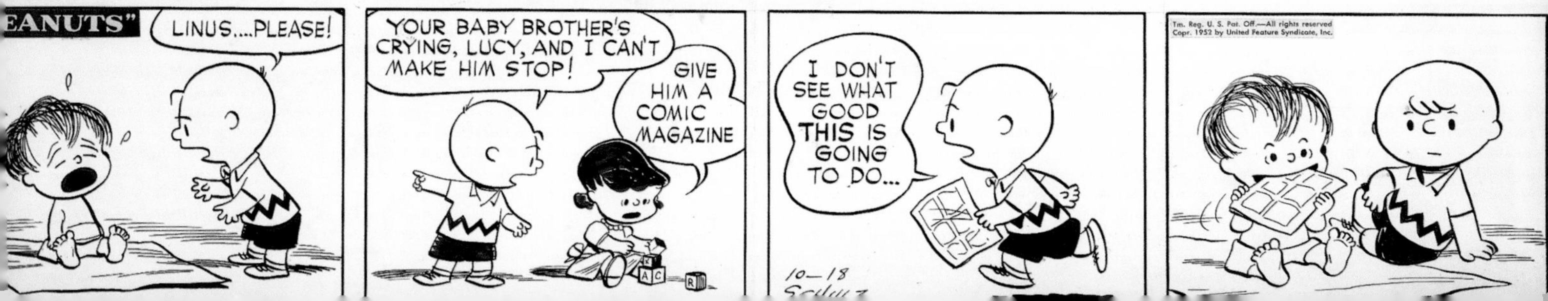
PEANUTS"
LINUS....PLEASE!
YOUR BABY BROTHER'S CRYING, LUCY, AND I CAN'T MAKE HIM STOP!
GIVE HIM A COMIC MAGAZINE
I DON'T SEE WHAT GOOD THIS IS GOING TO DO...
10-18
Tm. Reg. U. S. Pat. Off.—All rights reserved
Copr. 1952 by United Feature Syndicate, Inc.

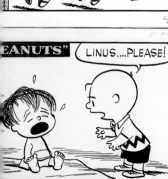

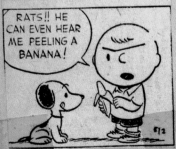

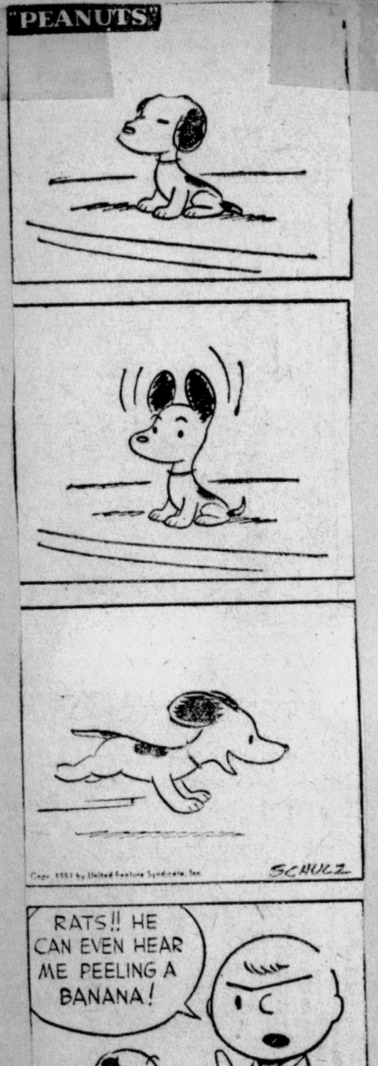
"PEANUTS"
Copr. 1951 by United Feature Syndicate, Inc.
SCHULZ
RATS!! HE CAN EVEN HEAR ME PEELING A BANANA!
5/2

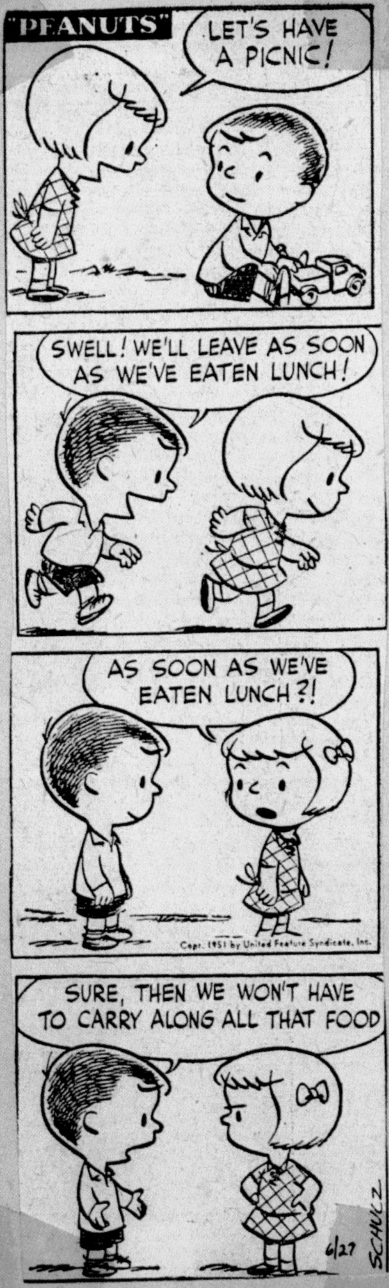
"PEANUTS"
LET'S HAVE A PICNIC!
SWELL! WE'LL LEAVE AS SOON AS WE'VE EATEN LUNCH!
AS SOON AS WE'VE EATEN LUNCH?!
Copr. 1951 by United Feature Syndicate, Inc.
SURE, THEN WE WON'T HAVE TO CARRY ALONG ALL THAT FOOD
6/27
SCHULZ

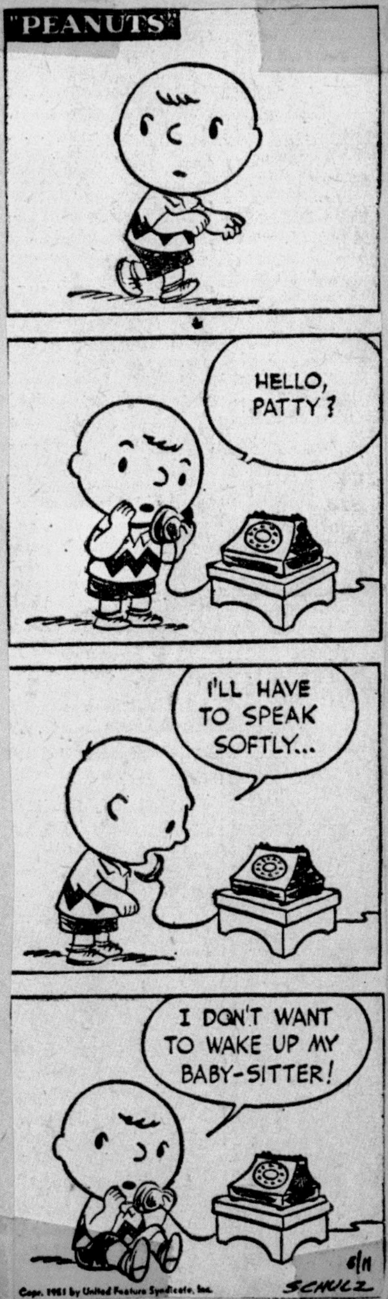
"PEANUTS"
HELLO, PATTY?
I'LL HAVE TO SPEAK SOFTLY...
I DON'T WANT TO WAKE UP MY BABY-SITTER!
6/11
Copr. 1951 by United Feature Syndicate, Inc.
SCHULZ

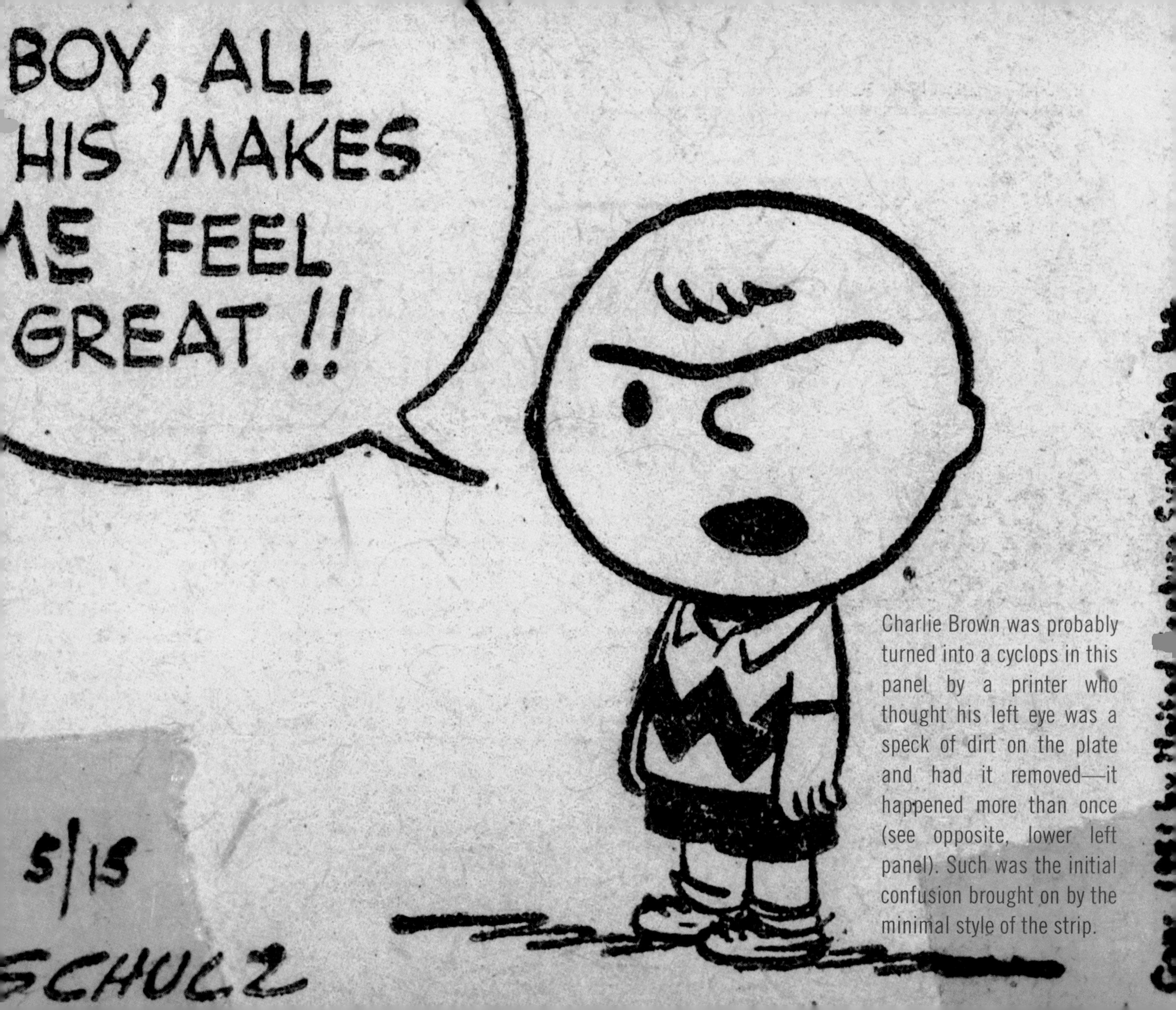

BOY, ALL
HIS MAKES
E FEEL
GREAT !!
5/15
SCHULZ

Charlie Brown was probably turned into a cyclops in this panel by a printer who thought his left eye was a speck of dirt on the plate and had it removed—it happened more than once (see opposite, lower left panel). Such was the initial confusion brought on by the minimal style of the strip.

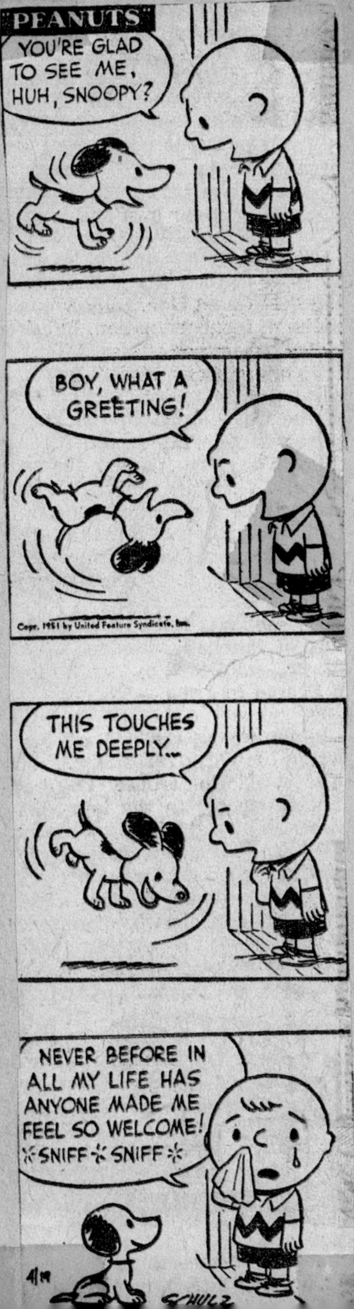
"PEANUTS"
YOU'RE GLAD TO SEE ME, HUH, SNOOPY?
BOY, WHAT A GREETING!
Copr. 1951 by United Feature Syndicate, Inc.
THIS TOUCHES ME DEEPLY...
NEVER BEFORE IN ALL MY LIFE HAS ANYONE MADE ME FEEL SO WELCOME! *SNIFF* *SNIFF*
4/19
SCHULZ

Only seven newspapers picked up the strip from the very beginning:

The Washington Post

The Chicago Tribune

Star Tribune of Minneapolis

The Morning Call, (Allentown, Pa.)

Bethlehem Globe-Times

The Denver Post

The Seattle Times

By 2000, the total was over 2,500.

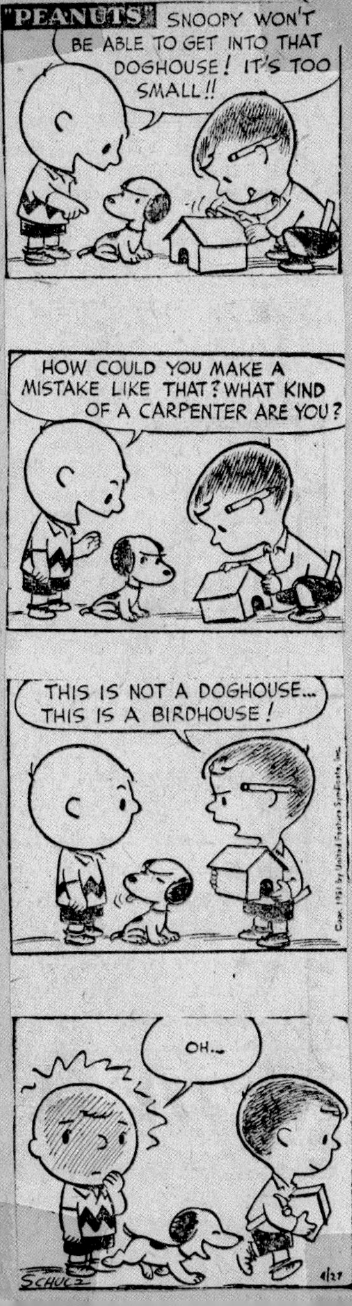
"PEANUTS"
SNOOPY WON'T BE ABLE TO GET INTO THAT DOGHOUSE! IT'S TOO SMALL!!
HOW COULD YOU MAKE A MISTAKE LIKE THAT? WHAT KIND OF A CARPENTER ARE YOU?
THIS IS NOT A DOGHOUSE... THIS IS A BIRDHOUSE!
OH...
SCHULZ
4/27

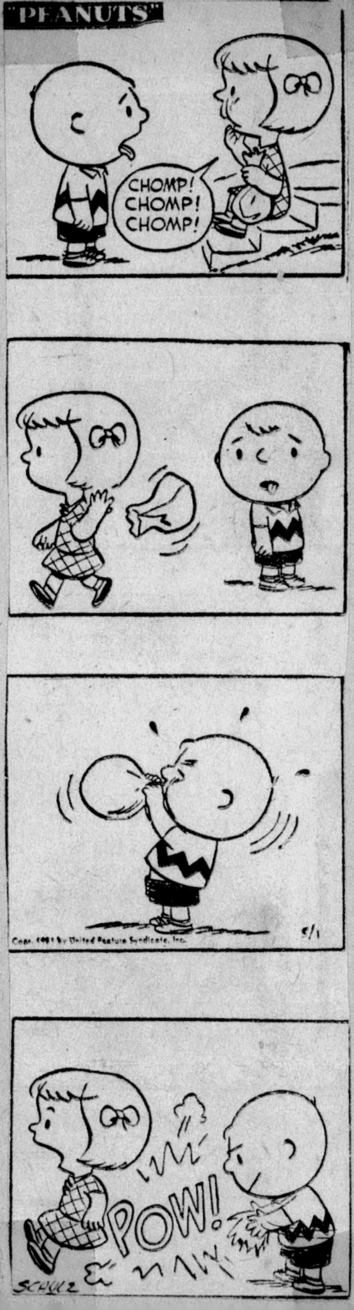
"PEANUTS"
CHOMP! CHOMP! CHOMP!
5/1
POW!
SCHULZ

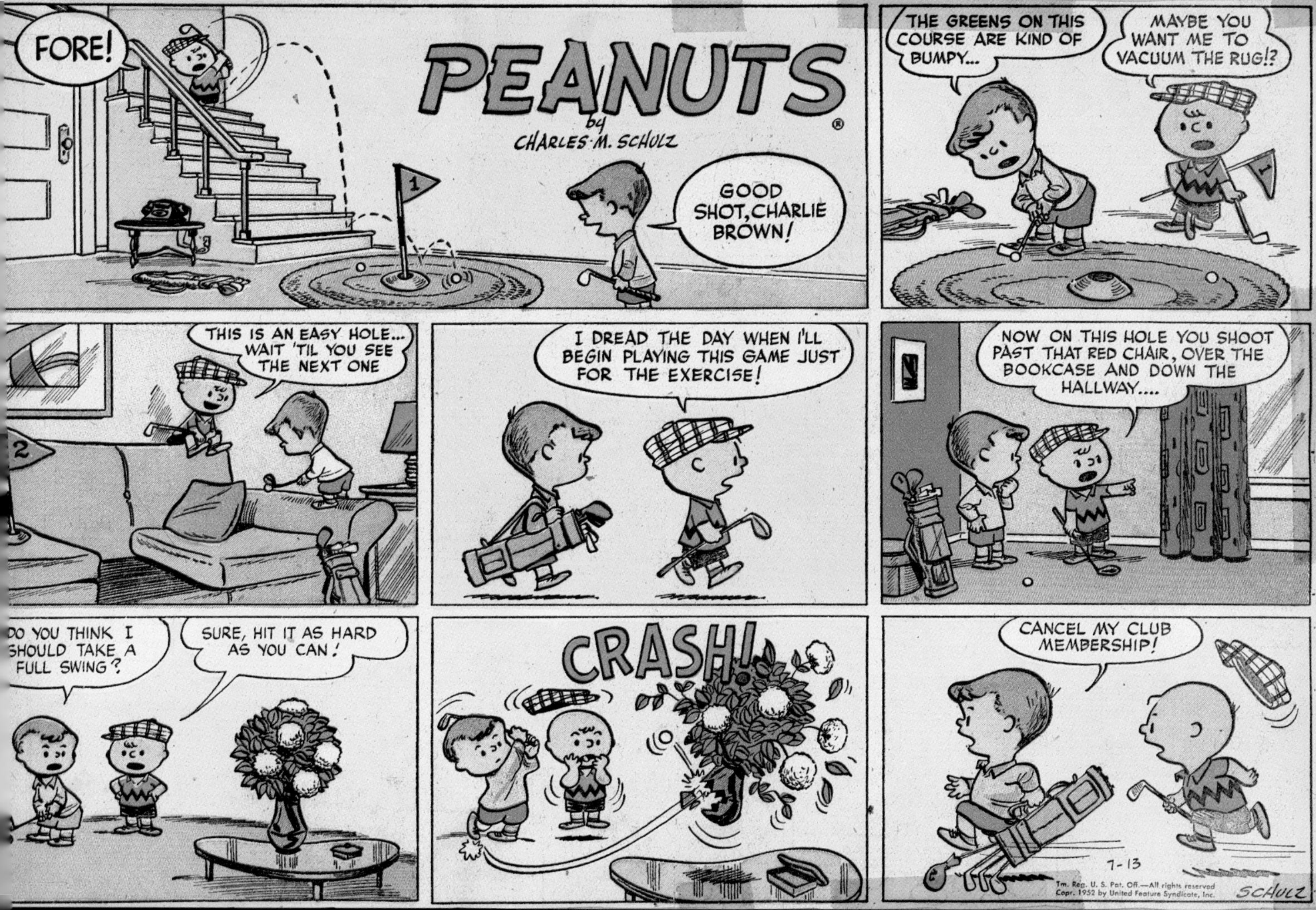
FORE!
PEANUTS
by CHARLES M. SCHULZ
GOOD SHOT, CHARLIE BROWN!
THE GREENS ON THIS COURSE ARE KIND OF BUMPY...
MAYBE YOU WANT ME TO VACUUM THE RUG!?
THIS IS AN EASY HOLE... WAIT 'TIL YOU SEE THE NEXT ONE
I DREAD THE DAY WHEN I'LL BEGIN PLAYING THIS GAME JUST FOR THE EXERCISE!
NOW ON THIS HOLE YOU SHOOT PAST THAT RED CHAIR, OVER THE BOOKCASE AND DOWN THE HALLWAY....
DO YOU THINK I SHOULD TAKE A FULL SWING?
SURE, HIT IT AS HARD AS YOU CAN!
CRASH!
CANCEL MY CLUB MEMBERSHIP!
7-13
Tm. Reg. U. S. Pat. Off.—All rights reserved Copr. 1952 by United Feature Syndicate, Inc.
SCHULZ

The first color Sunday strips appeared in 1952. Like the dailies, they were designed so they could be run several different ways, to accommodate varying formats of a host of newspapers. Sunday strips could run with just the bottom six panels by themselves, or with the accompanying top "title" panel. The top right panel was designed to be strictly optional—if there was space for it, fine. If not, it could be dropped without any significant loss to the storyline.

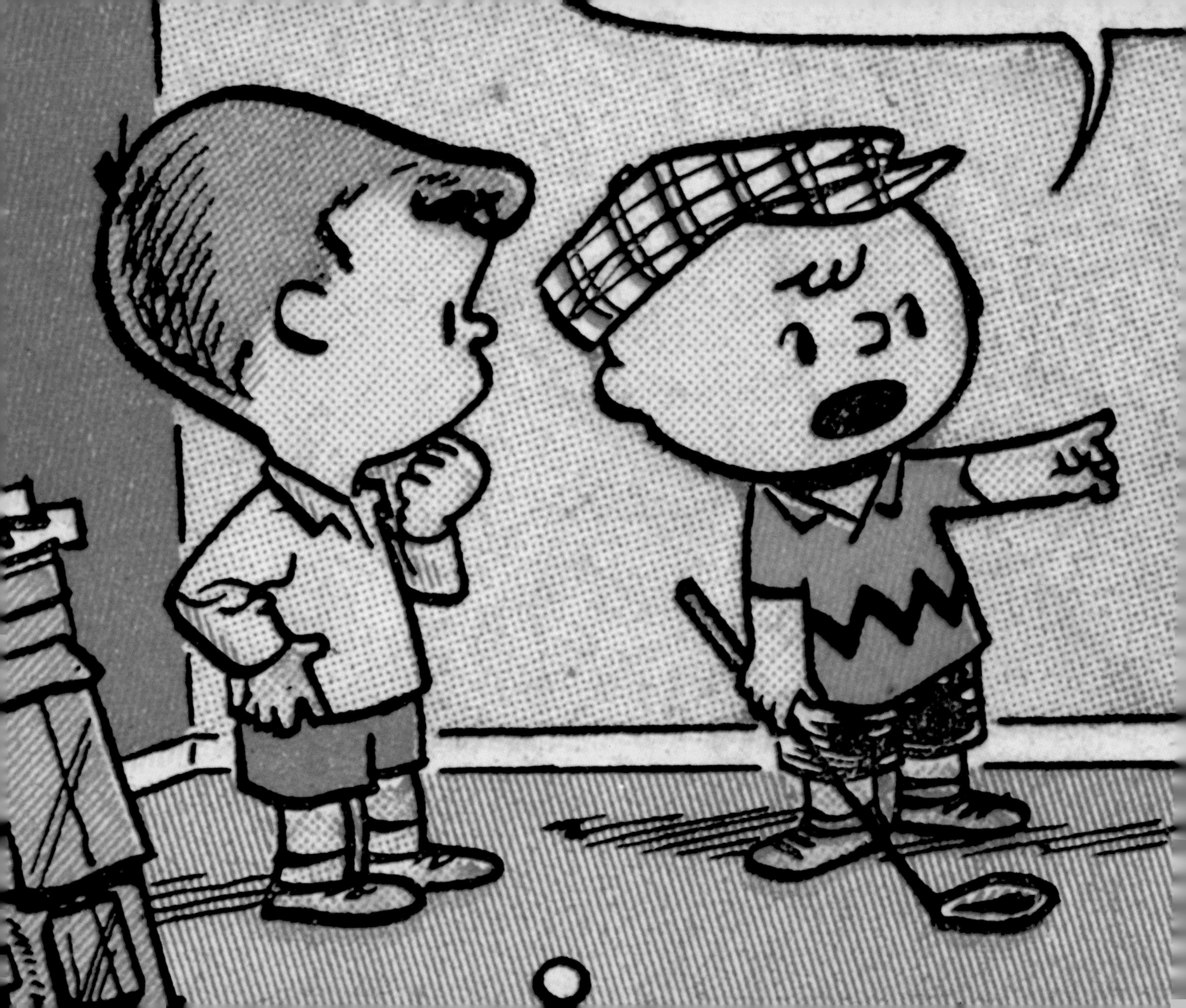

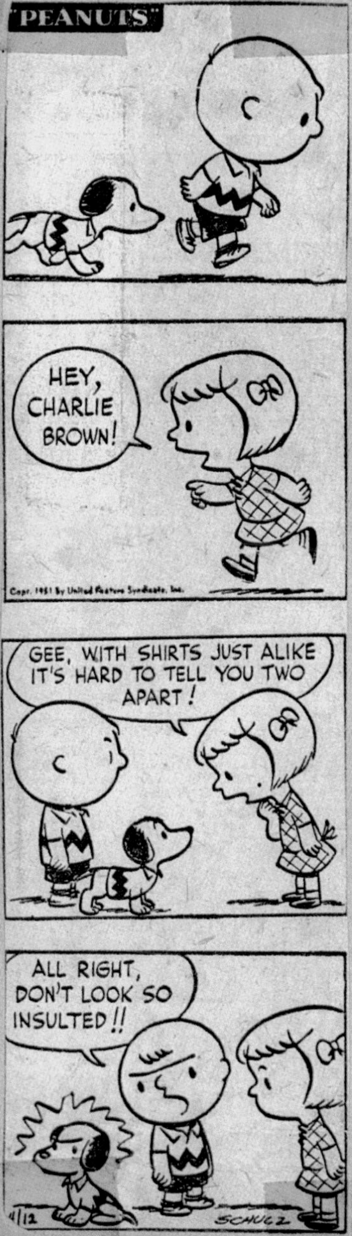
"PEANUTS"
HEY, CHARLIE BROWN!
Copr. 1951 by United Feature Syndicate, Inc.
GEE, WITH SHIRTS JUST ALIKE IT'S HARD TO TELL YOU TWO APART!
ALL RIGHT, DON'T LOOK SO INSULTED!!
4/12
SCHULZ

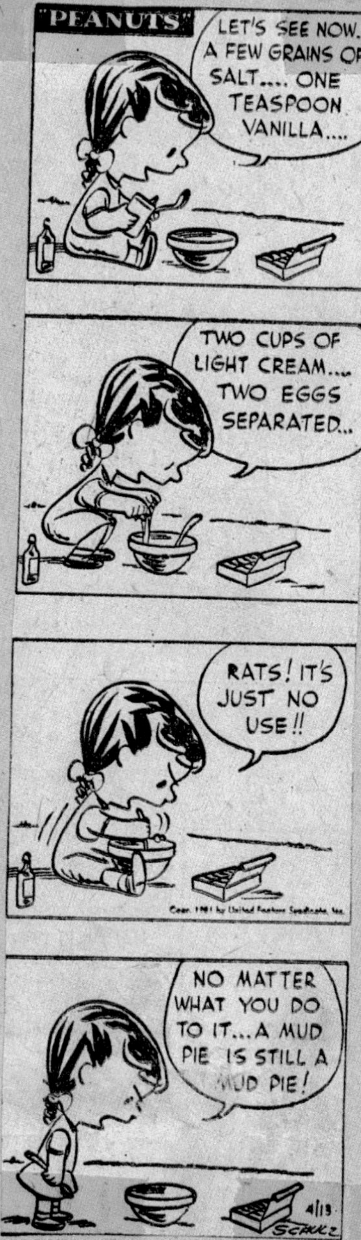
"PEANUTS"
LET'S SEE NOW... A FEW GRAINS OF SALT.... ONE TEASPOON VANILLA....
TWO CUPS OF LIGHT CREAM.... TWO EGGS SEPARATED...
RATS! IT'S JUST NO USE!!
Copr. 1951 by United Feature Syndicate, Inc.
NO MATTER WHAT YOU DO TO IT...A MUD PIE IS STILL A MUD PIE!
4/13
SCHULZ

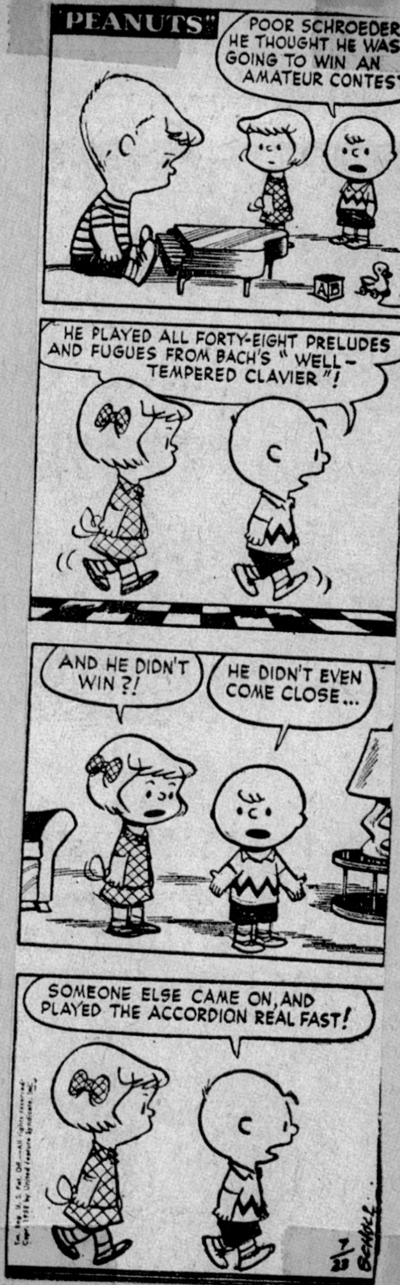
"PEANUTS"
POOR SCHROEDER... HE THOUGHT HE WAS GOING TO WIN AN AMATEUR CONTEST
HE PLAYED ALL FORTY-EIGHT PRELUDES AND FUGUES FROM BACH'S "WELL-TEMPERED CLAVIER"!
AND HE DIDN'T WIN?!
HE DIDN'T EVEN COME CLOSE...
SOMEONE ELSE CAME ON, AND PLAYED THE ACCORDION REAL FAST!
7/23
SCHULZ

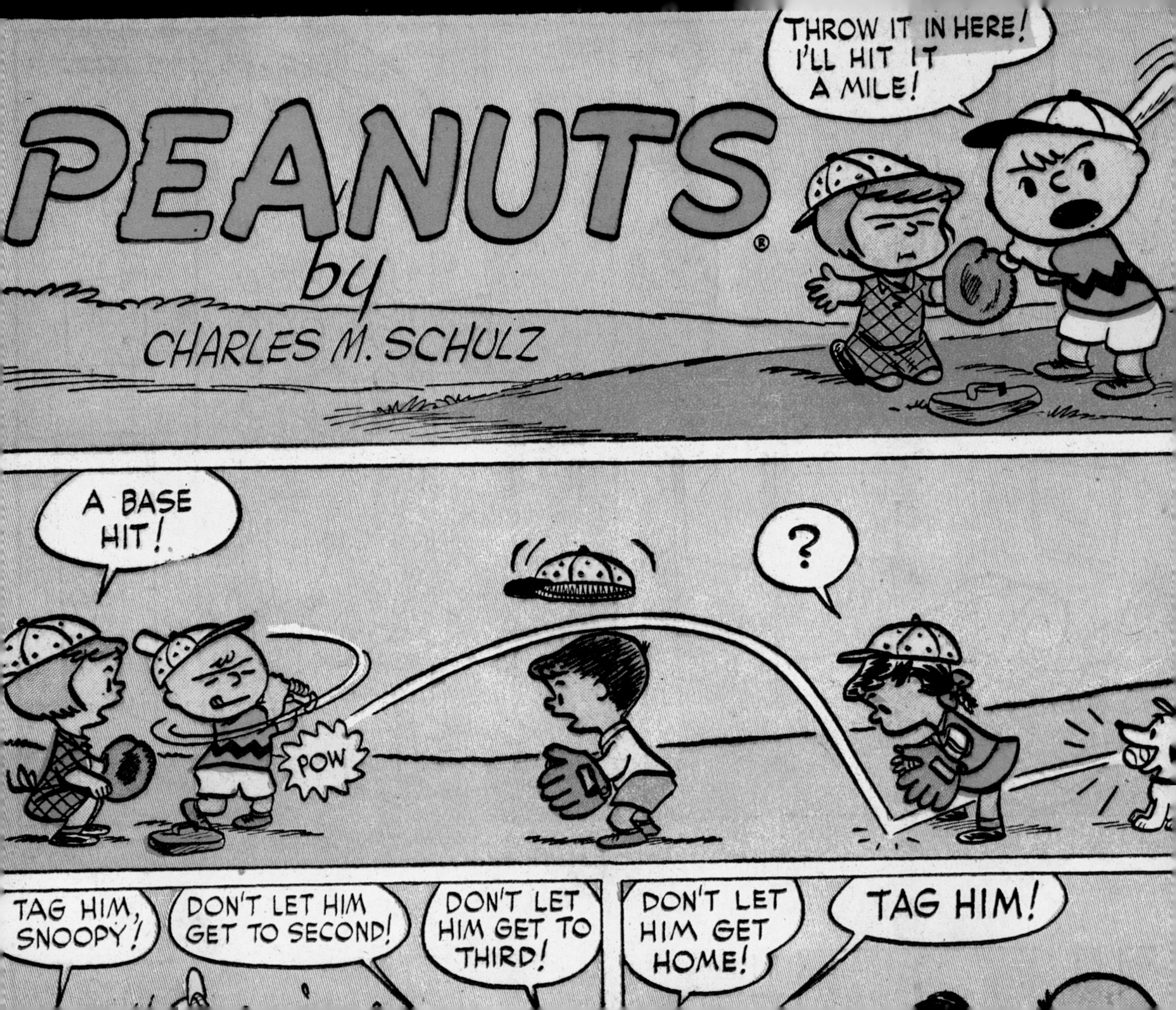
PEANUTS®
by
CHARLES M. SCHULZ
THROW IT IN HERE! I'LL HIT IT A MILE!
A BASE HIT!
POW
?
TAG HIM, SNOOPY!
DON'T LET HIM GET TO SECOND!
DON'T LET HIM GET TO THIRD!
DON'T LET HIM GET HOME!
TAG HIM!

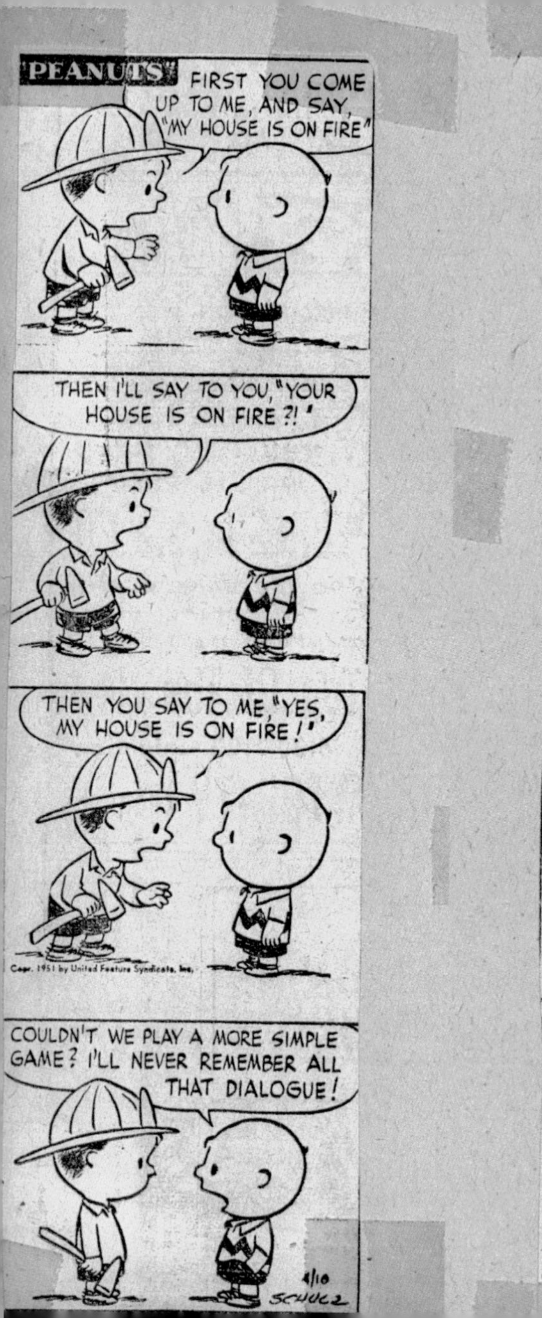
"PEANUTS"
FIRST YOU COME UP TO ME, AND SAY, "MY HOUSE IS ON FIRE"
THEN I'LL SAY TO YOU, "YOUR HOUSE IS ON FIRE ?!"
THEN YOU SAY TO ME, "YES, MY HOUSE IS ON FIRE!"
Copr. 1951 by United Feature Syndicate, Inc.
COULDN'T WE PLAY A MORE SIMPLE GAME? I'LL NEVER REMEMBER ALL THAT DIALOGUE!
SCHULZ

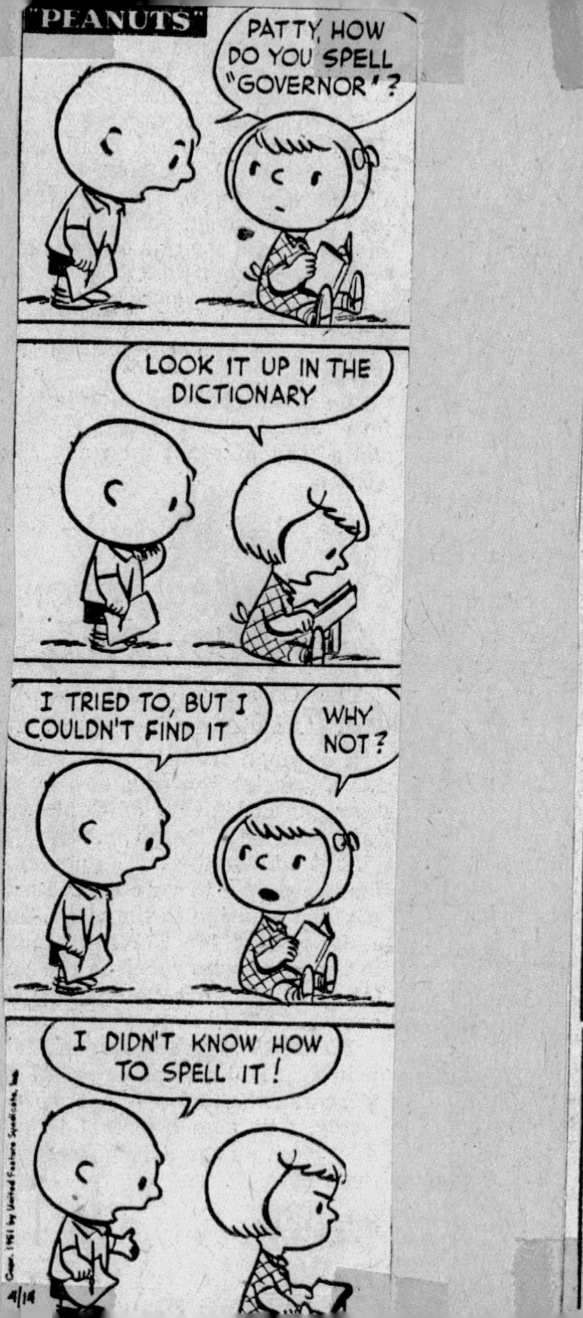
"PEANUTS"
PATTY, HOW DO YOU SPELL "GOVERNOR"?
LOOK IT UP IN THE DICTIONARY
I TRIED TO, BUT I COULDN'T FIND IT
WHY NOT?
I DIDN'T KNOW HOW TO SPELL IT!
Copr. 1951 by United Feature Syndicate, Inc.

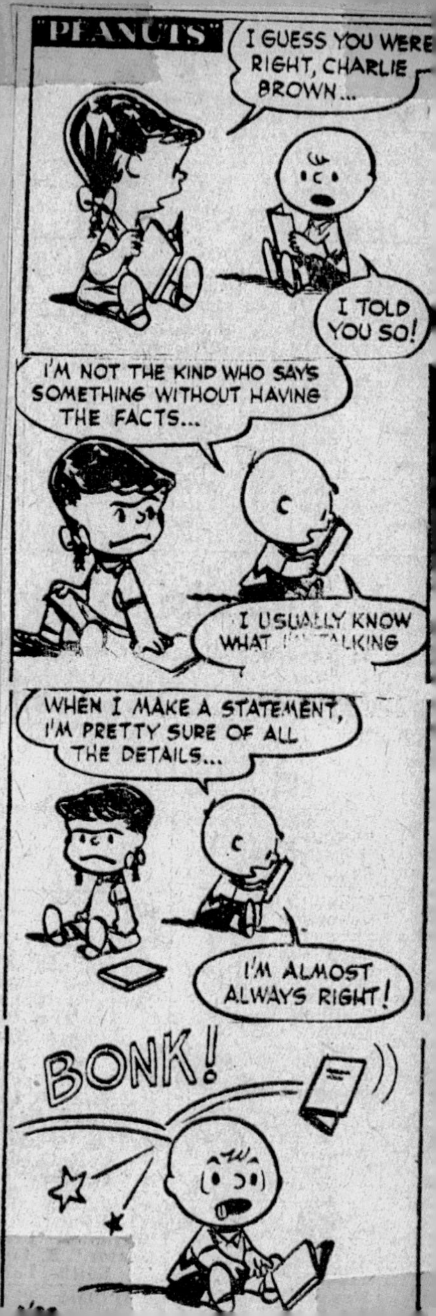
"PEANUTS"
I GUESS YOU WERE RIGHT, CHARLIE BROWN...
I TOLD YOU SO!
I'M NOT THE KIND WHO SAYS SOMETHING WITHOUT HAVING THE FACTS...
I USUALLY KNOW WHAT
TALKING
WHEN I MAKE A STATEMENT, I'M PRETTY SURE OF ALL THE DETAILS...
I'M ALMOST ALWAYS RIGHT!
BONK!

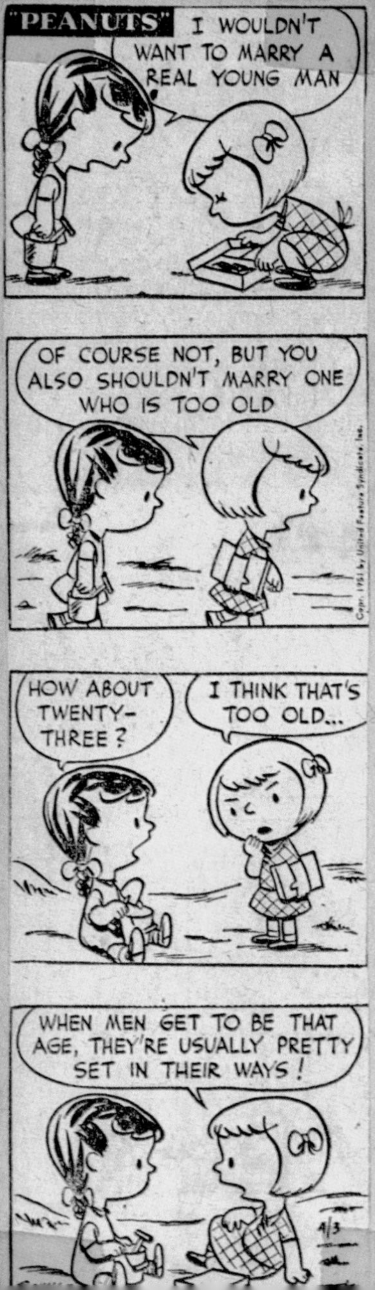
"PEANUTS"
I WOULDN'T WANT TO MARRY A REAL YOUNG MAN
OF COURSE NOT, BUT YOU ALSO SHOULDN'T MARRY ONE WHO IS TOO OLD
Copr. 1951 by United Feature Syndicate, Inc.
HOW ABOUT TWENTY-THREE?
I THINK THAT'S TOO OLD...
WHEN MEN GET TO BE THAT AGE, THEY'RE USUALLY PRETTY SET IN THEIR WAYS!
4/3

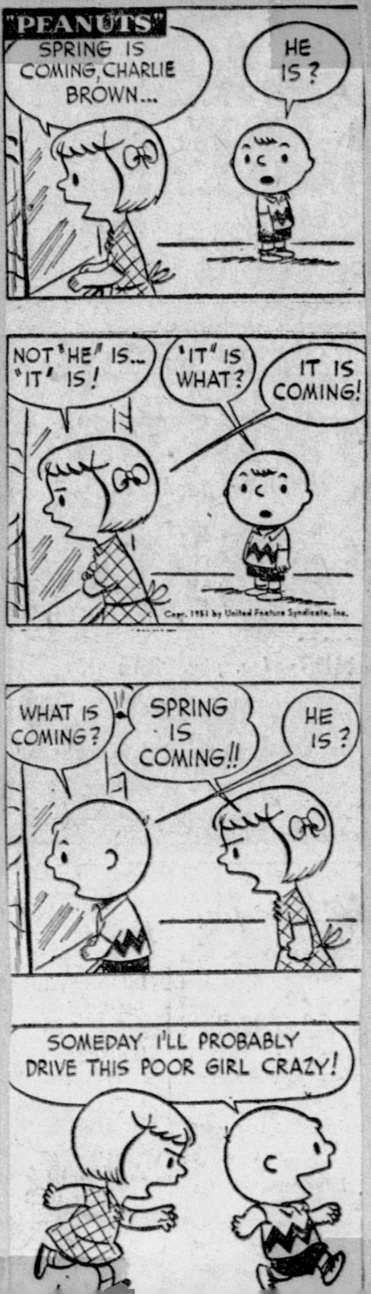
"PEANUTS"
SPRING IS COMING, CHARLIE BROWN...
HE IS?
NOT "HE" IS... "IT" IS!
"IT" IS WHAT?
IT IS COMING!
Copr. 1951 by United Feature Syndicate, Inc.
WHAT IS COMING?
SPRING IS COMING!!
HE IS?
SOMEDAY I'LL PROBABLY DRIVE THIS POOR GIRL CRAZY!

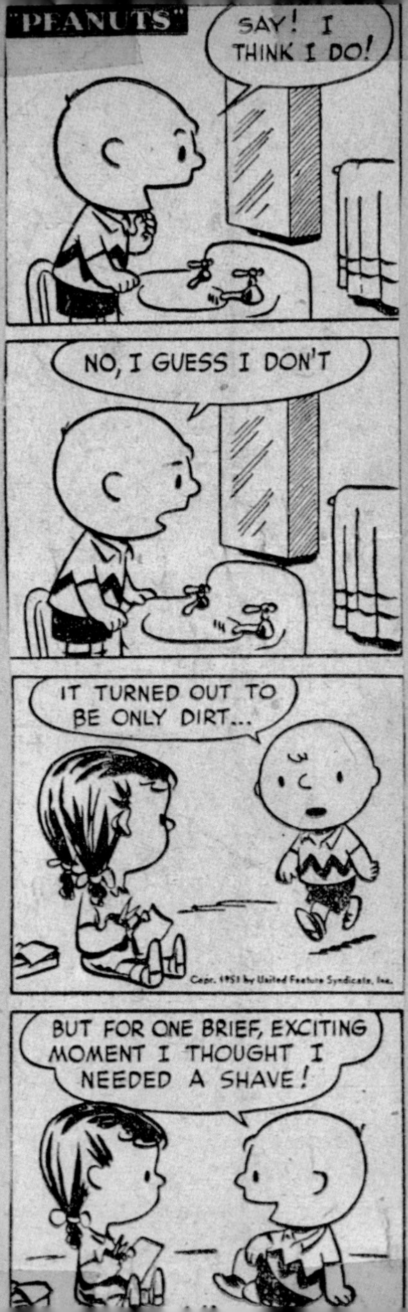
"PEANUTS"
SAY! I THINK I DO!
NO, I GUESS I DON'T
IT TURNED OUT TO BE ONLY DIRT...
Copr. 1951 by United Feature Syndicate, Inc.
BUT FOR ONE BRIEF, EXCITING MOMENT I THOUGHT I NEEDED A SHAVE!

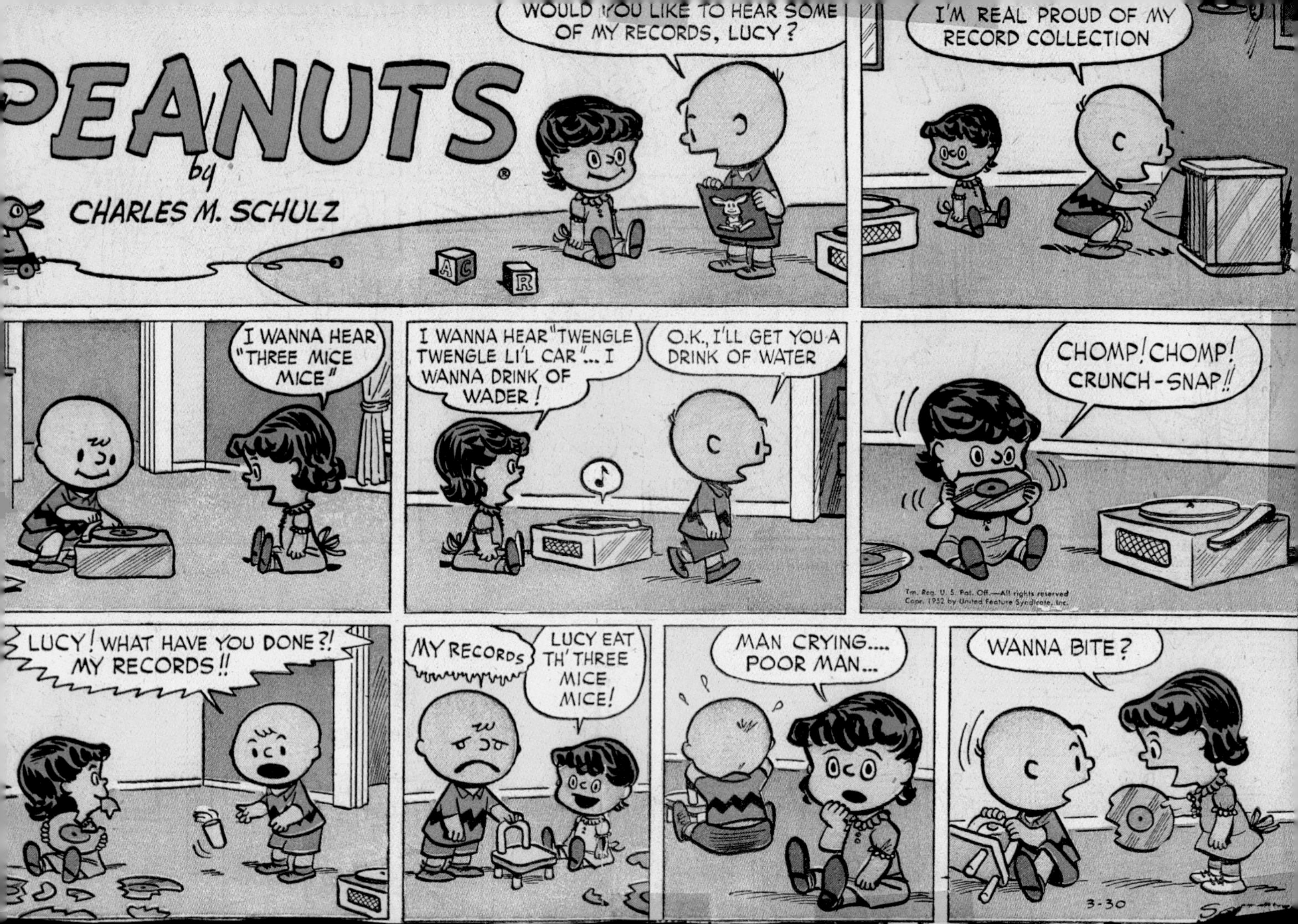
PEANUTS
by
CHARLES M. SCHULZ
WOULD YOU LIKE TO HEAR SOME OF MY RECORDS, LUCY?
I'M REAL PROUD OF MY RECORD COLLECTION
I WANNA HEAR "THREE MICE MICE"
I WANNA HEAR "TWENGLE TWENGLE LI'L CAR"... I WANNA DRINK OF WADER!
O.K., I'LL GET YOU A DRINK OF WATER
CHOMP! CHOMP! CRUNCH-SNAP!!
Tm. Reg. U. S. Pat. Off.—All rights reserved
Copr. 1952 by United Feature Syndicate, Inc.
LUCY! WHAT HAVE YOU DONE?! MY RECORDS!!
MY RECORDS
LUCY EAT TH' THREE MICE MICE!
MAN CRYING.... POOR MAN...
WANNA BITE?
3-30

Lucy first appeared in 1952 as a saucer-eyed baby, and a sweet-natured one at that.
Charlie Brown was often her baby-sitter and counselor in the early years. It didn't last long.

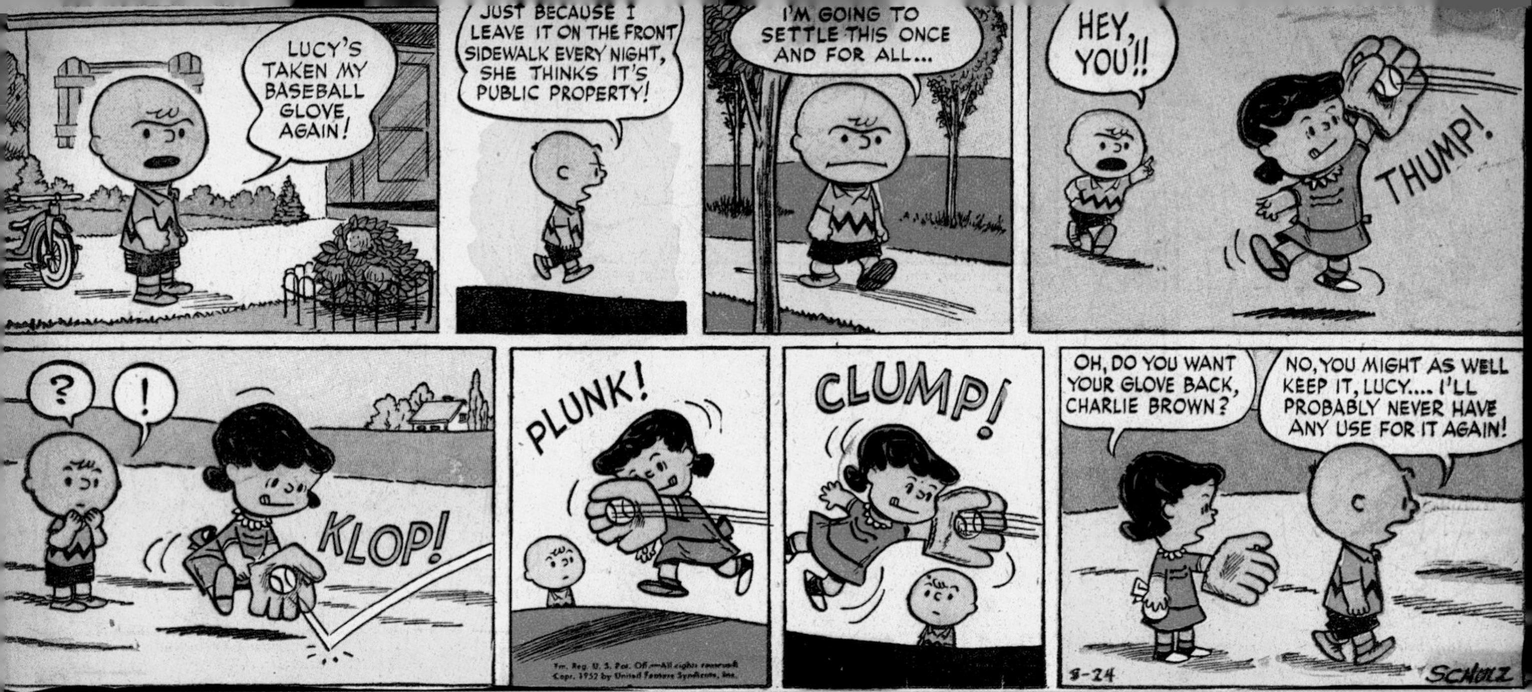
LUCY'S TAKEN MY BASEBALL GLOVE AGAIN!
JUST BECAUSE I LEAVE IT ON THE FRONT SIDEWALK EVERY NIGHT, SHE THINKS IT'S PUBLIC PROPERTY!
I'M GOING TO SETTLE THIS ONCE AND FOR ALL...
HEY, YOU!!
THUMP!
?
!
KLOP!
PLUNK!
CLUMP!
OH, DO YOU WANT YOUR GLOVE BACK, CHARLIE BROWN?
NO, YOU MIGHT AS WELL KEEP IT, LUCY.... I'LL PROBABLY NEVER HAVE ANY USE FOR IT AGAIN!
8-24
SCHULZ

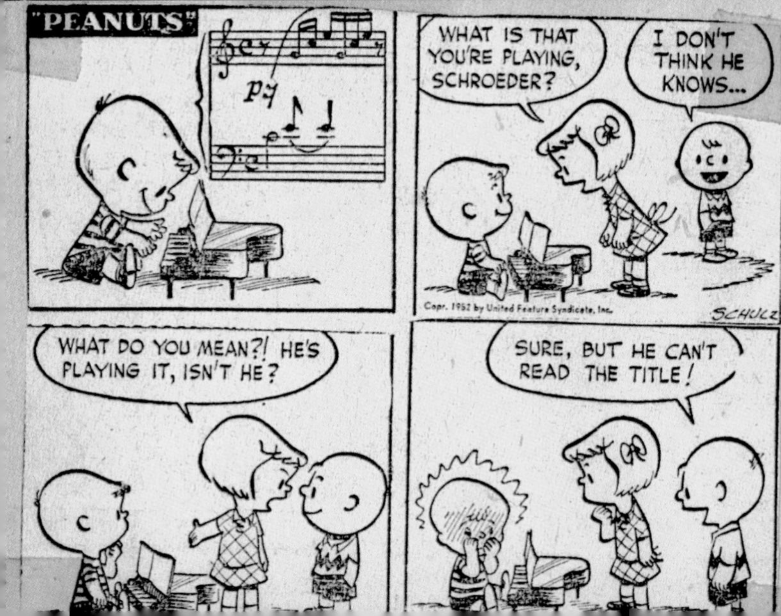
"PEANUTS"
WHAT IS THAT YOU'RE PLAYING, SCHROEDER?
I DON'T THINK HE KNOWS...
Copr. 1952 by United Feature Syndicate, Inc.
SCHULZ
WHAT DO YOU MEAN?! HE'S PLAYING IT, ISN'T HE?
SURE, BUT HE CAN'T READ THE TITLE!

Above: Lucy demonstrates an athletic skill in 1953 that would vanish in later years, when her baseball prowess would consist of watching in wonderment as fly balls drop at her feet or soar over her head.

Left: Schroeder's status as prodigy only goes so far.

Right: Charlie Brown's stint as William Tell has safety in mind.

Bottom: No good deed goes unpunished, as a typical Schulz punchline renders a lot of fraught anxiety ultimately misspent.

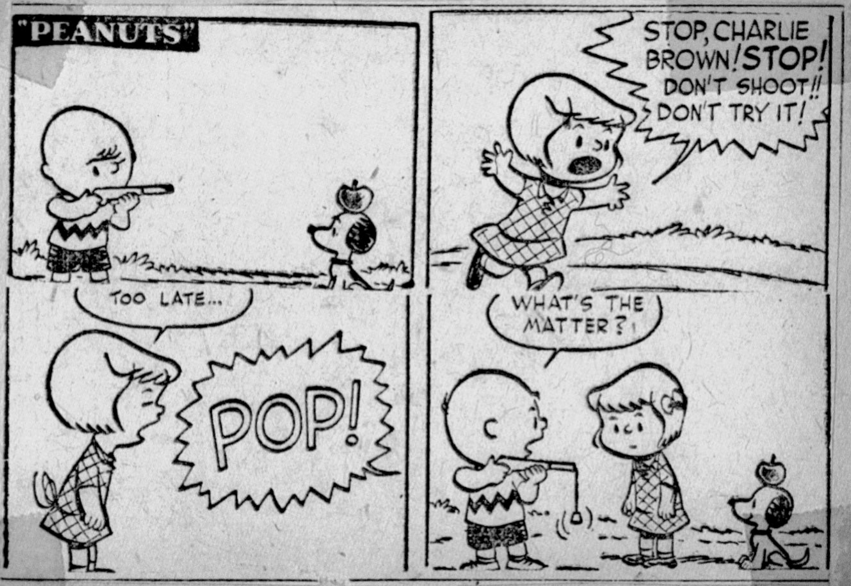
"PEANUTS"
STOP, CHARLIE BROWN! STOP! DON'T SHOOT!! DON'T TRY IT!
TOO LATE...
POP!
WHAT'S THE MATTER?

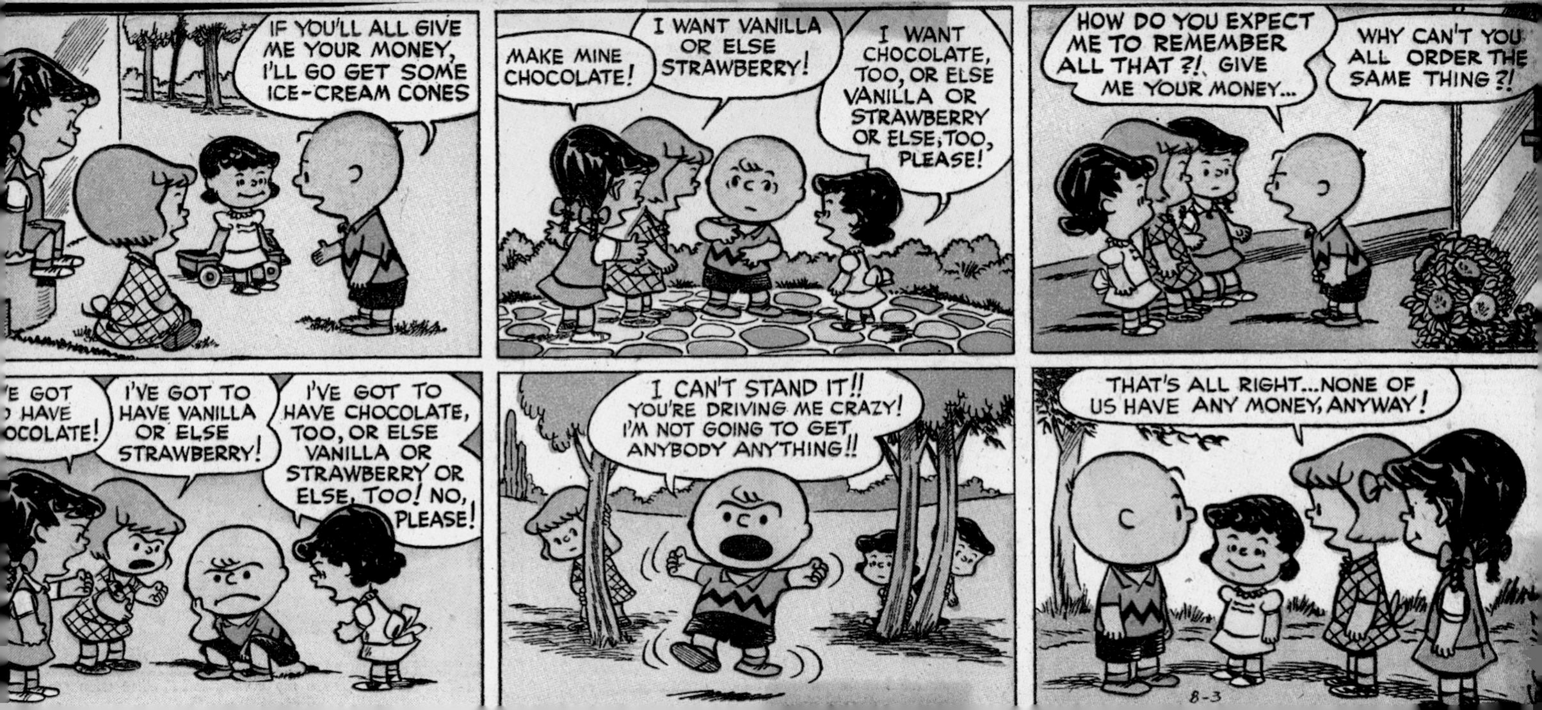
IF YOU'LL ALL GIVE ME YOUR MONEY, I'LL GO GET SOME ICE-CREAM CONES
MAKE MINE CHOCOLATE!
I WANT VANILLA OR ELSE STRAWBERRY!
I WANT CHOCOLATE, TOO, OR ELSE VANILLA OR STRAWBERRY OR ELSE, TOO, PLEASE!
HOW DO YOU EXPECT ME TO REMEMBER ALL THAT?! GIVE ME YOUR MONEY...
WHY CAN'T YOU ALL ORDER THE SAME THING?!
'E GOT HAVE OCOLATE!
I'VE GOT TO HAVE VANILLA OR ELSE STRAWBERRY!
I'VE GOT TO HAVE CHOCOLATE, TOO, OR ELSE VANILLA OR STRAWBERRY OR ELSE, TOO! NO, PLEASE!
I CAN'T STAND IT!! YOU'RE DRIVING ME CRAZY! I'M NOT GOING TO GET ANYBODY ANYTHING!!
THAT'S ALL RIGHT...NONE OF US HAVE ANY MONEY, ANYWAY!
8-3

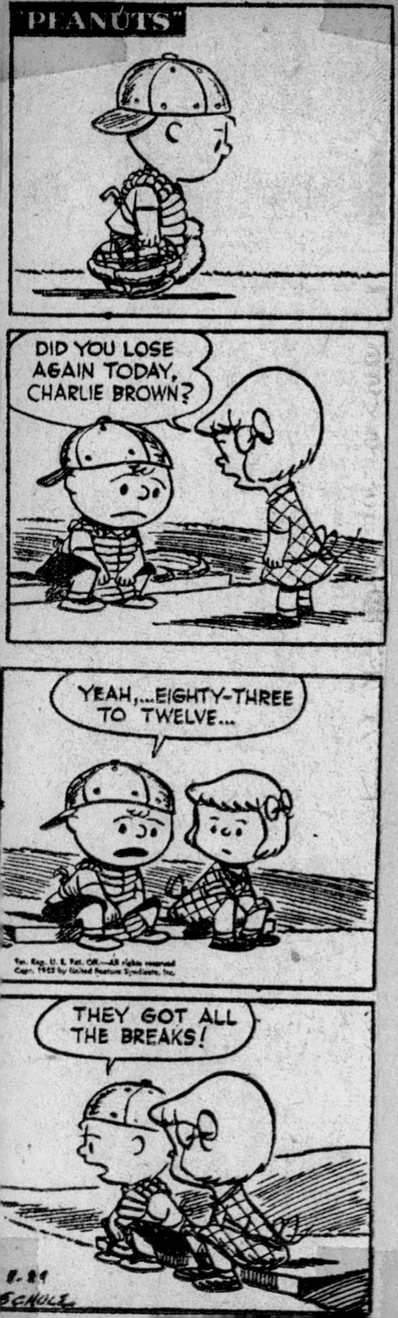
"PEANUTS"
DID YOU LOSE AGAIN TODAY, CHARLIE BROWN?
YEAH,...EIGHTY-THREE TO TWELVE...
THEY GOT ALL THE BREAKS!

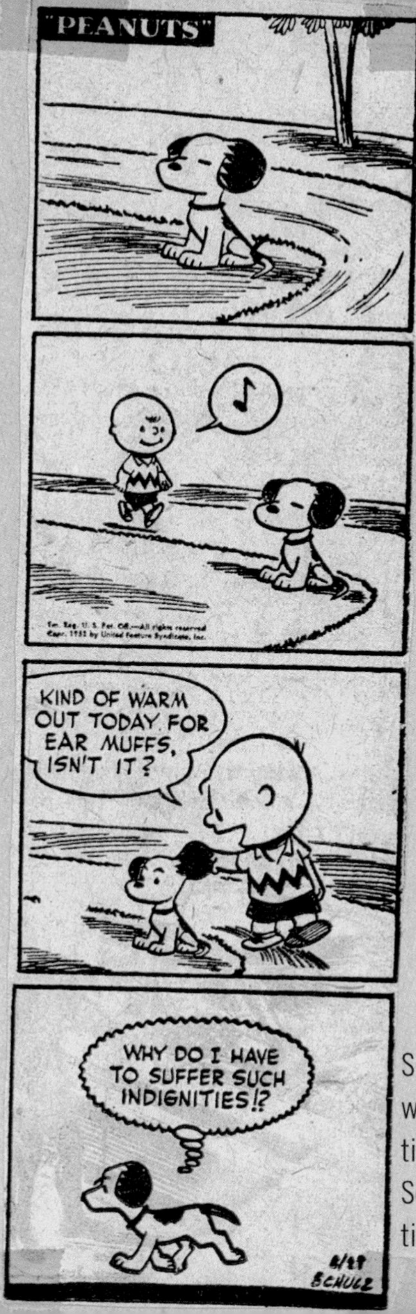
"PEANUTS"
KIND OF WARM OUT TODAY FOR EAR MUFFS, ISN'T IT?
WHY DO I HAVE TO SUFFER SUCH INDIGNITIES!?
SCHULZ

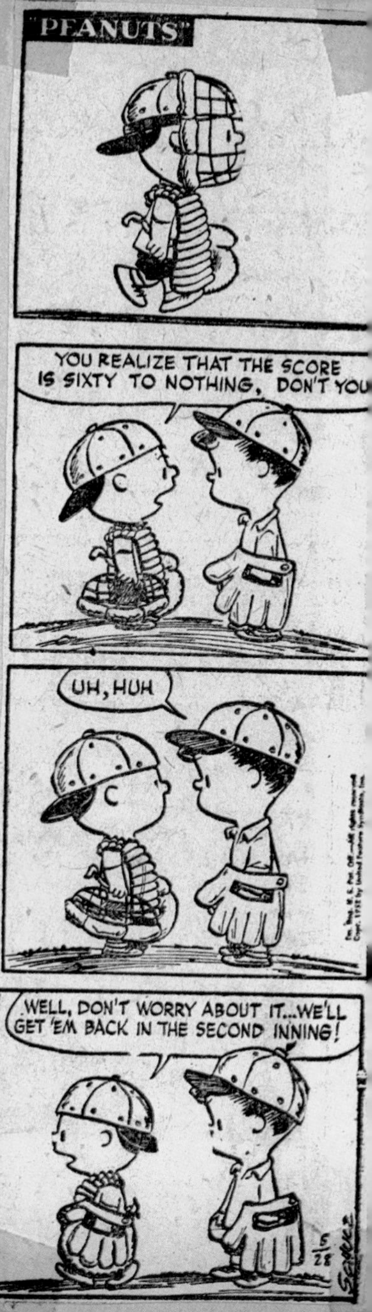
"PEANUTS"
YOU REALIZE THAT THE SCORE IS SIXTY TO NOTHING, DON'T YOU
UH, HUH
WELL, DON'T WORRY ABOUT IT...WE'LL GET 'EM BACK IN THE SECOND INNING!
5/28

Snoopy thinks a thought with words for the first time, 1951.
See opposite for the first time in color.

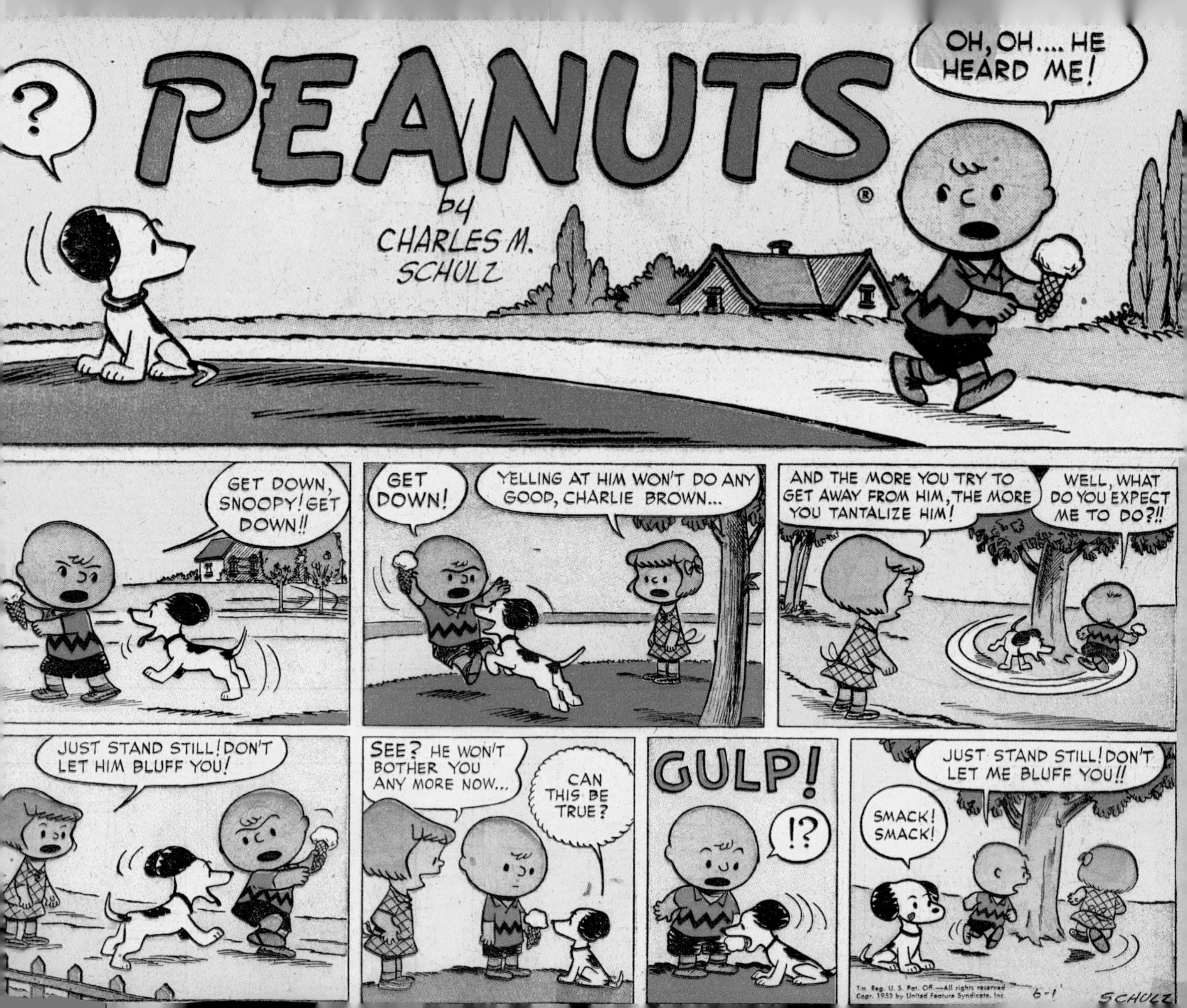
PEANUTS
by CHARLES M. SCHULZ
?
OH, OH.... HE HEARD ME!
GET DOWN, SNOOPY! GET DOWN!!
GET DOWN!
YELLING AT HIM WON'T DO ANY GOOD, CHARLIE BROWN...
AND THE MORE YOU TRY TO GET AWAY FROM HIM, THE MORE YOU TANTALIZE HIM!
WELL, WHAT DO YOU EXPECT ME TO DO?!!
JUST STAND STILL! DON'T LET HIM BLUFF YOU!
SEE? HE WON'T BOTHER YOU ANY MORE NOW...
CAN THIS BE TRUE?
GULP!
!?
JUST STAND STILL! DON'T LET ME BLUFF YOU!!
SMACK! SMACK!
T.m. Reg. U. S. Pat. Off.—All rights reserved Copr. 1952 by United Feature Syndicate, Inc.
6-1
SCHULZ

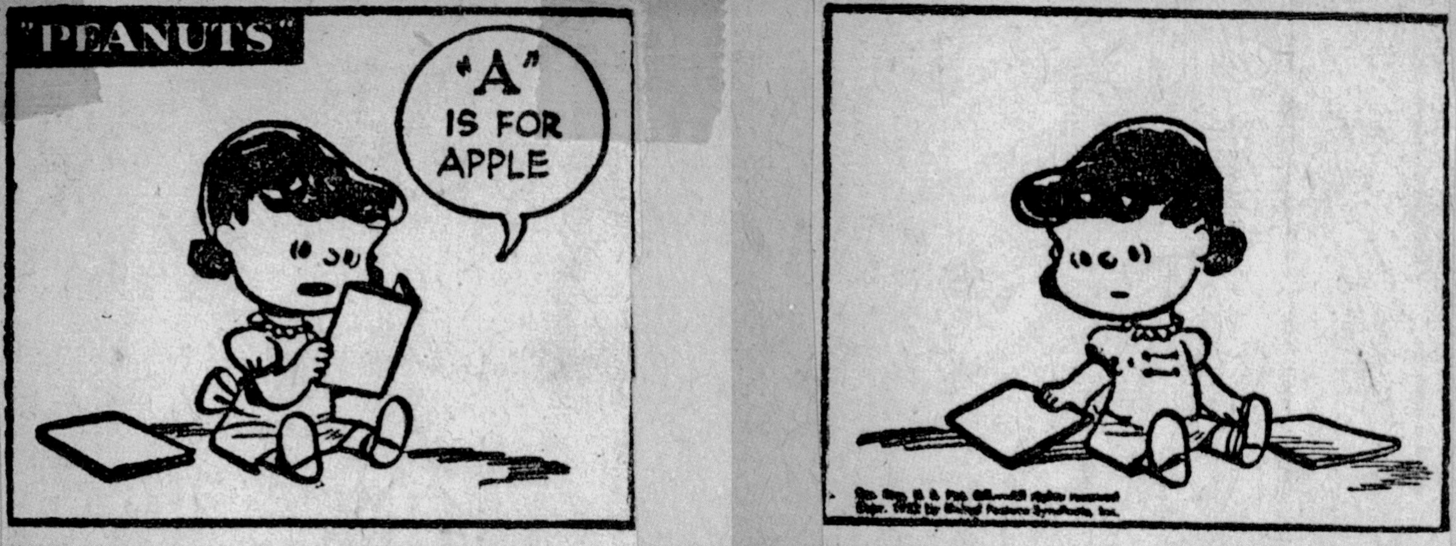
"PEANUTS"
"A" IS FOR APPLE

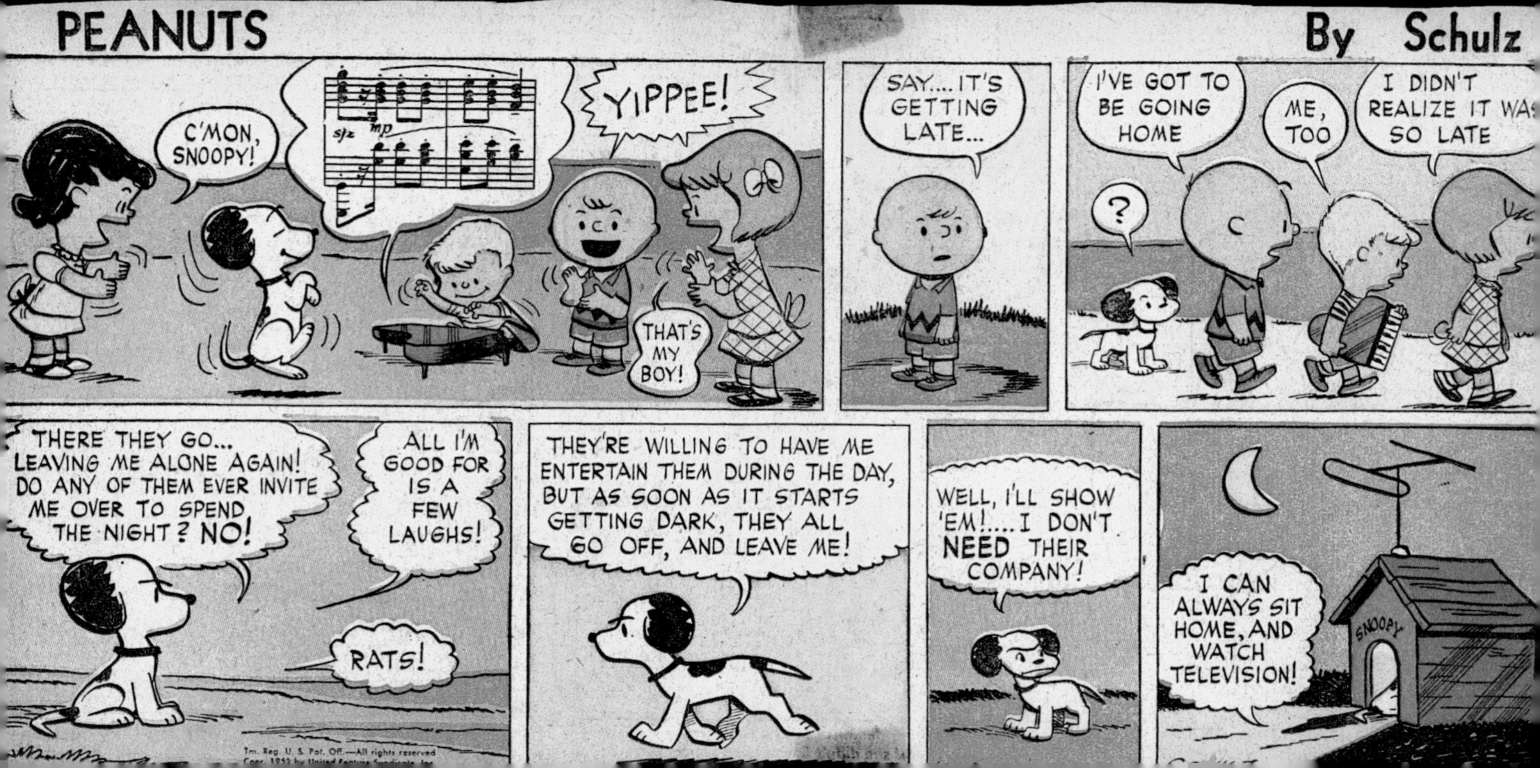
PEANUTS
By Schulz
C'MON, SNOOPY!
YIPPEE!
THAT'S MY BOY!
SAY.... IT'S GETTING LATE...
I'VE GOT TO BE GOING HOME
?
ME, TOO
I DIDN'T REALIZE IT WAS SO LATE
THERE THEY GO... LEAVING ME ALONE AGAIN! DO ANY OF THEM EVER INVITE ME OVER TO SPEND THE NIGHT? NO!
ALL I'M GOOD FOR IS A FEW LAUGHS!
RATS!
THEY'RE WILLING TO HAVE ME ENTERTAIN THEM DURING THE DAY, BUT AS SOON AS IT STARTS GETTING DARK, THEY ALL GO OFF, AND LEAVE ME!
WELL, I'LL SHOW 'EM!.... I DON'T NEED THEIR COMPANY!
I CAN ALWAYS SIT HOME, AND WATCH TELEVISION!
SNOOPY
Tm. Reg. U. S. Pat. Off.—All rights reserved

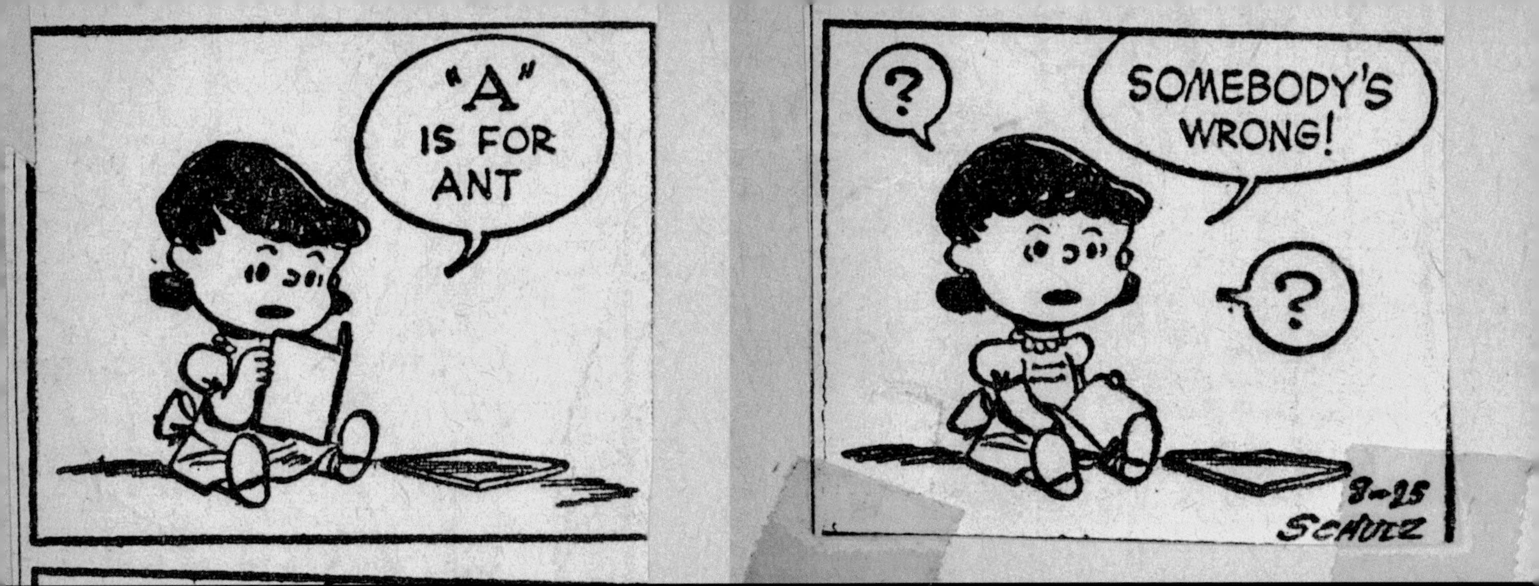
"A" IS FOR ANT
?
SOMEBODY'S WRONG!
?
8-25
SCHULZ

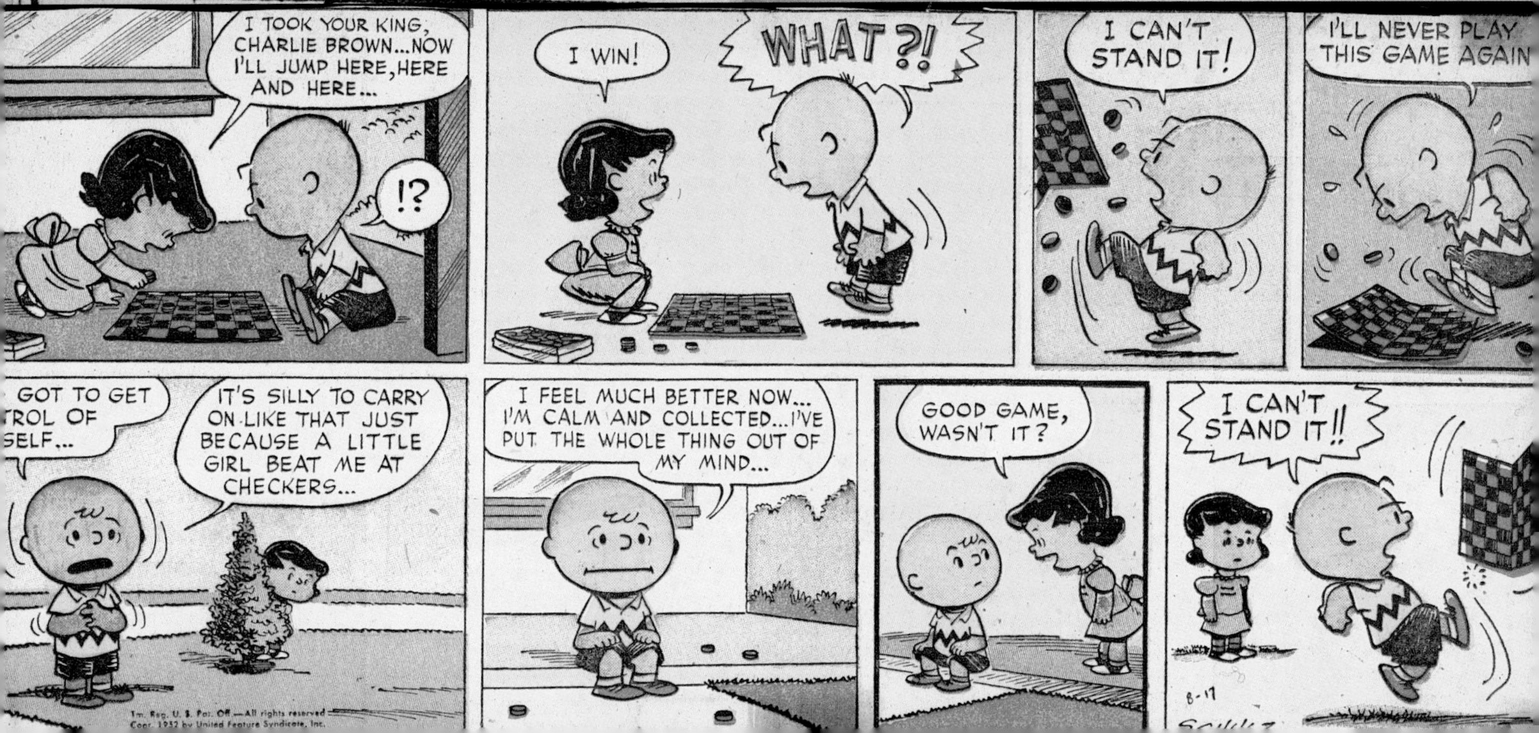
I TOOK YOUR KING, CHARLIE BROWN...NOW I'LL JUMP HERE, HERE AND HERE...
!?
I WIN!
WHAT?!
I CAN'T STAND IT!
I'LL NEVER PLAY THIS GAME AGAIN
GOT TO GET
TROL OF
SELF...
IT'S SILLY TO CARRY ON LIKE THAT JUST BECAUSE A LITTLE GIRL BEAT ME AT CHECKERS...
I FEEL MUCH BETTER NOW... I'M CALM AND COLLECTED...I'VE PUT THE WHOLE THING OUT OF MY MIND...
GOOD GAME, WASN'T IT?
I CAN'T STAND IT!!
8-17
Tm. Reg. U. S. Pat. Off.—All rights reserved
Copr. 1952 by United Feature Syndicate, Inc.

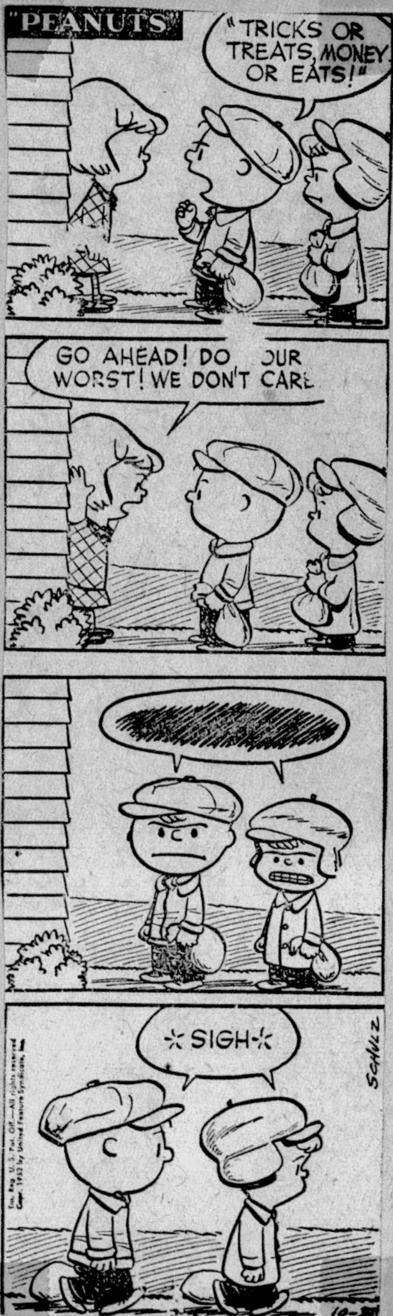
"PEANUTS"
"TRICKS OR TREATS, MONEY OR EATS!"
GO AHEAD! DO OUR WORST! WE DON'T CARE
☆SIGH☆
SCHULZ
Tm. Reg. U. S. Pat. Off.—All rights reserved
Copr. 1952 by United Feature Syndicate, Inc.
10-31

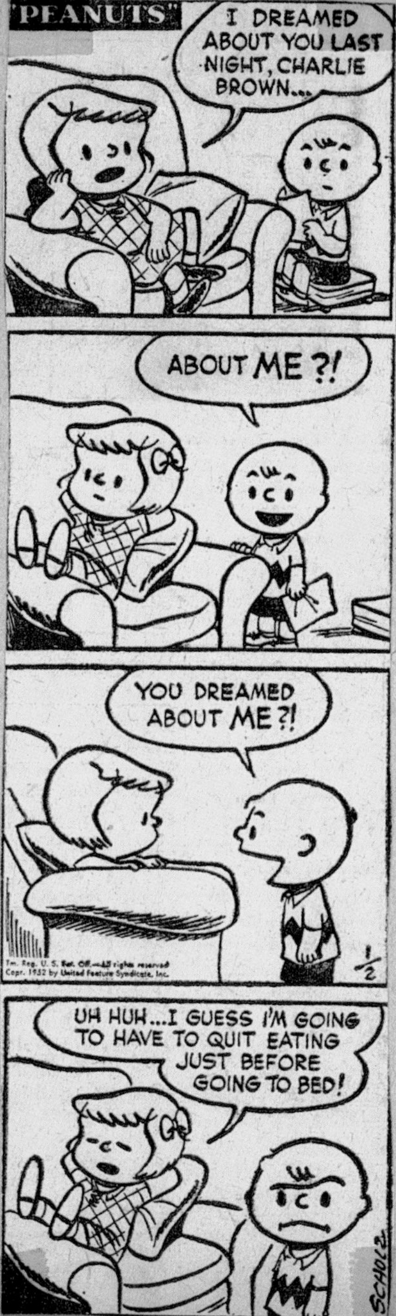
"PEANUTS"
I DREAMED ABOUT YOU LAST NIGHT, CHARLIE BROWN...
ABOUT ME?!
YOU DREAMED ABOUT ME?!
Tm. Reg. U. S. Pat. Off.—All rights reserved
Copr. 1952 by United Feature Syndicate, Inc.
1/2
UH HUH...I GUESS I'M GOING TO HAVE TO QUIT EATING JUST BEFORE GOING TO BED!
SCHULZ

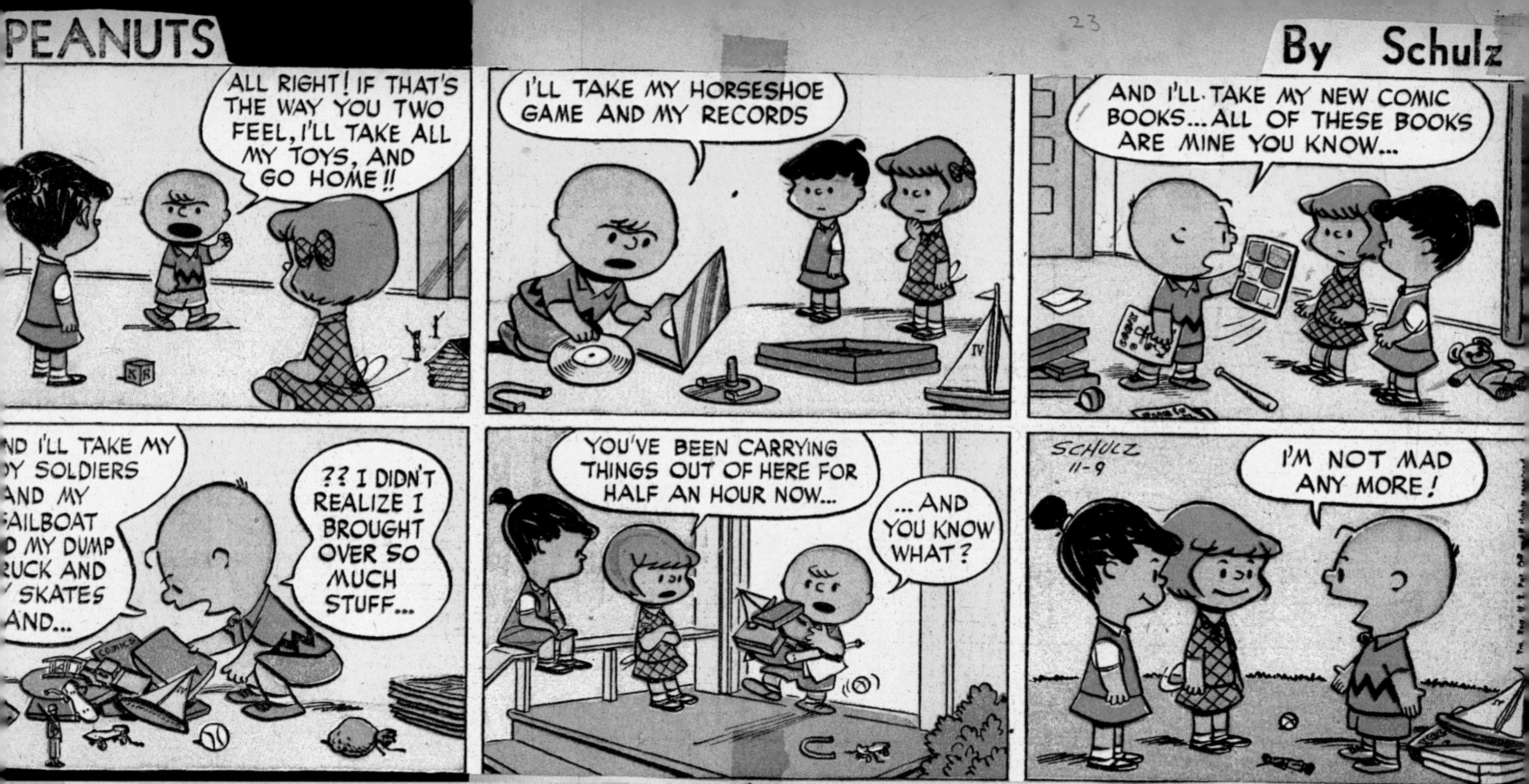
PEANUTS
By Schulz
ALL RIGHT! IF THAT'S THE WAY YOU TWO FEEL, I'LL TAKE ALL MY TOYS, AND GO HOME!!
I'LL TAKE MY HORSESHOE GAME AND MY RECORDS
AND I'LL TAKE MY NEW COMIC BOOKS... ALL OF THESE BOOKS ARE MINE YOU KNOW...
ND I'LL TAKE MY
SOLDIERS
AND MY
AILBOAT
D MY DUMP
RUCK AND
SKATES
AND...
?? I DIDN'T REALIZE I BROUGHT OVER SO MUCH STUFF...
YOU'VE BEEN CARRYING THINGS OUT OF HERE FOR HALF AN HOUR NOW...
...AND YOU KNOW WHAT?
SCHULZ 11-9
I'M NOT MAD ANY MORE!

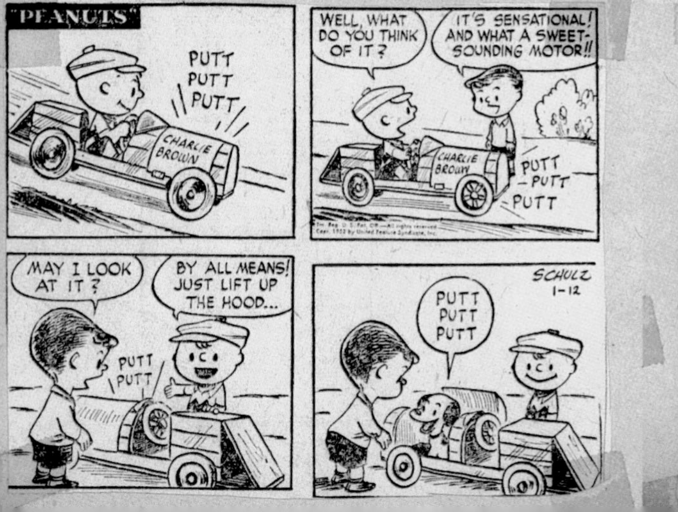
"PEANUTS"
PUTT PUTT PUTT
CHARLIE BROWN
WELL, WHAT DO YOU THINK OF IT?
IT'S SENSATIONAL! AND WHAT A SWEET-SOUNDING MOTOR!!
PUTT -PUTT PUTT
MAY I LOOK AT IT?
BY ALL MEANS! JUST LIFT UP THE HOOD...
PUTT PUTT
SCHULZ 1-12
PUTT PUTT PUTT

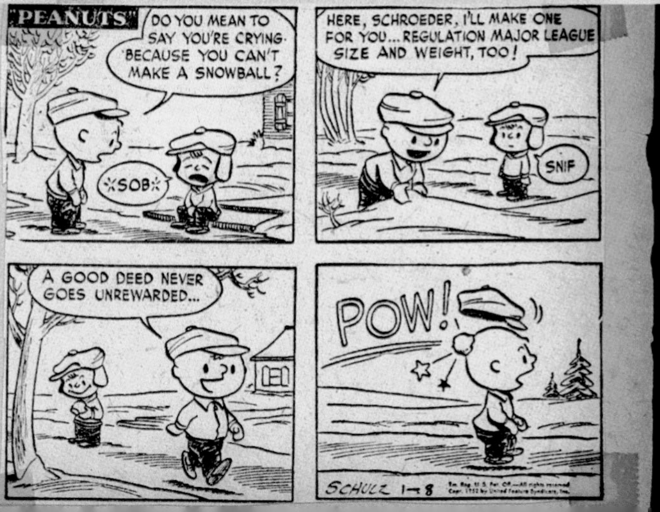
"PEANUTS"
DO YOU MEAN TO SAY YOU'RE CRYING BECAUSE YOU CAN'T MAKE A SNOWBALL?
SOB
HERE, SCHROEDER, I'LL MAKE ONE FOR YOU... REGULATION MAJOR LEAGUE SIZE AND WEIGHT, TOO!
SNIF
A GOOD DEED NEVER GOES UNREWARDED...
POW!
SCHULZ 1-8

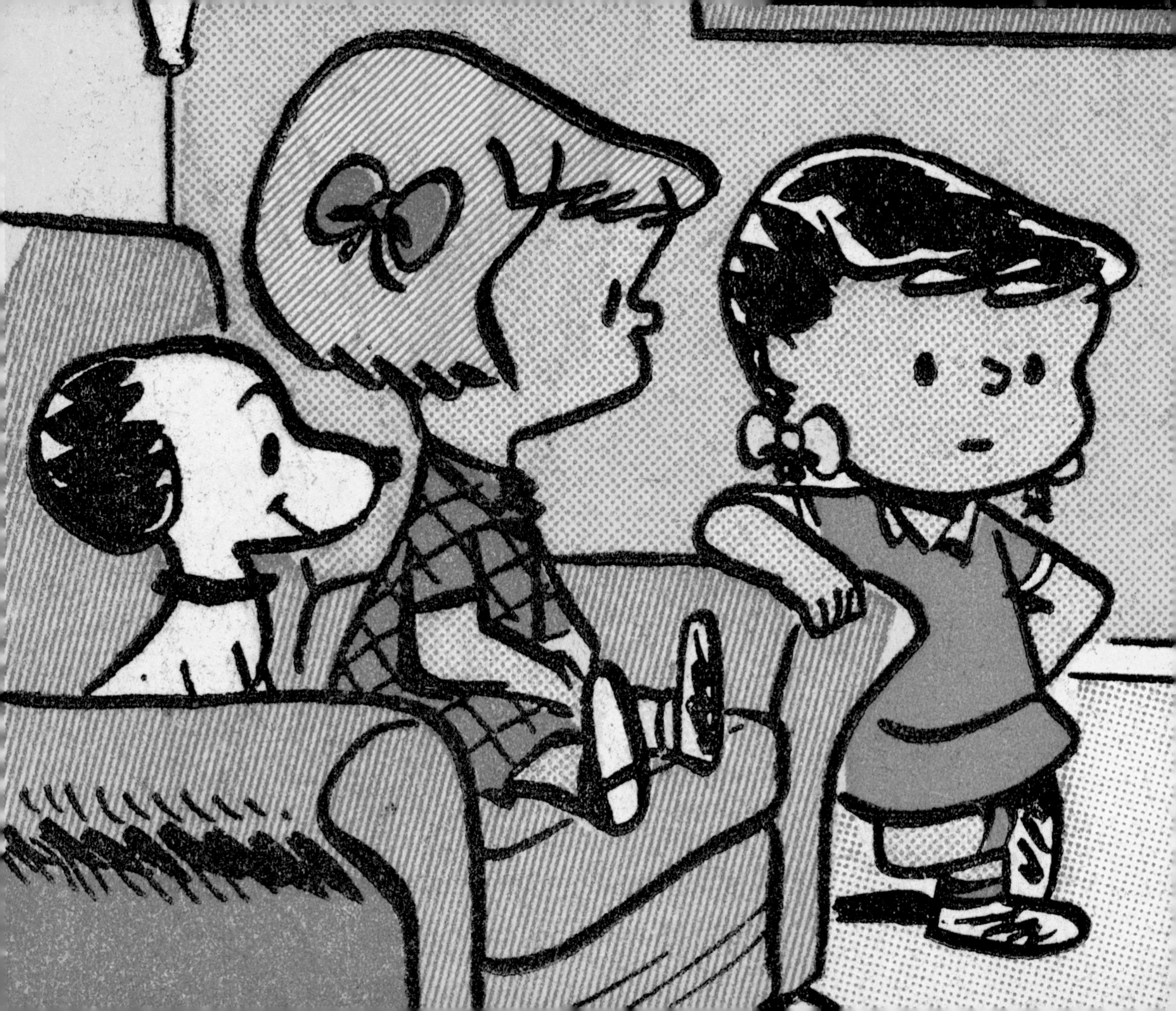

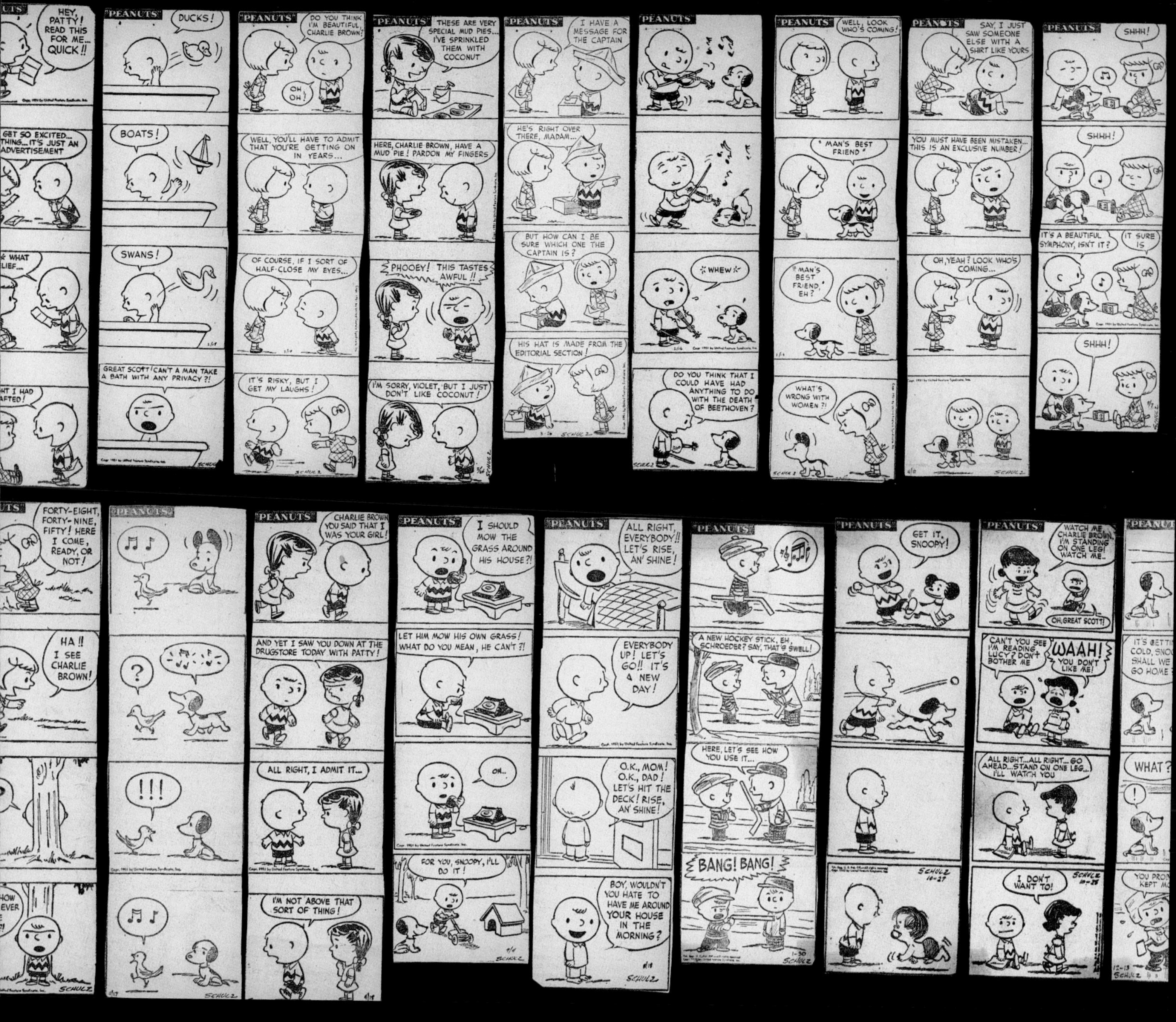
HEY, PATTY! READ THIS FOR ME... QUICK!!
ADVERTISEMENT
"PEANUTS"
DUCKS!
BOATS!
SWANS!
GREAT SCOTT! CAN'T A MAN TAKE A BATH WITH ANY PRIVACY?!
"PEANUTS"
DO YOU THINK I'M BEAUTIFUL, CHARLIE BROWN?
OH OH!
WELL, YOU'LL HAVE TO ADMIT THAT YOU'RE GETTING ON IN YEARS...
OF COURSE, IF I SORT OF HALF-CLOSE MY EYES...
IT'S RISKY, BUT I GET MY LAUGHS!
"PEANUTS"
THESE ARE VERY SPECIAL MUD PIES... I'VE SPRINKLED THEM WITH COCONUT
HERE, CHARLIE BROWN, HAVE A MUD PIE! PARDON MY FINGERS
PHOOEY! THIS TASTES AWFUL!!
I'M SORRY, VIOLET, BUT I JUST DON'T LIKE COCONUT!
"PEANUTS"
I HAVE A MESSAGE FOR THE CAPTAIN
HE'S RIGHT OVER THERE, MADAM...
BUT HOW CAN I BE SURE WHICH ONE THE CAPTAIN IS?
HIS HAT IS MADE FROM THE EDITORIAL SECTION!
"PEANUTS"
WHEW
DO YOU THINK THAT I COULD HAVE HAD ANYTHING TO DO WITH THE DEATH OF BEETHOVEN?
"PEANUTS"
WELL, LOOK WHO'S COMING!
"MAN'S BEST FRIEND"
"MAN'S BEST FRIEND," EH?
WHAT'S WRONG WITH WOMEN?!
"PEANUTS"
SAY, I JUST SAW SOMEONE ELSE WITH A SHIRT LIKE YOURS
YOU MUST HAVE BEEN MISTAKEN... THIS IS AN EXCLUSIVE NUMBER!
OH, YEAH? LOOK WHO'S COMING...
"PEANUTS"
SHHH!
SHHH!
IT'S A BEAUTIFUL SYMPHONY, ISN'T IT?
IT SURE IS
SHHH!
FORTY-EIGHT, FORTY-NINE, FIFTY! HERE I COME, READY, OR NOT!
HA!! I SEE CHARLIE BROWN!
"PEANUTS"
?
!!!
"PEANUTS"
CHARLIE BROWN YOU SAID THAT I WAS YOUR GIRL!
AND YET I SAW YOU DOWN AT THE DRUGSTORE TODAY WITH PATTY!
ALL RIGHT, I ADMIT IT...
I'M NOT ABOVE THAT SORT OF THING!
"PEANUTS"
I SHOULD MOW THE GRASS AROUND HIS HOUSE?!
LET HIM MOW HIS OWN GRASS! WHAT DO YOU MEAN, HE CAN'T?!
OH..
FOR YOU, SNOOPY, I'LL DO IT!
"PEANUTS"
ALL RIGHT, EVERYBODY!! LET'S RISE, AN' SHINE!
EVERYBODY UP! LET'S GO!! IT'S A NEW DAY!
O.K., MOM! O.K., DAD! LET'S HIT THE DECK! RISE, AN' SHINE!
BOY, WOULDN'T YOU HATE TO HAVE ME AROUND YOUR HOUSE IN THE MORNING?
"PEANUTS"
A NEW HOCKEY STICK, EH, SCHROEDER? SAY, THAT'S SWELL!
HERE, LET'S SEE HOW YOU USE IT...
BANG! BANG!
"PEANUTS"
GET IT, SNOOPY!
"PEANUTS"
WATCH ME CHARLIE BROWN. I'M STANDING ON ONE LEG! WATCH ME..
OH, GREAT SCOTT!
CAN'T YOU SEE I'M READING, LUCY? DON'T BOTHER ME
WAAH! YOU DON'T LIKE ME!
ALL RIGHT... ALL RIGHT... GO AHEAD... STAND ON ONE LEG! I'LL WATCH YOU
I DON'T WANT TO!
WHAT?
!
SCHULZ

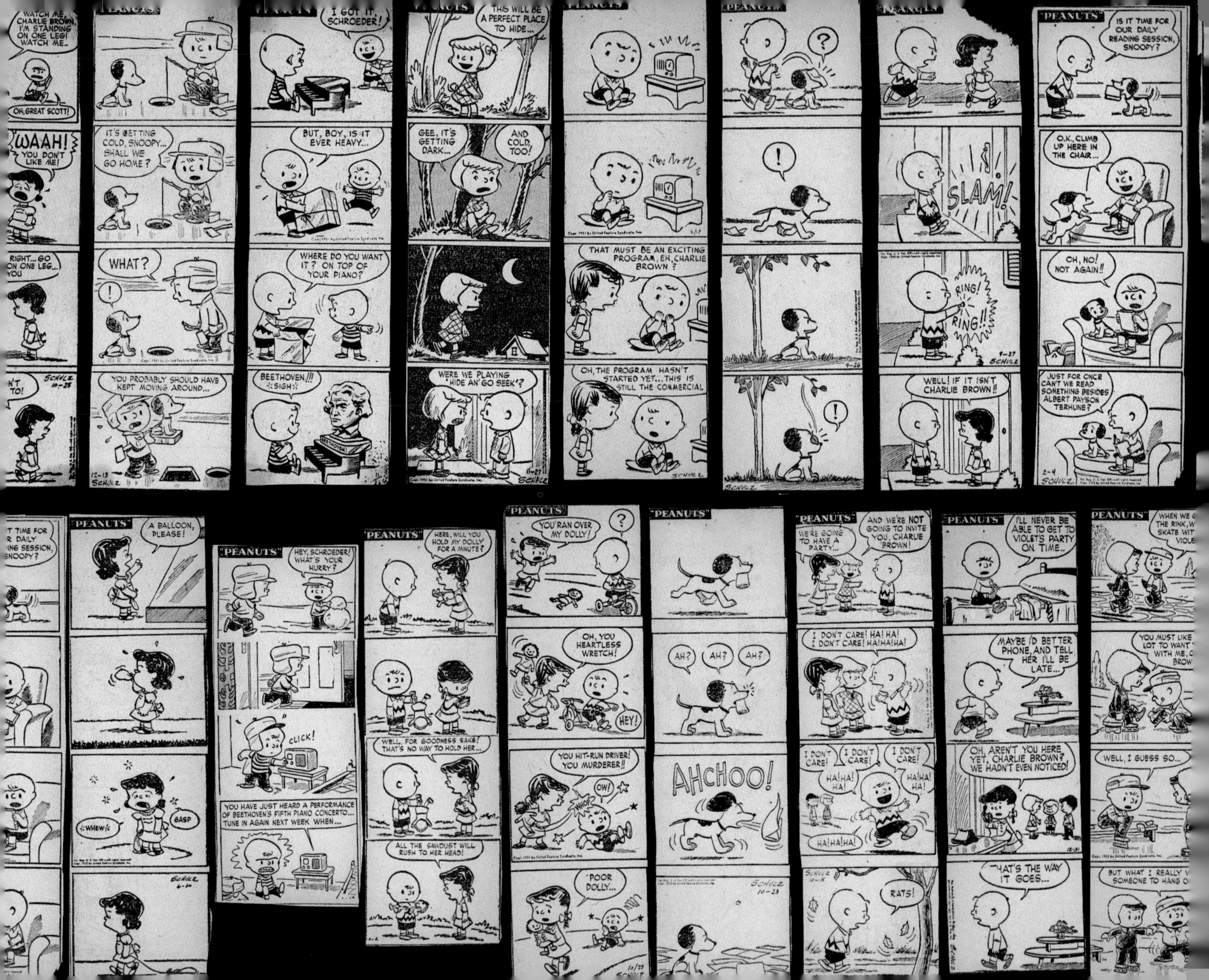

WATCH ME, CHARLIE BROWN, I'M STANDING ON ONE LEG! WATCH ME..
OH, GREAT SCOTT!
WAAH! YOU DON'T LIKE ME!
SCHULZ 10-28
IT'S GETTING COLD, SNOOPY... SHALL WE GO HOME?
WHAT?
!
YOU PROBABLY SHOULD HAVE KEPT MOVING AROUND...
12-13 SCHULZ
I GOT IT, SCHROEDER!
BUT, BOY, IS IT EVER HEAVY...
WHERE DO YOU WANT IT? ON TOP OF YOUR PIANO?
BEETHOVEN!!! *SIGH*
THIS WILL BE A PERFECT PLACE TO HIDE...
GEE, IT'S GETTING DARK...
AND COLD, TOO!
WERE WE PLAYING 'HIDE AN' GO SEEK'?
11-27 SCHULZ
THAT MUST BE AN EXCITING PROGRAM, EH, CHARLIE BROWN?
OH, THE PROGRAM HASN'T STARTED YET... THIS IS STILL THE COMMERCIAL
SCHULZ
?
!
9-26
!
SCHULZ
SLAM!
RING! RING!!
9-27 SCHULZ
WELL! IF IT ISN'T CHARLIE BROWN!!
IS IT TIME FOR OUR DAILY READING SESSION, SNOOPY?
O.K., CLIMB UP HERE IN THE CHAIR...
OH, NO! NOT AGAIN!!
JUST FOR ONCE CAN'T WE READ SOMETHING BESIDES ALBERT PAYSON TERHUNE?
2-4 SCHULZ
"PEANUTS"
A BALLOON, PLEASE!
WHEW
GASP
SCHULZ 6-10
"PEANUTS"
HEY, SCHROEDER! WHAT'S YOUR HURRY?
CLICK!
YOU HAVE JUST HEARD A PERFORMANCE OF BEETHOVEN'S FIFTH PIANO CONCERTO... TUNE IN AGAIN NEXT WEEK WHEN...
"PEANUTS"
HERE, WILL YOU HOLD MY DOLLY FOR A MINUTE?
WELL, FOR GOODNESS SAKE! THAT'S NO WAY TO HOLD HER...
ALL THE SAWDUST WILL RUSH TO HER HEAD!
"PEANUTS"
YOU RAN OVER MY DOLLY!
?
OH, YOU HEARTLESS WRETCH!
HEY!
YOU HIT-RUN DRIVER! YOU MURDERER!!
OW!
WHOP
POOR DOLLY...
10/27 SCHULZ
"PEANUTS"
AH?
AH?
AH?
AHCHOO!
SCHULZ 10-23
"PEANUTS"
WE'RE GOING TO HAVE A PARTY...
AND WE'RE NOT GOING TO INVITE YOU, CHARLIE BROWN!
I DON'T CARE! HA! HA! I DON'T CARE! HA!HA!HA!
I DON'T CARE!
I DON'T CARE!
I DON'T CARE!
HA! HA! HA!
HA! HA! HA!
HA!HA!HA!
SCHULZ 10-15
RATS!
"PEANUTS"
I'LL NEVER BE ABLE TO GET TO VIOLET'S PARTY ON TIME..
MAYBE I'D BETTER PHONE, AND TELL HER I'LL BE LATE...
OH, AREN'T YOU HERE YET, CHARLIE BROWN? WE HADN'T EVEN NOTICED!
12-31
THAT'S THE WAY IT GOES...
"PEANUTS"
WELL, I GUESS SO...

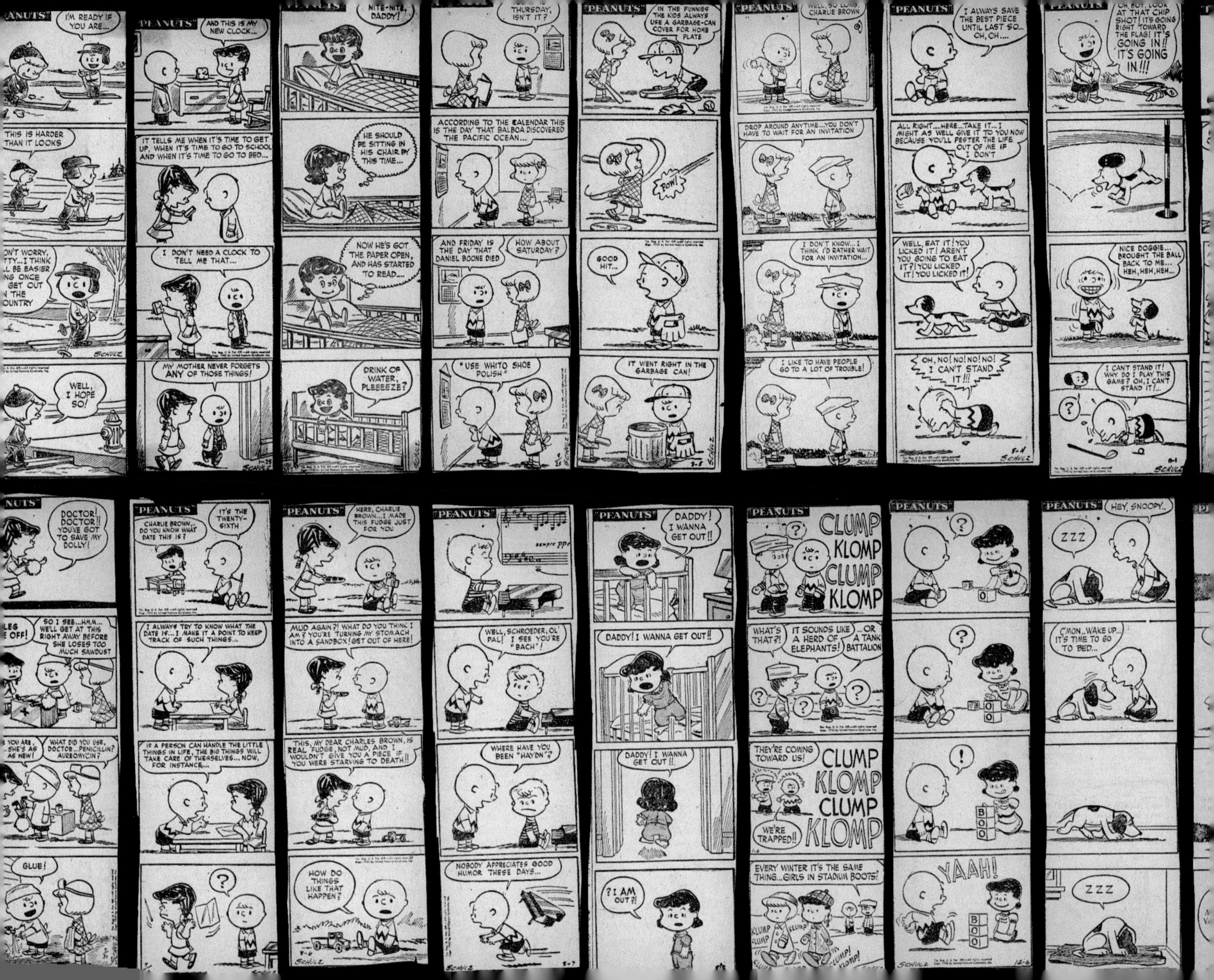
I'M READY IF YOU ARE...
THIS IS HARDER THAN IT LOOKS
WELL, I HOPE SO!
"PEANUTS"
AND THIS IS MY NEW CLOCK...
IT TELLS ME WHEN IT'S TIME TO GET UP, WHEN IT'S TIME TO GO TO SCHOOL AND WHEN IT'S TIME TO GO TO BED...
I DON'T NEED A CLOCK TO TELL ME THAT...
MY MOTHER NEVER FORGETS ANY OF THOSE THINGS!
SCHULZ
NITE-NITE, DADDY!
HE SHOULD BE SITTING IN HIS CHAIR BY THIS TIME...
NOW HE'S GOT THE PAPER OPEN, AND HAS STARTED TO READ...
DRINK OF WATER, PLEEEEZE?
THURSDAY, ISN'T IT?
ACCORDING TO THE CALENDAR THIS IS THE DAY THAT BALBOA DISCOVERED THE PACIFIC OCEAN...
AND FRIDAY IS THE DAY THAT DANIEL BOONE DIED
HOW ABOUT SATURDAY?
"USE WHITO SHOE POLISH"
"PEANUTS"
IN THE FUNNIES THE KIDS ALWAYS USE A GARBAGE-CAN COVER FOR HOME PLATE
POW!
GOOD HIT...
IT WENT RIGHT IN THE GARBAGE CAN!
"PEANUTS"
WELL, SO LONG, CHARLIE BROWN
DROP AROUND ANYTIME...YOU DON'T HAVE TO WAIT FOR AN INVITATION
I DON'T KNOW... I THINK I'D RATHER WAIT FOR AN INVITATION...
I LIKE TO HAVE PEOPLE GO TO A LOT OF TROUBLE!
"PEANUTS"
I ALWAYS SAVE THE BEST PIECE UNTIL LAST SO... OH, OH.....
ALL RIGHT....HERE...TAKE IT...I MIGHT AS WELL GIVE IT TO YOU NOW BECAUSE YOU'LL PESTER THE LIFE OUT OF ME IF I DON'T
WELL, EAT IT! YOU LICKED IT! AREN'T YOU GOING TO EAT IT?! YOU LICKED IT! YOU LICKED IT!
OH, NO! NO! NO! NO! I CAN'T STAND IT!!!
SCHULZ
OH, BOY, LOOK AT THAT CHIP SHOT! IT'S GOING RIGHT TOWARD THE FLAG! IT'S GOING IN!! IT'S GOING IN!!!
NICE DOGGIE... BROUGHT THE BALL BACK TO ME... HEH, HEH, HEH...
I CAN'T STAND IT! WHY DO I PLAY THIS GAME? OH, I CAN'T STAND IT!...
?
DOCTOR! DOCTOR!! YOU'VE GOT TO SAVE MY DOLLY!
SO I SEE...HMM... WE'LL GET AT THIS RIGHT AWAY BEFORE SHE LOSES TOO MUCH SAWDUST
WHAT DID YOU USE, DOCTOR...PENICILLIN? AUREOMYCIN?
GLUE!
"PEANUTS"
CHARLIE BROWN... DO YOU KNOW WHAT DATE THIS IS?
IT'S THE TWENTY-SIXTH
I ALWAYS TRY TO KNOW WHAT THE DATE IS... I MAKE IT A POINT TO KEEP TRACK OF SUCH THINGS...
IF A PERSON CAN HANDLE THE LITTLE THINGS IN LIFE, THE BIG THINGS WILL TAKE CARE OF THEMSELVES.... NOW, FOR INSTANCE...
?
"PEANUTS"
HERE, CHARLIE BROWN... I MADE THIS FUDGE JUST FOR YOU
MUD AGAIN?! WHAT DO YOU THINK I AM? YOU'RE TURNING MY STOMACH INTO A SANDBOX! GET OUT OF HERE!
THIS, MY DEAR CHARLES BROWN, IS REAL FUDGE, NOT MUD, AND I WOULDN'T GIVE YOU A PIECE IF YOU WERE STARVING TO DEATH!!
HOW DO THINGS LIKE THAT HAPPEN?
SCHULZ
"PEANUTS"
sempre ppp
WELL, SCHROEDER, OL' PAL! I SEE YOU'RE "BACH"!
WHERE HAVE YOU BEEN "HAYDN"?
NOBODY APPRECIATES GOOD HUMOR THESE DAYS...
SCHULZ
"PEANUTS"
DADDY! I WANNA GET OUT!!
DADDY! I WANNA GET OUT!!
DADDY! I WANNA GET OUT!!
?I AM OUT?!
"PEANUTS"
?
CLUMP KLOMP CLUMP KLOMP
WHAT'S THAT?!
IT SOUNDS LIKE A HERD OF ELEPHANTS!
...OR A TANK BATTALION
THEY'RE COMING TOWARD US!
CLUMP KLOMP CLUMP KLOMP
WE'RE TRAPPED!!
EVERY WINTER IT'S THE SAME THING...GIRLS IN STADIUM BOOTS!
KLUMP CLUMP KLUMP
CLUMP! KLOMP!
"PEANUTS"
?
?
!
BOO
YAAAH!
BOO
SCHULZ
"PEANUTS"
HEY, SNOOPY..
ZZZ
C'MON...WAKE UP... IT'S TIME TO GO TO BED...
ZZZ

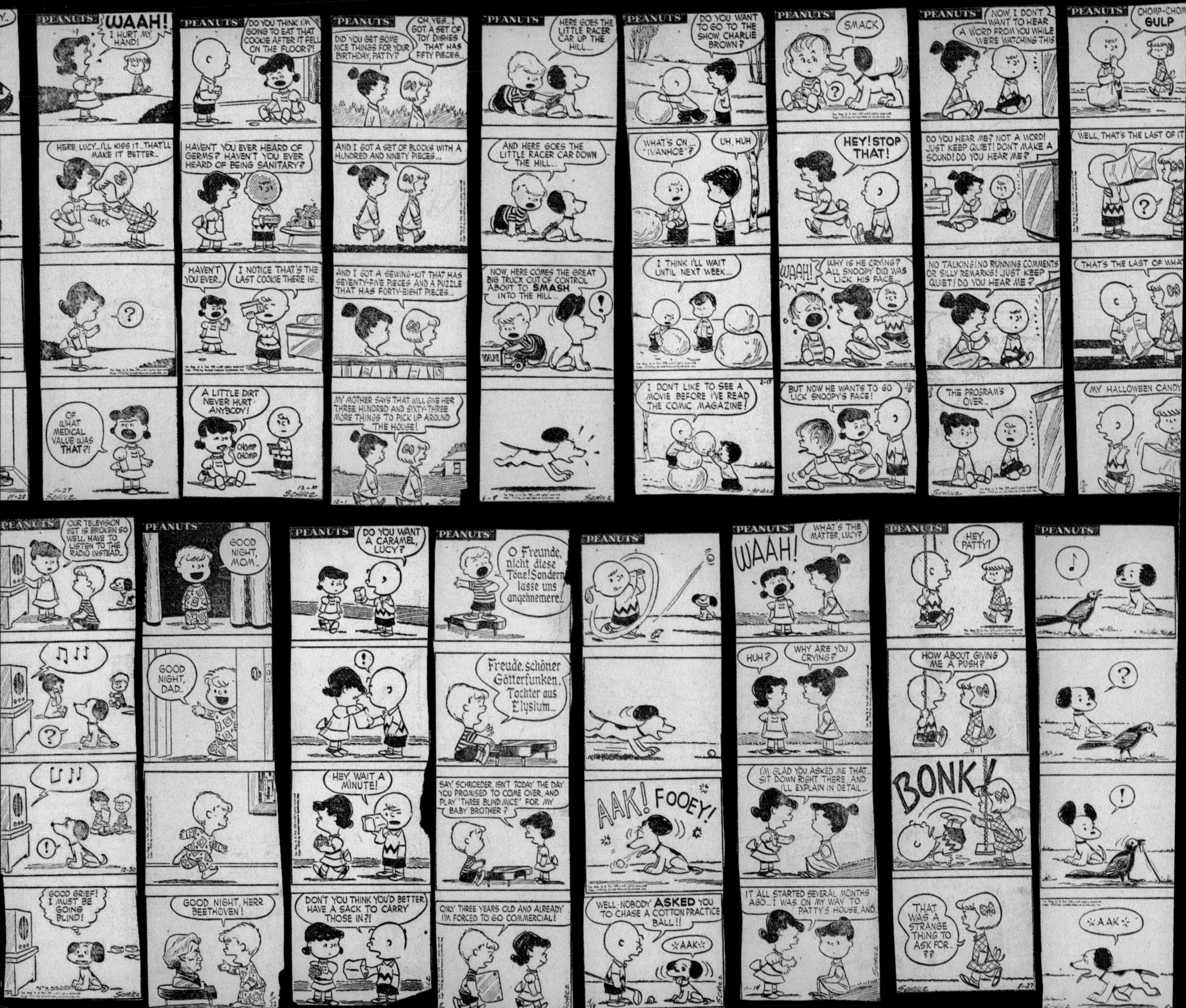
PEANUTS
WAAH! I HURT MY HAND!
HERE, LUCY...I'LL KISS IT...THAT'LL MAKE IT BETTER..
SMACK
?
OF WHAT MEDICAL VALUE WAS THAT?!
11-27
SCHULZ
PEANUTS
DO YOU THINK I'M GOING TO EAT THAT COOKIE AFTER IT FELL ON THE FLOOR?!
HAVEN'T YOU EVER HEARD OF GERMS? HAVEN'T YOU EVER HEARD OF BEING SANITARY?
HAVEN'T YOU EVER..
I NOTICE THAT'S THE LAST COOKIE THERE IS..
A LITTLE DIRT NEVER HURT ANYBODY!
CHOMP CHOMP
12-10
SCHULZ
PEANUTS
DID YOU GET SOME NICE THINGS FOR YOUR BIRTHDAY, PATTY?
OH, YES... I GOT A SET OF TOY DISHES THAT HAS FIFTY PIECES..
AND I GOT A SET OF BLOCKS WITH A HUNDRED AND NINETY PIECES...
AND I GOT A SEWING-KIT THAT HAS SEVENTY-FIVE PIECES AND A PUZZLE THAT HAS FORTY-EIGHT PIECES..
MY MOTHER SAYS THAT WILL GIVE HER THREE HUNDRED AND SIXTY-THREE MORE THINGS TO PICK UP AROUND THE HOUSE!
12-1
PEANUTS
HERE GOES THE LITTLE RACER CAR UP THE HILL...
AND HERE GOES THE LITTLE RACER CAR DOWN THE HILL...
NOW, HERE COMES THE GREAT BIG TRUCK OUT OF CONTROL ABOUT TO SMASH INTO THE HILL...
!
VAN
6-8
SCHULZ
PEANUTS
DO YOU WANT TO GO TO THE SHOW, CHARLIE BROWN?
WHAT'S ON... "IVANHOE"?
UH, HUH
I THINK I'LL WAIT UNTIL NEXT WEEK...
I DON'T LIKE TO SEE A MOVIE BEFORE I'VE READ THE COMIC MAGAZINE!
2-17
SCHULZ
PEANUTS
SMACK
?
HEY! STOP THAT!
WAAH!
WHY IS HE CRYING? ALL SNOOPY DID WAS LICK HIS FACE...
BUT NOW HE WANTS TO GO LICK SNOOPY'S FACE!
PEANUTS
NOW, I DON'T WANT TO HEAR A WORD FROM YOU WHILE WE'RE WATCHING THIS
DO YOU HEAR ME? NOT A WORD! JUST KEEP QUIET! DON'T MAKE A SOUND! DO YOU HEAR ME?
NO TALKING! NO RUNNING COMMENTS OR SILLY REMARKS! JUST KEEP QUIET! DO YOU HEAR ME?
THE PROGRAM'S OVER..
SCHULZ
PEANUTS
CHOMP-CHOMP GULP
WELL, THAT'S THE LAST OF IT
?
THAT'S THE LAST OF WHAT
MY HALLOWEEN CANDY
PEANUTS
OUR TELEVISION SET IS BROKEN SO WE'LL HAVE TO LISTEN TO THE RADIO INSTEAD..
?
!
GOOD GRIEF! I MUST BE GOING BLIND!
12-30
SCHULZ
PEANUTS
GOOD NIGHT, MOM..
GOOD NIGHT, DAD..
GOOD NIGHT, HERR BEETHOVEN!
PEANUTS
DO YOU WANT A CARAMEL, LUCY?
!
HEY, WAIT A MINUTE!
DON'T YOU THINK YOU'D BETTER HAVE A SACK TO CARRY THOSE IN?!
PEANUTS
O Freunde, nicht diese Töne! Sondern lasse uns angenehmere!..
Freude, schöner Götterfunken, Tochter aus Elysium..
SAY, SCHROEDER, ISN'T TODAY THE DAY YOU PROMISED TO COME OVER, AND PLAY "THREE BLIND MICE" FOR MY BABY BROTHER?
ONLY THREE YEARS OLD AND ALREADY I'M FORCED TO GO COMMERCIAL!
PEANUTS
AAK! FOOEY!
WELL, NOBODY ASKED YOU TO CHASE A COTTON PRACTICE BALL!!
AAK
SCHULZ
PEANUTS
WAAH!
WHAT'S THE MATTER, LUCY?
HUH?
WHY ARE YOU CRYING?
I'M GLAD YOU ASKED ME THAT.. SIT DOWN RIGHT THERE, AND I'LL EXPLAIN IN DETAIL..
IT ALL STARTED SEVERAL MONTHS AGO... I WAS ON MY WAY TO PATTY'S HOUSE, AND..
11-14
SCHULZ
PEANUTS
HEY, PATTY!
HOW ABOUT GIVING ME A PUSH?
BONK!
THAT WAS A STRANGE THING TO ASK FOR.. ??
SCHULZ
PEANUTS
?
!
AAK

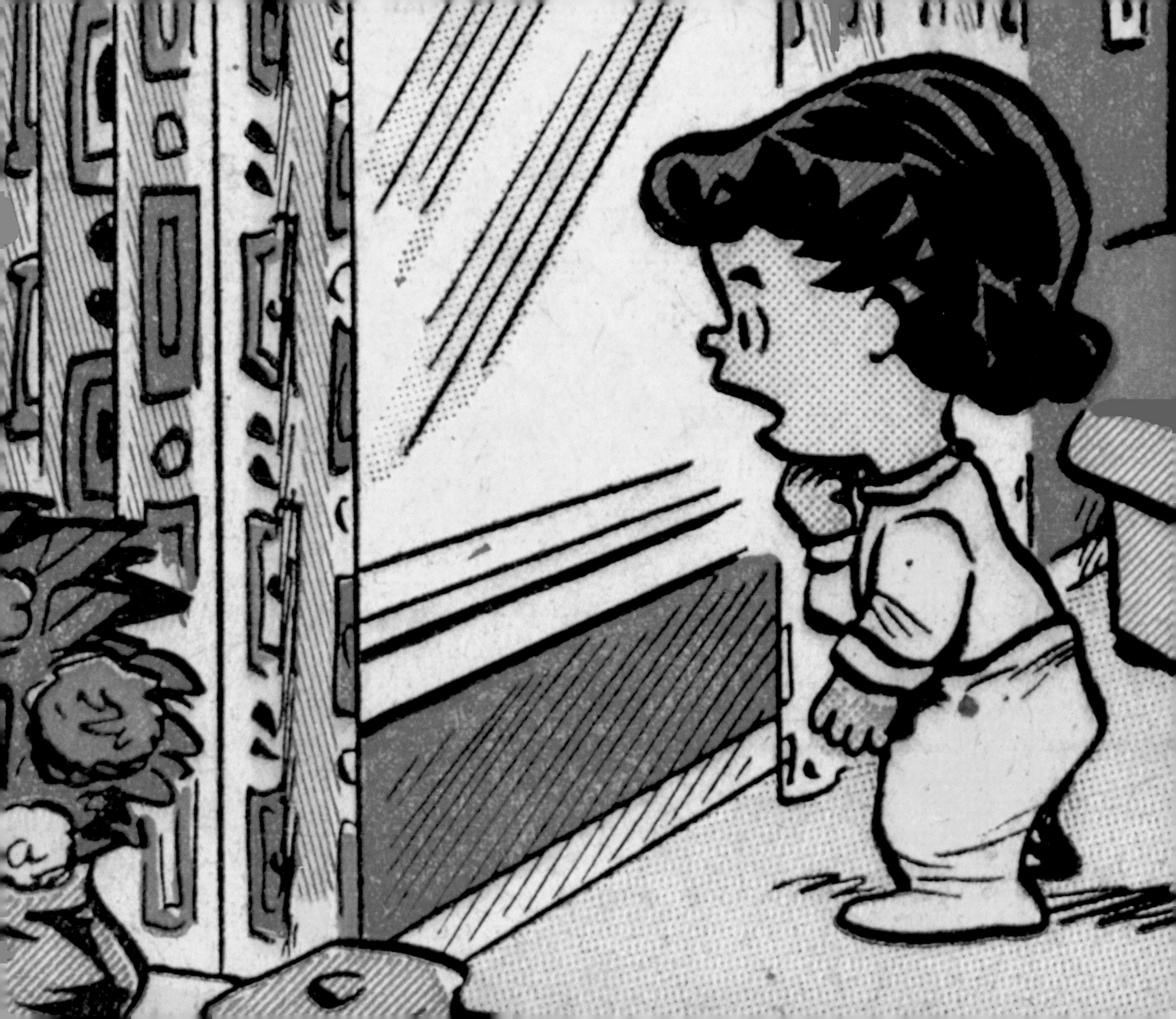

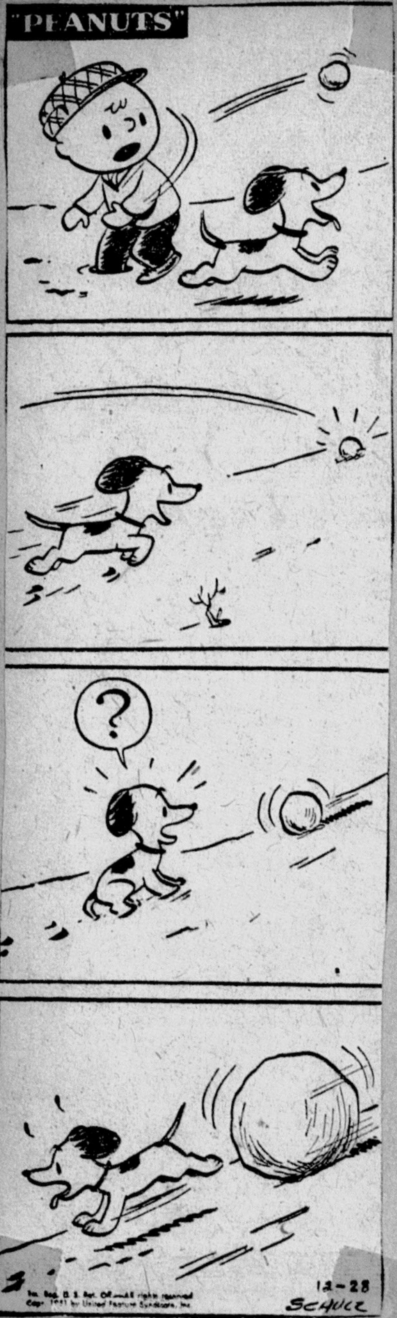
"PEANUTS"
?
12-28
SCHULZ

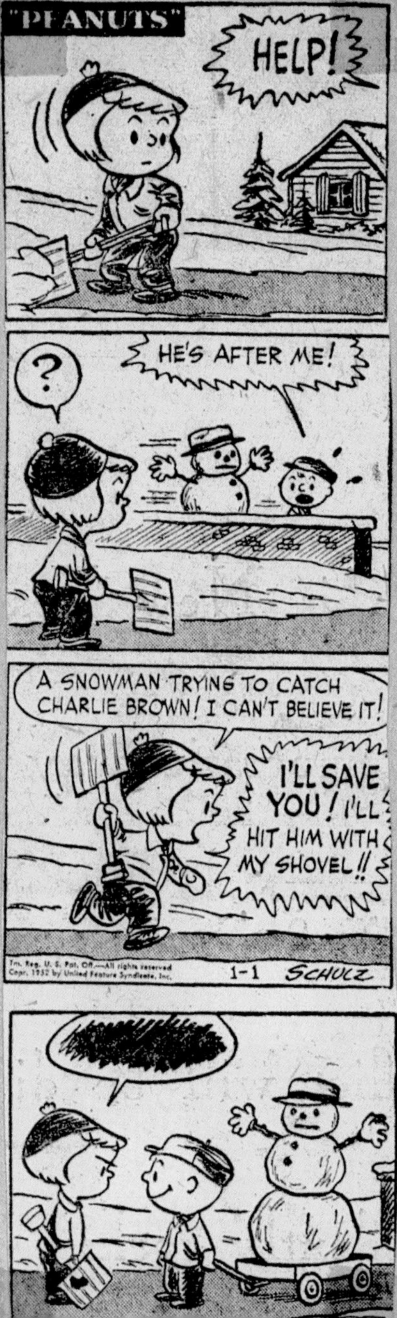
"PEANUTS"
HELP!
?
HE'S AFTER ME!
A SNOWMAN TRYING TO CATCH CHARLIE BROWN! I CAN'T BELIEVE IT!
I'LL SAVE YOU! I'LL HIT HIM WITH MY SHOVEL!!
Tm. Reg. U. S. Pat. Off.—All rights reserved
Copr. 1952 by United Feature Syndicate, Inc.
1-1
SCHULZ

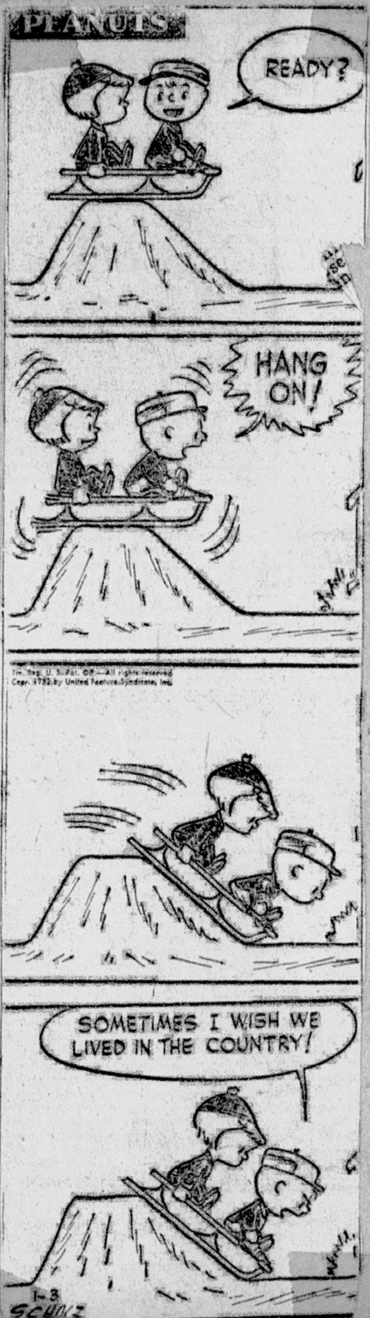
"PEANUTS"
READY?
HANG ON!
SOMETIMES I WISH WE LIVED IN THE COUNTRY!
1-3
SCHULZ

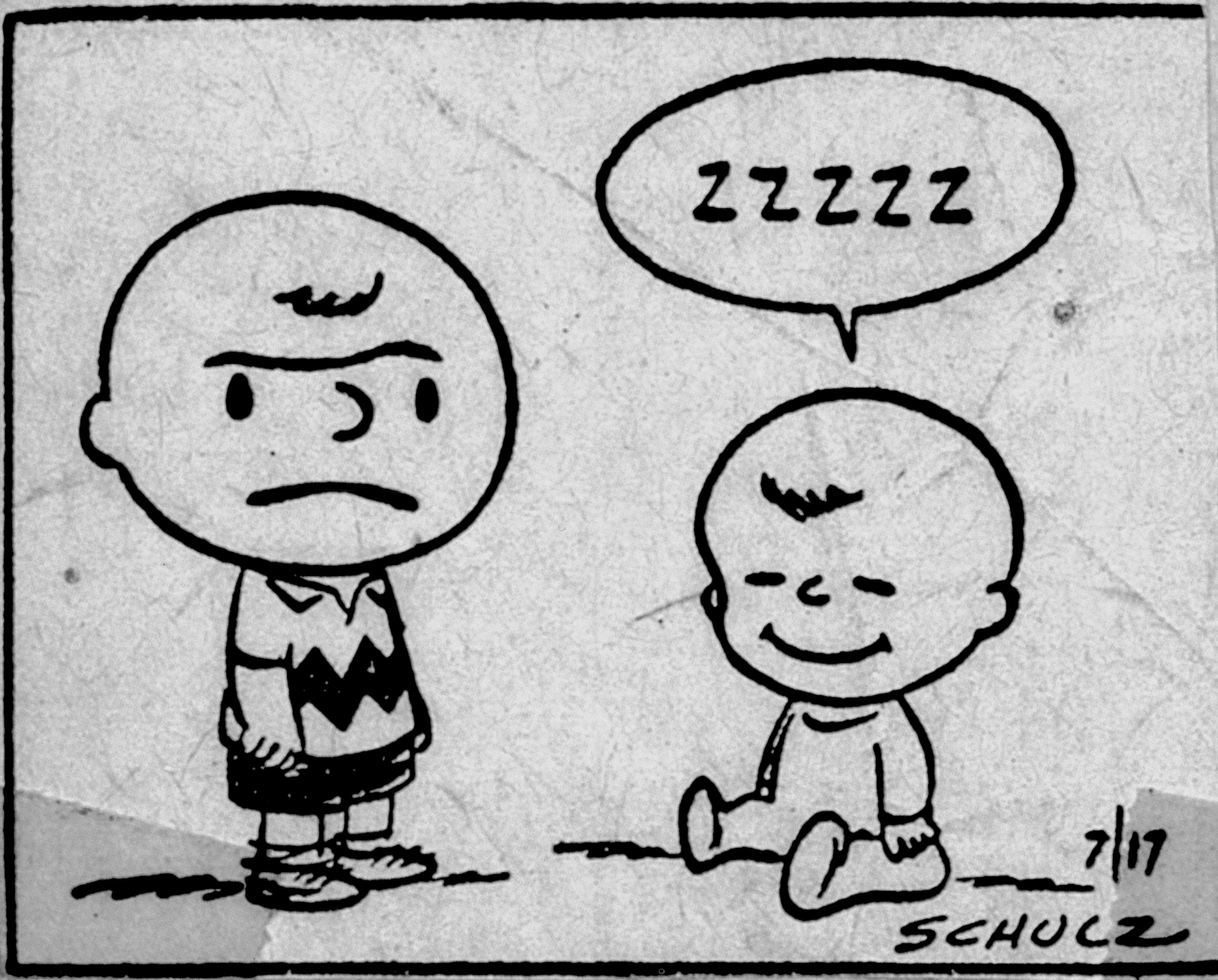
ZZZZZ
7/17
SCHULZ

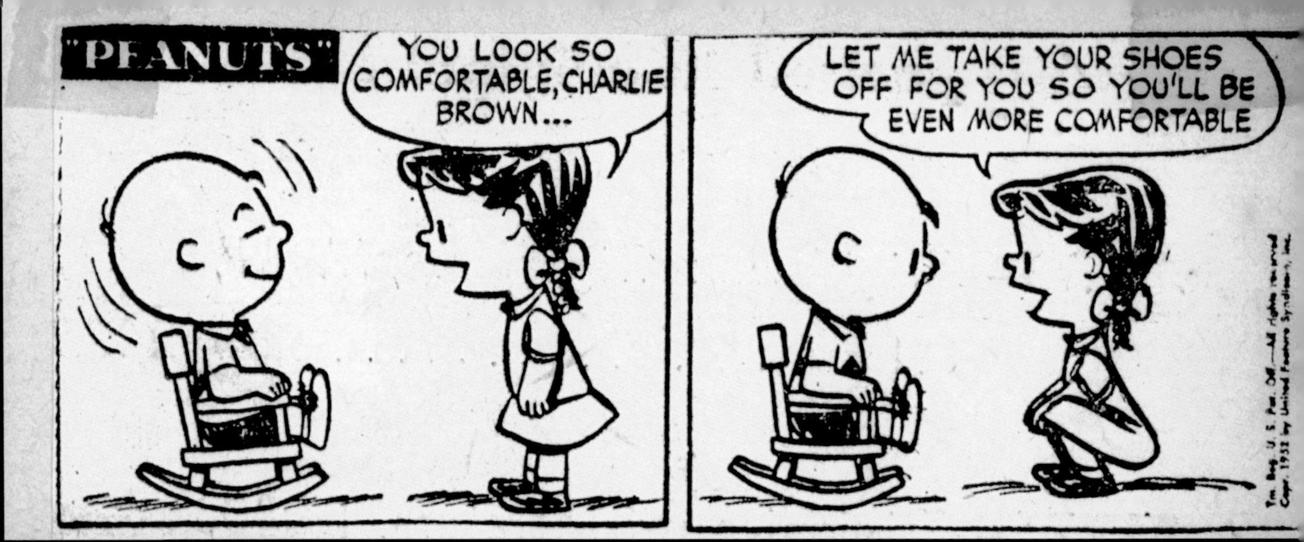
"PEANUTS"
YOU LOOK SO COMFORTABLE, CHARLIE BROWN...
LET ME TAKE YOUR SHOES OFF FOR YOU SO YOU'LL BE EVEN MORE COMFORTABLE
Tm. Reg. U. S. Pat. Off.—All rights reserved
Copr. 1952 by United Feature Syndicate, Inc.

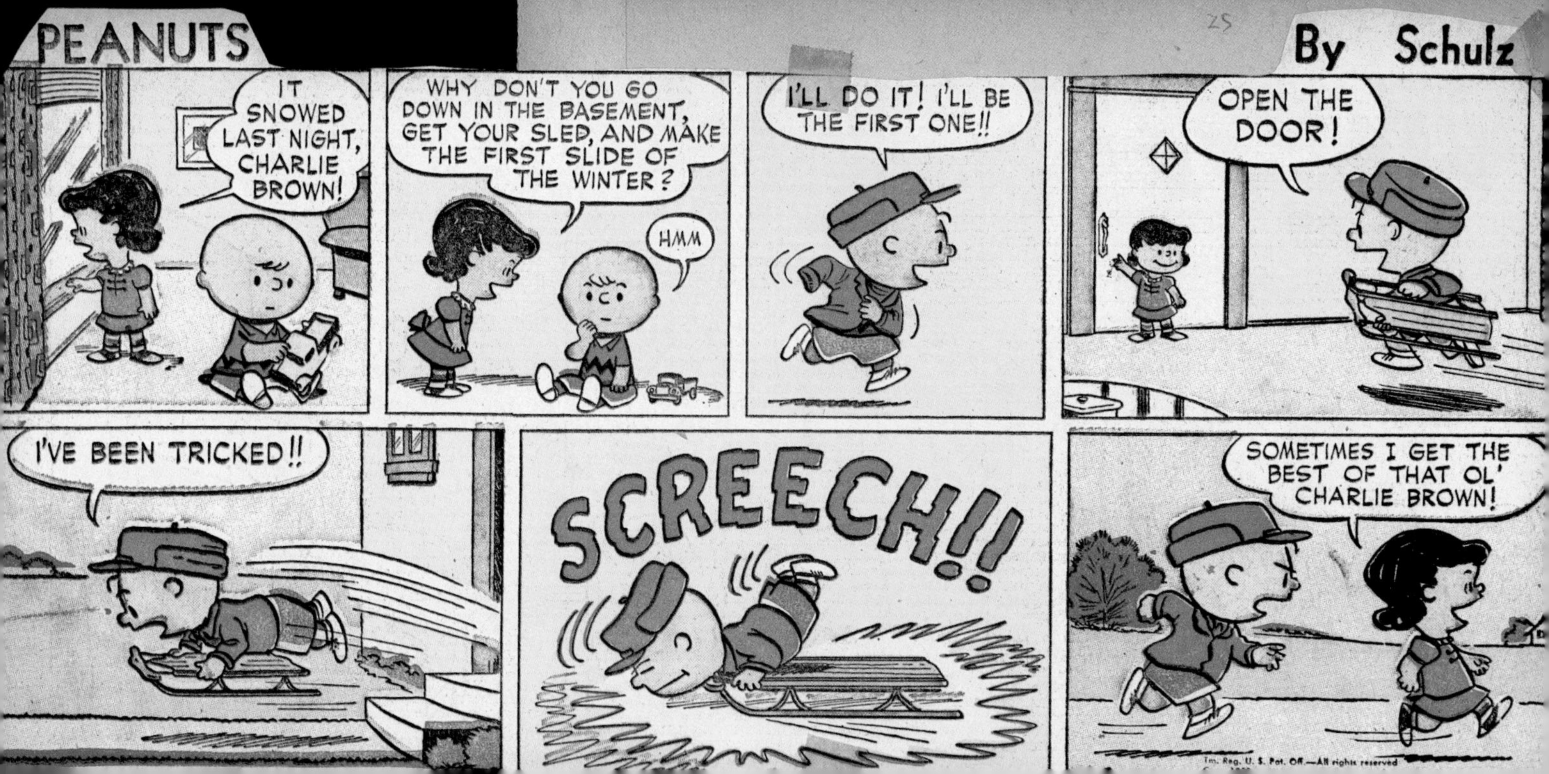
PEANUTS
By Schulz
IT SNOWED LAST NIGHT, CHARLIE BROWN!
WHY DON'T YOU GO DOWN IN THE BASEMENT, GET YOUR SLED, AND MAKE THE FIRST SLIDE OF THE WINTER?
HMM
I'LL DO IT! I'LL BE THE FIRST ONE!!
OPEN THE DOOR!
I'VE BEEN TRICKED!!
SCREECH!!
SOMETIMES I GET THE BEST OF THAT OL' CHARLIE BROWN!
Tm. Reg. U. S. Pat. Off.—All rights reserved

26

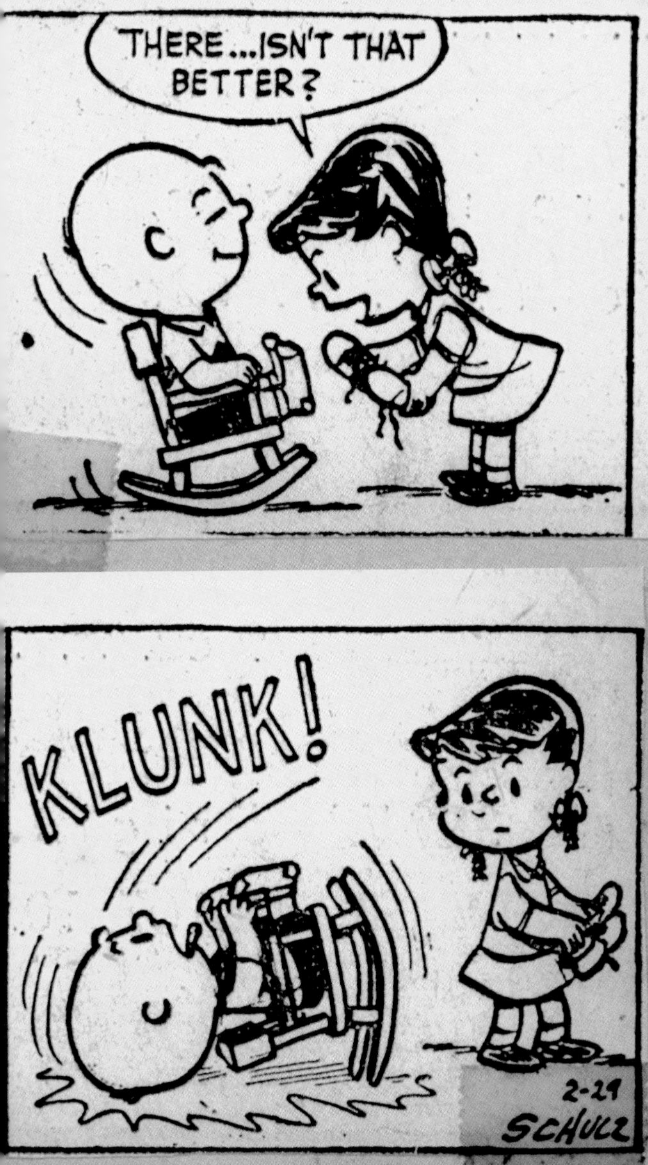
THERE...ISN'T THAT BETTER?
KLUNK!
2-29
SCHULZ

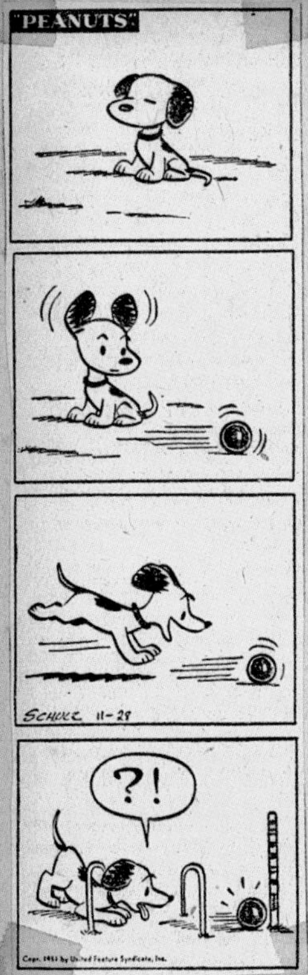
"PEANUTS"
SCHULZ 11-28
?!

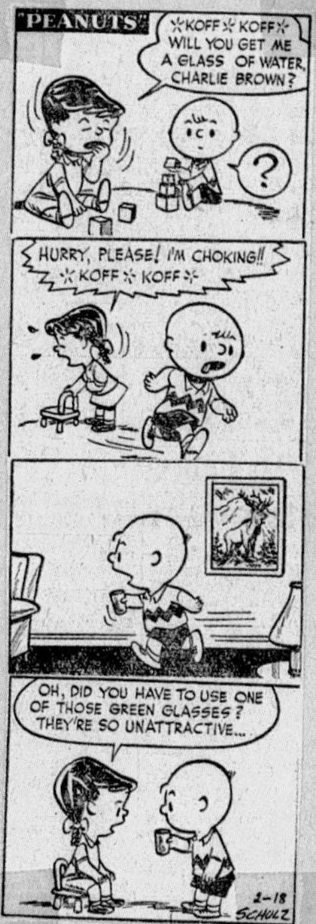
"PEANUTS"
KOFF *KOFF* WILL YOU GET ME A GLASS OF WATER, CHARLIE BROWN?
?
HURRY, PLEASE! I'M CHOKING!! *KOFF* *KOFF*
OH, DID YOU HAVE TO USE ONE OF THOSE GREEN GLASSES? THEY'RE SO UNATTRACTIVE...
2-18
SCHULZ

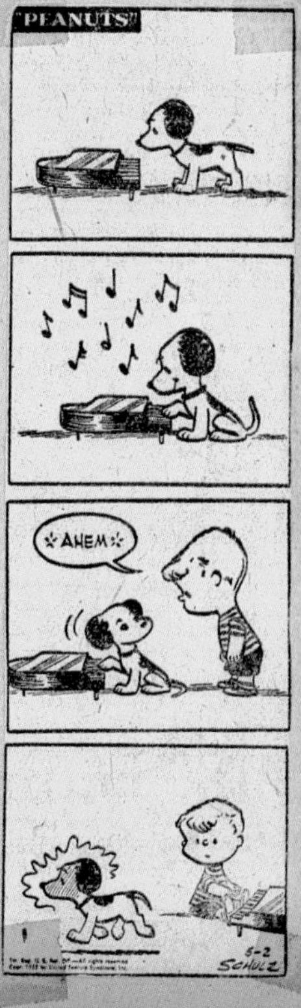
"PEANUTS"
AHEM
5-2
SCHULZ

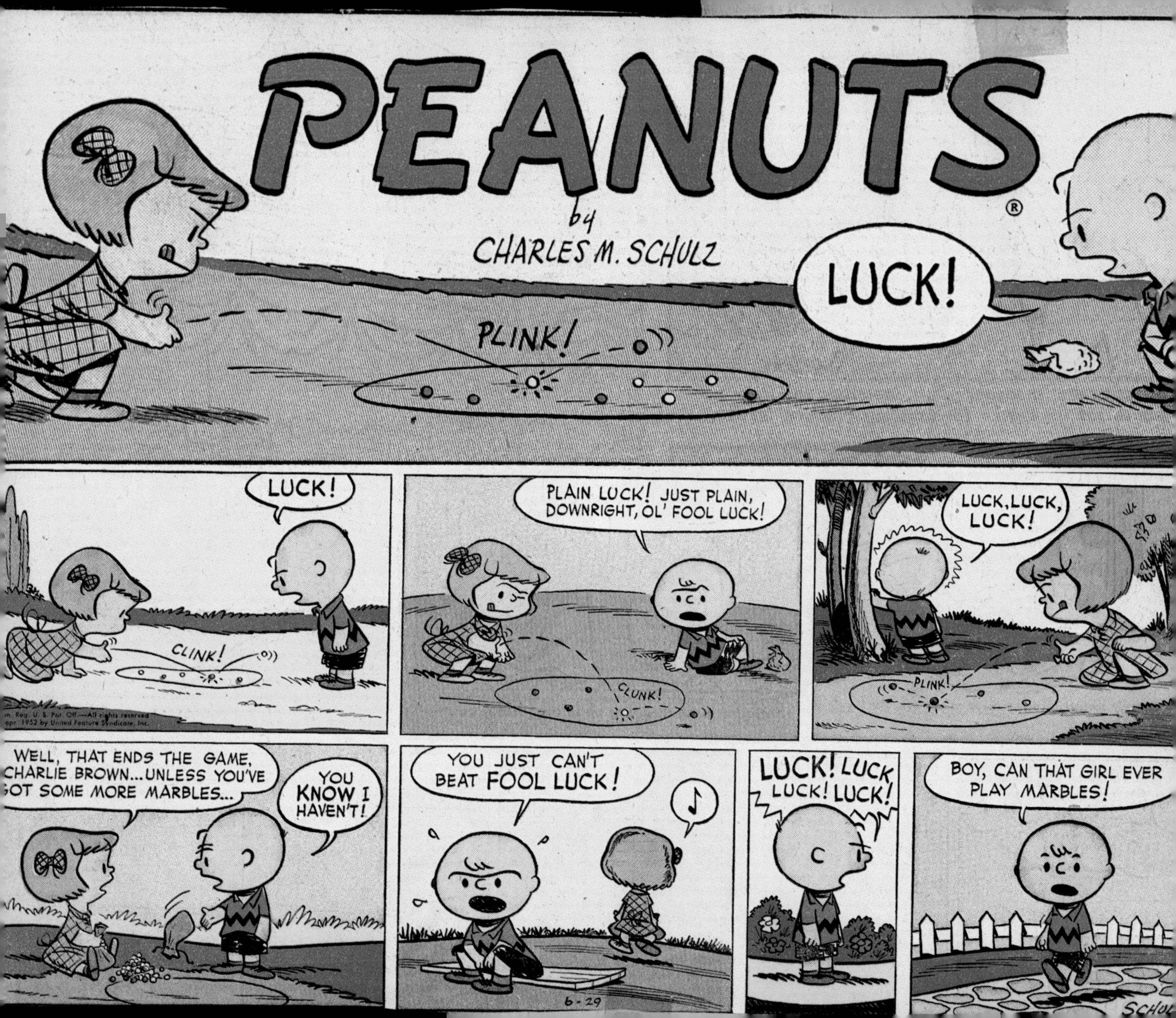
PEANUTS
by
CHARLES M. SCHULZ
PLINK!
LUCK!
LUCK!
CLINK!
PLAIN LUCK! JUST PLAIN, DOWNRIGHT, OL' FOOL LUCK!
CLUNK!
LUCK, LUCK, LUCK!
PLINK!
WELL, THAT ENDS THE GAME, CHARLIE BROWN...UNLESS YOU'VE GOT SOME MORE MARBLES...
YOU KNOW I HAVEN'T!
YOU JUST CAN'T BEAT FOOL LUCK!
♪
LUCK! LUCK LUCK! LUCK!
BOY, CAN THAT GIRL EVER PLAY MARBLES!
6-29

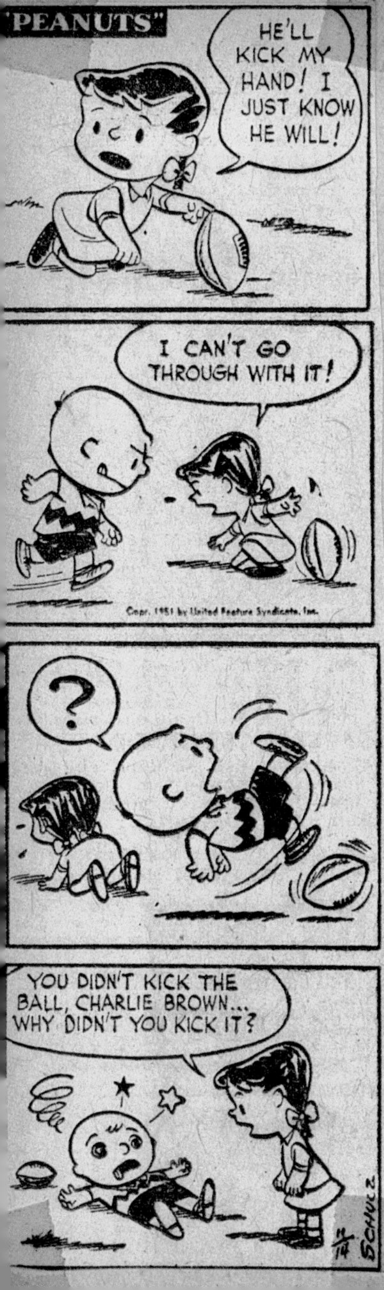
"PEANUTS"
HE'LL KICK MY HAND! I JUST KNOW HE WILL!
I CAN'T GO THROUGH WITH IT!
Copr. 1951 by United Feature Syndicate, Inc.
?
YOU DIDN'T KICK THE BALL, CHARLIE BROWN... WHY DIDN'T YOU KICK IT?
11/14
SCHULZ

Charlie Brown's first failed football kick was at the hands of Violet, not Lucy—on November 14, 1951. Where Lucy will be motivated by malice, Violet is just scared that she will be kicked by mistake, and balks at the last minute, leaving Charlie Brown to a fate that Lucy was to hand him throughout the duration of the strip.

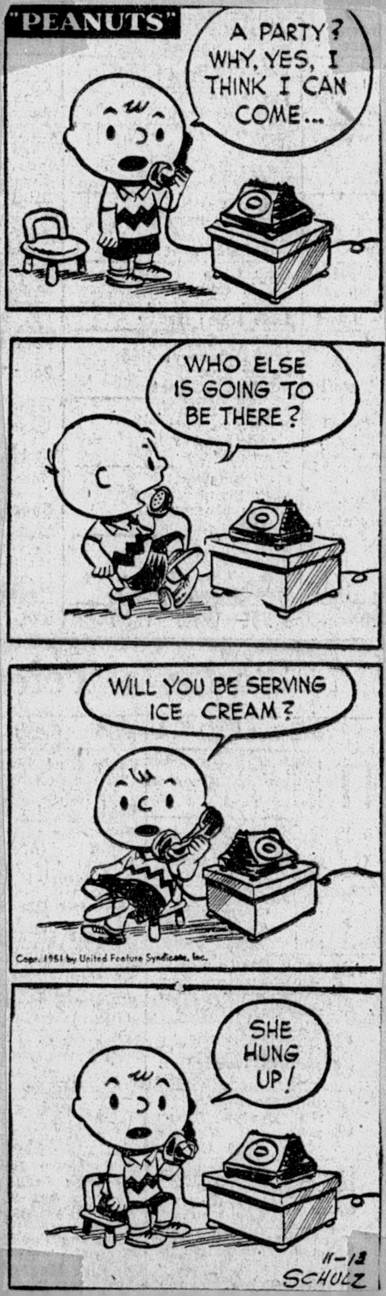
"PEANUTS"
A PARTY? WHY, YES, I THINK I CAN COME...
WHO ELSE IS GOING TO BE THERE?
WILL YOU BE SERVING ICE CREAM?
Copr. 1951 by United Feature Syndicate, Inc.
SHE HUNG UP!
11-13
SCHULZ

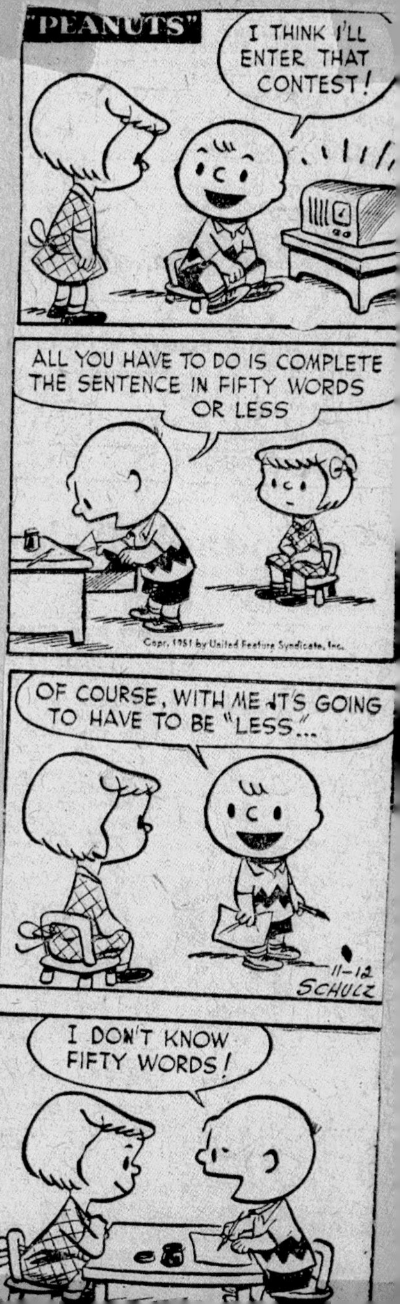
"PEANUTS"
I THINK I'LL ENTER THAT CONTEST!
ALL YOU HAVE TO DO IS COMPLETE THE SENTENCE IN FIFTY WORDS OR LESS
Copr. 1951 by United Feature Syndicate, Inc.
OF COURSE, WITH ME IT'S GOING TO HAVE TO BE "LESS"...
11-12
SCHULZ
I DON'T KNOW FIFTY WORDS!

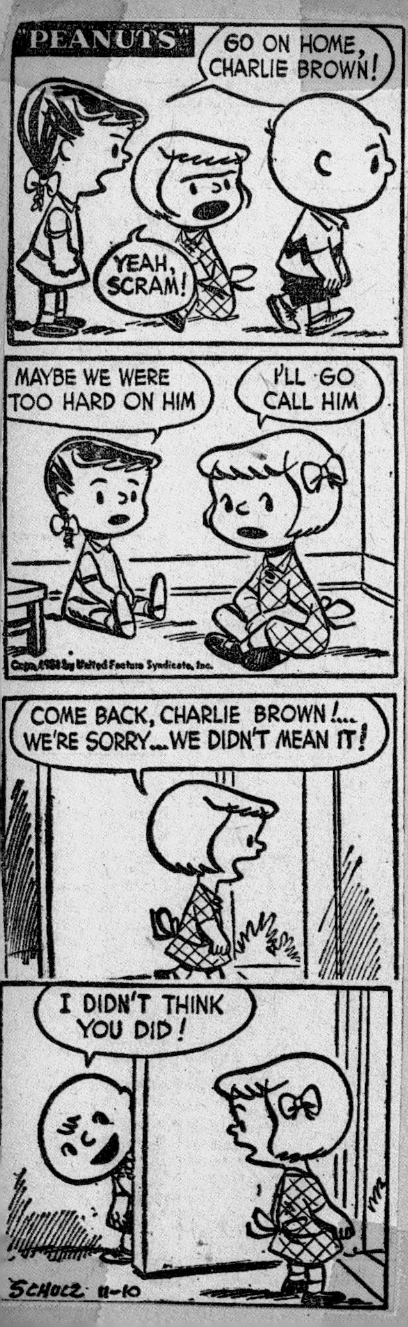
"PEANUTS"
GO ON HOME, CHARLIE BROWN!
YEAH, SCRAM!
MAYBE WE WERE TOO HARD ON HIM
I'LL GO CALL HIM
COME BACK, CHARLIE BROWN!... WE'RE SORRY... WE DIDN'T MEAN IT!
I DIDN'T THINK YOU DID!
SCHULZ 11-10

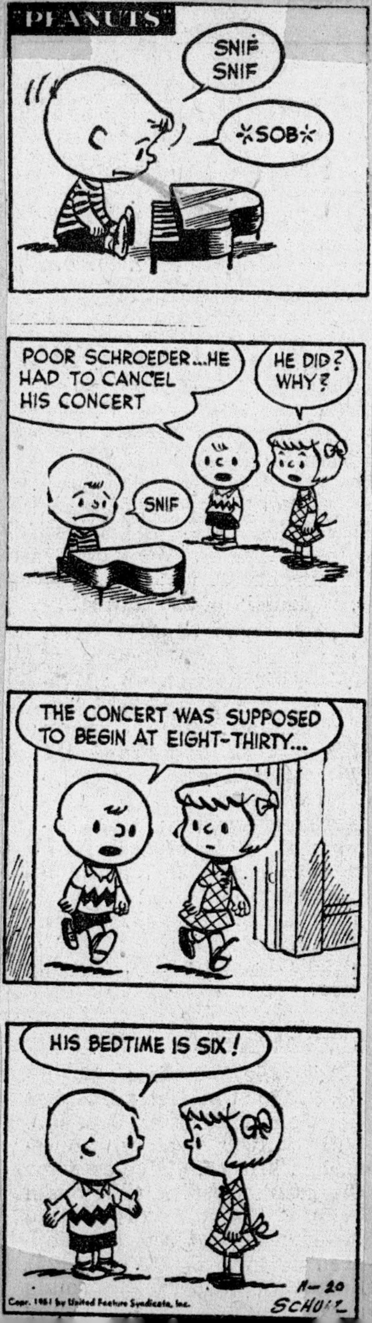
"PEANUTS"
SNIF SNIF
SOB
POOR SCHROEDER...HE HAD TO CANCEL HIS CONCERT
HE DID? WHY?
SNIF
THE CONCERT WAS SUPPOSED TO BEGIN AT EIGHT-THIRTY...
HIS BEDTIME IS SIX!
11-20
SCHULZ
Copr. 1951 by United Feature Syndicate, Inc.

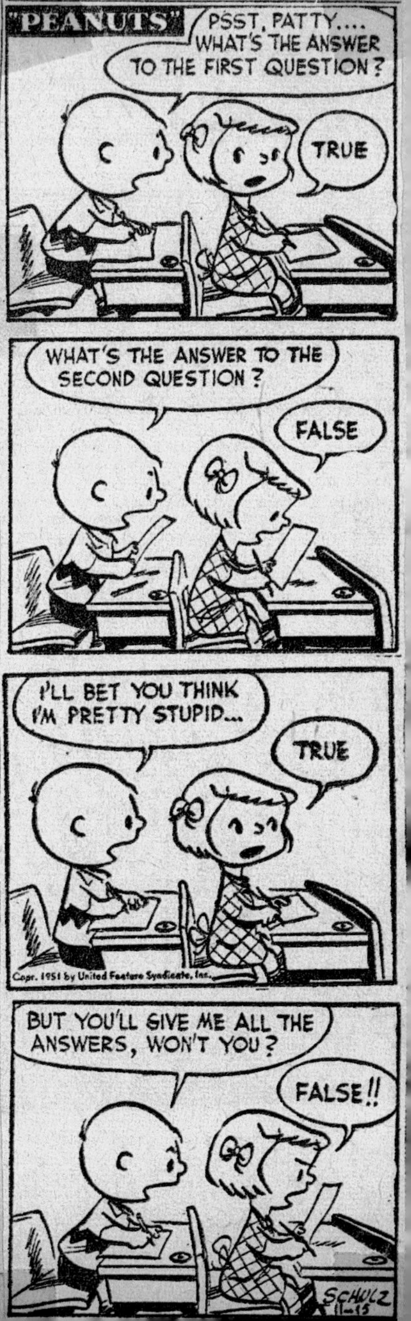
"PEANUTS"
PSST, PATTY.... WHAT'S THE ANSWER TO THE FIRST QUESTION?
TRUE
WHAT'S THE ANSWER TO THE SECOND QUESTION?
FALSE
I'LL BET YOU THINK I'M PRETTY STUPID...
TRUE
Copr. 1951 by United Feature Syndicate, Inc.
BUT YOU'LL GIVE ME ALL THE ANSWERS, WON'T YOU?
FALSE!!
SCHULZ 11-15

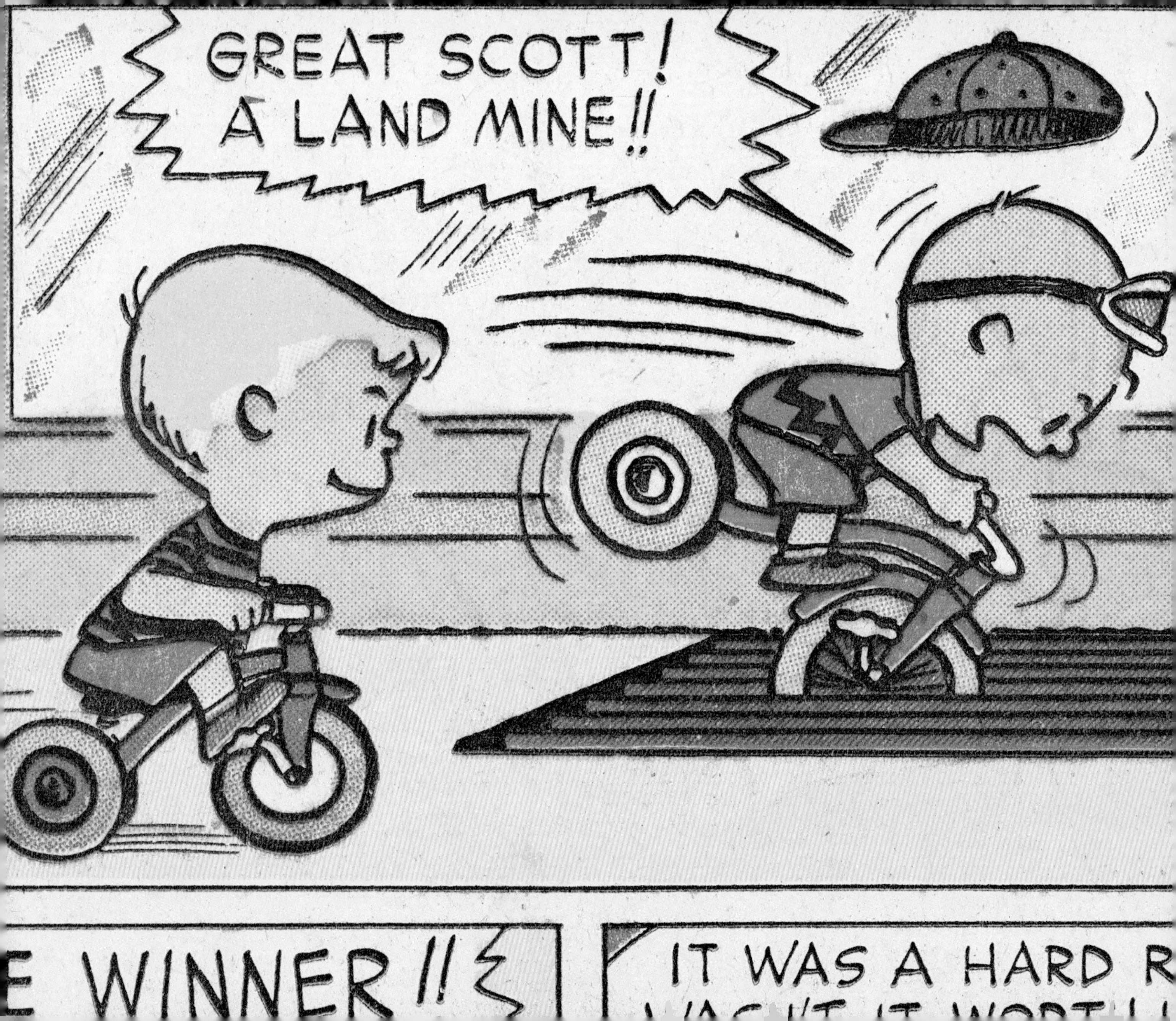
GREAT SCOTT!
A LAND MINE!!
E WINNER!!
IT WAS A HARD R

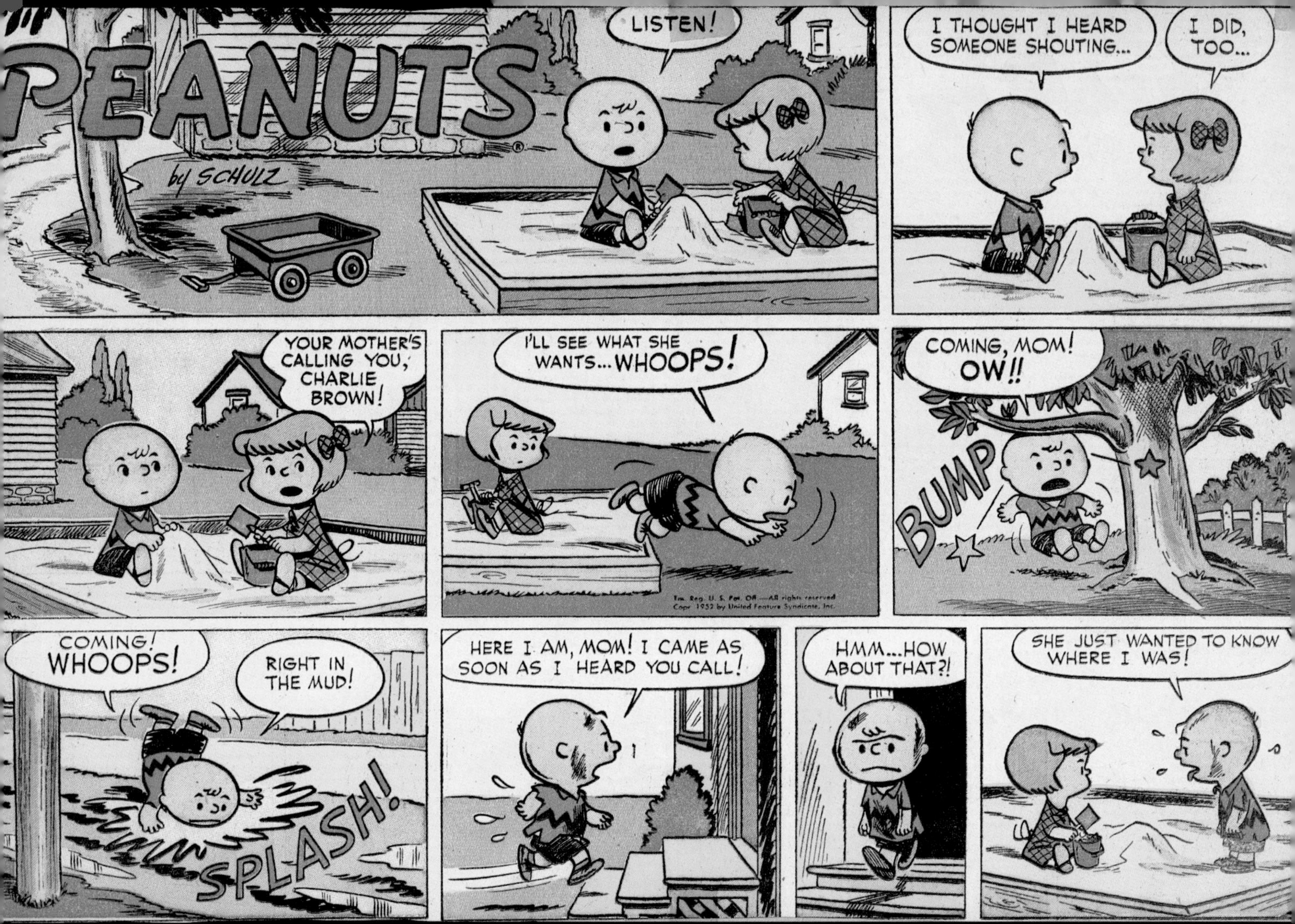
PEANUTS
by SCHULZ
LISTEN!
I THOUGHT I HEARD SOMEONE SHOUTING...
I DID, TOO...
YOUR MOTHER'S CALLING YOU, CHARLIE BROWN!
I'LL SEE WHAT SHE WANTS... WHOOPS!
Tm. Reg. U. S. Pat. Off.—All rights reserved Copr. 1952 by United Feature Syndicate, Inc.
COMING, MOM! OW!!
BUMP
COMING! WHOOPS!
RIGHT IN THE MUD!
SPLASH!
HERE I AM, MOM! I CAME AS SOON AS I HEARD YOU CALL!
HMM...HOW ABOUT THAT?!
SHE JUST WANTED TO KNOW WHERE I WAS!

"One of the main things to avoid is thinking too far ahead of yourself. Try to think of your daily episodes without concentrating too heavily on the overall theme of your comic feature. While you are concentrating on these daily episodes, trying to get the most humorous idea you can out of each, you will also be developing the personalities of your char-

"As your ideas develop personalities and as your personalities develop more ideas, the overall theme of your feature will then begin to take form. This really is the only practical way to develop a good solid comic-strip feature."

—Charles Schulz, from *Developing a Comic Strip*, 1959

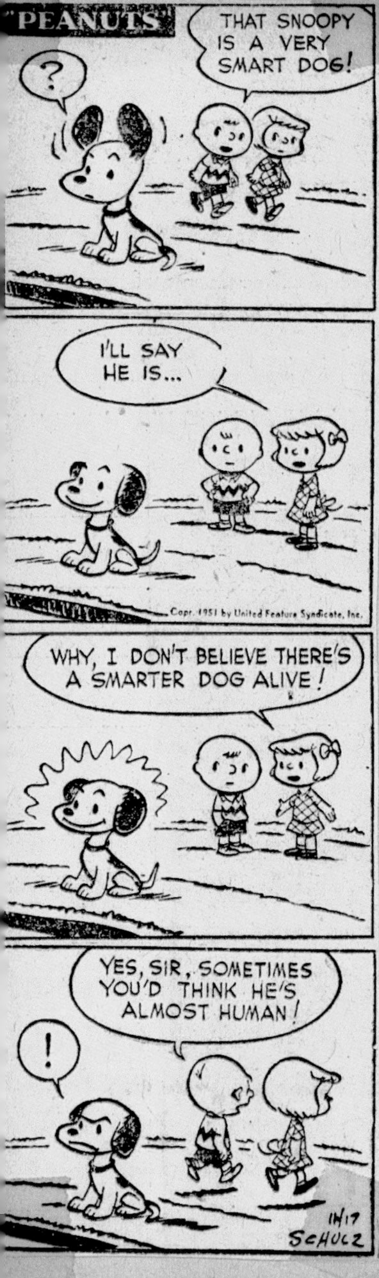
"PEANUTS"
THAT SNOOPY IS A VERY SMART DOG!
?
I'LL SAY HE IS...
Copr. 1951 by United Feature Syndicate, Inc.
WHY, I DON'T BELIEVE THERE'S A SMARTER DOG ALIVE!
YES, SIR, SOMETIMES YOU'D THINK HE'S ALMOST HUMAN!
!
11/17
SCHULZ

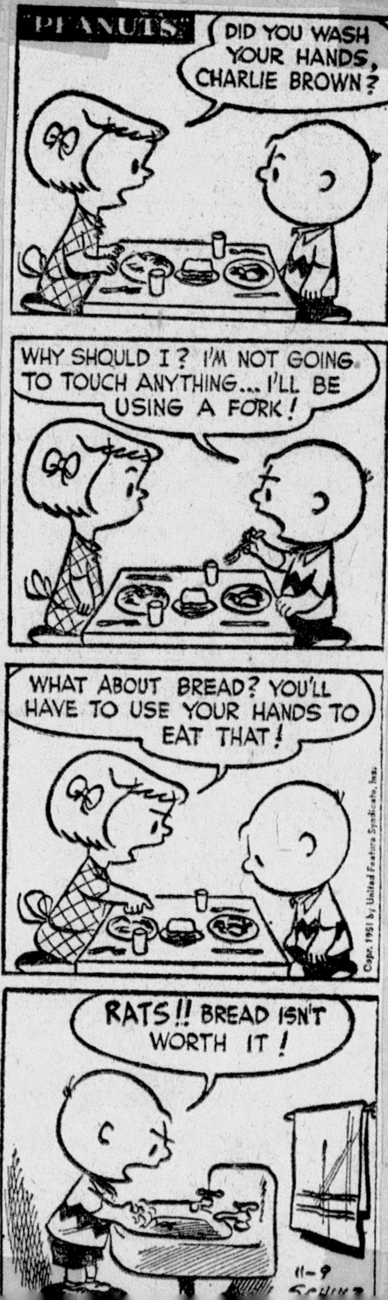
"PEANUTS"
DID YOU WASH YOUR HANDS, CHARLIE BROWN?
WHY SHOULD I? I'M NOT GOING TO TOUCH ANYTHING... I'LL BE USING A FORK!
WHAT ABOUT BREAD? YOU'LL HAVE TO USE YOUR HANDS TO EAT THAT!
Copr. 1951 by United Feature Syndicate, Inc.
RATS!! BREAD ISN'T WORTH IT!
11-9

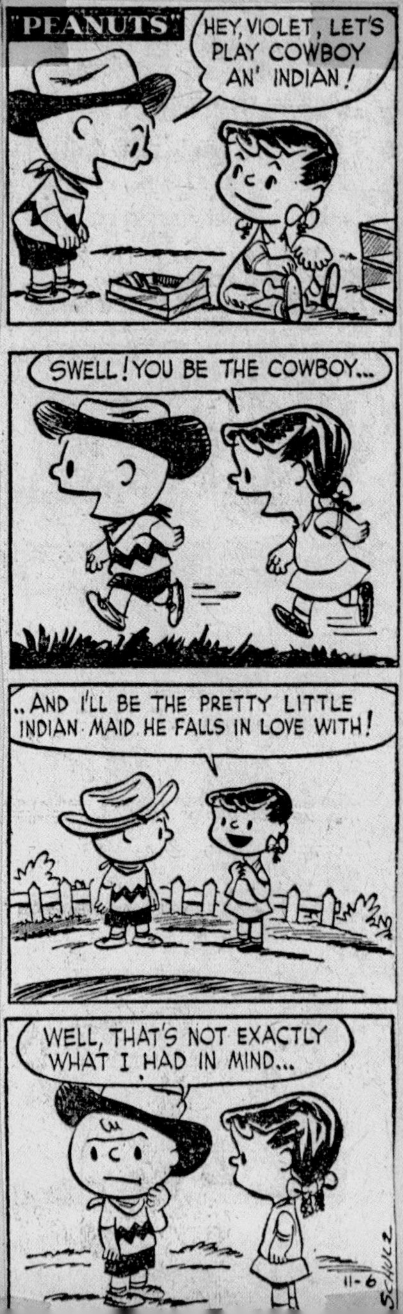
"PEANUTS"
HEY, VIOLET, LET'S PLAY COWBOY AN' INDIAN!
SWELL! YOU BE THE COWBOY...
..AND I'LL BE THE PRETTY LITTLE INDIAN MAID HE FALLS IN LOVE WITH!
WELL, THAT'S NOT EXACTLY WHAT I HAD IN MIND...
11-6
SCHULZ

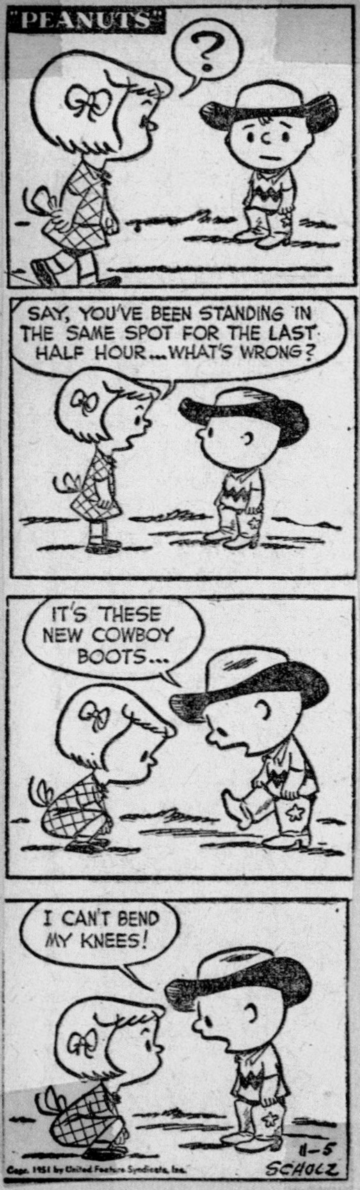
"PEANUTS"
?
SAY, YOU'VE BEEN STANDING IN THE SAME SPOT FOR THE LAST HALF HOUR...WHAT'S WRONG?
IT'S THESE NEW COWBOY BOOTS...
I CAN'T BEND MY KNEES!
11-5
Copr. 1951 by United Feature Syndicate, Inc.
SCHULZ

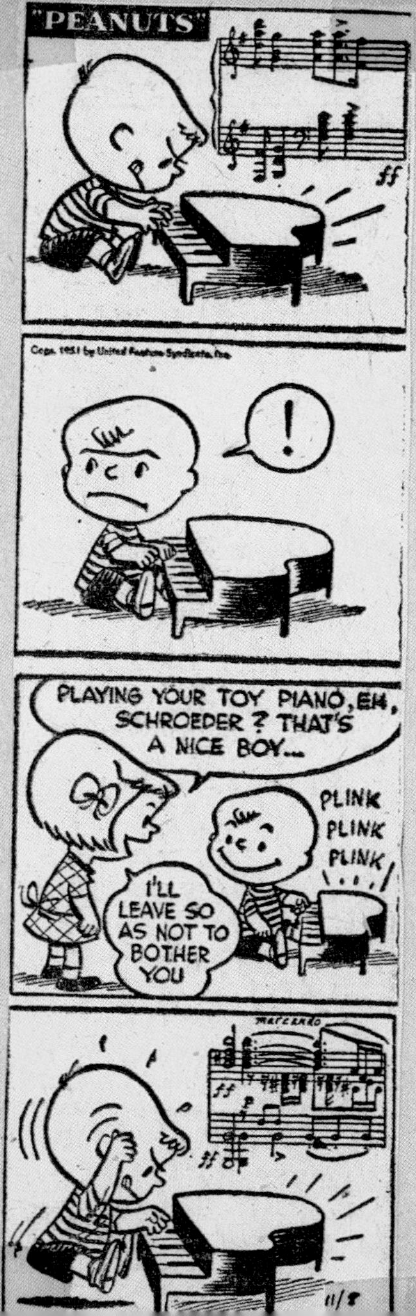
"PEANUTS"
ff
Copr. 1951 by United Feature Syndicate, Inc.
!
PLAYING YOUR TOY PIANO, EH, SCHROEDER? THAT'S A NICE BOY...
PLINK PLINK PLINK
I'LL LEAVE SO AS NOT TO BOTHER YOU
marcando
ff
11/8

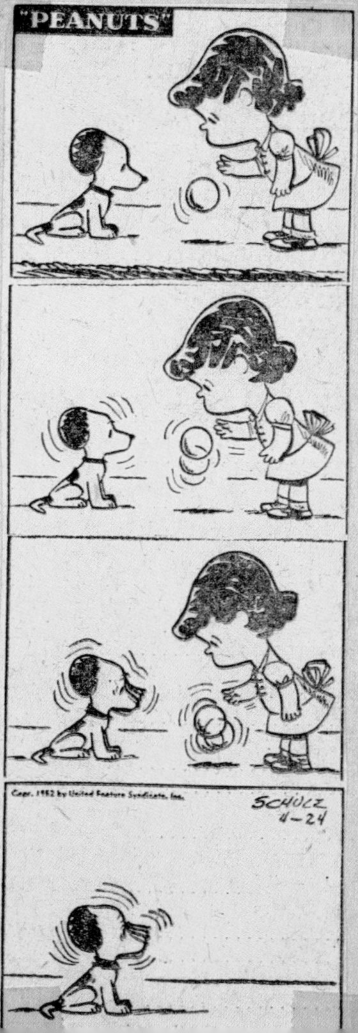
"PEANUTS"
Copr. 1952 by United Feature Syndicate, Inc.
SCHULZ 11-24

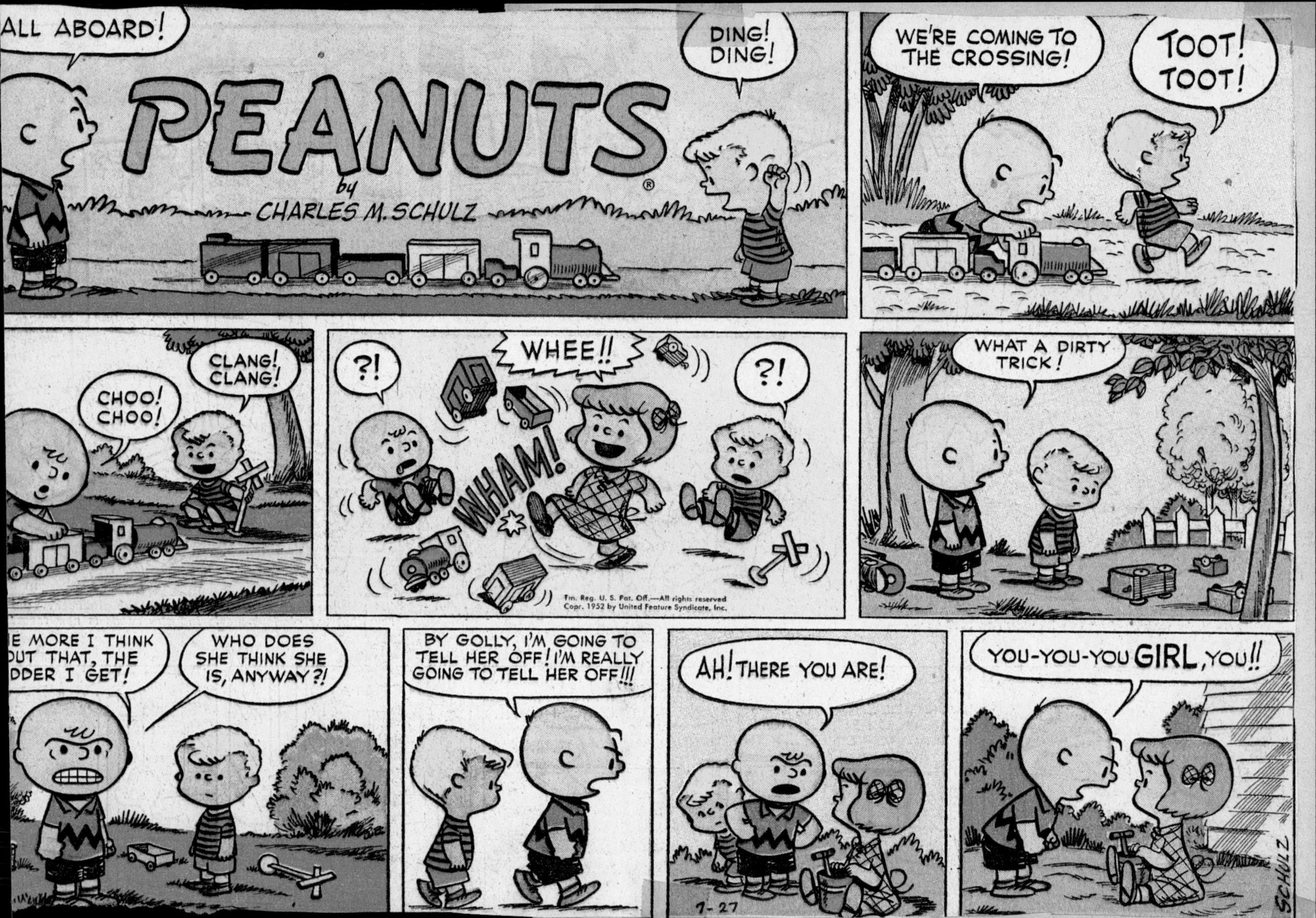
ALL ABOARD!
PEANUTS
by CHARLES M. SCHULZ
DING! DING!
WE'RE COMING TO THE CROSSING!
TOOT! TOOT!
CHOO! CHOO!
CLANG! CLANG!
?!
WHEE!!
?!
WHAM!
Tm. Reg. U. S. Pat. Off.—All rights reserved Copr. 1952 by United Feature Syndicate, Inc.
WHAT A DIRTY TRICK!
E MORE I THINK OUT THAT, THE DDER I GET!
WHO DOES SHE THINK SHE IS, ANYWAY?!
BY GOLLY, I'M GOING TO TELL HER OFF! I'M REALLY GOING TO TELL HER OFF!!!
AH! THERE YOU ARE!
7-27
YOU-YOU-YOU GIRL, YOU!!
SCHULZ

Grown-ups did not interest Schulz. And besides: "There was no room for adults. My strip, when it was given to me, was the size of four air-mail stamps. I just didn't have the room to draw [adults with the] kids." This literally provided *Peanuts* with a unique point of view. ". . . I brought the camera right down on level with the kids. I have never drawn the kids from an adult viewpoint, looking down on them."

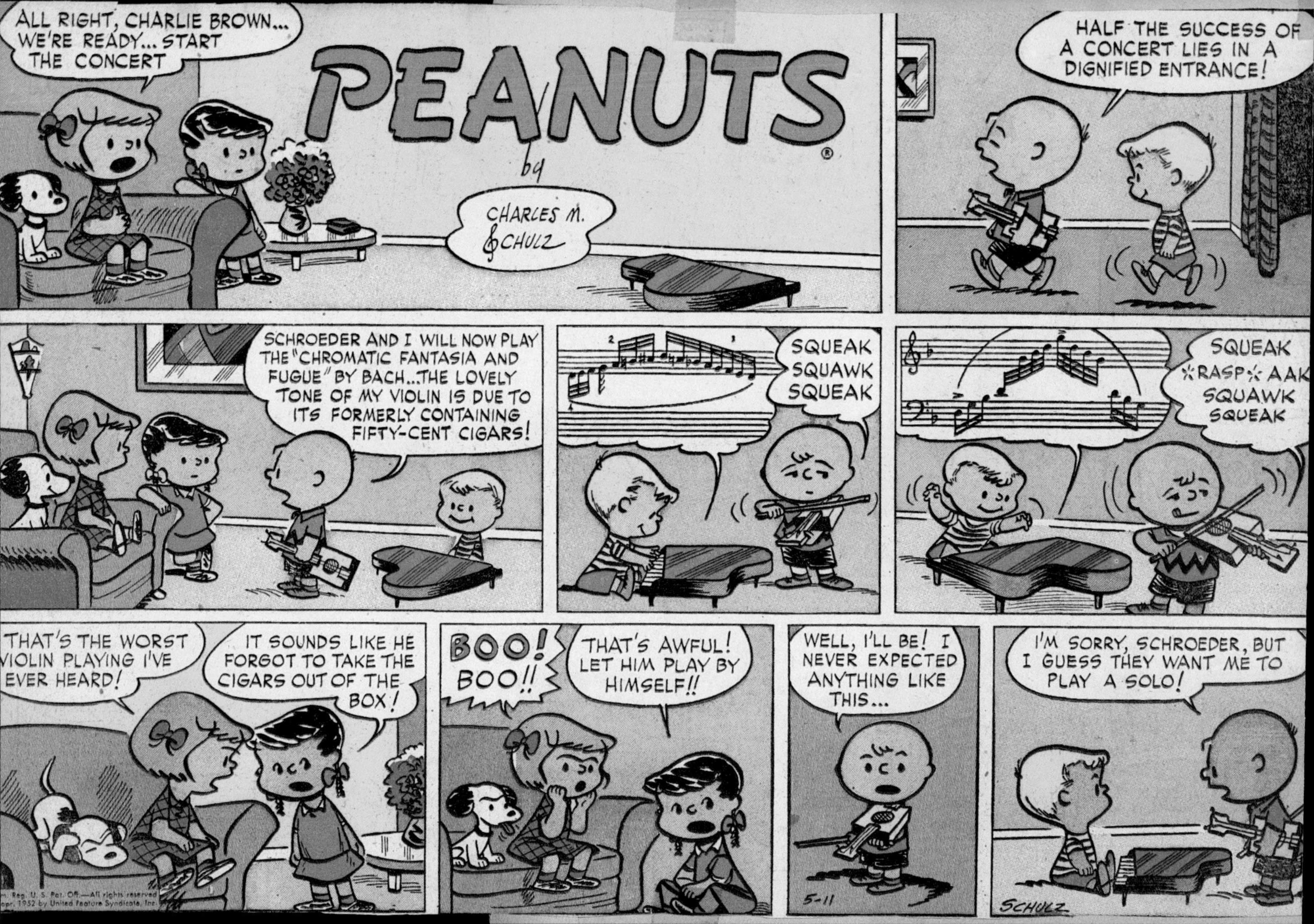

ALL RIGHT, CHARLIE BROWN... WE'RE READY... START THE CONCERT
PEANUTS
by
CHARLES M. SCHULZ
HALF THE SUCCESS OF A CONCERT LIES IN A DIGNIFIED ENTRANCE!
SCHROEDER AND I WILL NOW PLAY THE "CHROMATIC FANTASIA AND FUGUE" BY BACH...THE LOVELY TONE OF MY VIOLIN IS DUE TO ITS FORMERLY CONTAINING FIFTY-CENT CIGARS!
SQUEAK SQUAWK SQUEAK
SQUEAK *RASP* AAK SQUAWK SQUEAK
THAT'S THE WORST VIOLIN PLAYING I'VE EVER HEARD!
IT SOUNDS LIKE HE FORGOT TO TAKE THE CIGARS OUT OF THE BOX!
BOO! BOO!!
THAT'S AWFUL! LET HIM PLAY BY HIMSELF!!
WELL, I'LL BE! I NEVER EXPECTED ANYTHING LIKE THIS...
I'M SORRY, SCHROEDER, BUT I GUESS THEY WANT ME TO PLAY A SOLO!
Reg. U. S. Pat. Off.—All rights reserved
1952 by United Feature Syndicate, Inc.
5-11
SCHULZ

"I've never known much about art," Schulz said in a 1997 interview, "I've never been a student of art. To me, obtaining a comic strip was just the greatest thing in the world. To me. Because that's what I wanted, and that's what I knew I could do. I didn't think 'Well, a comic strip would be a good way to make a living so that someday I can be a painter.' I had no desire to do anything else."

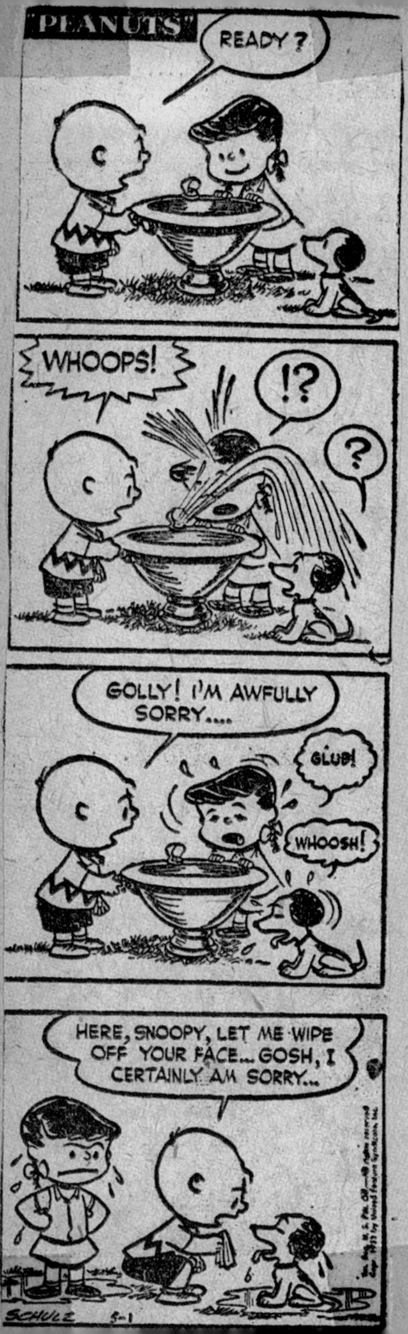
"PEANUTS"
READY?
WHOOPS!
!?
?
GOLLY! I'M AWFULLY SORRY....
GLUB!
WHOOSH!
HERE, SNOOPY, LET ME WIPE OFF YOUR FACE... GOSH, I CERTAINLY AM SORRY...
SCHULZ
5-1

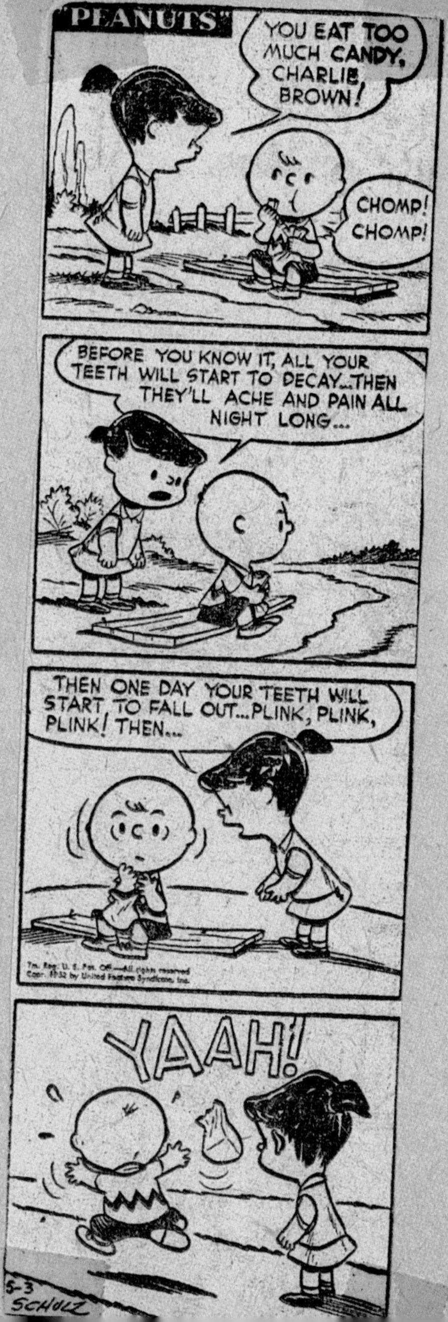
"PEANUTS"
YOU EAT TOO MUCH CANDY, CHARLIE BROWN!
CHOMP! CHOMP!
BEFORE YOU KNOW IT, ALL YOUR TEETH WILL START TO DECAY...THEN THEY'LL ACHE AND PAIN ALL NIGHT LONG...
THEN ONE DAY YOUR TEETH WILL START TO FALL OUT...PLINK, PLINK, PLINK! THEN...
Tm. Reg. U. S. Pat. Off.—All rights reserved
Copr. 1952 by United Feature Syndicate, Inc.
YAAH!
5-3
SCHULZ

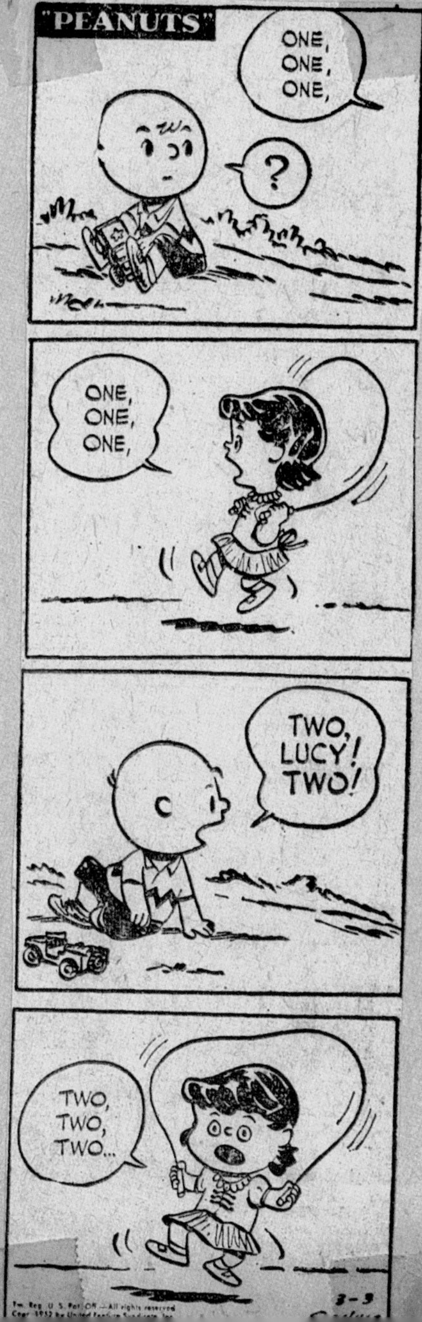
"PEANUTS"
ONE, ONE, ONE,
?
ONE, ONE, ONE,
TWO, LUCY! TWO!
TWO, TWO, TWO...

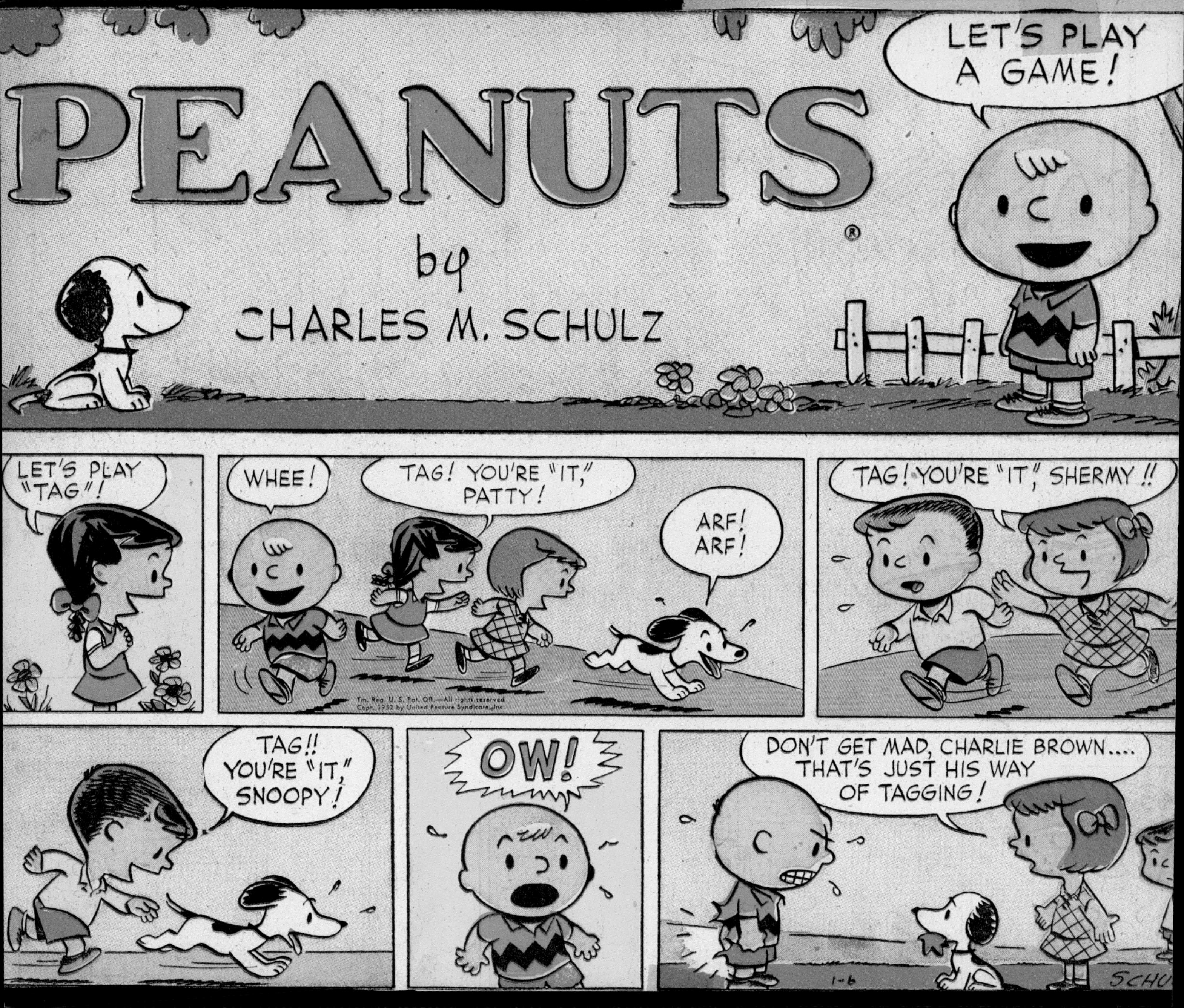
LET'S PLAY A GAME!
PEANUTS®
by CHARLES M. SCHULZ
LET'S PLAY "TAG"!
WHEE!
TAG! YOU'RE "IT," PATTY!
ARF! ARF!
Tm. Reg. U. S. Pat. Off.—All rights reserved Copr. 1952 by United Feature Syndicate, Inc.
TAG! YOU'RE "IT," SHERMY!!
TAG!! YOU'RE "IT," SNOOPY!
OW!
DON'T GET MAD, CHARLIE BROWN.... THAT'S JUST HIS WAY OF TAGGING!
1-6
SCHU

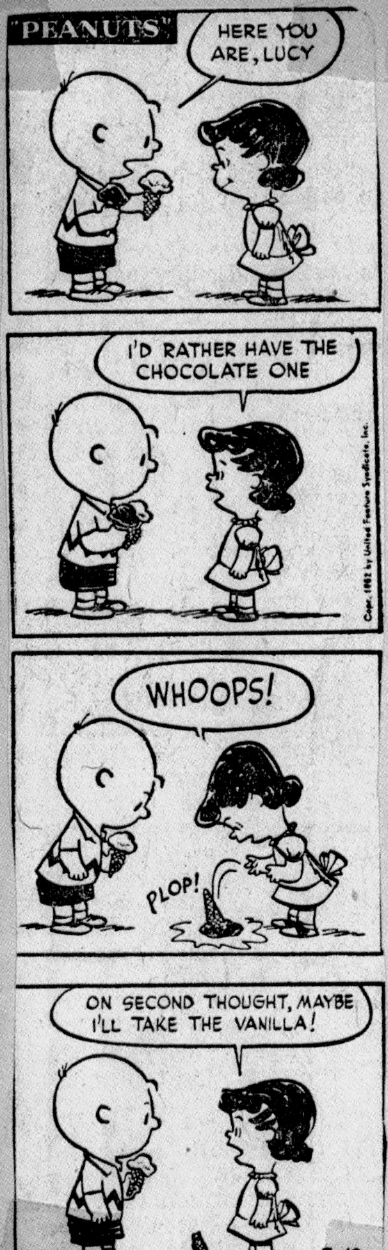
"PEANUTS"
HERE YOU ARE, LUCY
I'D RATHER HAVE THE CHOCOLATE ONE
Copr. 1952 by United Feature Syndicate, Inc.
WHOOPS!
PLOP!
ON SECOND THOUGHT, MAYBE I'LL TAKE THE VANILLA!
7-10
SCHULZ

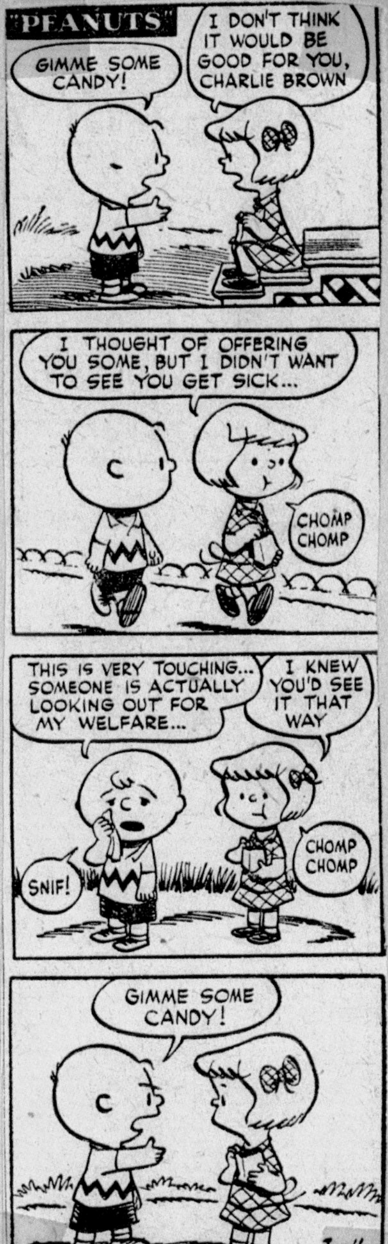
"PEANUTS"
GIMME SOME CANDY!
I DON'T THINK IT WOULD BE GOOD FOR YOU, CHARLIE BROWN
I THOUGHT OF OFFERING YOU SOME, BUT I DIDN'T WANT TO SEE YOU GET SICK...
CHOMP CHOMP
THIS IS VERY TOUCHING... SOMEONE IS ACTUALLY LOOKING OUT FOR MY WELFARE...
I KNEW YOU'D SEE IT THAT WAY
SNIF!
CHOMP CHOMP
GIMME SOME CANDY!
7-11
SCHULZ
Copr. 1952 by United Feature Syndicate, Inc.

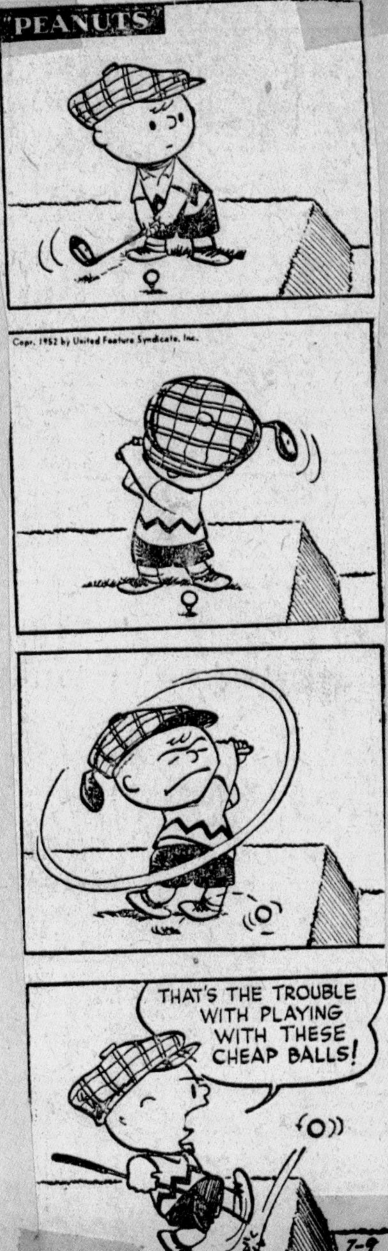
"PEANUTS"
Copr. 1952 by United Feature Syndicate, Inc.
THAT'S THE TROUBLE WITH PLAYING WITH THESE CHEAP BALLS!
7-9
SCHULZ

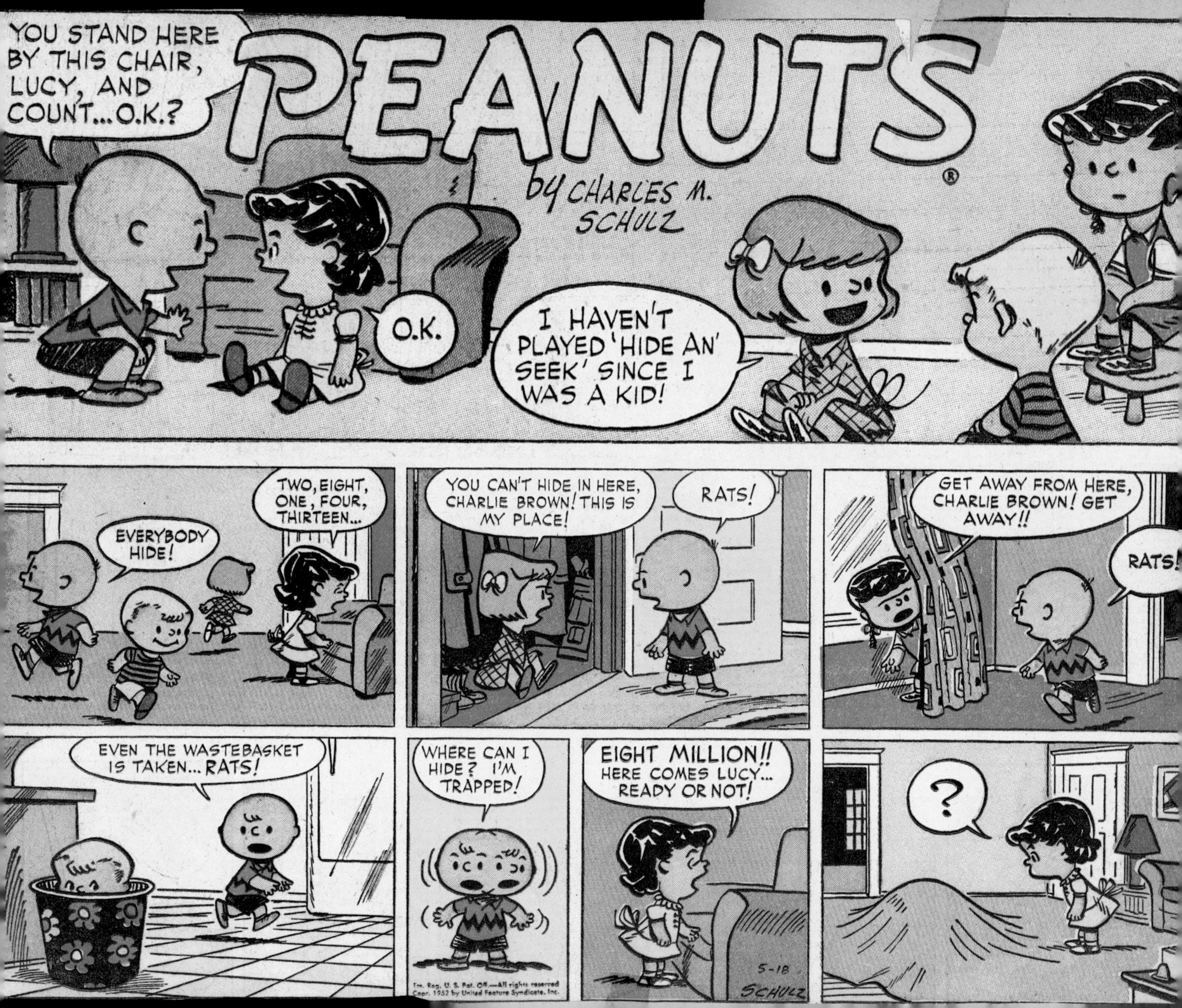
PEANUTS
by CHARLES M. SCHULZ
YOU STAND HERE BY THIS CHAIR, LUCY, AND COUNT...O.K.?
O.K.
I HAVEN'T PLAYED 'HIDE AN' SEEK' SINCE I WAS A KID!
EVERYBODY HIDE!
TWO, EIGHT, ONE, FOUR, THIRTEEN...
YOU CAN'T HIDE IN HERE, CHARLIE BROWN! THIS IS MY PLACE!
RATS!
GET AWAY FROM HERE, CHARLIE BROWN! GET AWAY!!
RATS!
EVEN THE WASTEBASKET IS TAKEN... RATS!
WHERE CAN I HIDE? I'M TRAPPED!
EIGHT MILLION!! HERE COMES LUCY... READY OR NOT!
?
Tm. Reg. U. S. Pat. Off.—All rights reserved Copr. 1952 by United Feature Syndicate, Inc.
5-18
SCHULZ

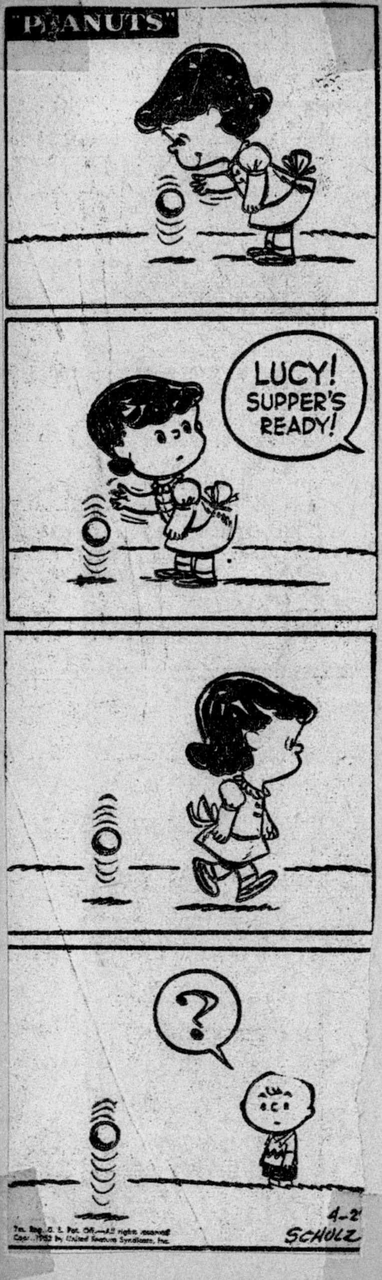
"PEANUTS"
LUCY! SUPPER'S READY!
?
4-2
SCHULZ

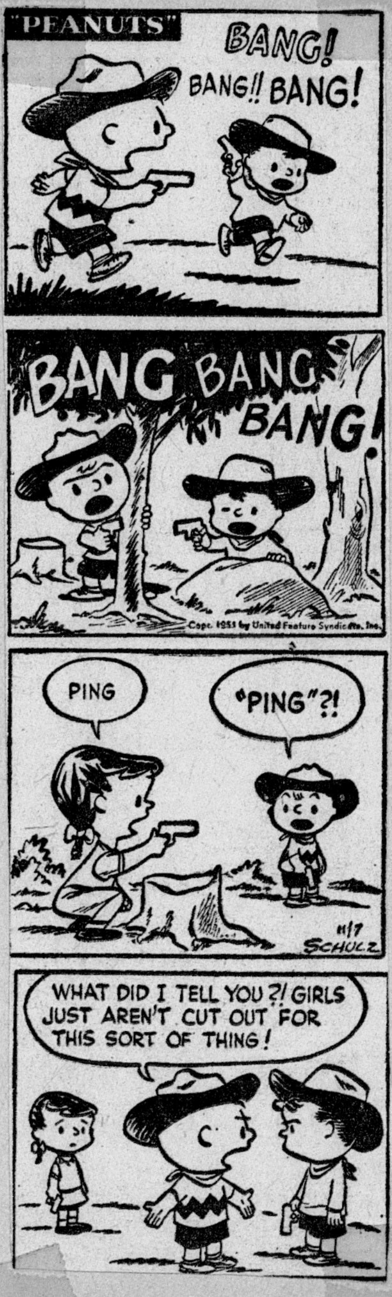
"PEANUTS"
BANG!
BANG!! BANG!
BANG BANG
BANG!
Copr. 1951 by United Feature Syndicate, Inc.
PING
"PING"?!
11/7
SCHULZ
WHAT DID I TELL YOU?! GIRLS JUST AREN'T CUT OUT FOR THIS SORT OF THING!

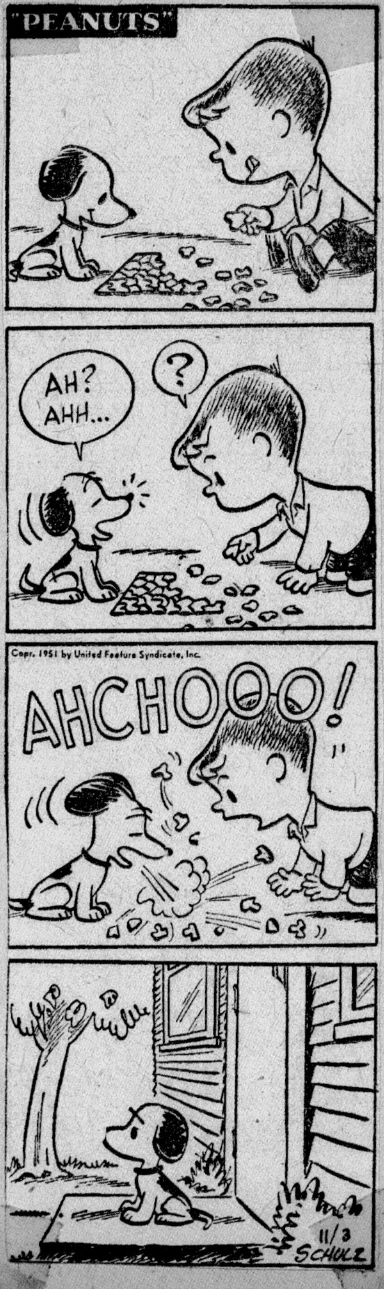
"PEANUTS"
AH? AHH...
?
Copr. 1951 by United Feature Syndicate, Inc.
AHCHOOO!
11/3
SCHULZ

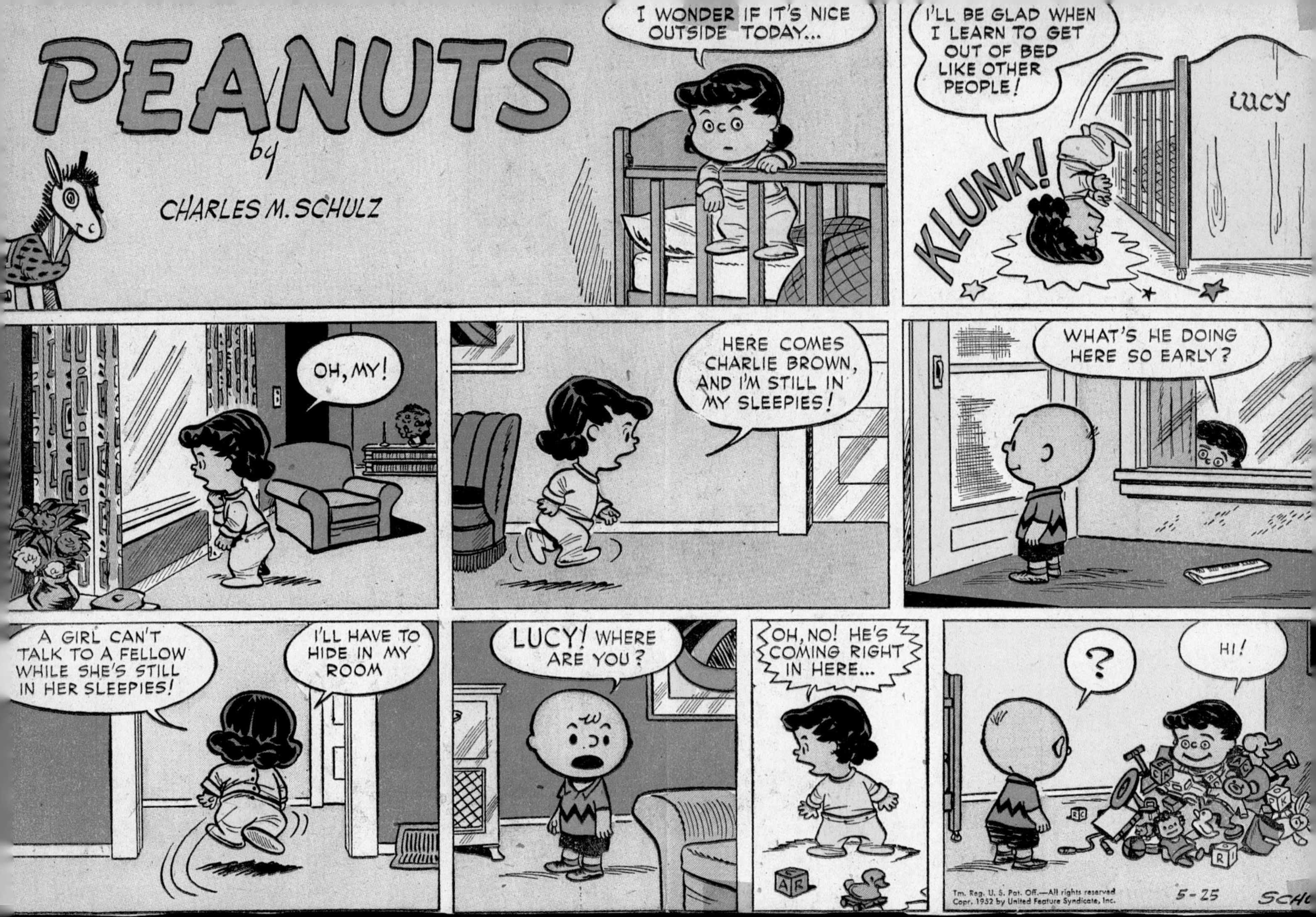
PEANUTS
by
CHARLES M. SCHULZ
I WONDER IF IT'S NICE OUTSIDE TODAY...
I'LL BE GLAD WHEN I LEARN TO GET OUT OF BED LIKE OTHER PEOPLE!
LUCY
KLUNK!
OH, MY!
HERE COMES CHARLIE BROWN, AND I'M STILL IN MY SLEEPIES!
WHAT'S HE DOING HERE SO EARLY?
A GIRL CAN'T TALK TO A FELLOW WHILE SHE'S STILL IN HER SLEEPIES!
I'LL HAVE TO HIDE IN MY ROOM
LUCY! WHERE ARE YOU?
OH, NO! HE'S COMING RIGHT IN HERE...
?
HI!
Tm. Reg. U. S. Pat. Off.—All rights reserved
Copr. 1952 by United Feature Syndicate, Inc.
5-25

"The humor that I introduced in 1950 was a very concise sort of humor. It grew out of magazine cartooning. I drew very brief incidents in the first *Peanuts* strips. Then as it began to grow and the characters developed, more conversation entered into it, and the characters themselves developed more intricate personalities. I grew away from drawing upon the actions of real little kids playing in sandboxes and riding tricycles." —1981

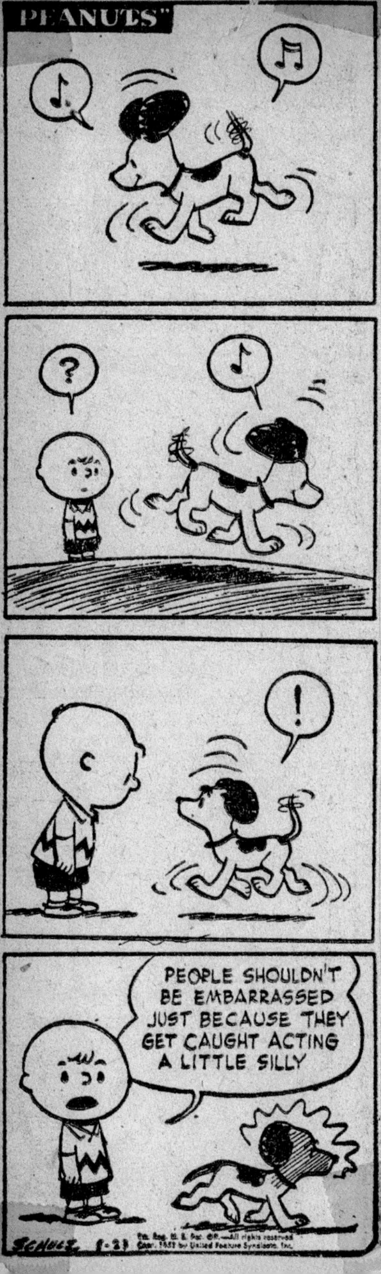
"PEANUTS"
?
!
PEOPLE SHOULDN'T BE EMBARRASSED JUST BECAUSE THEY GET CAUGHT ACTING A LITTLE SILLY
SCHULZ

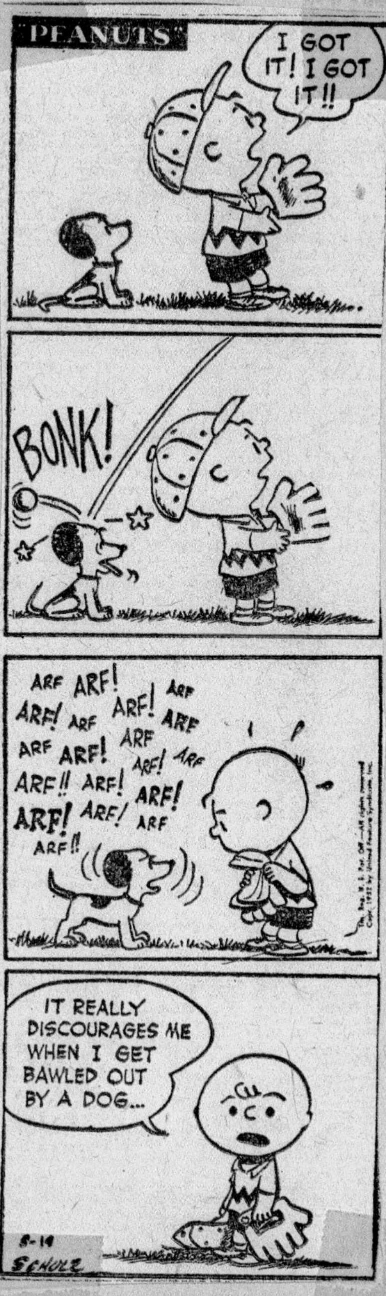
"PEANUTS"
I GOT IT! I GOT IT!!
BONK!
ARF ARF! ARF ARF! ARF ARF! ARF ARF ARF ARF! ARF ARF! ARF ARF!! ARF! ARF! ARF! ARF! ARF ARF!!
IT REALLY DISCOURAGES ME WHEN I GET BAWLED OUT BY A DOG...
SCHULZ

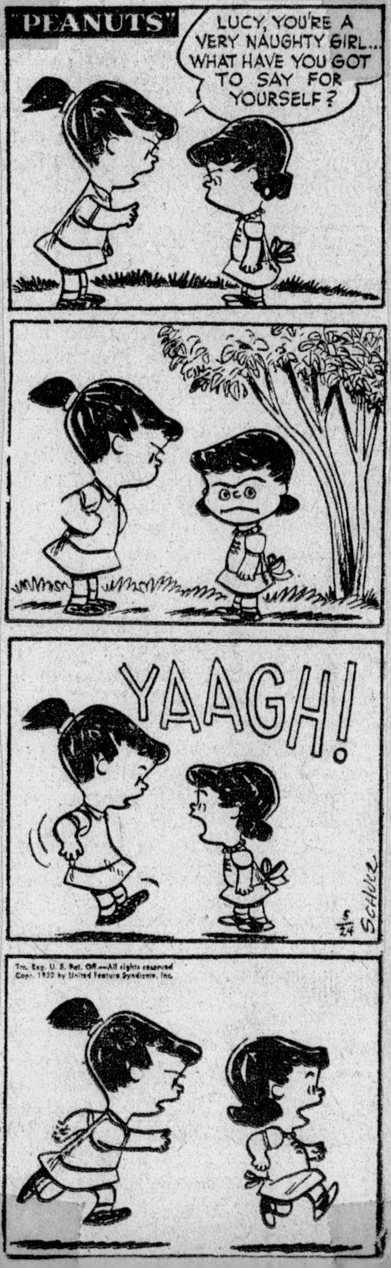
"PEANUTS"
LUCY, YOU'RE A VERY NAUGHTY GIRL... WHAT HAVE YOU GOT TO SAY FOR YOURSELF?
YAAGH!
SCHULZ

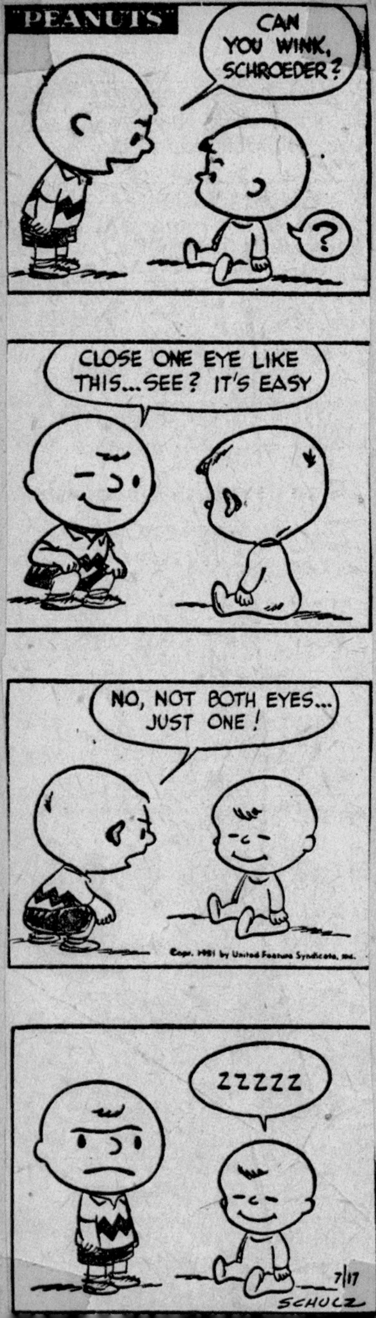
"PEANUTS"
CAN YOU WINK, SCHROEDER?
?
CLOSE ONE EYE LIKE THIS...SEE? IT'S EASY
NO, NOT BOTH EYES... JUST ONE!
Copr. 1951 by United Feature Syndicate, Inc.
ZZZZZ
7/17
SCHULZ

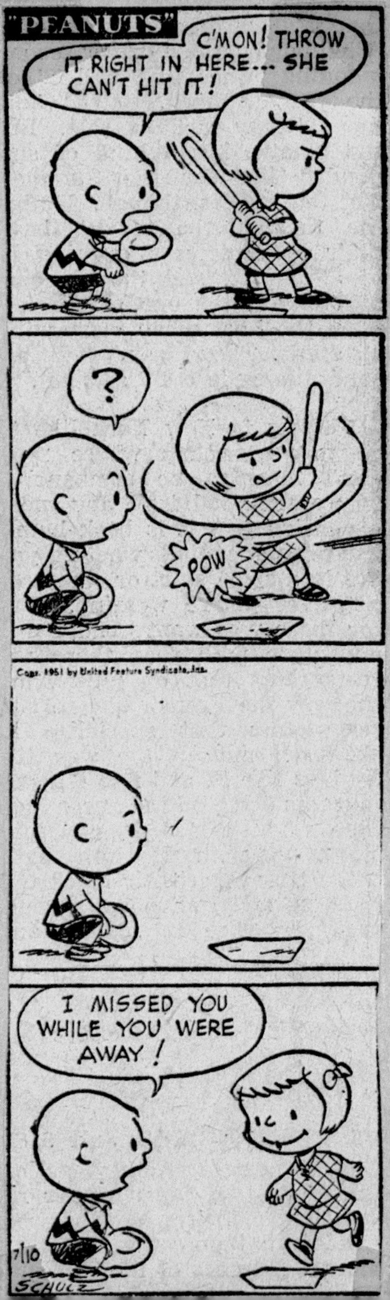
"PEANUTS"
C'MON! THROW IT RIGHT IN HERE... SHE CAN'T HIT IT!
?
POW
Copr. 1951 by United Feature Syndicate, Inc.
I MISSED YOU WHILE YOU WERE AWAY!
7/10
SCHULZ

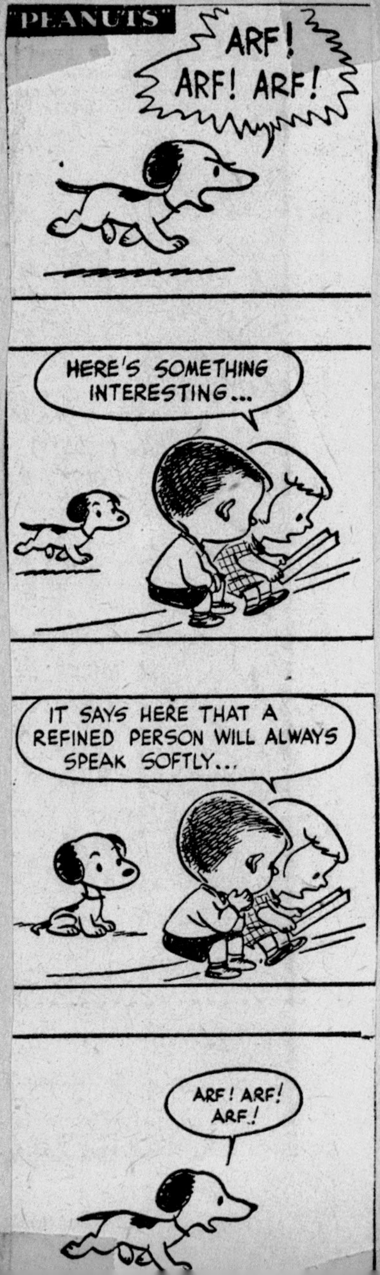
"PEANUTS"
ARF! ARF! ARF!
HERE'S SOMETHING INTERESTING...
IT SAYS HERE THAT A REFINED PERSON WILL ALWAYS SPEAK SOFTLY...
ARF! ARF! ARF!

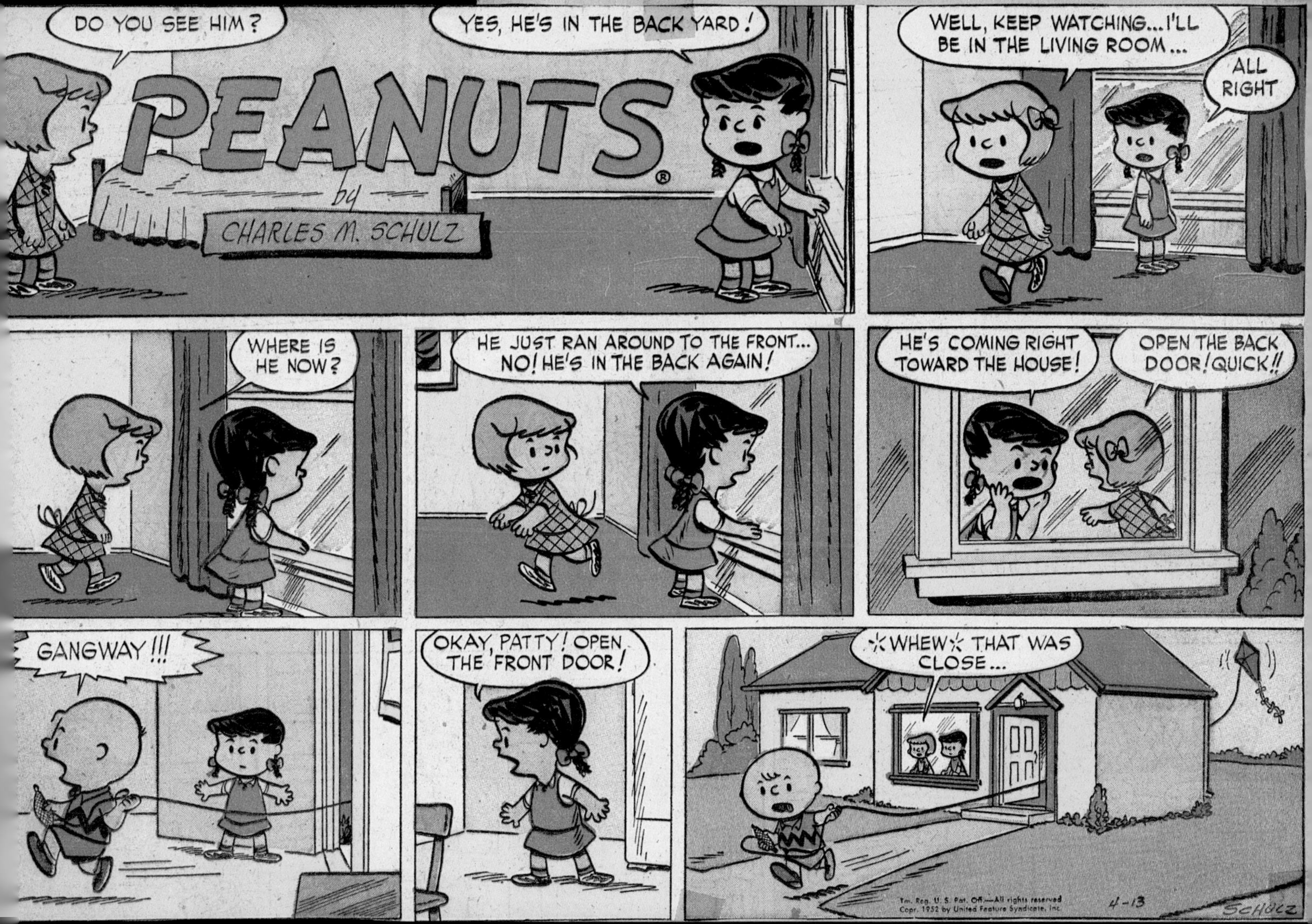
DO YOU SEE HIM?
YES, HE'S IN THE BACK YARD!
PEANUTS®
by CHARLES M. SCHULZ
WELL, KEEP WATCHING...I'LL BE IN THE LIVING ROOM...
ALL RIGHT
WHERE IS HE NOW?
HE JUST RAN AROUND TO THE FRONT... NO! HE'S IN THE BACK AGAIN!
HE'S COMING RIGHT TOWARD THE HOUSE!
OPEN THE BACK DOOR! QUICK!!
GANGWAY!!!
OKAY, PATTY! OPEN THE FRONT DOOR!
WHEW THAT WAS CLOSE...
Tm. Reg. U. S. Pat. Off.—All rights reserved
Copr. 1952 by United Feature Syndicate, Inc.
4-13
SCHULZ

In the years before the Kite-Eating Tree, Charlie Brown's problem wasn't getting his kite to fly, it was finding enough running room—a recycled *Li'l Folks* gag. The house is like something from Wonderland. From the inside it's huge, on the outside it's tiny. "When I went to St. Paul for the first time, I was struck by how much of the neighborhood of his youth shows up in the strip." recalled Paige Braddock, "The overhang and stairs of the front stoop that he often drew look just like his childhood house."

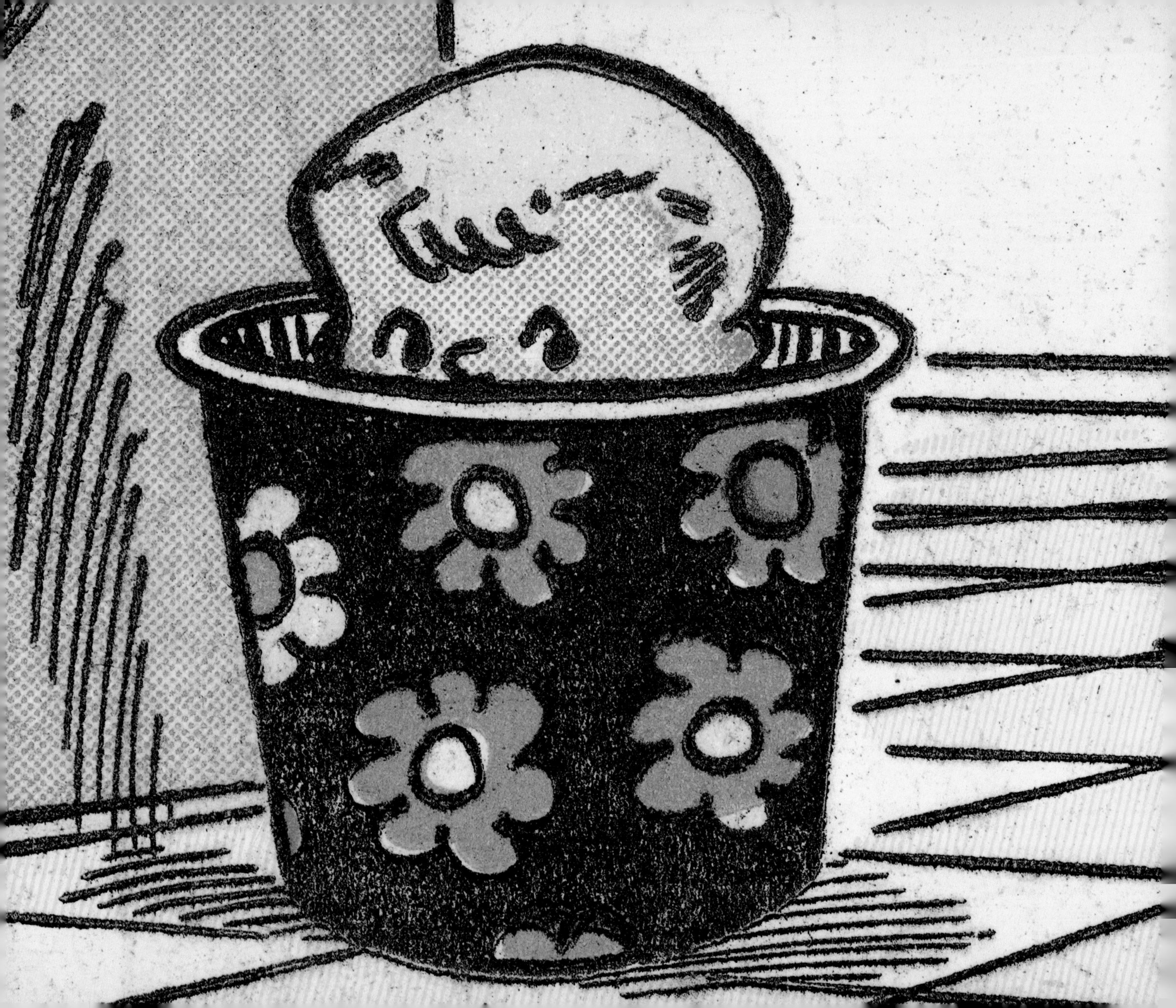

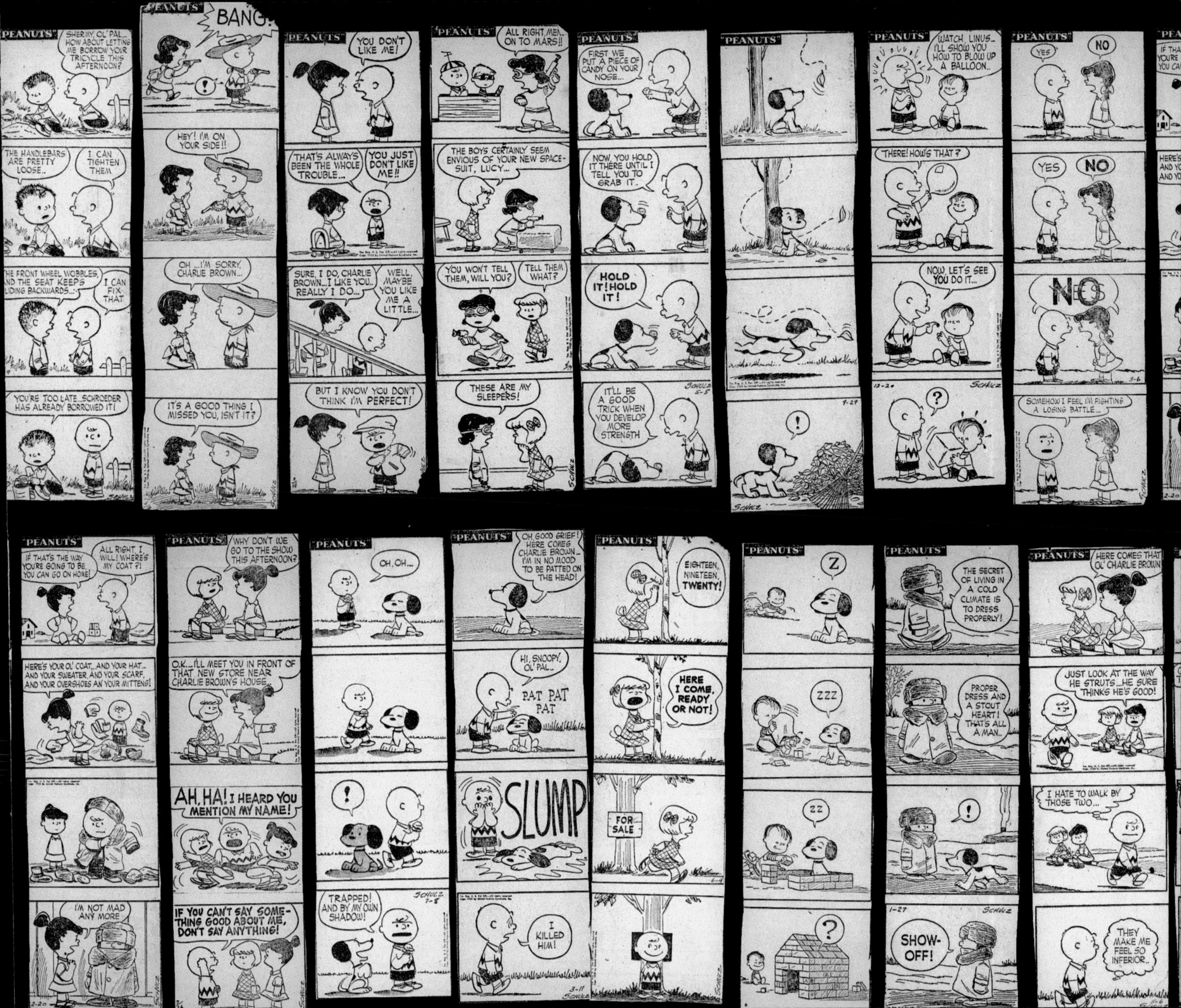
"PEANUTS"
SHERMY, OL' PAL.. HOW ABOUT LETTING ME BORROW YOUR TRICYCLE THIS AFTERNOON?
THE HANDLEBARS ARE PRETTY LOOSE..
I CAN TIGHTEN THEM
THE FRONT WHEEL WOBBLES, AND THE SEAT KEEPS SLIDING BACKWARDS...
I CAN FIX THAT
YOU'RE TOO LATE...SCHROEDER HAS ALREADY BORROWED IT!
SCHULZ
"PEANUTS"
BANG!
!
HEY! I'M ON YOUR SIDE!!
OH ...I'M SORRY, CHARLIE BROWN...
IT'S A GOOD THING I MISSED YOU, ISN'T IT?
SCHULZ
"PEANUTS"
YOU DON'T LIKE ME!
THAT'S ALWAYS BEEN THE WHOLE TROUBLE...
YOU JUST DON'T LIKE ME!!
SURE, I DO, CHARLIE BROWN...I LIKE YOU.. REALLY I DO...
WELL, MAYBE YOU LIKE ME A LITTLE...
BUT I KNOW YOU DON'T THINK I'M PERFECT!
SCHULZ
"PEANUTS"
ALL RIGHT, MEN.. ON TO MARS!!
THE BOYS CERTAINLY SEEM ENVIOUS OF YOUR NEW SPACE-SUIT, LUCY...
YOU WON'T TELL THEM, WILL YOU?
TELL THEM WHAT?
THESE ARE MY SLEEPERS!
SCHULZ
"PEANUTS"
FIRST WE PUT A PIECE OF CANDY ON YOUR NOSE...
NOW, YOU HOLD IT THERE UNTIL I TELL YOU TO GRAB IT..
HOLD IT! HOLD IT!
SCHULZ 5-5
IT'LL BE A GOOD TRICK WHEN YOU DEVELOP MORE STRENGTH
"PEANUTS"
SCHULZ
9-29
!
"PEANUTS"
WATCH LINUS.. I'LL SHOW YOU HOW TO BLOW UP A BALLOON..
THERE! HOW'S THAT?
NOW, LET'S SEE YOU DO IT...
3-6
12-2
SCHULZ
?
"PEANUTS"
YES
NO
YES
NO
NO
SOMEHOW I FEEL I'M FIGHTING A LOSING BATTLE...
SCHULZ
2-20
"PEANUTS"
IF THAT'S THE WAY YOU'RE GOING TO BE, YOU CAN GO ON HOME!
ALL RIGHT, I WILL! WHERE'S MY COAT?!
HERE'S YOUR OL' COAT...AND YOUR HAT... AND YOUR SWEATER, AND YOUR SCARF, AND YOUR OVERSHOES AN' YOUR MITTENS!
I'M NOT MAD ANY MORE
2-20
"PEANUTS"
WHY DON'T WE GO TO THE SHOW THIS AFTERNOON?
O.K....I'LL MEET YOU IN FRONT OF THAT NEW STORE NEAR CHARLIE BROWN'S HOUSE...
AH, HA! I HEARD YOU MENTION MY NAME!
IF YOU CAN'T SAY SOMETHING GOOD ABOUT ME, DON'T SAY ANYTHING!
SCHULZ
"PEANUTS"
OH, OH...
!
SCHULZ 7-8
TRAPPED! AND BY MY OWN SHADOW!
"PEANUTS"
OH, GOOD GRIEF! HERE COMES CHARLIE BROWN.. I'M IN NO MOOD TO BE PATTED ON THE HEAD!
HI, SNOOPY, OL' PAL...
PAT PAT PAT
SLUMP
I KILLED HIM!
3-11 SCHULZ
"PEANUTS"
EIGHTEEN, NINETEEN, TWENTY!
HERE I COME, READY OR NOT!
FOR SALE
6-4
SCHULZ
"PEANUTS"
Z
ZZZ
ZZ
?
"PEANUTS"
THE SECRET OF LIVING IN A COLD CLIMATE IS TO DRESS PROPERLY!
PROPER DRESS AND A STOUT HEART! THAT'S ALL A MAN..
!
1-27
SCHULZ
SHOW-OFF!
"PEANUTS"
HERE COMES THAT OL' CHARLIE BROWN
JUST LOOK AT THE WAY HE STRUTS...HE SURE THINKS HE'S GOOD!
I HATE TO WALK BY THOSE TWO...
THEY MAKE ME FEEL SO INFERIOR..

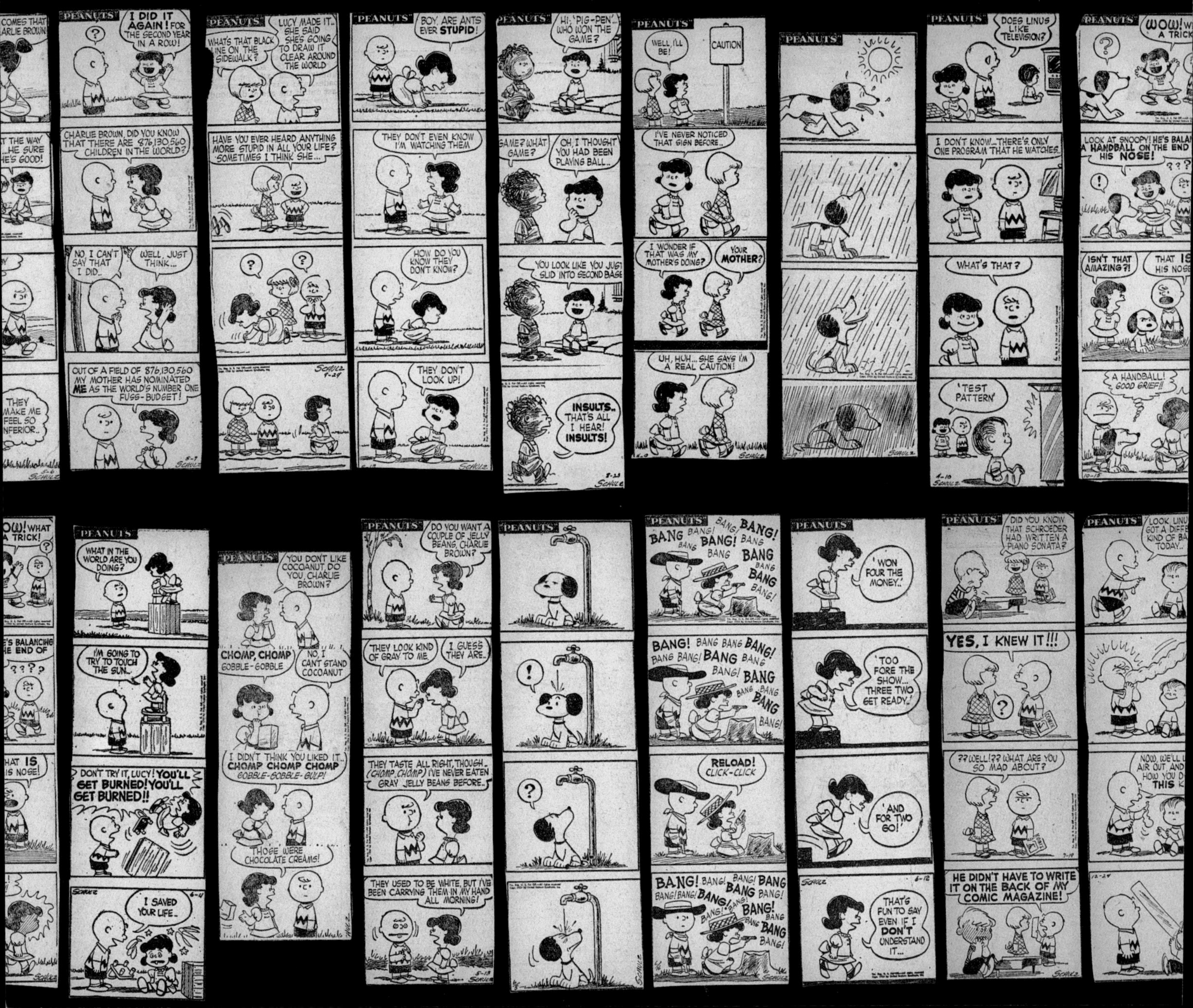

COMES THAT
ARLIE BROWN
T THE WAY
..HE SURE
HE'S GOOD!
THEY MAKE ME FEEL SO
NFERIOR..
PEANUTS
?
I DID IT AGAIN! FOR THE SECOND YEAR IN A ROW!
CHARLIE BROWN, DID YOU KNOW THAT THERE ARE 876,130,560 CHILDREN IN THE WORLD?
NO, I CAN'T SAY THAT I DID..
WELL, JUST THINK...
OUT OF A FIELD OF 876,130,560 MY MOTHER HAS NOMINATED ME AS THE WORLD'S NUMBER ONE FUSS-BUDGET!
PEANUTS
WHAT'S THAT BLACK LINE ON THE SIDEWALK?
LUCY MADE IT.. SHE SAID SHE'S GOING TO DRAW IT CLEAR AROUND THE WORLD
HAVE YOU EVER HEARD ANYTHING MORE STUPID IN ALL YOUR LIFE? SOMETIMES I THINK SHE...
?
?
PEANUTS
BOY, ARE ANTS EVER STUPID!
THEY DON'T EVEN KNOW I'M WATCHING THEM
HOW DO YOU KNOW THEY DON'T KNOW?
THEY DON'T LOOK UP!
PEANUTS
HI, 'PIG-PEN'... WHO WON THE GAME?
GAME? WHAT GAME?
OH, I THOUGHT YOU HAD BEEN PLAYING BALL...
YOU LOOK LIKE YOU JUST SLID INTO SECOND BASE
INSULTS.. THAT'S ALL I HEAR! INSULTS!
PEANUTS
WELL, I'LL BE!
CAUTION
I'VE NEVER NOTICED THAT SIGN BEFORE..
I WONDER IF THAT WAS MY MOTHER'S DOING?
YOUR MOTHER?
UH, HUH... SHE SAYS I'M A REAL CAUTION!
PEANUTS
PEANUTS
DOES LINUS LIKE TELEVISION?
I DON'T KNOW... THERE'S ONLY ONE PROGRAM THAT HE WATCHES.
WHAT'S THAT?
'TEST PATTERN'
PEANUTS
?
WOW! WH
A TRICK
LOOK AT SNOOPY! HE'S BALA
A HANDBALL ON THE END
HIS NOSE!
???
!
ISN'T THAT AMAZING?!
THAT IS
HIS NOSE
A HANDBALL! GOOD GRIEF!!
OW! WHAT
A TRICK!
?
E'S BALANCING
THE END OF
????
HAT IS
IS NOSE!
PEANUTS
WHAT IN THE WORLD ARE YOU DOING?
I'M GOING TO TRY TO TOUCH THE SUN..
DON'T TRY IT, LUCY! YOU'LL GET BURNED! YOU'LL GET BURNED!!
I SAVED YOUR LIFE..
PEANUTS
YOU DON'T LIKE COCOANUT, DO YOU, CHARLIE BROWN?
CHOMP, CHOMP GOBBLE-GOBBLE
NO, I CAN'T STAND COCOANUT
I DIDN'T THINK YOU LIKED IT.. CHOMP CHOMP CHOMP GOBBLE-GOBBLE-GULP!
THOSE WERE CHOCOLATE CREAMS!
PEANUTS
DO YOU WANT A COUPLE OF JELLY BEANS, CHARLIE BROWN?
THEY LOOK KIND OF GRAY TO ME
I GUESS THEY ARE..
THEY TASTE ALL RIGHT, THOUGH.. (CHOMP, CHOMP) I'VE NEVER EATEN GRAY JELLY BEANS BEFORE..
THEY USED TO BE WHITE, BUT I'VE BEEN CARRYING THEM IN MY HAND ALL MORNING!
PEANUTS
!
?
PEANUTS
BANG BANG! BANG! BANG! BANG BANG BANG BANG BANG BANG! BANG!
BANG! BANG BANG BANG! BANG BANG! BANG BANG BANG! BANG BANG BANG BANG BANG!
RELOAD! CLICK-CLICK
BANG! BANG! BANG! BANG BANG BANG! BANG! BANG! BANG! BANG! BANG! BANG BANG BANG!
PEANUTS
'WON FOUR THE MONEY.'
'TOO FORE THE SHOW... THREE TWO GET READY.'
'AND FOR TWO GO!'
THAT'S FUN TO SAY EVEN IF I DON'T UNDERSTAND IT...
PEANUTS
DID YOU KNOW THAT SCHROEDER HAD WRITTEN A PIANO SONATA?
YES, I KNEW IT!!!
?
?? WELL!?? WHAT ARE YOU SO MAD ABOUT?
HE DIDN'T HAVE TO WRITE IT ON THE BACK OF MY COMIC MAGAZINE!
PEANUTS
LOOK LINU
GOT A DIFFE
KIND OF BA
TODAY..
NOW, WE'LL
AIR OUT, AND
HOW YOU DO
THIS K

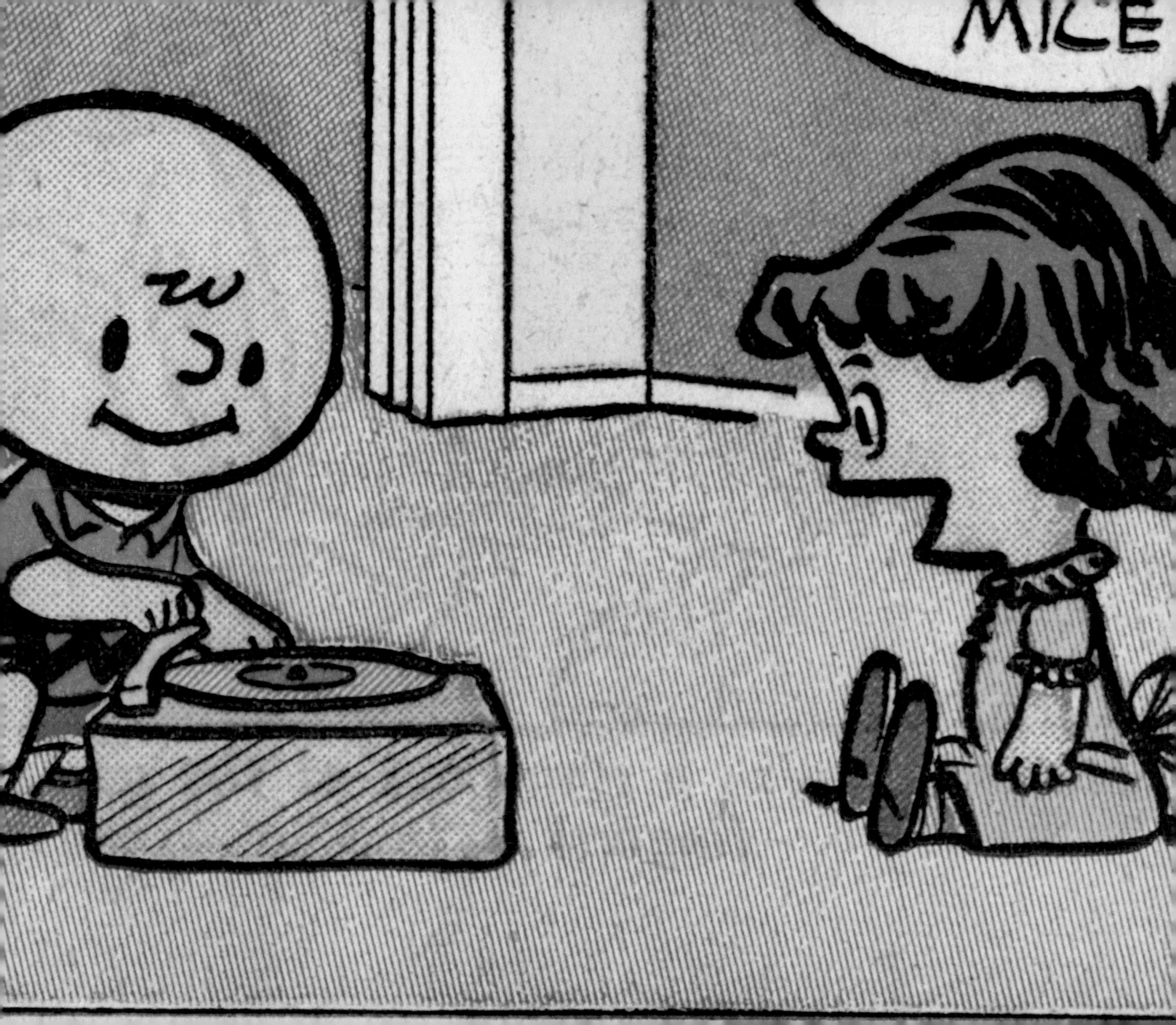
MICE

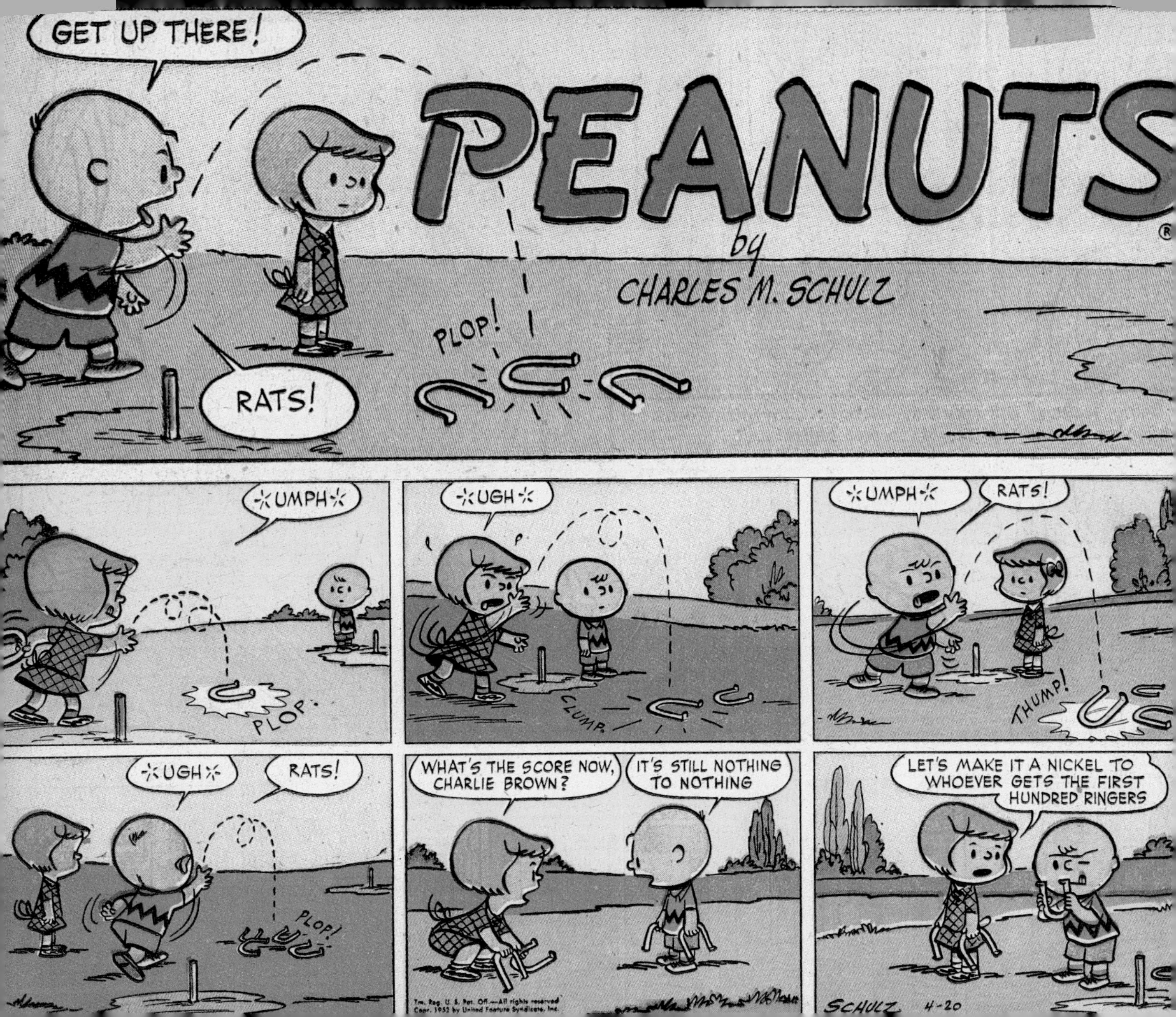
GET UP THERE!
PEANUTS
by CHARLES M. SCHULZ
RATS!
PLOP!
UMPH
PLOP
UGH
CLUMP
UMPH
RATS!
THUMP!
UGH
RATS!
PLOP!
WHAT'S THE SCORE NOW, CHARLIE BROWN?
IT'S STILL NOTHING TO NOTHING
Tm. Reg. U. S. Pat. Off.—All rights reserved Copr. 1952 by United Feature Syndicate, Inc.
LET'S MAKE IT A NICKEL TO WHOEVER GETS THE FIRST HUNDRED RINGERS
SCHULZ 4-20

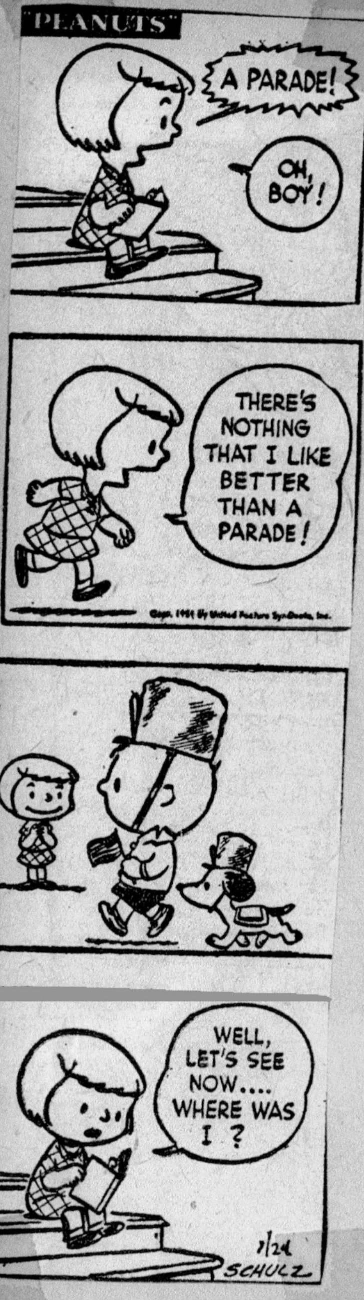
"PEANUTS"
A PARADE!
OH, BOY!
THERE'S NOTHING THAT I LIKE BETTER THAN A PARADE!
Copr. 1951 by United Feature Syndicate, Inc.
WELL, LET'S SEE NOW.... WHERE WAS I ?
7/24
SCHULZ

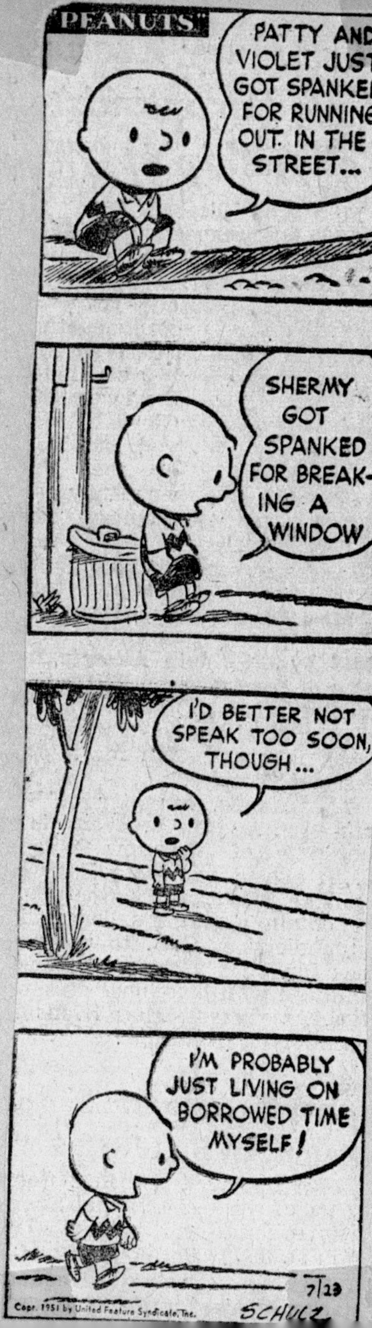
"PEANUTS"
PATTY AND VIOLET JUST GOT SPANKED FOR RUNNING OUT IN THE STREET...
SHERMY GOT SPANKED FOR BREAKING A WINDOW
I'D BETTER NOT SPEAK TOO SOON, THOUGH...
I'M PROBABLY JUST LIVING ON BORROWED TIME MYSELF!
7/23
Copr. 1951 by United Feature Syndicate, Inc.
SCHULZ

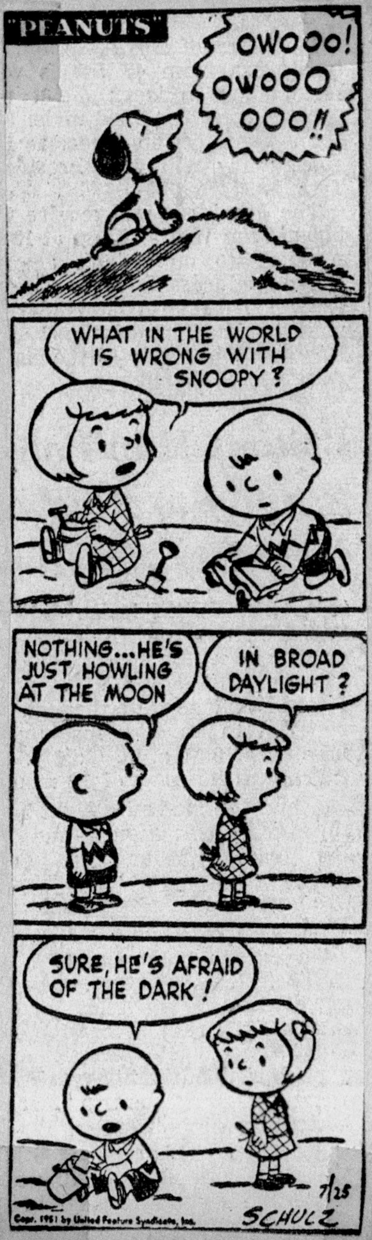
"PEANUTS"
OWOOO! OWOOO OOO!!
WHAT IN THE WORLD IS WRONG WITH SNOOPY?
NOTHING...HE'S JUST HOWLING AT THE MOON
IN BROAD DAYLIGHT?
SURE, HE'S AFRAID OF THE DARK!
7/25
Copr. 1951 by United Feature Syndicate, Inc.
SCHULZ

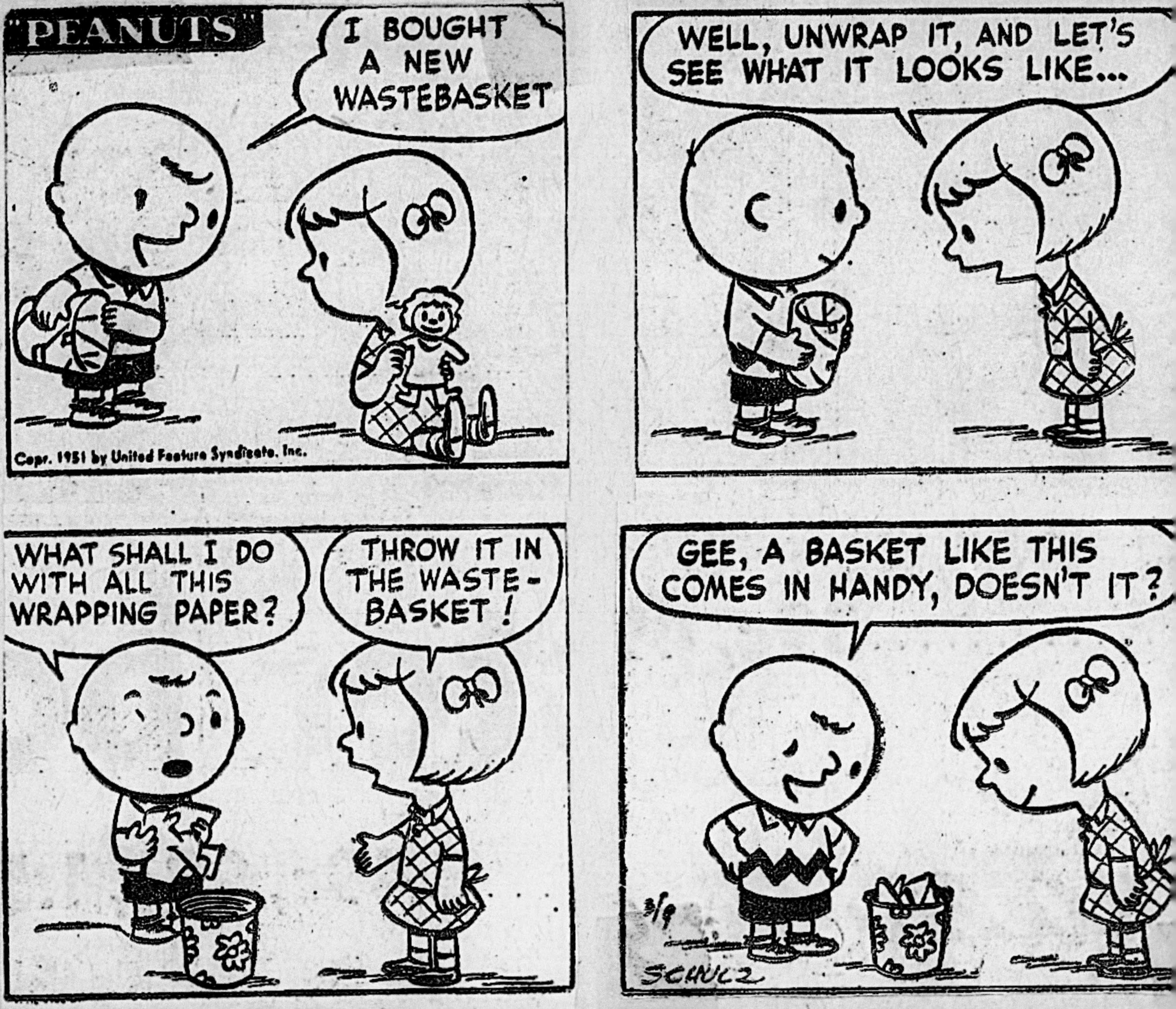
PEANUTS
I BOUGHT A NEW WASTEBASKET
Copr. 1951 by United Feature Syndicate, Inc.
WELL, UNWRAP IT, AND LET'S SEE WHAT IT LOOKS LIKE...
WHAT SHALL I DO WITH ALL THIS WRAPPING PAPER?
THROW IT IN THE WASTE-BASKET!
GEE, A BASKET LIKE THIS COMES IN HANDY, DOESN'T IT?
3/9
SCHULZ

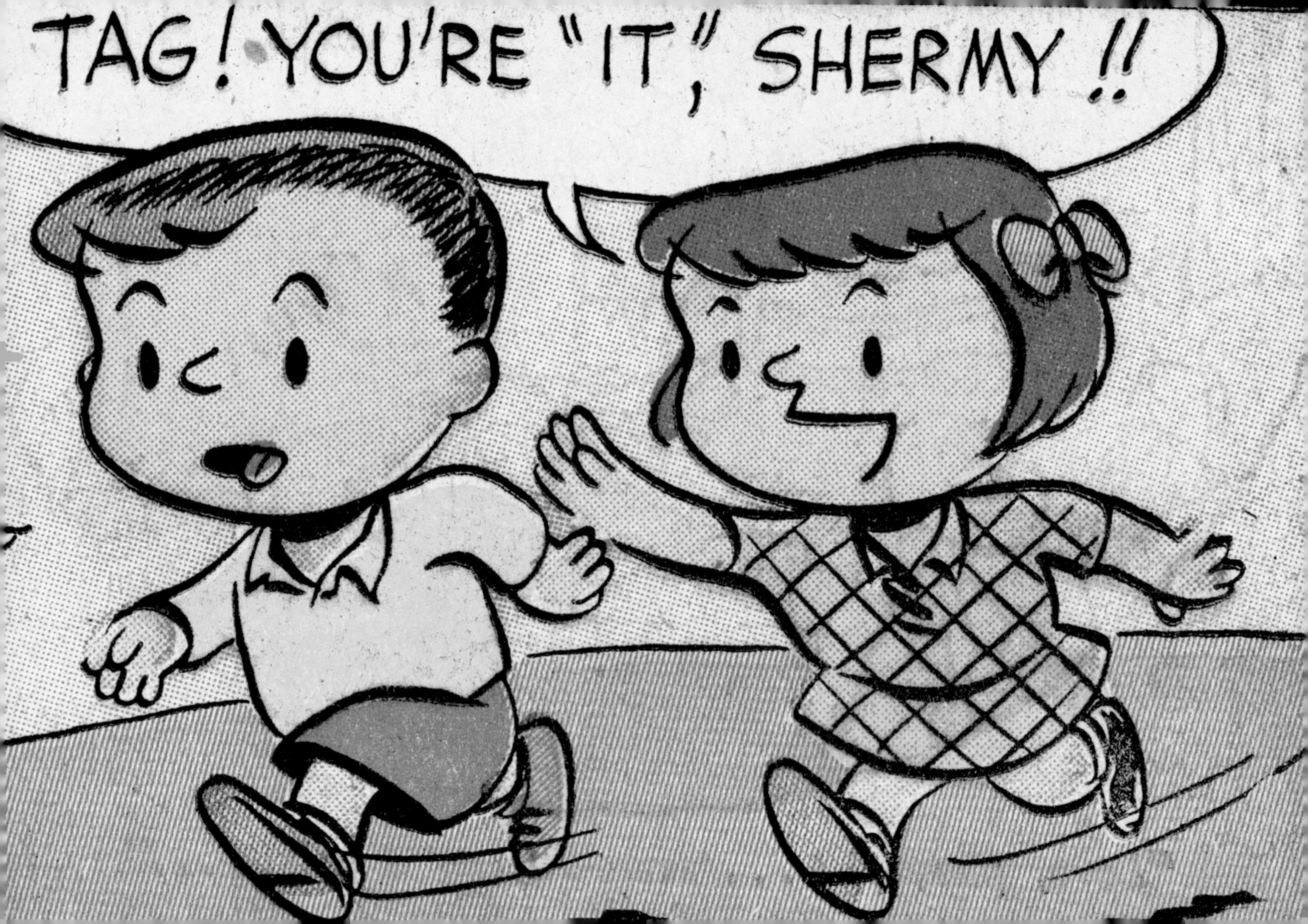
TAG! YOU'RE "IT," SHERMY!!

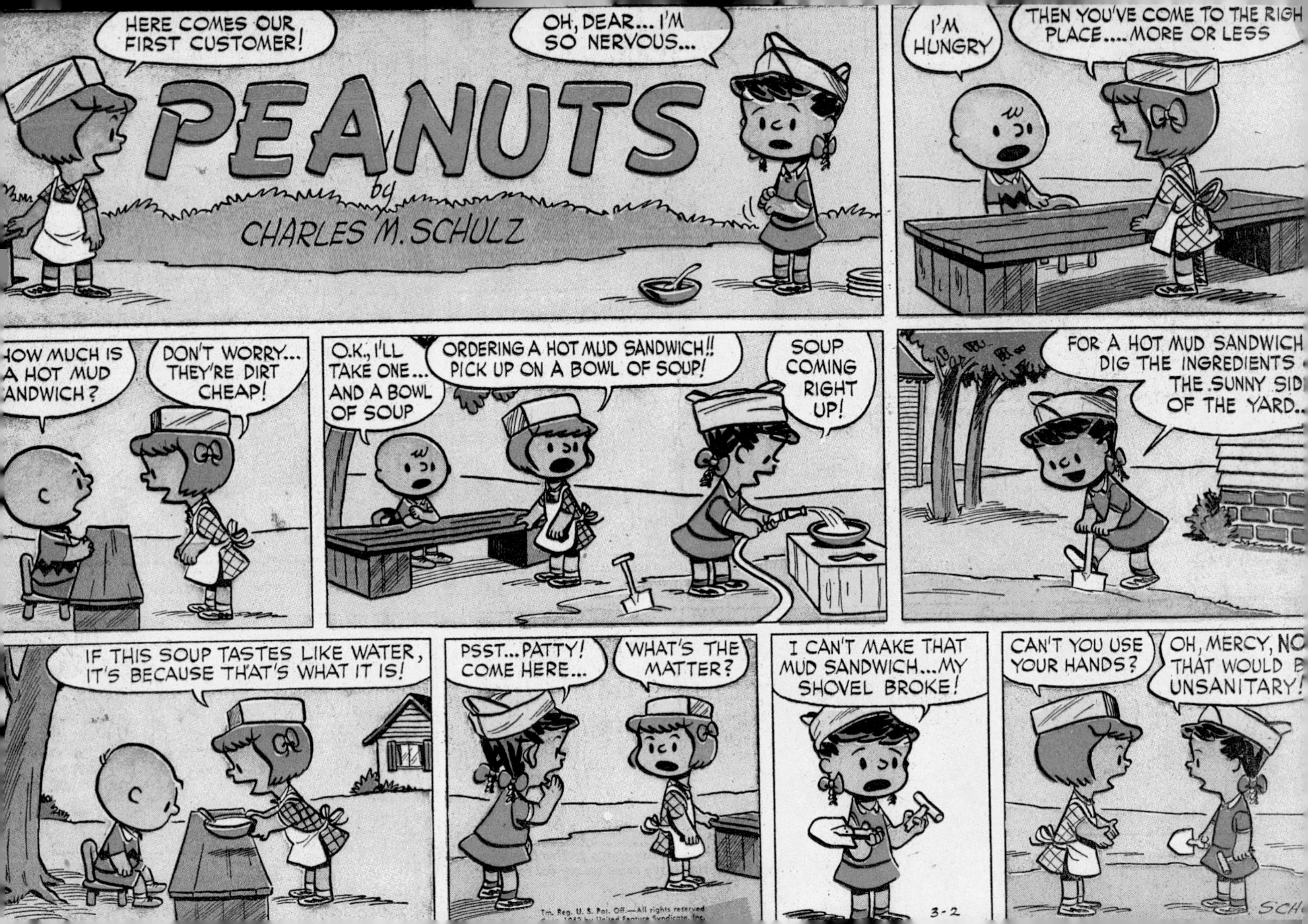

HERE COMES OUR FIRST CUSTOMER!
OH, DEAR... I'M SO NERVOUS...
PEANUTS
by CHARLES M. SCHULZ
I'M HUNGRY
THEN YOU'VE COME TO THE RIGH PLACE.... MORE OR LESS
HOW MUCH IS A HOT MUD ANDWICH?
DON'T WORRY... THEY'RE DIRT CHEAP!
O.K., I'LL TAKE ONE... AND A BOWL OF SOUP
ORDERING A HOT MUD SANDWICH!! PICK UP ON A BOWL OF SOUP!
SOUP COMING RIGHT UP!
FOR A HOT MUD SANDWICH DIG THE INGREDIENTS THE SUNNY SID OF THE YARD..
IF THIS SOUP TASTES LIKE WATER, IT'S BECAUSE THAT'S WHAT IT IS!
PSST... PATTY! COME HERE...
WHAT'S THE MATTER?
I CAN'T MAKE THAT MUD SANDWICH... MY SHOVEL BROKE!
CAN'T YOU USE YOUR HANDS?
OH, MERCY, NO THAT WOULD B UNSANITARY!
Tm. Reg. U. S. Pat. Off.—All rights reserved
3-2
SCH

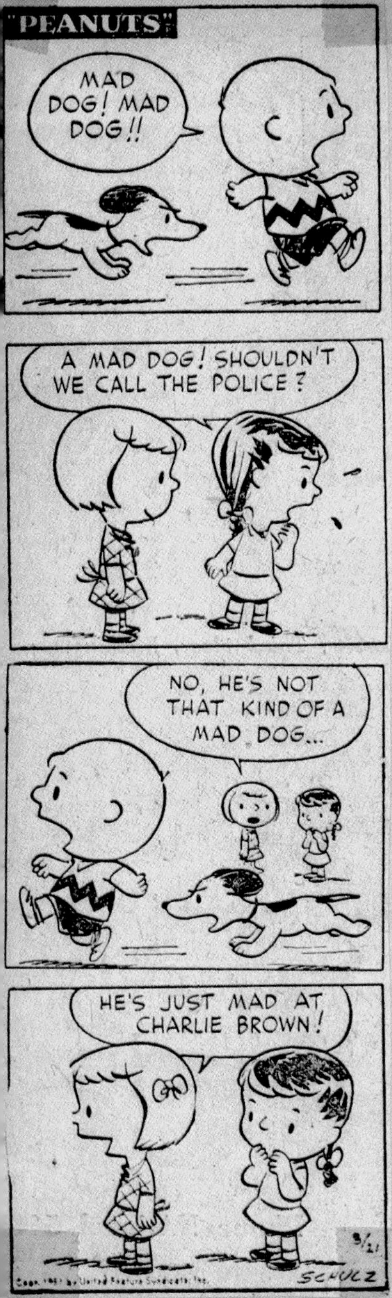
"PEANUTS"
MAD DOG! MAD DOG!!
A MAD DOG! SHOULDN'T WE CALL THE POLICE?
NO, HE'S NOT THAT KIND OF A MAD DOG...
HE'S JUST MAD AT CHARLIE BROWN!
3/21
SCHULZ

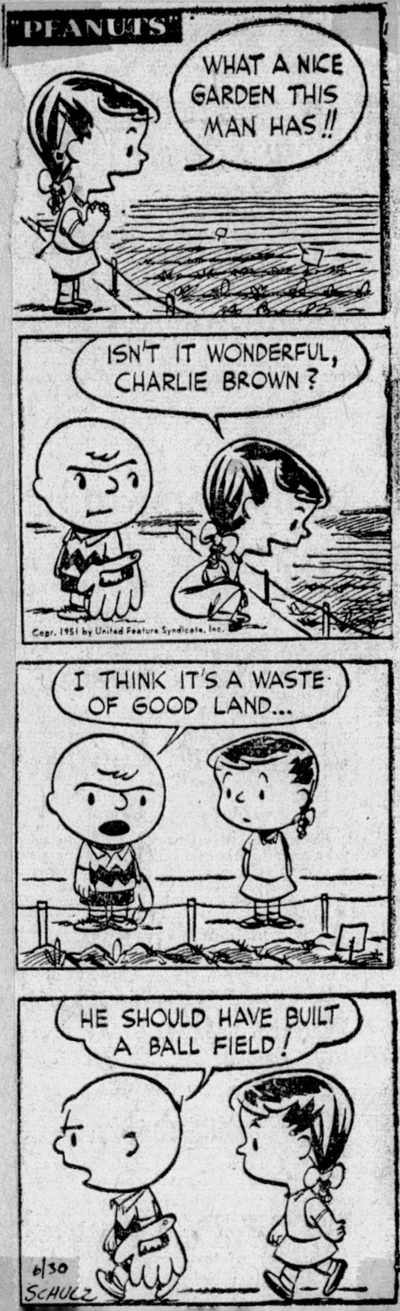
"PEANUTS"
WHAT A NICE GARDEN THIS MAN HAS!!
ISN'T IT WONDERFUL, CHARLIE BROWN?
Copr. 1951 by United Feature Syndicate, Inc.
I THINK IT'S A WASTE OF GOOD LAND...
HE SHOULD HAVE BUILT A BALL FIELD!
6/30
SCHULZ

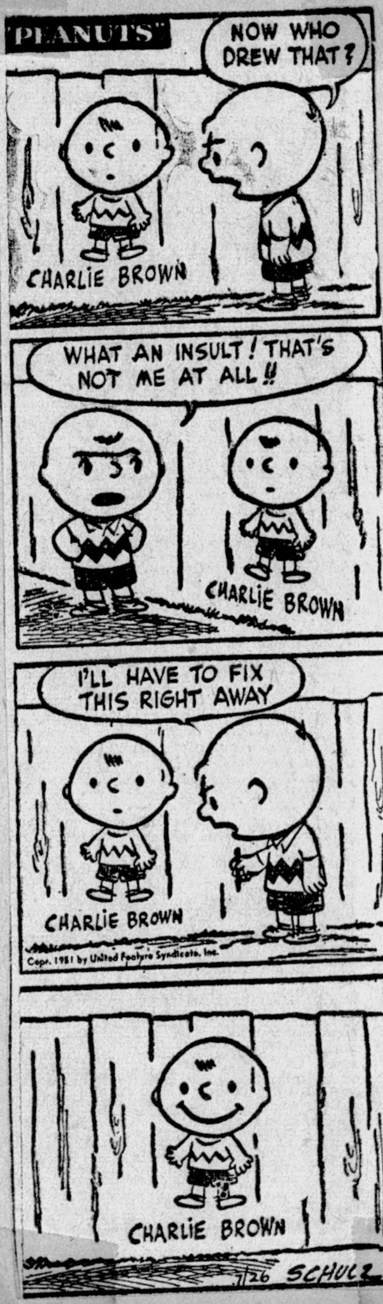
"PEANUTS"
NOW WHO DREW THAT?
CHARLIE BROWN
WHAT AN INSULT! THAT'S NOT ME AT ALL!!
CHARLIE BROWN
I'LL HAVE TO FIX THIS RIGHT AWAY
CHARLIE BROWN
Copr. 1951 by United Feature Syndicate, Inc.
CHARLIE BROWN
7/26
SCHULZ

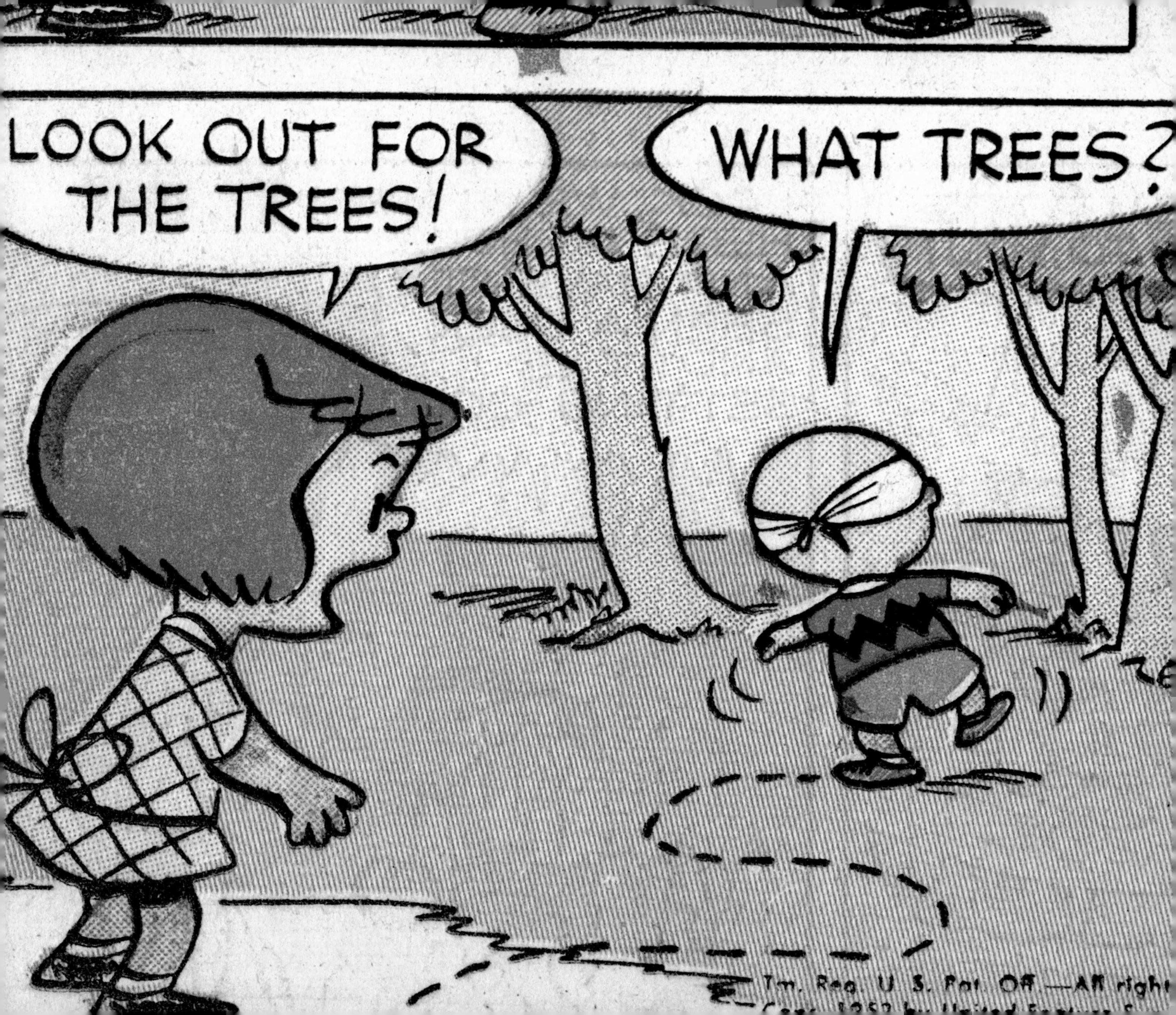
LOOK OUT FOR THE TREES!
WHAT TREES?

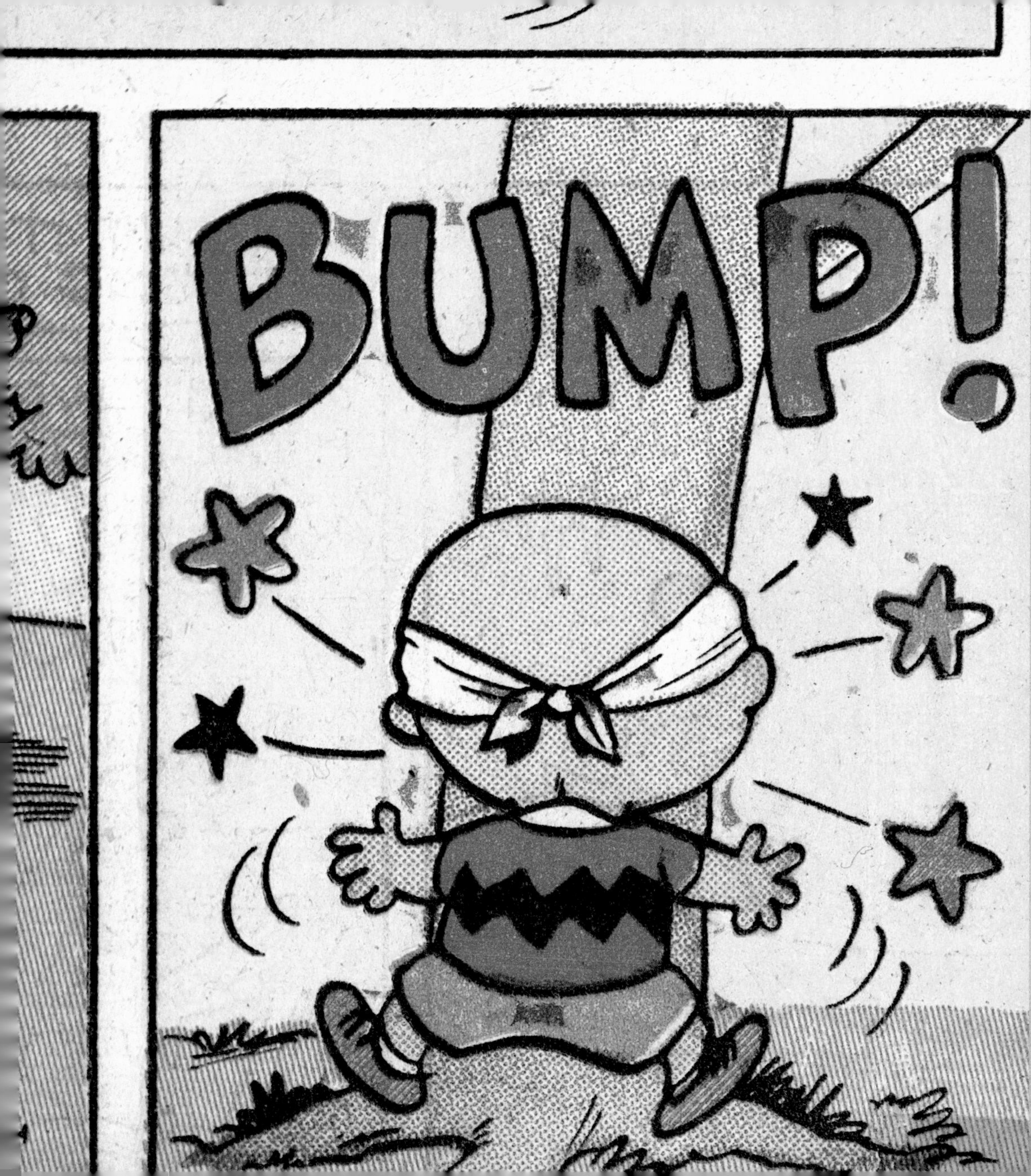
BUMP!

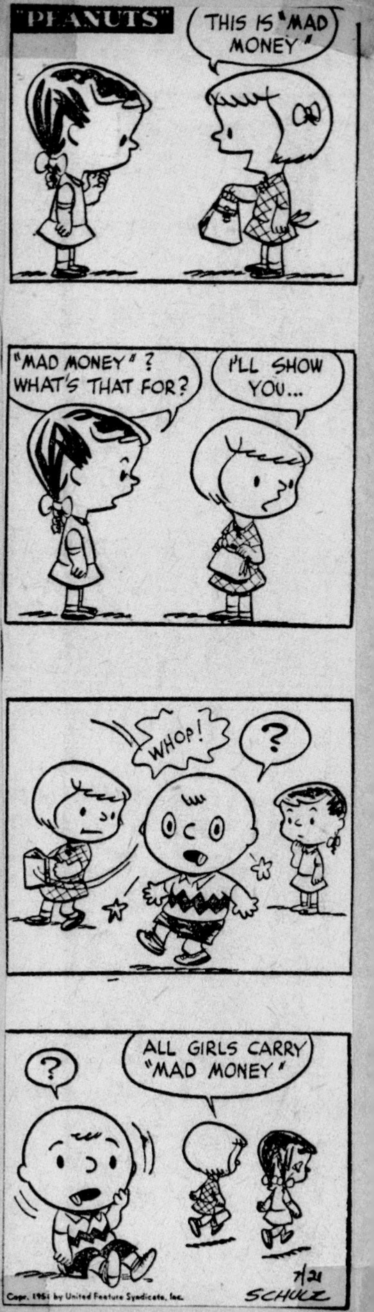
"PEANUTS"
THIS IS "MAD MONEY"
"MAD MONEY"? WHAT'S THAT FOR?
I'LL SHOW YOU...
WHOP!
?
?
ALL GIRLS CARRY "MAD MONEY"
7/21
Copr. 1951 by United Feature Syndicate, Inc.
SCHULZ

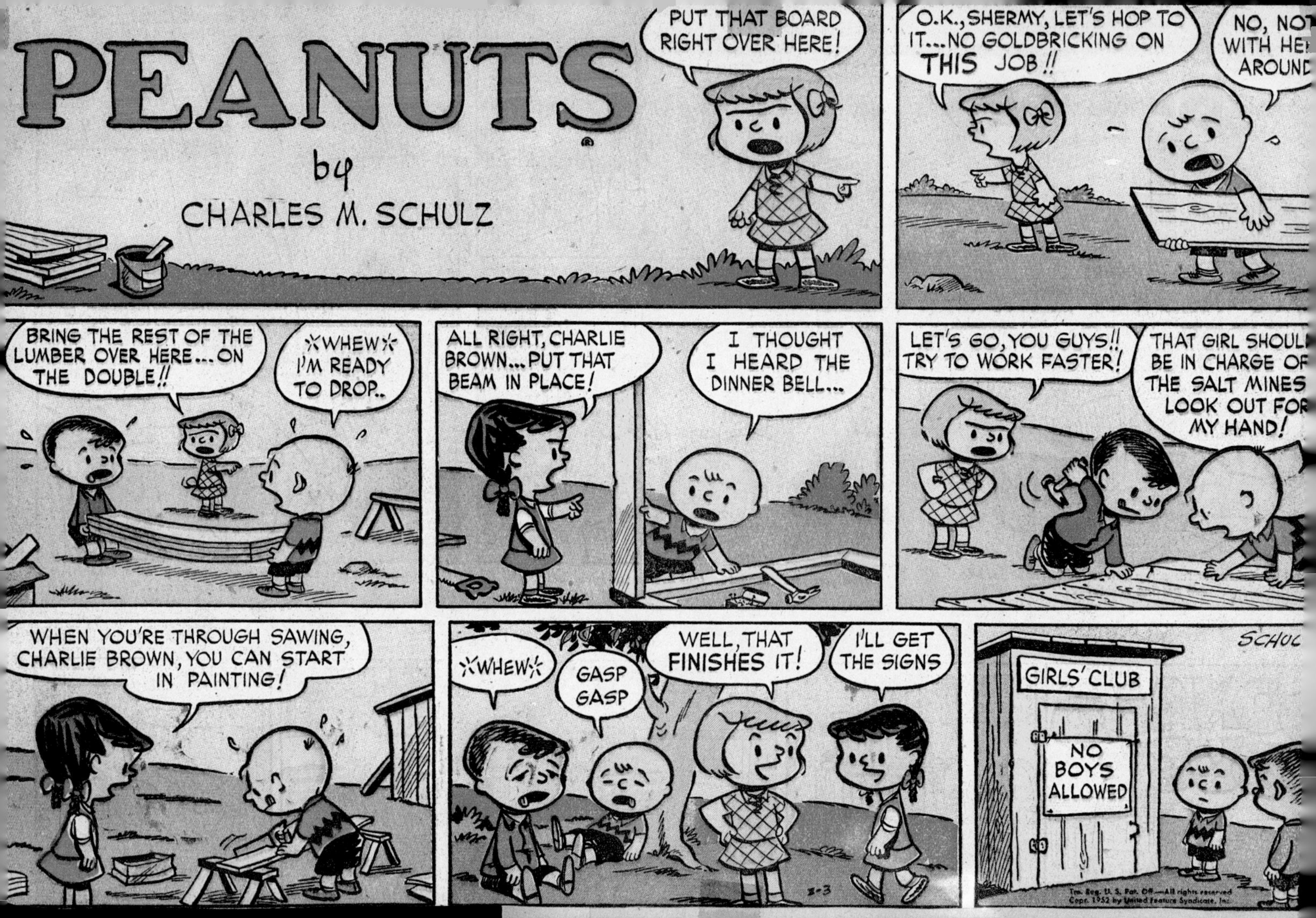
PEANUTS
by
CHARLES M. SCHULZ
PUT THAT BOARD RIGHT OVER HERE!
O.K., SHERMY, LET'S HOP TO IT...NO GOLDBRICKING ON THIS JOB!!
NO, NO WITH HE AROUN
BRING THE REST OF THE LUMBER OVER HERE...ON THE DOUBLE!!
WHEW I'M READY TO DROP..
ALL RIGHT, CHARLIE BROWN...PUT THAT BEAM IN PLACE!
I THOUGHT I HEARD THE DINNER BELL...
LET'S GO, YOU GUYS!! TRY TO WORK FASTER!
THAT GIRL SHOUL BE IN CHARGE OF THE SALT MINES LOOK OUT FOR MY HAND!
WHEN YOU'RE THROUGH SAWING, CHARLIE BROWN, YOU CAN START IN PAINTING!
WHEW
GASP GASP
WELL, THAT FINISHES IT!
I'LL GET THE SIGNS
GIRLS' CLUB
NO BOYS ALLOWED

With Lucy still a baby in 1953, someone had to boss the boys around, so Patty and Violet got the job. The ill-treatment of males by females was fair game in *Peanuts*, but *never* the other way around. Schulz said in 1967, "The supposedly weak people in the world are funny when they dominate the supposedly strong people. There is nothing funny about a little boy being mean to a little girl. That is simply not funny! But there is something funny about a little girl being mean to a little boy."

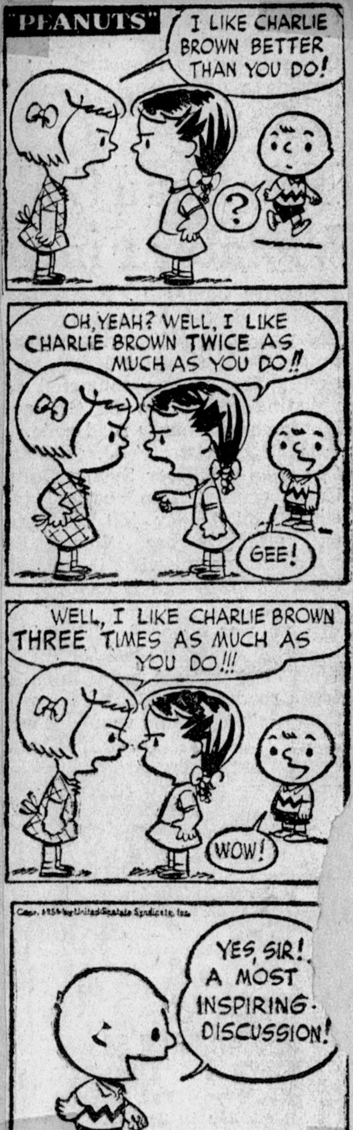
"PEANUTS"
I LIKE CHARLIE BROWN BETTER THAN YOU DO!
?
OH, YEAH? WELL, I LIKE CHARLIE BROWN TWICE AS MUCH AS YOU DO!!
GEE!
WELL, I LIKE CHARLIE BROWN THREE TIMES AS MUCH AS YOU DO!!!
WOW!
YES, SIR! A MOST INSPIRING DISCUSSION!
SCHULZ

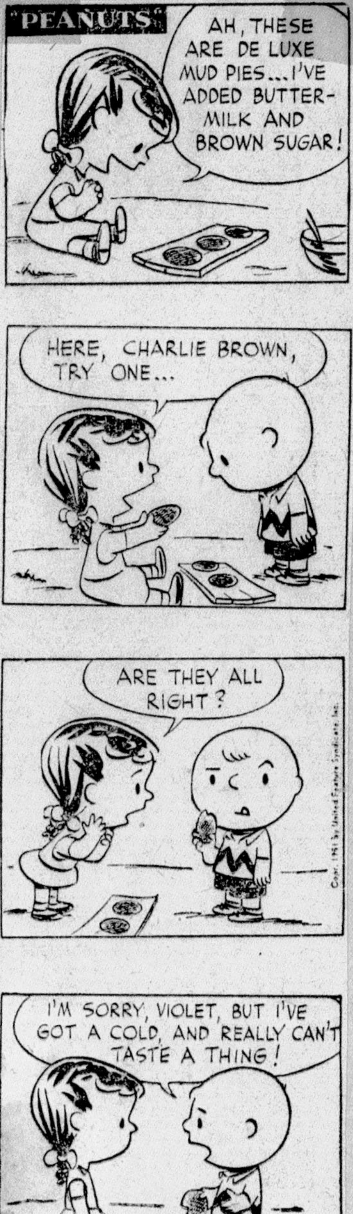
"PEANUTS"
AH, THESE ARE DE LUXE MUD PIES...I'VE ADDED BUTTER-MILK AND BROWN SUGAR!
HERE, CHARLIE BROWN, TRY ONE...
ARE THEY ALL RIGHT?
Copr. 1951 by United Feature Syndicate, Inc.
I'M SORRY, VIOLET, BUT I'VE GOT A COLD, AND REALLY CAN'T TASTE A THING!
3-31
SCHULZ

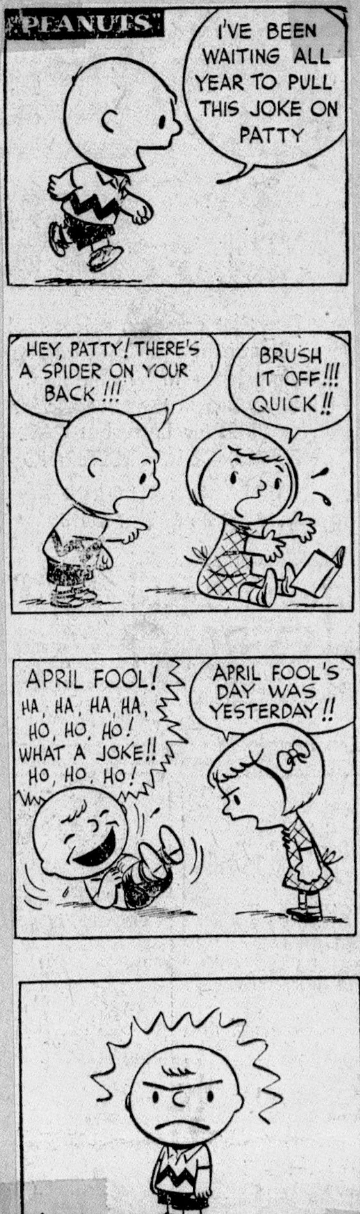
"PEANUTS"
I'VE BEEN WAITING ALL YEAR TO PULL THIS JOKE ON PATTY
HEY, PATTY! THERE'S A SPIDER ON YOUR BACK!!!
BRUSH IT OFF!!! QUICK!!
APRIL FOOL! HA, HA, HA, HA, HO, HO, HO! WHAT A JOKE!! HO, HO, HO!
APRIL FOOL'S DAY WAS YESTERDAY!!
Copr. 1951 by United Feature Syndicate, Inc.
SCHULZ

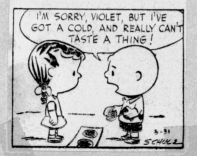

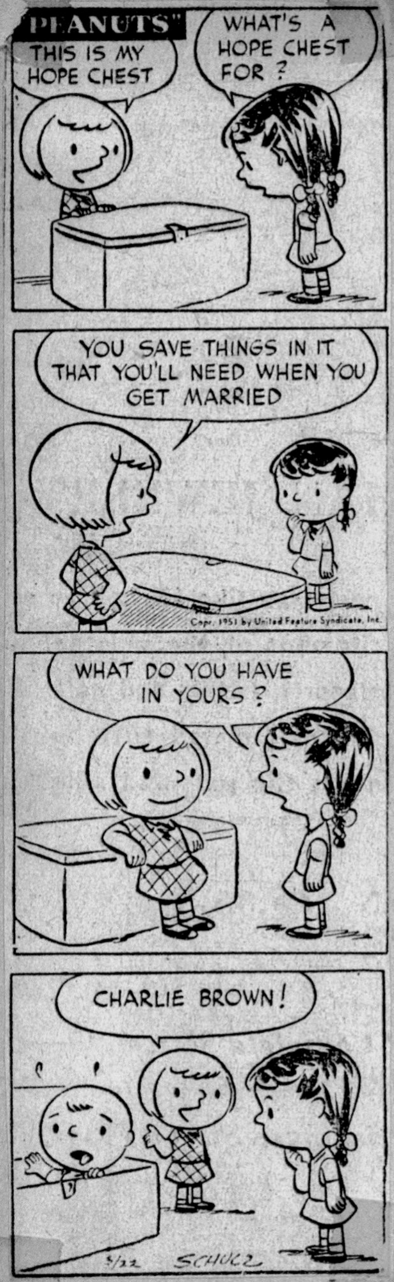
"PEANUTS"
THIS IS MY HOPE CHEST
WHAT'S A HOPE CHEST FOR ?
YOU SAVE THINGS IN IT THAT YOU'LL NEED WHEN YOU GET MARRIED
Copr. 1951 by United Feature Syndicate, Inc.
WHAT DO YOU HAVE IN YOURS ?
CHARLIE BROWN!
3/22 SCHULZ

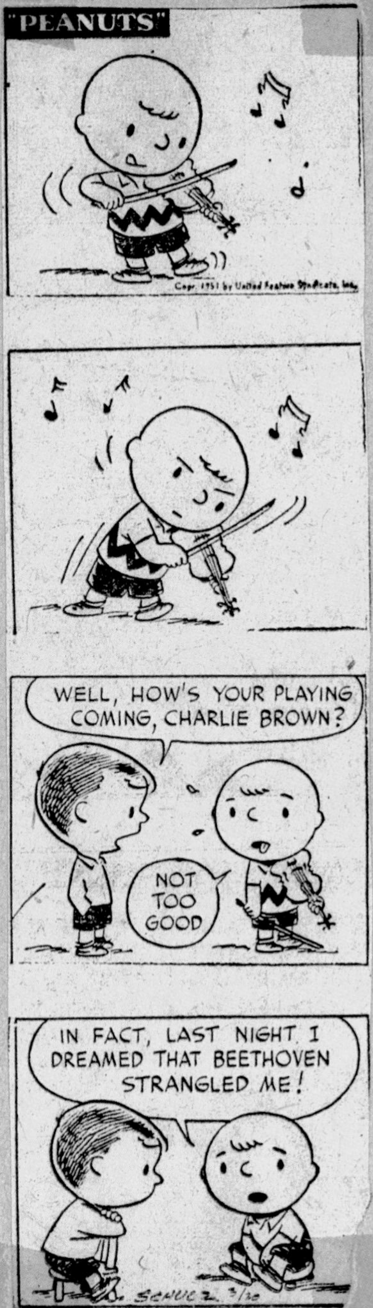
"PEANUTS"
Copr. 1951 by United Feature Syndicate, Inc.
WELL, HOW'S YOUR PLAYING COMING, CHARLIE BROWN?
NOT TOO GOOD
IN FACT, LAST NIGHT I DREAMED THAT BEETHOVEN STRANGLED ME!
SCHULZ 3/30

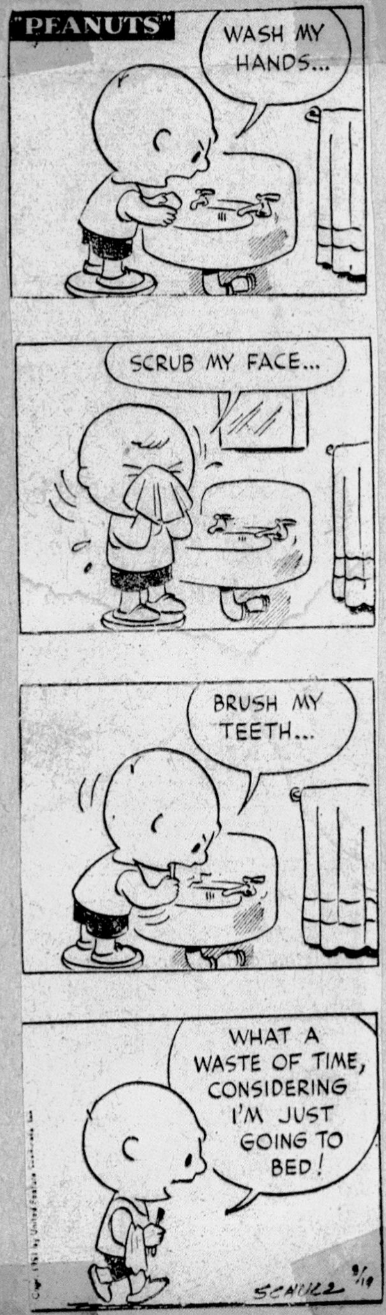
"PEANUTS"
WASH MY HANDS...
SCRUB MY FACE...
BRUSH MY TEETH...
WHAT A WASTE OF TIME, CONSIDERING I'M JUST GOING TO BED!
SCHULZ 9/19

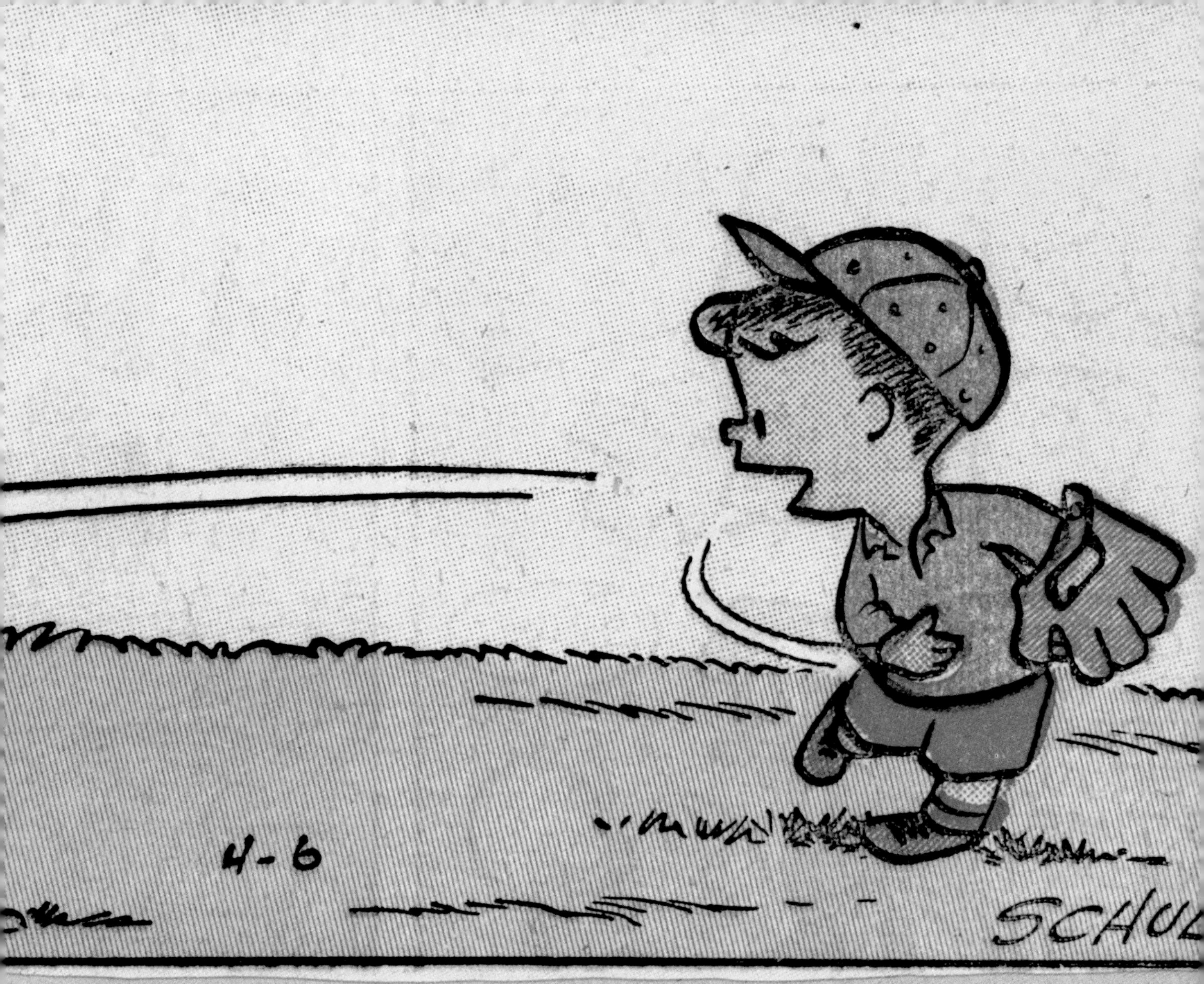
4-6
SCHUL

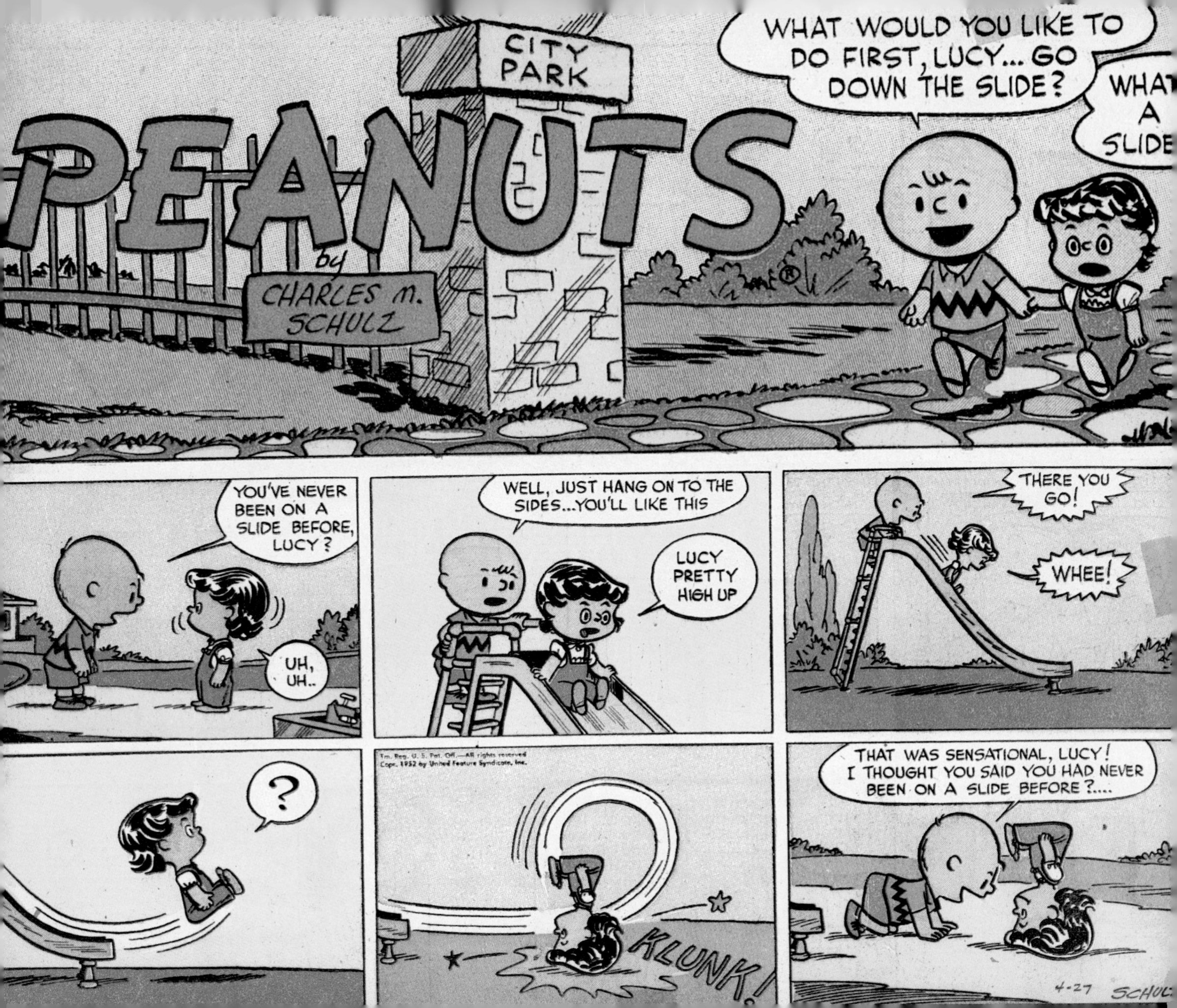
CITY PARK
PEANUTS
by CHARLES M. SCHULZ
WHAT WOULD YOU LIKE TO DO FIRST, LUCY... GO DOWN THE SLIDE?
WHAT A SLIDE
YOU'VE NEVER BEEN ON A SLIDE BEFORE, LUCY?
UH, UH..
WELL, JUST HANG ON TO THE SIDES...YOU'LL LIKE THIS
LUCY PRETTY HIGH UP
THERE YOU GO!
WHEE!
?
Tm. Reg. U. S. Pat. Off.—All rights reserved
Copr. 1952 by United Feature Syndicate, Inc.
KLUNK!
THAT WAS SENSATIONAL, LUCY! I THOUGHT YOU SAID YOU HAD NEVER BEEN ON A SLIDE BEFORE?....
4-27
SCHUL

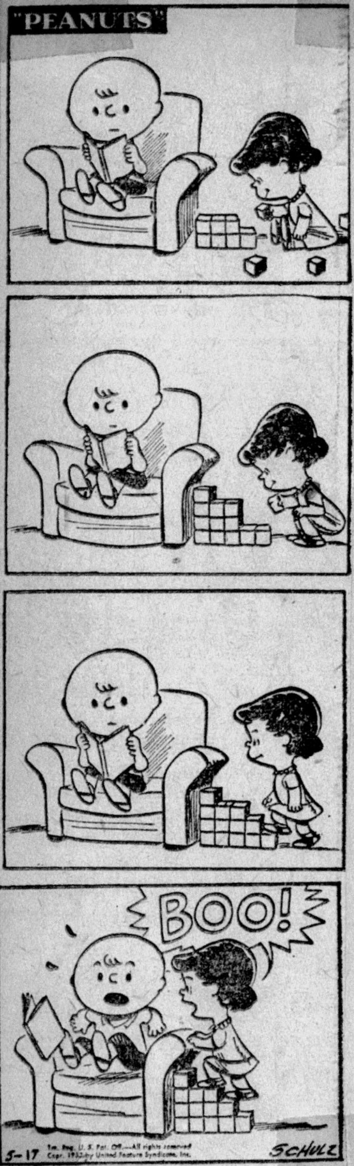
"PEANUTS"
BOO!
5-17
SCHULZ

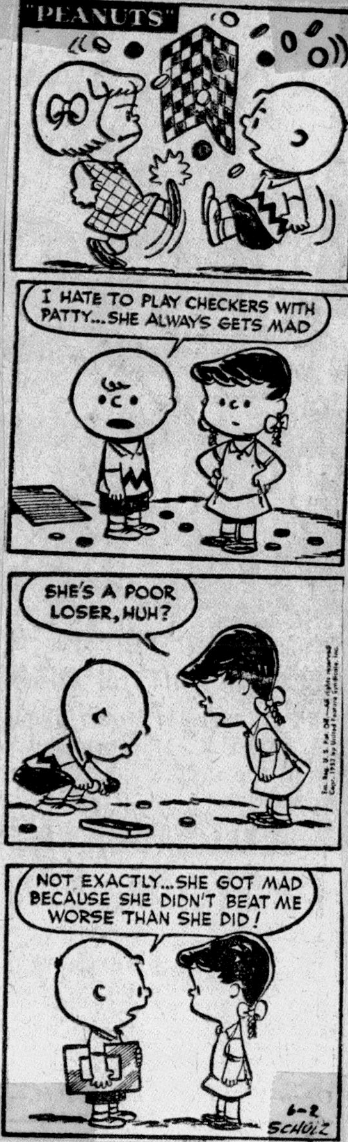
"PEANUTS"
I HATE TO PLAY CHECKERS WITH PATTY...SHE ALWAYS GETS MAD
SHE'S A POOR LOSER, HUH?
NOT EXACTLY...SHE GOT MAD BECAUSE SHE DIDN'T BEAT ME WORSE THAN SHE DID!
6-2
SCHULZ

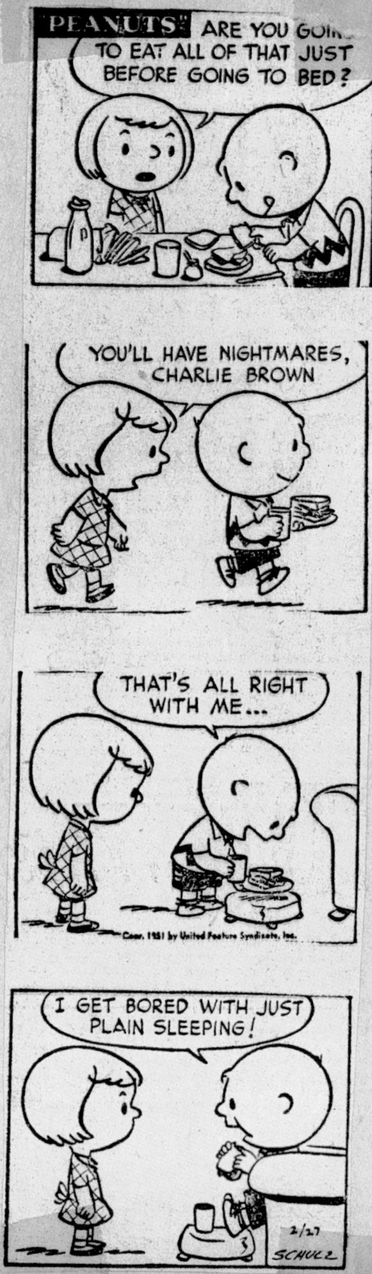
"PEANUTS"
ARE YOU GOI TO EAT ALL OF THAT JUST BEFORE GOING TO BED?
YOU'LL HAVE NIGHTMARES, CHARLIE BROWN
THAT'S ALL RIGHT WITH ME...
Copr. 1951 by United Feature Syndicate, Inc.
I GET BORED WITH JUST PLAIN SLEEPING!
2/27
SCHULZ

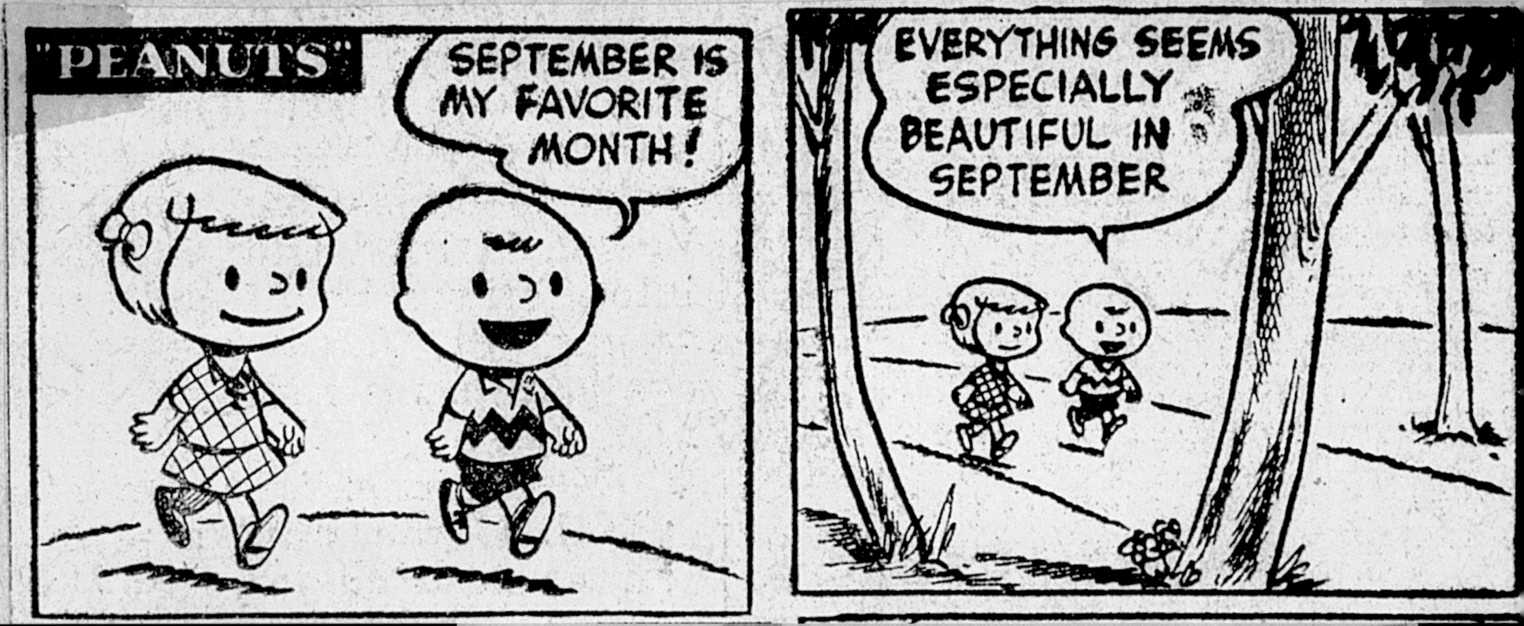
PEANUTS
SEPTEMBER IS MY FAVORITE MONTH!
EVERYTHING SEEMS ESPECIALLY BEAUTIFUL IN SEPTEMBER

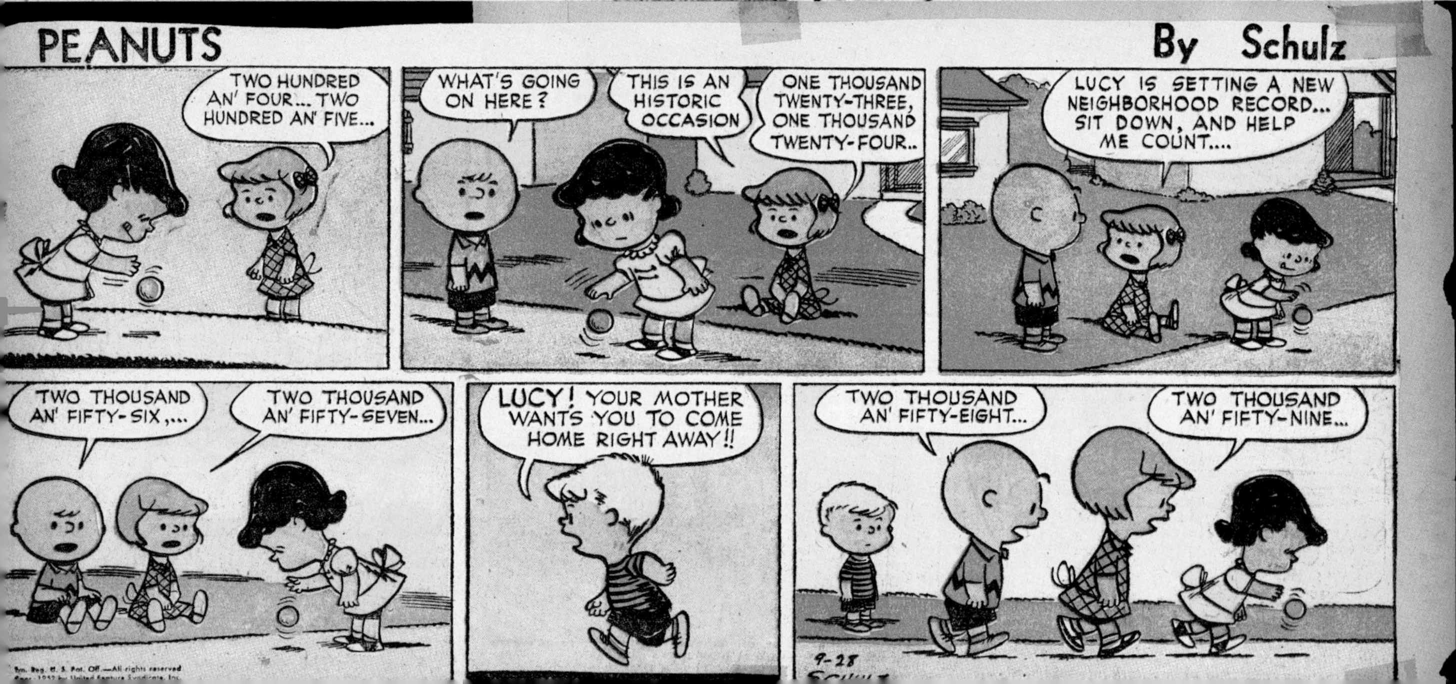
PEANUTS
By Schulz
TWO HUNDRED AN' FOUR... TWO HUNDRED AN' FIVE...
WHAT'S GOING ON HERE?
THIS IS AN HISTORIC OCCASION
ONE THOUSAND TWENTY-THREE, ONE THOUSAND TWENTY-FOUR..
LUCY IS SETTING A NEW NEIGHBORHOOD RECORD... SIT DOWN, AND HELP ME COUNT....
TWO THOUSAND AN' FIFTY-SIX,...
TWO THOUSAND AN' FIFTY-SEVEN...
LUCY! YOUR MOTHER WANTS YOU TO COME HOME RIGHT AWAY!!
TWO THOUSAND AN' FIFTY-EIGHT...
TWO THOUSAND AN' FIFTY-NINE...
9-28

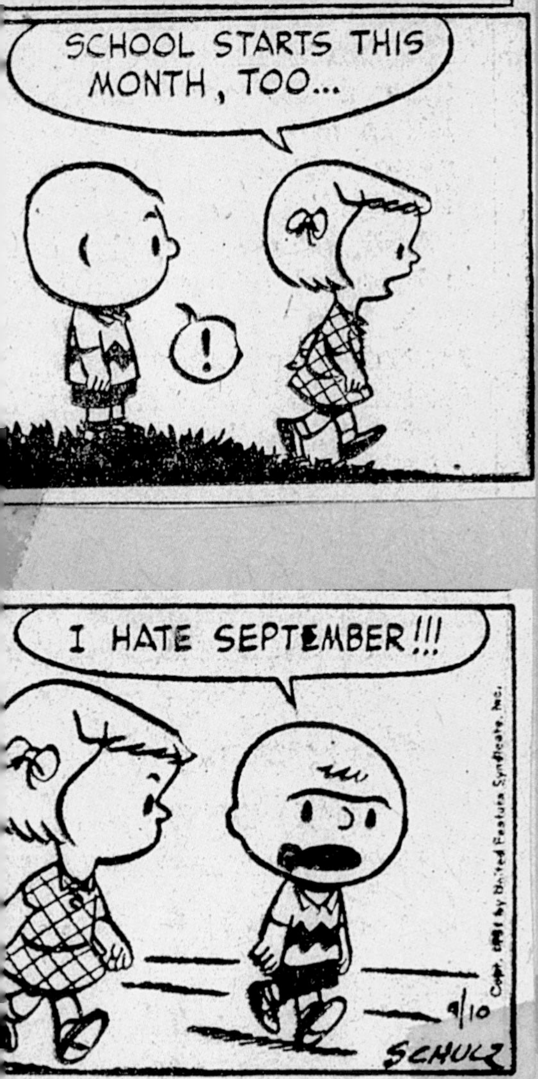
SCHOOL STARTS THIS MONTH, TOO...
I HATE SEPTEMBER!!!
Copr. 1951 by United Feature Syndicate, Inc.
9/10
SCHULZ

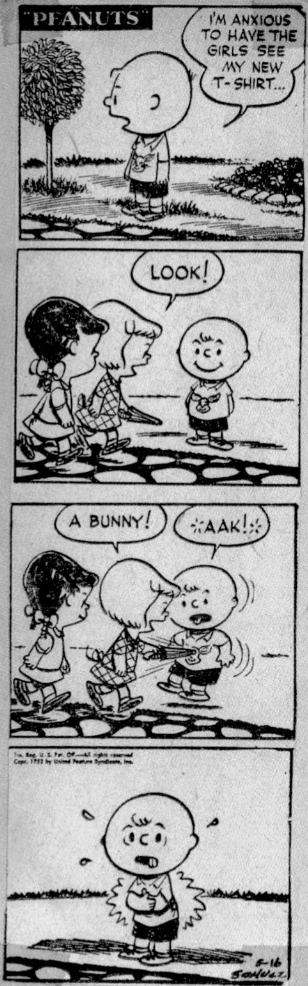
"PEANUTS"
I'M ANXIOUS TO HAVE THE GIRLS SEE MY NEW T-SHIRT...
LOOK!
A BUNNY!
AAK!
5-16
SCHULZ

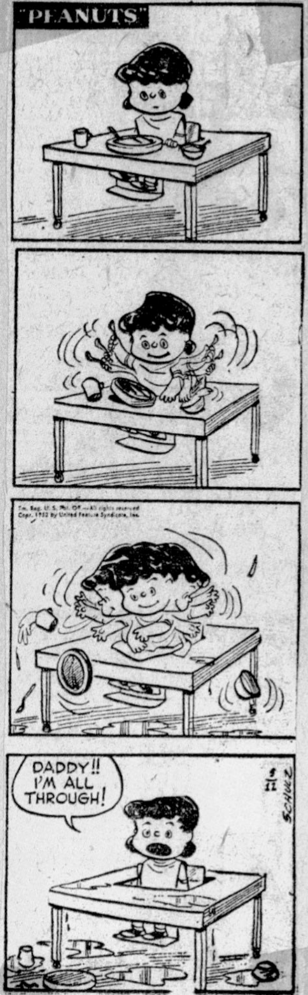
"PEANUTS"
DADDY!! I'M ALL THROUGH!
SCHULZ

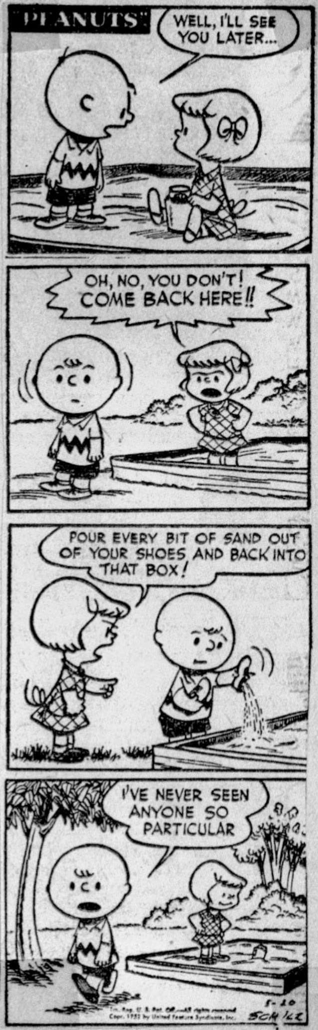
"PEANUTS"
WELL, I'LL SEE YOU LATER...
OH, NO, YOU DON'T! COME BACK HERE!!
POUR EVERY BIT OF SAND OUT OF YOUR SHOES AND BACK INTO THAT BOX!
I'VE NEVER SEEN ANYONE SO PARTICULAR
5-20
SCHULZ

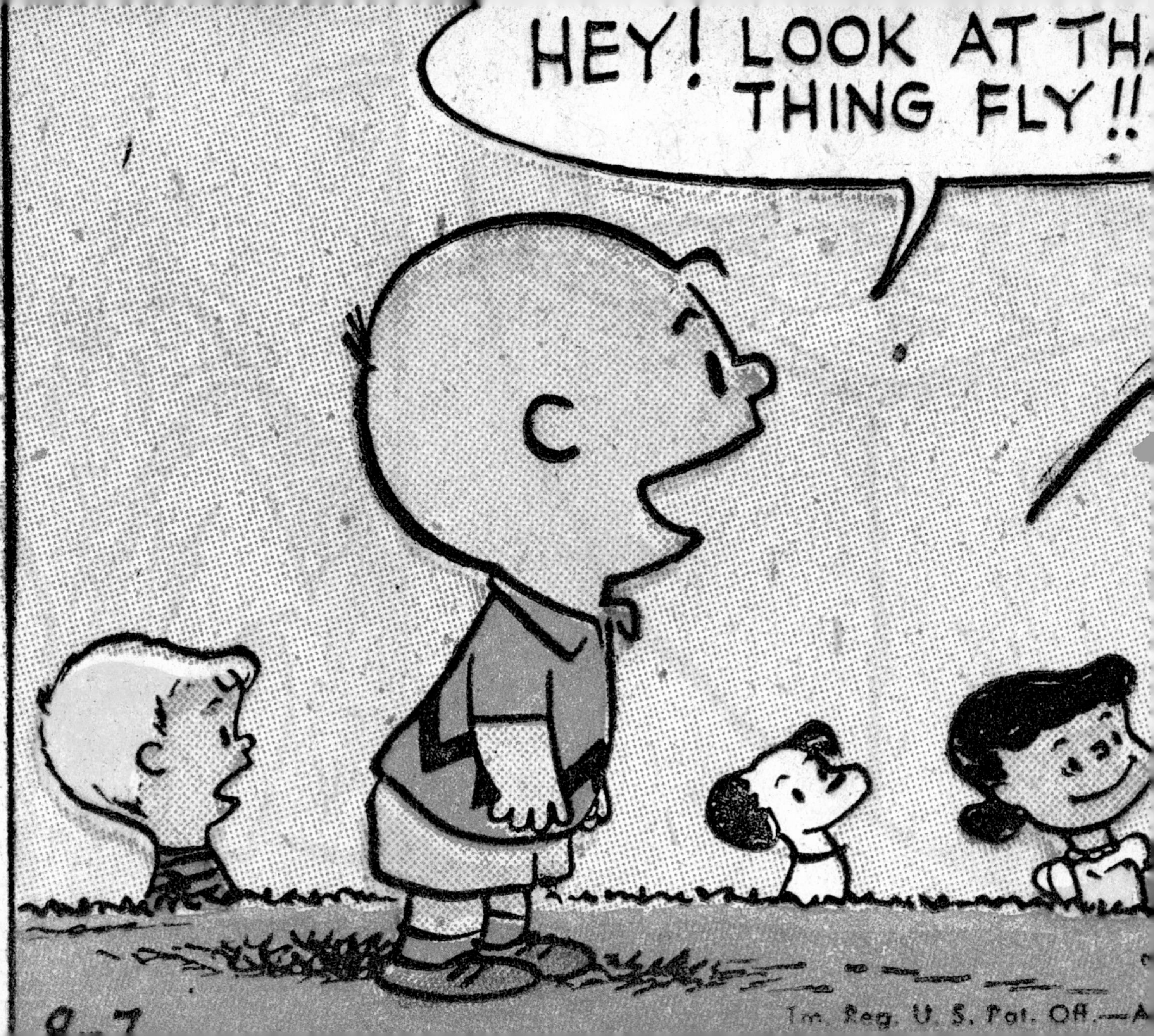
HEY! LOOK AT THA
THING FLY!!
Tm. Reg. U. S. Pat. Off.—A

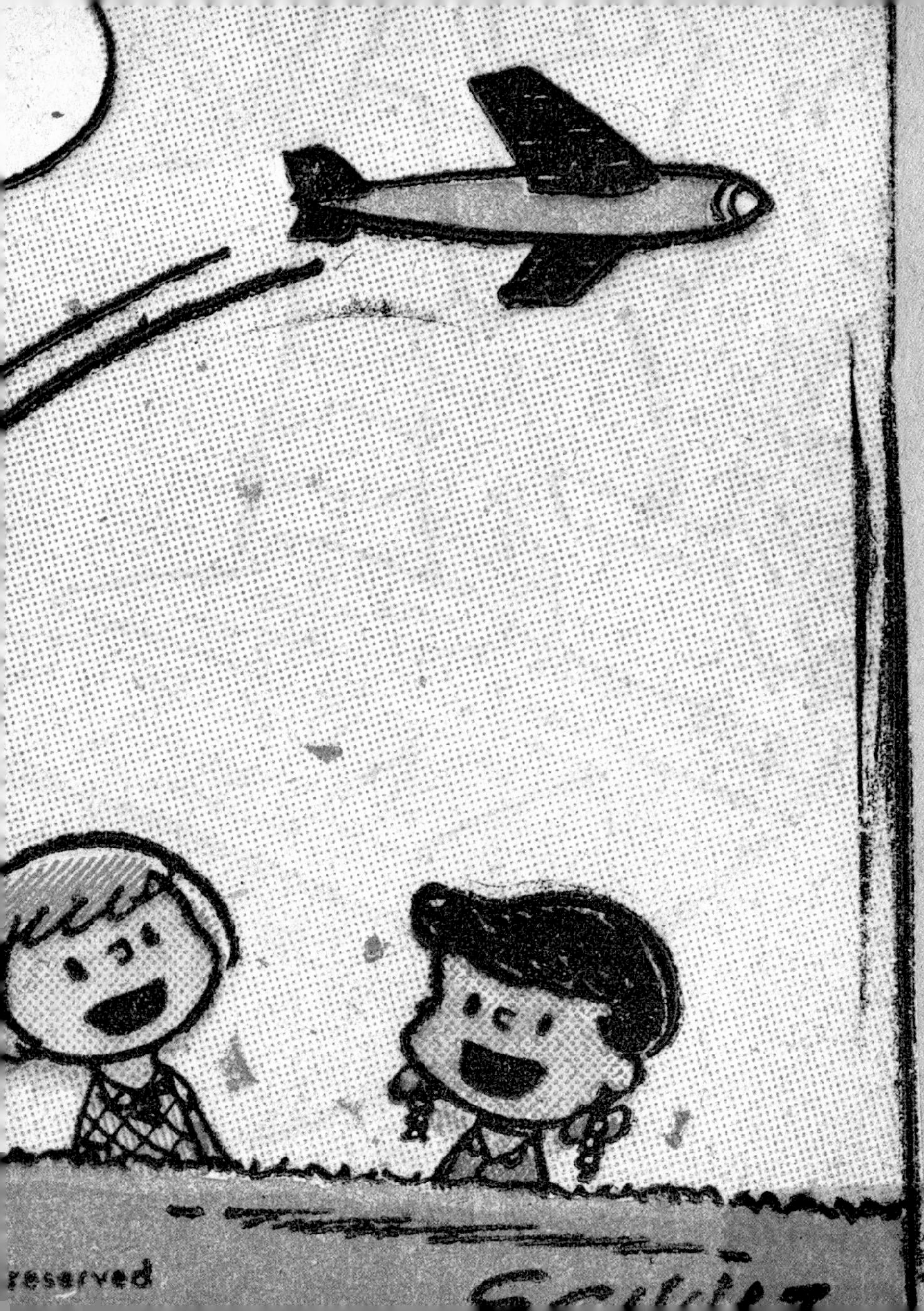

reserved

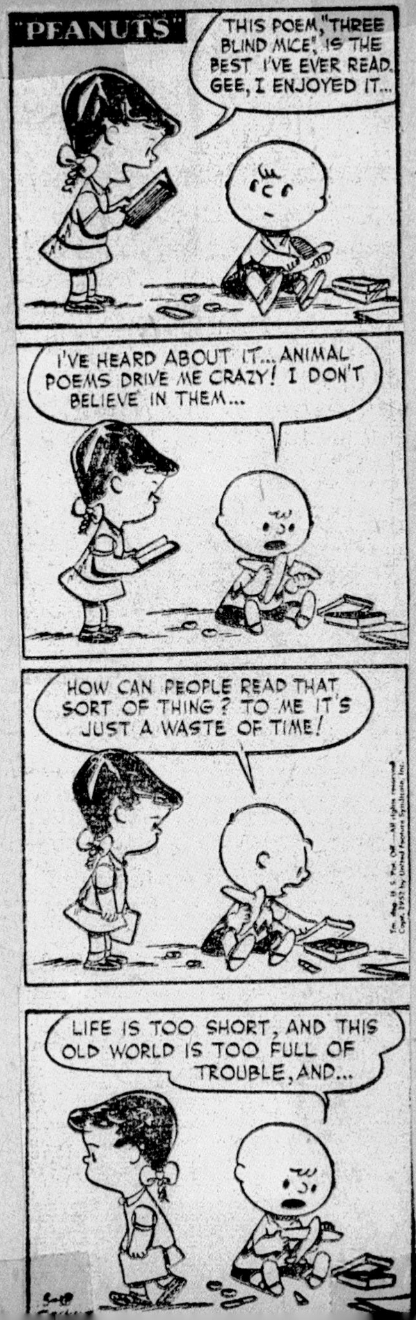

"PEANUTS"
THIS POEM, "THREE BLIND MICE," IS THE BEST I'VE EVER READ. GEE, I ENJOYED IT...
I'VE HEARD ABOUT IT... ANIMAL POEMS DRIVE ME CRAZY! I DON'T BELIEVE IN THEM...
HOW CAN PEOPLE READ THAT SORT OF THING? TO ME IT'S JUST A WASTE OF TIME!
LIFE IS TOO SHORT, AND THIS OLD WORLD IS TOO FULL OF TROUBLE, AND...

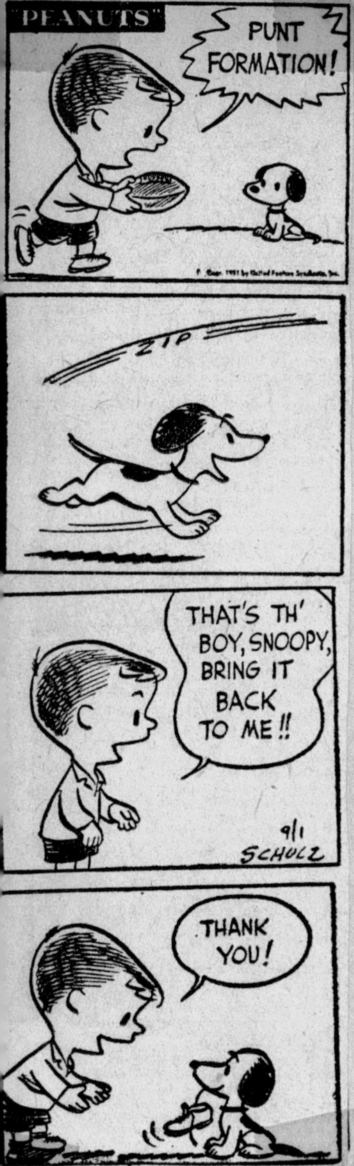
"PEANUTS"
PUNT FORMATION!
ZIP
THAT'S TH' BOY, SNOOPY, BRING IT BACK TO ME!!
9/1
SCHULZ
THANK YOU!

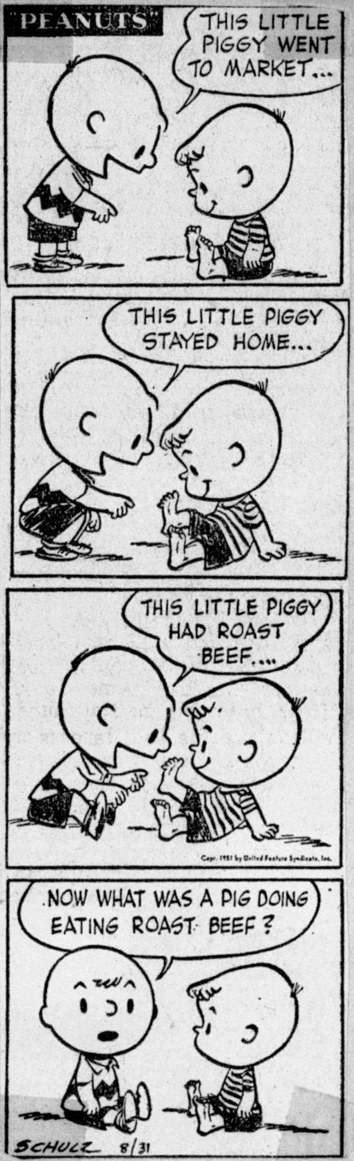
"PEANUTS"
THIS LITTLE PIGGY WENT TO MARKET...
THIS LITTLE PIGGY STAYED HOME...
THIS LITTLE PIGGY HAD ROAST BEEF....
NOW WHAT WAS A PIG DOING EATING ROAST BEEF?
SCHULZ 8/31

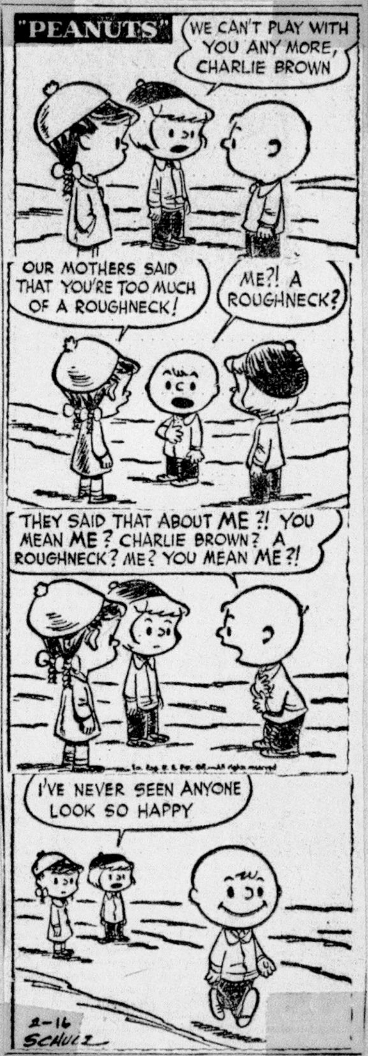
"PEANUTS"
WE CAN'T PLAY WITH YOU ANY MORE, CHARLIE BROWN
OUR MOTHERS SAID THAT YOU'RE TOO MUCH OF A ROUGHNECK!
ME?! A ROUGHNECK?
THEY SAID THAT ABOUT ME?! YOU MEAN ME? CHARLIE BROWN? A ROUGHNECK? ME? YOU MEAN ME?!
I'VE NEVER SEEN ANYONE LOOK SO HAPPY
2-16
SCHULZ

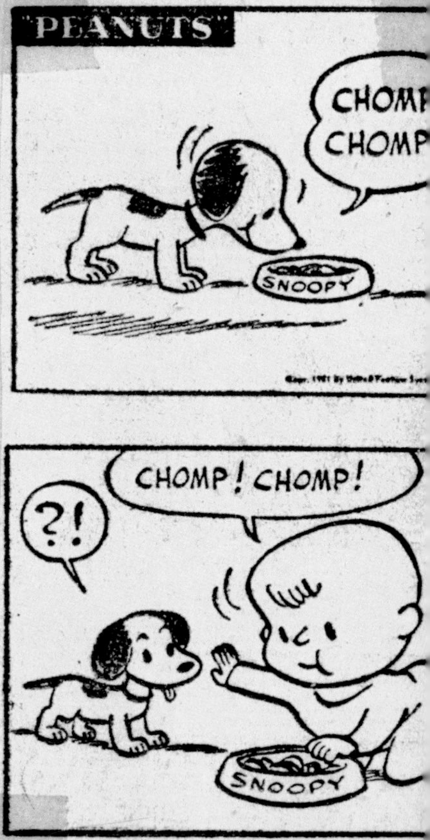
"PEANUTS"
CHOMP CHOMP
SNOOPY
CHOMP! CHOMP!
?!
SNOOPY

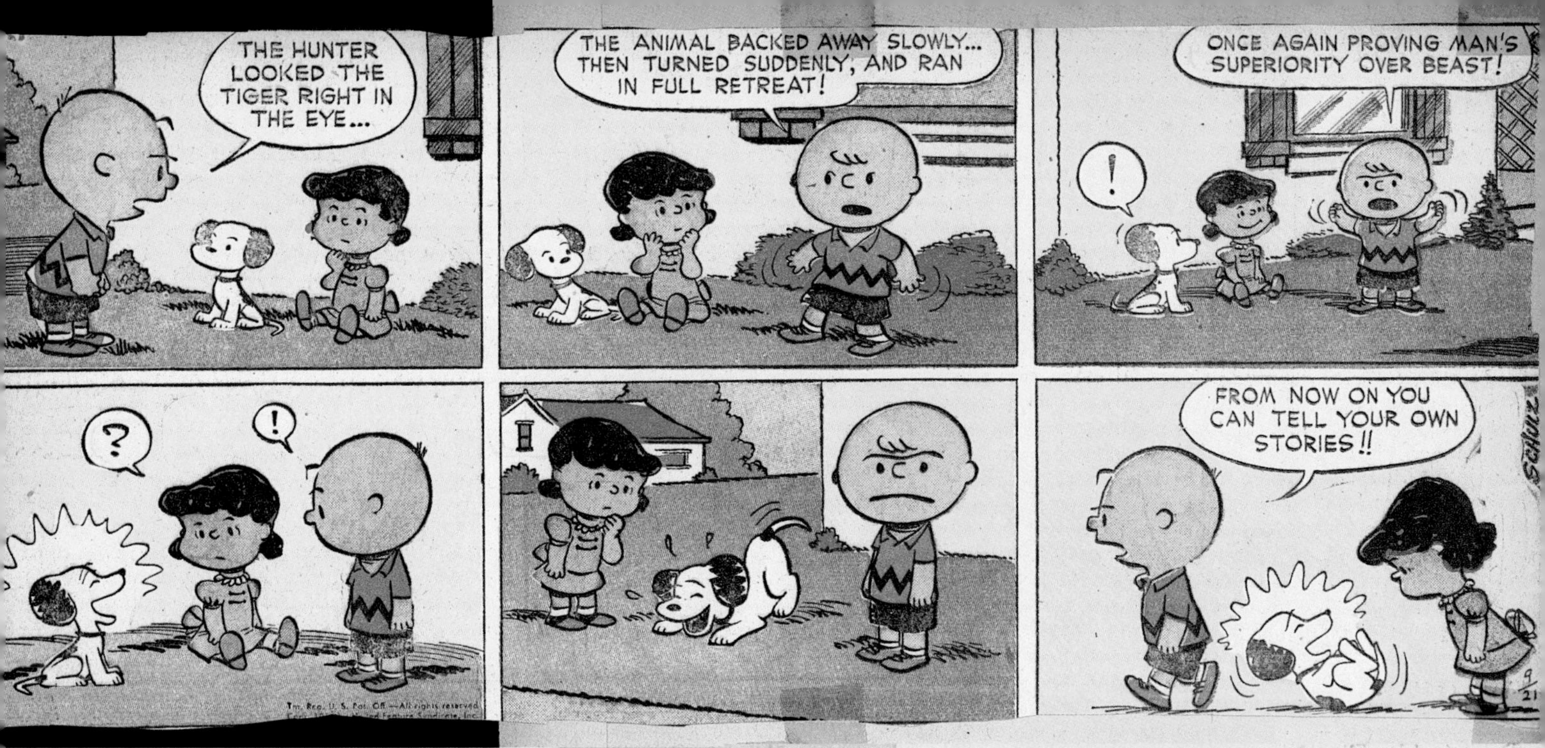
THE HUNTER LOOKED THE TIGER RIGHT IN THE EYE...
THE ANIMAL BACKED AWAY SLOWLY... THEN TURNED SUDDENLY, AND RAN IN FULL RETREAT!
ONCE AGAIN PROVING MAN'S SUPERIORITY OVER BEAST!
!
?
!
FROM NOW ON YOU CAN TELL YOUR OWN STORIES!!
SCHULZ
9/21

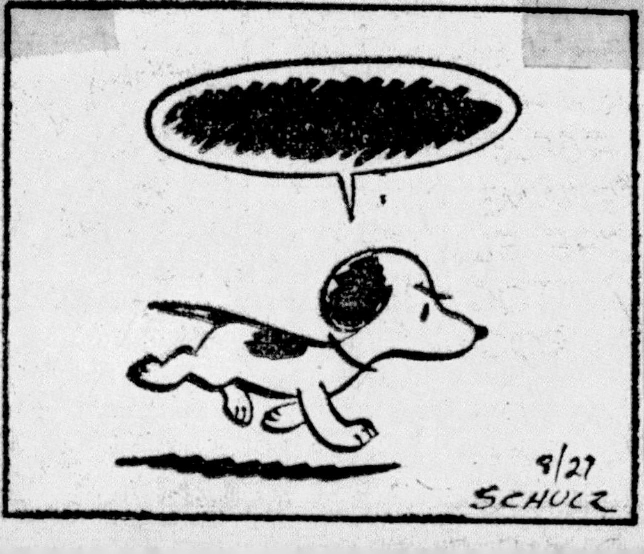
9/27
SCHULZ

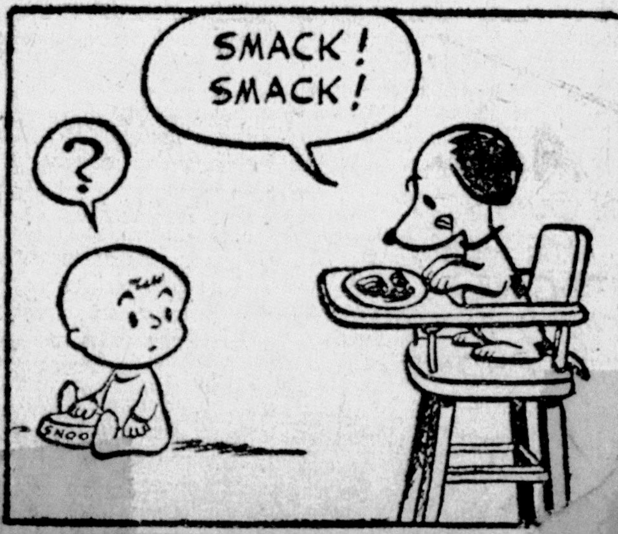
SMACK! SMACK!
?
SNOO

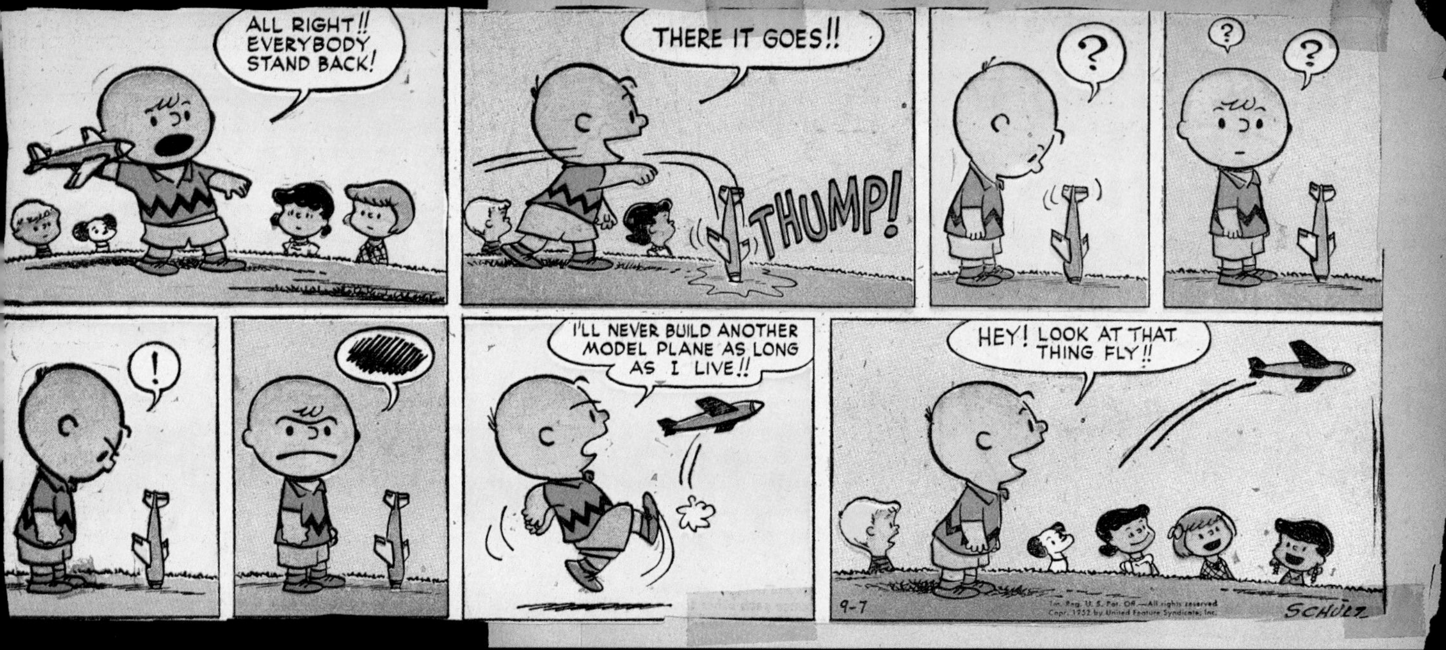
ALL RIGHT!! EVERYBODY STAND BACK!
THERE IT GOES!!
THUMP!
?
?
?
!
I'LL NEVER BUILD ANOTHER MODEL PLANE AS LONG AS I LIVE!!
HEY! LOOK AT THAT THING FLY!!
9-7
Tm. Reg. U. S. Pat. Off.—All rights reserved
Copr. 1952 by United Feature Syndicate, Inc.
SCHULZ

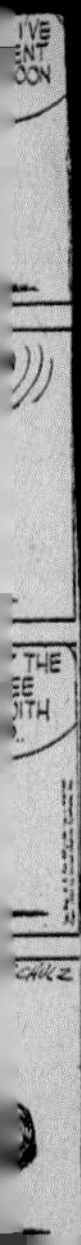

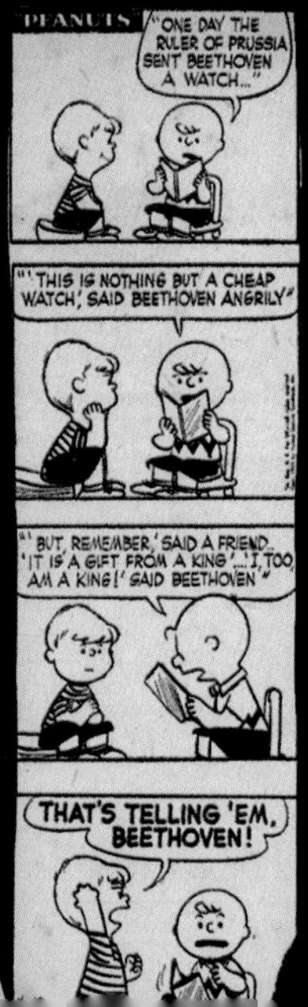
"PEANUTS"
"ONE DAY THE RULER OF PRUSSIA SENT BEETHOVEN A WATCH..."
"'THIS IS NOTHING BUT A CHEAP WATCH,' SAID BEETHOVEN ANGRILY"
"'BUT, REMEMBER,' SAID A FRIEND.. 'IT IS A GIFT FROM A KING'...'I, TOO, AM A KING!' SAID BEETHOVEN"
THAT'S TELLING 'EM, BEETHOVEN!

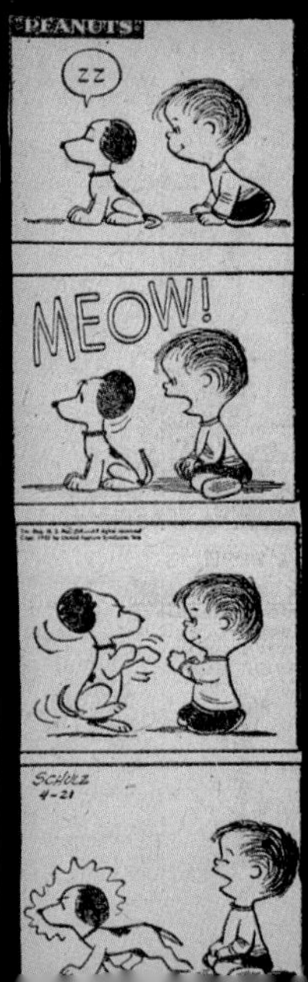
"PEANUTS"
ZZ
MEOW!
4-21

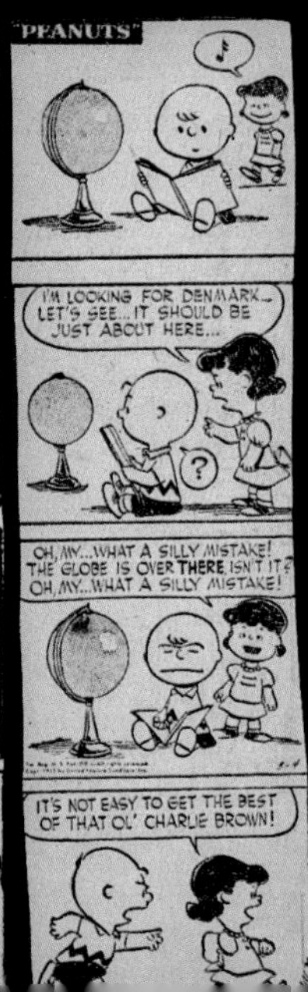
"PEANUTS"
I'M LOOKING FOR DENMARK.. LET'S SEE...IT SHOULD BE JUST ABOUT HERE...
?
OH, MY...WHAT A SILLY MISTAKE! THE GLOBE IS OVER THERE, ISN'T IT? OH, MY...WHAT A SILLY MISTAKE!
IT'S NOT EASY TO GET THE BEST OF THAT OL' CHARLIE BROWN!

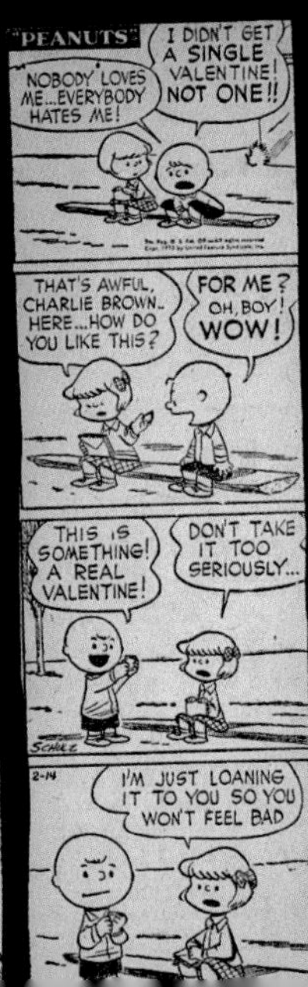
"PEANUTS"
NOBODY LOVES ME...EVERYBODY HATES ME!
I DIDN'T GET A SINGLE VALENTINE! NOT ONE!!
THAT'S AWFUL, CHARLIE BROWN.. HERE...HOW DO YOU LIKE THIS?
FOR ME? OH, BOY! WOW!
THIS IS SOMETHING! A REAL VALENTINE!
DON'T TAKE IT TOO SERIOUSLY...
2-14
I'M JUST LOANING IT TO YOU SO YOU WON'T FEEL BAD

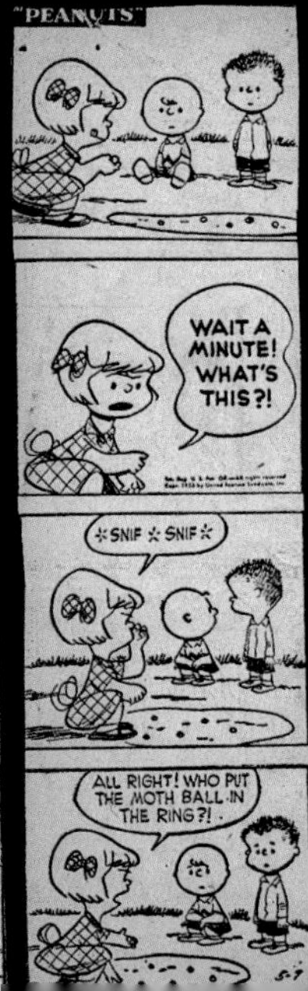
"PEANUTS"
WAIT A MINUTE! WHAT'S THIS?!
SNIF SNIF
ALL RIGHT! WHO PUT THE MOTH BALL IN THE RING?!
5-7

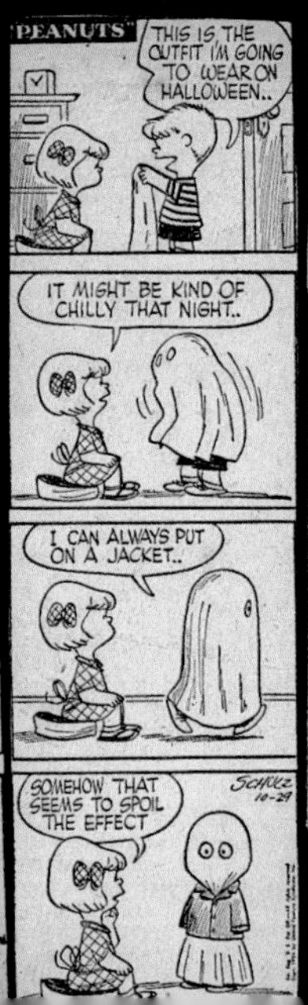
"PEANUTS"
THIS IS THE OUTFIT I'M GOING TO WEAR ON HALLOWEEN..
IT MIGHT BE KIND OF CHILLY THAT NIGHT..
I CAN ALWAYS PUT ON A JACKET..
SOMEHOW THAT SEEMS TO SPOIL THE EFFECT
SCHULZ 10-29

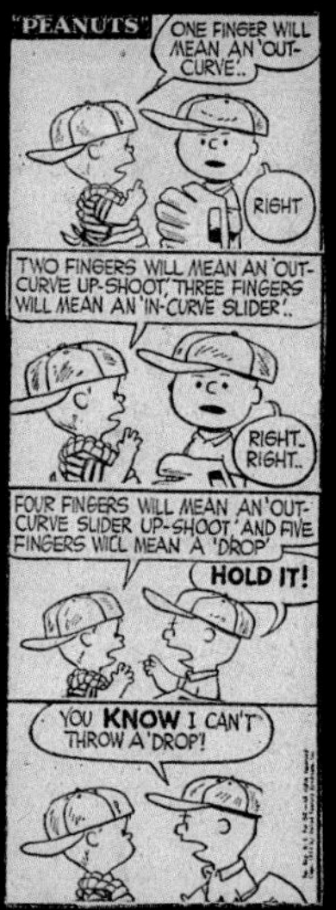
"PEANUTS"
ONE FINGER WILL MEAN AN 'OUT-CURVE'..
RIGHT
TWO FINGERS WILL MEAN AN 'OUT-CURVE UP-SHOOT,' THREE FINGERS WILL MEAN AN 'IN-CURVE SLIDER'..
RIGHT. RIGHT..
FOUR FINGERS WILL MEAN AN 'OUT-CURVE SLIDER UP-SHOOT,' AND FIVE FINGERS WILL MEAN A 'DROP'
HOLD IT!
YOU KNOW I CAN'T THROW A 'DROP'!

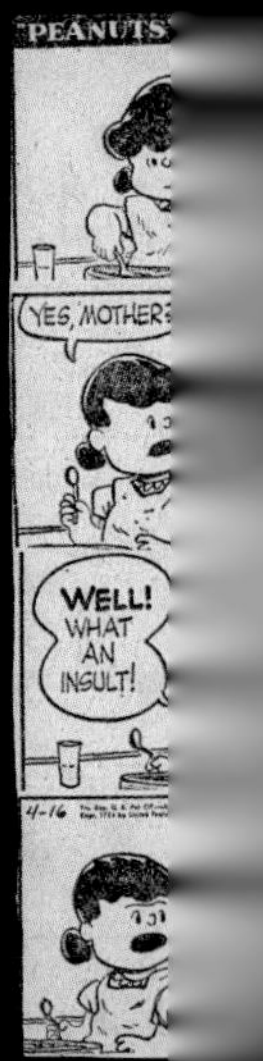
"PEANUTS"
YES, MOTHER
WELL! WHAT AN INSULT!
4-16

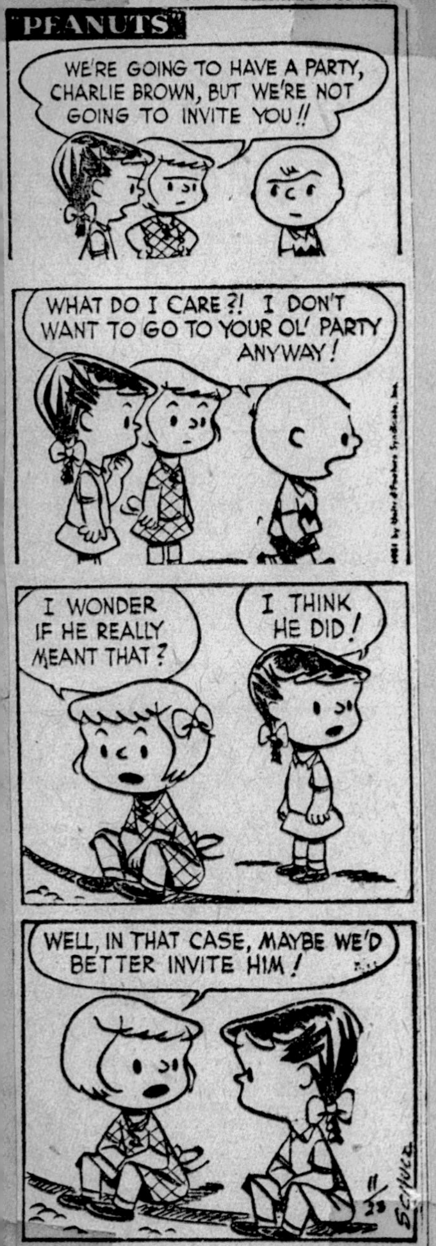
"PEANUTS"
WE'RE GOING TO HAVE A PARTY, CHARLIE BROWN, BUT WE'RE NOT GOING TO INVITE YOU!!
WHAT DO I CARE?! I DON'T WANT TO GO TO YOUR OL' PARTY ANYWAY!
I WONDER IF HE REALLY MEANT THAT?
I THINK HE DID!
WELL, IN THAT CASE, MAYBE WE'D BETTER INVITE HIM!
11/23
SCHULZ

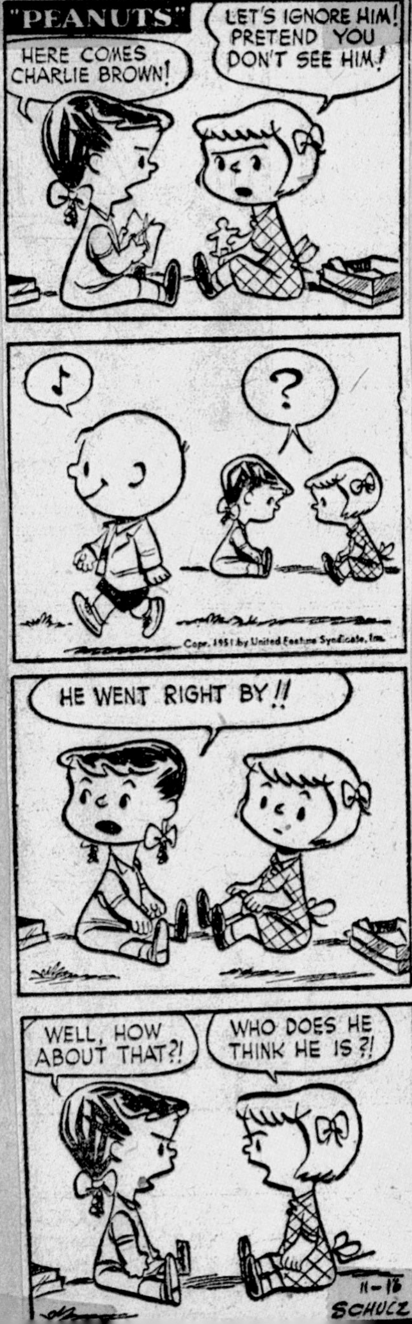
"PEANUTS"
HERE COMES CHARLIE BROWN!
LET'S IGNORE HIM! PRETEND YOU DON'T SEE HIM!
♪
?
Copr. 1951 by United Feature Syndicate, Inc.
HE WENT RIGHT BY!!
WELL, HOW ABOUT THAT?!
WHO DOES HE THINK HE IS?!
11-16
SCHULZ

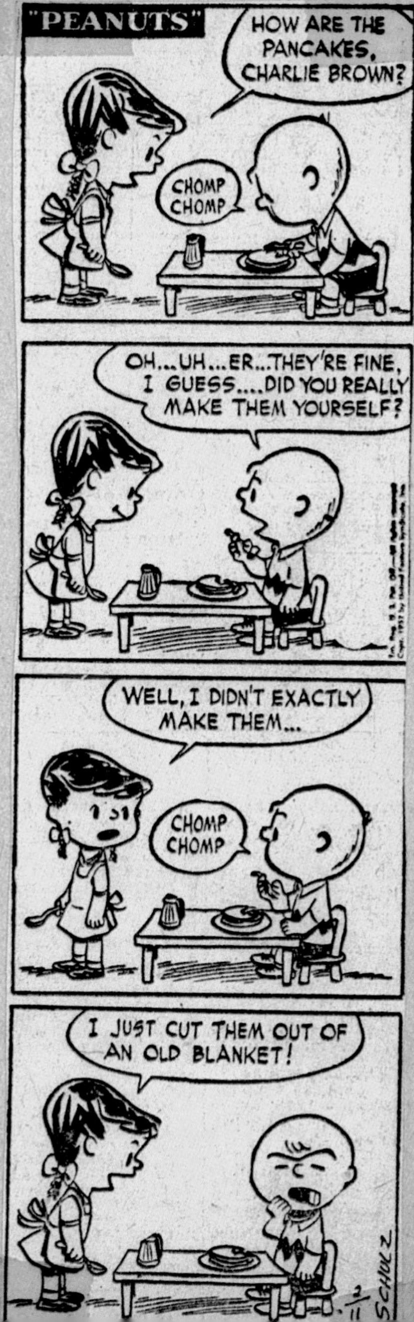
"PEANUTS"
HOW ARE THE PANCAKES, CHARLIE BROWN?
CHOMP CHOMP
OH...UH...ER...THEY'RE FINE, I GUESS....DID YOU REALLY MAKE THEM YOURSELF?
WELL, I DIDN'T EXACTLY MAKE THEM...
CHOMP CHOMP
I JUST CUT THEM OUT OF AN OLD BLANKET!
2/11
SCHULZ

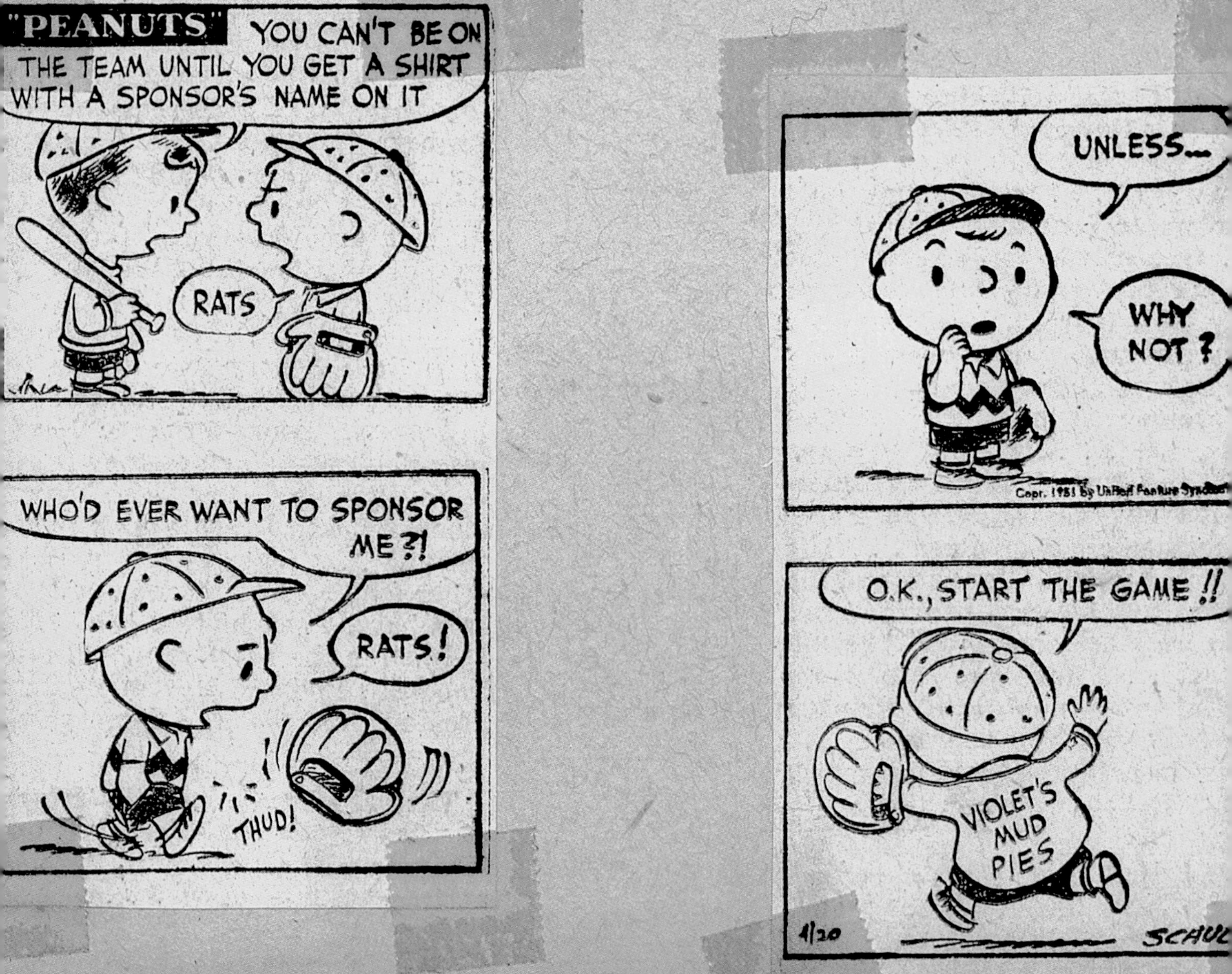
"PEANUTS"
YOU CAN'T BE ON THE TEAM UNTIL YOU GET A SHIRT WITH A SPONSOR'S NAME ON IT
RATS
WHO'D EVER WANT TO SPONSOR ME?!
RATS!
THUD!
UNLESS...
WHY NOT?
Copr. 1951 by United Feature Syndicate
O.K., START THE GAME!!
VIOLET'S MUD PIES
4/20
SCHUL

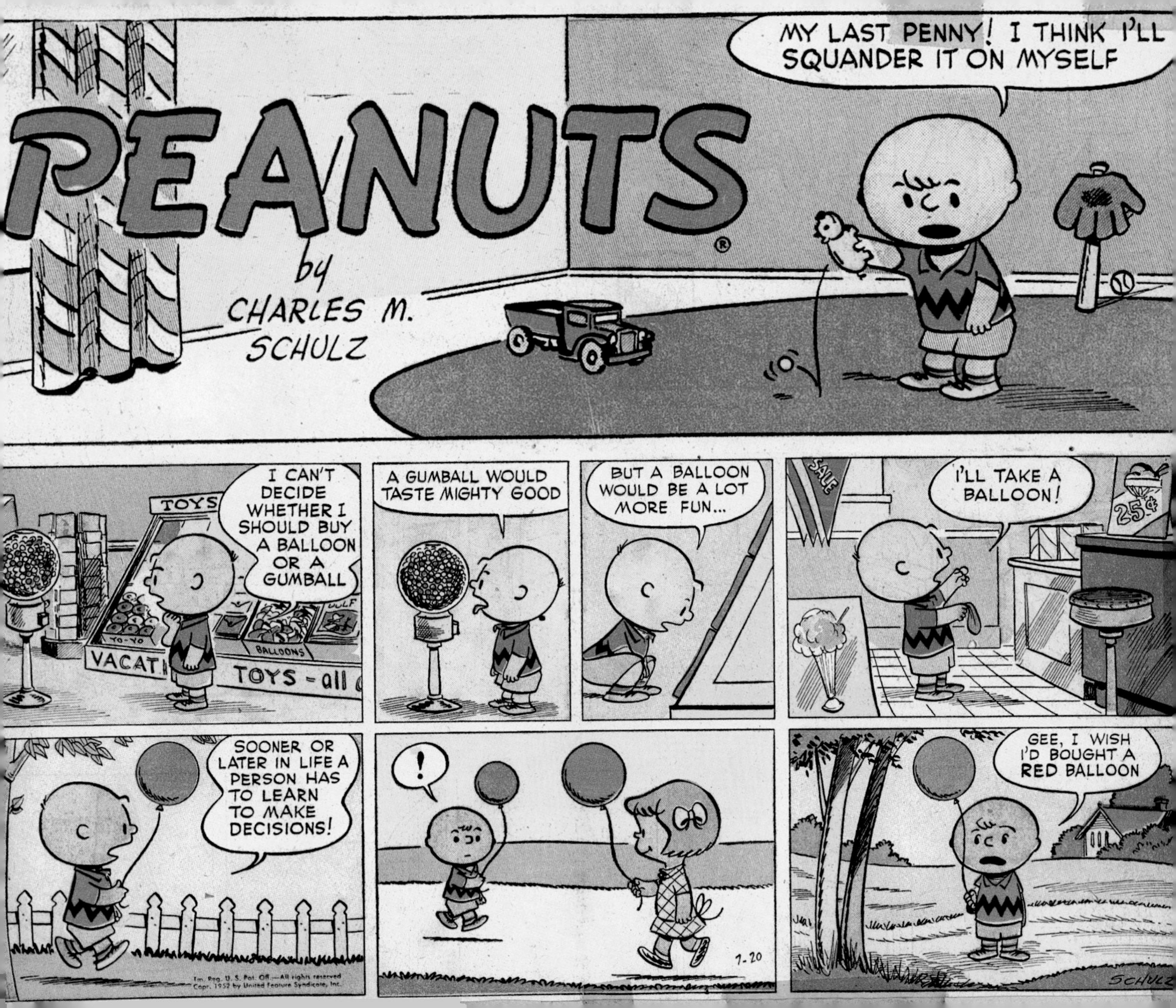

PEANUTS
by CHARLES M. SCHULZ
MY LAST PENNY! I THINK I'LL SQUANDER IT ON MYSELF
TOYS
YO-YO
BALLOONS
VACAT
TOYS - all
I CAN'T DECIDE WHETHER I SHOULD BUY A BALLOON OR A GUMBALL
A GUMBALL WOULD TASTE MIGHTY GOOD
BUT A BALLOON WOULD BE A LOT MORE FUN...
SALE
25¢
I'LL TAKE A BALLOON!
SOONER OR LATER IN LIFE A PERSON HAS TO LEARN TO MAKE DECISIONS!
Tm. Reg. U. S. Pat. Off.—All rights reserved
Copr. 1952 by United Feature Syndicate, Inc.
!
7-20
GEE, I WISH I'D BOUGHT A RED BALLOON
SCHULZ

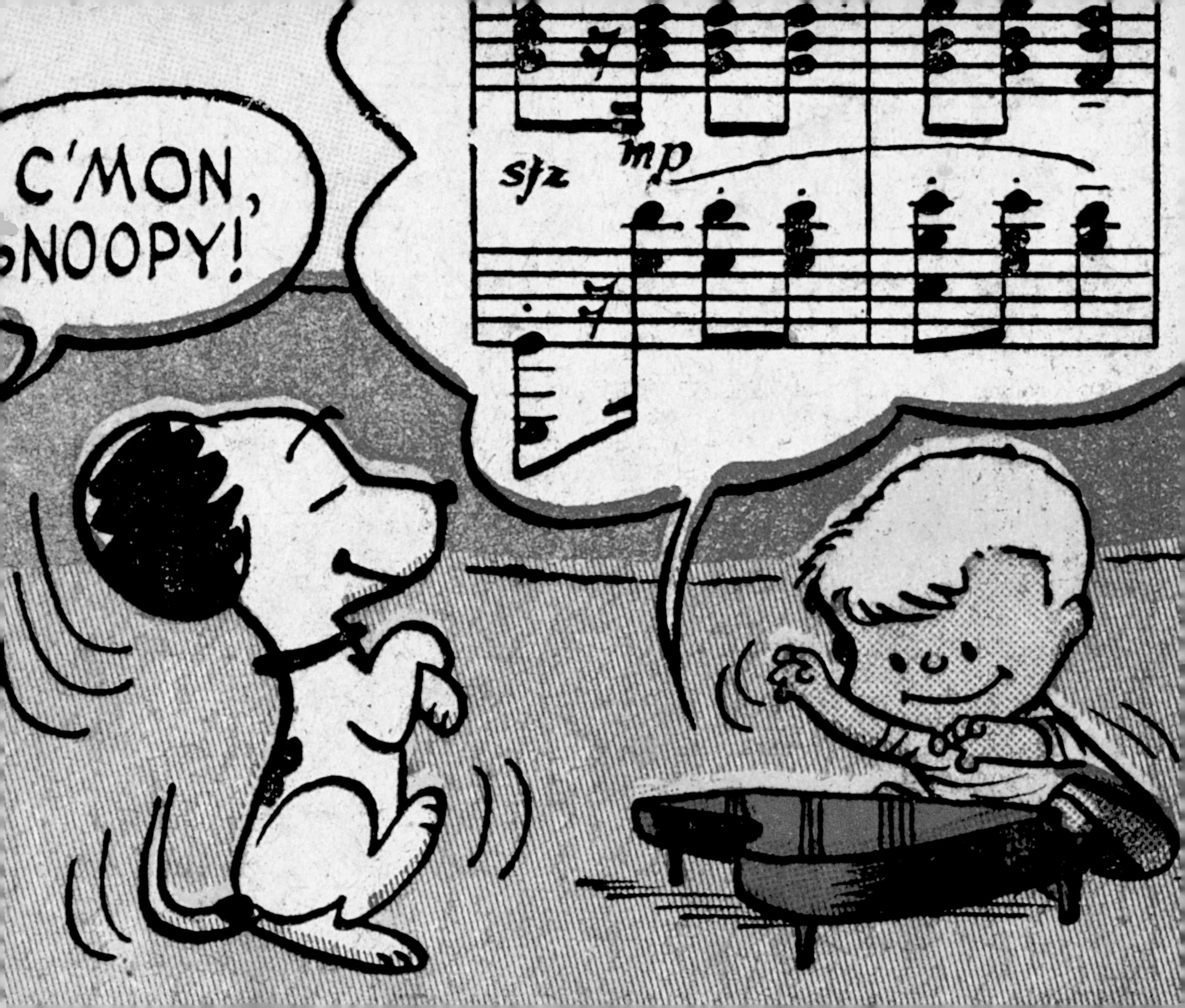
C'MON, SNOOPY!
sfz
mp

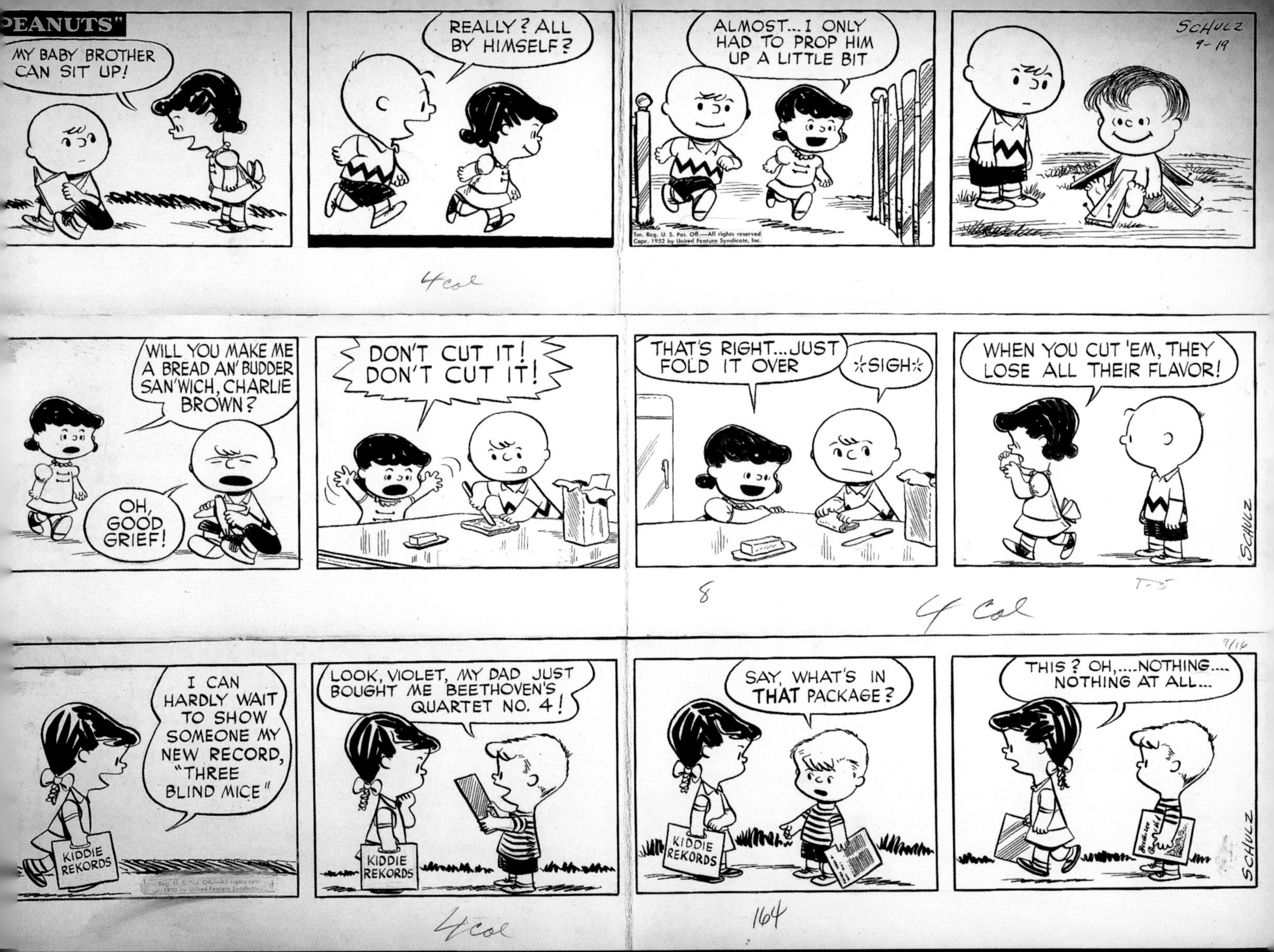
PEANUTS
MY BABY BROTHER CAN SIT UP!
REALLY? ALL BY HIMSELF?
ALMOST... I ONLY HAD TO PROP HIM UP A LITTLE BIT
Tm. Reg. U. S. Pat. Off.—All rights reserved Copr. 1952 by United Feature Syndicate, Inc.
SCHULZ 9-19
4 col
WILL YOU MAKE ME A BREAD AN' BUDDER SAN'WICH, CHARLIE BROWN?
OH, GOOD GRIEF!
DON'T CUT IT! DON'T CUT IT!
THAT'S RIGHT... JUST FOLD IT OVER
SIGH
WHEN YOU CUT 'EM, THEY LOSE ALL THEIR FLAVOR!
SCHULZ
4 Col
I CAN HARDLY WAIT TO SHOW SOMEONE MY NEW RECORD, "THREE BLIND MICE"
KIDDIE REKORDS
LOOK, VIOLET, MY DAD JUST BOUGHT ME BEETHOVEN'S QUARTET NO. 4!
KIDDIE REKORDS
SAY, WHAT'S IN THAT PACKAGE?
KIDDIE REKORDS
THIS? OH,....NOTHING.... NOTHING AT ALL...
SCHULZ
4 col
164

Linus, Lucy's baby brother, was introduced in September 1952, top. Charlie Brown still played a paternal role regarding Lucy, middle, and through Schroeder the idea of cultural snobbism was introduced, bottom.

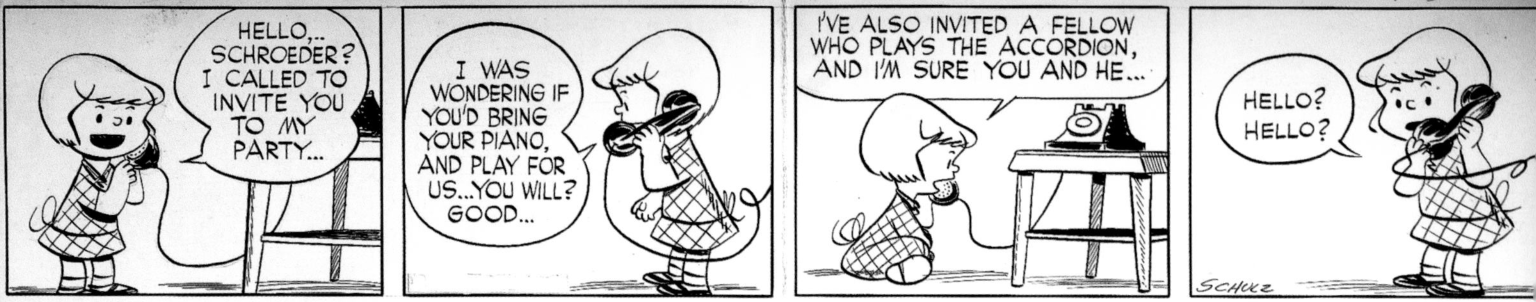
HELLO,.. SCHROEDER? I CALLED TO INVITE YOU TO MY PARTY...
I WAS WONDERING IF YOU'D BRING YOUR PIANO, AND PLAY FOR US...YOU WILL? GOOD...
I'VE ALSO INVITED A FELLOW WHO PLAYS THE ACCORDION, AND I'M SURE YOU AND HE...
HELLO? HELLO?
SCHULZ

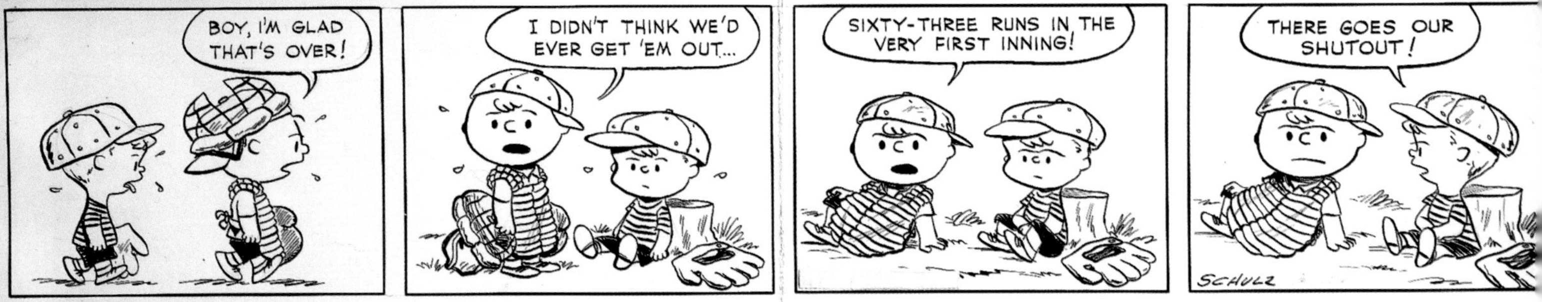
BOY, I'M GLAD THAT'S OVER!
I DIDN'T THINK WE'D EVER GET 'EM OUT...
SIXTY-THREE RUNS IN THE VERY FIRST INNING!
THERE GOES OUR SHUTOUT!
SCHULZ

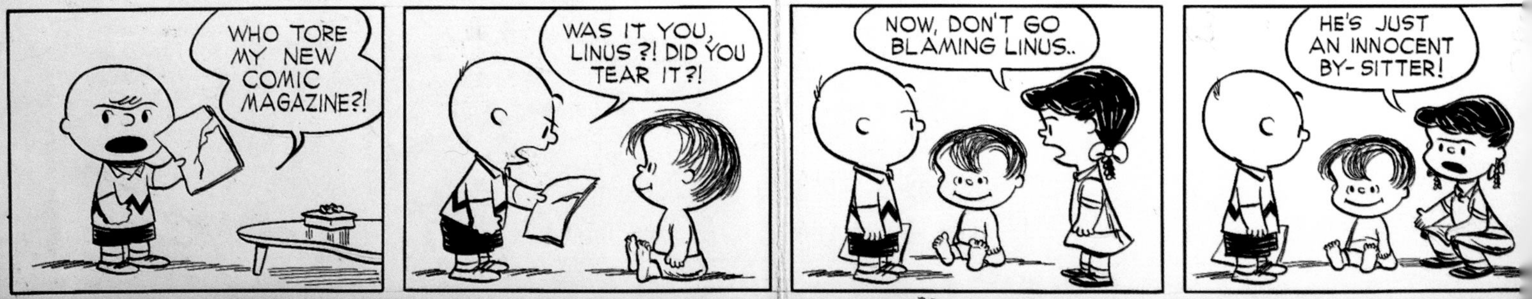
WHO TORE MY NEW COMIC MAGAZINE?!
WAS IT YOU, LINUS?! DID YOU TEAR IT?!
NOW, DON'T GO BLAMING LINUS..
HE'S JUST AN INNOCENT BY-SITTER!

Opposite, bottom: The concept of Charlotte Braun in 1954—a sort of female counterpart to Charlie Brown—came and went very quickly, and has become just another snippet of *Peanuts* trivia. The rigors of producing 365 cartoons a year meant that some of the ideas were bound to be better than others, but also forced Schulz to generate new material constantly, decide what worked, and proceed accordingly. In this case that meant discarding Charlotte, but keeping her voice—and eventually giving it to Lucy.

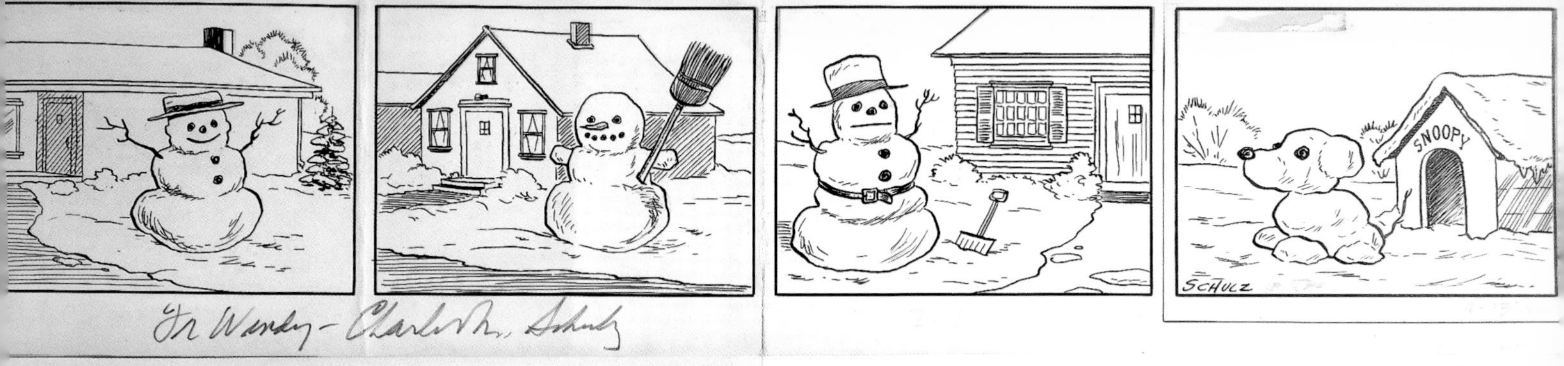
SNOOPY
SCHULZ
To Wendy – Charles M. Schulz

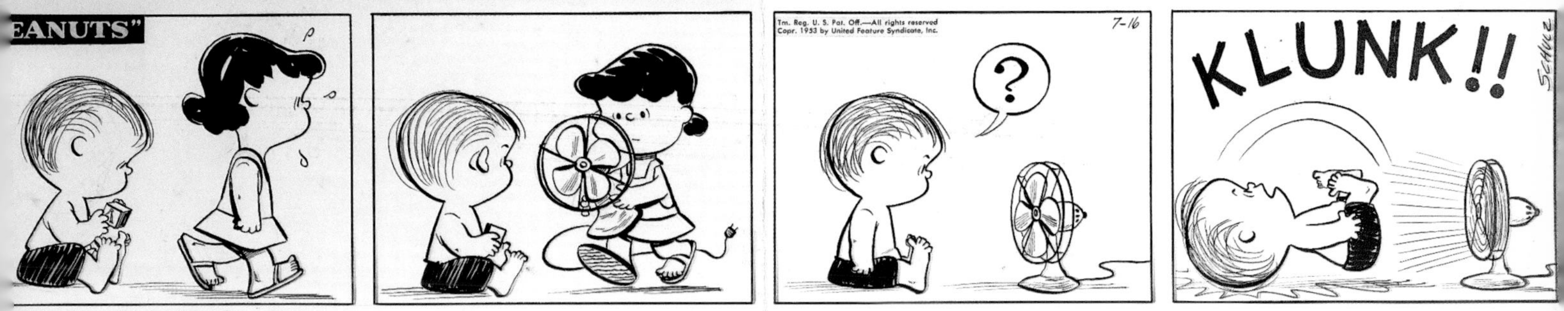
EANUTS"
Tm. Reg. U. S. Pat. Off.—All rights reserved Copr. 1953 by United Feature Syndicate, Inc.
7-16
?
KLUNK!!
SCHULZ

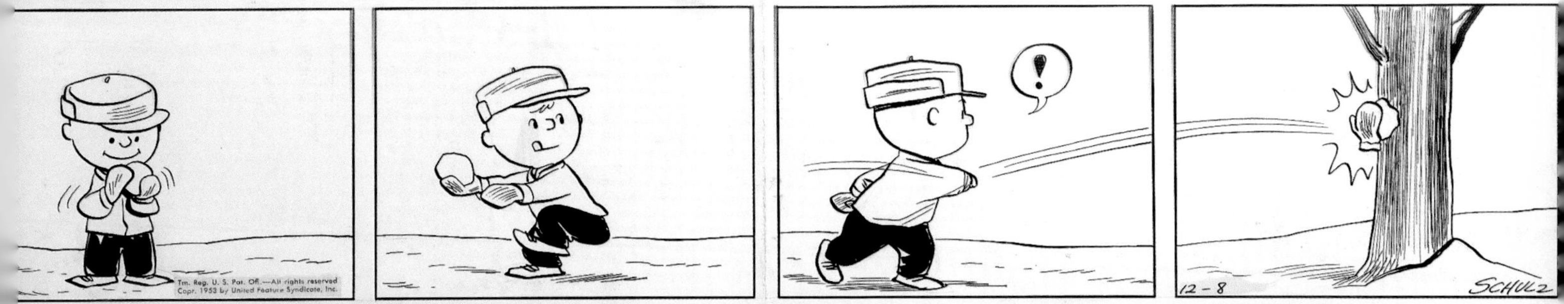
Tm. Reg. U. S. Pat. Off.—All rights reserved Copr. 1953 by United Feature Syndicate, Inc.
!
12-8
SCHULZ

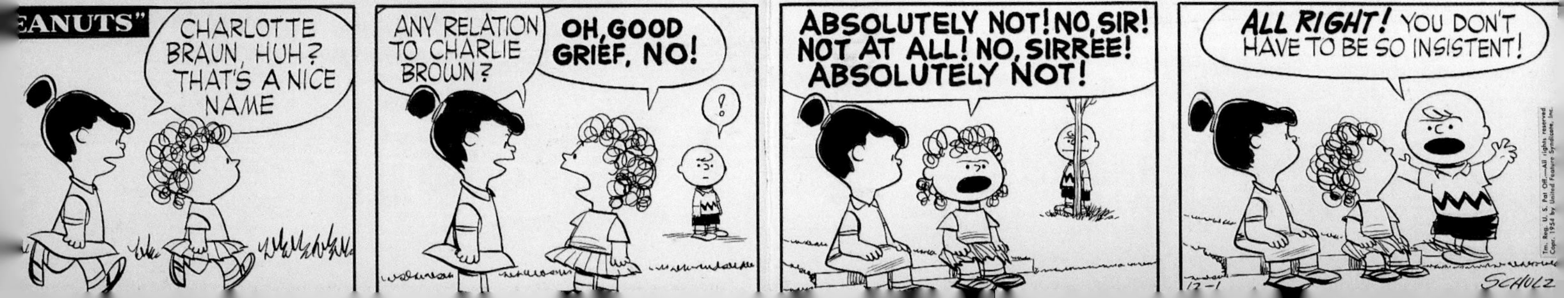
EANUTS"
CHARLOTTE BRAUN, HUH? THAT'S A NICE NAME
ANY RELATION TO CHARLIE BROWN?
OH, GOOD GRIEF, NO!
!
ABSOLUTELY NOT! NO, SIR! NOT AT ALL! NO, SIRREE! ABSOLUTELY NOT!
ALL RIGHT! YOU DON'T HAVE TO BE SO INSISTENT!
Tm. Reg. U. S. Pat. Off.—All rights reserved Copr. 1954 by United Feature Syndicate, Inc.
12-1
SCHULZ

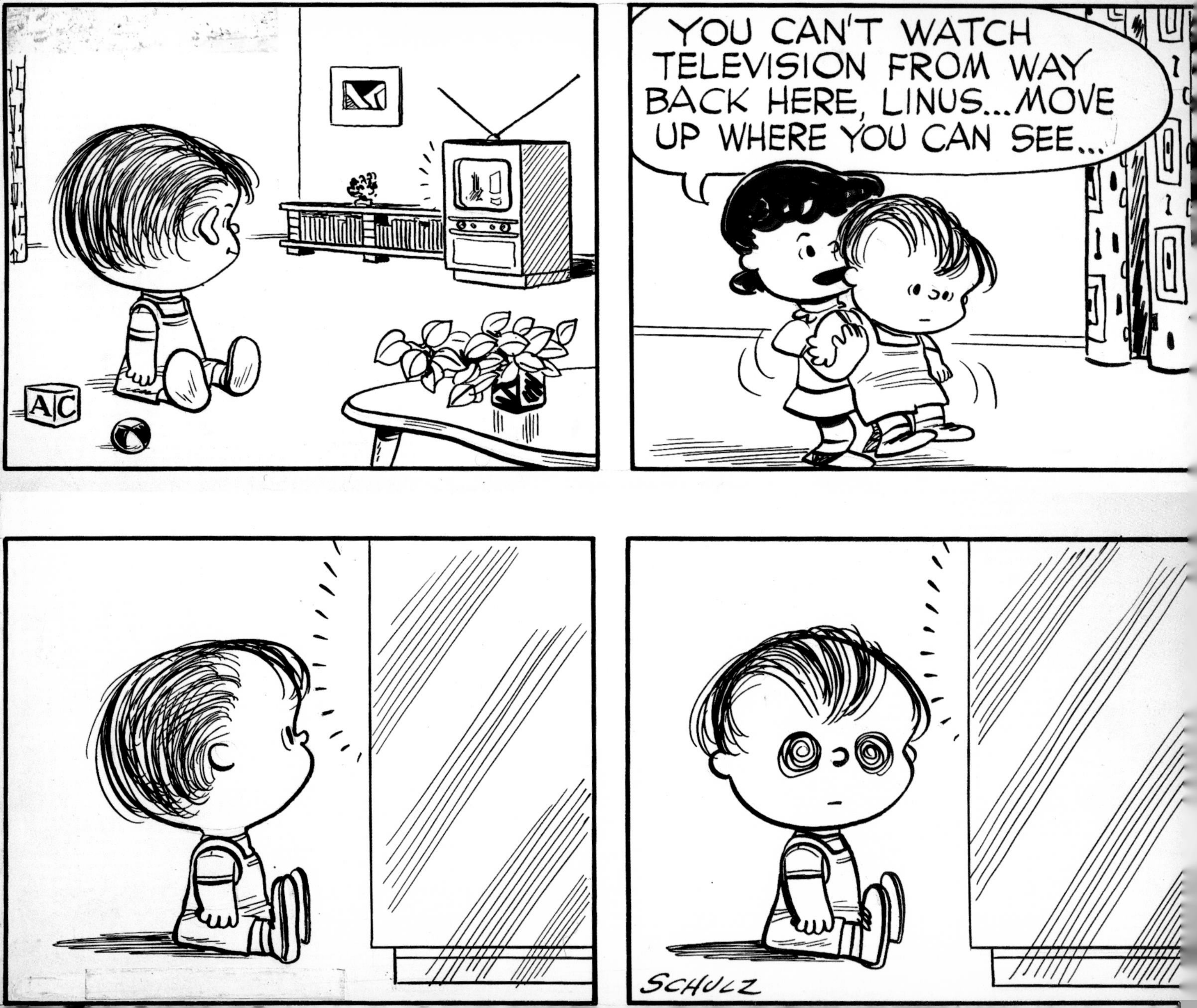
YOU CAN'T WATCH TELEVISION FROM WAY BACK HERE, LINUS...MOVE UP WHERE YOU CAN SEE...
SCHULZ

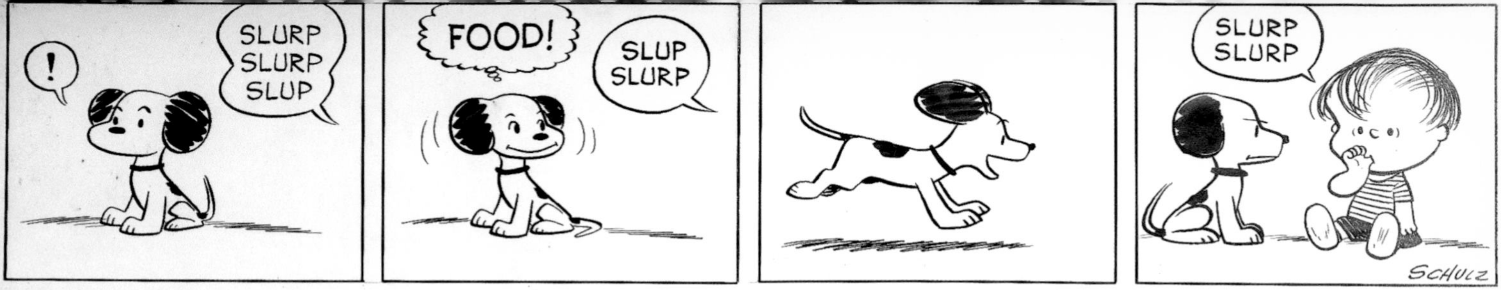
!
SLURP SLURP SLUP
FOOD!
SLUP SLURP
SLURP SLURP
SCHULZ

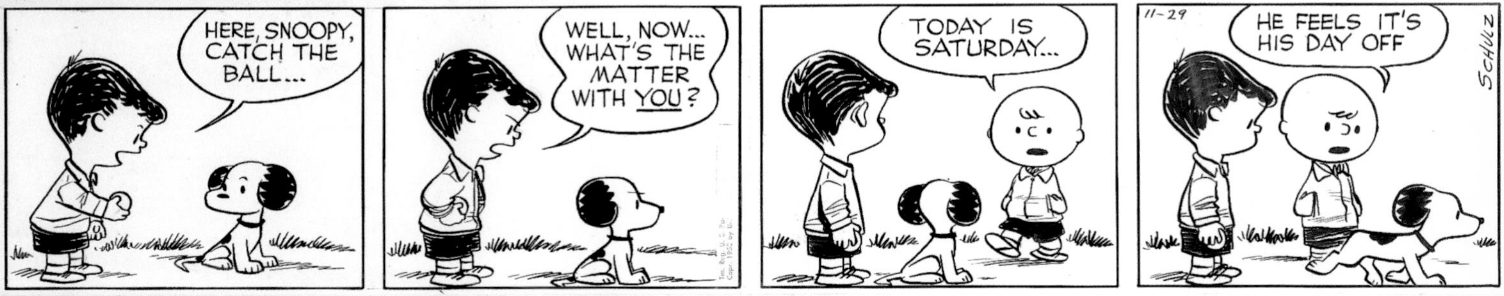
HERE, SNOOPY, CATCH THE BALL...
WELL, NOW... WHAT'S THE MATTER WITH YOU?
TODAY IS SATURDAY...
11-29
HE FEELS IT'S HIS DAY OFF
SCHULZ

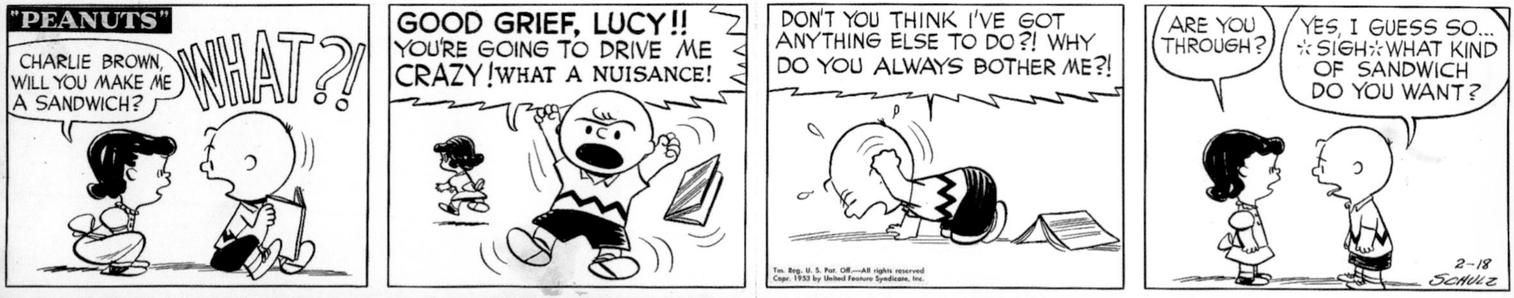
"PEANUTS"
CHARLIE BROWN, WILL YOU MAKE ME A SANDWICH?
WHAT?!
GOOD GRIEF, LUCY!! YOU'RE GOING TO DRIVE ME CRAZY! WHAT A NUISANCE!
DON'T YOU THINK I'VE GOT ANYTHING ELSE TO DO?! WHY DO YOU ALWAYS BOTHER ME?!
Tm. Reg. U. S. Pat. Off.—All rights reserved Copr. 1953 by United Feature Syndicate, Inc.
ARE YOU THROUGH?
YES, I GUESS SO... ☆SIGH☆ WHAT KIND OF SANDWICH DO YOU WANT?
2-18
SCHULZ

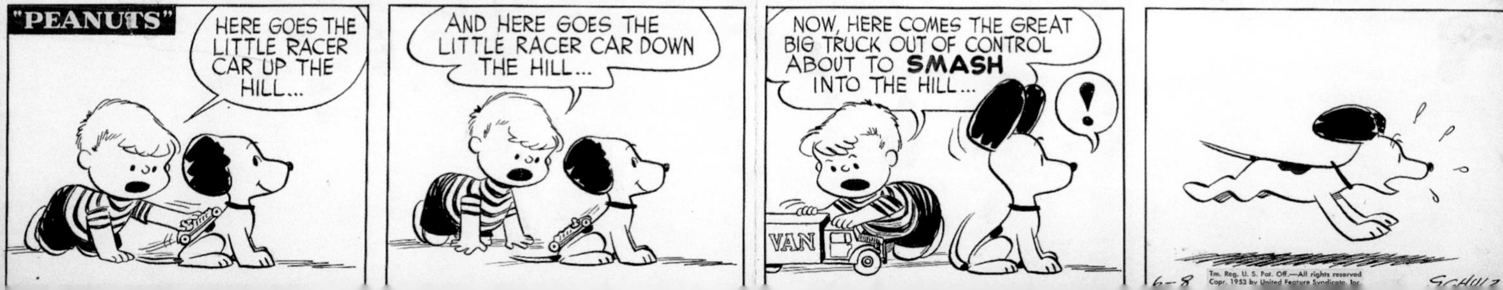
"PEANUTS"
HERE GOES THE LITTLE RACER CAR UP THE HILL...
AND HERE GOES THE LITTLE RACER CAR DOWN THE HILL...
NOW, HERE COMES THE GREAT BIG TRUCK OUT OF CONTROL ABOUT TO SMASH INTO THE HILL...
!
VAN
6-8
Tm. Reg. U. S. Pat. Off.—All rights reserved Copr. 1953 by United Feature Syndicate, Inc.
SCHULZ

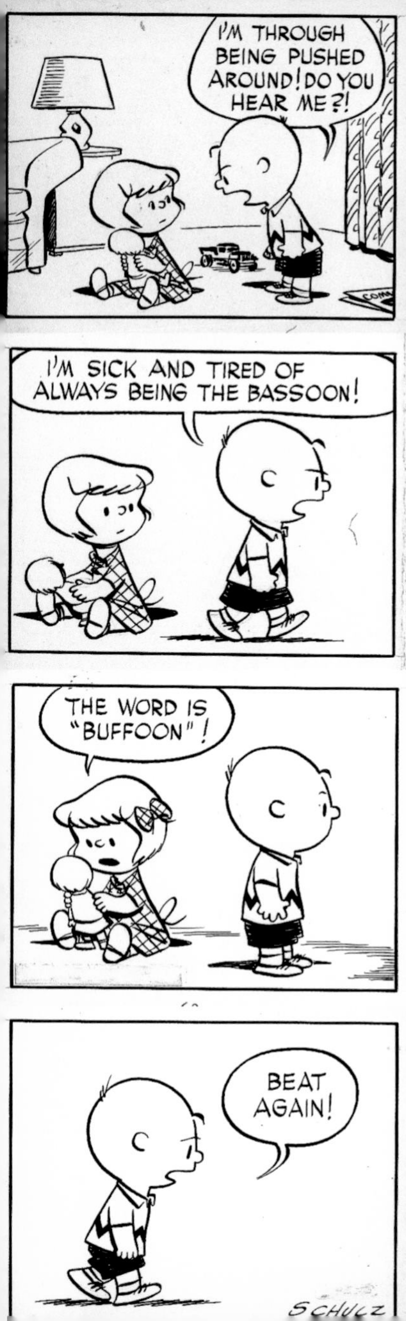
I'M THROUGH BEING PUSHED AROUND! DO YOU HEAR ME?!
I'M SICK AND TIRED OF ALWAYS BEING THE BASSOON!
THE WORD IS "BUFFOON"!
BEAT AGAIN!
SCHULZ

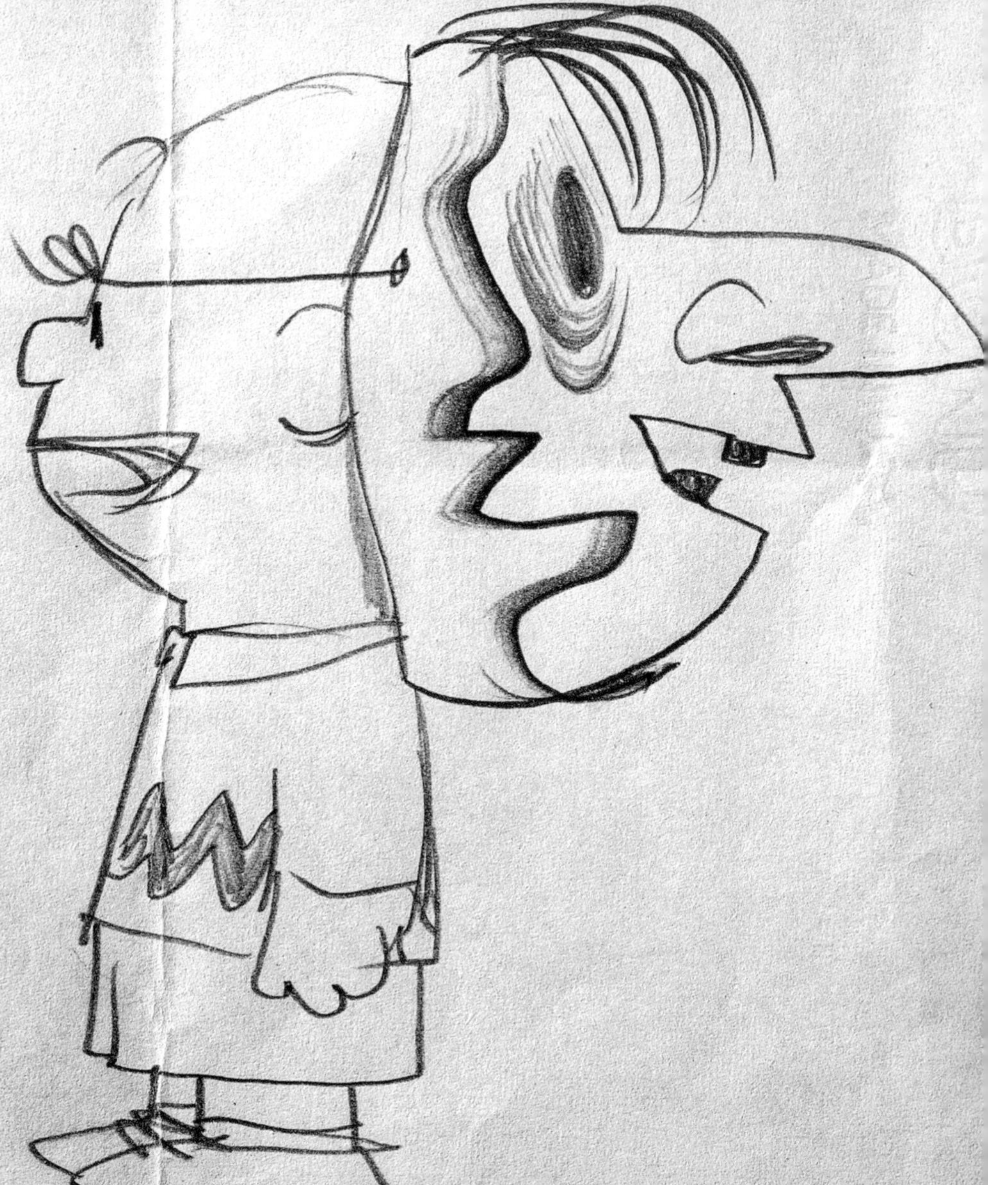

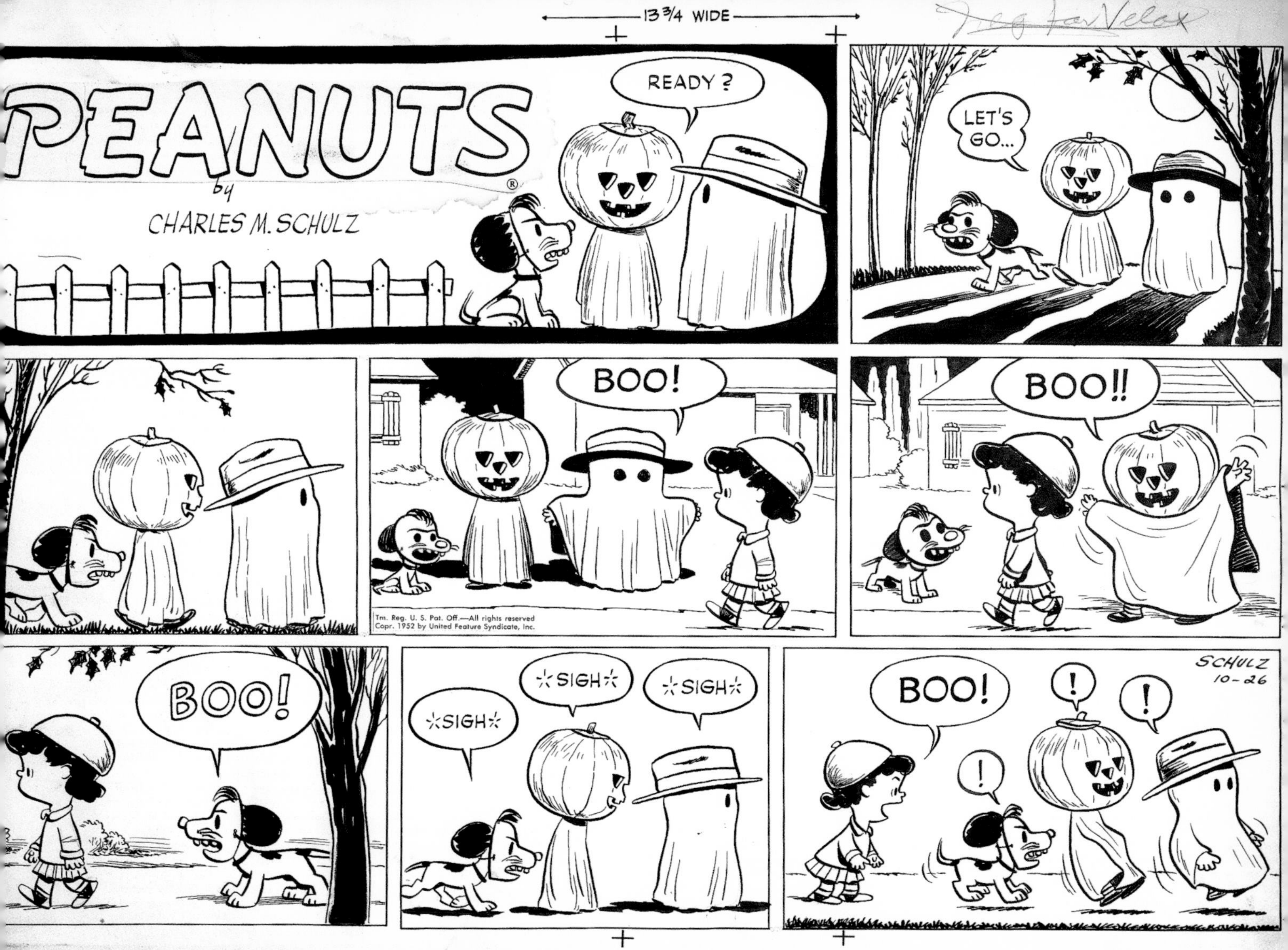
13 3/4 WIDE
PEANUTS
by
CHARLES M. SCHULZ
READY?
LET'S GO...
BOO!
Tm. Reg. U. S. Pat. Off.—All rights reserved
Copr. 1952 by United Feature Syndicate, Inc.
BOO!!
BOO!
SIGH
SIGH
SIGH
SCHULZ
10-26
BOO!
!
!
!

Snoopy often "thought" words, but he never actually spoke them, with the possible exception of this Sunday strip from 1953. The "pumpkin-headed" kid must be Charlie Brown, but who's wearing the hat? Opposite: Picasso was one of Schulz's favorite artists, and this undated sketch of Charlie Brown (probably mid-1950s) appears to bear his influence.

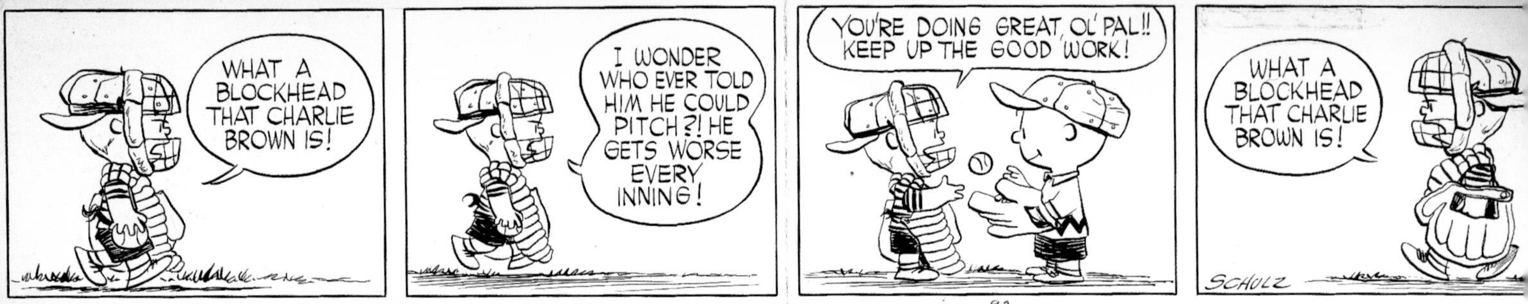
WHAT A BLOCKHEAD THAT CHARLIE BROWN IS!
I WONDER WHO EVER TOLD HIM HE COULD PITCH?! HE GETS WORSE EVERY INNING!
YOU'RE DOING GREAT, OL' PAL!! KEEP UP THE GOOD WORK!
WHAT A BLOCKHEAD THAT CHARLIE BROWN IS!
SCHULZ

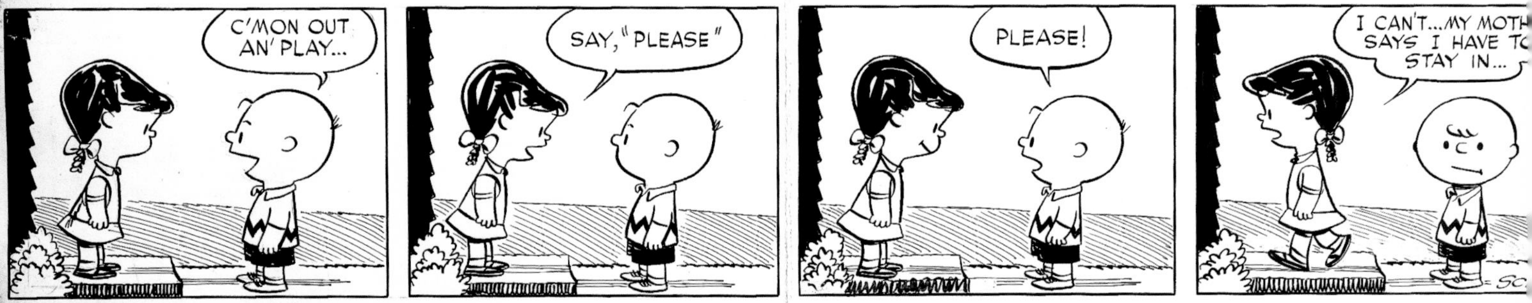
C'MON OUT AN' PLAY...
SAY, "PLEASE"
PLEASE!

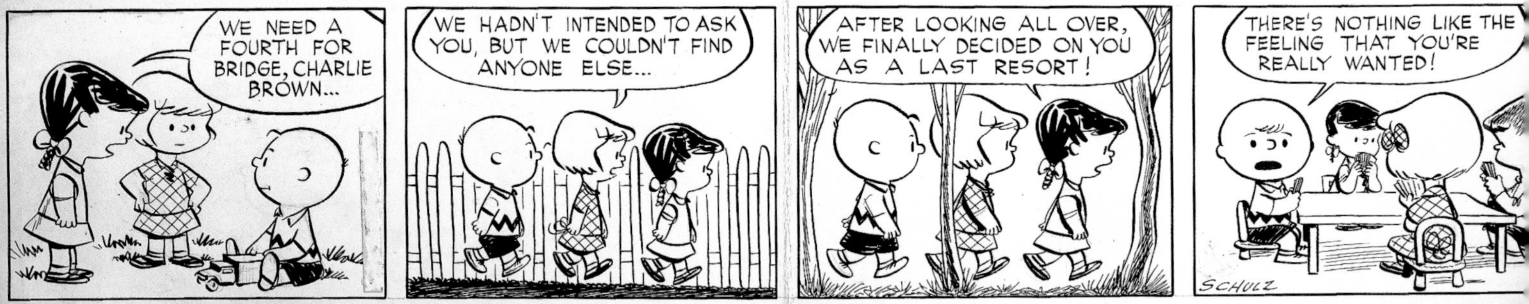
WE NEED A FOURTH FOR BRIDGE, CHARLIE BROWN...
WE HADN'T INTENDED TO ASK YOU, BUT WE COULDN'T FIND ANYONE ELSE...
AFTER LOOKING ALL OVER, WE FINALLY DECIDED ON YOU AS A LAST RESORT!
THERE'S NOTHING LIKE THE FEELING THAT YOU'RE REALLY WANTED!
SCHULZ

Compare the last panel in the above middle strip (1953) to the opposite page (1955). In the mid-50s Charlie Brown's head started to become less of a perfect oval (slightly wider at the bottom) and smaller in proportion to the rest of his body; and his eyes and "hair" sat higher on his face. This trend would continue through the 60s and on, giving him an increasingly mature, less baby-like appearance.

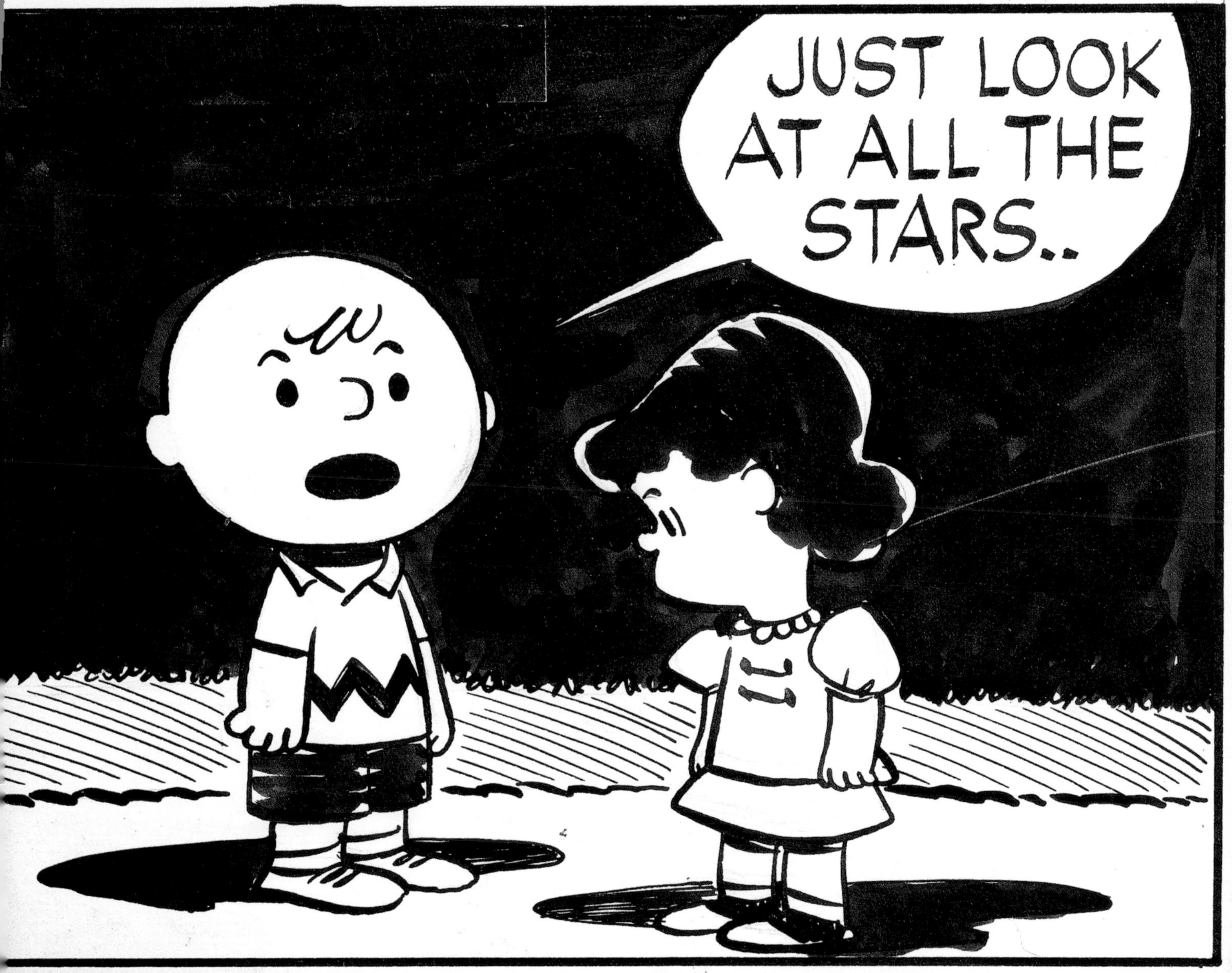
JUST LOOK AT ALL THE STARS..

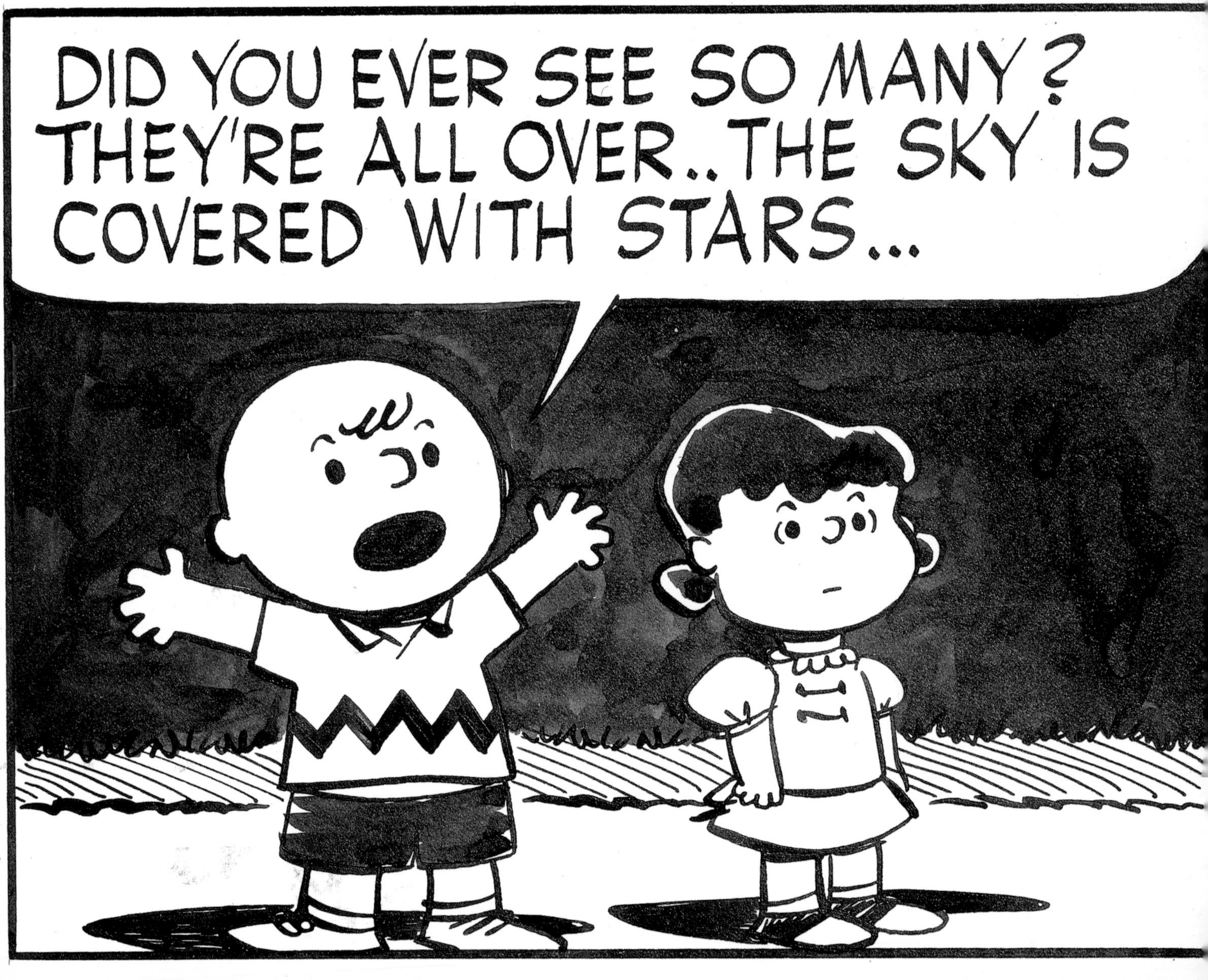
DID YOU EVER SEE SO MANY? THEY'RE ALL OVER.. THE SKY IS COVERED WITH STARS...

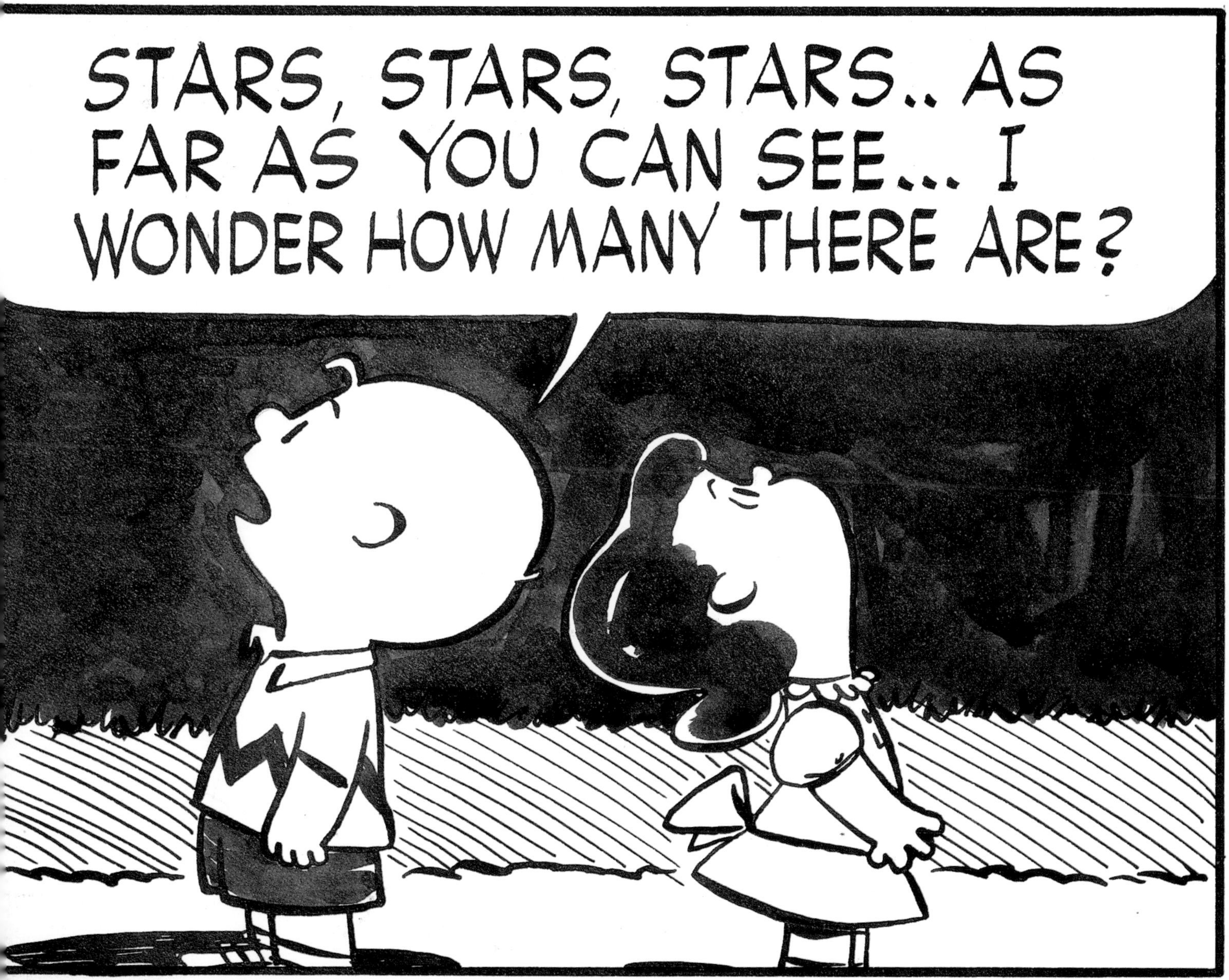
STARS, STARS, STARS.. AS FAR AS YOU CAN SEE... I WONDER HOW MANY THERE ARE?

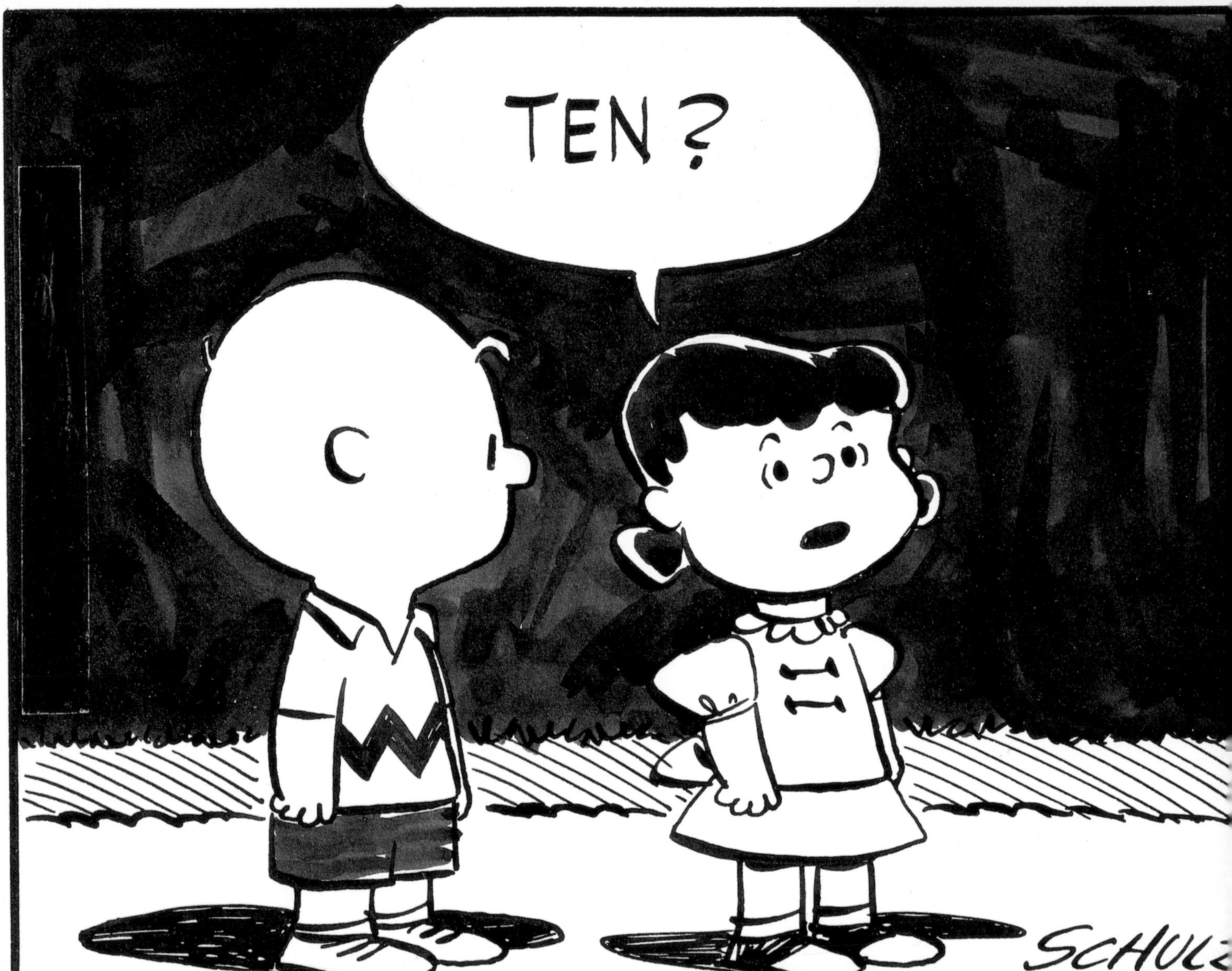
TEN?
SCHULZ

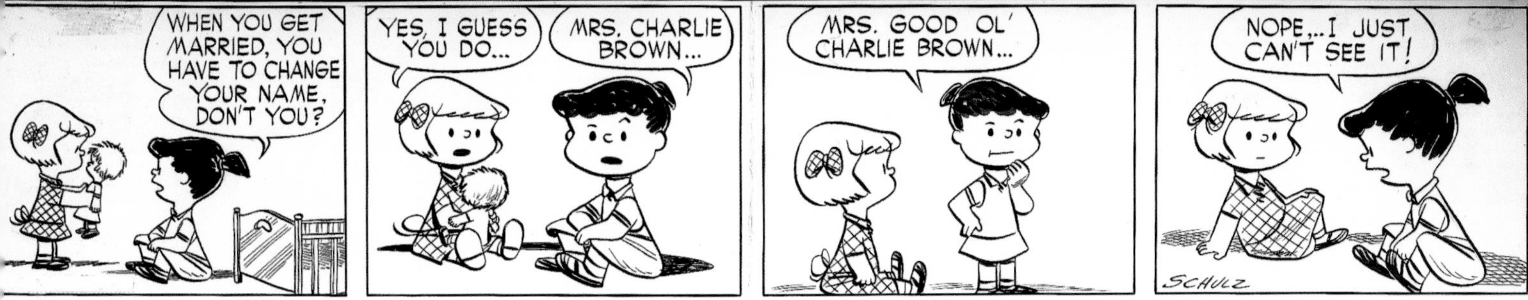
WHEN YOU GET MARRIED, YOU HAVE TO CHANGE YOUR NAME, DON'T YOU?
YES, I GUESS YOU DO...
MRS. CHARLIE BROWN...
MRS. GOOD OL' CHARLIE BROWN...
NOPE,...I JUST CAN'T SEE IT!
SCHULZ

26 4 Col

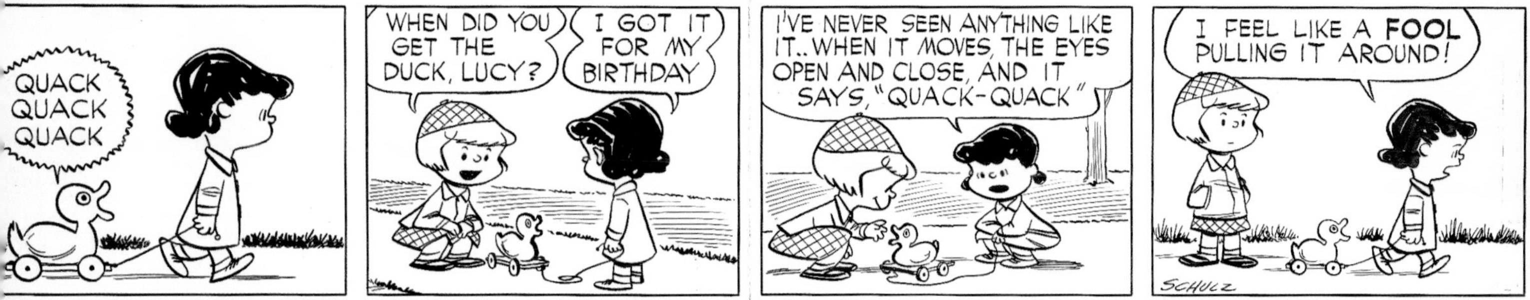
QUACK QUACK QUACK
WHEN DID YOU GET THE DUCK, LUCY?
I GOT IT FOR MY BIRTHDAY
I'VE NEVER SEEN ANYTHING LIKE IT..WHEN IT MOVES, THE EYES OPEN AND CLOSE, AND IT SAYS, "QUACK-QUACK"
I FEEL LIKE A **FOOL** PULLING IT AROUND!
SCHULZ

41

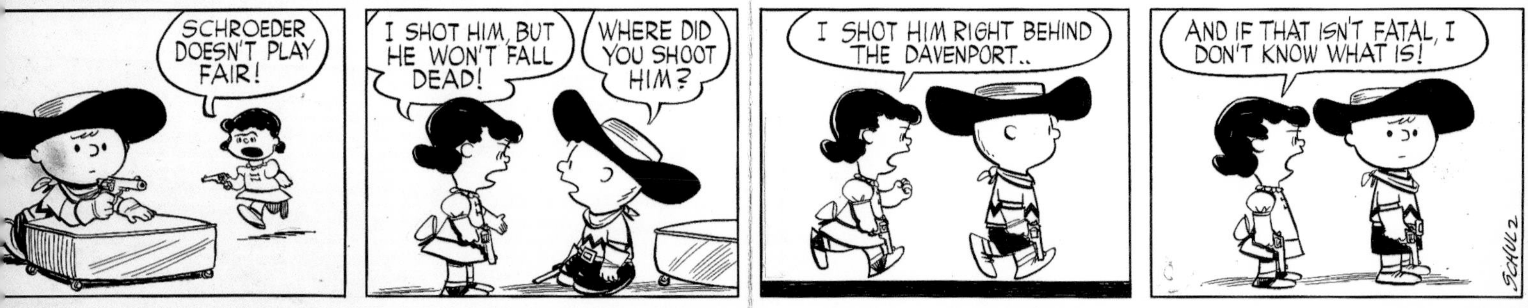
SCHROEDER DOESN'T PLAY FAIR!
I SHOT HIM, BUT HE WON'T FALL DEAD!
WHERE DID YOU SHOOT HIM?
I SHOT HIM RIGHT BEHIND THE DAVENPORT..
AND IF THAT ISN'T FATAL, I DON'T KNOW WHAT IS!
SCHULZ

17⁰

Schroeder's interest in music actually began with Charlie Brown. "The very first year the strip began I was looking through this book on music, and it showed a portion of Beethoven's Ninth in it, so I drew a cartoon of Charlie Brown singing this. I thought it looked kind of neat, showing these complicated notes coming out of the mouth of this comic-strip character, and I thought about it some more, and then I thought 'Why not have one of the little kids play a toy piano? Why not have Schroeder, who had just come into the strip as a baby, play it? That's how it all started. If I had known that it would work as well, I would have planned it more carefully." Schulz always drew all of the sheet music in the strip by hand.

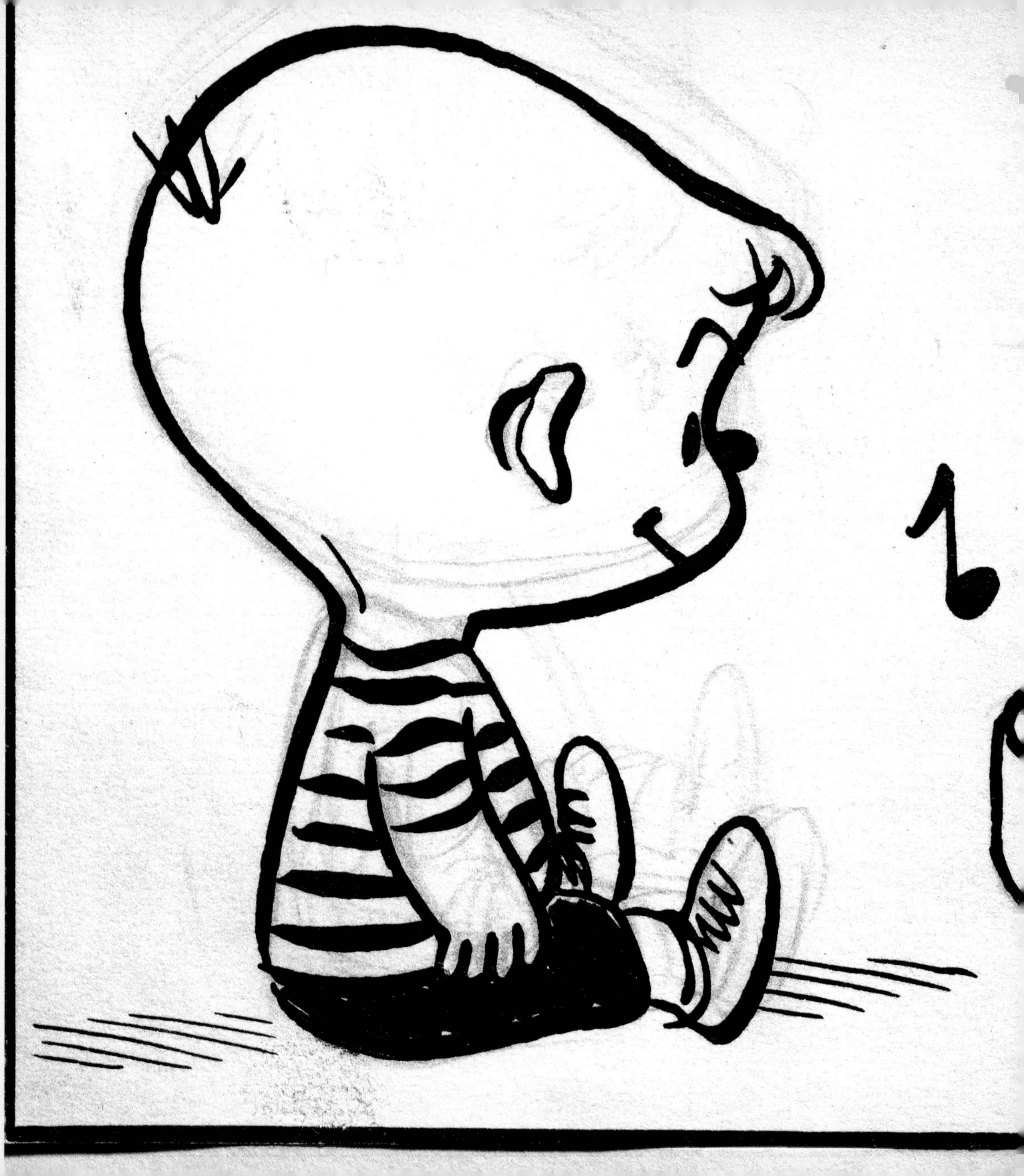

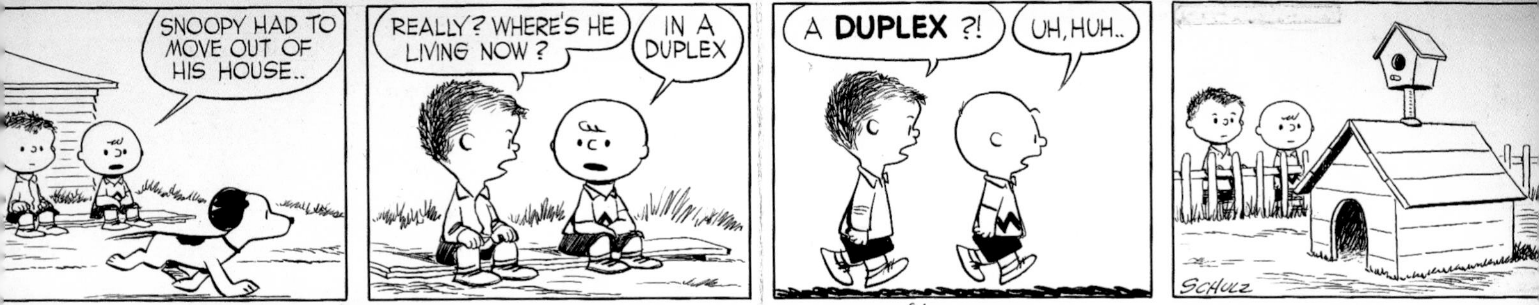
SNOOPY HAD TO MOVE OUT OF HIS HOUSE..
REALLY? WHERE'S HE LIVING NOW?
IN A DUPLEX
A **DUPLEX** ?!
UH, HUH..
SCHULZ

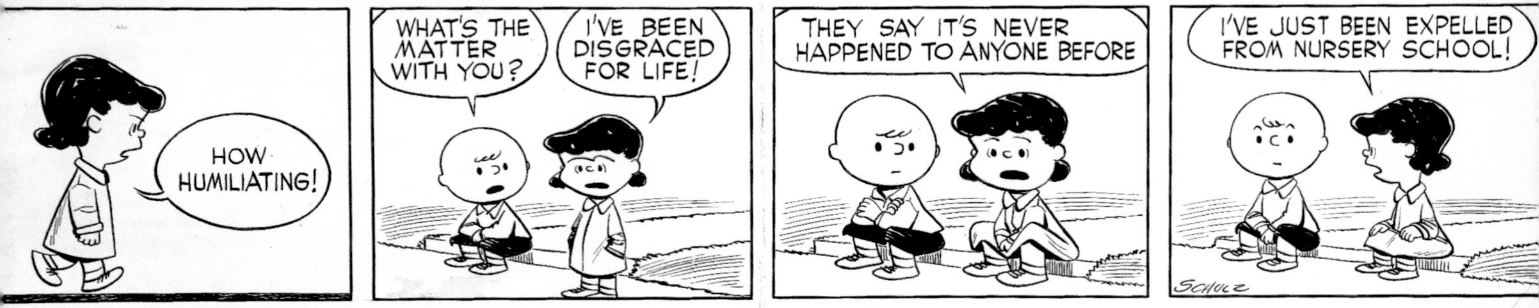
HOW HUMILIATING!
WHAT'S THE MATTER WITH YOU?
I'VE BEEN DISGRACED FOR LIFE!
THEY SAY IT'S NEVER HAPPENED TO ANYONE BEFORE
I'VE JUST BEEN EXPELLED FROM NURSERY SCHOOL!
SCHULZ

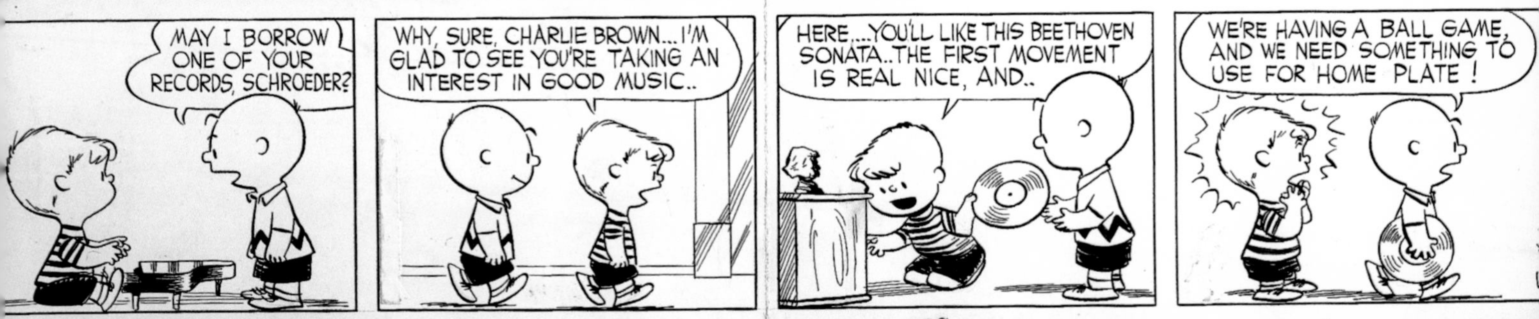
MAY I BORROW ONE OF YOUR RECORDS, SCHROEDER?
WHY, SURE, CHARLIE BROWN... I'M GLAD TO SEE YOU'RE TAKING AN INTEREST IN GOOD MUSIC..
HERE,...YOU'LL LIKE THIS BEETHOVEN SONATA..THE FIRST MOVEMENT IS REAL NICE, AND..
WE'RE HAVING A BALL GAME, AND WE NEED SOMETHING TO USE FOR HOME PLATE!

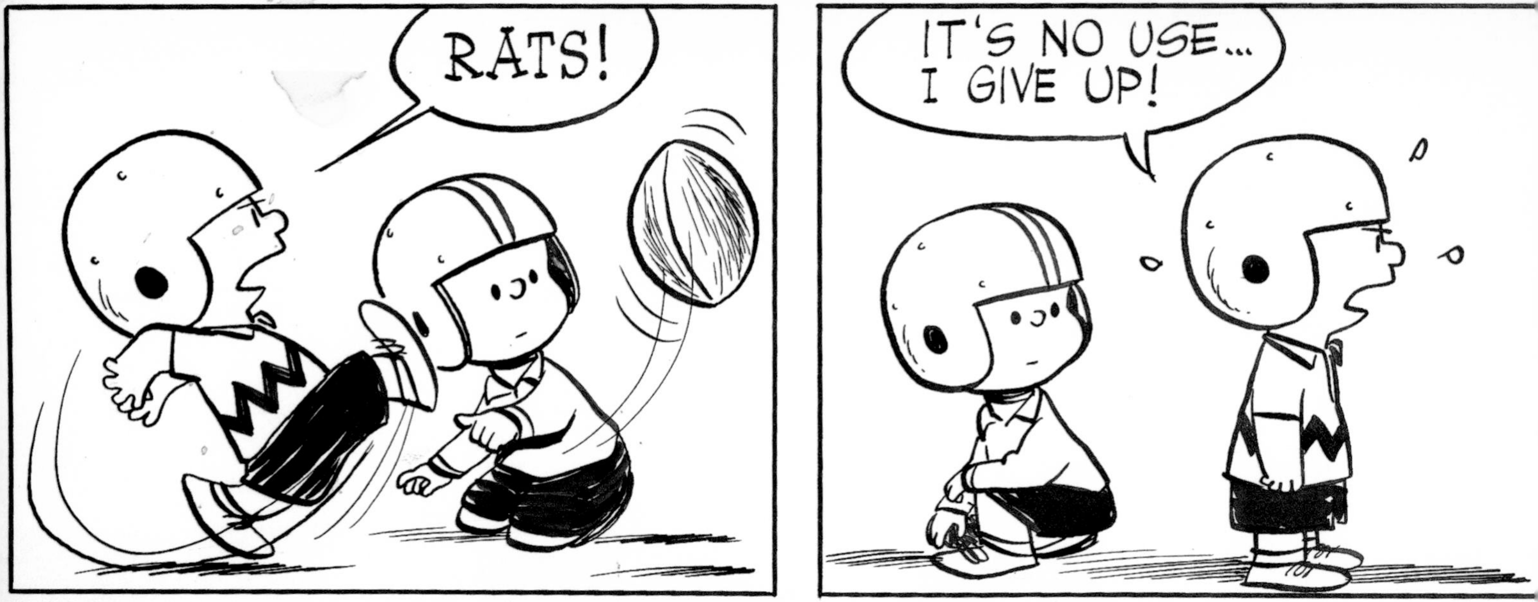
RATS!
IT'S NO USE...
I GIVE UP!

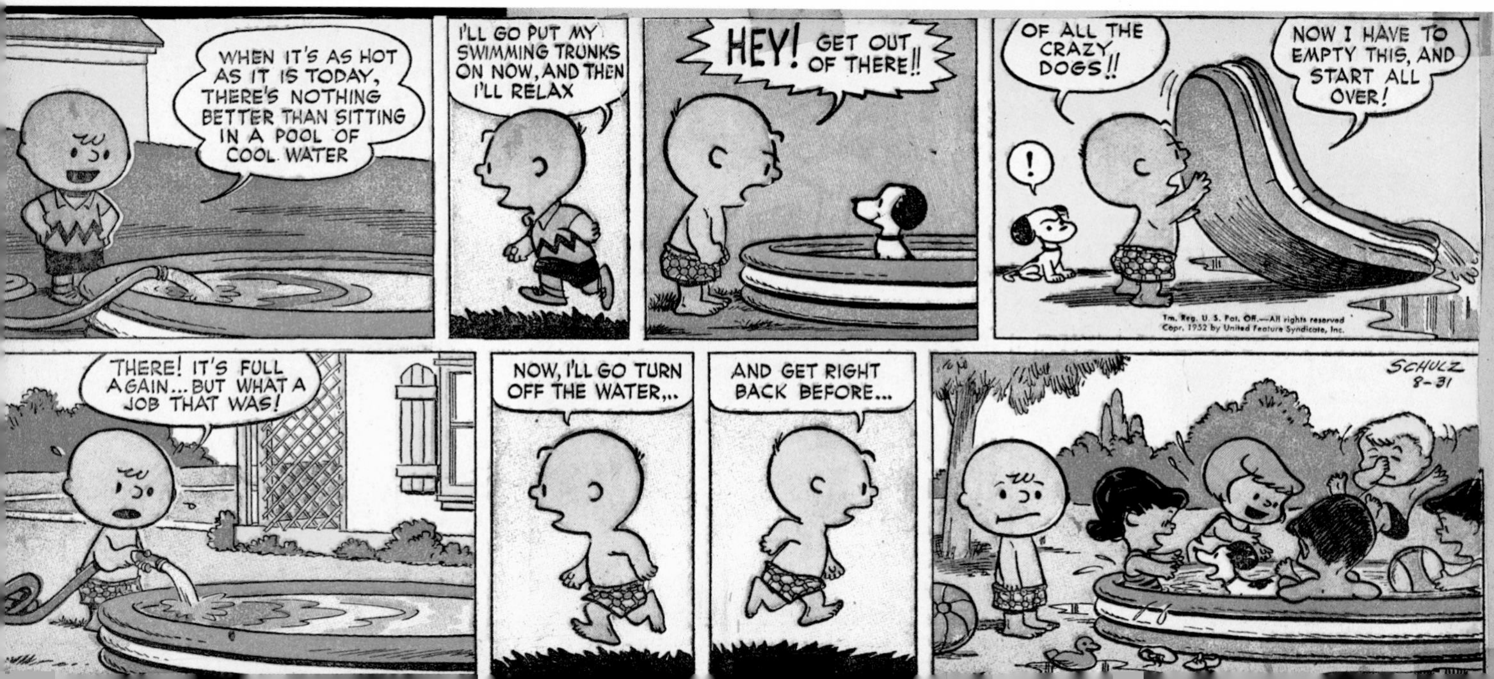
WHEN IT'S AS HOT AS IT IS TODAY, THERE'S NOTHING BETTER THAN SITTING IN A POOL OF COOL WATER
I'LL GO PUT MY SWIMMING TRUNKS ON NOW, AND THEN I'LL RELAX
HEY! GET OUT OF THERE!!
OF ALL THE CRAZY DOGS!!
!
NOW I HAVE TO EMPTY THIS, AND START ALL OVER!
Tm. Reg. U. S. Pat. Off.—All rights reserved Copr. 1952 by United Feature Syndicate, Inc.
THERE! IT'S FULL AGAIN... BUT WHAT A JOB THAT WAS!
NOW, I'LL GO TURN OFF THE WATER,..
AND GET RIGHT BACK BEFORE...
SCHULZ 8-31

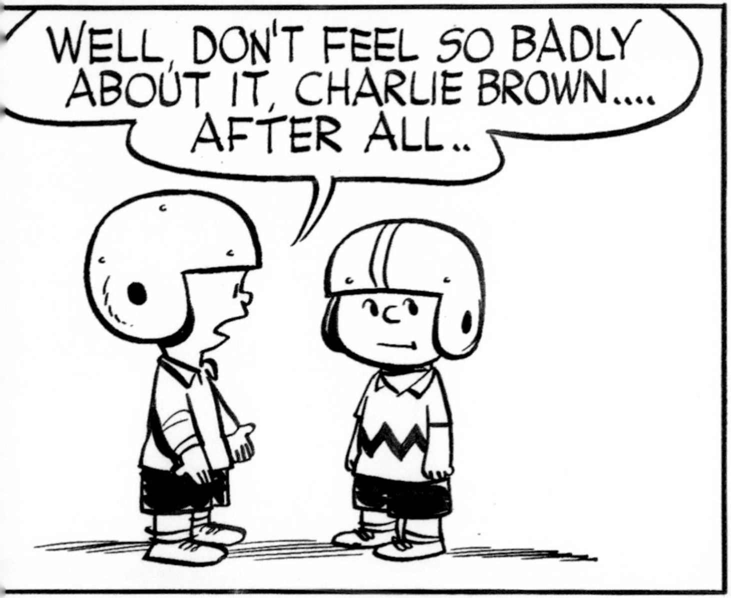
WELL, DON'T FEEL SO BADLY ABOUT IT, CHARLIE BROWN.... AFTER ALL..

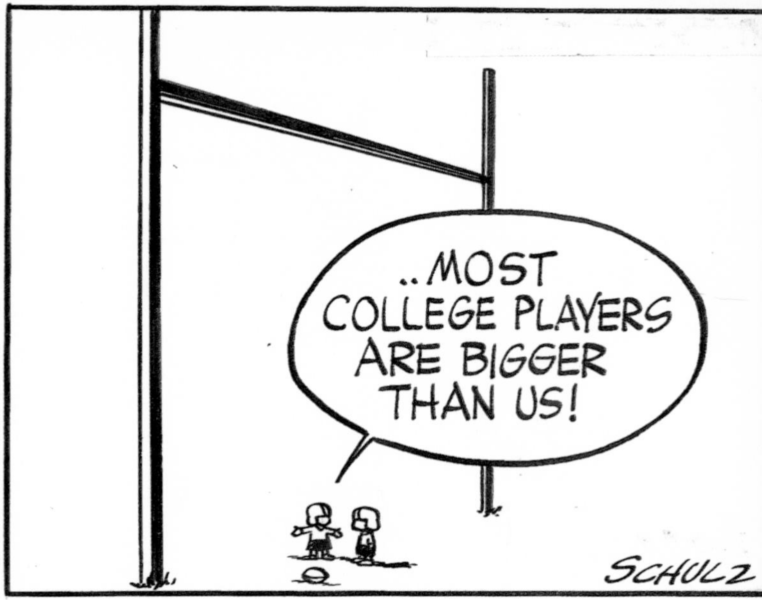
..MOST COLLEGE PLAYERS ARE BIGGER THAN US!
SCHULZ

Schulz's original ending for this mid-1950s strip (below right) probably wasn't dramatic enough. The much more extreme solution (top right) was pasted on top of it, something he rarely did. At least (with Lucy nowhere in the vicinity) Charlie Brown got to kick the football.

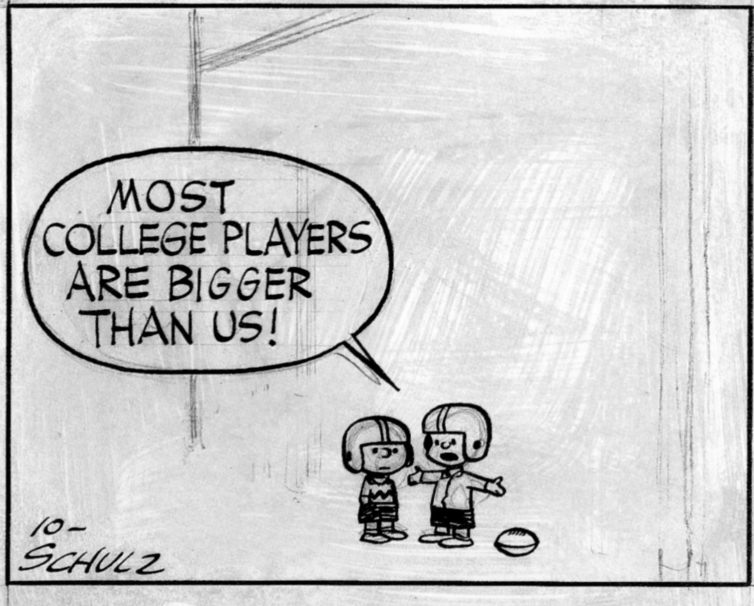
MOST COLLEGE PLAYERS ARE BIGGER THAN US!
SCHULZ

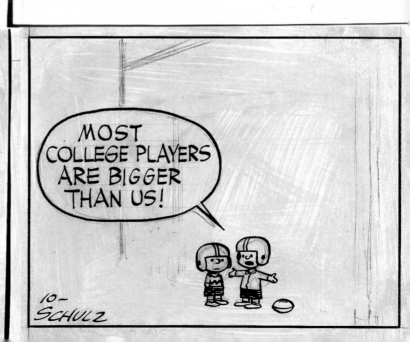

4 col

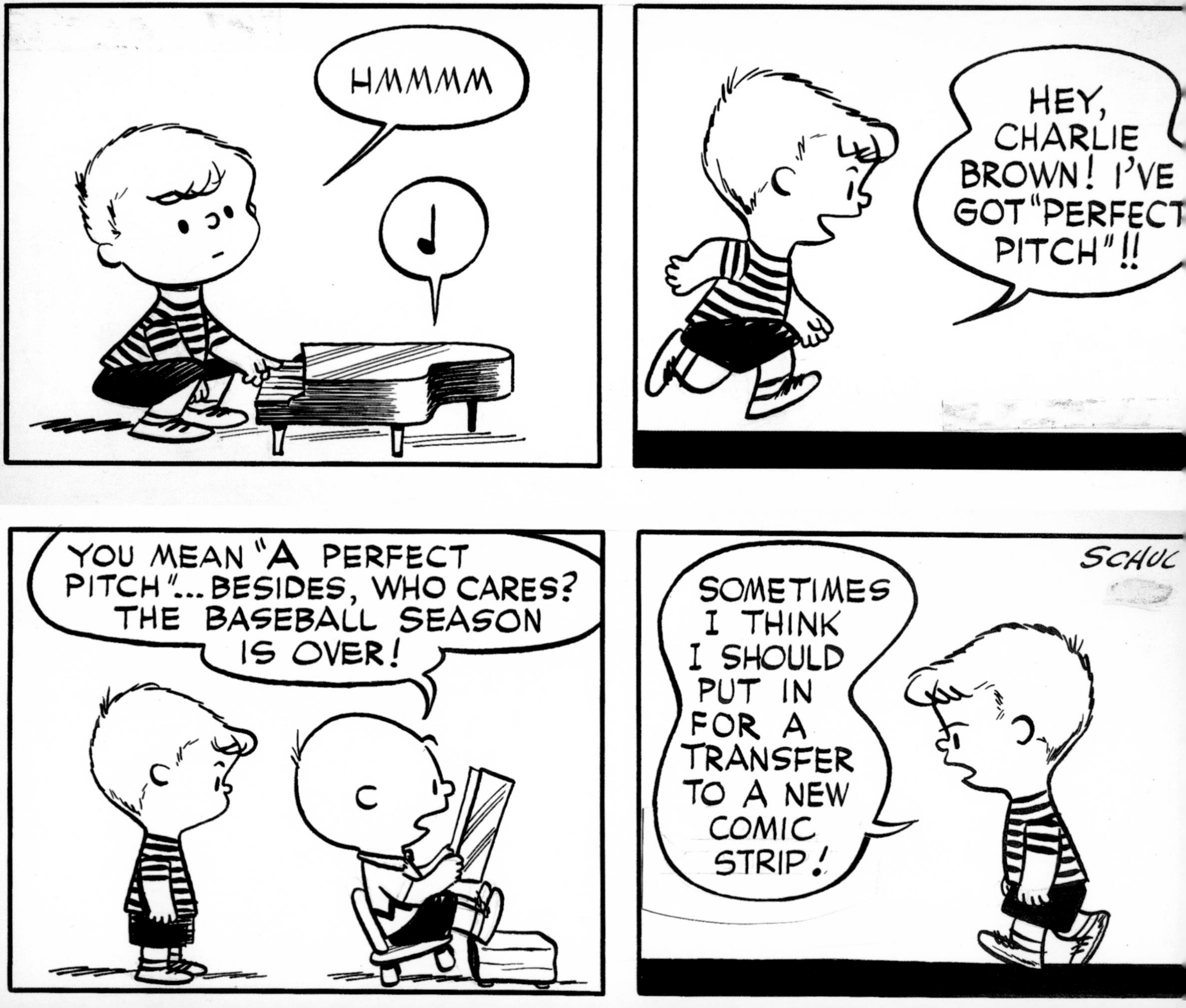
HMMMM
HEY, CHARLIE BROWN! I'VE GOT "PERFECT PITCH"!!
YOU MEAN "A PERFECT PITCH"... BESIDES, WHO CARES? THE BASEBALL SEASON IS OVER!
SOMETIMES I THINK I SHOULD PUT IN FOR A TRANSFER TO A NEW COMIC STRIP!
SCHUL

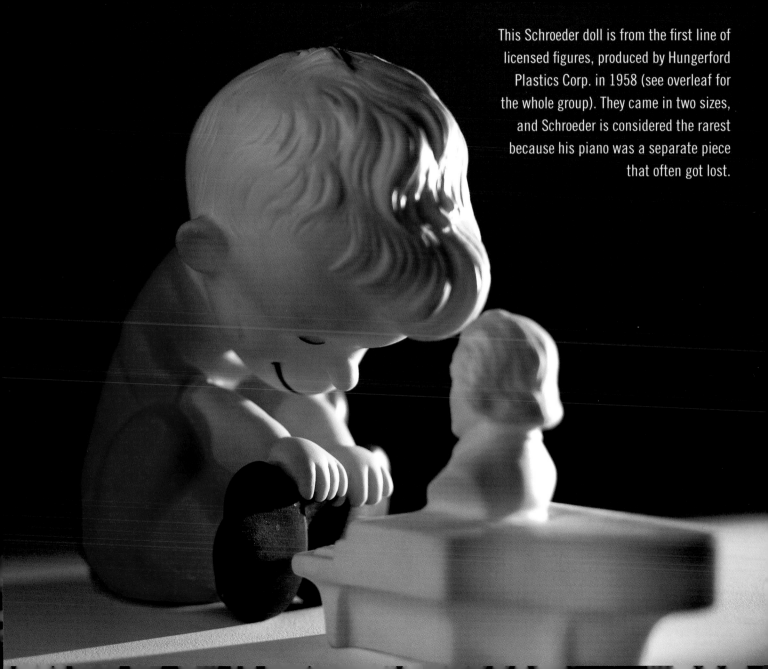

This Schroeder doll is from the first line of licensed figures, produced by Hungerford Plastics Corp. in 1958 (see overleaf for the whole group). They came in two sizes, and Schroeder is considered the rarest because his piano was a separate piece that often got lost.

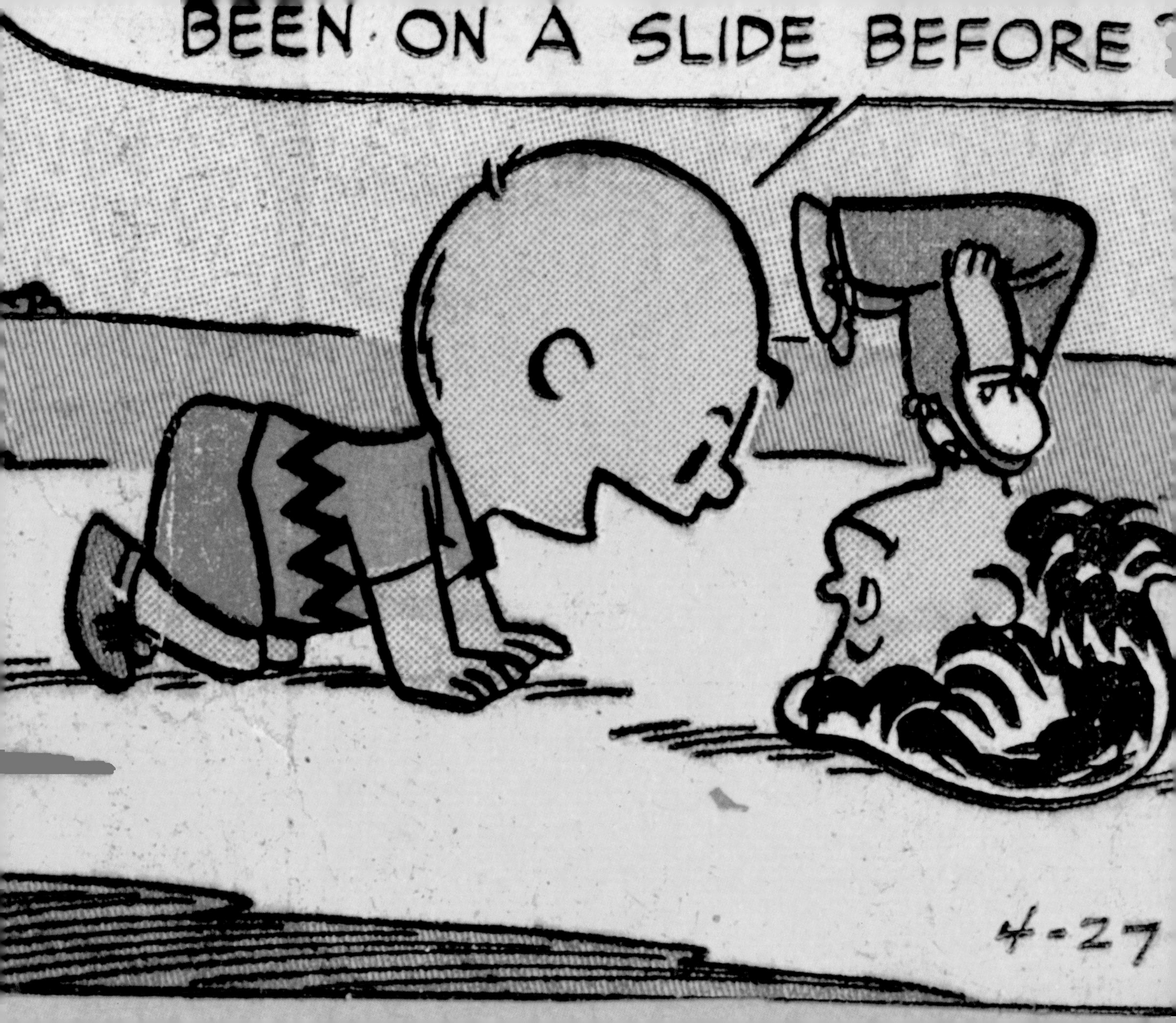
BEEN ON A SLIDE BEFORE?
4-27

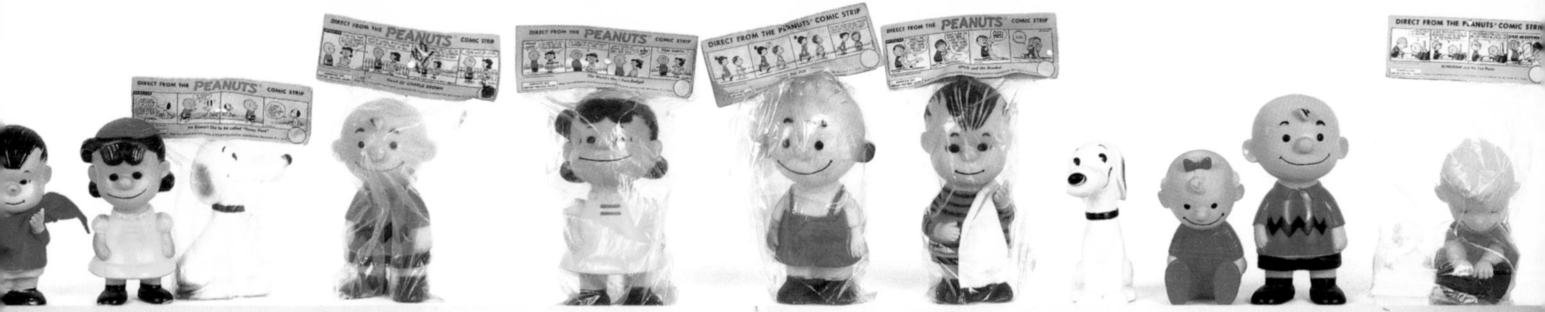

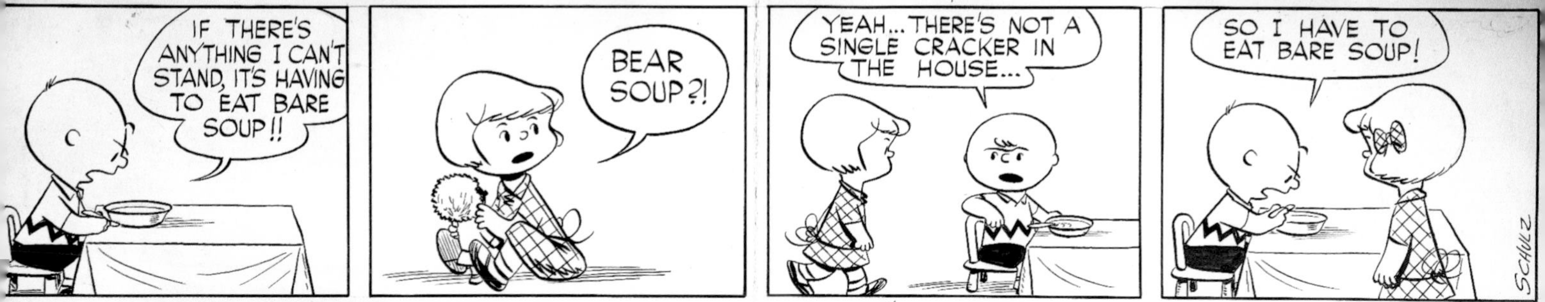

IF THERE'S ANYTHING I CAN'T STAND, IT'S HAVING TO EAT BARE SOUP!!
BEAR SOUP?!
YEAH... THERE'S NOT A SINGLE CRACKER IN THE HOUSE...
SO I HAVE TO EAT BARE SOUP!
SCHULZ

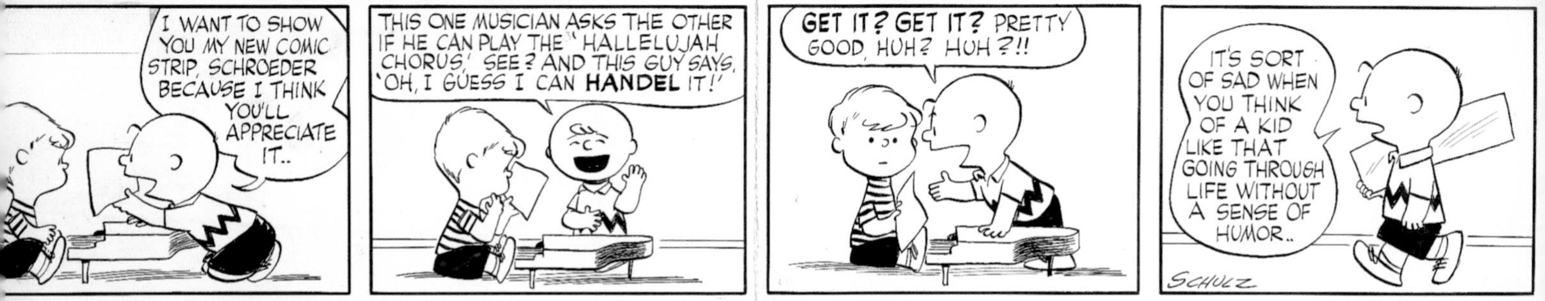

I WANT TO SHOW YOU MY NEW COMIC STRIP, SCHROEDER BECAUSE I THINK YOU'LL APPRECIATE IT..
THIS ONE MUSICIAN ASKS THE OTHER IF HE CAN PLAY THE "HALLELUJAH CHORUS," SEE? AND THIS GUY SAYS, 'OH, I GUESS I CAN HANDEL IT!'
GET IT? GET IT? PRETTY GOOD, HUH? HUH?!!
IT'S SORT OF SAD WHEN YOU THINK OF A KID LIKE THAT GOING THROUGH LIFE WITHOUT A SENSE OF HUMOR..
SCHULZ

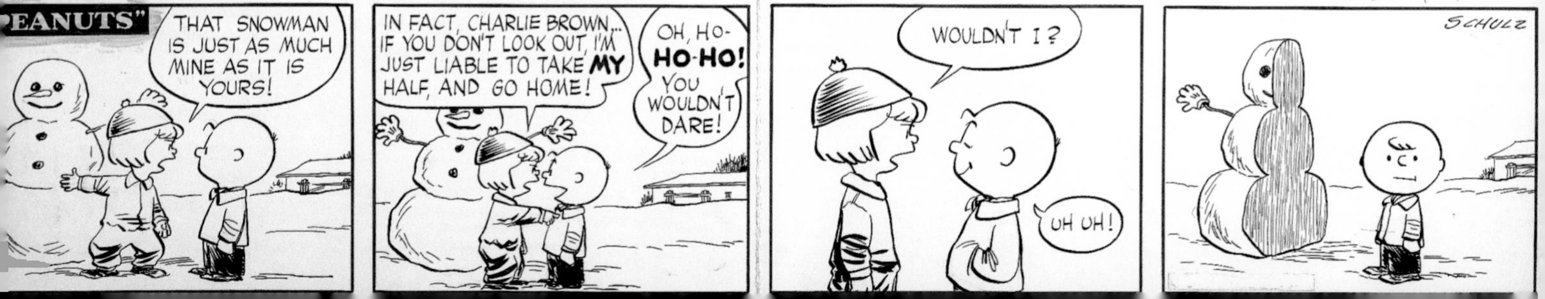

EANUTS"
THAT SNOWMAN IS JUST AS MUCH MINE AS IT IS YOURS!
IN FACT, CHARLIE BROWN... IF YOU DON'T LOOK OUT, I'M JUST LIABLE TO TAKE MY HALF, AND GO HOME!
OH, HO-HO-HO! YOU WOULDN'T DARE!
WOULDN'T I?
UH OH!
SCHULZ

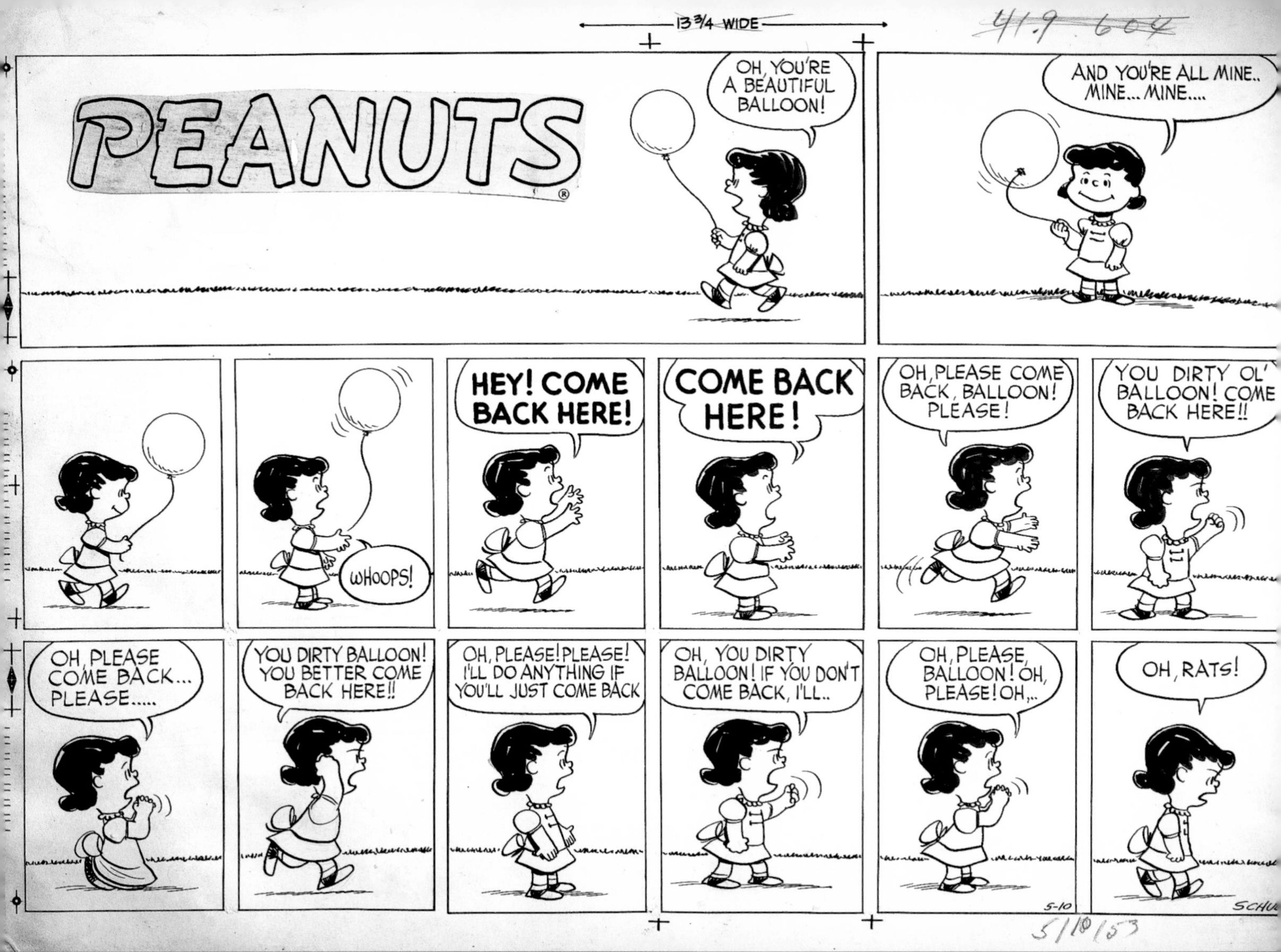
13 3/4 WIDE
41.9 604
PEANUTS
OH, YOU'RE A BEAUTIFUL BALLOON!
AND YOU'RE ALL MINE.. MINE... MINE....
WHOOPS!
HEY! COME BACK HERE!
COME BACK HERE!
OH, PLEASE COME BACK, BALLOON! PLEASE!
YOU DIRTY OL' BALLOON! COME BACK HERE!!
OH, PLEASE COME BACK... PLEASE.....
YOU DIRTY BALLOON! YOU BETTER COME BACK HERE!!
OH, PLEASE! PLEASE! I'LL DO ANYTHING IF YOU'LL JUST COME BACK
OH, YOU DIRTY BALLOON! IF YOU DON'T COME BACK, I'LL..
OH, PLEASE, BALLOON! OH, PLEASE! OH,..
OH, RATS!
5-10
SCHU
5/10/53

Lucy's days as a charming baby were short-lived. Only a few years after her introduction in 1952, she grew to the same age as the other characters and became their peer. By the end of the 1950s she was the female star of the strip. Schulz found far more possibilities for her than for Violet or Patty, who all but vanished by the end of the 1960s.

Schulz said in 1966: "Little girls of that age are smarter than little boys and Lucy knows it better than most little girls. But she's not as smart as she thinks she is. Beneath the surface there's something tender. But perhaps if you scratched deeper you'd find she's even worse than she seems."

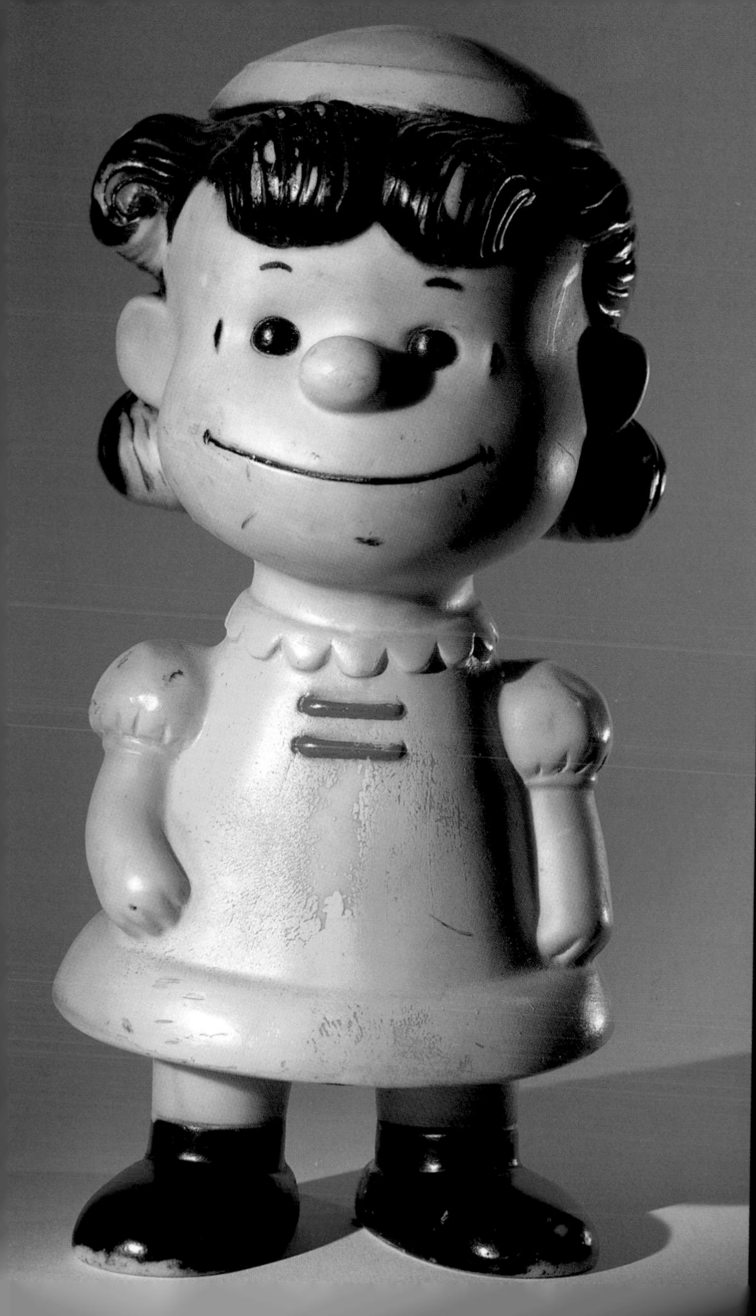

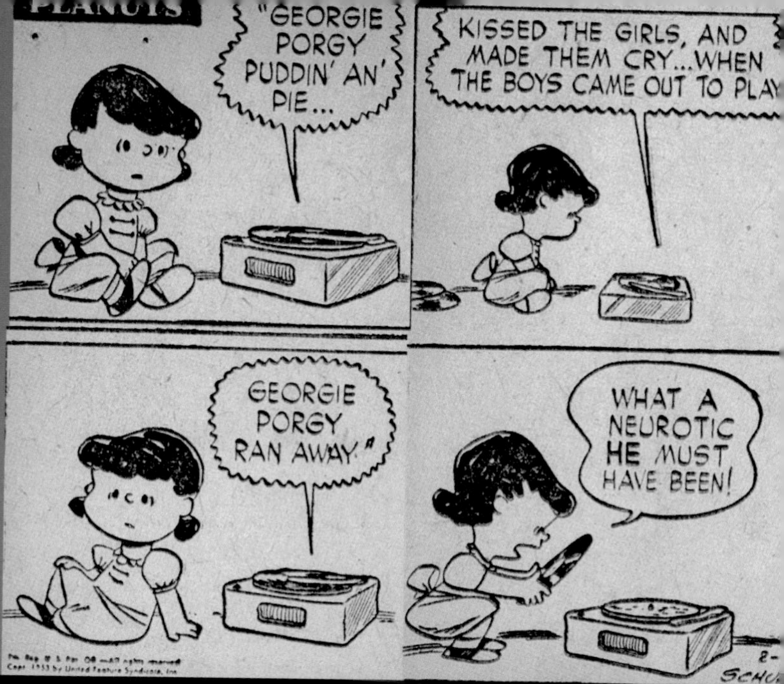
"GEORGIE PORGY PUDDIN' AN' PIE...
KISSED THE GIRLS, AND MADE THEM CRY...WHEN THE BOYS CAME OUT TO PLAY
GEORGIE PORGY RAN AWAY."
WHAT A NEUROTIC HE MUST HAVE BEEN!

In what *has* to be the first use of the word "neurotic" in a daily comic strip (1954), Lucy calls a spade a spade. "You have to give her credit, though," Schulz said in a 1967 interview, "she has a way of cutting right down to the truth. This is one of her good points." And there aren't many. "Lucy is not a favorite [of mine] because I don't especially like her, that's all. But she *works*, and a central comic-strip character is not only one who fills his role very well, but who will provide ideas by the very nature of his personality. This is why Charlie Brown, Linus, Snoopy, and Lucy appear more than the others. Their personalities are so broad and flexible that they provide more ideas."

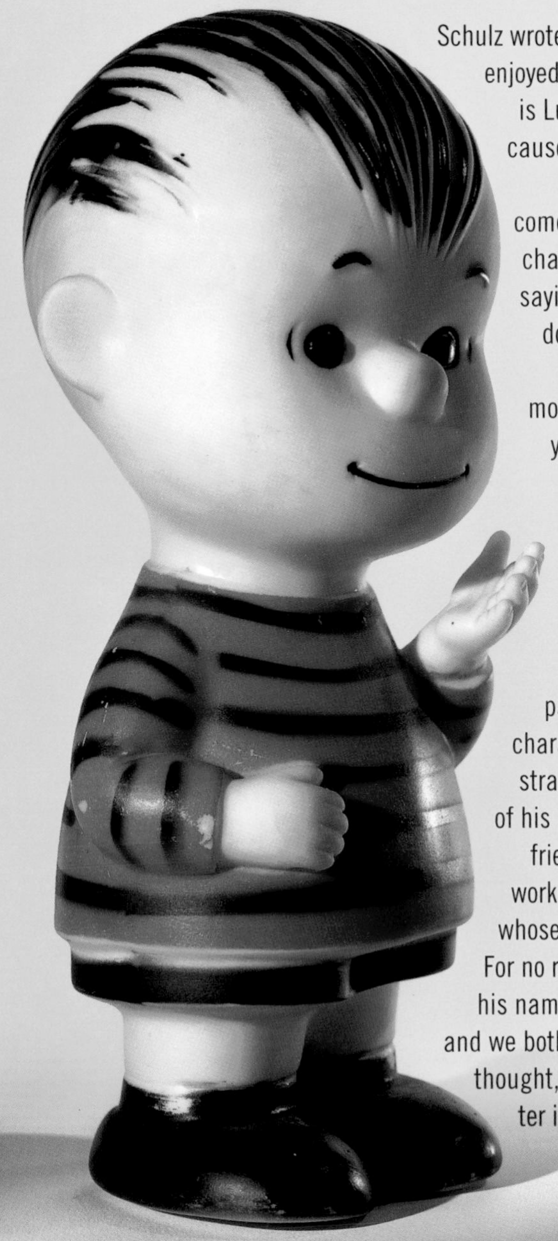

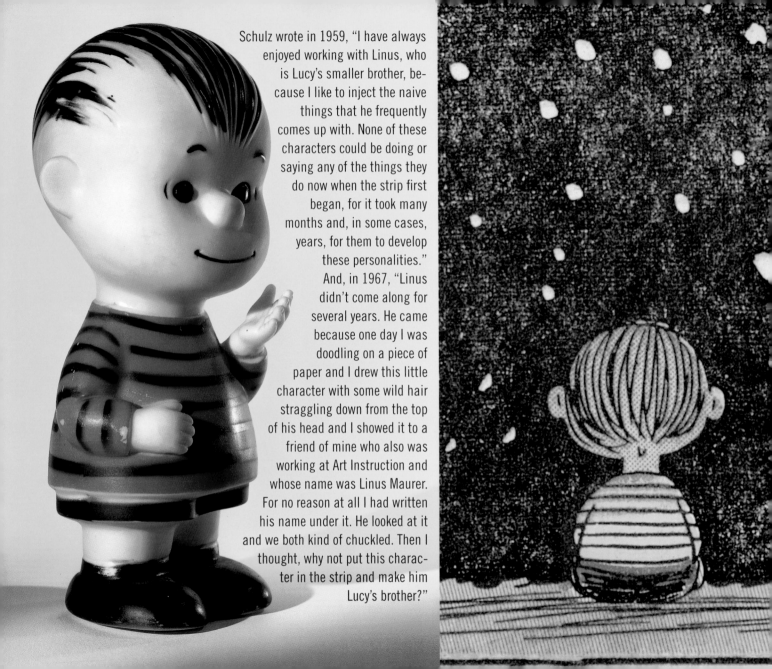

Schulz wrote in 1959, "I have always enjoyed working with Linus, who is Lucy's smaller brother, because I like to inject the naive things that he frequently comes up with. None of these characters could be doing or saying any of the things they do now when the strip first began, for it took many months and, in some cases, years, for them to develop these personalities."

And, in 1967, "Linus didn't come along for several years. He came because one day I was doodling on a piece of paper and I drew this little character with some wild hair straggling down from the top of his head and I showed it to a friend of mine who also was working at Art Instruction and whose name was Linus Maurer. For no reason at all I had written his name under it. He looked at it and we both kind of chuckled. Then I thought, why not put this character in the strip and make him Lucy's brother?"

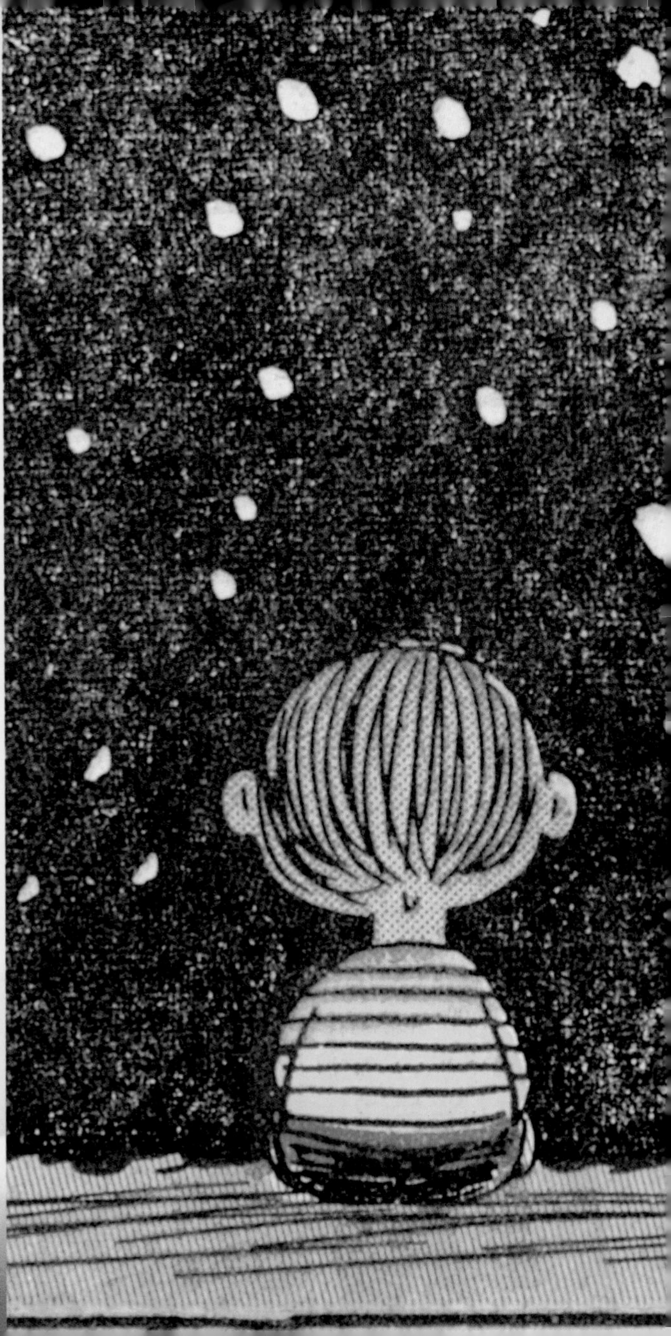

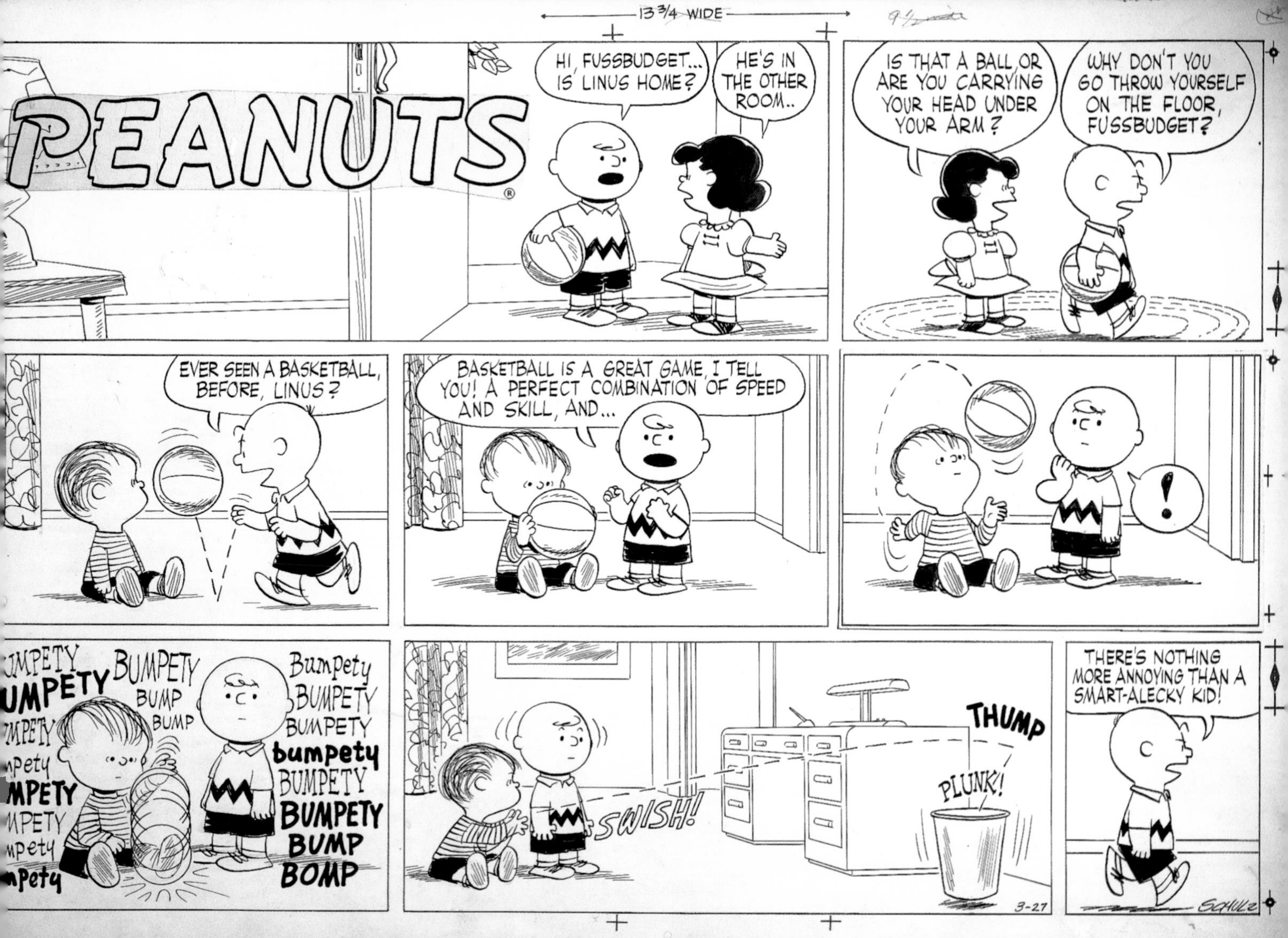
13 3/4 WIDE
PEANUTS
HI, FUSSBUDGET... IS LINUS HOME?
HE'S IN THE OTHER ROOM..
IS THAT A BALL OR ARE YOU CARRYING YOUR HEAD UNDER YOUR ARM?
WHY DON'T YOU GO THROW YOURSELF ON THE FLOOR, FUSSBUDGET?
EVER SEEN A BASKETBALL, BEFORE, LINUS?
BASKETBALL IS A GREAT GAME, I TELL YOU! A PERFECT COMBINATION OF SPEED AND SKILL, AND...
!
BUMPETY
BUMP
BUMP
Bumpety
BUMPETY
BUMPETY
bumpety
BUMPETY
BUMPETY
BUMP
BOMP
SWISH!
THUMP
PLUNK!
3-27
THERE'S NOTHING MORE ANNOYING THAN A SMART-ALECKY KID!
SCHULZ

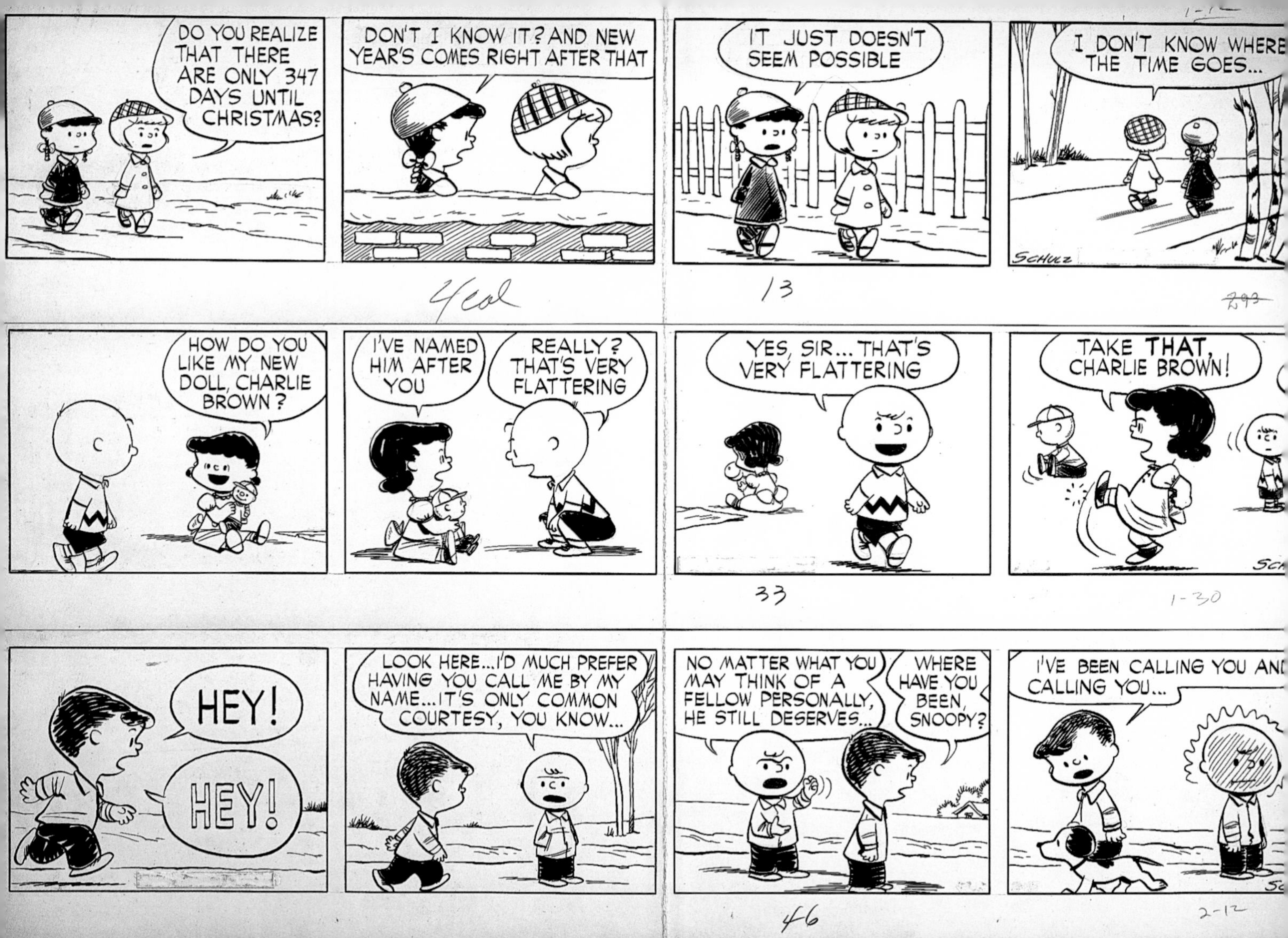
DO YOU REALIZE THAT THERE ARE ONLY 347 DAYS UNTIL CHRISTMAS?
DON'T I KNOW IT? AND NEW YEAR'S COMES RIGHT AFTER THAT
IT JUST DOESN'T SEEM POSSIBLE
I DON'T KNOW WHERE THE TIME GOES...
SCHULZ
HOW DO YOU LIKE MY NEW DOLL, CHARLIE BROWN?
I'VE NAMED HIM AFTER YOU
REALLY? THAT'S VERY FLATTERING
YES, SIR... THAT'S VERY FLATTERING
TAKE THAT, CHARLIE BROWN!
HEY!
HEY!
LOOK HERE...I'D MUCH PREFER HAVING YOU CALL ME BY MY NAME...IT'S ONLY COMMON COURTESY, YOU KNOW...
NO MATTER WHAT YOU MAY THINK OF A FELLOW PERSONALLY, HE STILL DESERVES...
WHERE HAVE YOU BEEN, SNOOPY?
I'VE BEEN CALLING YOU AND CALLING YOU...

Though it was first and foremost a newspaper strip, the popularity of *Peanuts* made its appearance in comic books inevitable. In 1952, *Peanuts* strips began appearing in such titles as *Tip Top Comics* and *United Comics*, comic books published by United Feature featuring its properties. The only time Schulz ever relinquished creating comics that featured his characters was for Dell and Gold Key comic books in the late 1950s and early 1960s, "Because it gave me a chance to have a couple of

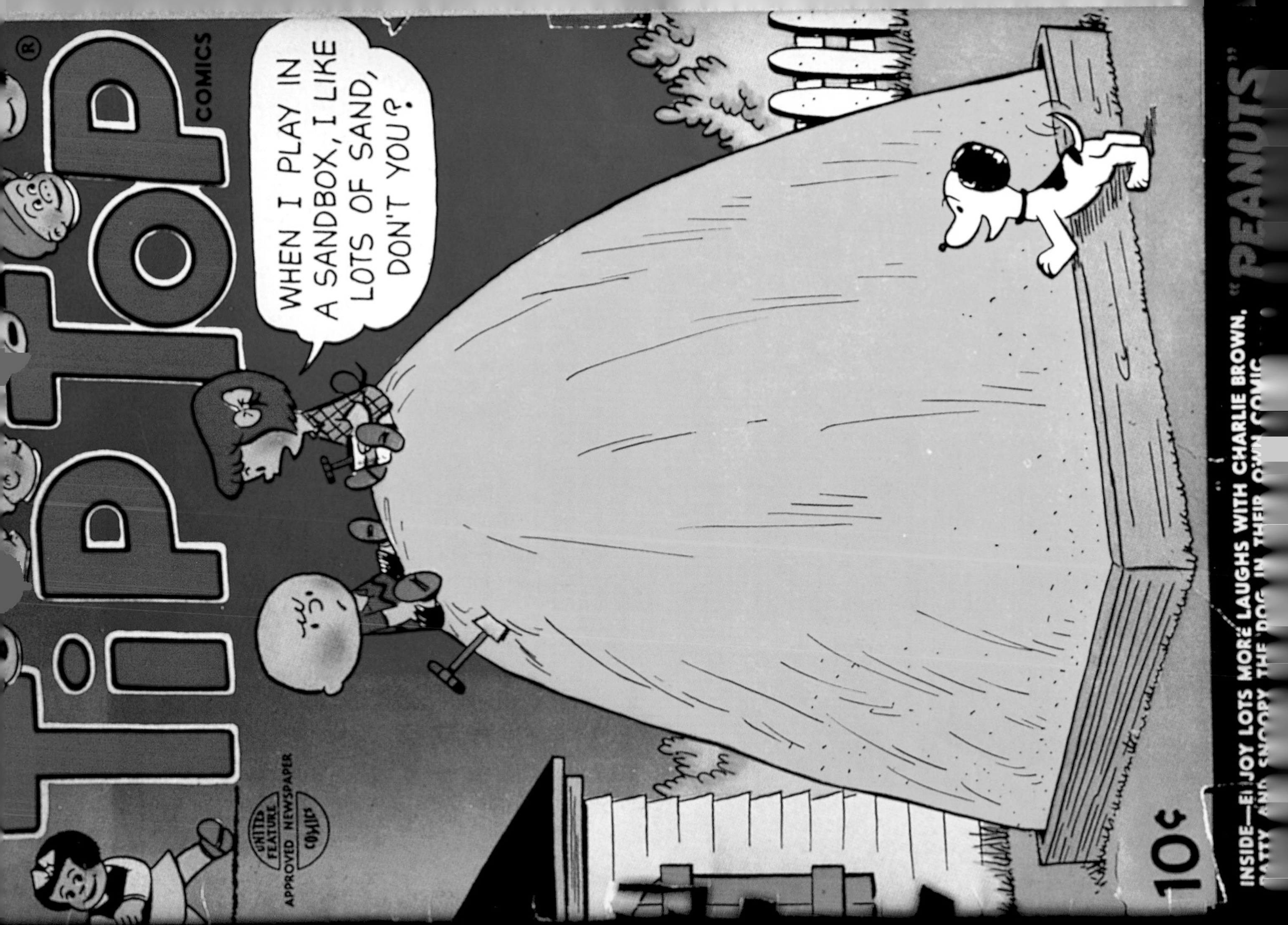
TIP TOP COMICS
WHEN I PLAY IN A SANDBOX, I LIKE LOTS OF SAND, DON'T YOU?
UNITED FEATURE COMICS
APPROVED NEWSPAPER
10¢
INSIDE—ENJOY LOTS MORE LAUGHS WITH CHARLIE BROWN,
"PEANUTS"

friends do something." he said, in 1997. Namely Jim Sasseville and Dale Hale, two friends from Art Instruction that Schulz had brought with him to California. Schulz was adamant that he never used assistants on the strip, and considered the comic book stories to be completely separate from it. The real re-print life of *Peanuts* was not to be comics, but paperback books. First published in 1952 by Rinehart and Co., to date there are over an astonishing 200 million *Peanuts* strip collections in print.

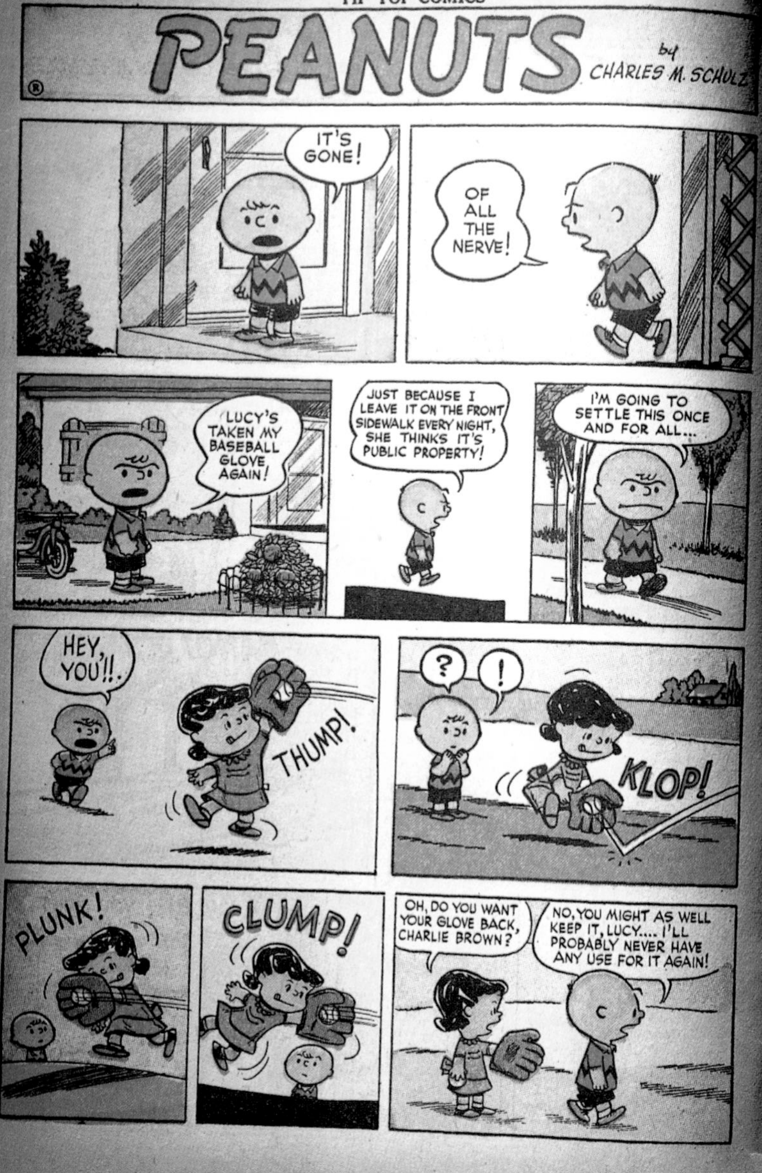
PEANUTS
by CHARLES M. SCHULZ
IT'S GONE!
OF ALL THE NERVE!
LUCY'S TAKEN MY BASEBALL GLOVE AGAIN!
JUST BECAUSE I LEAVE IT ON THE FRONT SIDEWALK EVERY NIGHT, SHE THINKS IT'S PUBLIC PROPERTY!
I'M GOING TO SETTLE THIS ONCE AND FOR ALL...
HEY, YOU!!
THUMP!
?
!
KLOP!
PLUNK!
CLUMP!
OH, DO YOU WANT YOUR GLOVE BACK, CHARLIE BROWN?
NO, YOU MIGHT AS WELL KEEP IT, LUCY.... I'LL PROBABLY NEVER HAVE ANY USE FOR IT AGAIN!

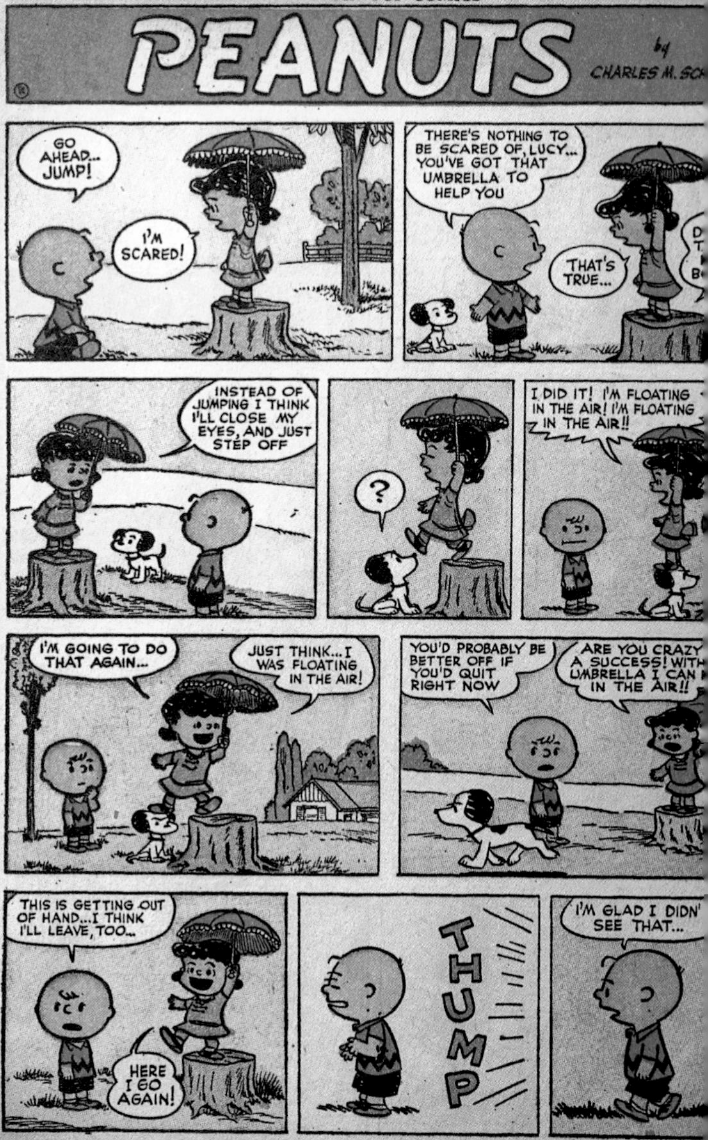
PEANUTS
by CHARLES M. SC
GO AHEAD... JUMP!
I'M SCARED!
THERE'S NOTHING TO BE SCARED OF, LUCY... YOU'VE GOT THAT UMBRELLA TO HELP YOU
THAT'S TRUE...
INSTEAD OF JUMPING I THINK I'LL CLOSE MY EYES, AND JUST STEP OFF
?
I DID IT! I'M FLOATING IN THE AIR! I'M FLOATING IN THE AIR!!
I'M GOING TO DO THAT AGAIN...
JUST THINK... I WAS FLOATING IN THE AIR!
YOU'D PROBABLY BE BETTER OFF IF YOU'D QUIT RIGHT NOW
ARE YOU CRAZY
A SUCCESS! WITH
UMBRELLA I CAN
IN THE AIR!!
THIS IS GETTING OUT OF HAND... I THINK I'LL LEAVE, TOO...
HERE I GO AGAIN!
THUMP
I'M GLAD I DIDN'
SEE THAT...

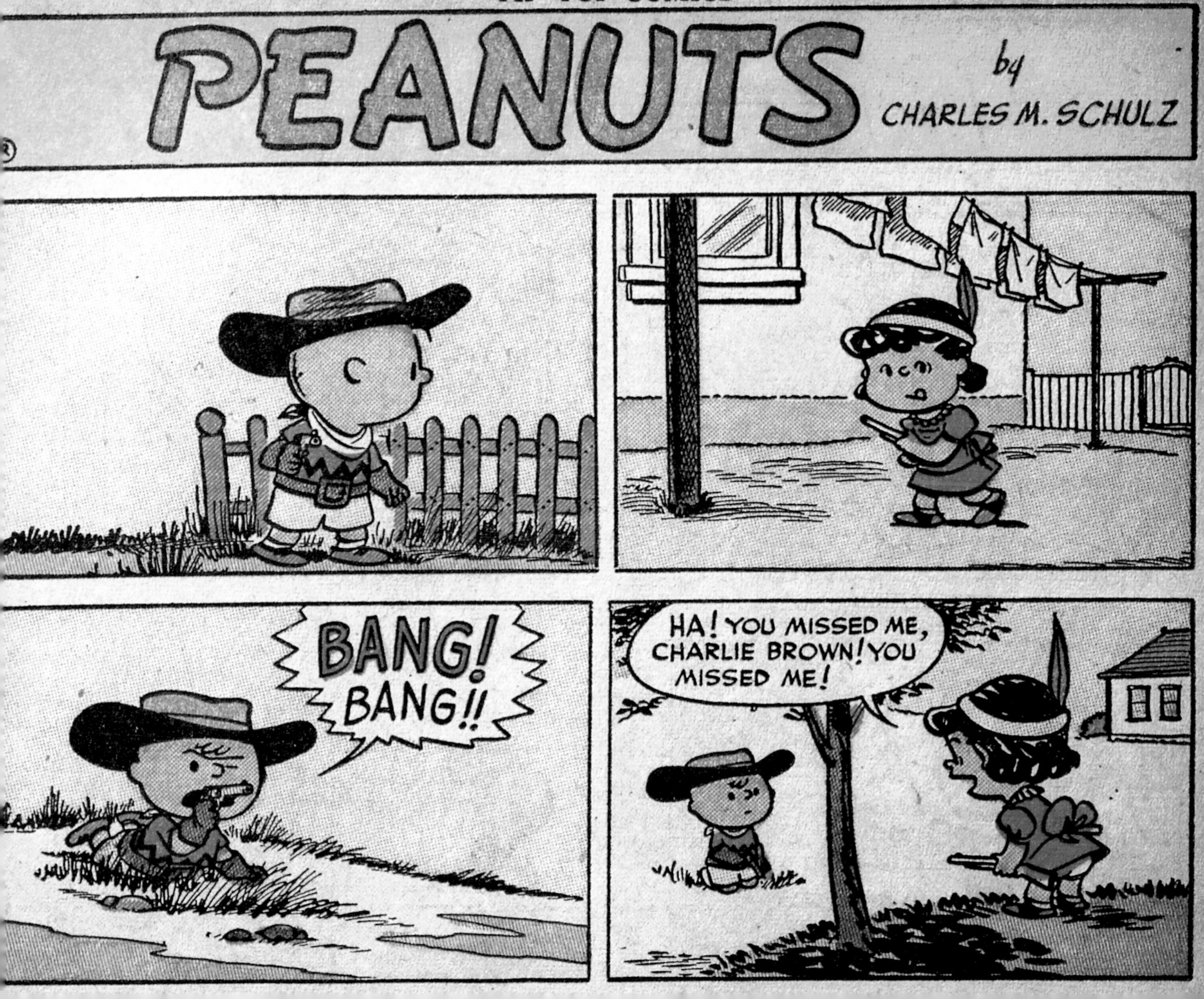
PEANUTS
by CHARLES M. SCHULZ
BANG! BANG!!
HA! YOU MISSED ME, CHARLIE BROWN! YOU MISSED ME!

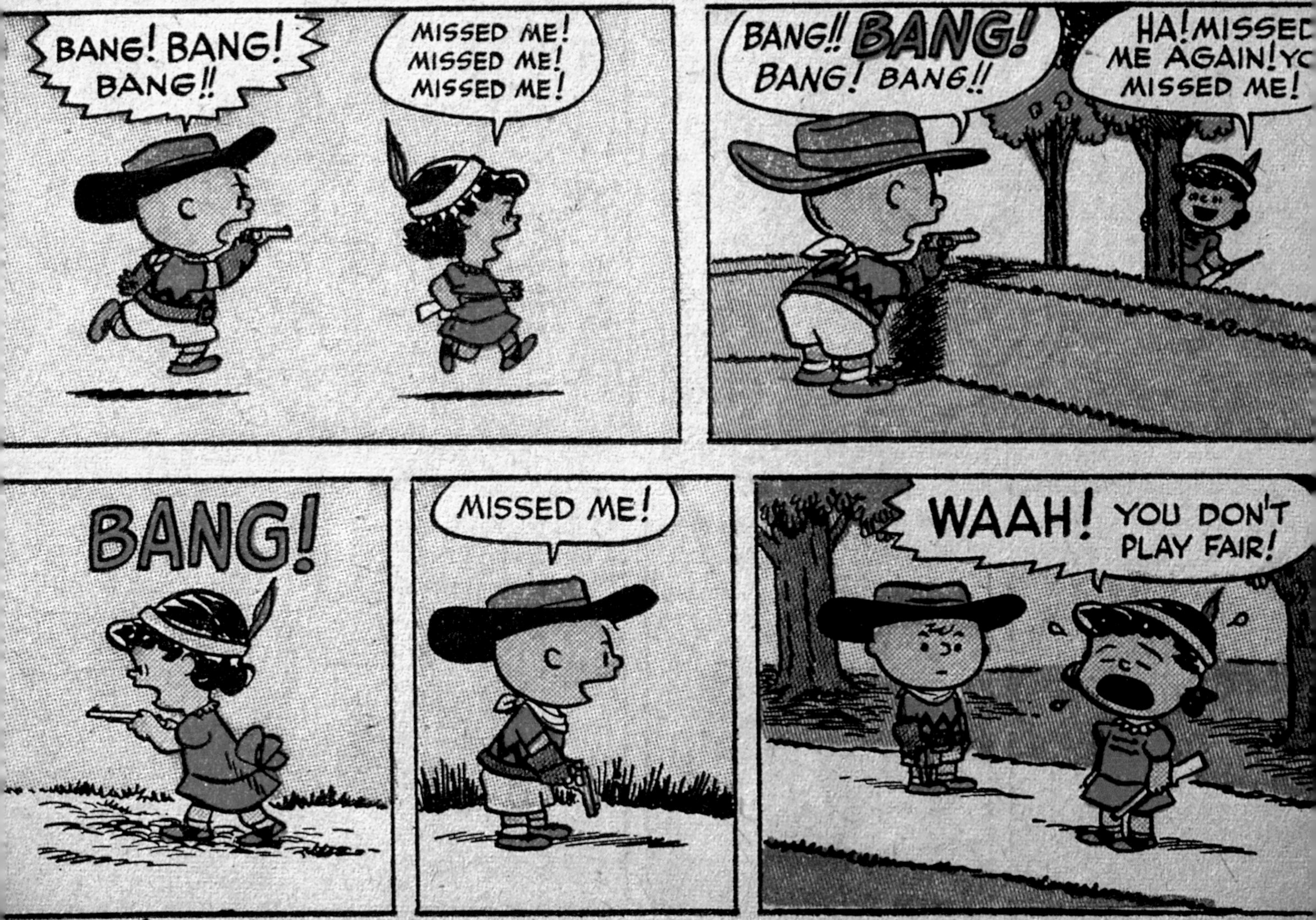

BANG! BANG! BANG!!
MISSED ME! MISSED ME! MISSED ME!
BANG!! BANG! BANG! BANG!!
HA! MISSED ME AGAIN! YO MISSED ME!
BANG!
MISSED ME!
WAAH! YOU DON'T PLAY FAIR!

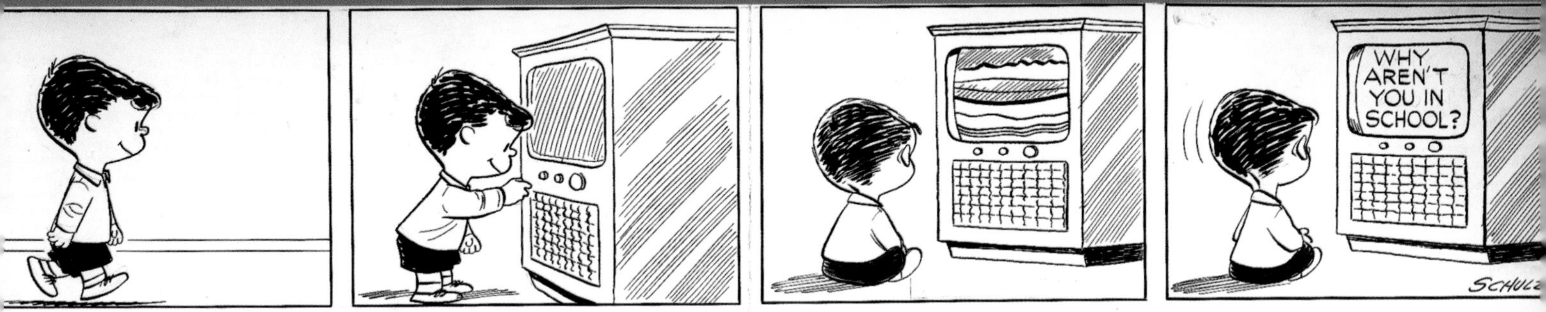
WHY AREN'T YOU IN SCHOOL?
SCHULZ

34 1-7

4 col 8 9-7

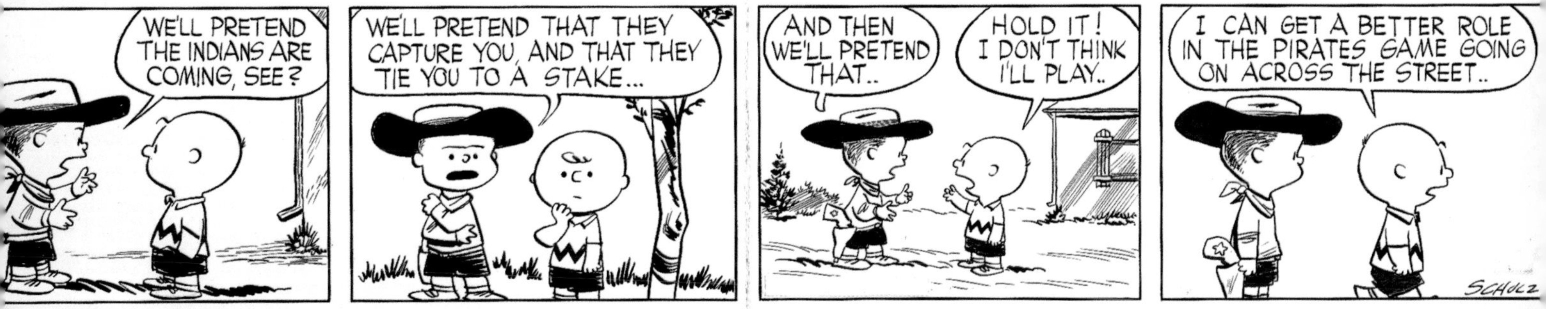
WE'LL PRETEND THE INDIANS ARE COMING, SEE?
WE'LL PRETEND THAT THEY CAPTURE YOU, AND THAT THEY TIE YOU TO A STAKE...
AND THEN WE'LL PRETEND THAT..
HOLD IT! I DON'T THINK I'LL PLAY..
I CAN GET A BETTER ROLE IN THE PIRATES GAME GOING ON ACROSS THE STREET..
SCHULZ

160 28

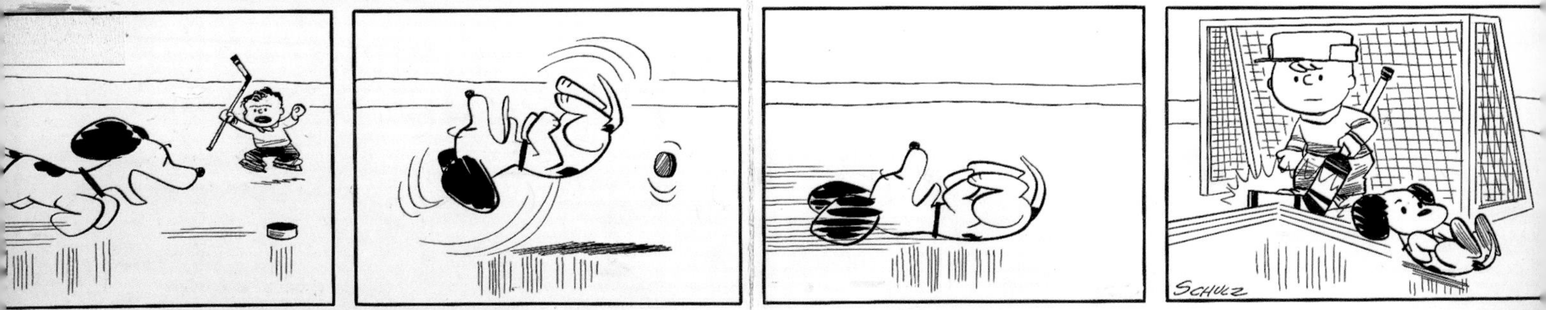
SCHULZ

27 1-28

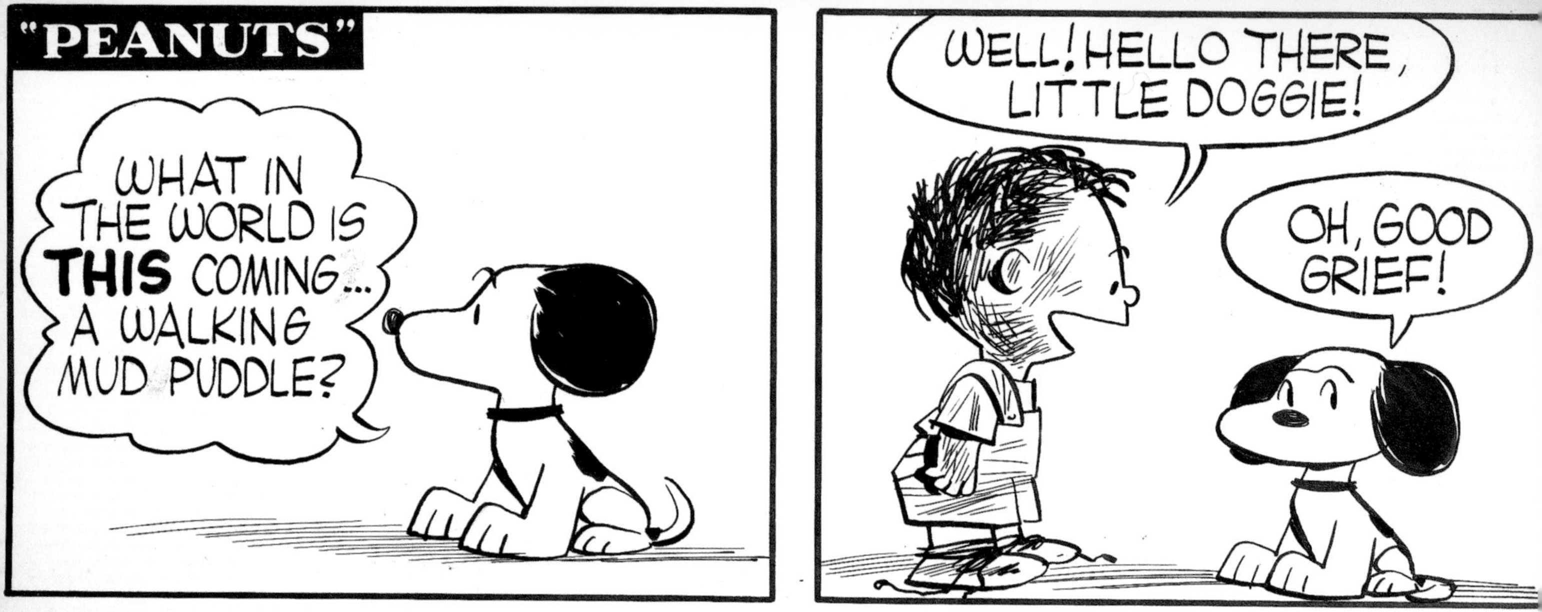
"PEANUTS"
WHAT IN THE WORLD IS **THIS** COMING... A WALKING MUD PUDDLE?
WELL! HELLO THERE, LITTLE DOGGIE!
OH, GOOD GRIEF!

The fact that Snoopy seems to be "speaking" here, rather than "thinking" in a thought balloon, is most likely just an oversight.

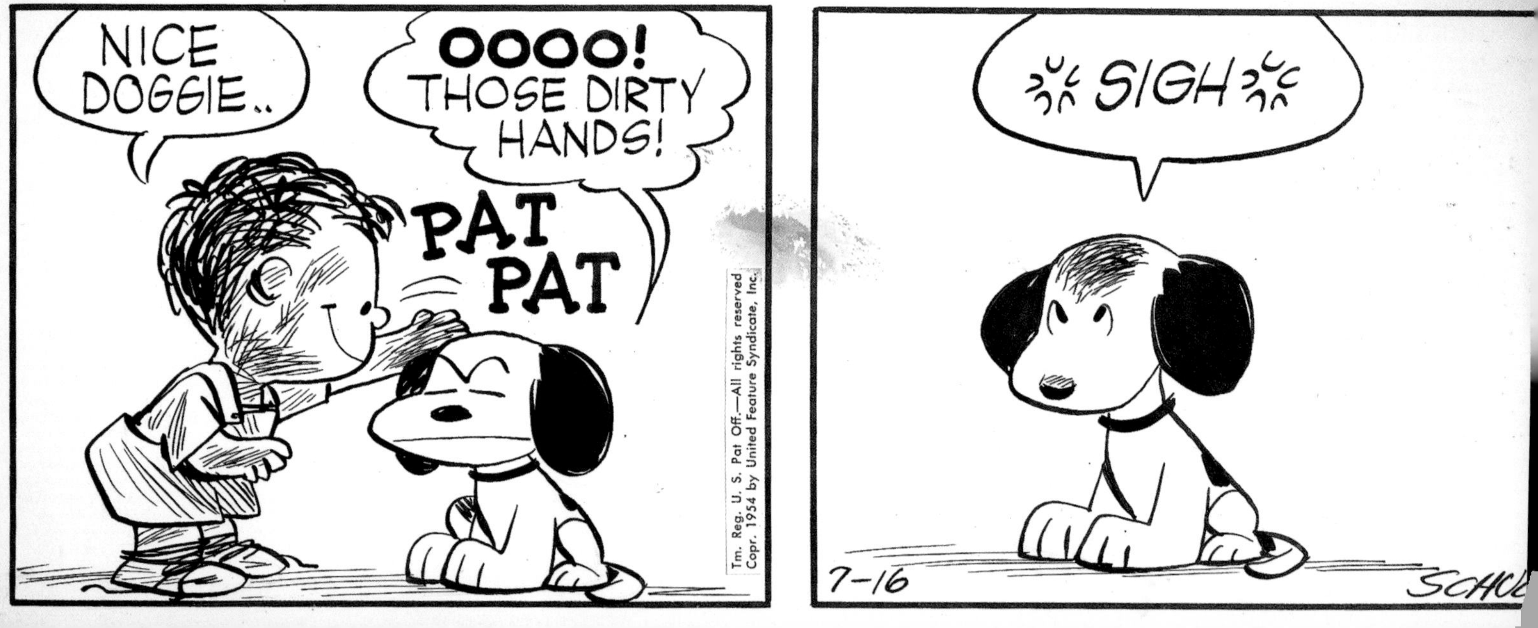
NICE DOGGIE..
OOOO! THOSE DIRTY HANDS!
PAT
PAT
Tm. Reg. U. S. Pat Off.—All rights reserved
Copr. 1954 by United Feature Syndicate, Inc.
SIGH
7-16

When asked in an interview in 1977 if he ever created a character who became more popular than he would have liked, Schulz surprisingly answered Pig-Pen. "Everybody kind of likes Pig-Pen. I don't like to draw him. He's only useful if you have him involved in dust and being dirty. I don't have many ideas on that; I ran out of them. People are always asking 'Why don't you draw Pig-Pen?' "

Introduced in July of 1954, Pig-Pen was a kind of vaudevillian figure who existed solely to become filthy. Somehow, a lot of people related to that—like the sensation of a pebble caught in your shoe feeling like a boulder.

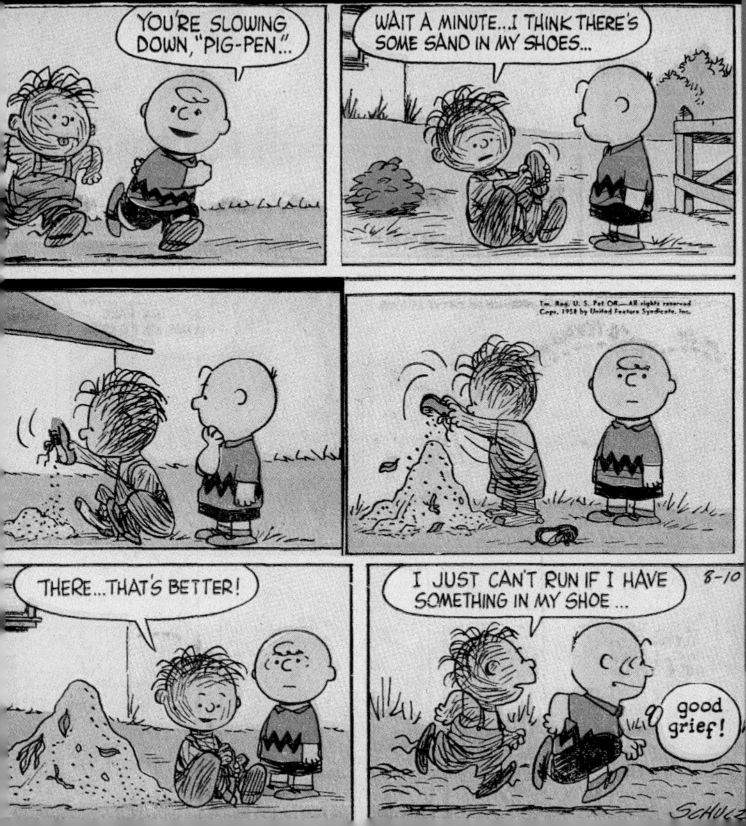
YOU'RE SLOWING DOWN, "PIG-PEN"...
WAIT A MINUTE...I THINK THERE'S SOME SAND IN MY SHOES...
Tm. Reg. U. S. Pat. Off.—All rights reserved Copr. 1958 by United Feature Syndicate, Inc.
THERE...THAT'S BETTER!
I JUST CAN'T RUN IF I HAVE SOMETHING IN MY SHOE...
8-10
good grief!
SCHULZ

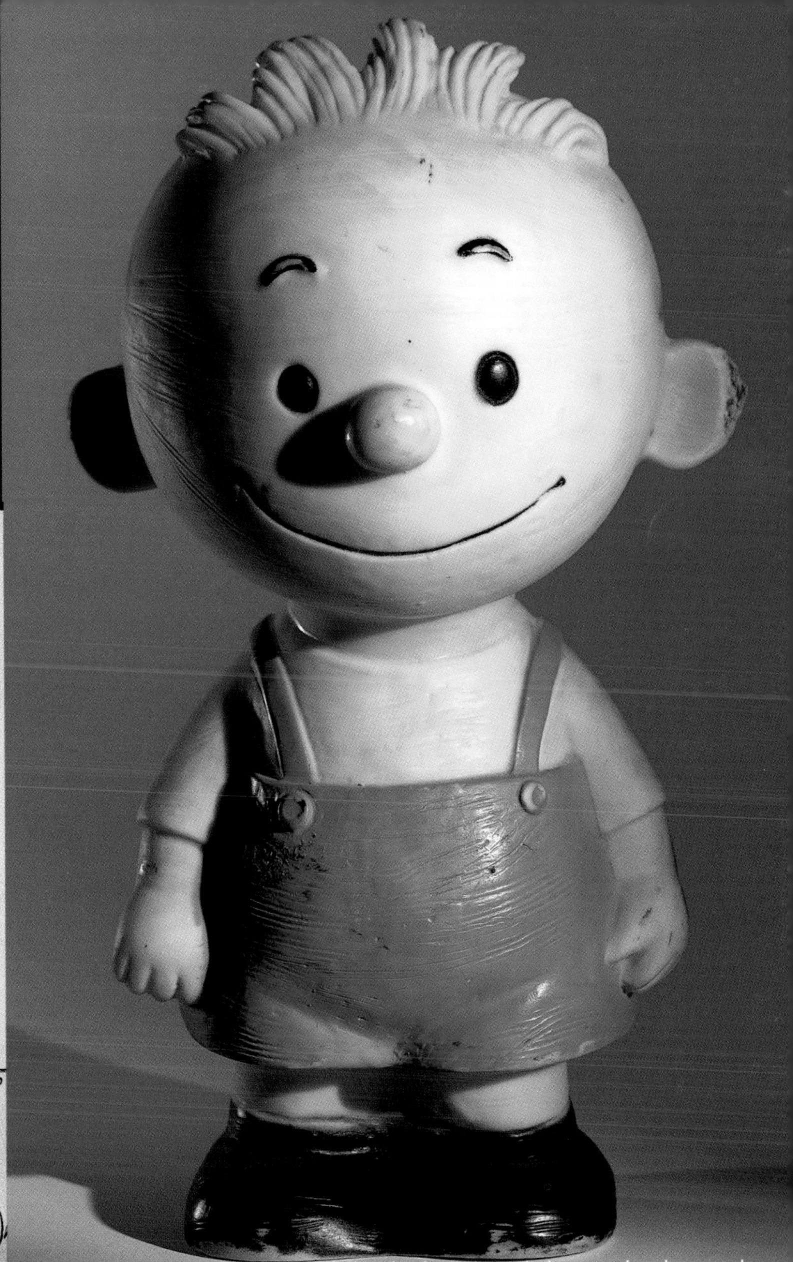

This 1958 Hungerford Pig-Pen doll arrived on store shelves, curiously enough, clean as a whistle—probably a marketing decision.

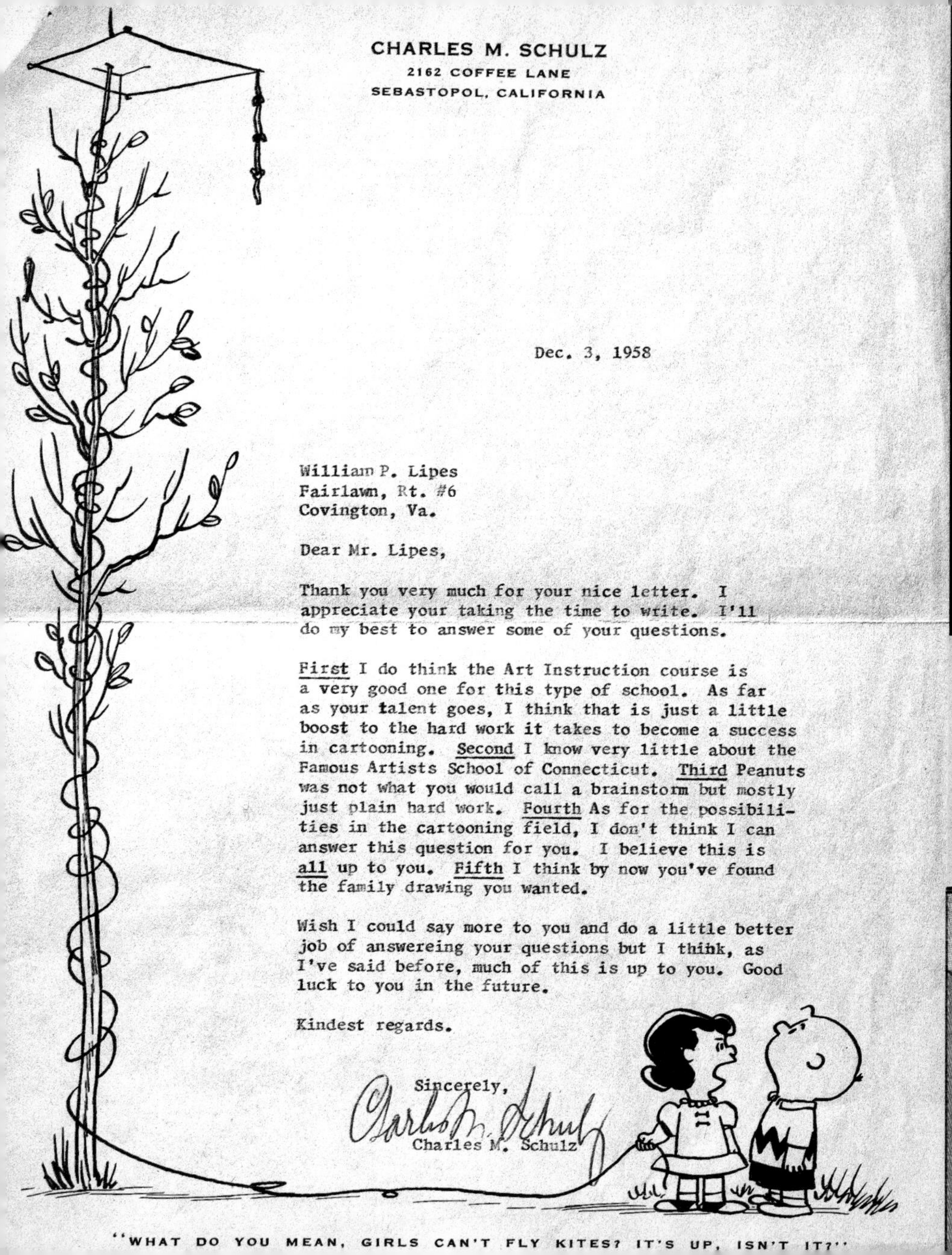

CHARLES M. SCHULZ
2162 COFFEE LANE
SEBASTOPOL, CALIFORNIA

Dec. 3, 1958

William P. Lipes
Fairlawn, Rt. #6
Covington, Va.

Dear Mr. Lipes,

Thank you very much for your nice letter. I appreciate your taking the time to write. I'll do my best to answer some of your questions.

First I do think the Art Instruction course is a very good one for this type of school. As far as your talent goes, I think that is just a little boost to the hard work it takes to become a success in cartooning. Second I know very little about the Famous Artists School of Connecticut. Third Peanuts was not what you would call a brainstorm but mostly just plain hard work. Fourth As for the possibilities in the cartooning field, I don't think I can answer this question for you. I believe this is all up to you. Fifth I think by now you've found the family drawing you wanted.

Wish I could say more to you and do a little better job of answereing your questions but I think, as I've said before, much of this is up to you. Good luck to you in the future.

Kindest regards.

Sincerely,

Charles M. Schulz

''WHAT DO YOU MEAN, GIRLS CAN'T FLY KITES? IT'S UP, ISN'T IT?''

Left: Schulz encourages a fan, on stationery that features the Kite Eating Tree, one of Charlie Brown's greatest nemeses.

Opposite: Schulz did not draw this comic book story, from *Tip Top Comics*, 1958. Note how oddly wrong it feels to have what is usually contained in four or six panels go on for pages. Also, it shows just how deceptively simple Schulz's style is and yet impossible to copy.

Below: It simply isn't meant to be. Charlie Brown finally gets his kite to fly and the sheer impossibility of it causes spontaneous combustion. 1958.

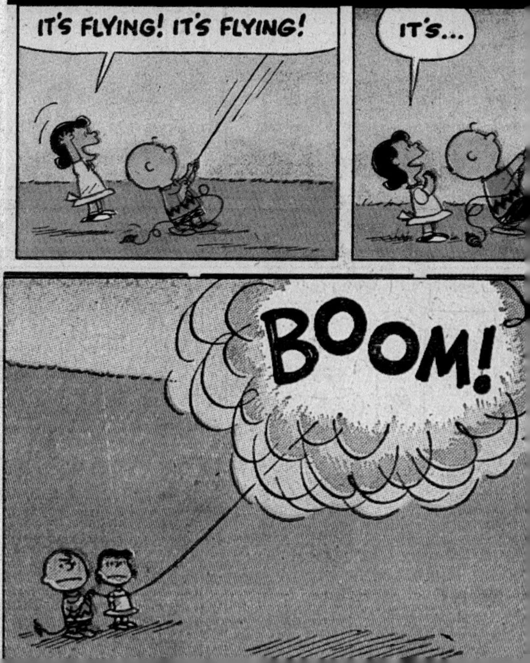
IT'S FLYING! IT'S FLYING!
IT'S...
BOOM!

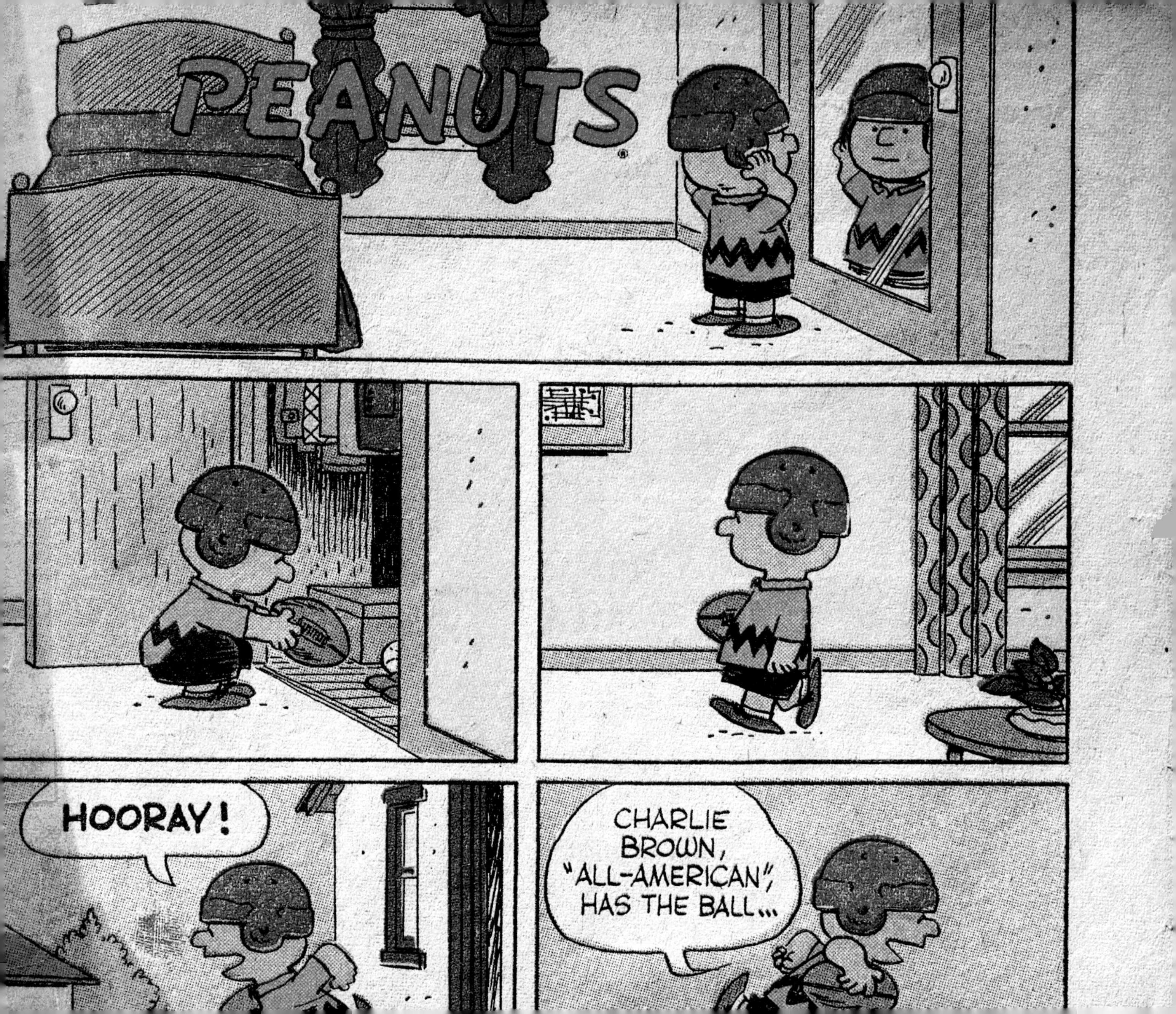
PEANUTS
HOORAY!
CHARLIE BROWN, "ALL-AMERICAN", HAS THE BALL...

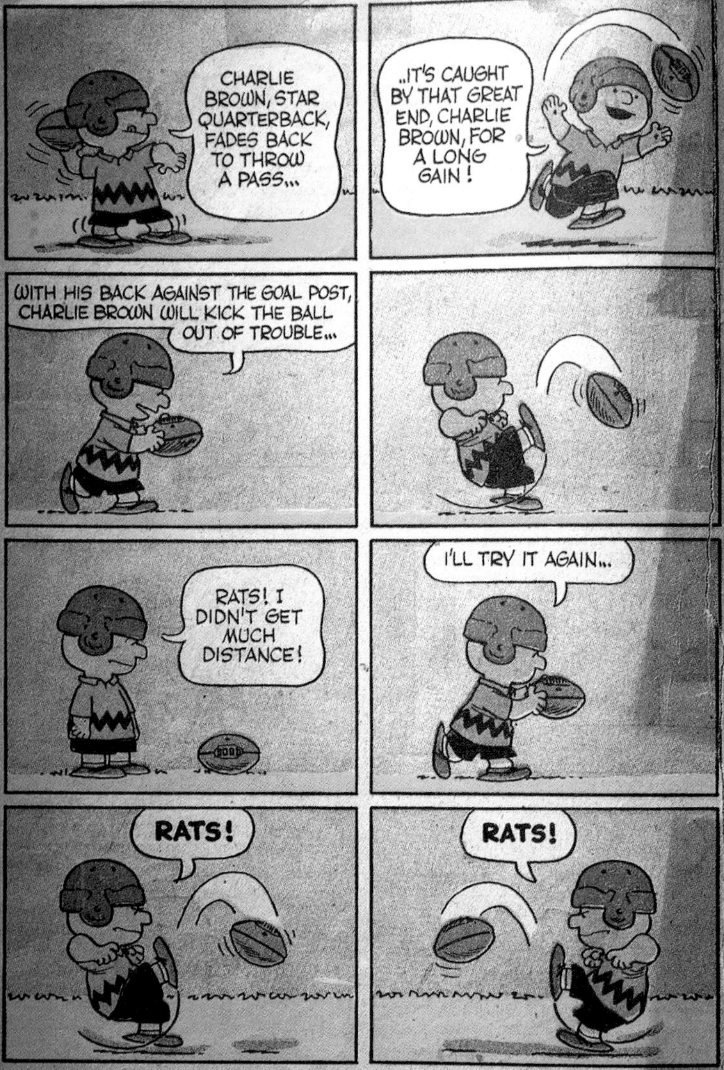
CHARLIE BROWN, STAR QUARTERBACK, FADES BACK TO THROW A PASS...
..IT'S CAUGHT BY THAT GREAT END, CHARLIE BROWN, FOR A LONG GAIN!
WITH HIS BACK AGAINST THE GOAL POST, CHARLIE BROWN WILL KICK THE BALL OUT OF TROUBLE...
RATS! I DIDN'T GET MUCH DISTANCE!
I'LL TRY IT AGAIN...
RATS!
RATS!

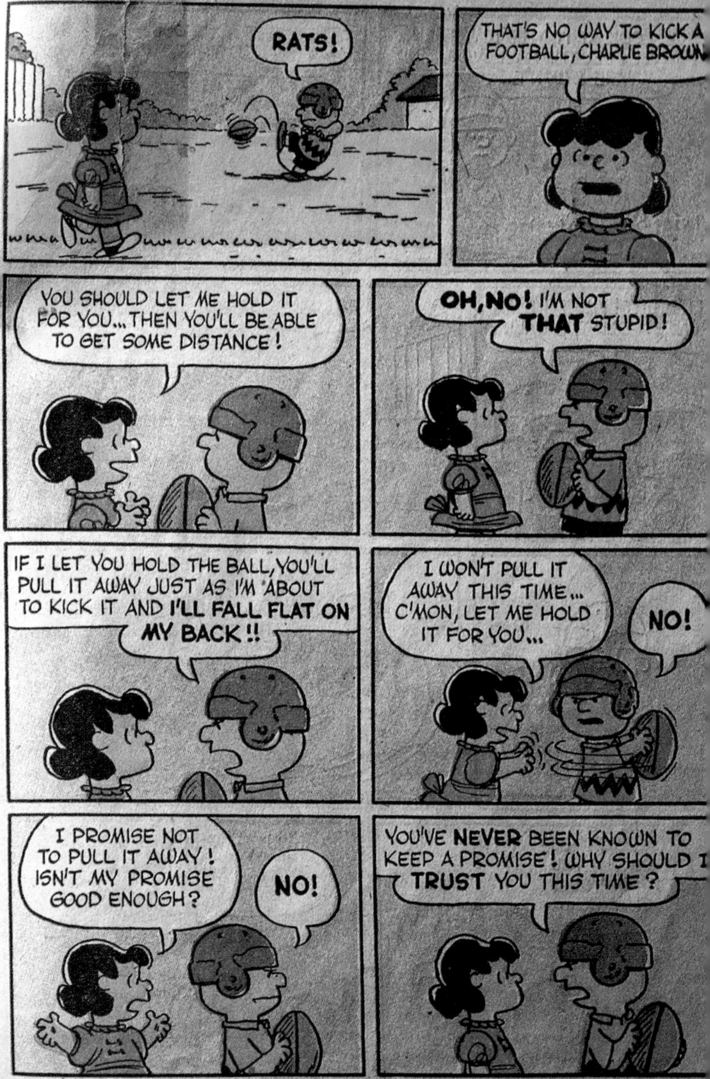
RATS!
THAT'S NO WAY TO KICK A FOOTBALL, CHARLIE BROWN
YOU SHOULD LET ME HOLD IT FOR YOU... THEN YOU'LL BE ABLE TO GET SOME DISTANCE!
OH, NO! I'M NOT THAT STUPID!
IF I LET YOU HOLD THE BALL, YOU'LL PULL IT AWAY JUST AS I'M ABOUT TO KICK IT AND I'LL FALL FLAT ON MY BACK!!
I WON'T PULL IT AWAY THIS TIME... C'MON, LET ME HOLD IT FOR YOU...
NO!
I PROMISE NOT TO PULL IT AWAY! ISN'T MY PROMISE GOOD ENOUGH?
NO!
YOU'VE NEVER BEEN KNOWN TO KEEP A PROMISE! WHY SHOULD I TRUST YOU THIS TIME?

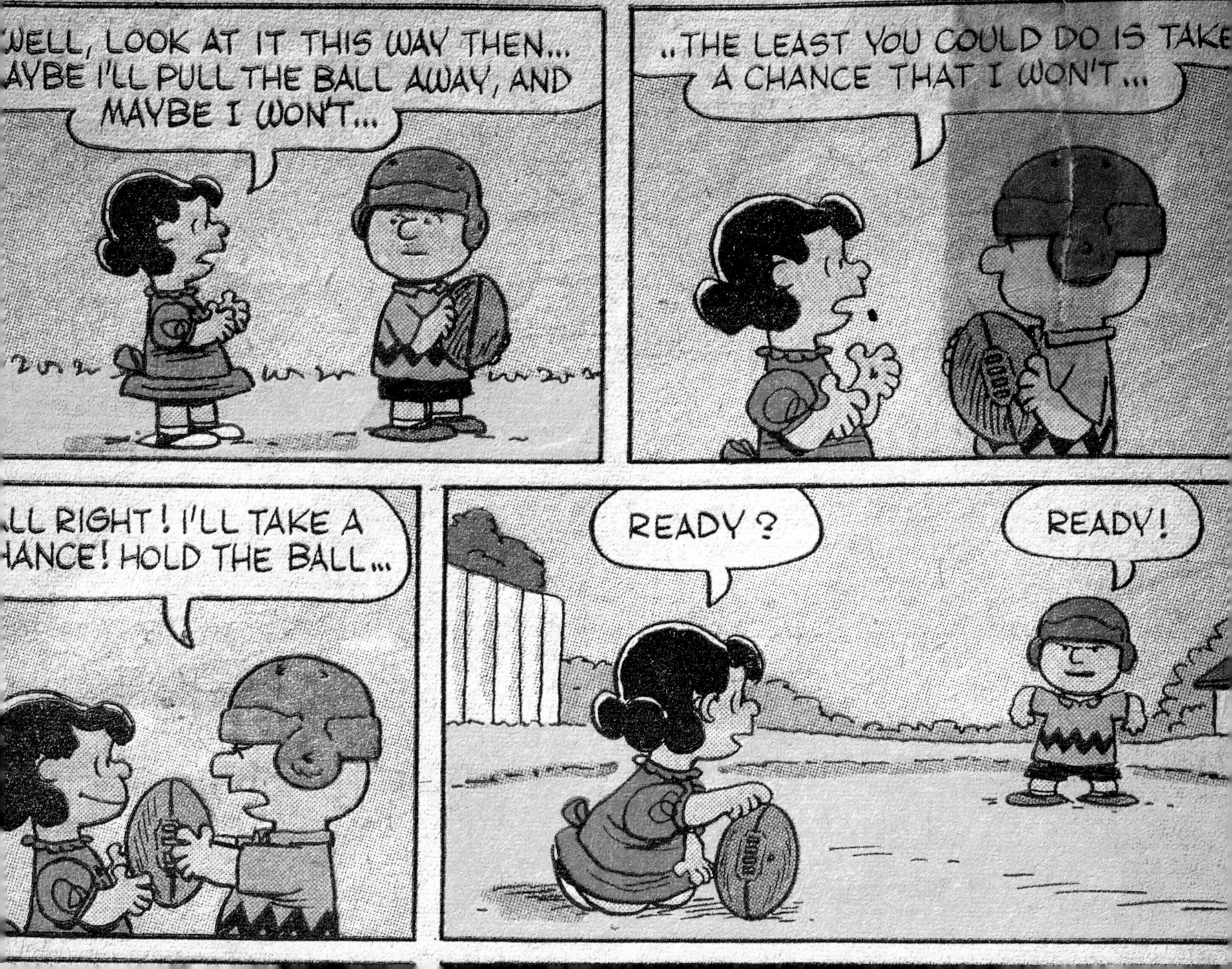

WELL, LOOK AT IT THIS WAY THEN... AYBE I'LL PULL THE BALL AWAY, AND MAYBE I WON'T...
..THE LEAST YOU COULD DO IS TAKE A CHANCE THAT I WON'T...
LL RIGHT! I'LL TAKE A HANCE! HOLD THE BALL...
READY?
READY!

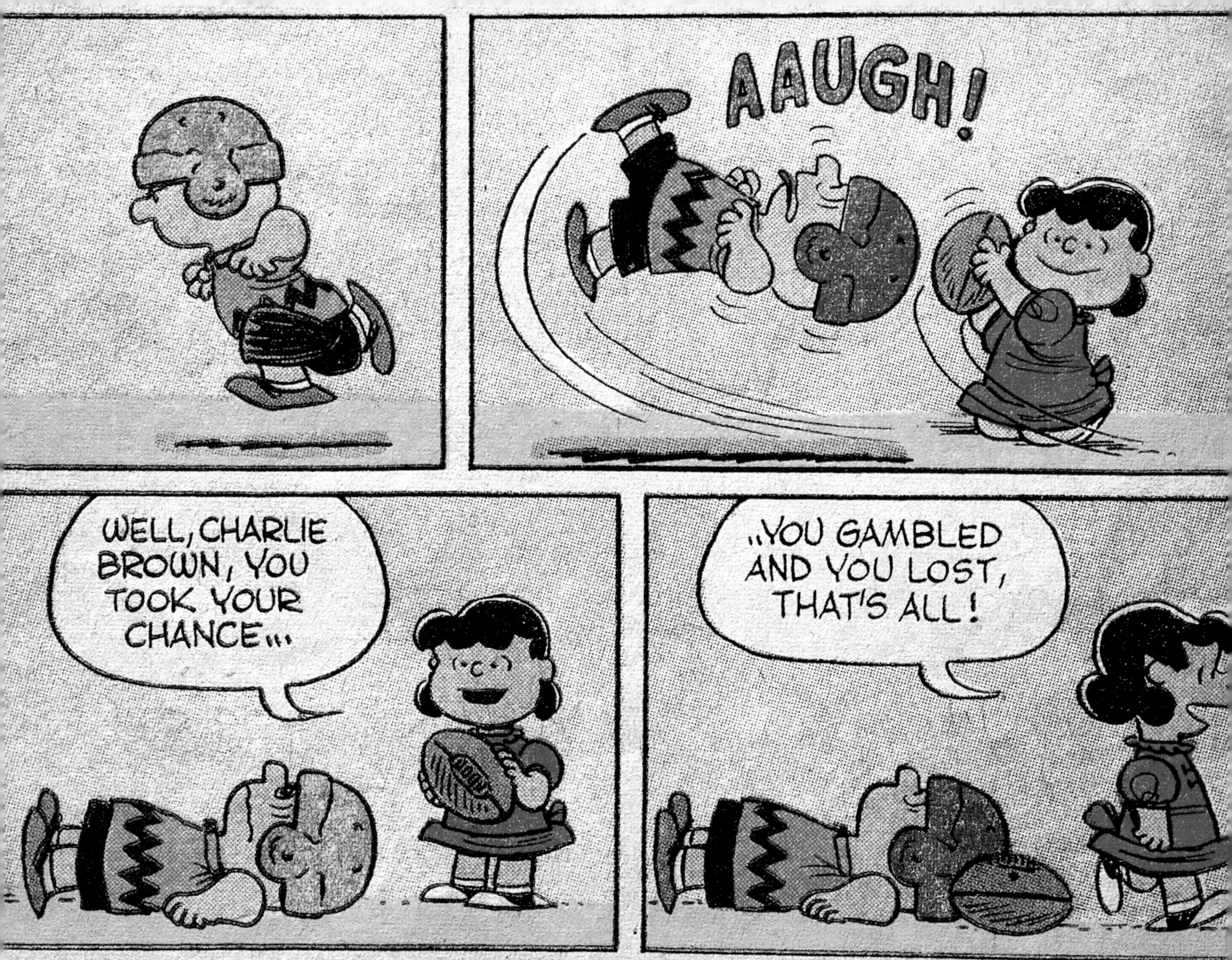
AAUGH!
WELL, CHARLIE BROWN, YOU TOOK YOUR CHANCE...
..YOU GAMBLED AND YOU LOST, THAT'S ALL!

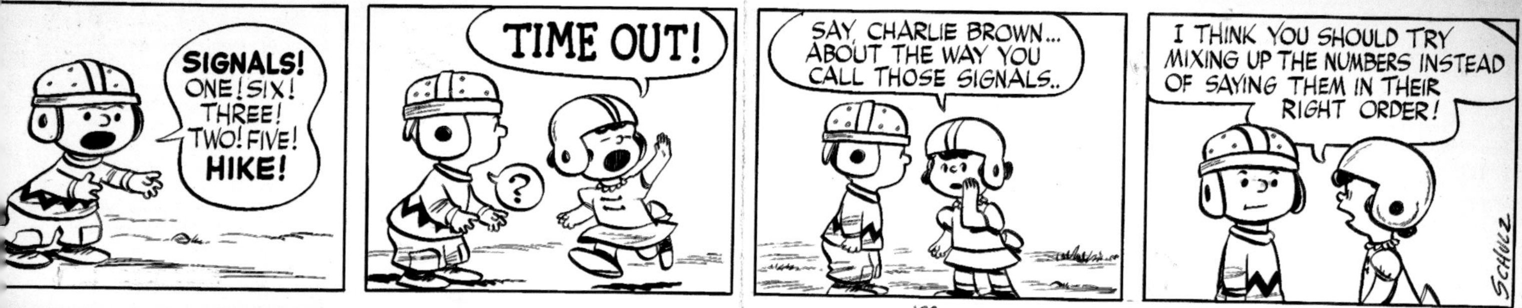
SIGNALS! ONE! SIX! THREE! TWO! FIVE! HIKE!
TIME OUT!
?
SAY, CHARLIE BROWN... ABOUT THE WAY YOU CALL THOSE SIGNALS..
I THINK YOU SHOULD TRY MIXING UP THE NUMBERS INSTEAD OF SAYING THEM IN THEIR RIGHT ORDER!
SCHULZ

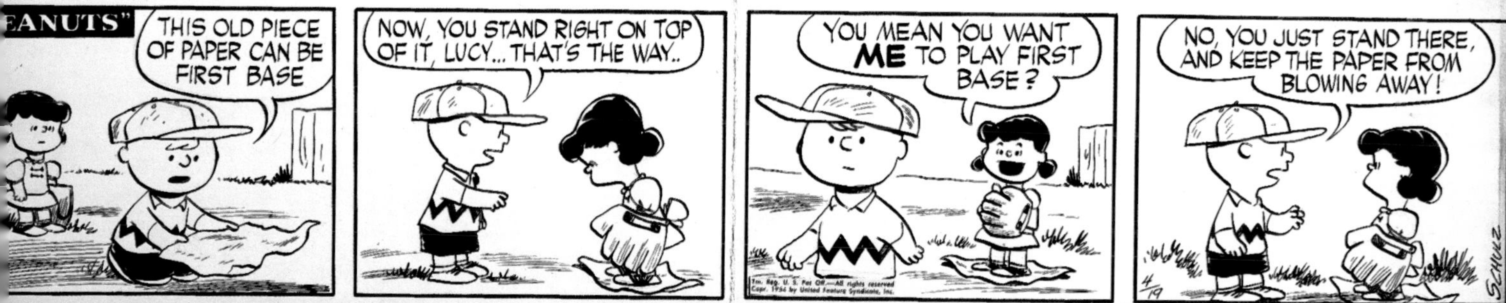
EANUTS"
THIS OLD PIECE OF PAPER CAN BE FIRST BASE
NOW, YOU STAND RIGHT ON TOP OF IT, LUCY... THAT'S THE WAY..
YOU MEAN YOU WANT ME TO PLAY FIRST BASE?
Tm. Reg. U. S. Pat. Off.—All rights reserved Copr. 1954 by United Feature Syndicate, Inc.
NO, YOU JUST STAND THERE, AND KEEP THE PAPER FROM BLOWING AWAY!
4/19
SCHULZ

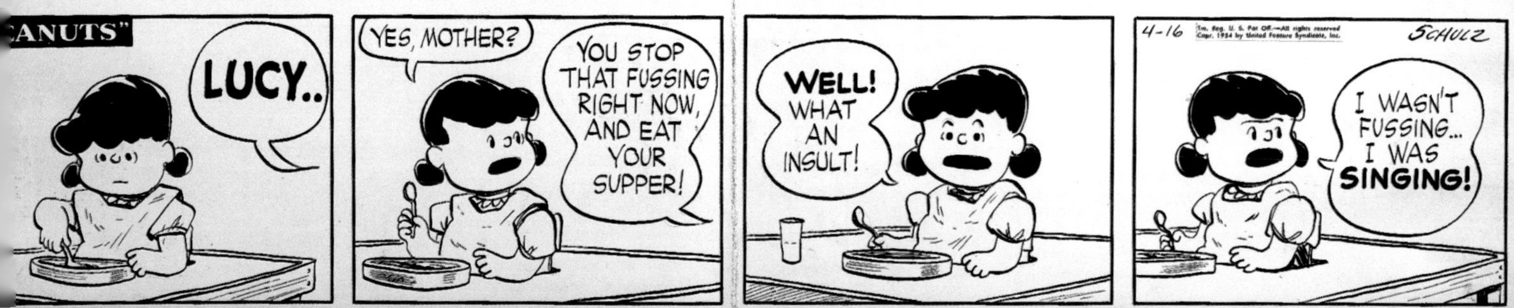
ANUTS"
LUCY..
YES, MOTHER?
YOU STOP THAT FUSSING RIGHT NOW, AND EAT YOUR SUPPER!
WELL! WHAT AN INSULT!
4-16
Tm. Reg. U. S. Pat. Off.—All rights reserved Copr. 1954 by United Feature Syndicate, Inc.
SCHULZ
I WASN'T FUSSING... I WAS SINGING!

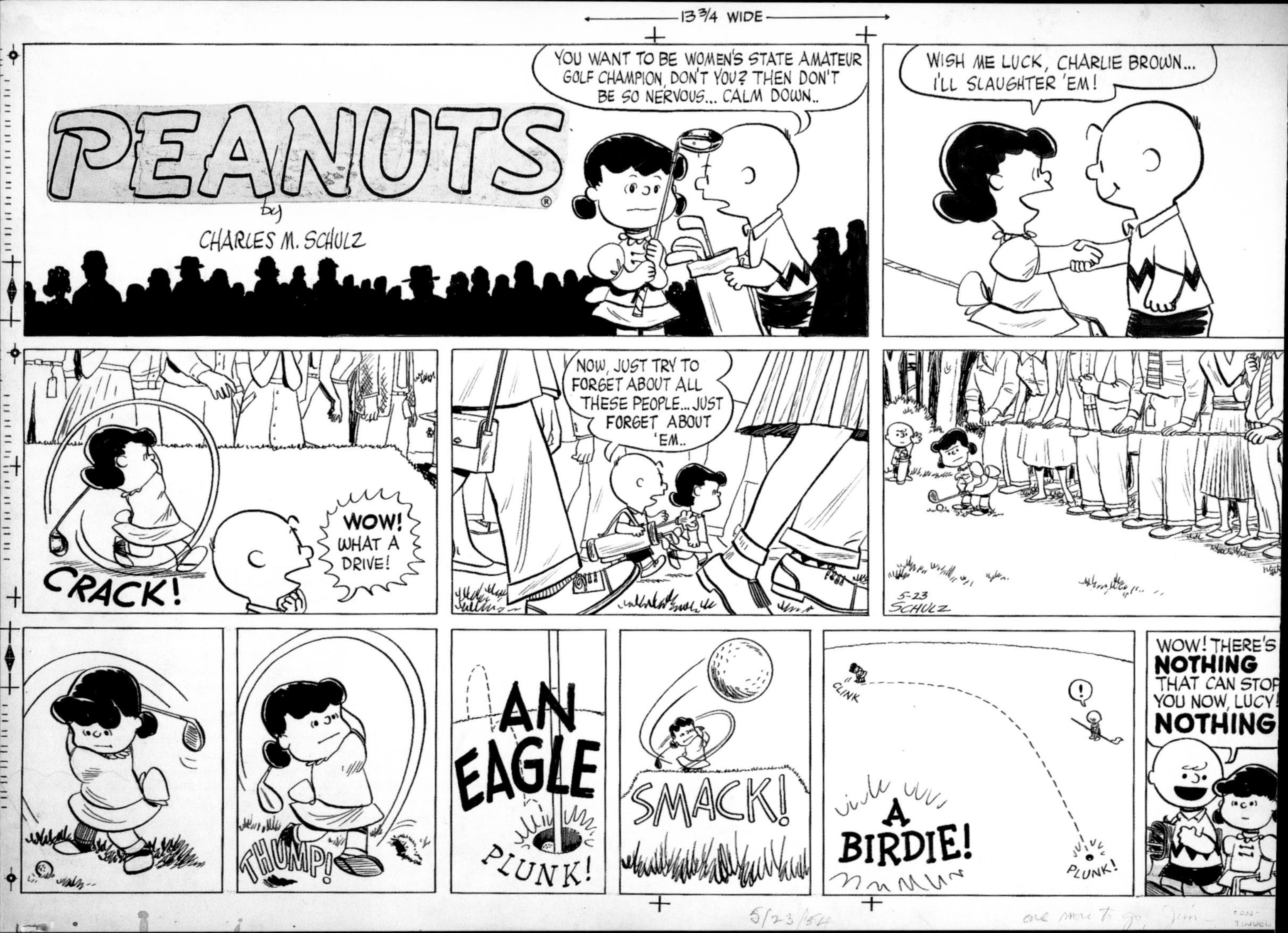
13 3/4 WIDE
PEANUTS
by CHARLES M. SCHULZ
YOU WANT TO BE WOMEN'S STATE AMATEUR GOLF CHAMPION, DON'T YOU? THEN DON'T BE SO NERVOUS... CALM DOWN..
WISH ME LUCK, CHARLIE BROWN... I'LL SLAUGHTER 'EM!
CRACK!
WOW! WHAT A DRIVE!
NOW, JUST TRY TO FORGET ABOUT ALL THESE PEOPLE... JUST FORGET ABOUT 'EM..
5-23 SCHULZ
THUMP!
AN EAGLE
PLUNK!
SMACK!
CLINK
!
A BIRDIE!
PLUNK!
WOW! THERE'S NOTHING THAT CAN STOP YOU NOW, LUCY! NOTHING
5/23/54

This Sunday strip from 1954 is reprinted here for the first time. Schulz apparently considered it a failed experiment and never had it collected in a book. It's one of a four-part series of Sunday strips featuring Charlie Brown and Lucy at a golf tournament with—gasp!—adults. Schulz took Charlie Brown's advice and chose to forget about them.

Opposite, top: Undated Art Instruction Inc. Christmas card from th mid-1950s, featuring the work of its star pupil and instructor.

Opposite, bottom: The use of repetition in this holiday strip from 195 heightens the sense of Linus's anxiety. In the end, threats will mak you remember *anything*.

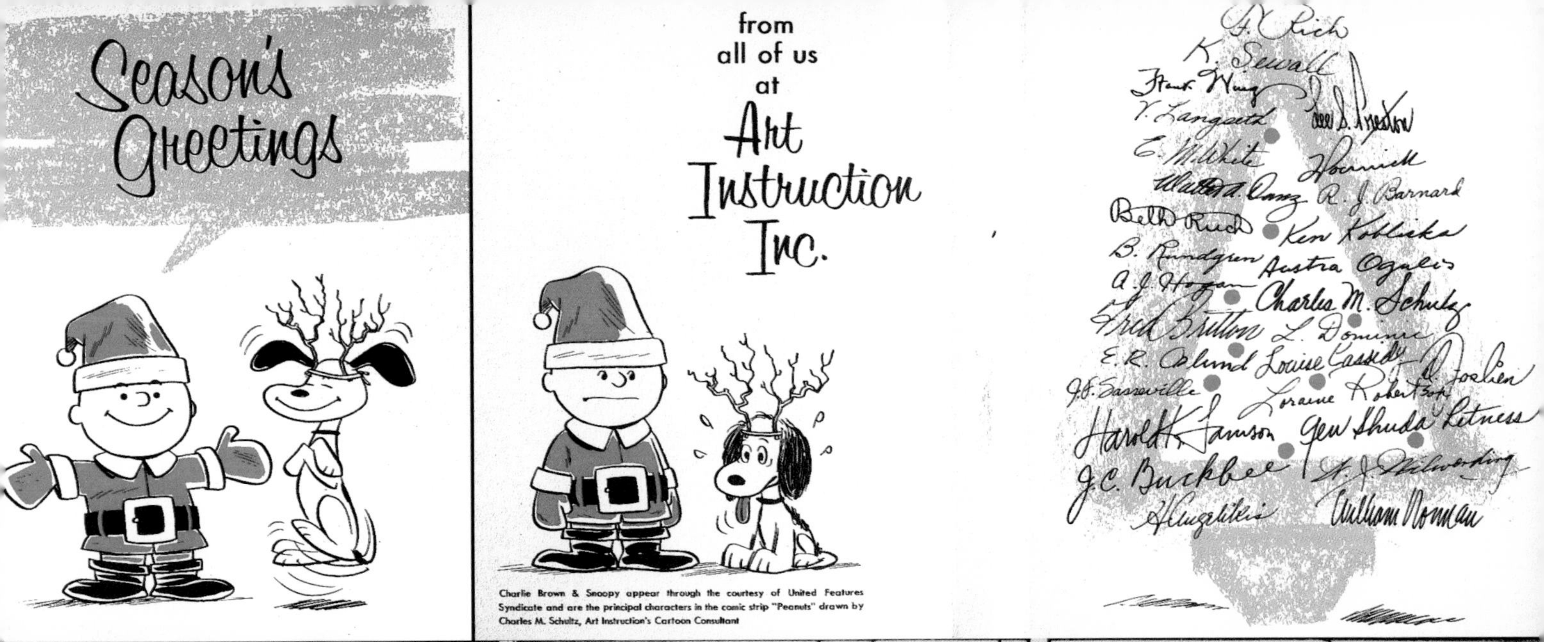
Season's Greetings
from all of us at Art Instruction Inc.
Charlie Brown & Snoopy appear through the courtesy of United Features Syndicate and are the principal characters in the comic strip "Peanuts" drawn by Charles M. Schultz, Art Instruction's Cartoon Consultant
Charles M. Schulz

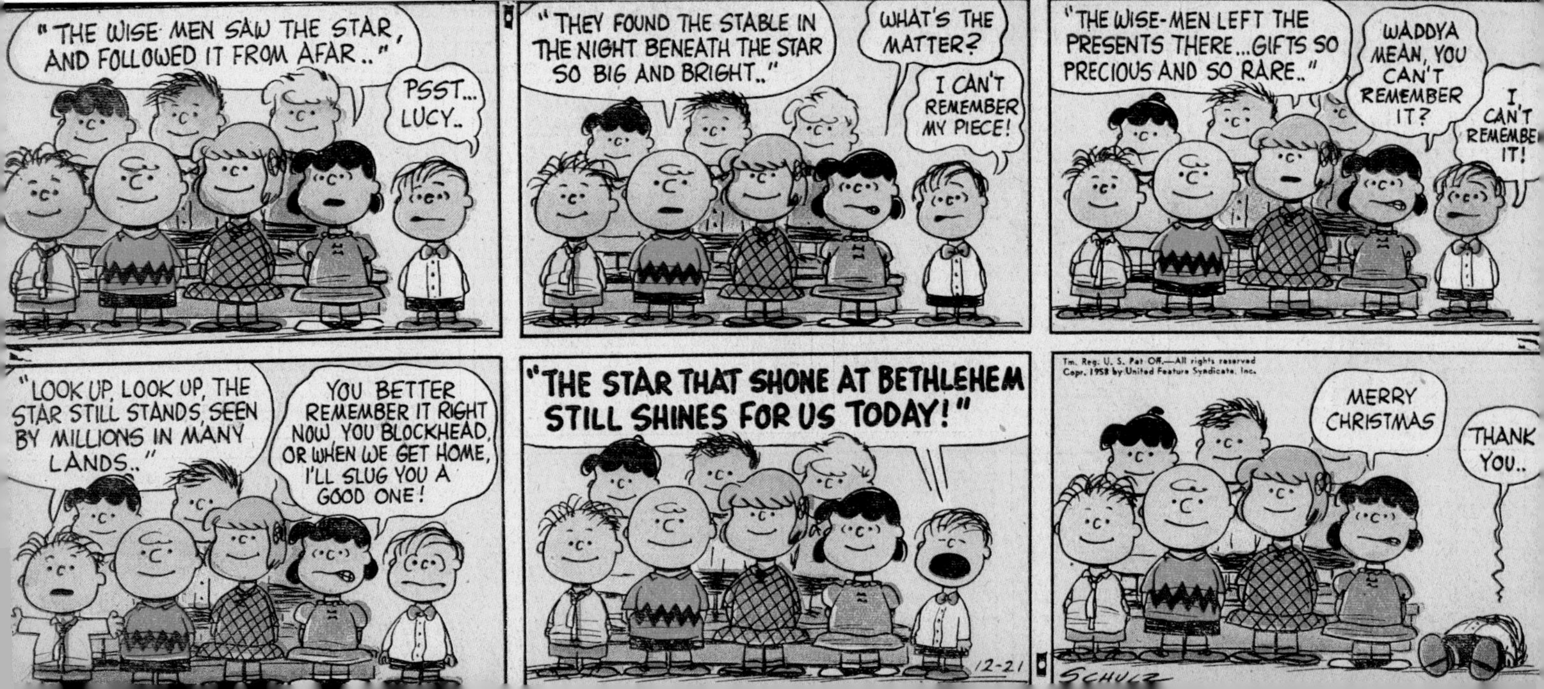
"THE WISE MEN SAW THE STAR, AND FOLLOWED IT FROM AFAR.."
PSST... LUCY..
"THEY FOUND THE STABLE IN THE NIGHT BENEATH THE STAR SO BIG AND BRIGHT.."
WHAT'S THE MATTER?
I CAN'T REMEMBER MY PIECE!
"THE WISE-MEN LEFT THE PRESENTS THERE...GIFTS SO PRECIOUS AND SO RARE.."
WADDYA MEAN, YOU CAN'T REMEMBER IT?
I CAN'T REMEMBE IT!
"LOOK UP, LOOK UP, THE STAR STILL STANDS, SEEN BY MILLIONS IN MANY LANDS.."
YOU BETTER REMEMBER IT RIGHT NOW YOU BLOCKHEAD, OR WHEN WE GET HOME, I'LL SLUG YOU A GOOD ONE!
"THE STAR THAT SHONE AT BETHLEHEM STILL SHINES FOR US TODAY!"
12-21
Tm. Reg. U. S. Pat Off.—All rights reserved
Copr. 1958 by United Feature Syndicate, Inc.
MERRY CHRISTMAS
THANK YOU..
SCHULZ

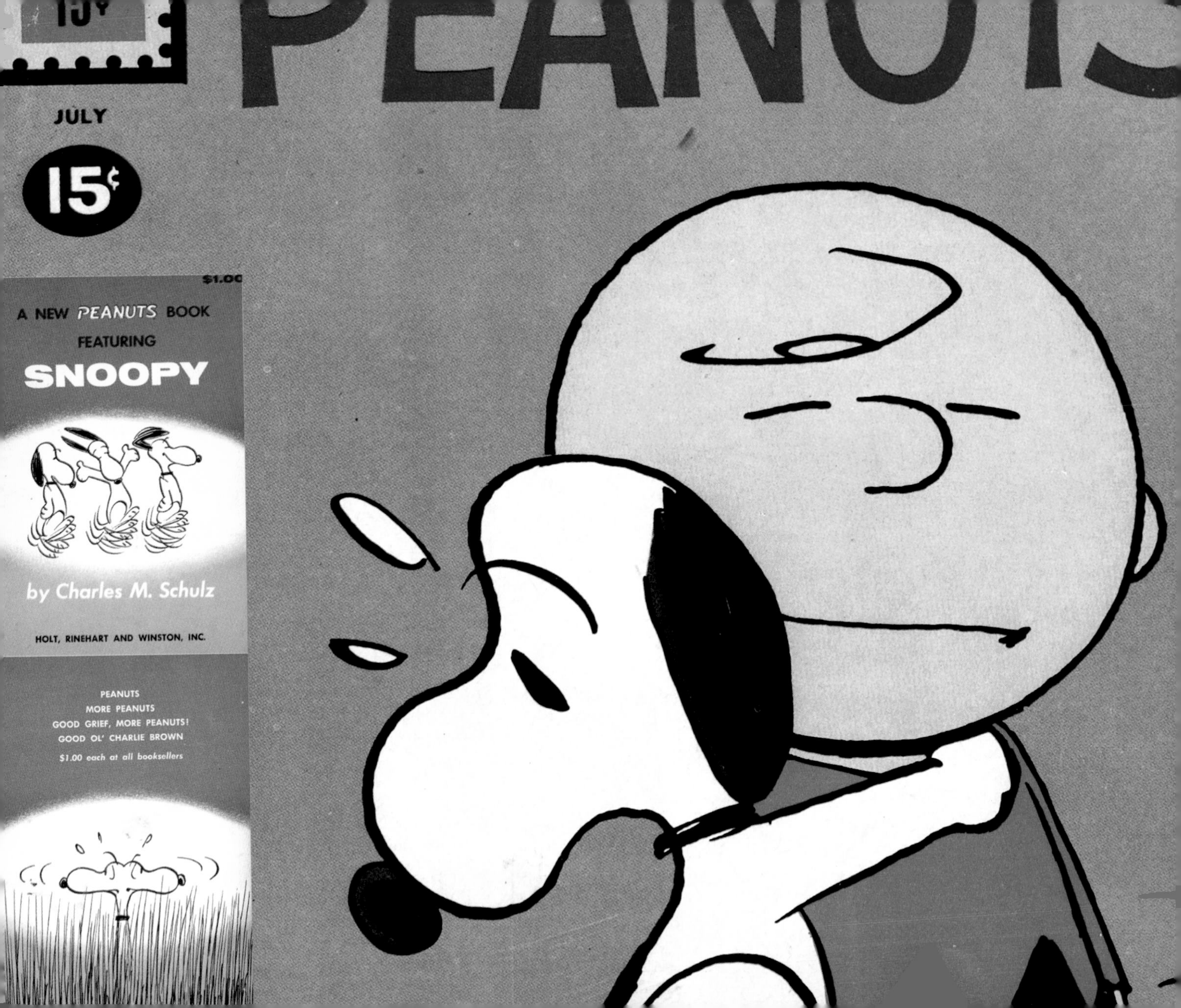
JULY
15¢
A NEW PEANUTS BOOK
FEATURING
SNOOPY
by Charles M. Schulz
HOLT, RINEHART AND WINSTON, INC.
PEANUTS
MORE PEANUTS
GOOD GRIEF, MORE PEANUTS!
GOOD OL' CHARLIE BROWN
$1.00 each at all booksellers

Opposite: Snoopy hangs onto Charlie Brown for dear life on this Dell Comics cover from 1961. Though he didn't do the stories inside, Schulz did draw all the covers.

Opposite, below left: One of the first of many books of collected strips issued by Rinehart.

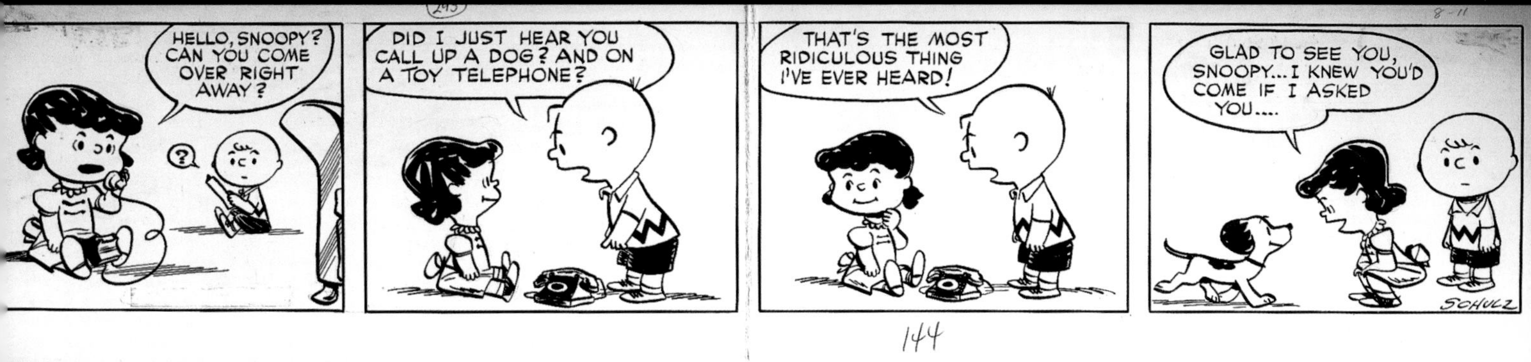
HELLO, SNOOPY? CAN YOU COME OVER RIGHT AWAY?
?
DID I JUST HEAR YOU CALL UP A DOG? AND ON A TOY TELEPHONE?
THAT'S THE MOST RIDICULOUS THING I'VE EVER HEARD!
GLAD TO SEE YOU, SNOOPY... I KNEW YOU'D COME IF I ASKED YOU....
SCHULZ
144

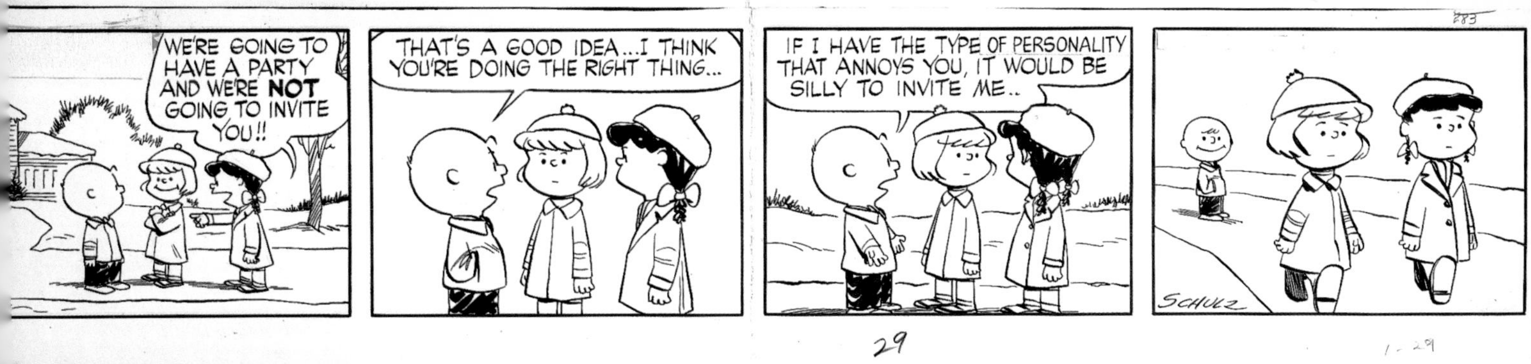
WE'RE GOING TO HAVE A PARTY AND WE'RE **NOT** GOING TO INVITE YOU!!
THAT'S A GOOD IDEA...I THINK YOU'RE DOING THE RIGHT THING...
IF I HAVE THE TYPE OF PERSONALITY THAT ANNOYS YOU, IT WOULD BE SILLY TO INVITE ME..
SCHULZ
29

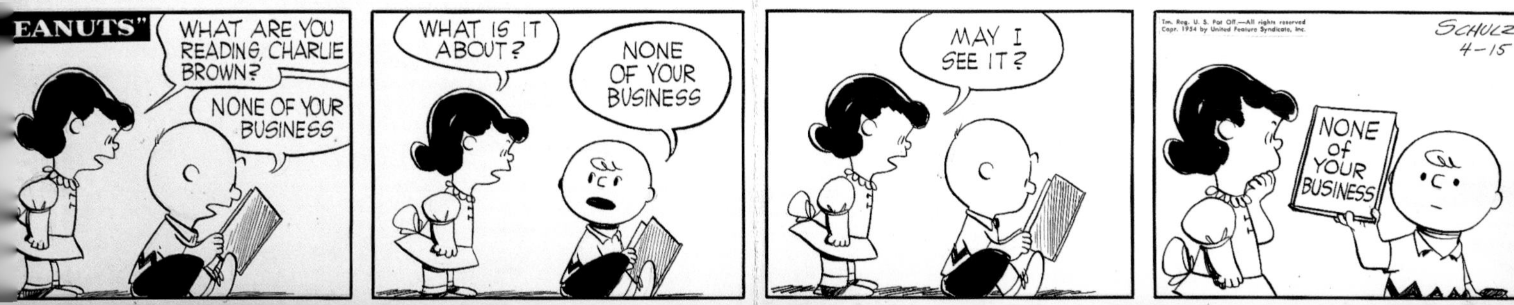
EANUTS"
WHAT ARE YOU READING, CHARLIE BROWN?
NONE OF YOUR BUSINESS
WHAT IS IT ABOUT?
NONE OF YOUR BUSINESS
MAY I SEE IT?
Tm. Reg. U. S. Pat. Off.—All rights reserved Copr. 1954 by United Feature Syndicate, Inc.
SCHULZ 4-15
NONE of YOUR BUSINESS

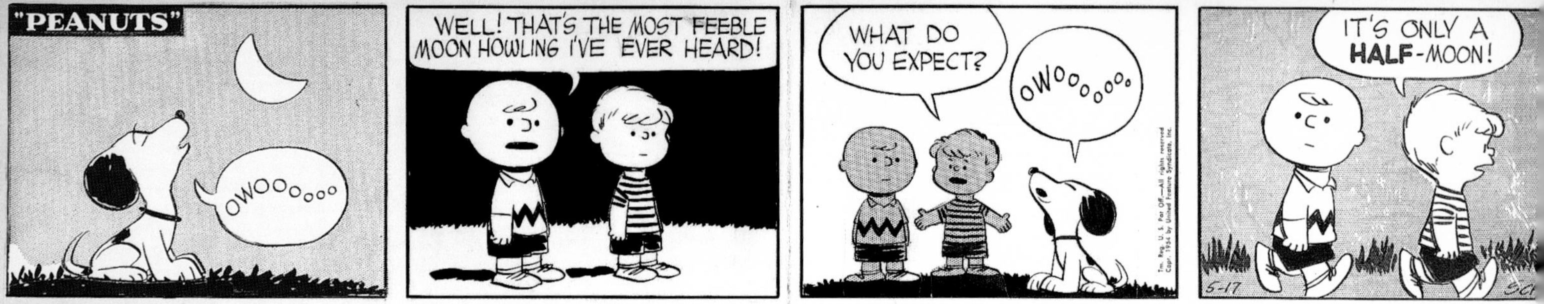
"PEANUTS"
OWOOOoooo
WELL! THAT'S THE MOST FEEBLE MOON HOWLING I'VE EVER HEARD!
WHAT DO YOU EXPECT?
OWOooooooo
Tm. Reg. U. S. Pat. Off.—All rights reserved Copr. 1954 by United Feature Syndicate, Inc.
IT'S ONLY A HALF-MOON!
5-17

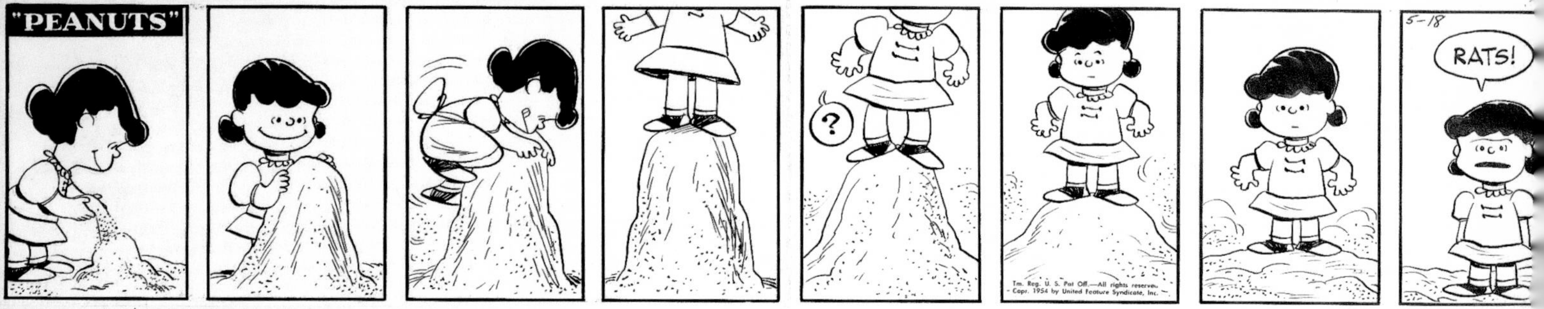
"PEANUTS"
?
Tm. Reg. U. S. Pat. Off.—All rights reserved Copr. 1954 by United Feature Syndicate, Inc.
5-18
RATS!

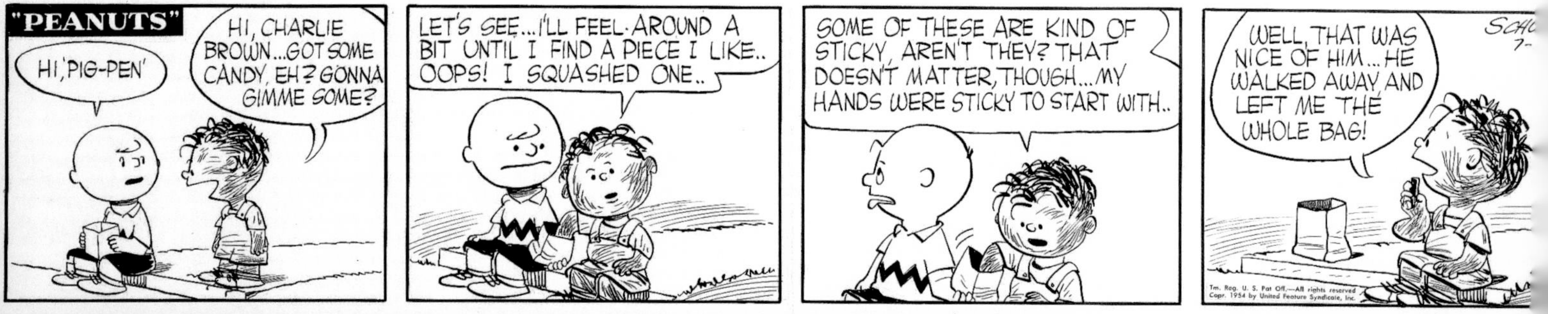
"PEANUTS"
HI, 'PIG-PEN'
HI, CHARLIE BROWN...GOT SOME CANDY, EH? GONNA GIMME SOME?
LET'S SEE...I'LL FEEL AROUND A BIT UNTIL I FIND A PIECE I LIKE.. OOPS! I SQUASHED ONE..
SOME OF THESE ARE KIND OF STICKY, AREN'T THEY? THAT DOESN'T MATTER, THOUGH...MY HANDS WERE STICKY TO START WITH..
WELL, THAT WAS NICE OF HIM...HE WALKED AWAY, AND LEFT ME THE WHOLE BAG!
Tm. Reg. U. S. Pat. Off.—All rights reserved Copr. 1954 by United Feature Syndicate, Inc.

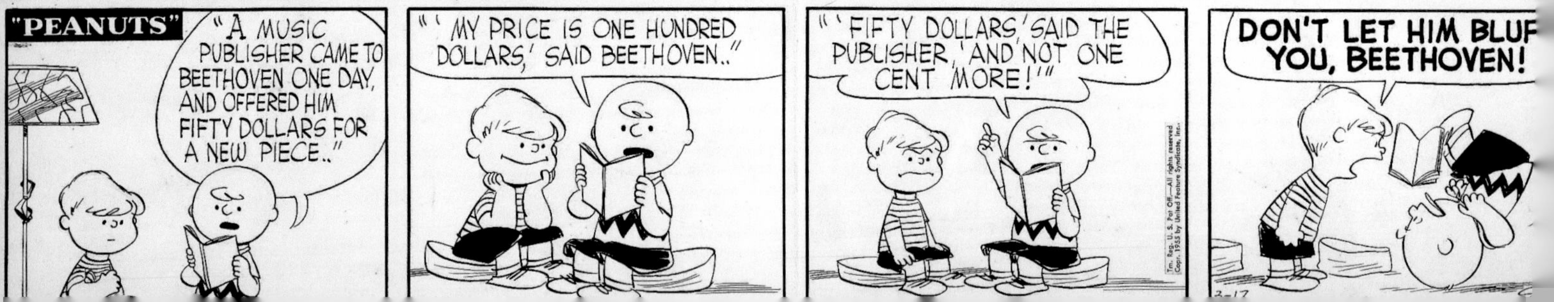
"PEANUTS"
"A MUSIC PUBLISHER CAME TO BEETHOVEN ONE DAY, AND OFFERED HIM FIFTY DOLLARS FOR A NEW PIECE.."
"'MY PRICE IS ONE HUNDRED DOLLARS,' SAID BEETHOVEN.."
"'FIFTY DOLLARS,' SAID THE PUBLISHER, 'AND NOT ONE CENT MORE!'"
Tm. Reg. U. S. Pat. Off.—All rights reserved Copr. 1955 by United Feature Syndicate, Inc.
DON'T LET HIM BLUF YOU, BEETHOVEN!

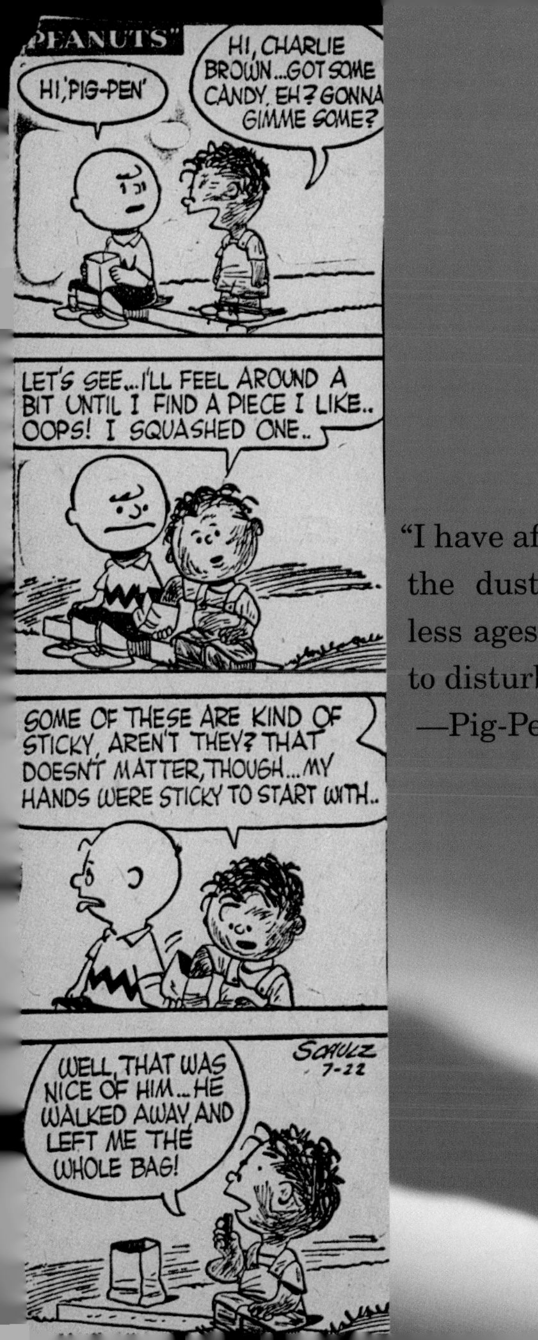
PEANUTS
HI, 'PIG-PEN'
HI, CHARLIE BROWN...GOT SOME CANDY, EH? GONNA GIMME SOME?
LET'S SEE...I'LL FEEL AROUND A BIT UNTIL I FIND A PIECE I LIKE.. OOPS! I SQUASHED ONE..
SOME OF THESE ARE KIND OF STICKY, AREN'T THEY? THAT DOESN'T MATTER, THOUGH...MY HANDS WERE STICKY TO START WITH..
WELL, THAT WAS NICE OF HIM...HE WALKED AWAY, AND LEFT ME THE WHOLE BAG!
SCHULZ 7-22

"I have affixed to me the dust of countless ages. Who am I to disturb history?"
—Pig-Pen, 1955

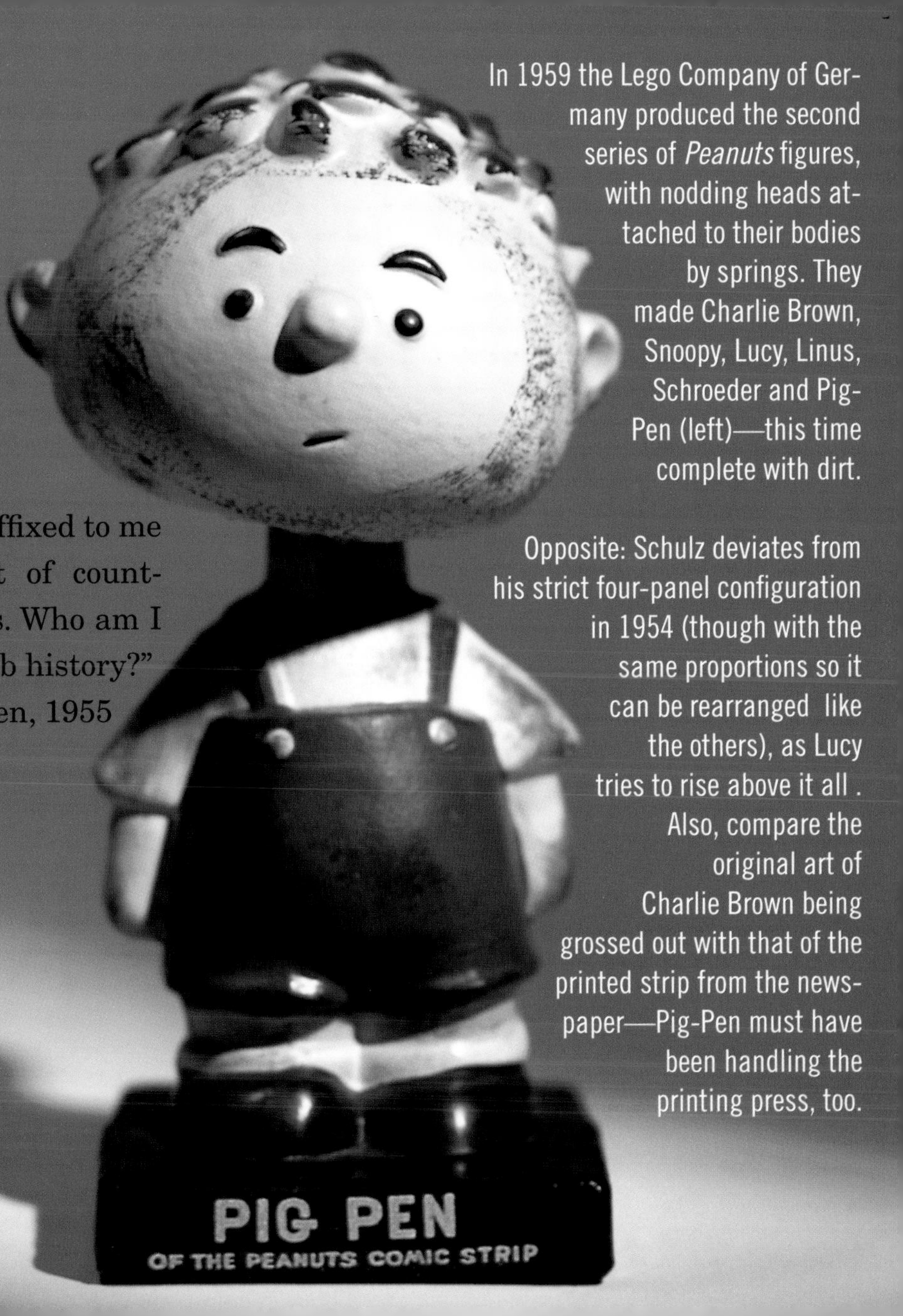
PIG PEN
OF THE PEANUTS COMIC STRIP

In 1959 the Lego Company of Germany produced the second series of *Peanuts* figures, with nodding heads attached to their bodies by springs. They made Charlie Brown, Snoopy, Lucy, Linus, Schroeder and Pig-Pen (left)—this time complete with dirt.

Opposite: Schulz deviates from his strict four-panel configuration in 1954 (though with the same proportions so it can be rearranged like the others), as Lucy tries to rise above it all. Also, compare the original art of Charlie Brown being grossed out with that of the printed strip from the newspaper—Pig-Pen must have been handling the printing press, too.

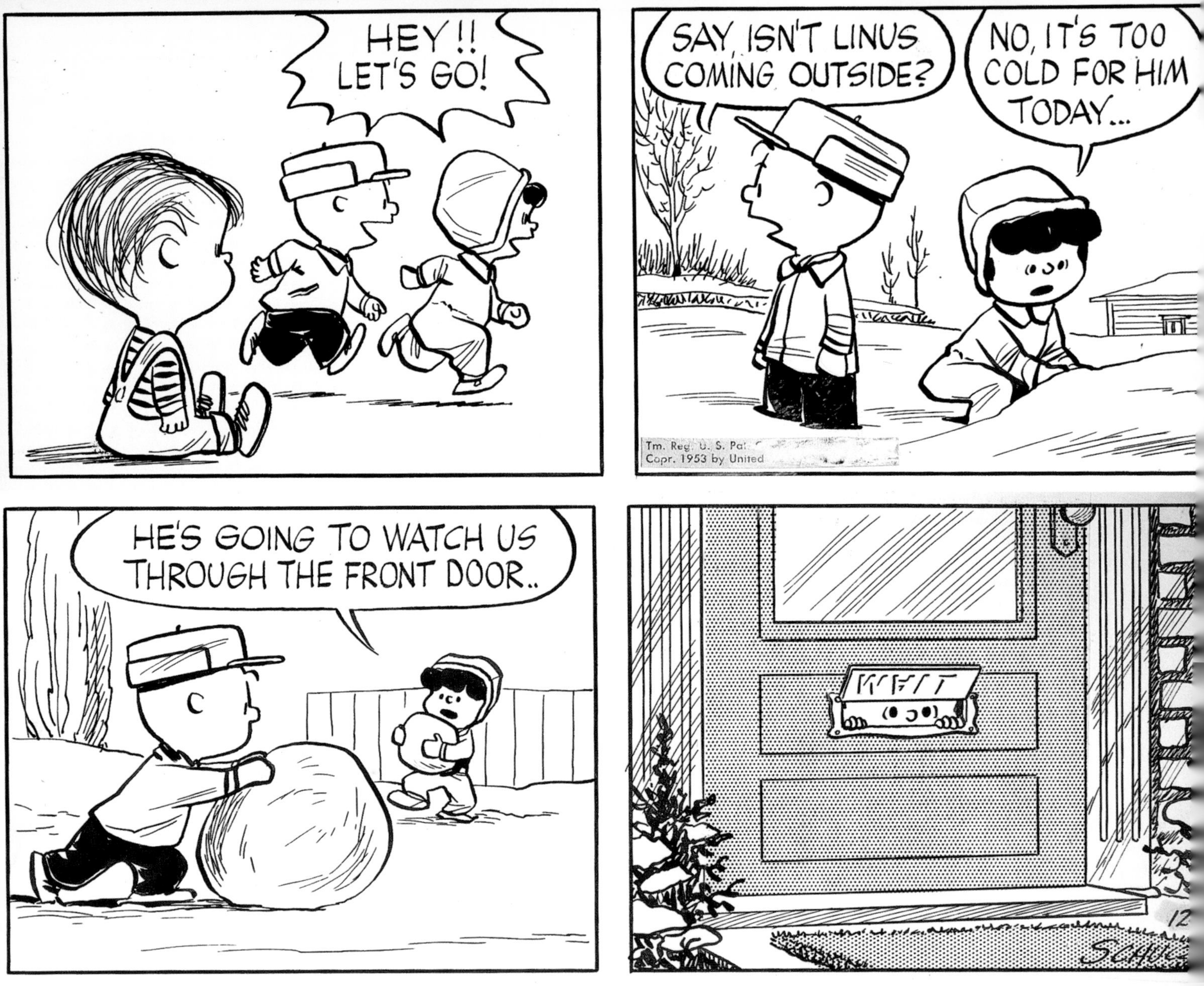
HEY!! LET'S GO!
SAY, ISN'T LINUS COMING OUTSIDE?
NO, IT'S TOO COLD FOR HIM TODAY...
Tm. Reg. U. S. Pat.
Copr. 1953 by United
HE'S GOING TO WATCH US THROUGH THE FRONT DOOR..

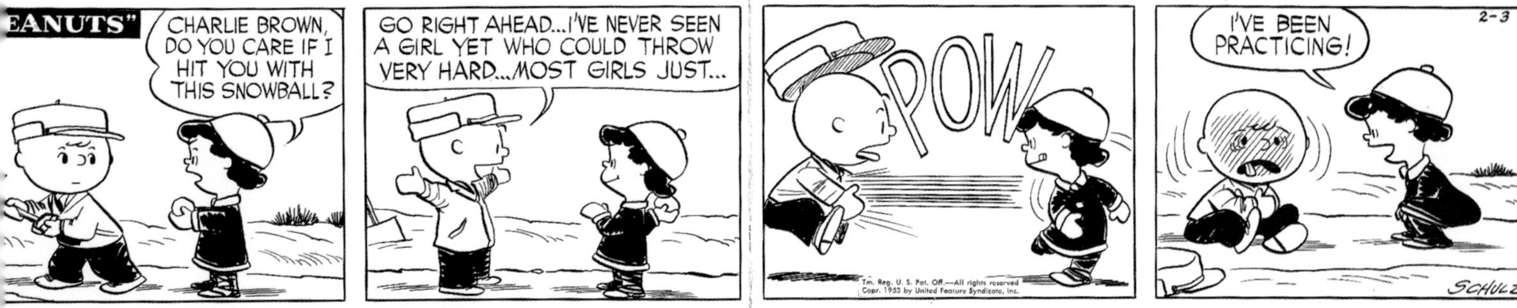
EANUTS"
CHARLIE BROWN, DO YOU CARE IF I HIT YOU WITH THIS SNOWBALL?
GO RIGHT AHEAD...I'VE NEVER SEEN A GIRL YET WHO COULD THROW VERY HARD...MOST GIRLS JUST...
POW
Tm. Reg. U. S. Pat. Off.—All rights reserved Copr. 1953 by United Feature Syndicate, Inc.
2-3
I'VE BEEN PRACTICING!
SCHULZ

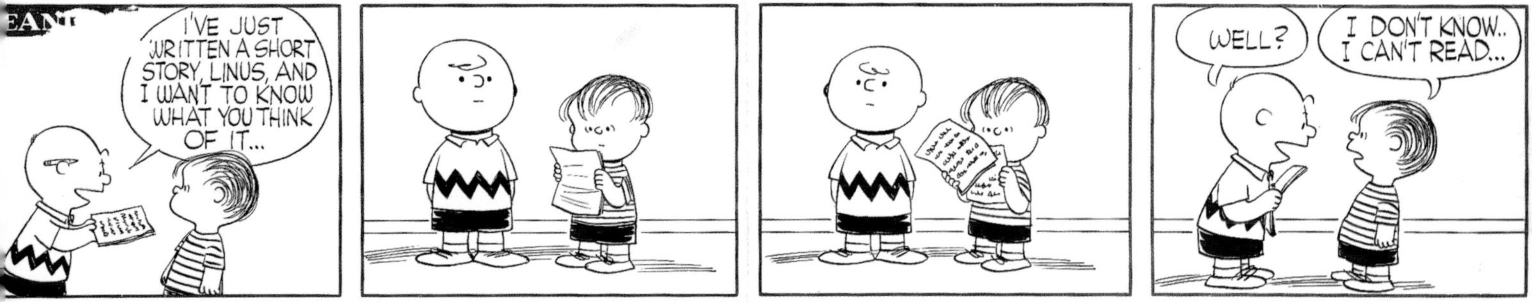
I'VE JUST WRITTEN A SHORT STORY, LINUS, AND I WANT TO KNOW WHAT YOU THINK OF IT...
WELL?
I DON'T KNOW.. I CAN'T READ...

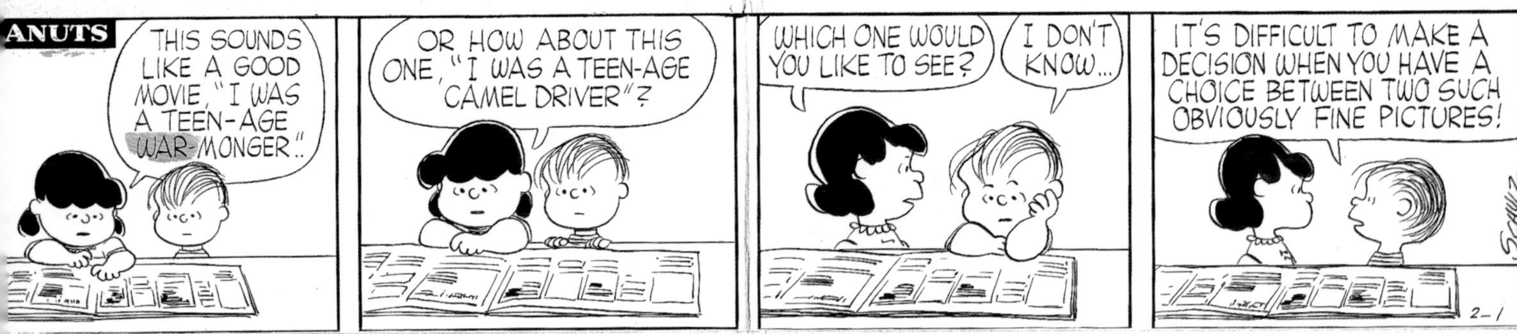
ANUTS
THIS SOUNDS LIKE A GOOD MOVIE, "I WAS A TEEN-AGE WAR-MONGER"!
OR HOW ABOUT THIS ONE, "I WAS A TEEN-AGE CAMEL DRIVER"?
WHICH ONE WOULD YOU LIKE TO SEE?
I DON'T KNOW...
IT'S DIFFICULT TO MAKE A DECISION WHEN YOU HAVE A CHOICE BETWEEN TWO SUCH OBVIOUSLY FINE PICTURES!
SCHULZ
2-1

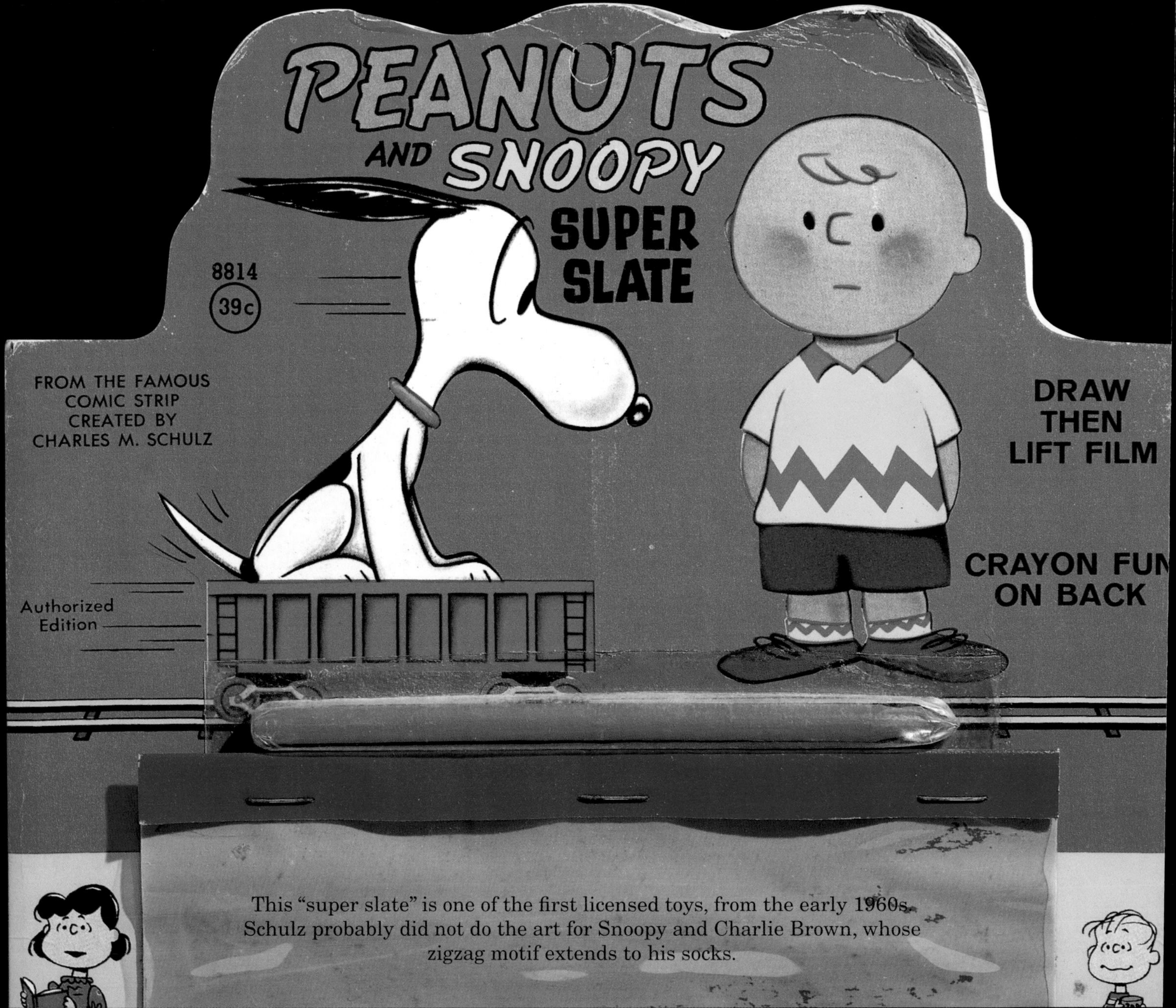
PEANUTS
AND SNOOPY
SUPER SLATE
8814
39c
FROM THE FAMOUS COMIC STRIP CREATED BY CHARLES M. SCHULZ
DRAW THEN LIFT FILM
CRAYON FUN ON BACK
Authorized Edition

This "super slate" is one of the first licensed toys, from the early 1960s. Schulz probably did not do the art for Snoopy and Charlie Brown, whose zigzag motif extends to his socks.

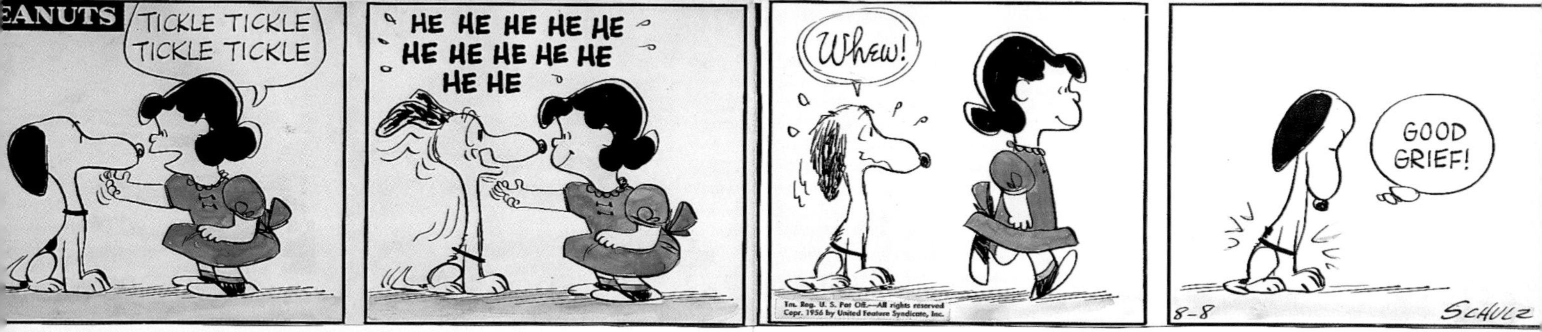
EANUTS
TICKLE TICKLE TICKLE TICKLE
HE HE HE HE HE HE HE HE HE HE HE HE
Whew!
Tm. Reg. U. S. Pat Off.—All rights reserved Copr. 1956 by United Feature Syndicate, Inc.
GOOD GRIEF!
8-8
SCHULZ

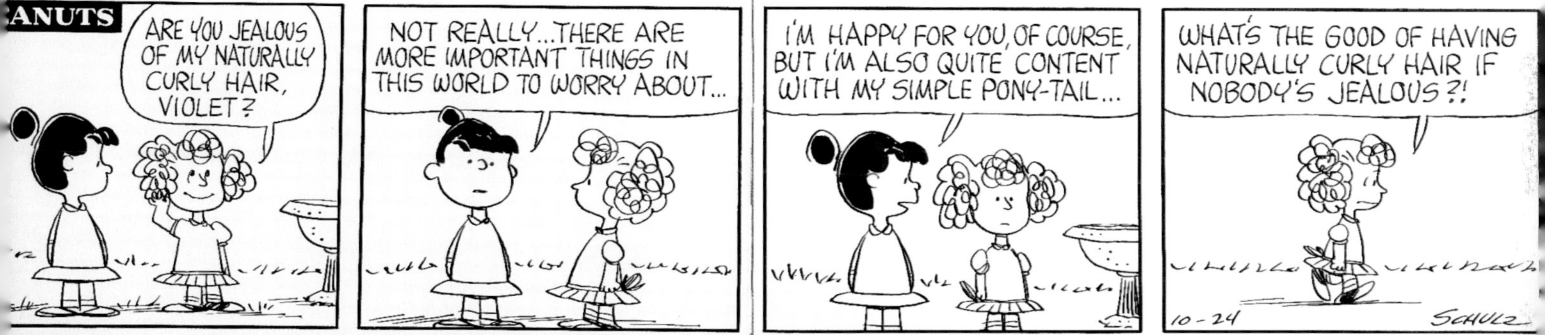
EANUTS
ARE YOU JEALOUS OF MY NATURALLY CURLY HAIR, VIOLET?
NOT REALLY...THERE ARE MORE IMPORTANT THINGS IN THIS WORLD TO WORRY ABOUT...
I'M HAPPY FOR YOU, OF COURSE, BUT I'M ALSO QUITE CONTENT WITH MY SIMPLE PONY-TAIL...
WHAT'S THE GOOD OF HAVING NATURALLY CURLY HAIR IF NOBODY'S JEALOUS?!
10-24
SCHULZ

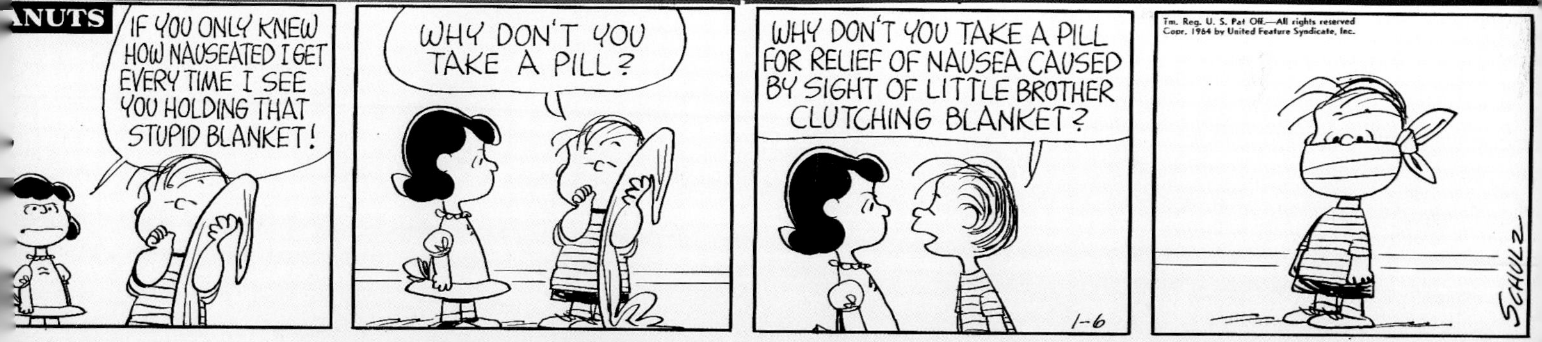
ANUTS
IF YOU ONLY KNEW HOW NAUSEATED I GET EVERY TIME I SEE YOU HOLDING THAT STUPID BLANKET!
WHY DON'T YOU TAKE A PILL?
WHY DON'T YOU TAKE A PILL FOR RELIEF OF NAUSEA CAUSED BY SIGHT OF LITTLE BROTHER CLUTCHING BLANKET?
1-6
Tm. Reg. U. S. Pat Off.—All rights reserved Copr. 1964 by United Feature Syndicate, Inc.
SCHULZ

7½ wide + 9½ wide So. H1683 350/276

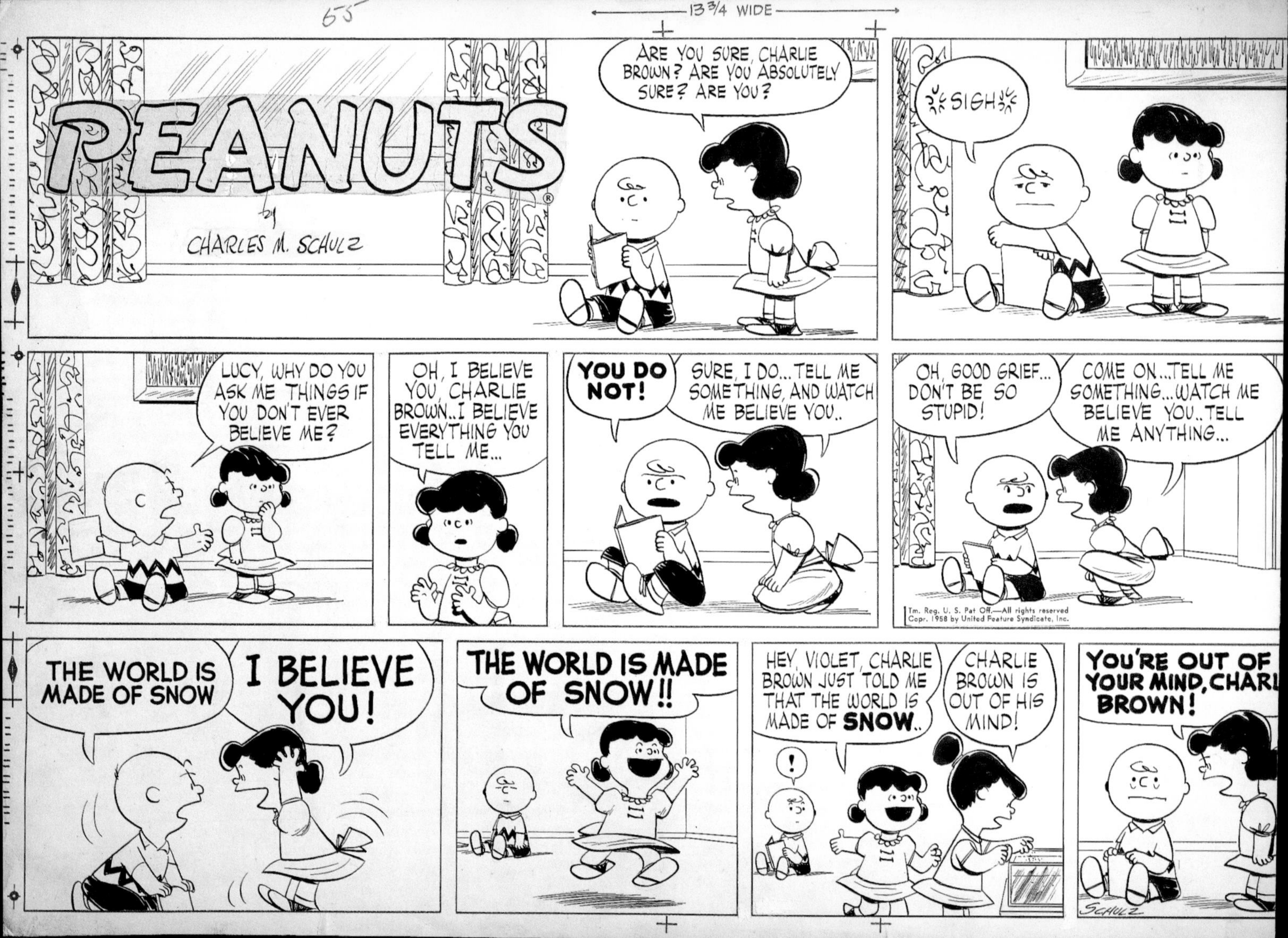

65
13 3/4 WIDE
PEANUTS
by CHARLES M. SCHULZ
ARE YOU SURE, CHARLIE BROWN? ARE YOU ABSOLUTELY SURE? ARE YOU?
SIGH
LUCY, WHY DO YOU ASK ME THINGS IF YOU DON'T EVER BELIEVE ME?
OH, I BELIEVE YOU, CHARLIE BROWN..I BELIEVE EVERYTHING YOU TELL ME...
YOU DO NOT!
SURE, I DO...TELL ME SOMETHING, AND WATCH ME BELIEVE YOU..
OH, GOOD GRIEF... DON'T BE SO STUPID!
COME ON...TELL ME SOMETHING...WATCH ME BELIEVE YOU..TELL ME ANYTHING...
Tm. Reg. U. S. Pat Off.—All rights reserved Copr. 1958 by United Feature Syndicate, Inc.
THE WORLD IS MADE OF SNOW
I BELIEVE YOU!
THE WORLD IS MADE OF SNOW!!
HEY, VIOLET, CHARLIE BROWN JUST TOLD ME THAT THE WORLD IS MADE OF SNOW..
!
CHARLIE BROWN IS OUT OF HIS MIND!
YOU'RE OUT OF YOUR MIND, CHARL BROWN!
SCHULZ

At first Lucy wasn't any worse than her friends Violet and Patty, all of whom took delight in tormenting Charlie Brown when the mood struck. But at some point Lucy pulled ahead of the pack and then *no one* was safe (above right, 1958). Schulz claimed that Lucy was the outlet for the darker nature of his personality. One of the scariest things about her was the ease with which she could shift from friendly to venomous. Just like real people.

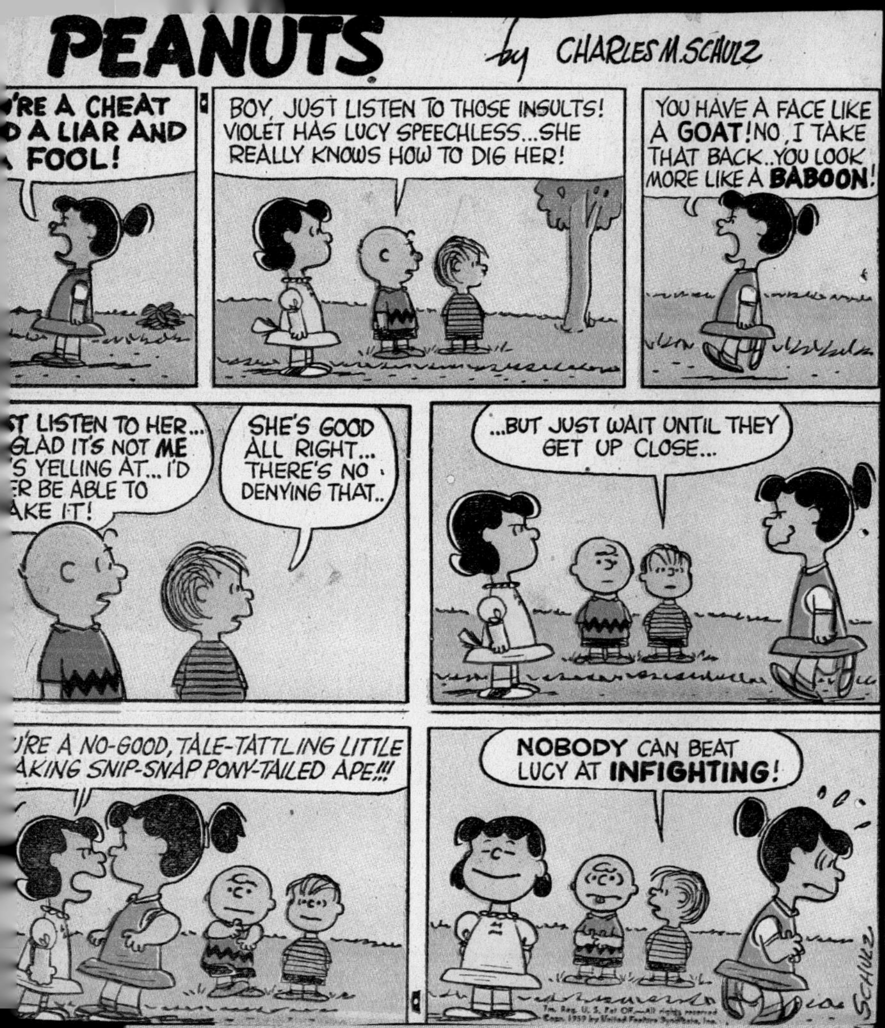
PEANUTS
by CHARLES M. SCHULZ
'RE A CHEAT
D A LIAR AND
FOOL!
BOY, JUST LISTEN TO THOSE INSULTS! VIOLET HAS LUCY SPEECHLESS...SHE REALLY KNOWS HOW TO DIG HER!
YOU HAVE A FACE LIKE A GOAT! NO, I TAKE THAT BACK..YOU LOOK MORE LIKE A BABOON!
ST LISTEN TO HER...
GLAD IT'S NOT ME
'S YELLING AT... I'D
ER BE ABLE TO
AKE IT!
SHE'S GOOD ALL RIGHT... THERE'S NO DENYING THAT..
...BUT JUST WAIT UNTIL THEY GET UP CLOSE...
'RE A NO-GOOD, TALE-TATTLING LITTLE
AKING SNIP-SNAP PONY-TAILED APE!!!
NOBODY CAN BEAT LUCY AT INFIGHTING!
SCHULZ

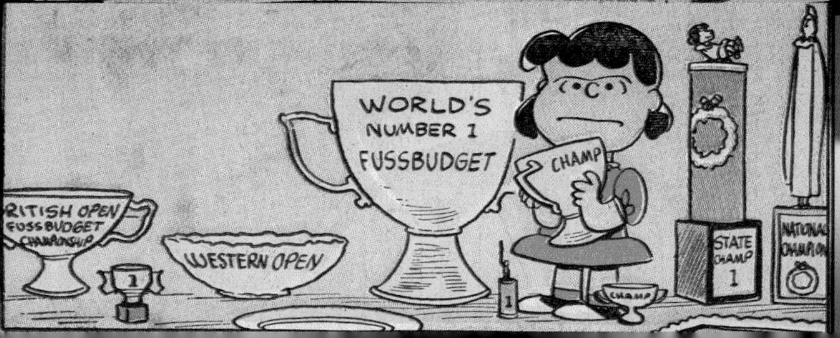
WORLD'S NUMBER 1 FUSSBUDGET
CHAMP
RITISH OPEN FUSSBUDGET CHAMPIONSHIP
WESTERN OPEN
STATE CHAMP 1
NATIONAL CHAMPION
CHAMP

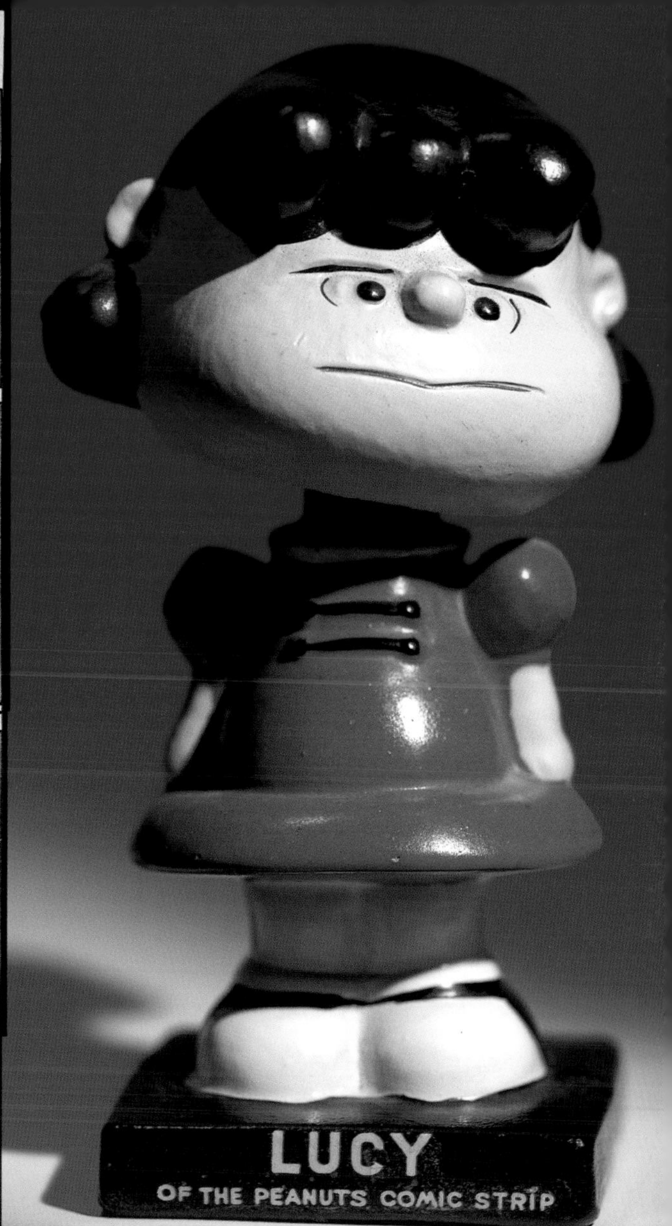
LUCY
OF THE PEANUTS COMIC STRIP

The Lucy "nodder" figure (1959) is unusual because she actually looks crabby. Licensees tended to produce "happy" versions of the characters.

The Ford Motor Company was the first major advertising licensee for the *Peanuts* characters in 1959, but it was more than that—it spawned the first animated versions of the characters, which led to a lifelong partnership between Schulz and animator Bill Melendez.

Melendez was at Playhouse Pictures, a cartoon studio that mostly made commercials and listed Ford as its biggest client. A Melendez-animated Charlie Brown made his TV debut in 1959, on ads for the Ford Falcon, and the rest of the gang soon followed—all in black and white.

Not long after, documentary producer Lee Mendelson was putting together a short film called *A Boy Named Charlie Brown* and wanted an animated sequence. He brought on Melendez, and with Schulz, they formed a team that put together *A Charlie Brown Christmas* in 1964. More than thirty animated specials followed, in as many years.

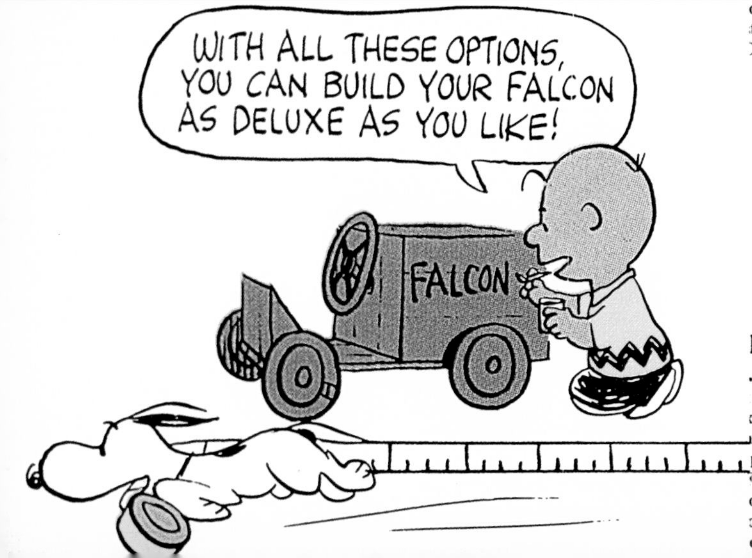

WITH ALL THESE OPTIONS, YOU CAN BUILD YOUR FALCON AS DELUXE AS YOU LIKE!
FALCON

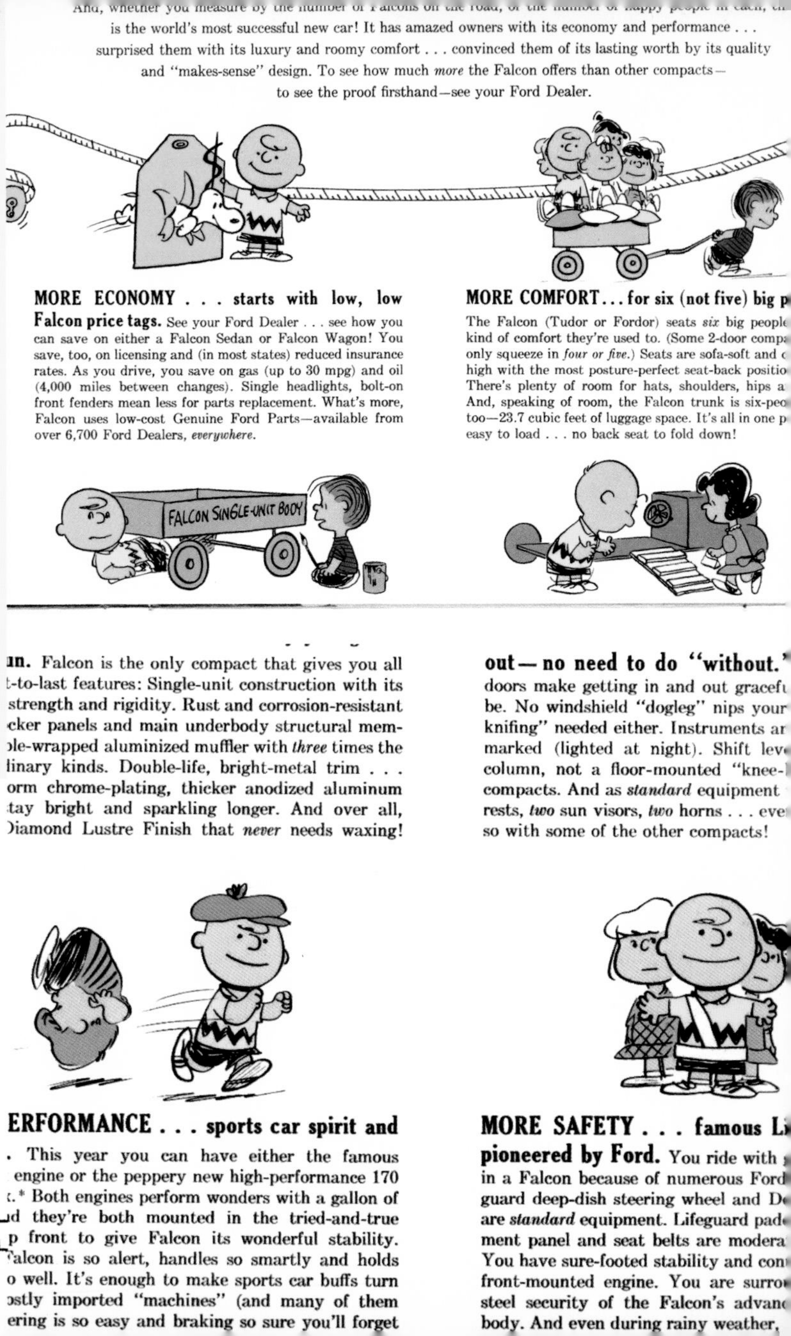

is the world's most successful new car! It has amazed owners with its economy and performance . . . surprised them with its luxury and roomy comfort . . . convinced them of its lasting worth by its quality and "makes-sense" design. To see how much *more* the Falcon offers than other compacts—to see the proof firsthand—see your Ford Dealer.

MORE ECONOMY . . . starts with low, low Falcon price tags. See your Ford Dealer . . . see how you can save on either a Falcon Sedan or Falcon Wagon! You save, too, on licensing and (in most states) reduced insurance rates. As you drive, you save on gas (up to 30 mpg) and oil (4,000 miles between changes). Single headlights, bolt-on front fenders mean less for parts replacement. What's more, Falcon uses low-cost Genuine Ford Parts—available from over 6,700 Ford Dealers, *everywhere.*

MORE COMFORT . . . for six (not five) big p
The Falcon (Tudor or Fordor) seats *six* big people kind of comfort they're used to. (Some 2-door comp only squeeze in *four or five.*) Seats are sofa-soft and high with the most posture-perfect seat-back positio There's plenty of room for hats, shoulders, hips a And, speaking of room, the Falcon trunk is six-peo too—23.7 cubic feet of luggage space. It's all in one p easy to load . . . no back seat to fold down!

FALCON SINGLE-UNIT BODY

in. Falcon is the only compact that gives you all t-to-last features: Single-unit construction with its strength and rigidity. Rust and corrosion-resistant cker panels and main underbody structural memble-wrapped aluminized muffler with *three* times the linary kinds. Double-life, bright-metal trim . . . orm chrome-plating, thicker anodized aluminum tay bright and sparkling longer. And over all, Diamond Lustre Finish that *never* needs waxing!

out—no need to do "without." doors make getting in and out gracef be. No windshield "dogleg" nips your knifing" needed either. Instruments ar marked (lighted at night). Shift lev column, not a floor-mounted "knee- compacts. And as *standard* equipment rests, *two* sun visors, *two* horns . . . eve so with some of the other compacts!

ERFORMANCE . . . sports car spirit and . This year you can have either the famous engine or the peppery new high-performance 170 .* Both engines perform wonders with a gallon of d they're both mounted in the tried-and-true p front to give Falcon its wonderful stability. Falcon is so alert, handles so smartly and holds o well. It's enough to make sports car buffs turn ostly imported "machines" (and many of them ering is so easy and braking so sure you'll forget

MORE SAFETY . . . famous Li pioneered by Ford. You ride with in a Falcon because of numerous Ford guard deep-dish steering wheel and D are *standard* equipment. Lifeguard pad ment panel and seat belts are modera You have sure-footed stability and con front-mounted engine. You are surro steel security of the Falcon's advan body. And even during rainy weather,

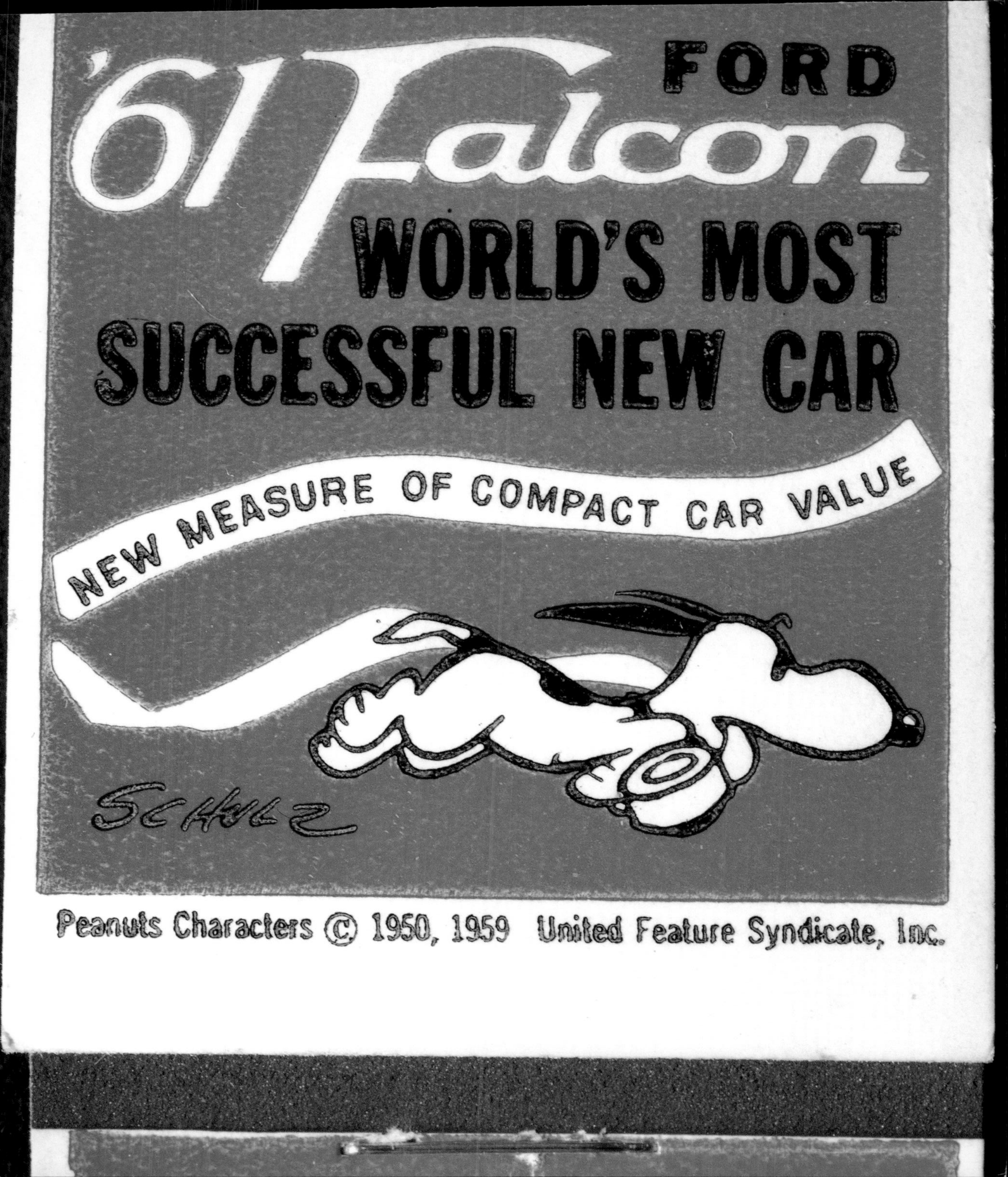
FORD
'61 Falcon
WORLD'S MOST
SUCCESSFUL NEW CAR
NEW MEASURE OF COMPACT CAR VALUE
SCHULZ
Peanuts Characters © 1950, 1959 United Feature Syndicate, Inc.

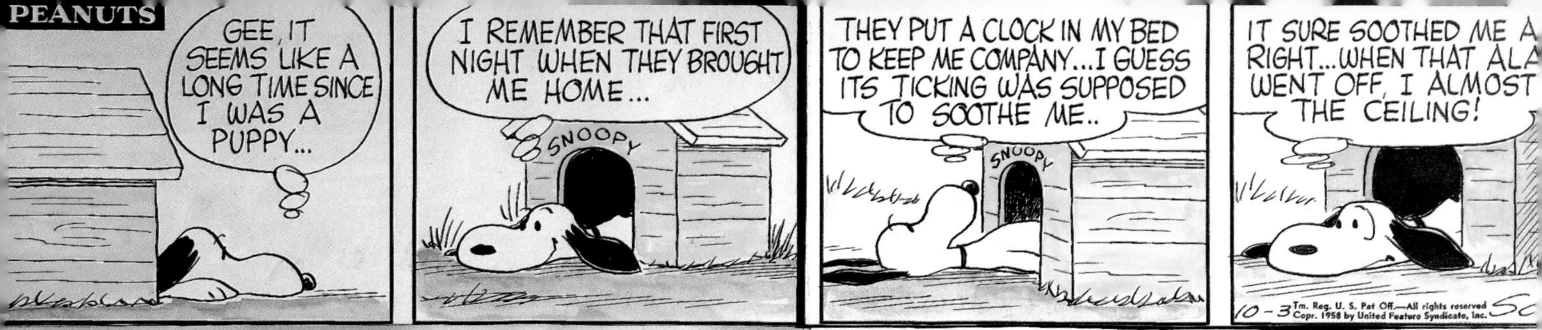
PEANUTS
GEE, IT SEEMS LIKE A LONG TIME SINCE I WAS A PUPPY...
I REMEMBER THAT FIRST NIGHT WHEN THEY BROUGHT ME HOME...
SNOOPY
THEY PUT A CLOCK IN MY BED TO KEEP ME COMPANY...I GUESS ITS TICKING WAS SUPPOSED TO SOOTHE ME..
SNOOPY
IT SURE SOOTHED ME A RIGHT...WHEN THAT ALA WENT OFF, I ALMOST THE CEILING!
10-3
Tm. Reg. U. S. Pat Off.—All rights reserved Copr. 1958 by United Feature Syndicate, Inc.

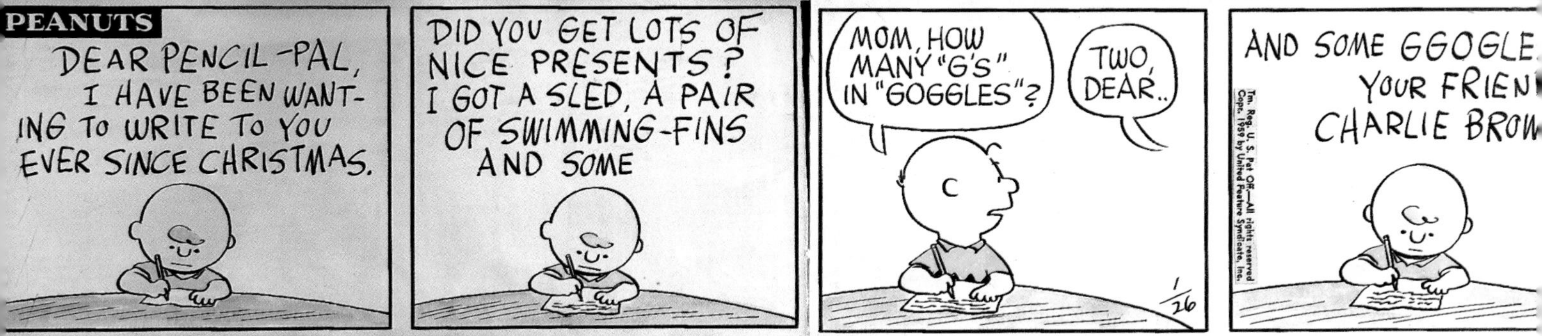
PEANUTS
DEAR PENCIL-PAL, I HAVE BEEN WANTING TO WRITE TO YOU EVER SINCE CHRISTMAS.
DID YOU GET LOTS OF NICE PRESENTS? I GOT A SLED, A PAIR OF SWIMMING-FINS AND SOME
MOM, HOW MANY "G'S" IN "GOGGLES"?
TWO, DEAR..
1/26
Tm. Reg. U. S. Pat Off.—All rights reserved Copr. 1959 by United Feature Syndicate, Inc.
AND SOME GGOGLE. YOUR FRIEN CHARLIE BROW

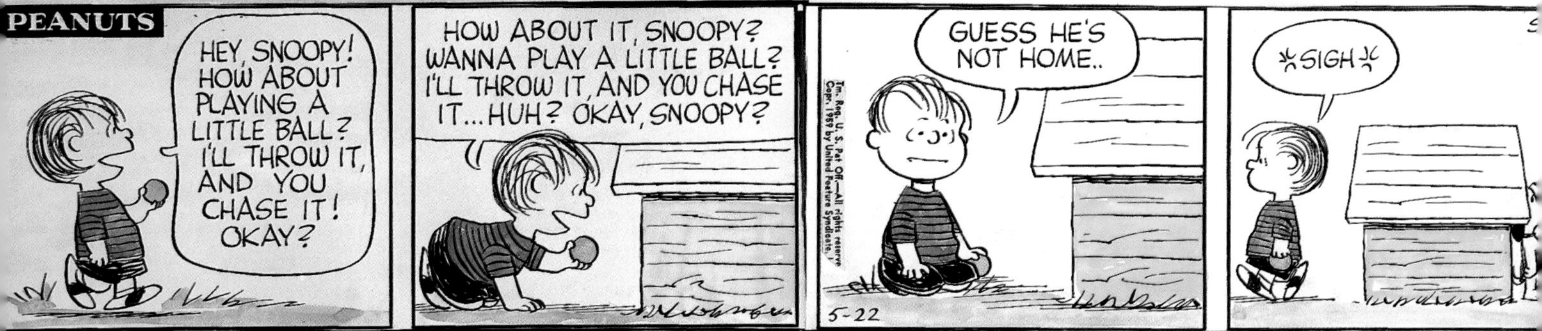
PEANUTS
HEY, SNOOPY! HOW ABOUT PLAYING A LITTLE BALL? I'LL THROW IT, AND YOU CHASE IT! OKAY?
HOW ABOUT IT, SNOOPY? WANNA PLAY A LITTLE BALL? I'LL THROW IT, AND YOU CHASE IT...HUH? OKAY, SNOOPY?
Tm. Reg. U. S. Pat Off.—All rights reserve Copr. 1959 by United Feature Syndicate,
GUESS HE'S NOT HOME..
5-22
SIGH

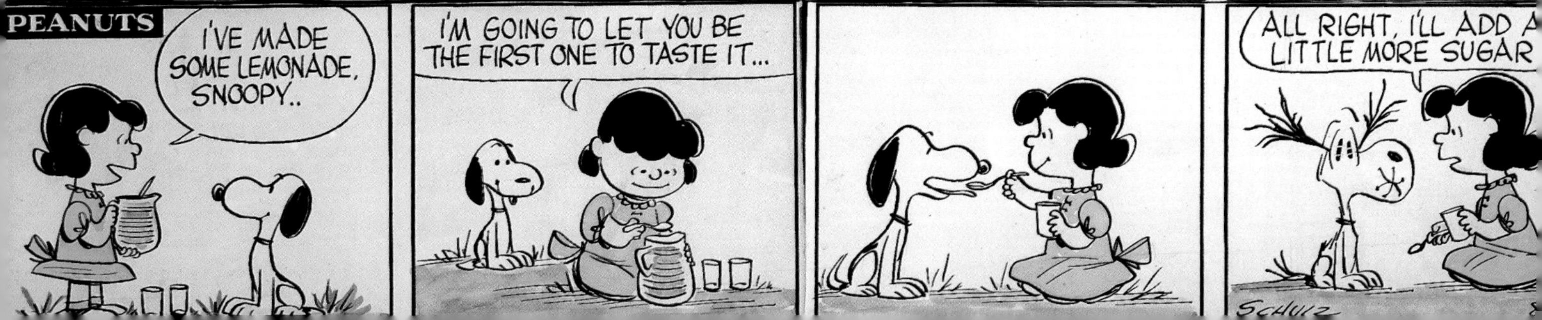
PEANUTS
I'VE MADE SOME LEMONADE, SNOOPY..
I'M GOING TO LET YOU BE THE FIRST ONE TO TASTE IT...
ALL RIGHT, I'LL ADD A LITTLE MORE SUGAR
SCHULZ

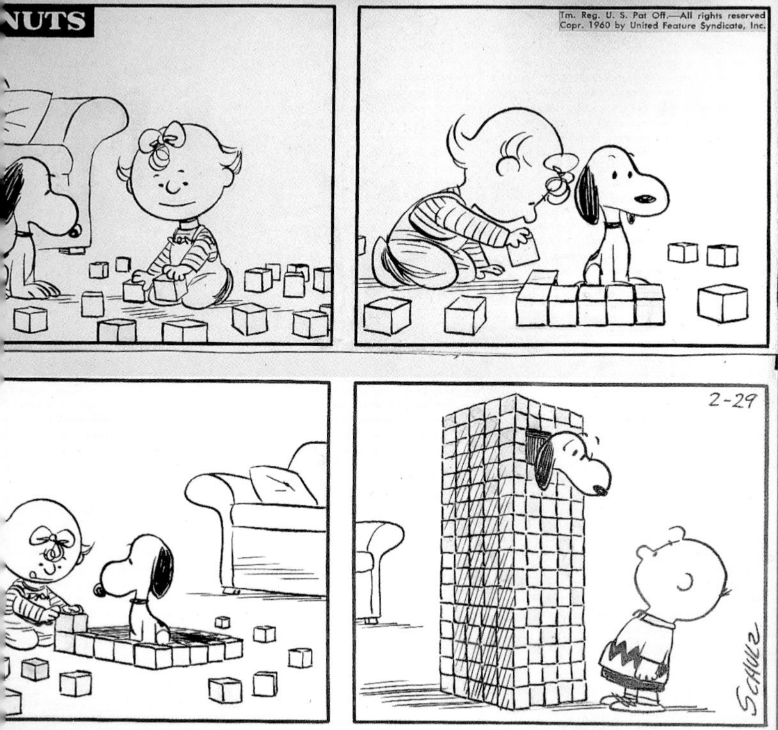
NUTS
Tm. Reg. U. S. Pat Off.—All rights reserved
Copr. 1960 by United Feature Syndicate, Inc.
2-29
SCHULZ

The arrival of Charlie Brown's little sister Sally in June 1959 (and her first appearance that August) changed the dynamic of his life as a loner—at least in his own home. At first he was almost fatherly with her, as he was with Lucy. And like Lucy, Sally didn't stay a baby for long. Soon she'd learn to walk, talk, and develop a crush on Linus, much to his chagrin. She also made demands on her big brother, like this example from the early 1990s:

Sally: "School starts next week. I need you to test me on my multiplication tables."
Charlie Brown: "Okay, how much is five times eight?"
Sally: "Who cares?"
Charlie Brown: "I think you're ready."

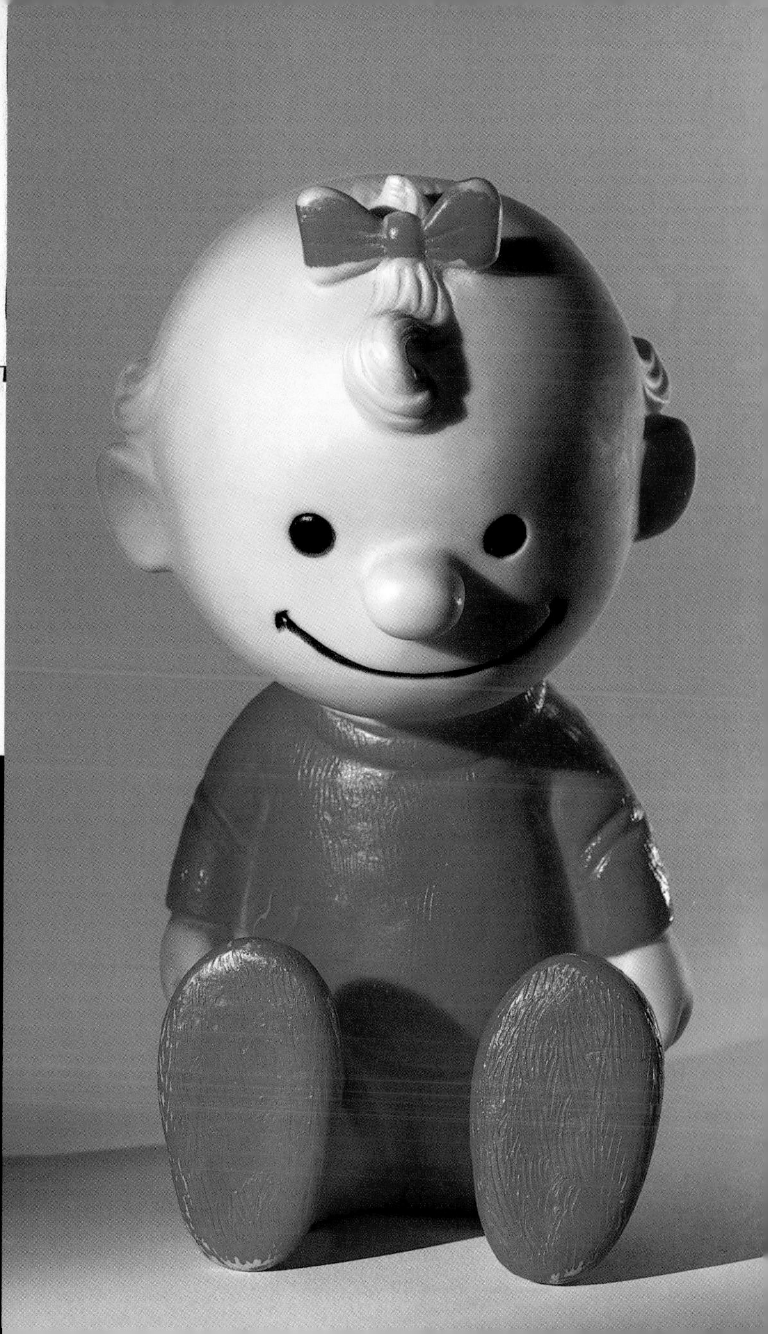

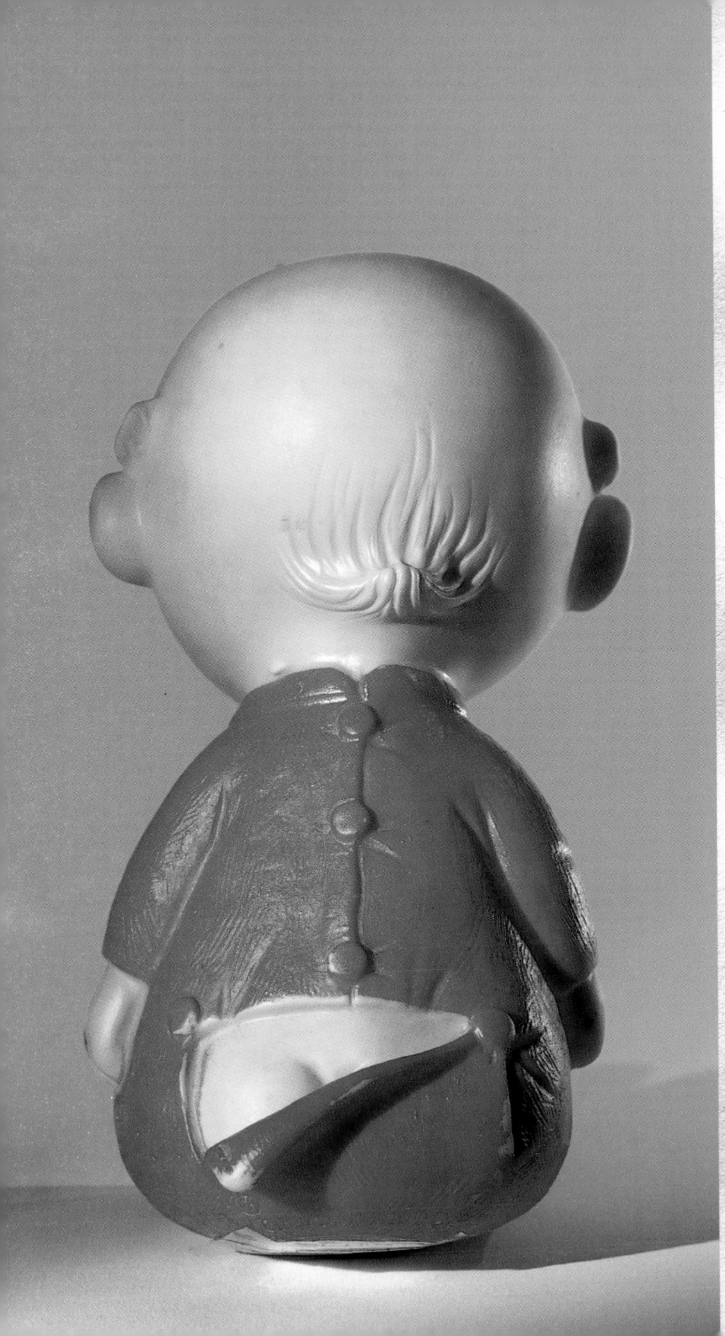

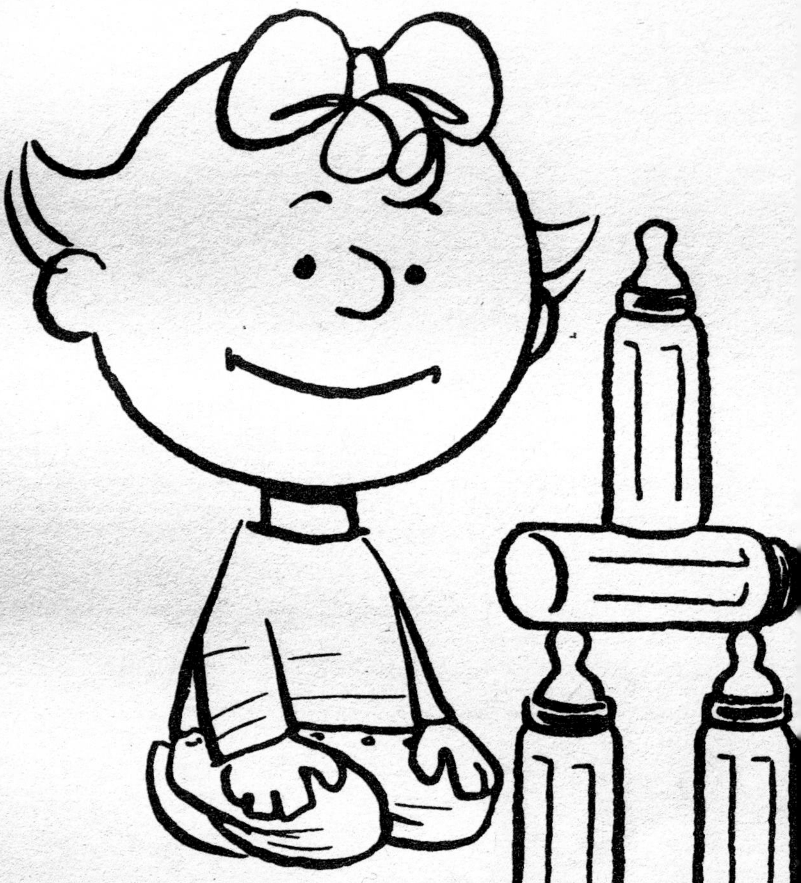

by Charles M. Schulz

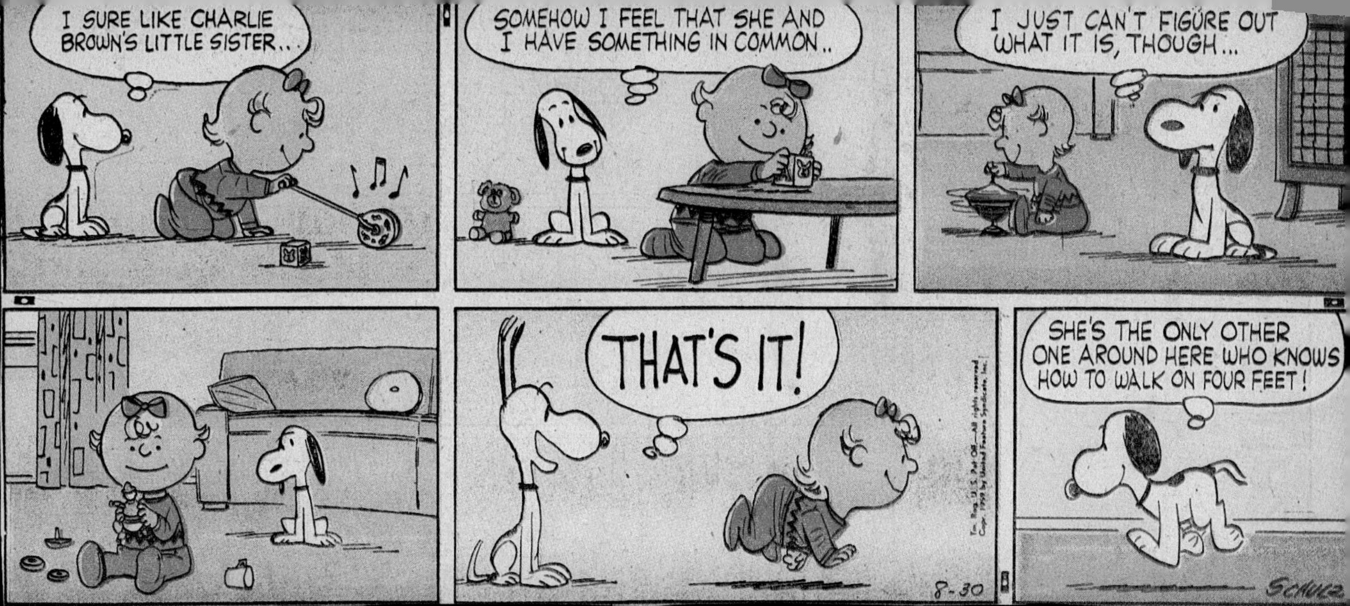
I SURE LIKE CHARLIE BROWN'S LITTLE SISTER..
SOMEHOW I FEEL THAT SHE AND I HAVE SOMETHING IN COMMON..
I JUST CAN'T FIGURE OUT WHAT IT IS, THOUGH...
THAT'S IT!
Tm. Reg. U.S. Pat. Off.—All rights reserved
Copr. 1959 by United Feature Syndicate, Inc.
8-30
SHE'S THE ONLY OTHER ONE AROUND HERE WHO KNOWS HOW TO WALK ON FOUR FEET!
SCHULZ

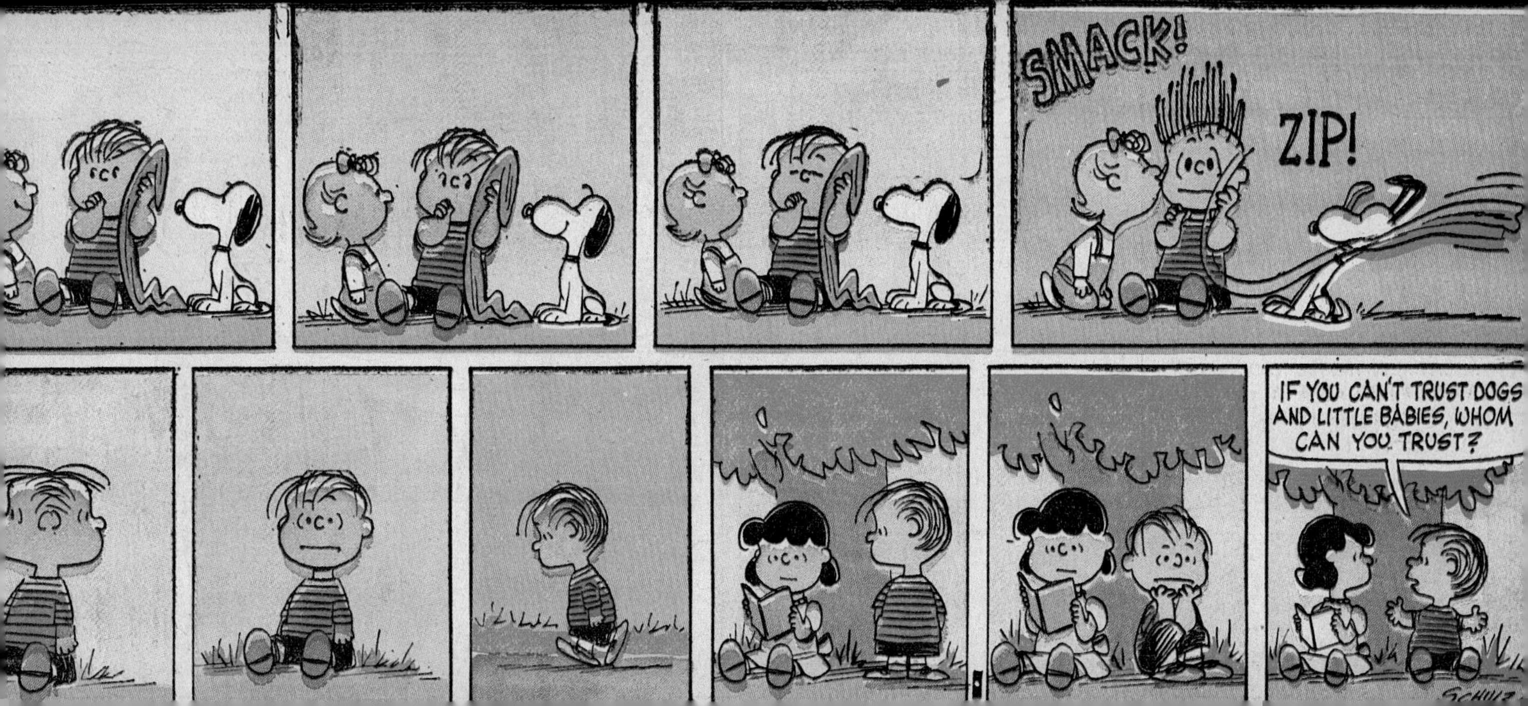
SMACK!
ZIP!
IF YOU CAN'T TRUST DOGS AND LITTLE BABIES, WHOM CAN YOU TRUST?
SCHULZ

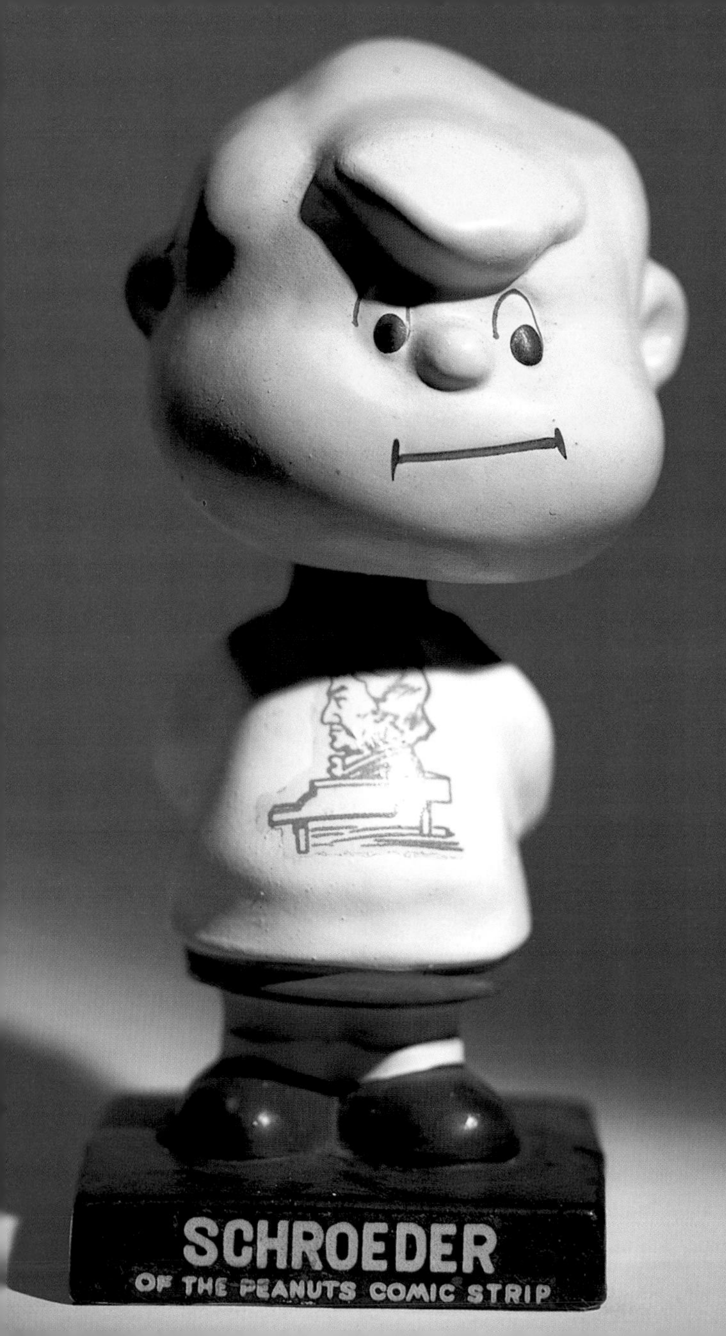
SCHROEDER
OF THE PEANUTS COMIC STRIP

Peanuts **thrives** on unrequited love: Charlie Brown's for the Little Red-haired Girl, Sally's for Linus, Linus's for his teacher Miss Othmar, and of course, Lucy's for Schroeder. For over thirty years she lay back, leaned on his piano, and threw herself at him.

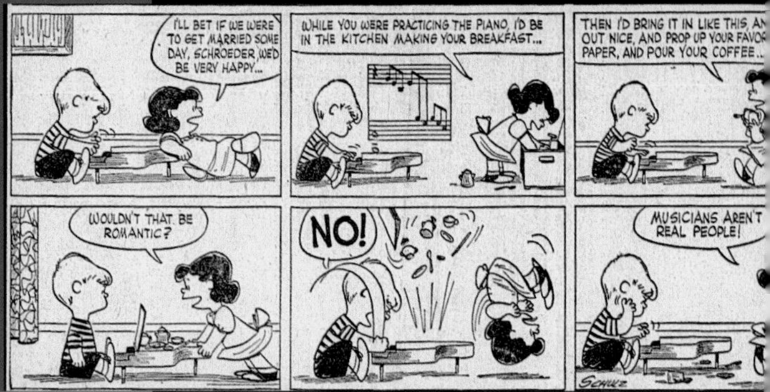
I'LL BET IF WE WERE TO GET MARRIED SOME DAY, SCHROEDER, WE'D BE VERY HAPPY...
WHILE YOU WERE PRACTICING THE PIANO, I'D BE IN THE KITCHEN MAKING YOUR BREAKFAST...
THEN I'D BRING IT IN LIKE THIS,
OUT NICE, AND PROP UP YOUR
PAPER, AND POUR YOUR COFFEE...
WOULDN'T THAT BE ROMANTIC?
NO!
MUSICIANS AREN'T REAL PEOPLE!
SCHULZ

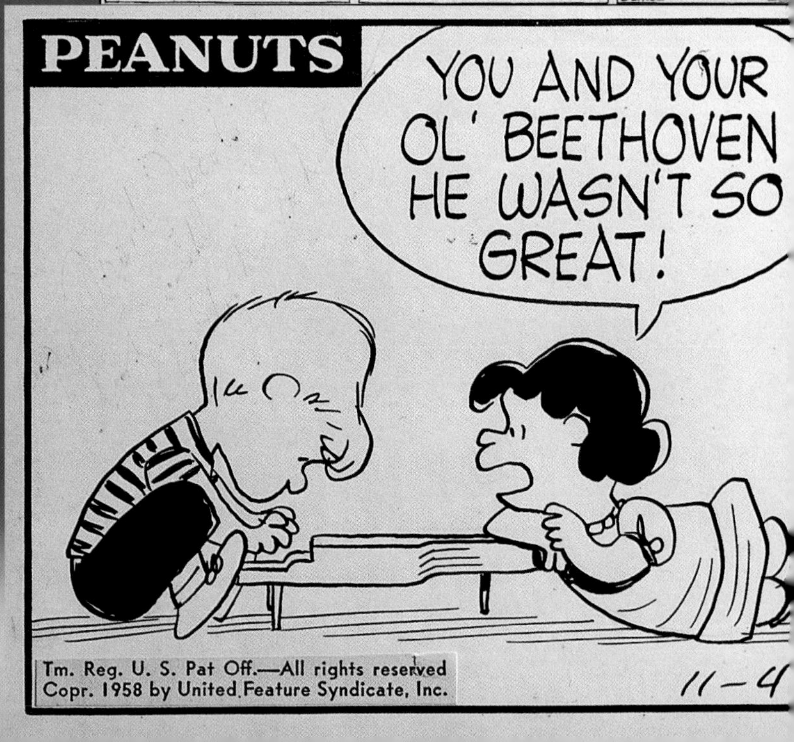
PEANUTS
YOU AND YOUR OL' BEETHOVEN HE WASN'T SO GREAT!
Tm. Reg. U. S. Pat Off.—All rights reserved
Copr. 1958 by United Feature Syndicate, Inc.
11-4

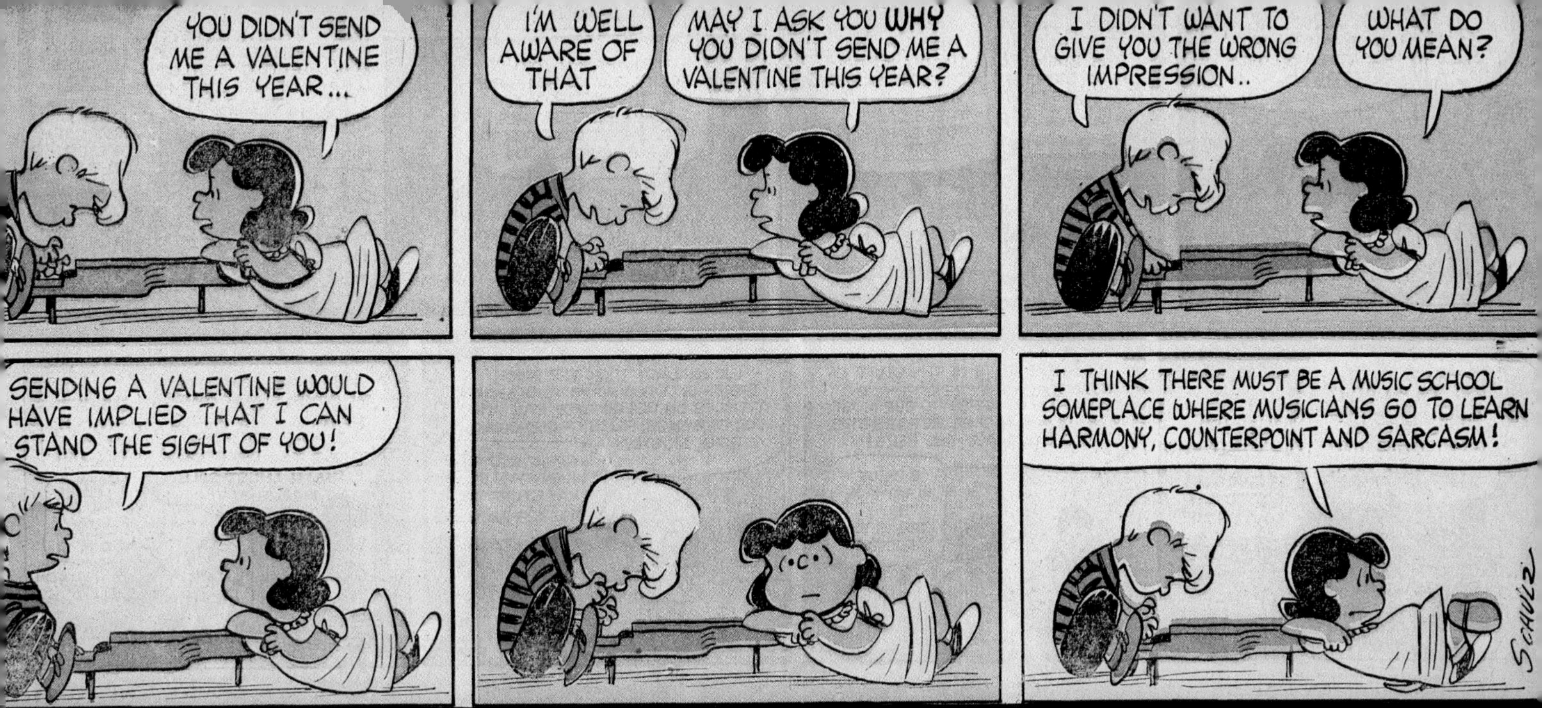
YOU DIDN'T SEND ME A VALENTINE THIS YEAR...
I'M WELL AWARE OF THAT
MAY I ASK YOU **WHY** YOU DIDN'T SEND ME A VALENTINE THIS YEAR?
I DIDN'T WANT TO GIVE YOU THE WRONG IMPRESSION..
WHAT DO YOU MEAN?
SENDING A VALENTINE WOULD HAVE IMPLIED THAT I CAN STAND THE SIGHT OF YOU!
I THINK THERE MUST BE A MUSIC SCHOOL SOMEPLACE WHERE MUSICIANS GO TO LEARN HARMONY, COUNTERPOINT AND SARCASM!
SCHULZ

As with so much else in the strip, her lack of success was part of any reader's own life. And it gave Lucy a much-needed soft spot that made her sympathetic. At least in *this* situation.

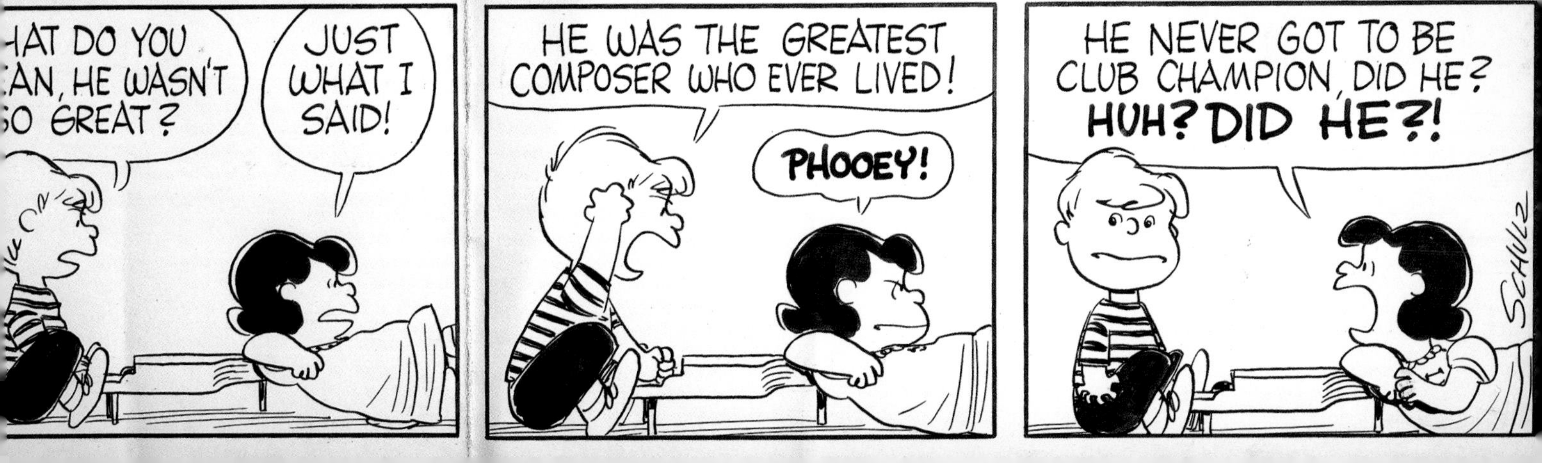
HAT DO YOU AN, HE WASN'T O GREAT?
JUST WHAT I SAID!
HE WAS THE GREATEST COMPOSER WHO EVER LIVED!
PHOOEY!
HE NEVER GOT TO BE CLUB CHAMPION, DID HE? HUH? DID HE?!
SCHULZ

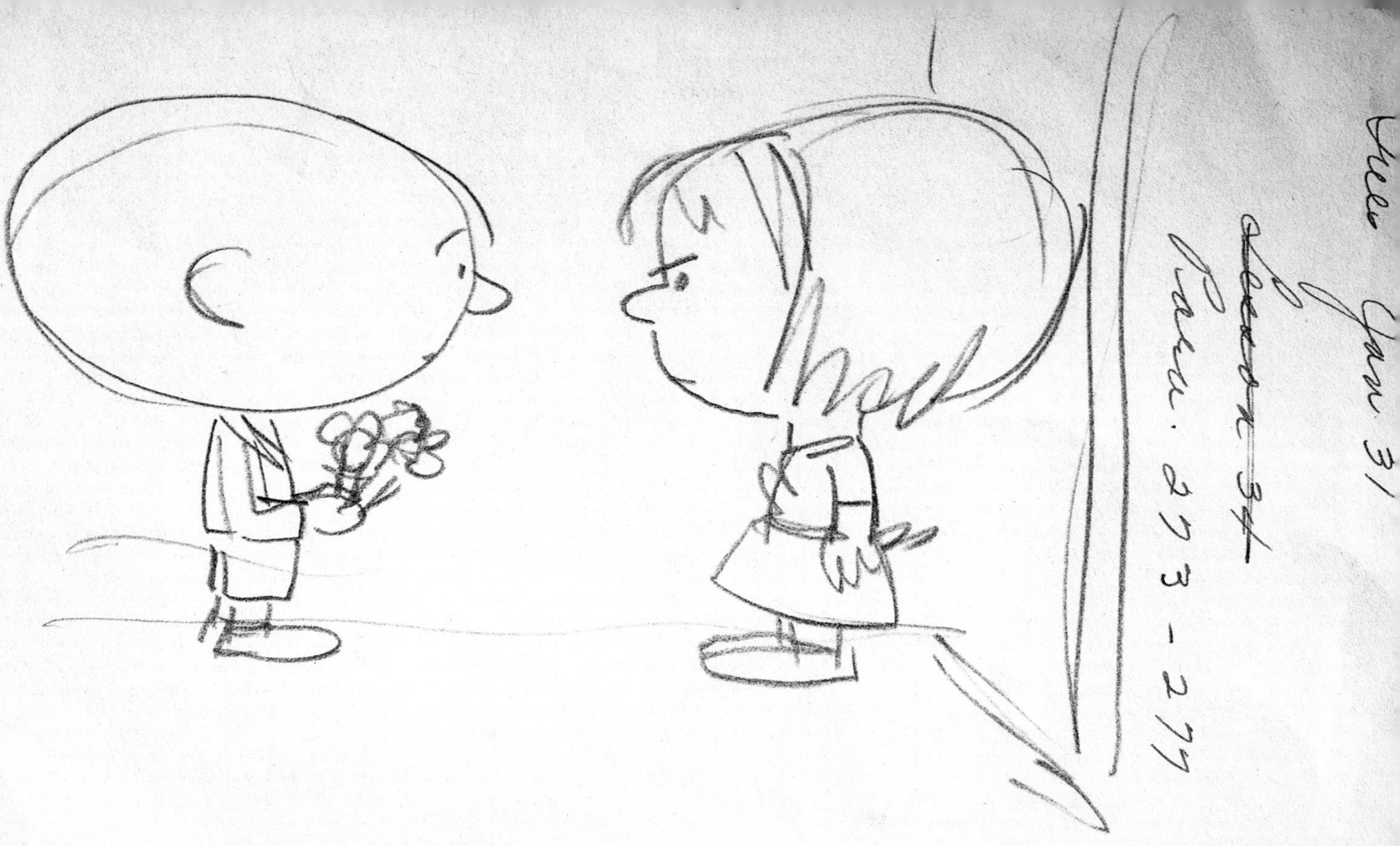

This is the only known drawing by Schulz of the Little Red-Haired Girl, from 1950. In 1947 Donna Johnson began working in the accounting department of Art Instruction Inc. Schulz became smitten, and a long romance ensued. When he proposed, however, she refused him and married fireman Allan Wold instead. Schulz was devastated, but he remained friends with her for the rest of his life, and he drew on his unfulfilled love to produce one of the most poignant storylines in *Peanuts*.

The device of never actually seeing the Little Red-Haired Girl brilliantly underscored Charlie Brown's hopeless longing for her. And besides, as Schulz admitted in 1997, "I could never draw her to satisfy the readers' impression of what she's probably like."

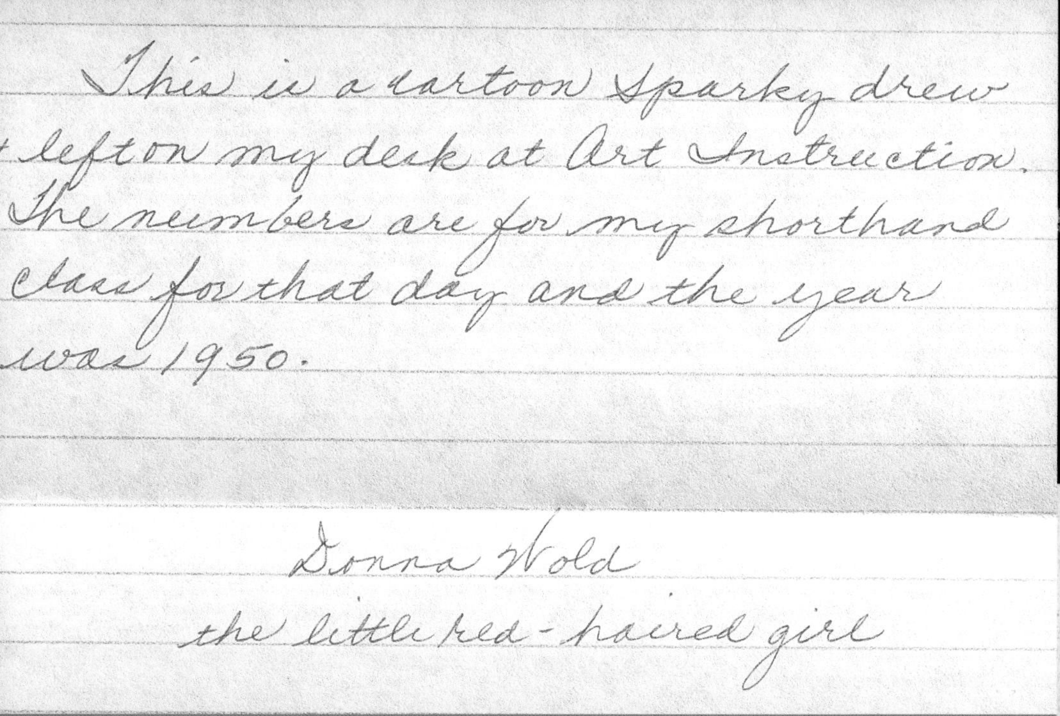

This is a cartoon Sparky drew
+ left on my desk at Art Instruction.
The numbers are for my shorthand
class for that day and the year
was 1950.

Donna Wold
the little red-haired girl

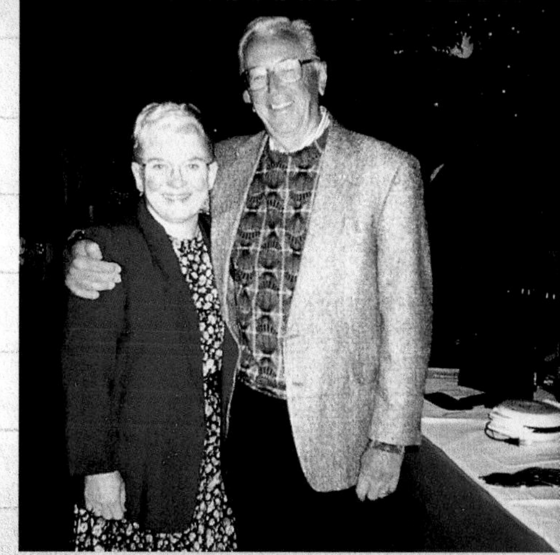

This note to a Peanuts collector explains the numbers scrawled on the drawing on the opposite page.

Above, right: Schulz and Donna Wold in the 1980s.

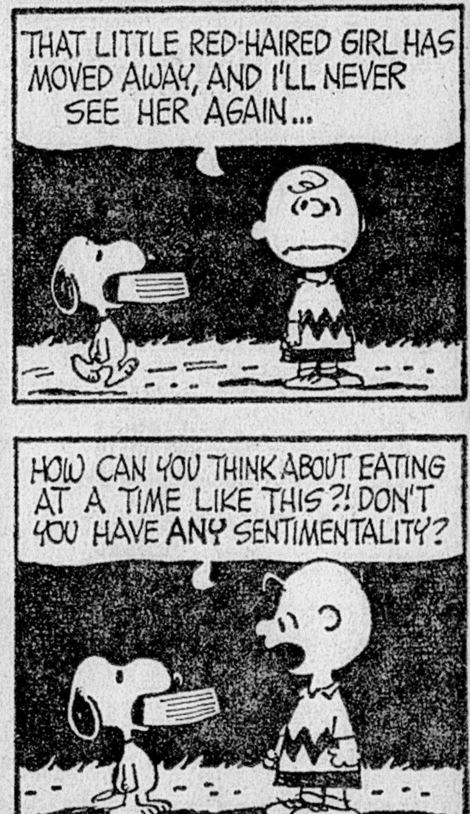

THAT LITTLE RED-HAIRED GIRL HAS MOVED AWAY, AND I'LL NEVER SEE HER AGAIN...
HOW CAN YOU THINK ABOUT EATING AT A TIME LIKE THIS?! DON'T YOU HAVE ANY SENTIMENTALITY?

"They say that opposites attract . . . She's really something and I'm really nothing . . . How opposite can you get?"

—Charlie Brown, 1963

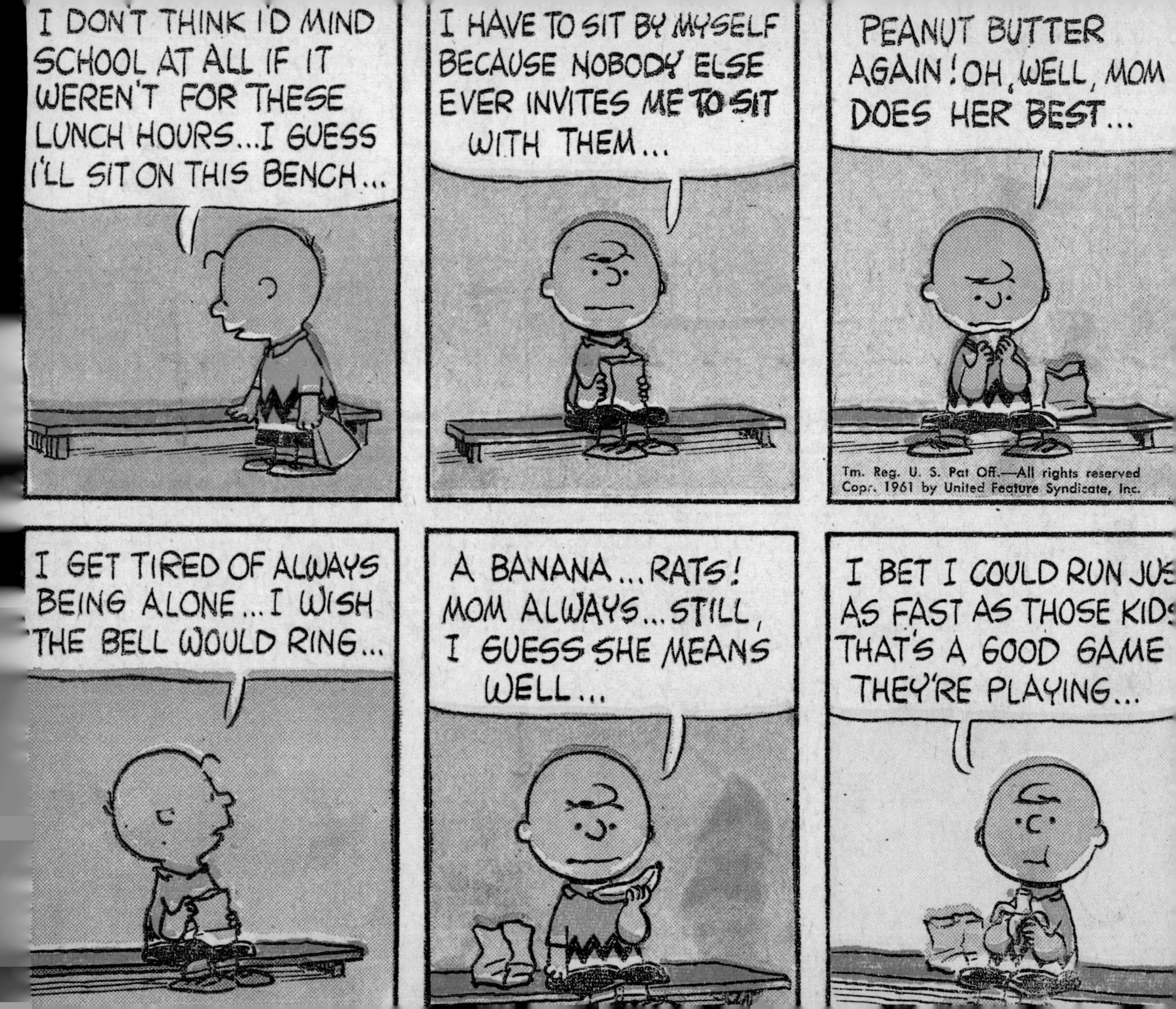

I DON'T THINK I'D MIND SCHOOL AT ALL IF IT WEREN'T FOR THESE LUNCH HOURS...I GUESS I'LL SIT ON THIS BENCH...
I HAVE TO SIT BY MYSELF BECAUSE NOBODY ELSE EVER INVITES ME TO SIT WITH THEM...
PEANUT BUTTER AGAIN! OH, WELL, MOM DOES HER BEST...
Tm. Reg. U. S. Pat Off.—All rights reserved
Copr. 1961 by United Feature Syndicate, Inc.
I GET TIRED OF ALWAYS BEING ALONE...I WISH THE BELL WOULD RING...
A BANANA...RATS! MOM ALWAYS...STILL, I GUESS SHE MEANS WELL...
I BET I COULD RUN JU AS FAST AS THOSE KID THAT'S A GOOD GAME THEY'RE PLAYING...

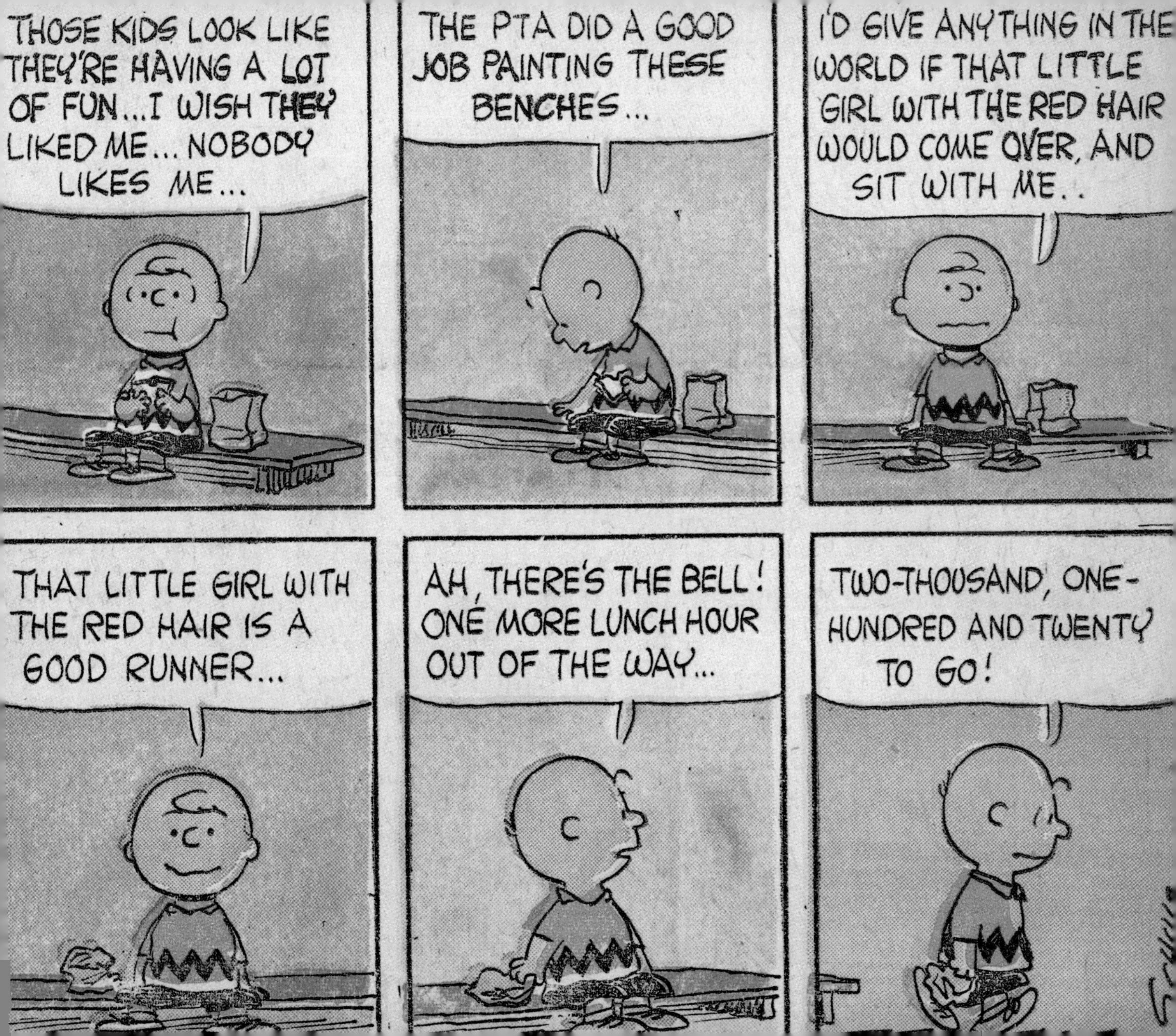
THOSE KIDS LOOK LIKE THEY'RE HAVING A LOT OF FUN...I WISH THEY LIKED ME... NOBODY LIKES ME...
THE PTA DID A GOOD JOB PAINTING THESE BENCHES...
I'D GIVE ANYTHING IN THE WORLD IF THAT LITTLE GIRL WITH THE RED HAIR WOULD COME OVER, AND SIT WITH ME..
THAT LITTLE GIRL WITH THE RED HAIR IS A GOOD RUNNER...
AH, THERE'S THE BELL! ONE MORE LUNCH HOUR OUT OF THE WAY...
TWO-THOUSAND, ONE-HUNDRED AND TWENTY TO GO!

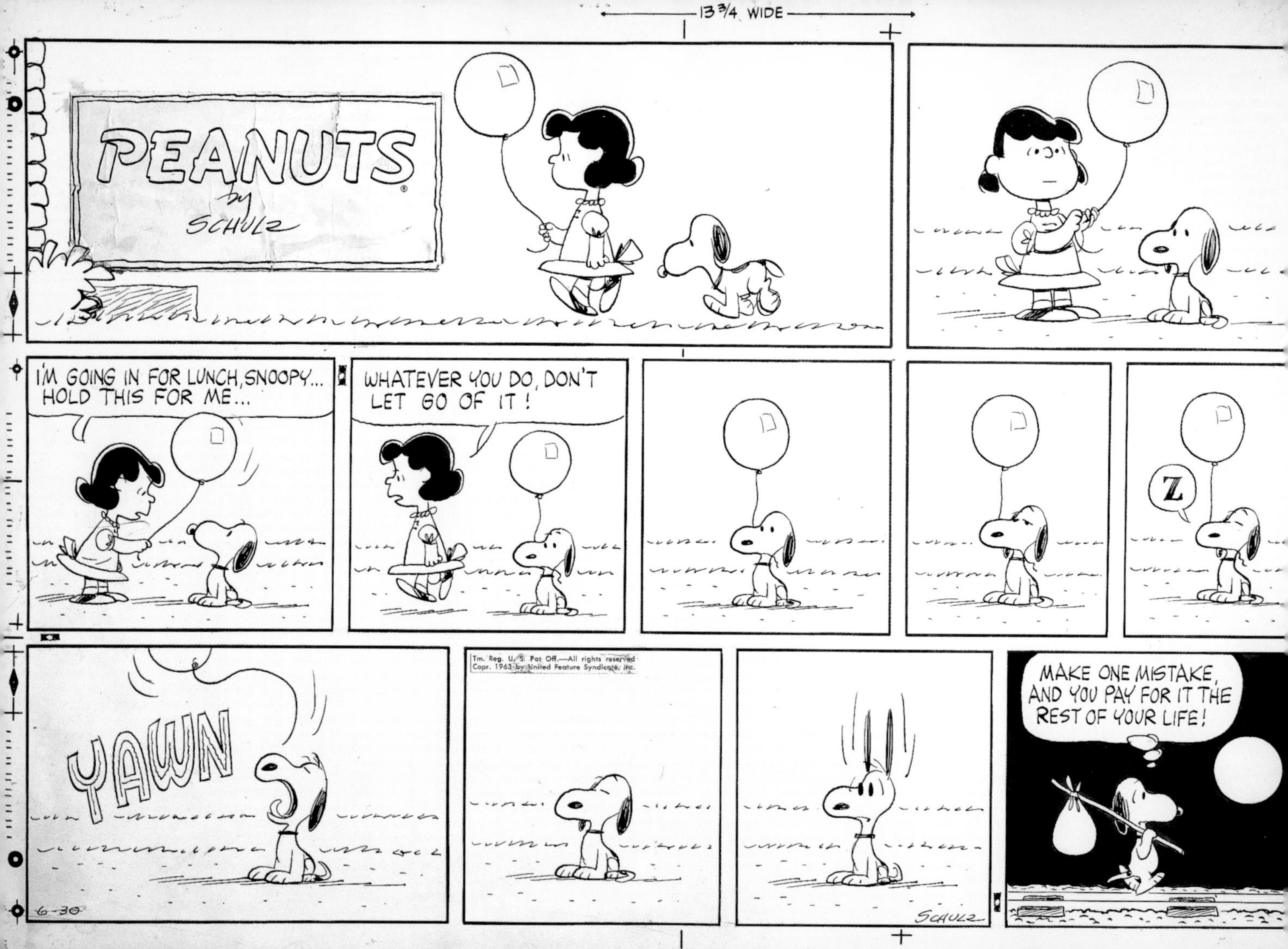
13 3/4 WIDE
PEANUTS
by SCHULZ
I'M GOING IN FOR LUNCH, SNOOPY... HOLD THIS FOR ME...
WHATEVER YOU DO, DON'T LET GO OF IT!
Z
YAWN
Tm. Reg. U. S. Pat. Off.—All rights reserved
Copr. 1963 by United Feature Syndicate, Inc.
SCHULZ
MAKE ONE MISTAKE, AND YOU PAY FOR IT THE REST OF YOUR LIFE!
6-30

"Right from the very beginning, we established that Snoopy as a dog who could understand all of the things which the children were saying to him. He also has a very highly developed sense of intelligence and frequently resents the things the children say about him. He definitely has a mind of his own, and expresses it in thoughts and action." —C. M. S., 1959

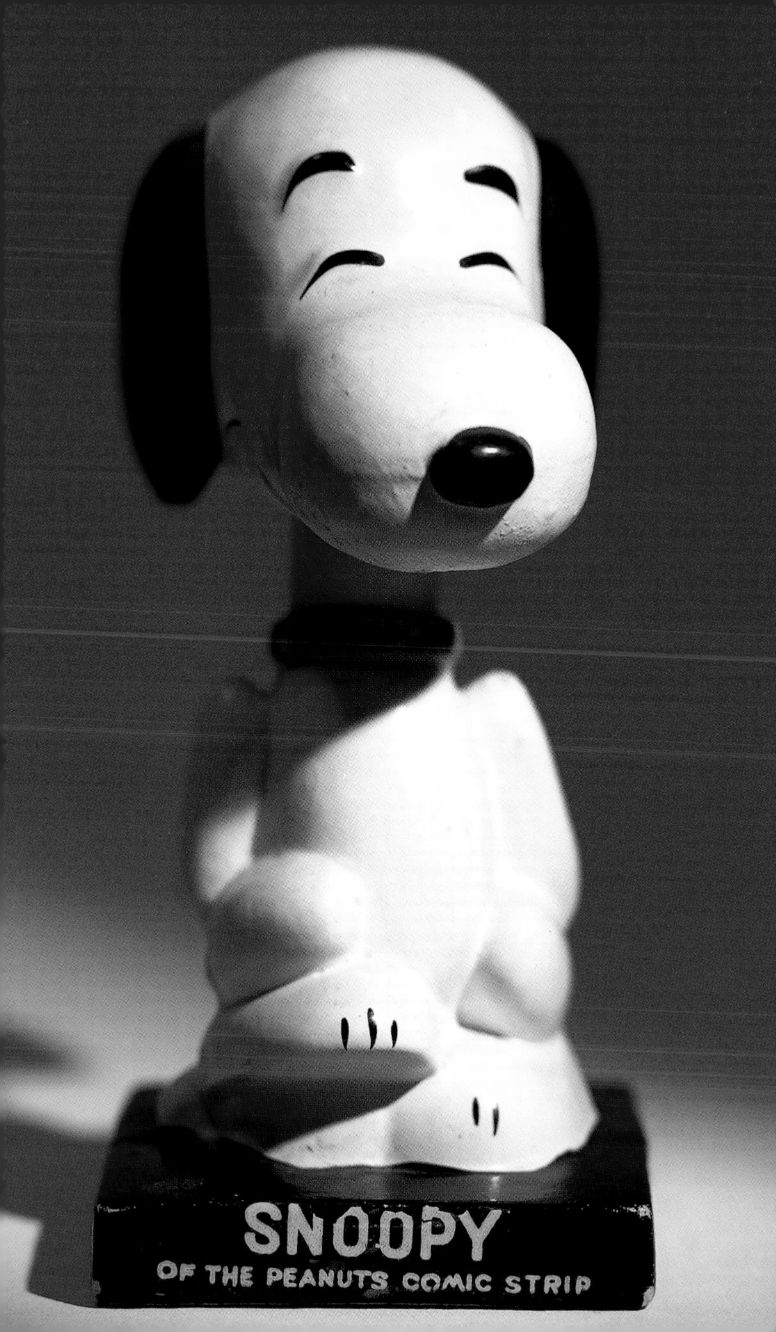
SNOOPY
OF THE PEANUTS COMIC STRIP

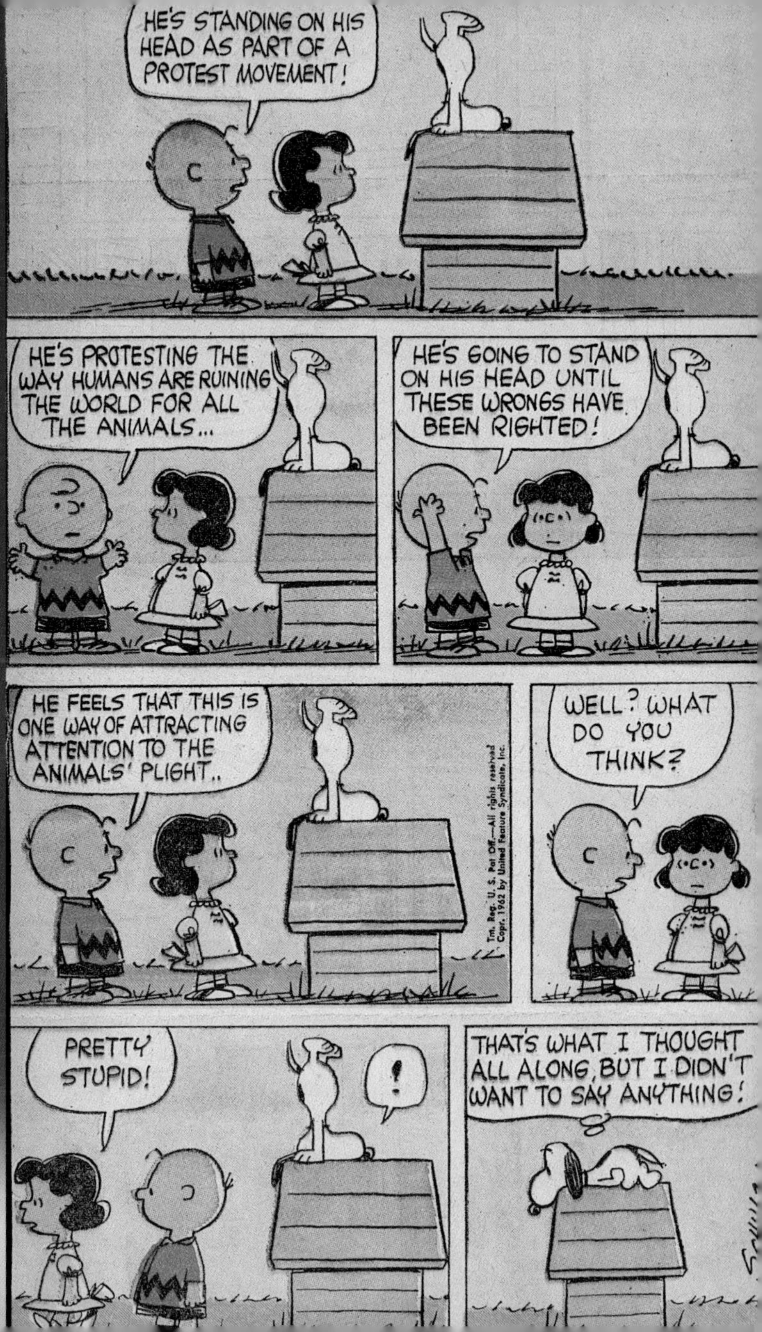
HE'S STANDING ON HIS HEAD AS PART OF A PROTEST MOVEMENT!
HE'S PROTESTING THE WAY HUMANS ARE RUINING THE WORLD FOR ALL THE ANIMALS...
HE'S GOING TO STAND ON HIS HEAD UNTIL THESE WRONGS HAVE BEEN RIGHTED!
HE FEELS THAT THIS IS ONE WAY OF ATTRACTING ATTENTION TO THE ANIMALS' PLIGHT..
Tm. Reg. U. S. Pat. Off.—All rights reserved
Copr. 1962 by United Feature Syndicate, Inc.
WELL? WHAT DO YOU THINK?
PRETTY STUPID!
!
THAT'S WHAT I THOUGHT ALL ALONG, BUT I DIDN'T WANT TO SAY ANYTHING!

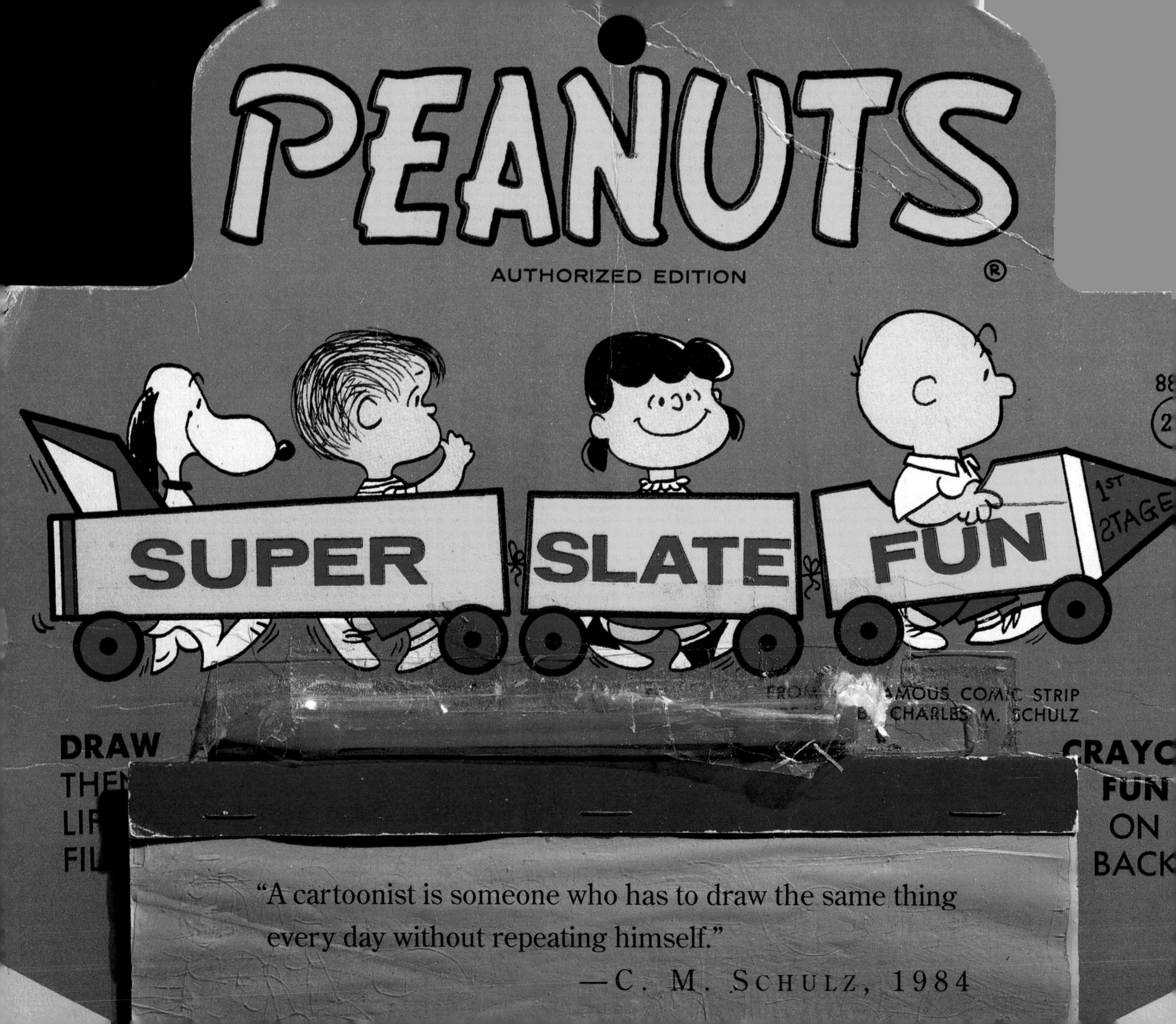
PEANUTS
AUTHORIZED EDITION
SUPER
SLATE
FUN
1ST STAGE
CHARLES M. SCHULZ
DRAW
ON
BACK

"A cartoonist is someone who has to draw the same thing every day without repeating himself."

—C. M. SCHULZ, 1984

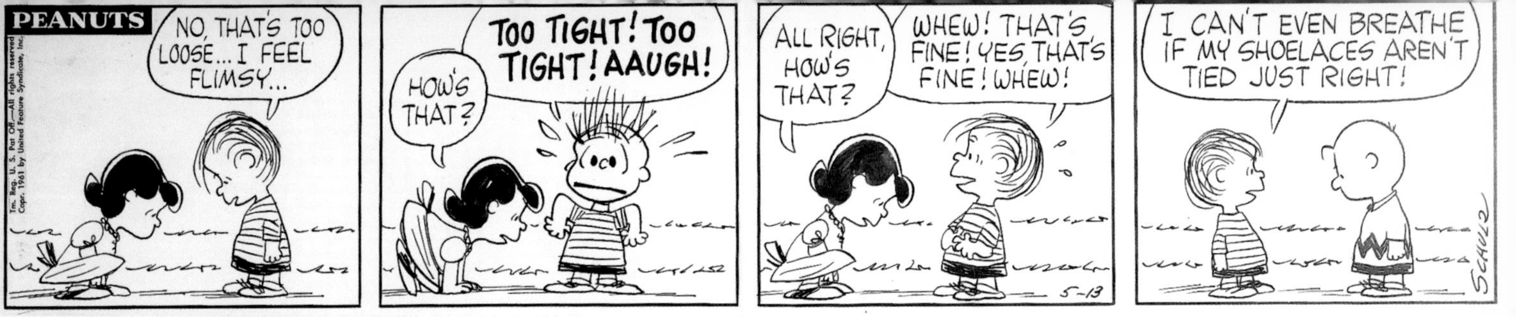
PEANUTS
Tm. Reg. U. S. Pat Off.—All rights reserved Copr. 1961 by United Feature Syndicate, Inc.
NO, THAT'S TOO LOOSE... I FEEL FLIMSY...
HOW'S THAT?
TOO TIGHT! TOO TIGHT! AAUGH!
ALL RIGHT, HOW'S THAT?
WHEW! THAT'S FINE! YES, THAT'S FINE! WHEW!
5-13
I CAN'T EVEN BREATHE IF MY SHOELACES AREN'T TIED JUST RIGHT!
SCHULZ

To Judy with every best wish – Charles M. Schulz

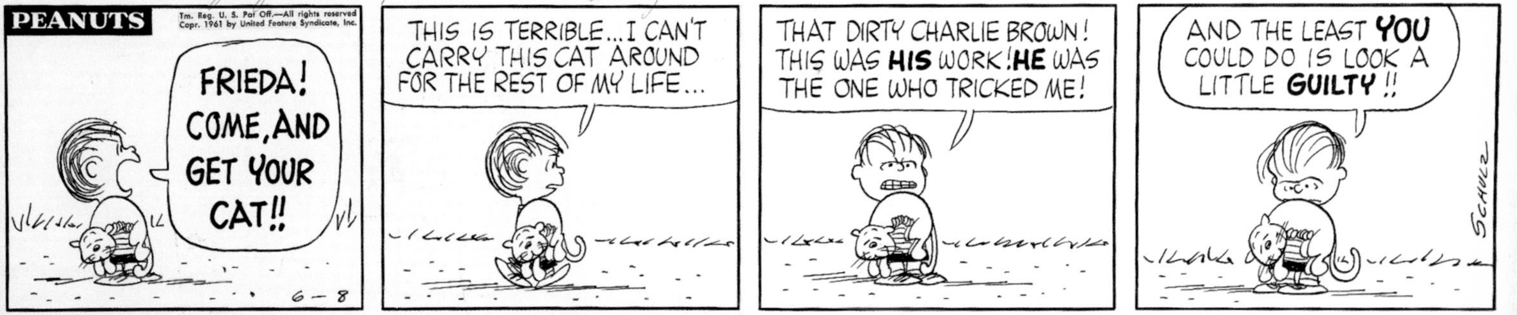
PEANUTS
Tm. Reg. U. S. Pat Off.—All rights reserved Copr. 1961 by United Feature Syndicate, Inc.
FRIEDA! COME, AND GET YOUR CAT!!
6-8
THIS IS TERRIBLE... I CAN'T CARRY THIS CAT AROUND FOR THE REST OF MY LIFE...
THAT DIRTY CHARLIE BROWN! THIS WAS HIS WORK! HE WAS THE ONE WHO TRICKED ME!
AND THE LEAST YOU COULD DO IS LOOK A LITTLE GUILTY!!
SCHULZ

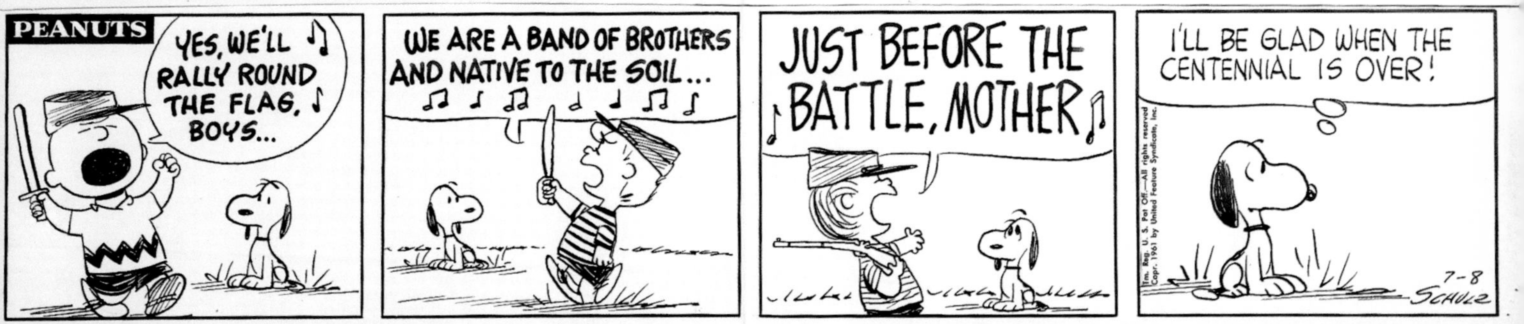
PEANUTS
YES, WE'LL RALLY ROUND THE FLAG, BOYS...
WE ARE A BAND OF BROTHERS AND NATIVE TO THE SOIL...
JUST BEFORE THE BATTLE, MOTHER
Tm. Reg. U. S. Pat Off.—All rights reserved Copr. 1961 by United Feature Syndicate, Inc.
I'LL BE GLAD WHEN THE CENTENNIAL IS OVER!
7-8
SCHULZ

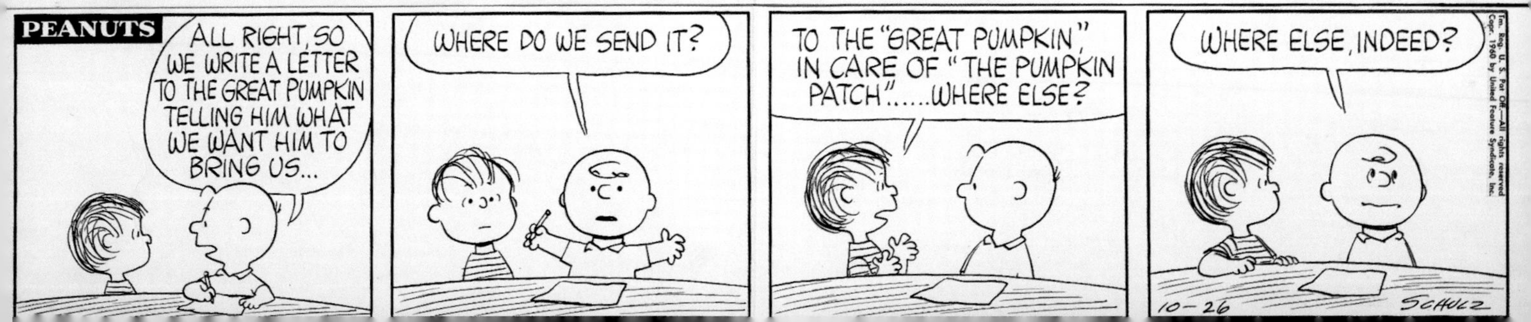
PEANUTS
ALL RIGHT, SO WE WRITE A LETTER TO THE GREAT PUMPKIN TELLING HIM WHAT WE WANT HIM TO BRING US...
WHERE DO WE SEND IT?
TO THE "GREAT PUMPKIN," IN CARE OF "THE PUMPKIN PATCH".....WHERE ELSE?
WHERE ELSE, INDEED?
Tm. Reg. U. S. Pat Off.—All rights reserved Copr. 1960 by United Feature Syndicate, Inc.
10-26
SCHULZ

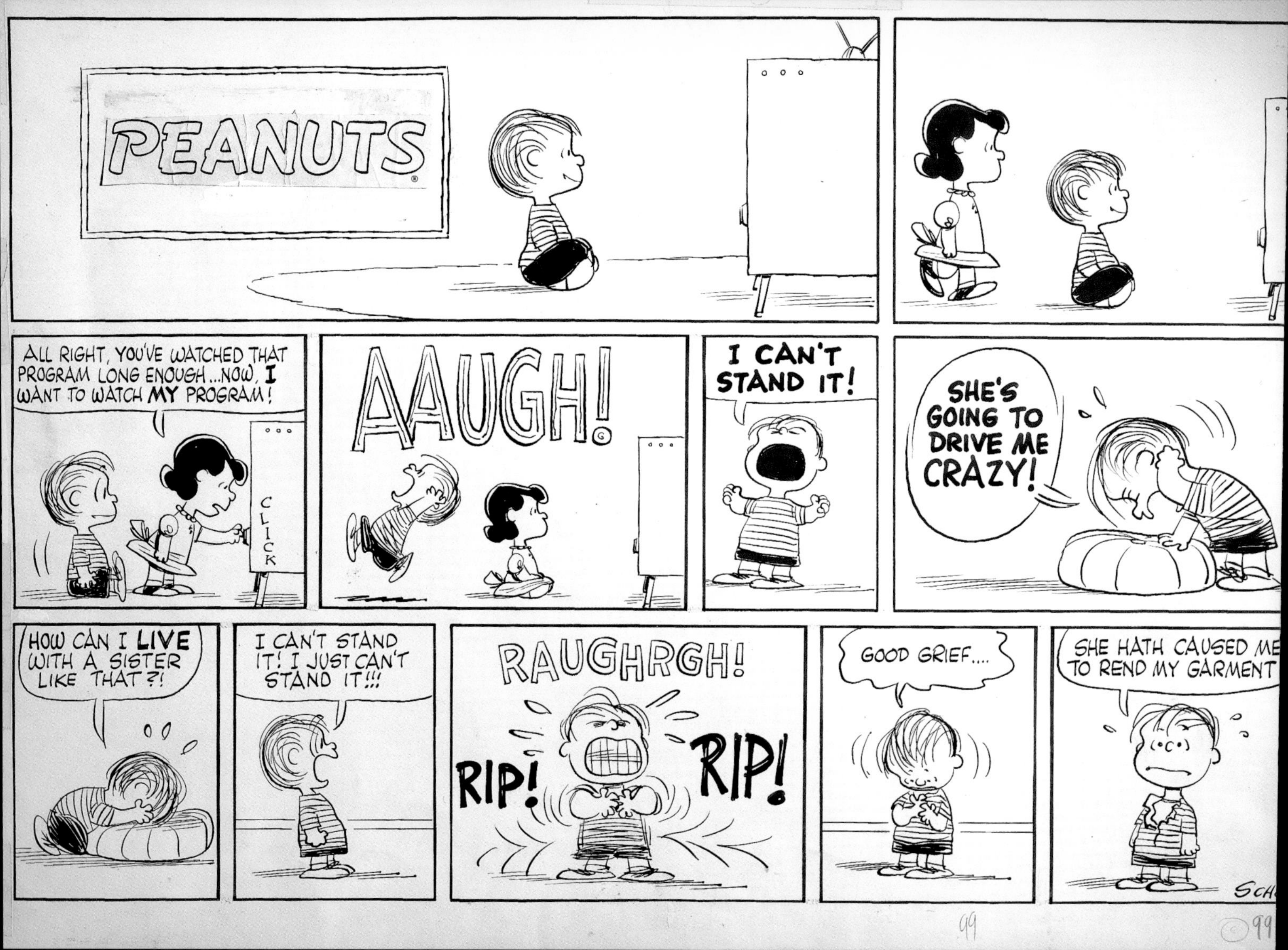
PEANUTS
ALL RIGHT, YOU'VE WATCHED THAT PROGRAM LONG ENOUGH...NOW, I WANT TO WATCH MY PROGRAM!
CLICK
AAUGH!
I CAN'T STAND IT!
SHE'S GOING TO DRIVE ME CRAZY!
HOW CAN I LIVE WITH A SISTER LIKE THAT?!
I CAN'T STAND IT! I JUST CAN'T STAND IT!!!
RAUGHRGH!
RIP!
RIP!
GOOD GRIEF....
SHE HATH CAUSED ME TO REND MY GARMENT

Opposite, right: Linus and his security blanket, on a wall plaque from the mid 1960s. Schulz said in 1977 "[The security blanket] came, of course, from our first three children. And again it wasn't plotted very carefully at first because I think even Charlie Brown had a blanket in one or two sequences. But it worked out well, and that is probably the single best thing that I ever thought of. 'Security blanket' is now in the dictionary."

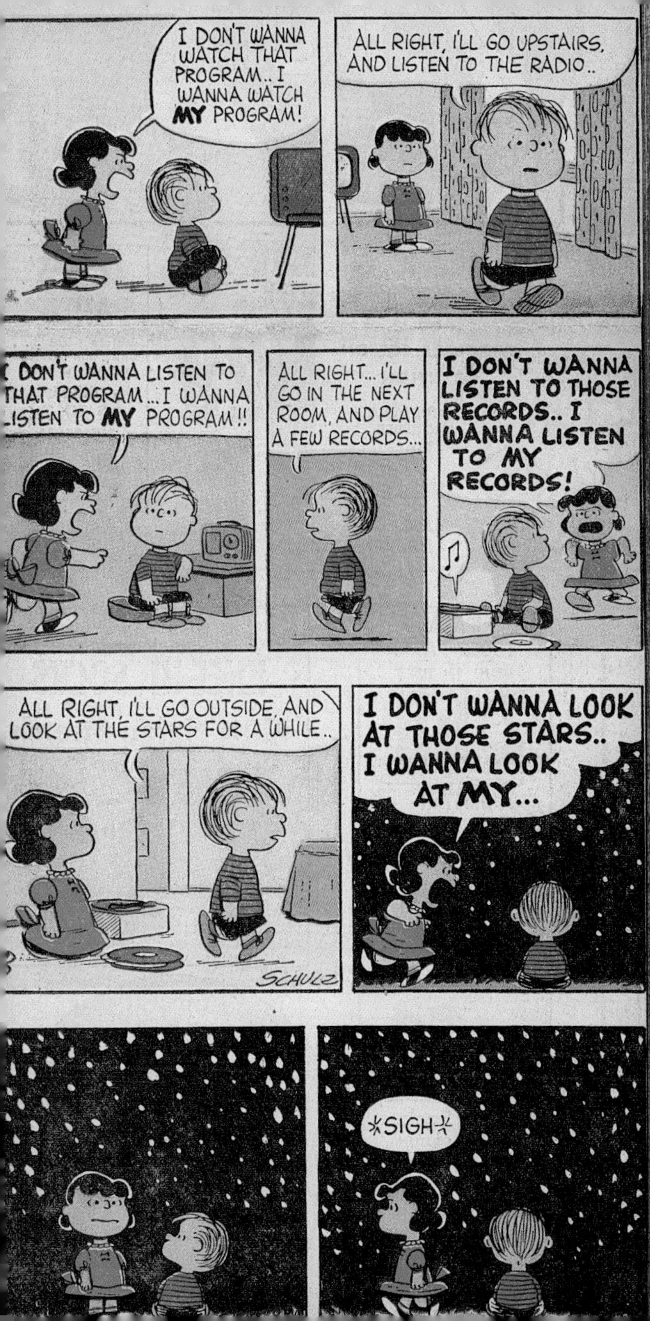
I DON'T WANNA WATCH THAT PROGRAM.. I WANNA WATCH MY PROGRAM!
ALL RIGHT, I'LL GO UPSTAIRS, AND LISTEN TO THE RADIO..
I DON'T WANNA LISTEN TO THAT PROGRAM... I WANNA LISTEN TO MY PROGRAM!!
ALL RIGHT... I'LL GO IN THE NEXT ROOM, AND PLAY A FEW RECORDS...
I DON'T WANNA LISTEN TO THOSE RECORDS.. I WANNA LISTEN TO MY RECORDS!
ALL RIGHT, I'LL GO OUTSIDE, AND LOOK AT THE STARS FOR A WHILE..
I DON'T WANNA LOOK AT THOSE STARS.. I WANNA LOOK AT MY...
SCHULZ
SIGH

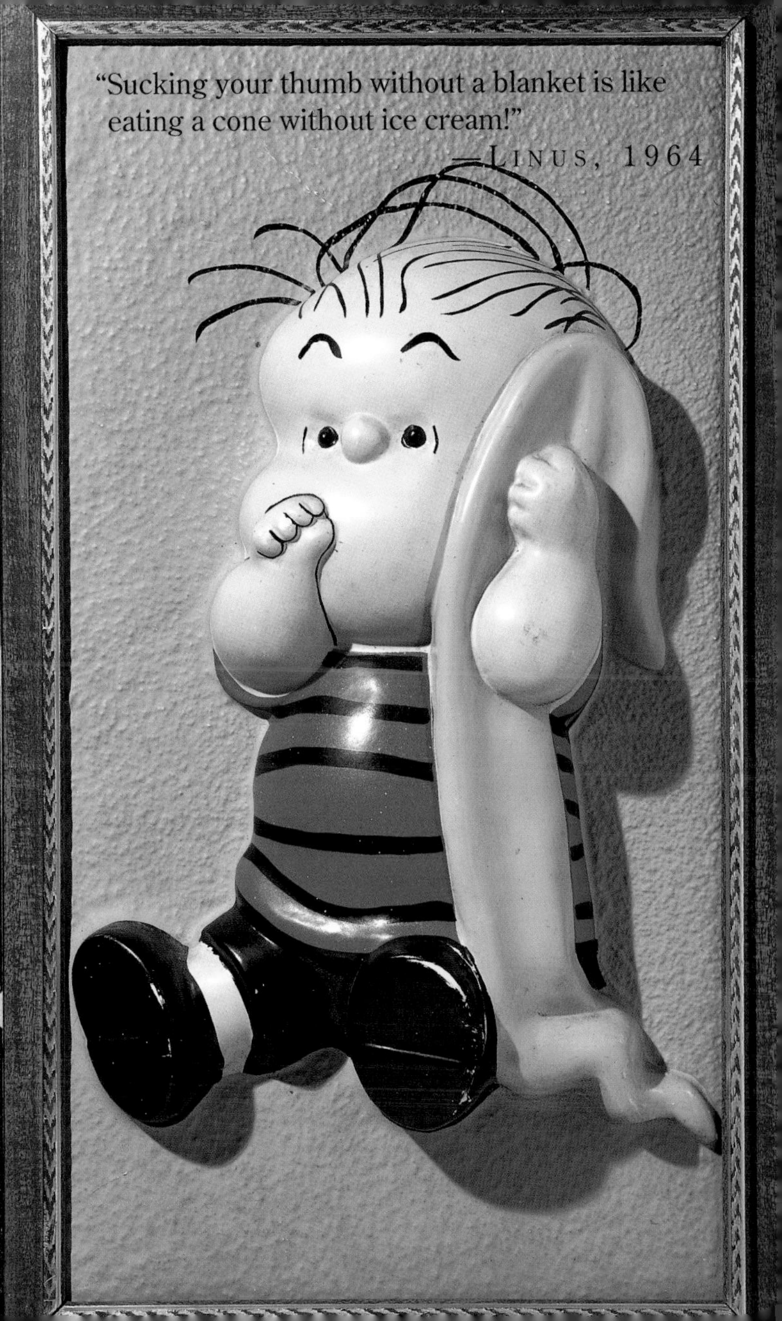

"Sucking your thumb without a blanket is like eating a cone without ice cream!"

—Linus, 1964

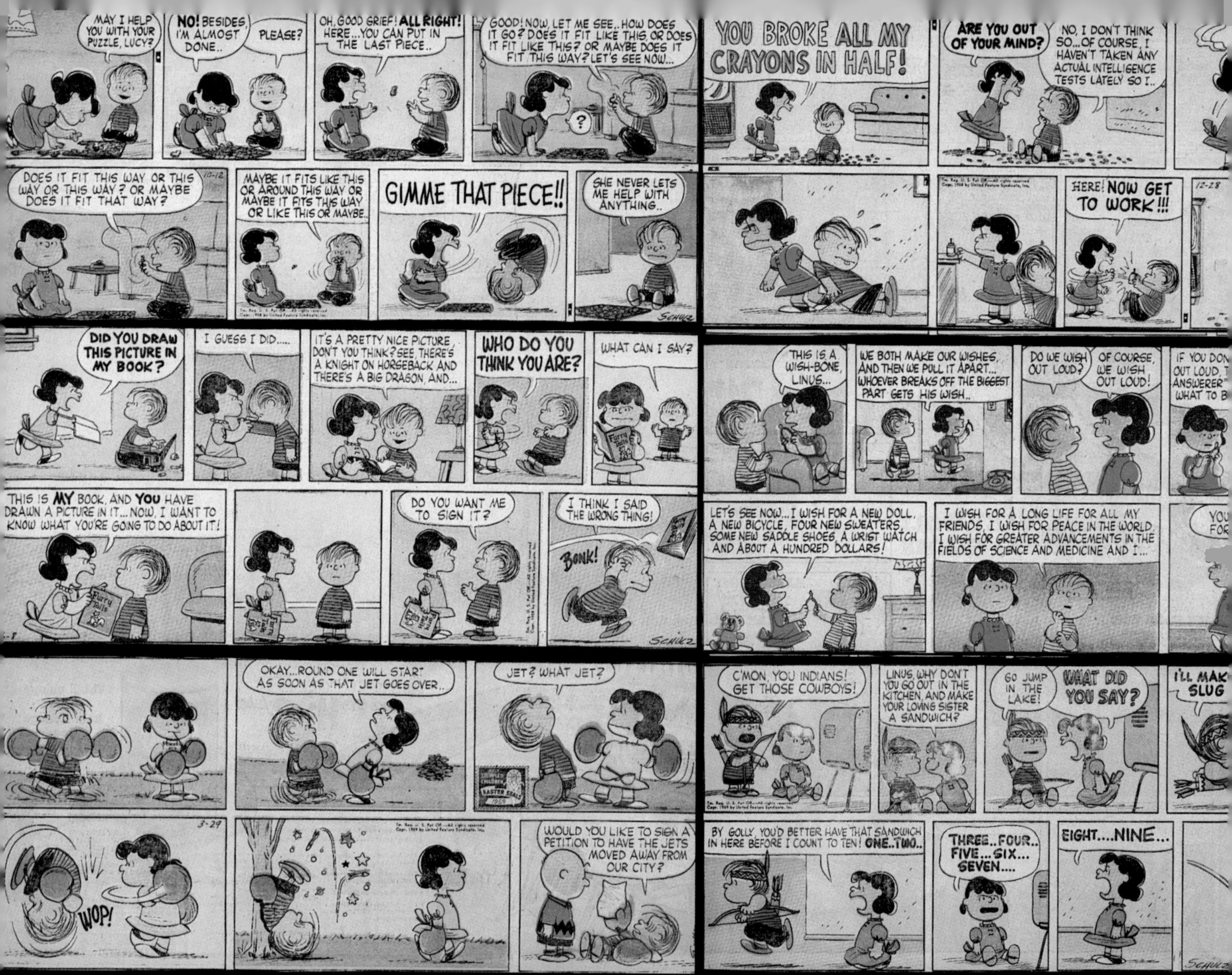
MAY I HELP YOU WITH YOUR PUZZLE, LUCY?
NO! BESIDES, I'M ALMOST DONE..
PLEASE?
OH, GOOD GRIEF! ALL RIGHT! HERE...YOU CAN PUT IN THE LAST PIECE..
GOOD! NOW, LET ME SEE.. HOW DOES IT GO? DOES IT FIT LIKE THIS, OR DOES IT FIT LIKE THIS? OR MAYBE DOES IT FIT THIS WAY? LET'S SEE NOW...
?
DOES IT FIT THIS WAY OR THIS WAY OR THIS WAY? OR MAYBE DOES IT FIT THAT WAY?
MAYBE IT FITS LIKE THIS OR AROUND THIS WAY OR MAYBE IT FITS THIS WAY OR LIKE THIS OR MAYBE..
GIMME THAT PIECE!!
SHE NEVER LETS ME HELP WITH ANYTHING..
DID YOU DRAW THIS PICTURE IN MY BOOK?
I GUESS I DID.....
IT'S A PRETTY NICE PICTURE, DON'T YOU THINK? SEE, THERE'S A KNIGHT ON HORSEBACK AND THERE'S A BIG DRAGON, AND...
WHO DO YOU THINK YOU ARE?
WHAT CAN I SAY?
THIS IS MY BOOK, AND YOU HAVE DRAWN A PICTURE IN IT...NOW, I WANT TO KNOW WHAT YOU'RE GOING TO DO ABOUT IT!
DO YOU WANT ME TO SIGN IT?
I THINK I SAID THE WRONG THING!
BONK!
OKAY...ROUND ONE WILL START AS SOON AS THAT JET GOES OVER..
JET? WHAT JET?
WOP!
WOULD YOU LIKE TO SIGN A PETITION TO HAVE THE JETS MOVED AWAY FROM OUR CITY?
YOU BROKE ALL MY CRAYONS IN HALF!
ARE YOU OUT OF YOUR MIND?
NO, I DON'T THINK SO...OF COURSE, I HAVEN'T TAKEN ANY ACTUAL INTELLIGENCE TESTS LATELY SO I..
HERE! NOW GET TO WORK!!!
THIS IS A WISH-BONE, LINUS...
WE BOTH MAKE OUR WISHES, AND THEN WE PULL IT APART... WHOEVER BREAKS OFF THE BIGGEST PART GETS HIS WISH..
DO WE WISH OUT LOUD?
OF COURSE, WE WISH OUT LOUD!
LET'S SEE NOW...I WISH FOR A NEW DOLL, A NEW BICYCLE, FOUR NEW SWEATERS, SOME NEW SADDLE SHOES, A WRIST WATCH AND ABOUT A HUNDRED DOLLARS!
I WISH FOR A LONG LIFE FOR ALL MY FRIENDS, I WISH FOR PEACE IN THE WORLD, I WISH FOR GREATER ADVANCEMENTS IN THE FIELDS OF SCIENCE AND MEDICINE AND I...
C'MON, YOU INDIANS! GET THOSE COWBOYS!
LINUS, WHY DON'T YOU GO OUT IN THE KITCHEN, AND MAKE YOUR LOVING SISTER A SANDWICH?
GO JUMP IN THE LAKE!
WHAT DID YOU SAY?
BY GOLLY, YOU'D BETTER HAVE THAT SANDWICH IN HERE BEFORE I COUNT TO TEN! ONE..TWO..
THREE..FOUR.. FIVE...SIX... SEVEN....
EIGHT....NINE...
SCHULZ

Of the torment Lucy puts Linus through, Schulz said in 1997, "You know, the kids in the strip—it's kind of a parody of the cruelty that exists among children. Because they are struggling to survive."

Opposite. An undated sketch, probably from the mid 1960s, of an unusually retaliatory L

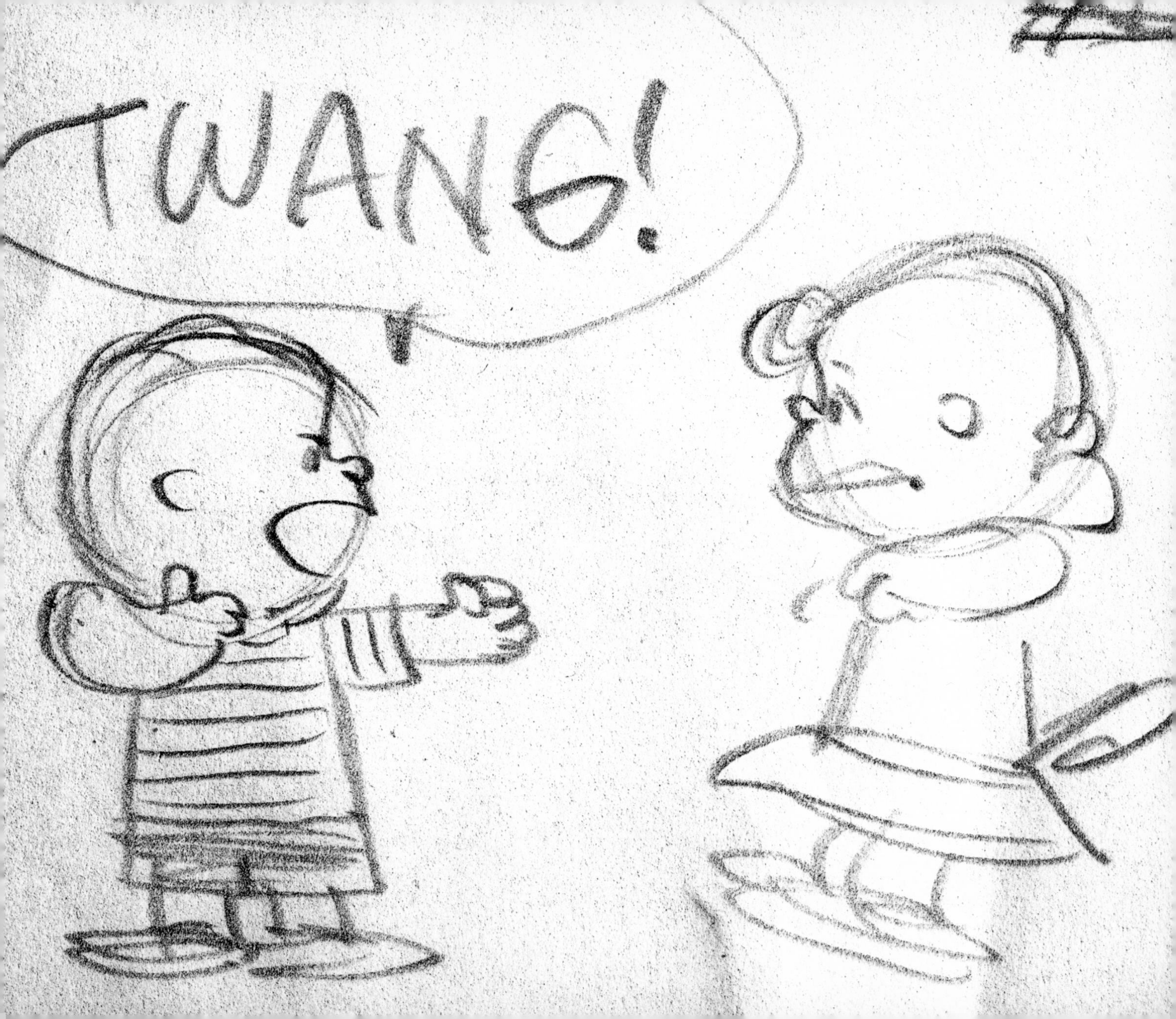
TWANG!

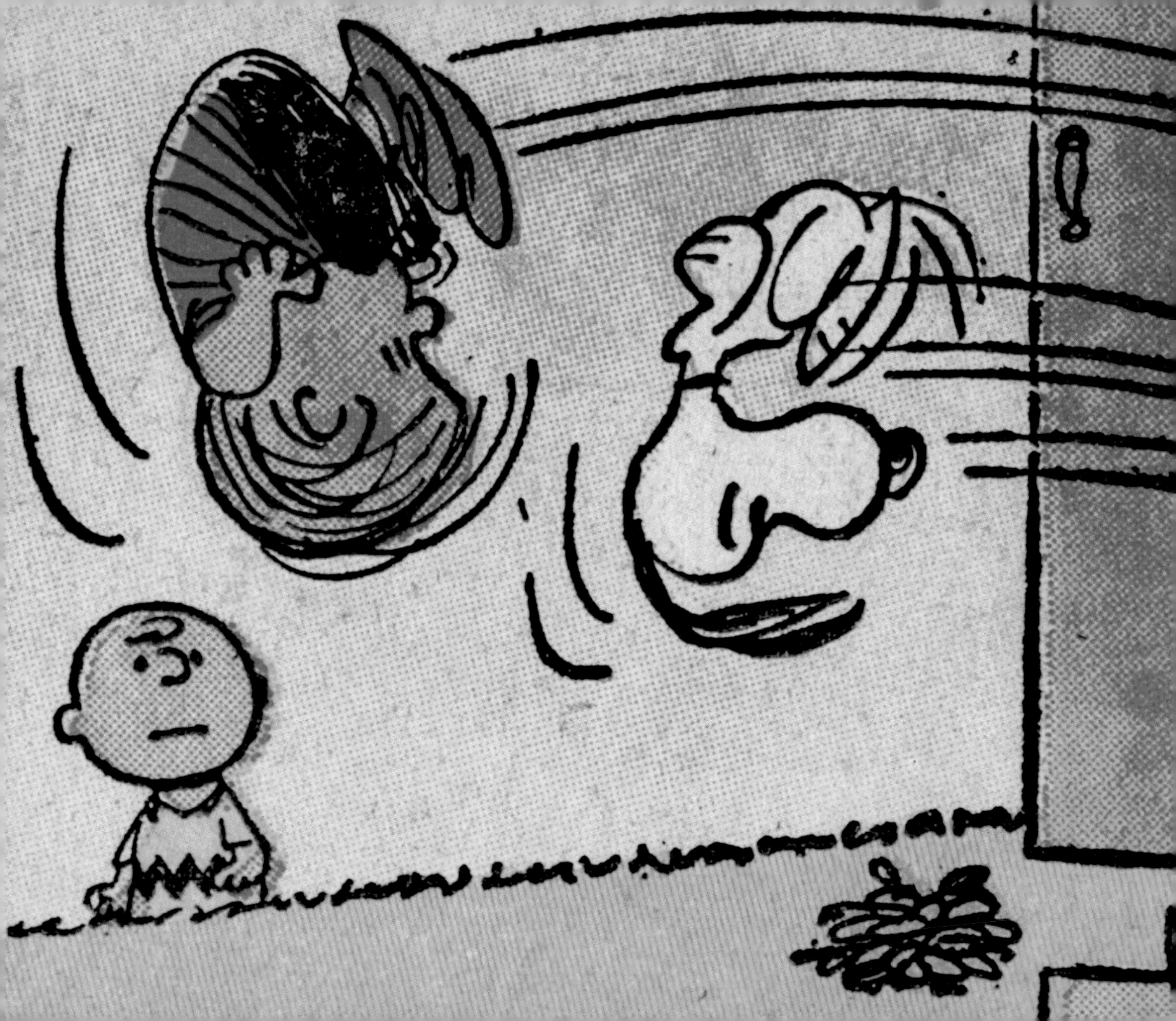

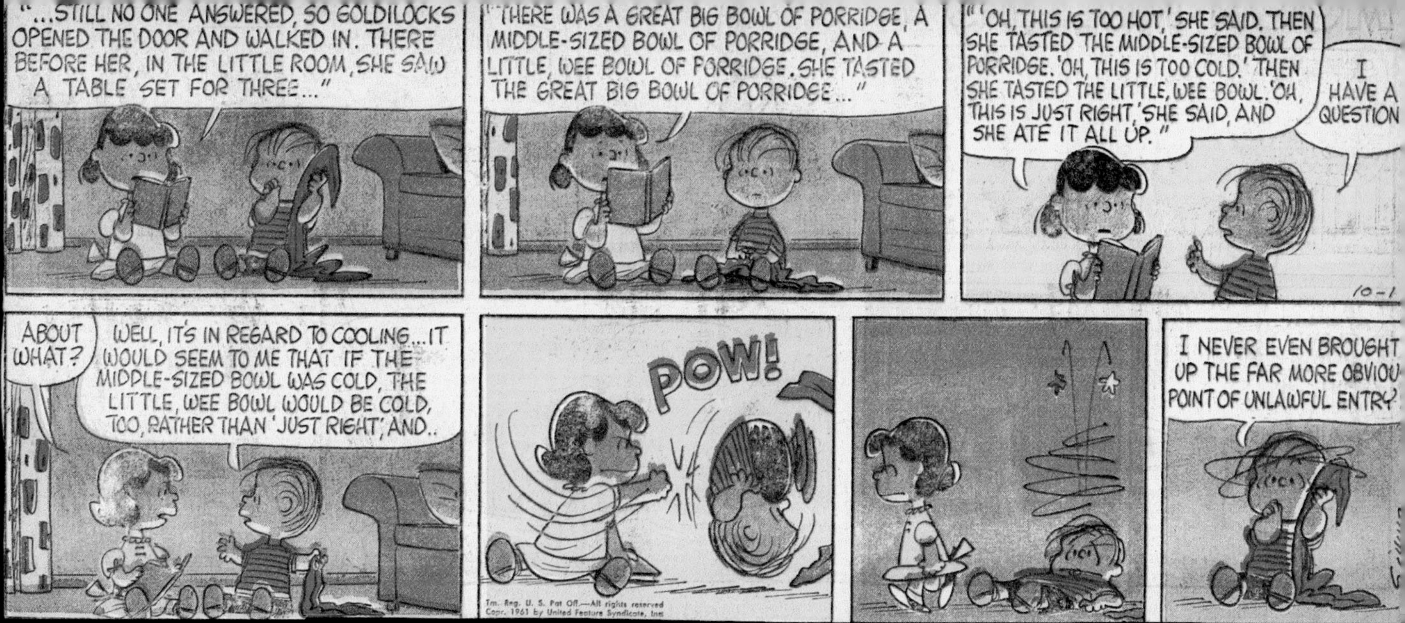
"...STILL NO ONE ANSWERED, SO GOLDILOCKS OPENED THE DOOR AND WALKED IN. THERE BEFORE HER, IN THE LITTLE ROOM, SHE SAW A TABLE SET FOR THREE..."
"THERE WAS A GREAT BIG BOWL OF PORRIDGE, A MIDDLE-SIZED BOWL OF PORRIDGE, AND A LITTLE, WEE BOWL OF PORRIDGE. SHE TASTED THE GREAT BIG BOWL OF PORRIDGE..."
"'OH, THIS IS TOO HOT,' SHE SAID. THEN SHE TASTED THE MIDDLE-SIZED BOWL OF PORRIDGE. 'OH, THIS IS TOO COLD.' THEN SHE TASTED THE LITTLE, WEE BOWL. 'OH, THIS IS JUST RIGHT,' SHE SAID, AND SHE ATE IT ALL UP."
I HAVE A QUESTION
10-1
ABOUT WHAT?
WELL, IT'S IN REGARD TO COOLING...IT WOULD SEEM TO ME THAT IF THE MIDDLE-SIZED BOWL WAS COLD, THE LITTLE, WEE BOWL WOULD BE COLD, TOO, RATHER THAN 'JUST RIGHT,' AND..
POW!
Tm. Reg. U. S. Pat Off.—All rights reserved Copr. 1961 by United Feature Syndicate, Inc.
I NEVER EVEN BROUGHT UP THE FAR MORE OBVIOU POINT OF UNLAWFUL ENTRY

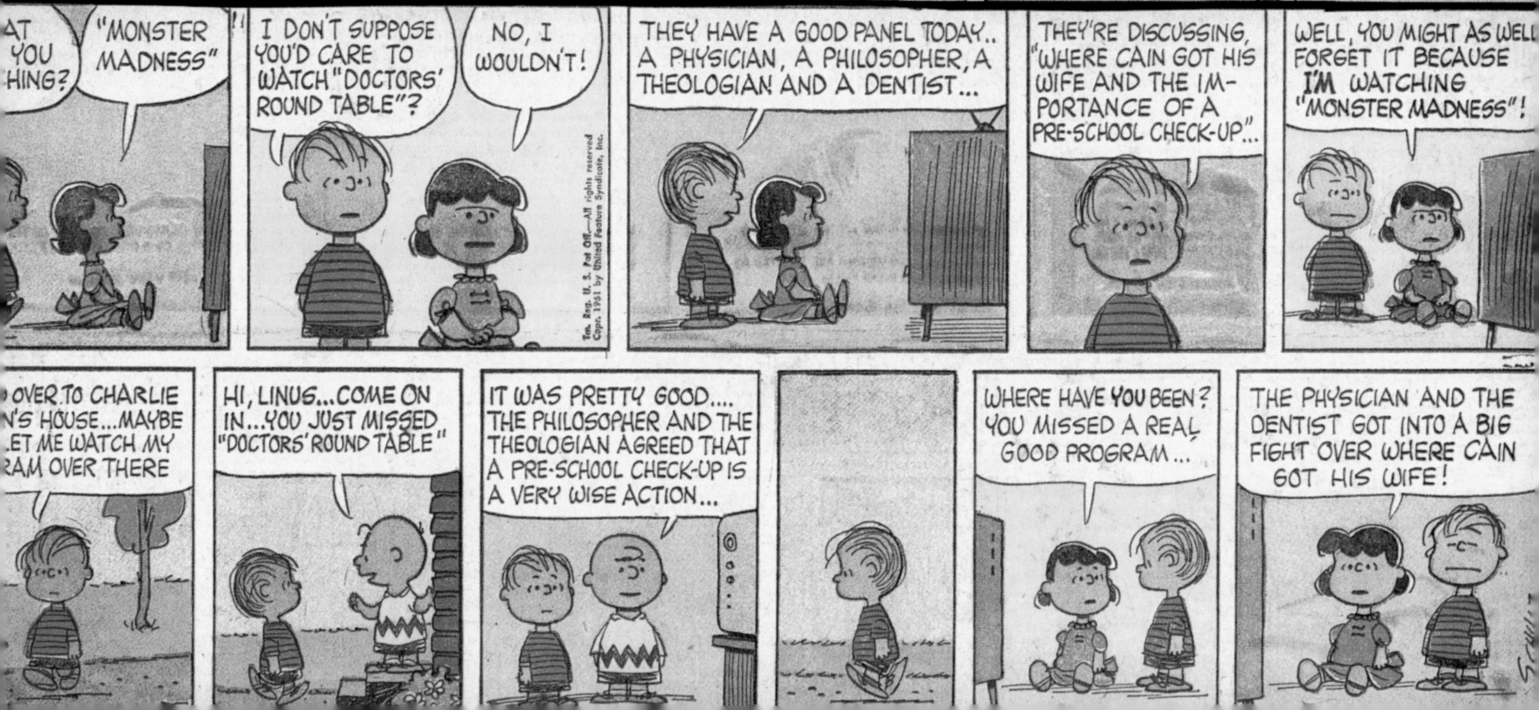
AT YOU HING?
"MONSTER MADNESS"
I DON'T SUPPOSE YOU'D CARE TO WATCH "DOCTORS' ROUND TABLE"?
NO, I WOULDN'T!
Tm. Reg. U. S. Pat. Off.—All rights reserved Copr. 1961 by United Feature Syndicate, Inc.
THEY HAVE A GOOD PANEL TODAY.. A PHYSICIAN, A PHILOSOPHER, A THEOLOGIAN AND A DENTIST...
THEY'RE DISCUSSING, "WHERE CAIN GOT HIS WIFE AND THE IMPORTANCE OF A PRE-SCHOOL CHECK-UP"...
WELL, YOU MIGHT AS WELL FORGET IT BECAUSE I'M WATCHING "MONSTER MADNESS"!
OVER TO CHARLIE N'S HOUSE...MAYBE LET ME WATCH MY RAM OVER THERE
HI, LINUS...COME ON IN...YOU JUST MISSED "DOCTORS' ROUND TABLE"
IT WAS PRETTY GOOD.... THE PHILOSOPHER AND THE THEOLOGIAN AGREED THAT A PRE-SCHOOL CHECK-UP IS A VERY WISE ACTION...
WHERE HAVE YOU BEEN? YOU MISSED A REAL GOOD PROGRAM...
THE PHYSICIAN AND THE DENTIST GOT INTO A BIG FIGHT OVER WHERE CAIN GOT HIS WIFE!

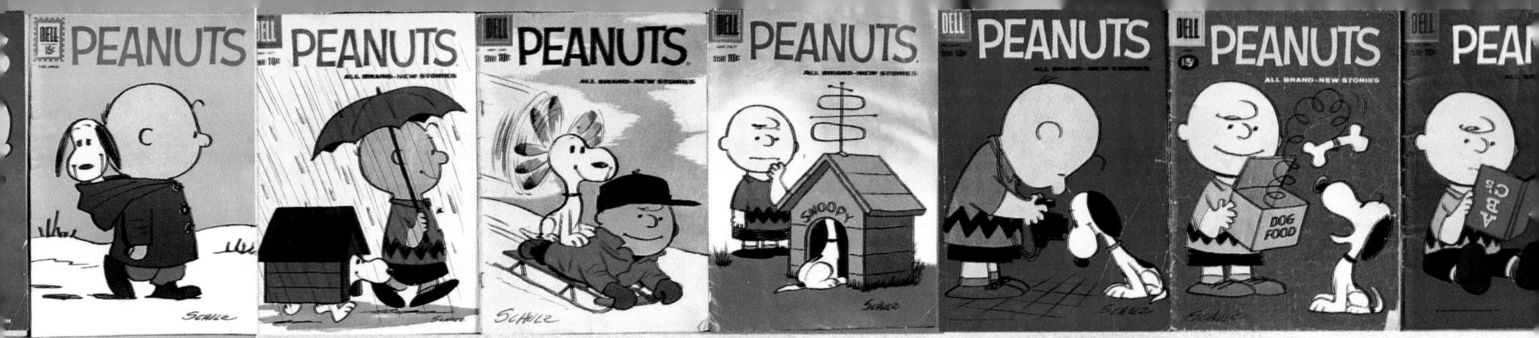
DELL
PEANUTS
ALL BRAND-NEW STORIES
SNOOPY
DOG FOOD
SCHULZ

Comic book covers for Dell, early 1960s.

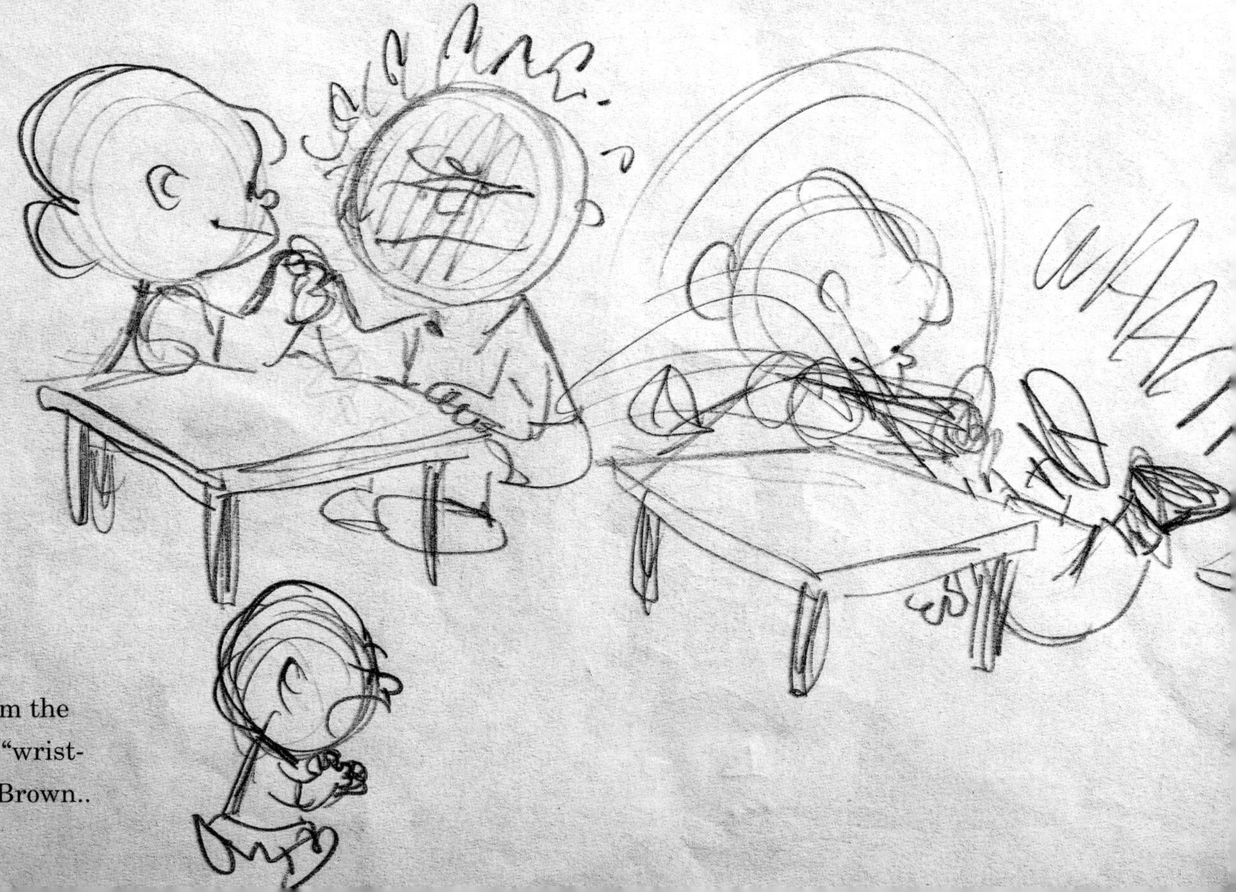

Undated sketch from the mid-1950s of Lucy "wrist-wrestling" Charlie Brown..

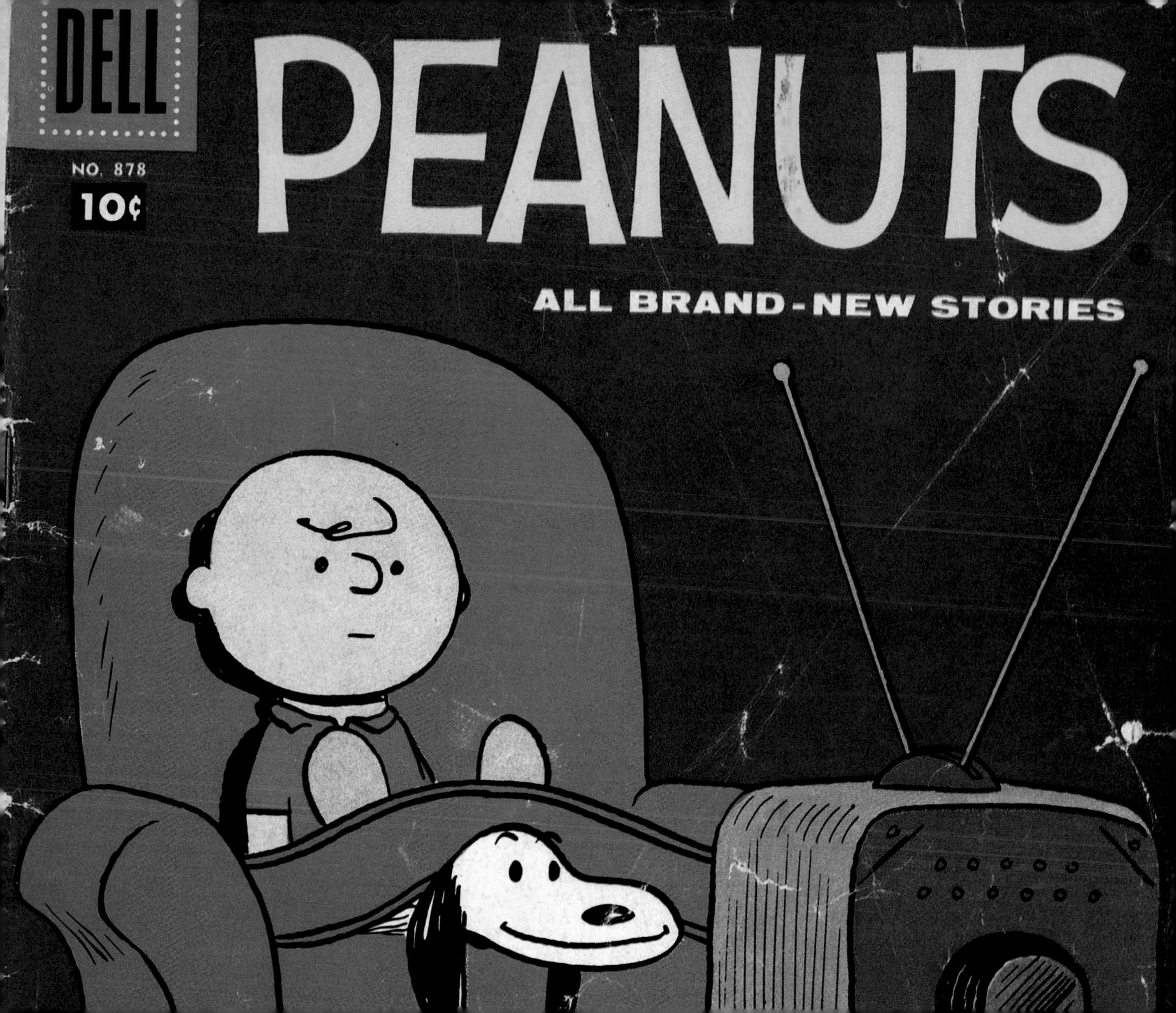
DELL
NO. 878
10¢
PEANUTS
ALL BRAND-NEW STORIES

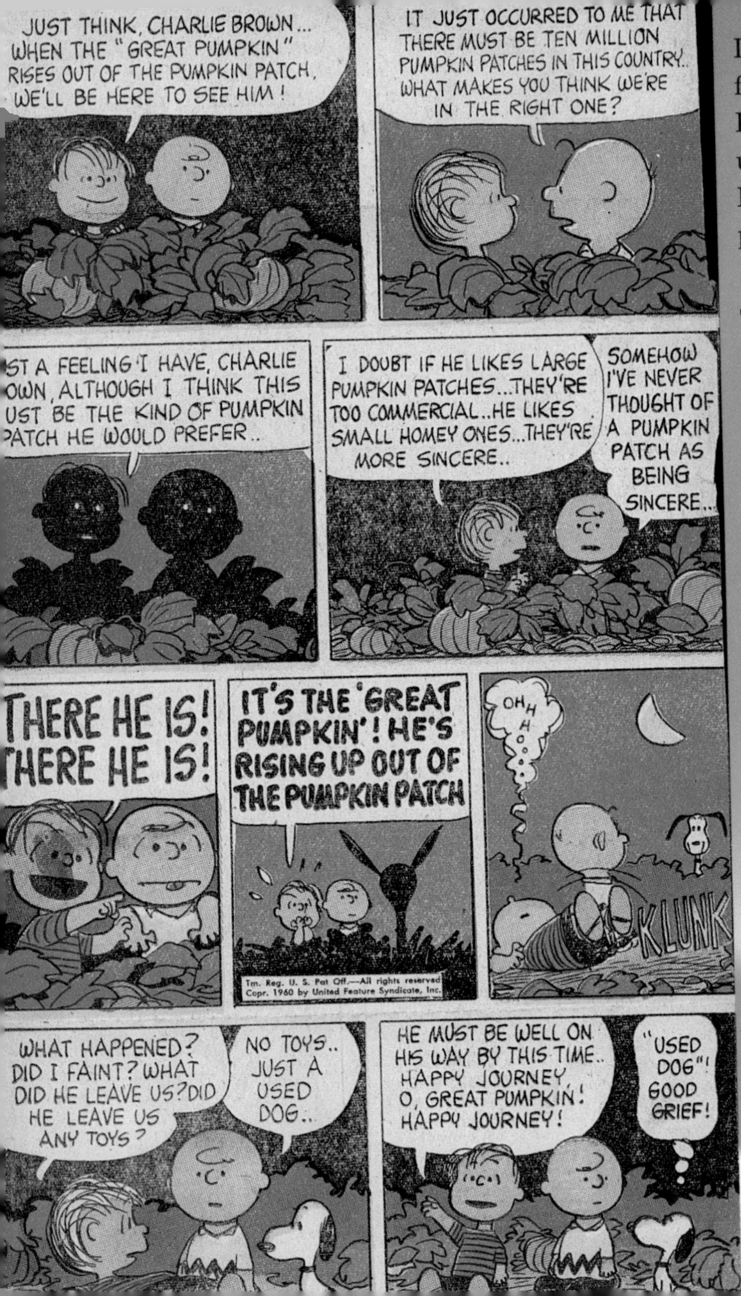
JUST THINK, CHARLIE BROWN... WHEN THE "GREAT PUMPKIN" RISES OUT OF THE PUMPKIN PATCH, WE'LL BE HERE TO SEE HIM!
IT JUST OCCURRED TO ME THAT THERE MUST BE TEN MILLION PUMPKIN PATCHES IN THIS COUNTRY.. WHAT MAKES YOU THINK WE'RE IN THE RIGHT ONE?
ST A FEELING I HAVE, CHARLIE OWN, ALTHOUGH I THINK THIS UST BE THE KIND OF PUMPKIN PATCH HE WOULD PREFER..
I DOUBT IF HE LIKES LARGE PUMPKIN PATCHES...THEY'RE TOO COMMERCIAL..HE LIKES SMALL HOMEY ONES...THEY'RE MORE SINCERE..
SOMEHOW I'VE NEVER THOUGHT OF A PUMPKIN PATCH AS BEING SINCERE..
THERE HE IS! THERE HE IS!
IT'S THE 'GREAT PUMPKIN'! HE'S RISING UP OUT OF THE PUMPKIN PATCH
Tm. Reg. U. S. Pat Off.—All rights reserved Copr. 1960 by United Feature Syndicate, Inc.
OHHHOOO
KLUNK
WHAT HAPPENED? DID I FAINT? WHAT DID HE LEAVE US? DID HE LEAVE US ANY TOYS?
NO TOYS.. JUST A USED DOG..
HE MUST BE WELL ON HIS WAY BY THIS TIME.. HAPPY JOURNEY, O, GREAT PUMPKIN! HAPPY JOURNEY!
"USED DOG"! GOOD GRIEF!

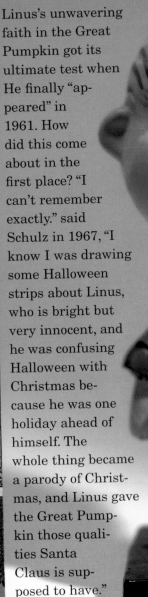

Linus's unwavering faith in the Great Pumpkin got its ultimate test when He finally "appeared" in 1961. How did this come about in the first place? "I can't remember exactly." said Schulz in 1967, "I know I was drawing some Halloween strips about Linus, who is bright but very innocent, and he was confusing Halloween with Christmas because he was one holiday ahead of himself. The whole thing became a parody of Christmas, and Linus gave the Great Pumpkin those qualities Santa Claus is supposed to have."

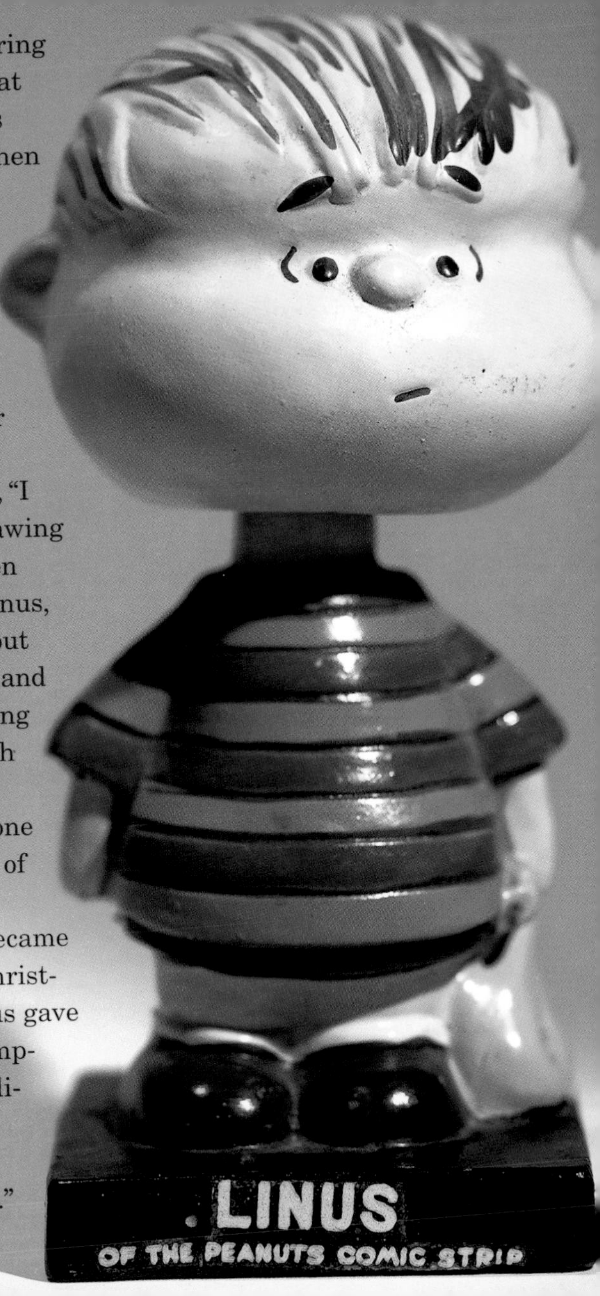
LINUS
OF THE PEANUTS COMIC STRIP

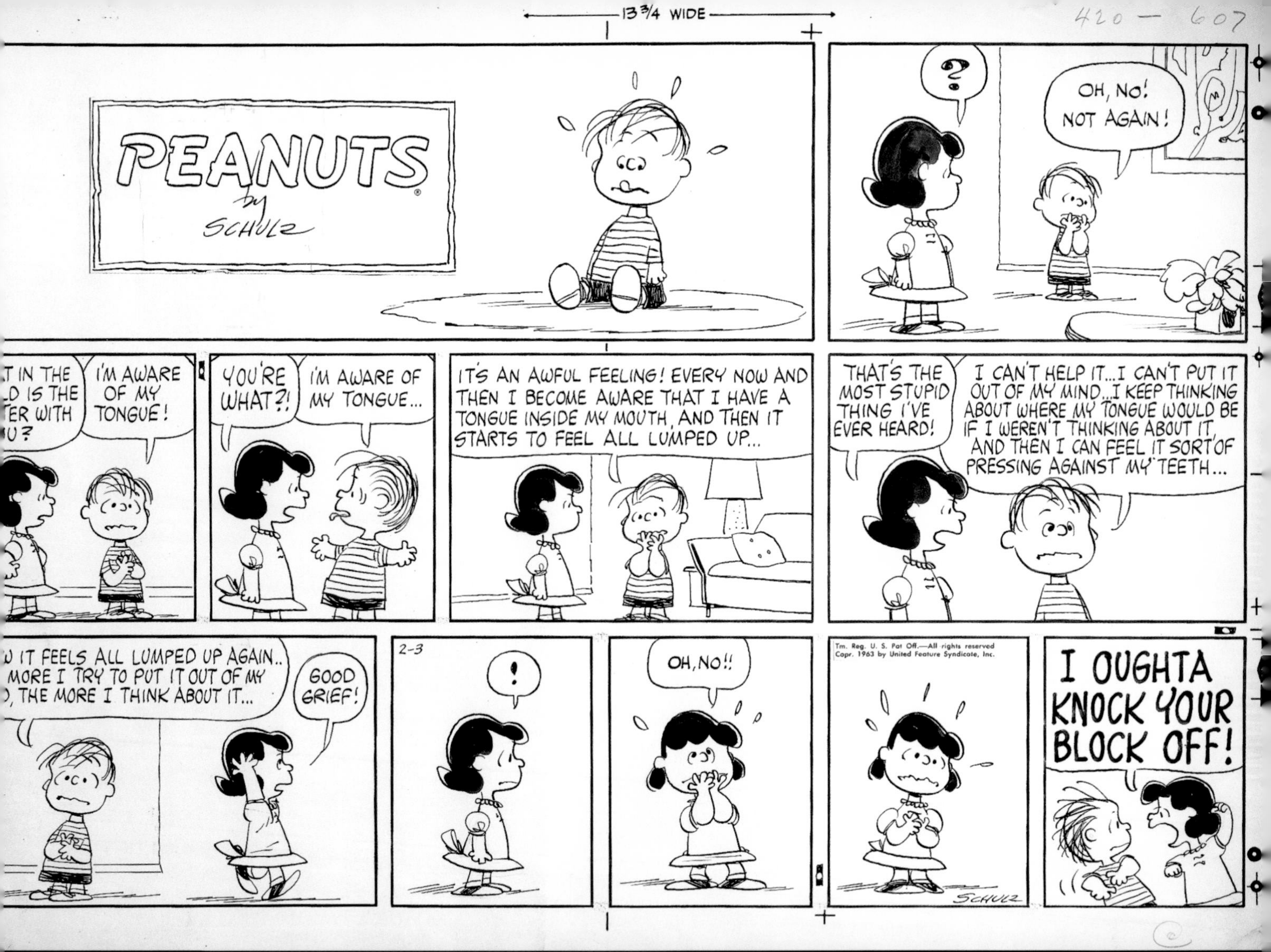
13 3/4 WIDE
420 — 607
PEANUTS
by SCHULZ
?
OH, NO! NOT AGAIN!
T IN THE D IS THE TER WITH U?
I'M AWARE OF MY TONGUE!
YOU'RE WHAT?!
I'M AWARE OF MY TONGUE...
IT'S AN AWFUL FEELING! EVERY NOW AND THEN I BECOME AWARE THAT I HAVE A TONGUE INSIDE MY MOUTH, AND THEN IT STARTS TO FEEL ALL LUMPED UP...
THAT'S THE MOST STUPID THING I'VE EVER HEARD!
I CAN'T HELP IT...I CAN'T PUT IT OUT OF MY MIND...I KEEP THINKING ABOUT WHERE MY TONGUE WOULD BE IF I WEREN'T THINKING ABOUT IT, AND THEN I CAN FEEL IT SORT OF PRESSING AGAINST MY TEETH...
W IT FEELS ALL LUMPED UP AGAIN.. MORE I TRY TO PUT IT OUT OF MY , THE MORE I THINK ABOUT IT...
GOOD GRIEF!
2-3
!
OH, NO!!
Tm. Reg. U. S. Pat Off.—All rights reserved Copr. 1963 by United Feature Syndicate, Inc.
SCHULZ
I OUGHTA KNOCK YOUR BLOCK OFF!

One of the delights of *Peanuts* is its total unpredictability. "I don't think it's necessary for every reader to understand every strip that you draw," Schulz said in 1981. Above: in a wonderfully bizarre idea from 1965, Lucy doesn't understand

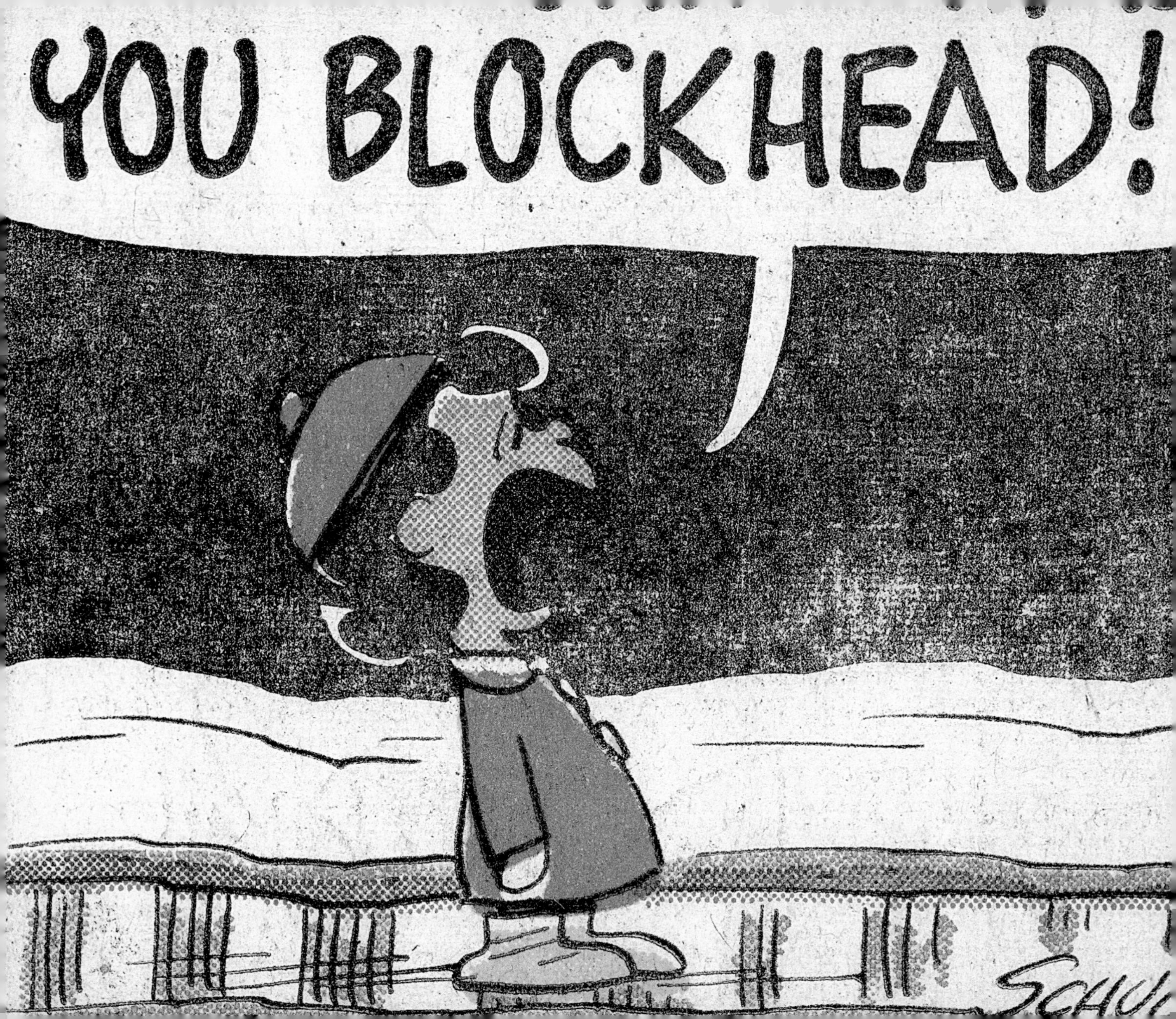
YOU BLOCKHEAD!

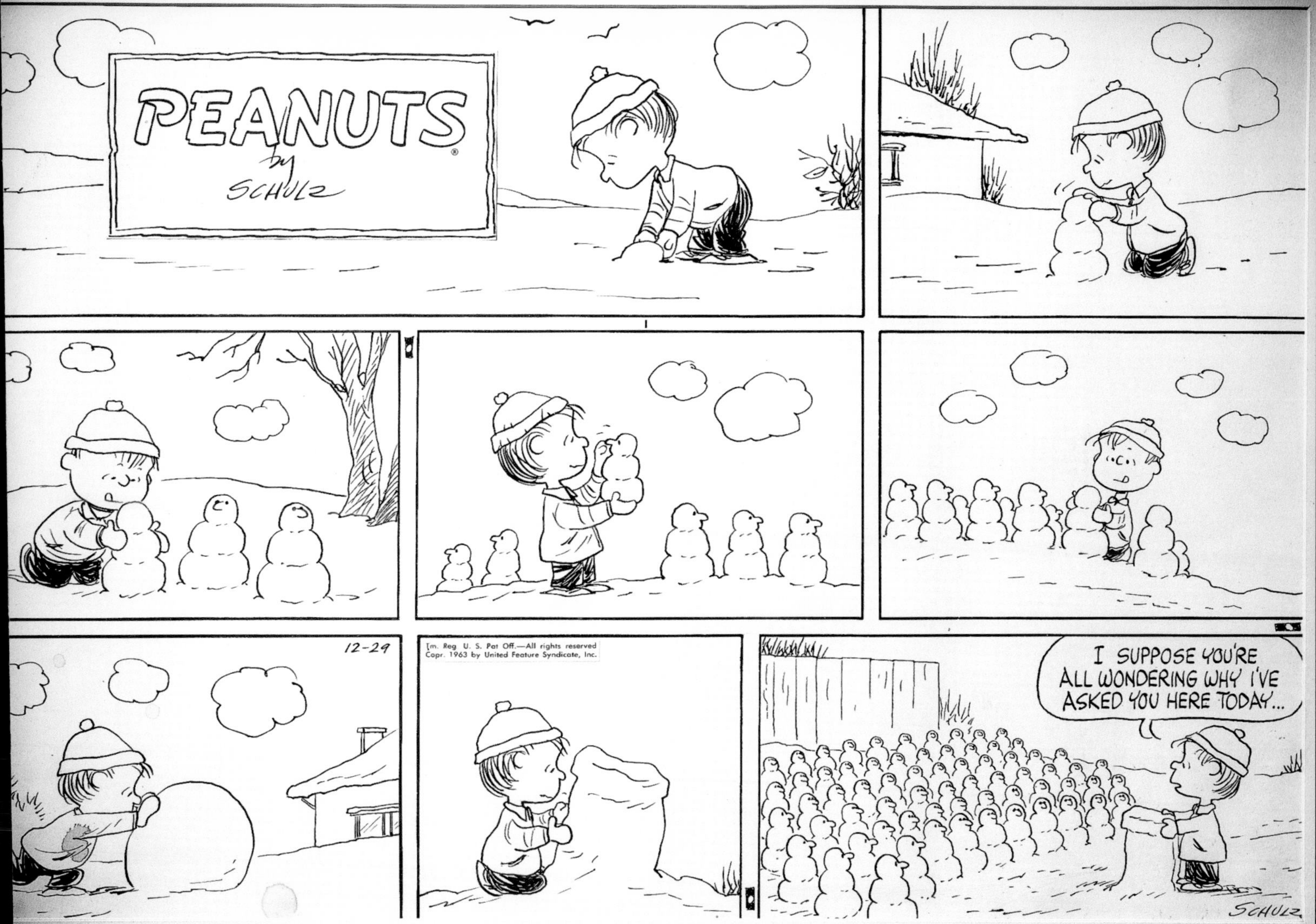
PEANUTS
by
SCHULZ
12-29
Tm. Reg U. S. Pat Off.—All rights reserved
Copr. 1963 by United Feature Syndicate, Inc.
I SUPPOSE YOU'RE ALL WONDERING WHY I'VE ASKED YOU HERE TODAY...
SCHULZ

"The fussier Lucy became, the more ideas she gave me. Her persecution of poor Linus, after he came along, accounted for years and years of ideas." —C.M. SCHULZ, 1998

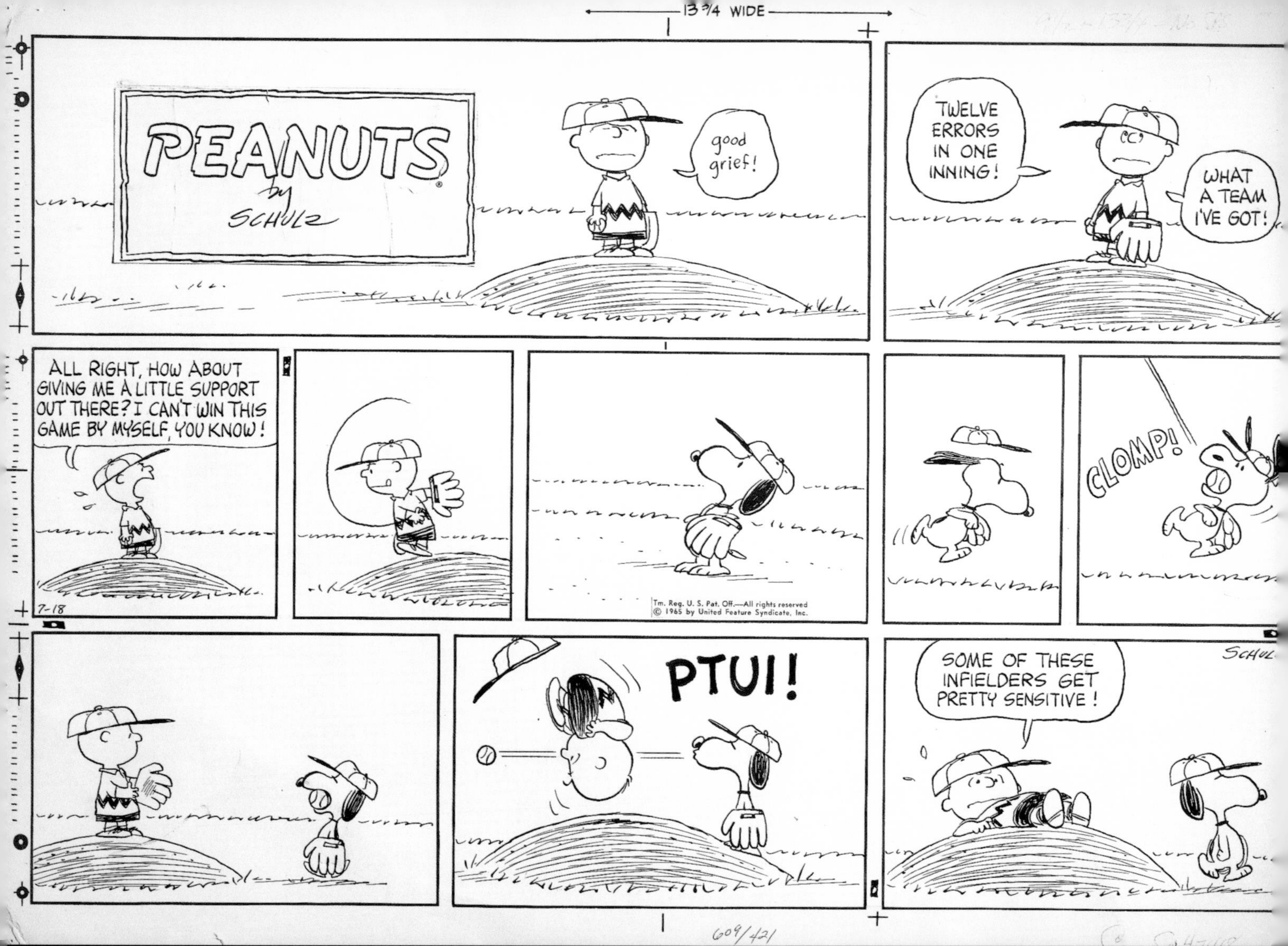
13 3/4 WIDE
PEANUTS
by SCHULZ
good grief!
TWELVE ERRORS IN ONE INNING!
WHAT A TEAM I'VE GOT!
ALL RIGHT, HOW ABOUT GIVING ME A LITTLE SUPPORT OUT THERE? I CAN'T WIN THIS GAME BY MYSELF, YOU KNOW!
7-18
Tm. Reg. U. S. Pat. Off.—All rights reserved
© 1965 by United Feature Syndicate, Inc.
CLOMP!
PTUI!
SOME OF THESE INFIELDERS GET PRETTY SENSITIVE!
SCHULZ
609/421

Opposite: Even Linus's 1960 bid to "run away" from home is criticized by Lucy, and it's up to Charlie Brown to save the day. The panels without dialogue are particularly effective—you can practically *hear* the relief in Linus's head

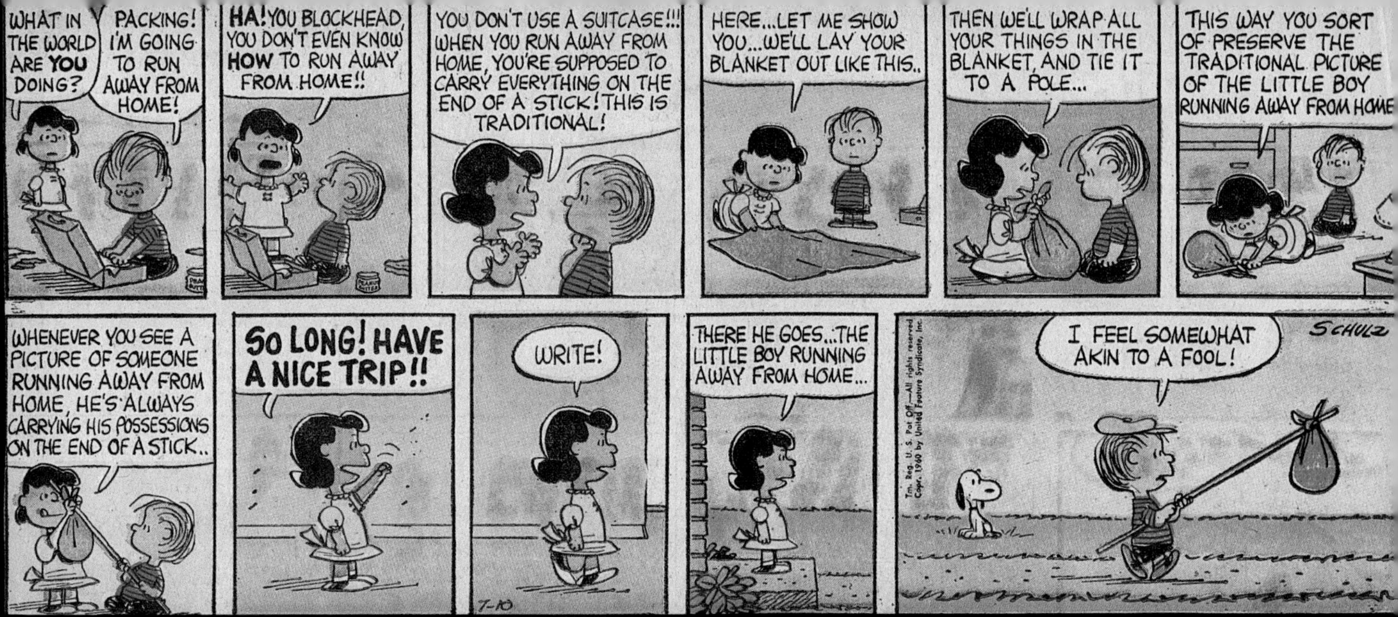
WHAT IN THE WORLD ARE YOU DOING?
PACKING! I'M GOING TO RUN AWAY FROM HOME!
HA! YOU BLOCKHEAD, YOU DON'T EVEN KNOW HOW TO RUN AWAY FROM HOME!!
YOU DON'T USE A SUITCASE!!! WHEN YOU RUN AWAY FROM HOME, YOU'RE SUPPOSED TO CARRY EVERYTHING ON THE END OF A STICK! THIS IS TRADITIONAL!
HERE...LET ME SHOW YOU...WE'LL LAY YOUR BLANKET OUT LIKE THIS..
THEN WE'LL WRAP ALL YOUR THINGS IN THE BLANKET, AND TIE IT TO A POLE...
THIS WAY YOU SORT OF PRESERVE THE TRADITIONAL PICTURE OF THE LITTLE BOY RUNNING AWAY FROM HOME
WHENEVER YOU SEE A PICTURE OF SOMEONE RUNNING AWAY FROM HOME, HE'S ALWAYS CARRYING HIS POSSESSIONS ON THE END OF A STICK..
SO LONG! HAVE A NICE TRIP!!
7-10
WRITE!
THERE HE GOES...THE LITTLE BOY RUNNING AWAY FROM HOME...
Tm. Reg. U. S. Pat. Off.—All rights reserved Copr. 1960 by United Feature Syndicate, Inc.
SCHULZ
I FEEL SOMEWHAT AKIN TO A FOOL!

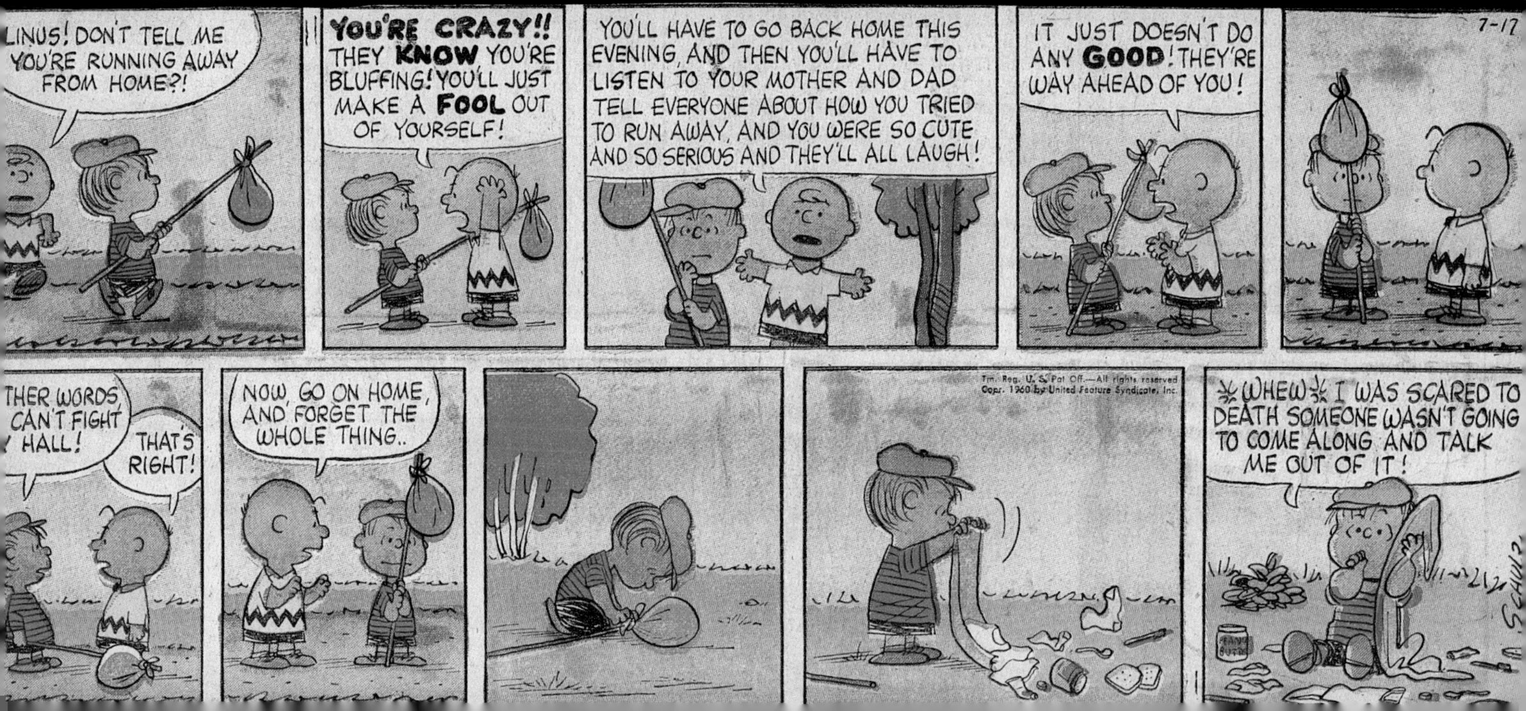
LINUS! DON'T TELL ME YOU'RE RUNNING AWAY FROM HOME?!
YOU'RE CRAZY!! THEY KNOW YOU'RE BLUFFING! YOU'LL JUST MAKE A FOOL OUT OF YOURSELF!
YOU'LL HAVE TO GO BACK HOME THIS EVENING, AND THEN YOU'LL HAVE TO LISTEN TO YOUR MOTHER AND DAD TELL EVERYONE ABOUT HOW YOU TRIED TO RUN AWAY, AND YOU WERE SO CUTE AND SO SERIOUS AND THEY'LL ALL LAUGH!
IT JUST DOESN'T DO ANY GOOD! THEY'RE WAY AHEAD OF YOU!
7-17
THER WORDS, CAN'T FIGHT HALL!
THAT'S RIGHT!
NOW, GO ON HOME, AND FORGET THE WHOLE THING..
Tm. Reg. U. S. Pat. Off.—All rights reserved Copr. 1960 by United Feature Syndicate, Inc.
WHEW! I WAS SCARED TO DEATH SOMEONE WASN'T GOING TO COME ALONG AND TALK ME OUT OF IT!
SCHULZ

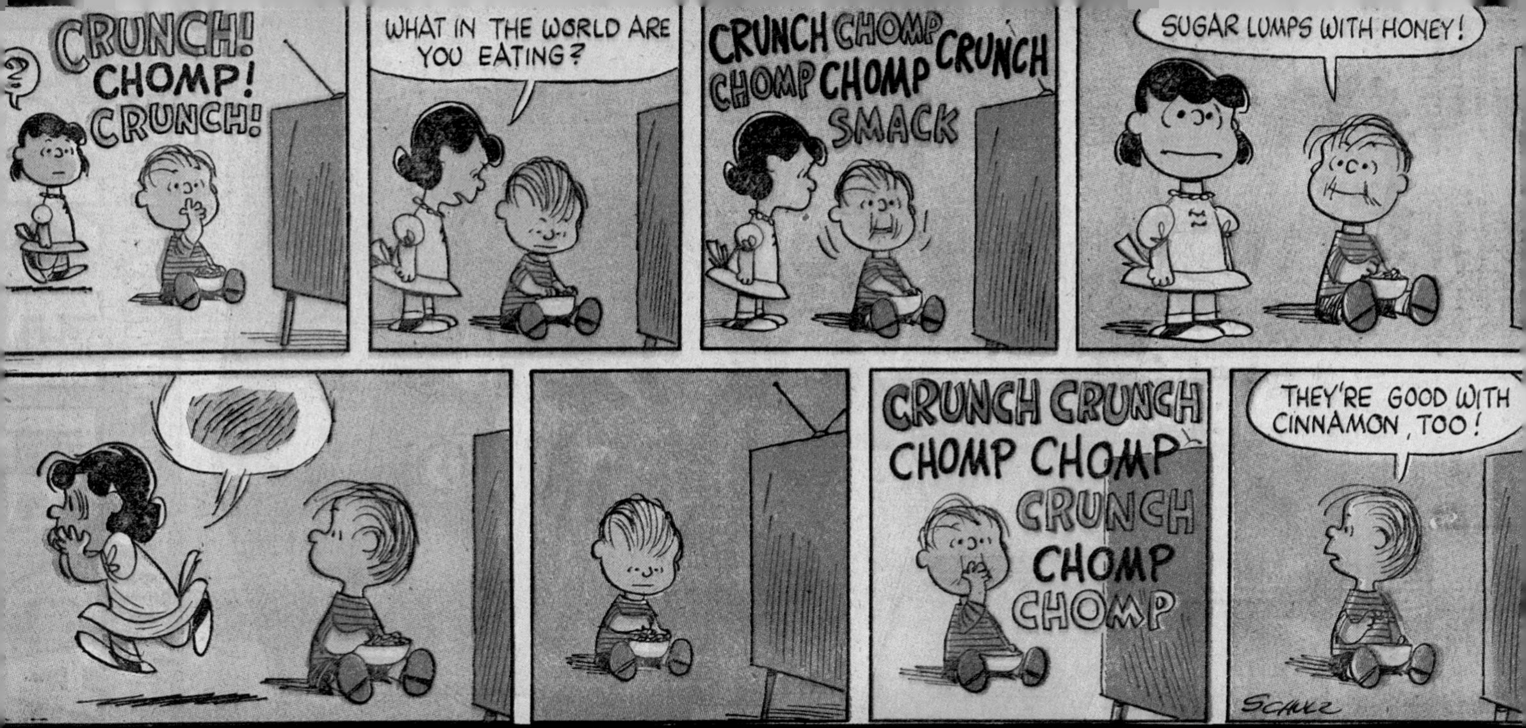
CRUNCH! CHOMP! CRUNCH!
?
WHAT IN THE WORLD ARE YOU EATING?
CRUNCH CHOMP CRUNCH CHOMP CHOMP SMACK
SUGAR LUMPS WITH HONEY!
CRUNCH CRUNCH CHOMP CHOMP CRUNCH CHOMP CHOMP
THEY'RE GOOD WITH CINNAMON, TOO!
SCHULZ

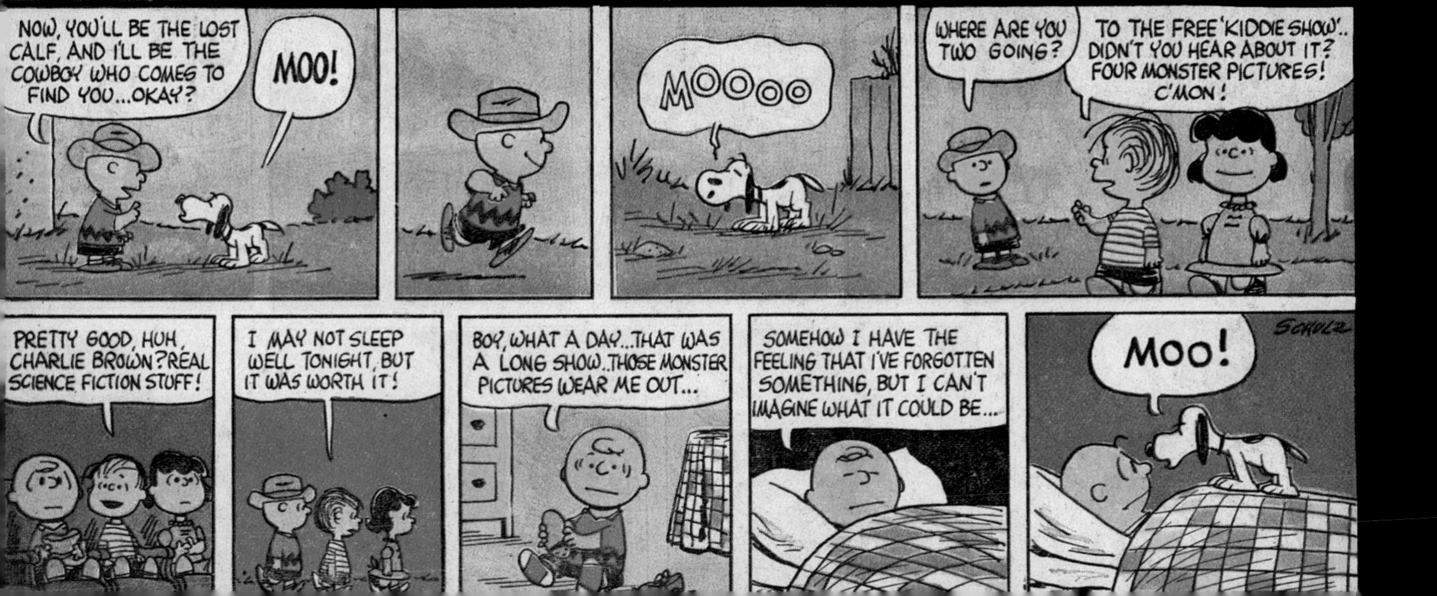
NOW, YOU'LL BE THE LOST CALF, AND I'LL BE THE COWBOY WHO COMES TO FIND YOU...OKAY?
MOO!
MOOOOO
WHERE ARE YOU TWO GOING?
TO THE FREE 'KIDDIE SHOW'.. DIDN'T YOU HEAR ABOUT IT? FOUR MONSTER PICTURES! C'MON!
PRETTY GOOD, HUH, CHARLIE BROWN? REAL SCIENCE FICTION STUFF!
I MAY NOT SLEEP WELL TONIGHT, BUT IT WAS WORTH IT!
BOY, WHAT A DAY...THAT WAS A LONG SHOW..THOSE MONSTER PICTURES WEAR ME OUT...
SOMEHOW I HAVE THE FEELING THAT I'VE FORGOTTEN SOMETHING, BUT I CAN'T IMAGINE WHAT IT COULD BE...
SCHULZ
MOO!

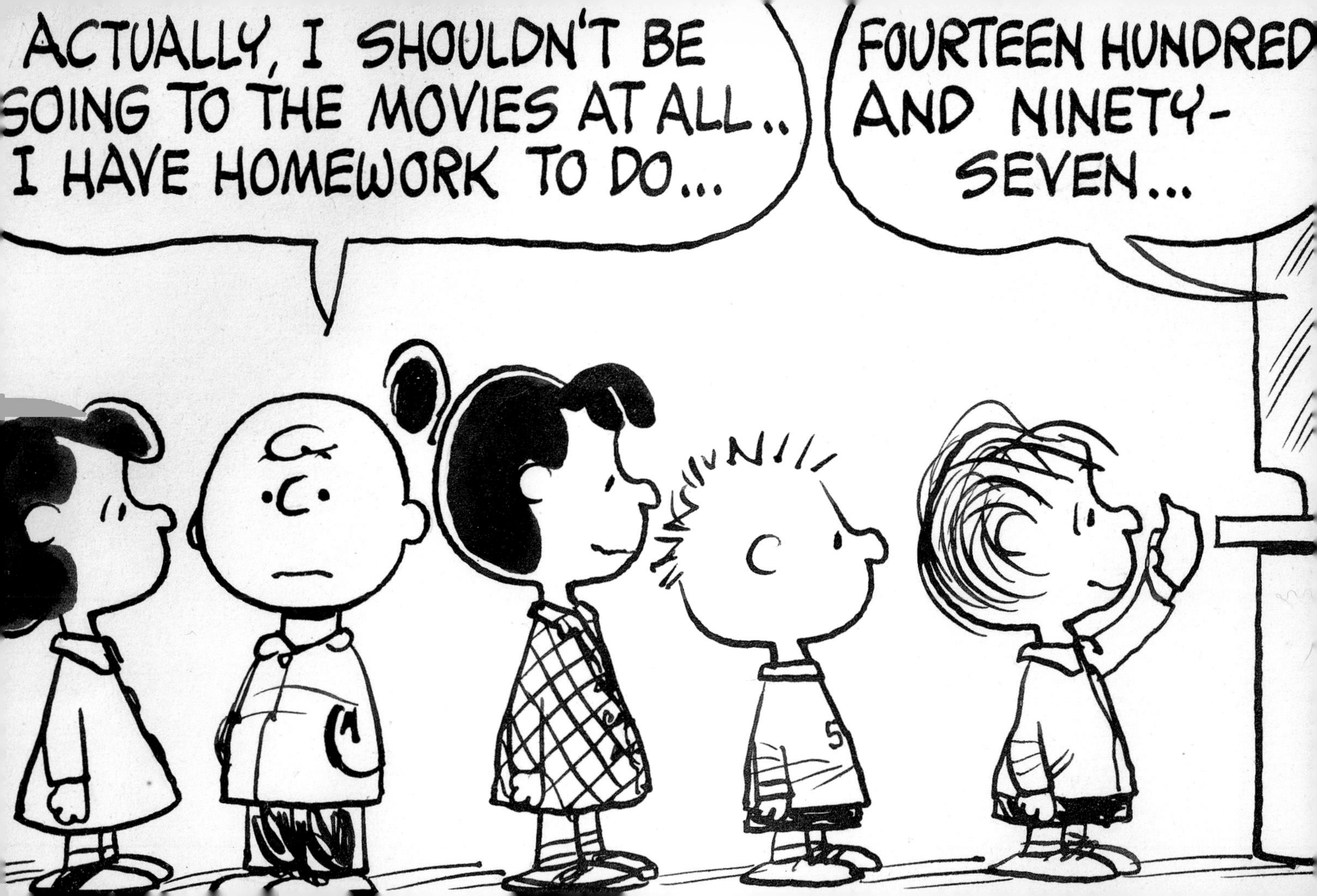
ACTUALLY, I SHOULDN'T BE GOING TO THE MOVIES AT ALL.. I HAVE HOMEWORK TO DO...
FOURTEEN HUNDRED AND NINETY-SEVEN...

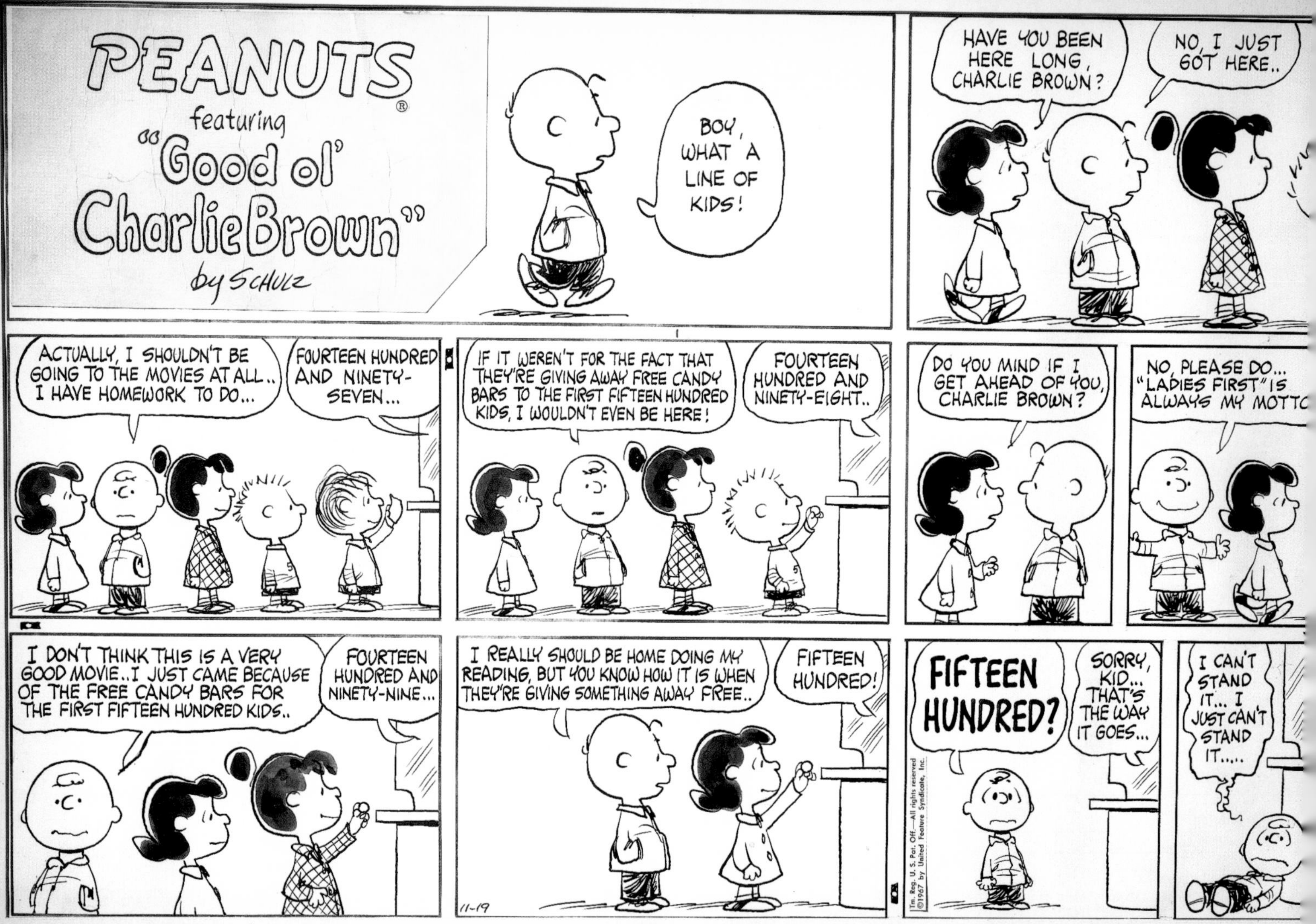
PEANUTS®
featuring "Good ol' Charlie Brown"
by SCHULZ
BOY, WHAT A LINE OF KIDS!
HAVE YOU BEEN HERE LONG, CHARLIE BROWN?
NO, I JUST GOT HERE..
ACTUALLY, I SHOULDN'T BE GOING TO THE MOVIES AT ALL.. I HAVE HOMEWORK TO DO...
FOURTEEN HUNDRED AND NINETY-SEVEN...
IF IT WEREN'T FOR THE FACT THAT THEY'RE GIVING AWAY FREE CANDY BARS TO THE FIRST FIFTEEN HUNDRED KIDS, I WOULDN'T EVEN BE HERE!
FOURTEEN HUNDRED AND NINETY-EIGHT..
DO YOU MIND IF I GET AHEAD OF YOU, CHARLIE BROWN?
NO, PLEASE DO... "LADIES FIRST" IS ALWAYS MY MOTTO
I DON'T THINK THIS IS A VERY GOOD MOVIE.. I JUST CAME BECAUSE OF THE FREE CANDY BARS FOR THE FIRST FIFTEEN HUNDRED KIDS..
FOURTEEN HUNDRED AND NINETY-NINE...
I REALLY SHOULD BE HOME DOING MY READING, BUT YOU KNOW HOW IT IS WHEN THEY'RE GIVING SOMETHING AWAY FREE..
FIFTEEN HUNDRED!
11-19
Tm. Reg. U. S. Pat. Off.—All rights reserved ©1967 by United Feature Syndicate, Inc.
FIFTEEN HUNDRED?
SORRY, KID... THAT'S THE WAY IT GOES...
I CAN'T STAND IT... I JUST CAN'T STAND IT.....

"Charlie Brown's personality goes in several directions. Most of the time he is quite depressed because of the feelings of other people about him, but at the same time he has a certain amount of arrogance. Generally, however, he is wholly struck down by the remarks of the other characters, especially Lucy. She represents all of the cold-blooded, self-sufficient people in this world who do not feel that it is at all necessary ever to say anything kind about anyone." —from Schulz's *Developing a Comic Strip*, 1959

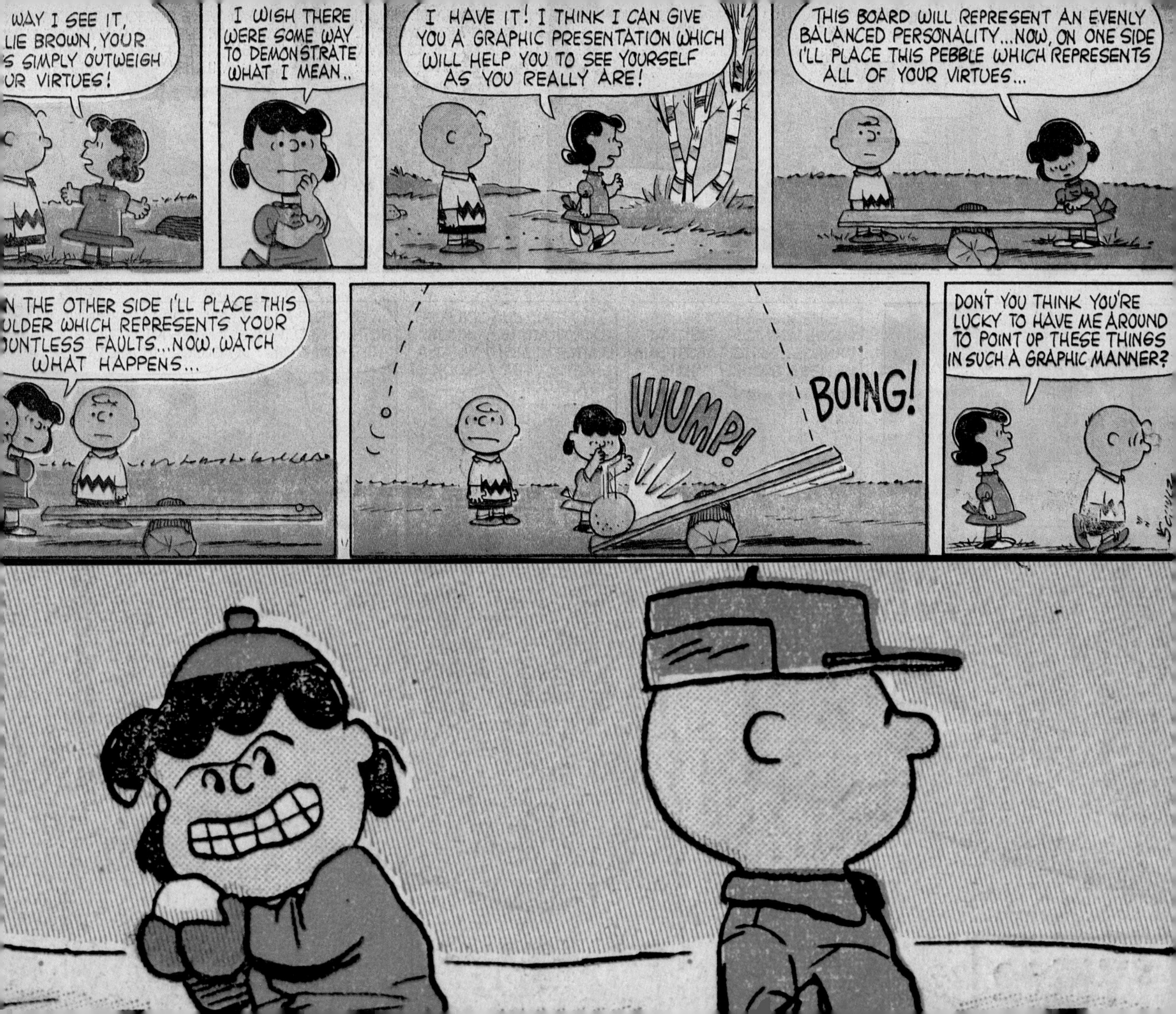
WAY I SEE IT, LIE BROWN, YOUR S SIMPLY OUTWEIGH UR VIRTUES!
I WISH THERE WERE SOME WAY TO DEMONSTRATE WHAT I MEAN..
I HAVE IT! I THINK I CAN GIVE YOU A GRAPHIC PRESENTATION WHICH WILL HELP YOU TO SEE YOURSELF AS YOU REALLY ARE!
THIS BOARD WILL REPRESENT AN EVENLY BALANCED PERSONALITY...NOW, ON ONE SIDE I'LL PLACE THIS PEBBLE WHICH REPRESENTS ALL OF YOUR VIRTUES...
N THE OTHER SIDE I'LL PLACE THIS ULDER WHICH REPRESENTS YOUR UNTLESS FAULTS...NOW, WATCH WHAT HAPPENS...
WUMP!
BOING!
DON'T YOU THINK YOU'RE LUCKY TO HAVE ME AROUND TO POINT UP THESE THINGS IN SUCH A GRAPHIC MANNER?

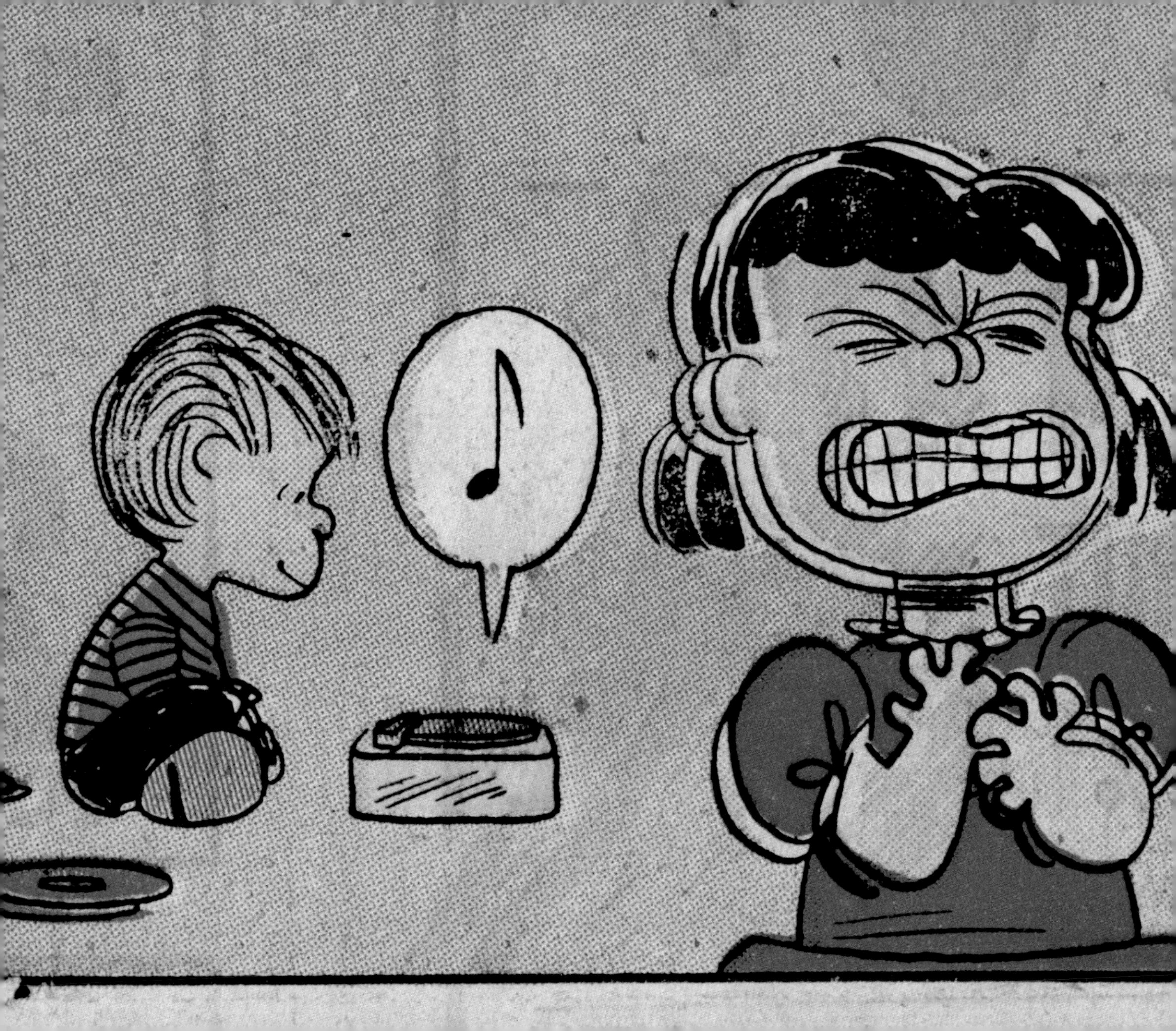

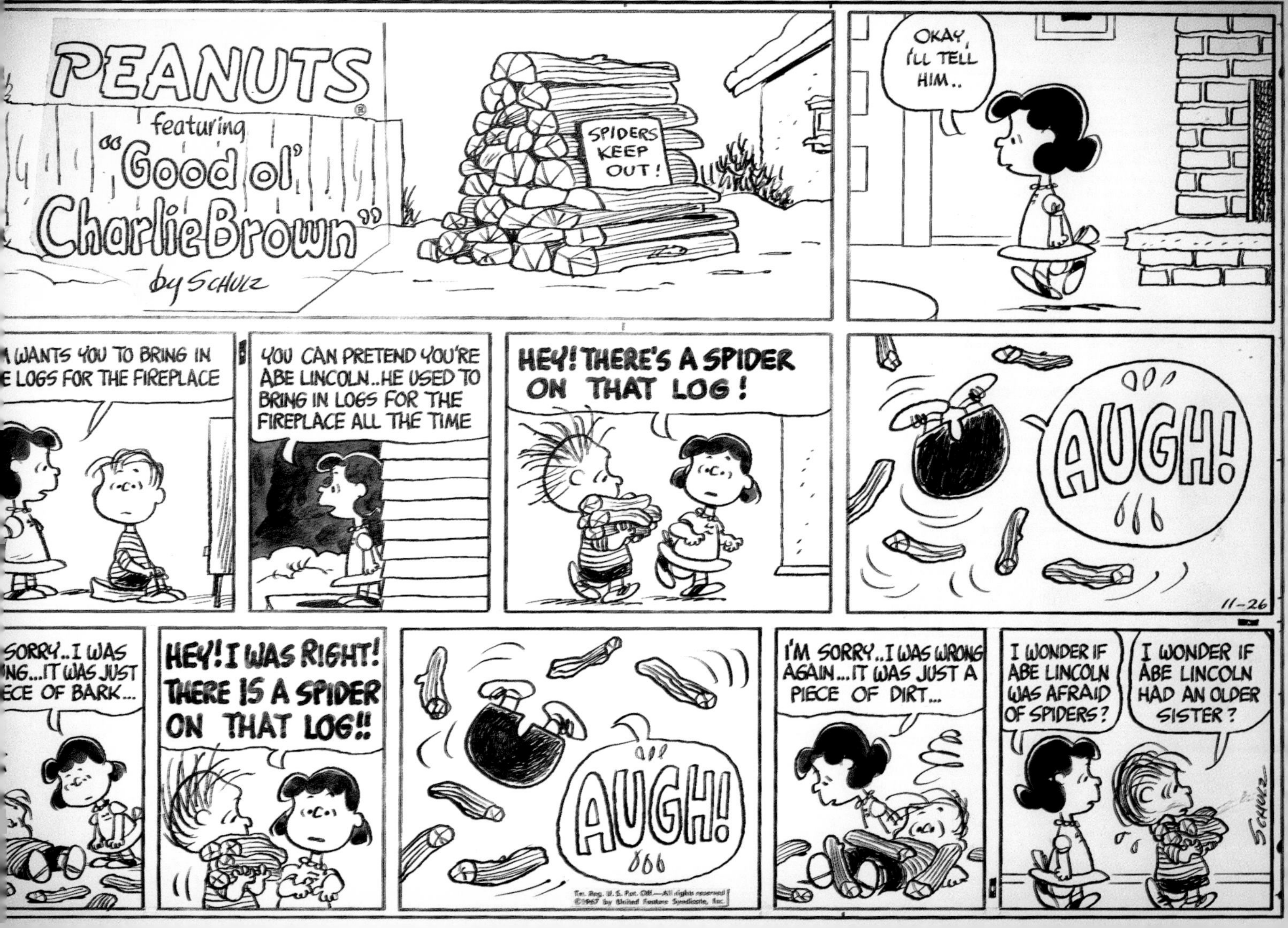
PEANUTS
featuring "Good ol' Charlie Brown"
by SCHULZ
SPIDERS KEEP OUT!
OKAY, I'LL TELL HIM..
1 WANTS YOU TO BRING IN
E LOGS FOR THE FIREPLACE
YOU CAN PRETEND YOU'RE ABE LINCOLN..HE USED TO BRING IN LOGS FOR THE FIREPLACE ALL THE TIME
HEY! THERE'S A SPIDER ON THAT LOG!
AUGH!
11-26
SORRY..I WAS
NG...IT WAS JUST
ECE OF BARK...
HEY! I WAS RIGHT! THERE IS A SPIDER ON THAT LOG!!
AUGH!
Tm. Reg. U. S. Pat. Off.—All rights reserved ©1967 by United Feature Syndicate, Inc.
I'M SORRY..I WAS WRONG AGAIN...IT WAS JUST A PIECE OF DIRT...
I WONDER IF ABE LINCOLN WAS AFRAID OF SPIDERS?
I WONDER IF ABE LINCOLN HAD AN OLDER SISTER?
SCHULZ

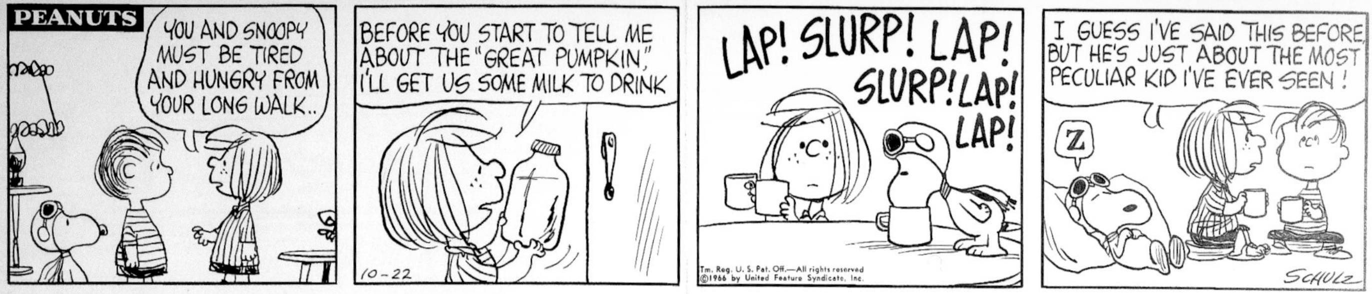
PEANUTS
YOU AND SNOOPY MUST BE TIRED AND HUNGRY FROM YOUR LONG WALK..
BEFORE YOU START TO TELL ME ABOUT THE "GREAT PUMPKIN," I'LL GET US SOME MILK TO DRINK
10-22
LAP! SLURP! LAP! SLURP! LAP! LAP!
Tm. Reg. U. S. Pat. Off.—All rights reserved ©1966 by United Feature Syndicate, Inc.
I GUESS I'VE SAID THIS BEFORE, BUT HE'S JUST ABOUT THE MOST PECULIAR KID I'VE EVER SEEN!
Z
SCHULZ

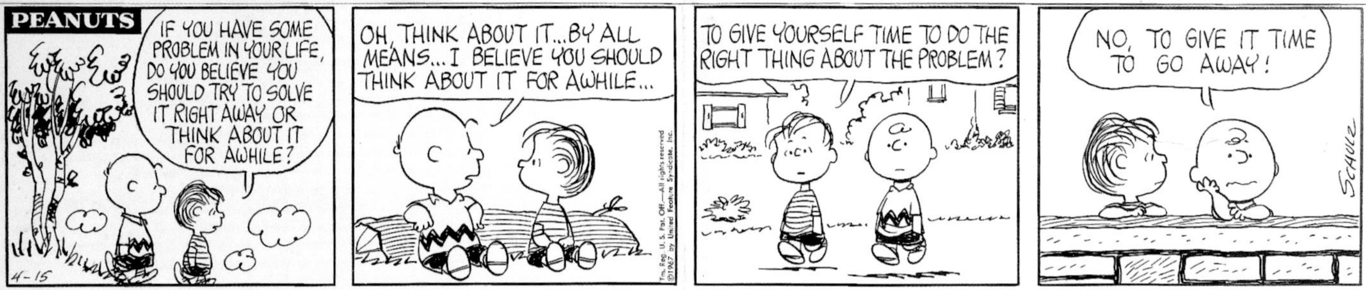
PEANUTS
IF YOU HAVE SOME PROBLEM IN YOUR LIFE, DO YOU BELIEVE YOU SHOULD TRY TO SOLVE IT RIGHT AWAY OR THINK ABOUT IT FOR AWHILE?
4-15
OH, THINK ABOUT IT...BY ALL MEANS...I BELIEVE YOU SHOULD THINK ABOUT IT FOR AWHILE...
Tm. Reg. U. S. Pat. Off.—All rights reserved ©1967 by United Feature Syndicate, Inc.
TO GIVE YOURSELF TIME TO DO THE RIGHT THING ABOUT THE PROBLEM?
NO, TO GIVE IT TIME TO GO AWAY!
SCHULZ

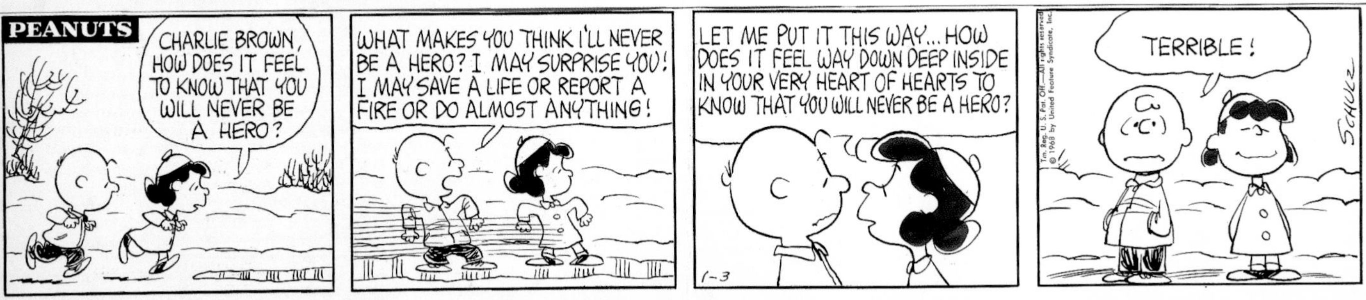
PEANUTS
CHARLIE BROWN, HOW DOES IT FEEL TO KNOW THAT YOU WILL NEVER BE A HERO?
WHAT MAKES YOU THINK I'LL NEVER BE A HERO? I MAY SURPRISE YOU! I MAY SAVE A LIFE OR REPORT A FIRE OR DO ALMOST ANYTHING!
LET ME PUT IT THIS WAY...HOW DOES IT FEEL WAY DOWN DEEP INSIDE IN YOUR VERY HEART OF HEARTS TO KNOW THAT YOU WILL NEVER BE A HERO?
1-3
Tm. Reg. U. S. Pat. Off.—All rights reserved © 1968 by United Feature Syndicate, Inc.
TERRIBLE!
SCHULZ

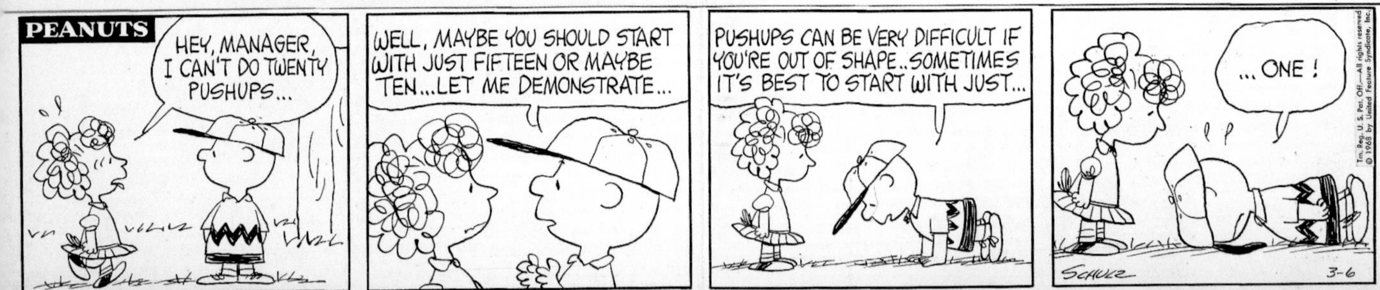
PEANUTS
HEY, MANAGER, I CAN'T DO TWENTY PUSHUPS...
WELL, MAYBE YOU SHOULD START WITH JUST FIFTEEN OR MAYBE TEN...LET ME DEMONSTRATE...
PUSHUPS CAN BE VERY DIFFICULT IF YOU'RE OUT OF SHAPE..SOMETIMES IT'S BEST TO START WITH JUST...
SCHULZ
...ONE!
3-6
Tm. Reg. U. S. Pat. Off.—All rights reserved © 1968 by United Feature Syndicate, Inc.

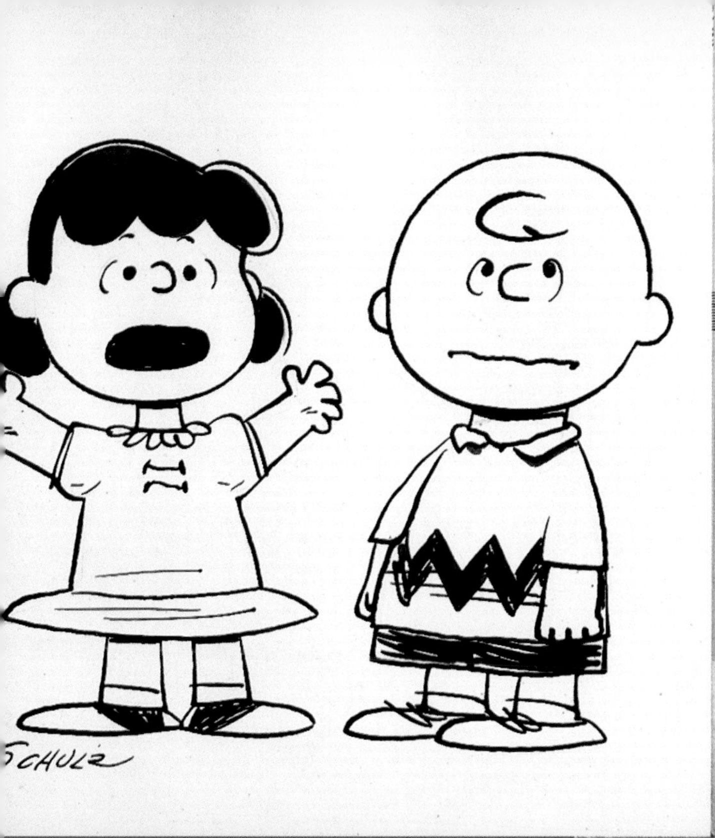
SCHULZ

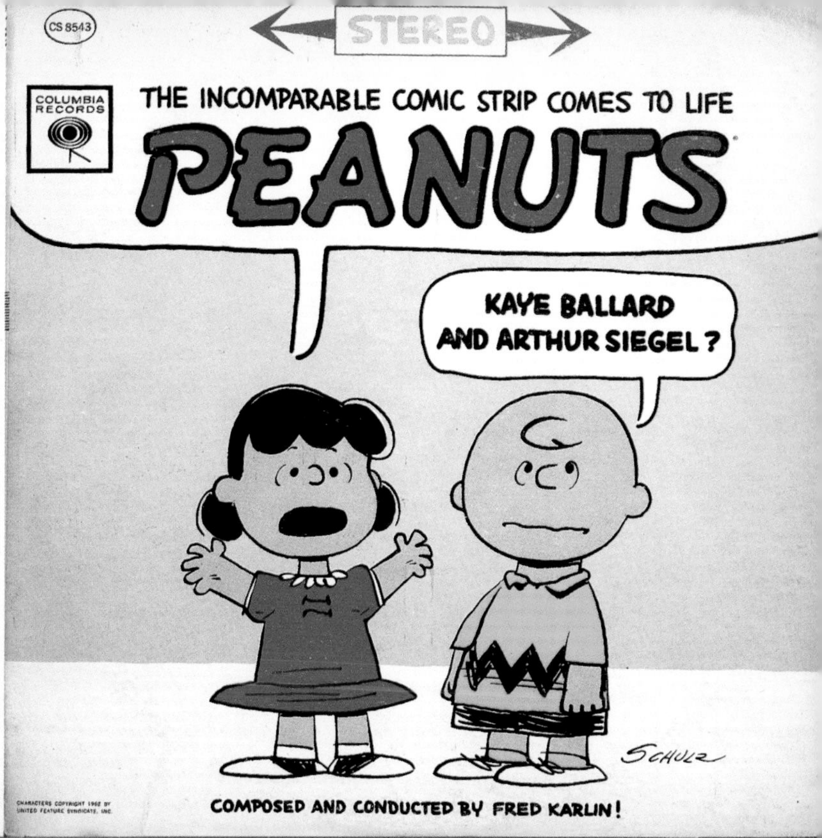
CS 8543
STEREO
COLUMBIA RECORDS
THE INCOMPARABLE COMIC STRIP COMES TO LIFE
PEANUTS
KAYE BALLARD AND ARTHUR SIEGEL ?
SCHULZ
CHARACTERS COPYRIGHT 1962 BY UNITED FEATURE SYNDICATE, INC.
COMPOSED AND CONDUCTED BY FRED KARLIN!

Kaye Ballard, of "The Mothers-in-Law" fame, recorded the first *Peanuts* record album for Columbia in the early 1960s.

Selchow and Richtor Co. made the first game featuring all the *Peanuts* characters in 1967.

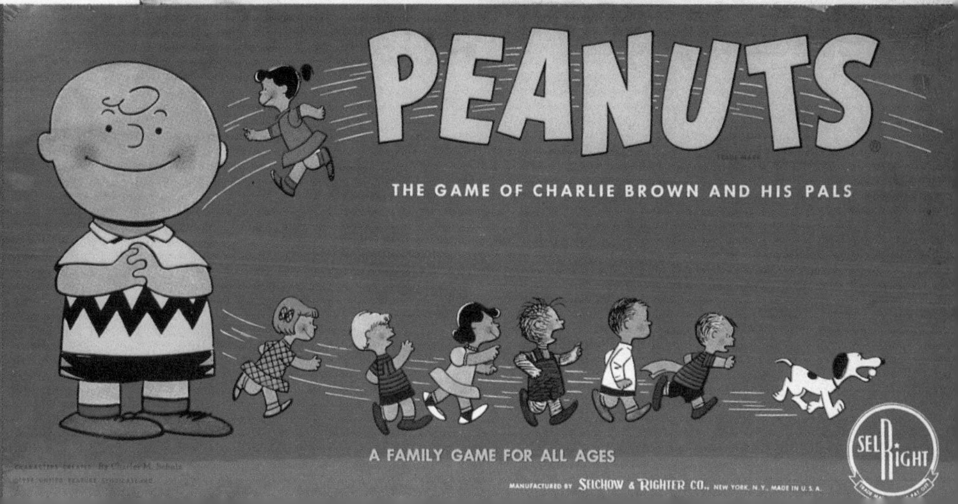
PEANUTS
THE GAME OF CHARLIE BROWN AND HIS PALS
A FAMILY GAME FOR ALL AGES
MANUFACTURED BY SELCHOW & RIGHTER CO., NEW YORK, N.Y., MADE IN U.S.A.
SELRIGHT

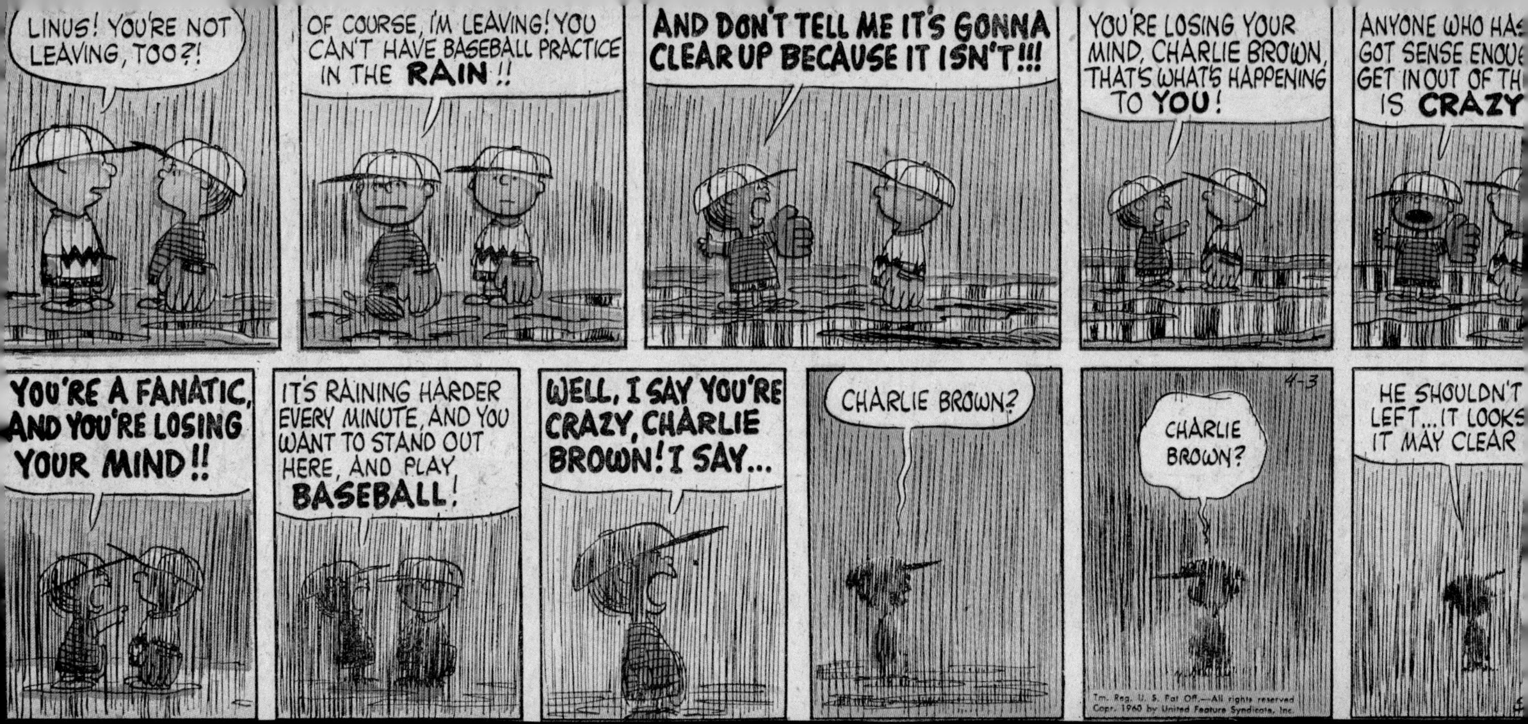
LINUS! YOU'RE NOT LEAVING, TOO?!
OF COURSE, I'M LEAVING! YOU CAN'T HAVE BASEBALL PRACTICE IN THE RAIN!!
AND DON'T TELL ME IT'S GONNA CLEAR UP BECAUSE IT ISN'T!!!
YOU'RE LOSING YOUR MIND, CHARLIE BROWN, THAT'S WHAT'S HAPPENING TO YOU!
ANYONE WHO HAS GOT SENSE ENOU GET IN OUT OF TH IS CRAZY
YOU'RE A FANATIC, AND YOU'RE LOSING YOUR MIND!!
IT'S RAINING HARDER EVERY MINUTE, AND YOU WANT TO STAND OUT HERE, AND PLAY BASEBALL!
WELL, I SAY YOU'RE CRAZY, CHARLIE BROWN! I SAY...
CHARLIE BROWN?
CHARLIE BROWN?
HE SHOULDN'T LEFT...IT LOOKS IT MAY CLEAR
Tm. Reg. U. S. Pat. Off.—All rights reserved Copr. 1960 by United Feature Syndicate, Inc.

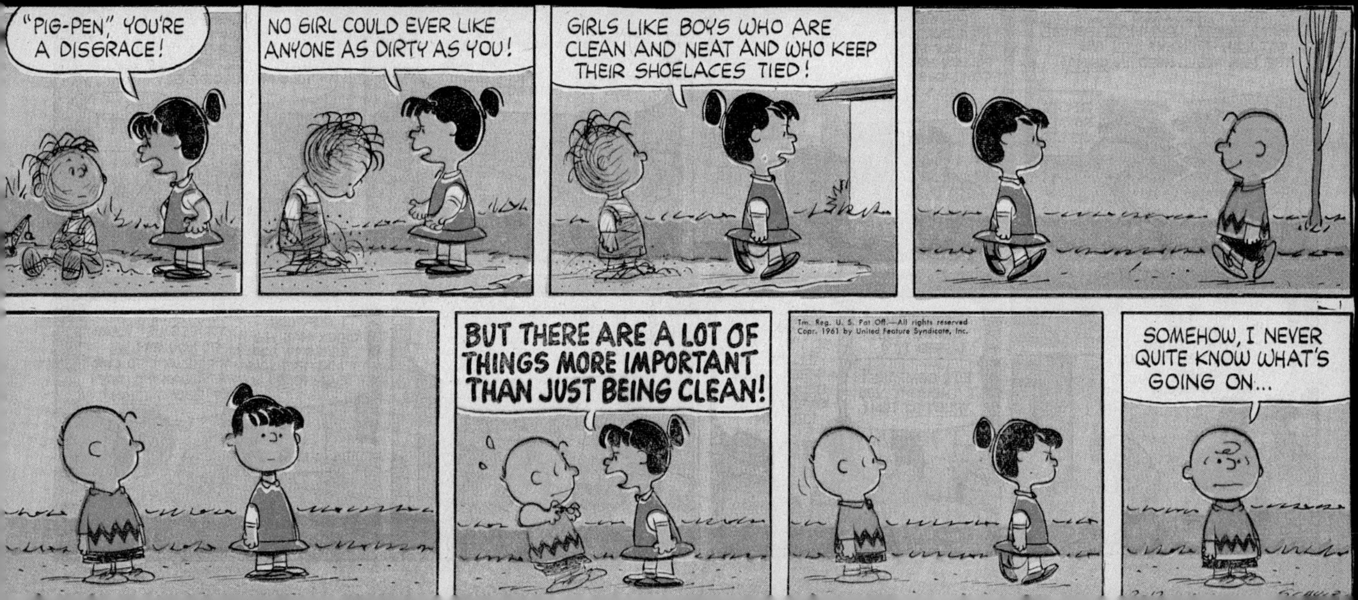
"PIG-PEN," YOU'RE A DISGRACE!
NO GIRL COULD EVER LIKE ANYONE AS DIRTY AS YOU!
GIRLS LIKE BOYS WHO ARE CLEAN AND NEAT AND WHO KEEP THEIR SHOELACES TIED!
BUT THERE ARE A LOT OF THINGS MORE IMPORTANT THAN JUST BEING CLEAN!
Tm. Reg. U. S. Pat. Off.—All rights reserved Copr. 1961 by United Feature Syndicate, Inc.
SOMEHOW, I NEVER QUITE KNOW WHAT'S GOING ON...

Non-sequiturs always made for great comedy. Charlie Brown uttered this punchline (left) a *lot*.

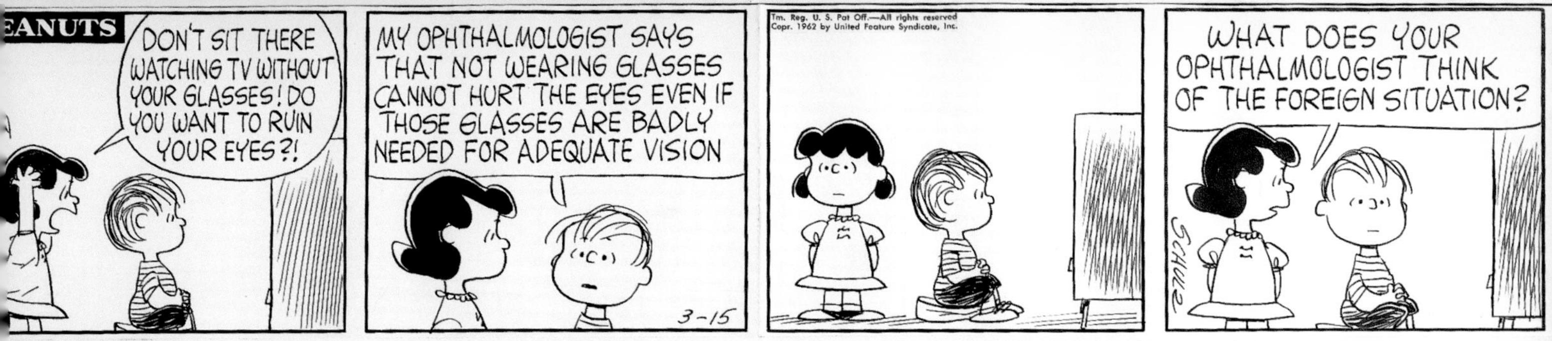
PEANUTS
DON'T SIT THERE WATCHING TV WITHOUT YOUR GLASSES! DO YOU WANT TO RUIN YOUR EYES?!
MY OPHTHALMOLOGIST SAYS THAT NOT WEARING GLASSES CANNOT HURT THE EYES EVEN IF THOSE GLASSES ARE BADLY NEEDED FOR ADEQUATE VISION
3-15
Tm. Reg. U. S. Pat Off.—All rights reserved
Copr. 1962 by United Feature Syndicate, Inc.
WHAT DOES YOUR OPHTHALMOLOGIST THINK OF THE FOREIGN SITUATION?
SCHULZ

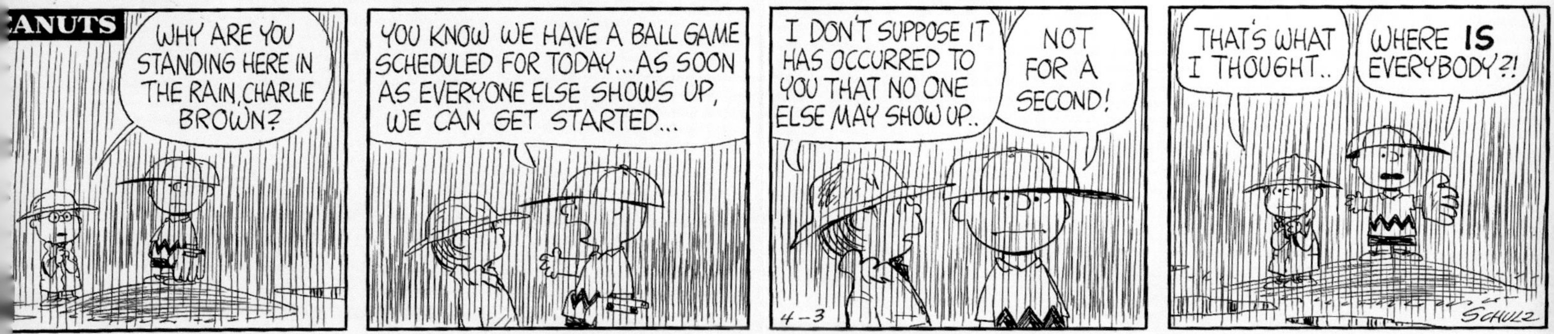
PEANUTS
WHY ARE YOU STANDING HERE IN THE RAIN, CHARLIE BROWN?
YOU KNOW WE HAVE A BALL GAME SCHEDULED FOR TODAY...AS SOON AS EVERYONE ELSE SHOWS UP, WE CAN GET STARTED...
I DON'T SUPPOSE IT HAS OCCURRED TO YOU THAT NO ONE ELSE MAY SHOW UP..
NOT FOR A SECOND!
4-3
THAT'S WHAT I THOUGHT..
WHERE IS EVERYBODY?!
SCHULZ

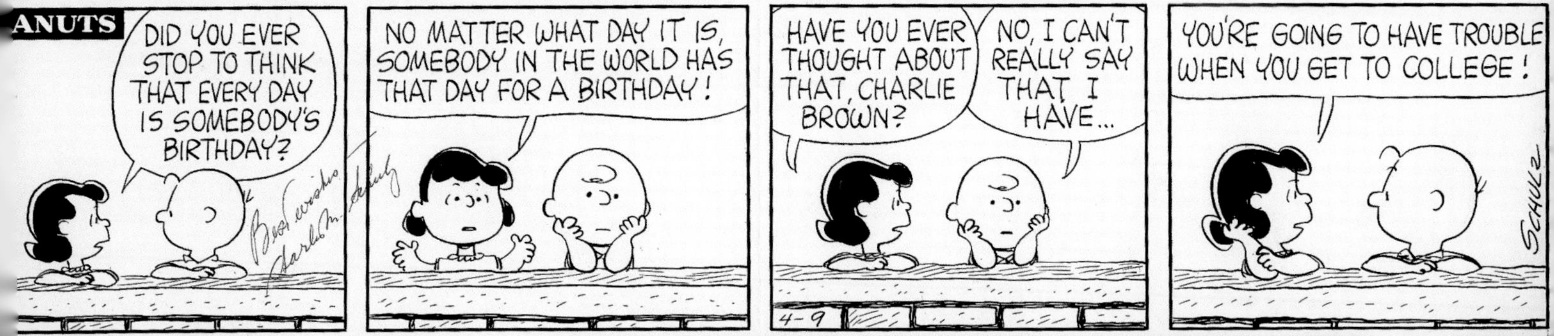
PEANUTS
DID YOU EVER STOP TO THINK THAT EVERY DAY IS SOMEBODY'S BIRTHDAY?
Best wishes
Charles M. Schulz
NO MATTER WHAT DAY IT IS, SOMEBODY IN THE WORLD HAS THAT DAY FOR A BIRTHDAY!
HAVE YOU EVER THOUGHT ABOUT THAT, CHARLIE BROWN?
NO, I CAN'T REALLY SAY THAT I HAVE...
4-9
YOU'RE GOING TO HAVE TROUBLE WHEN YOU GET TO COLLEGE!
SCHULZ

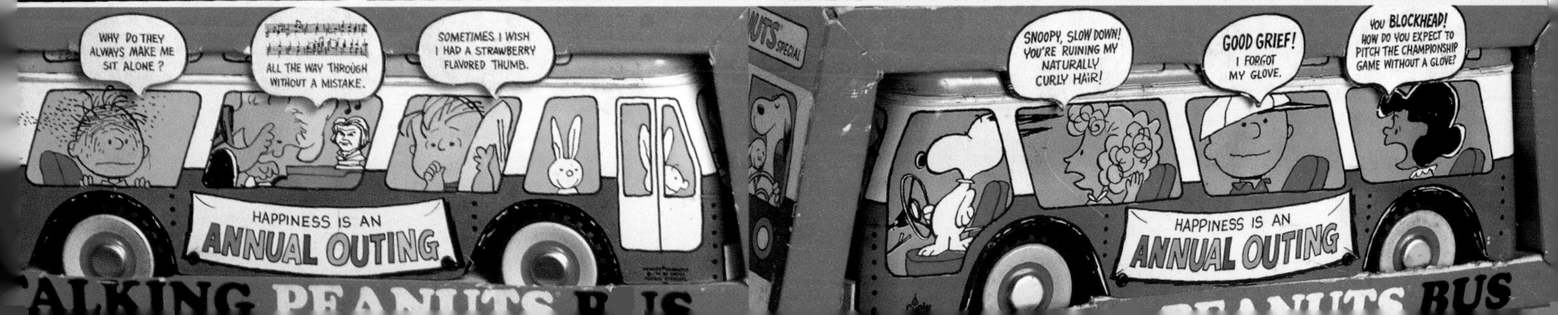
WHY DO THEY ALWAYS MAKE ME SIT ALONE?
ALL THE WAY THROUGH WITHOUT A MISTAKE.
SOMETIMES I WISH I HAD A STRAWBERRY FLAVORED THUMB.
HAPPINESS IS AN ANNUAL OUTING
SNOOPY, SLOW DOWN! YOU'RE RUINING MY NATURALLY CURLY HAIR!
GOOD GRIEF! I FORGOT MY GLOVE.
YOU BLOCKHEAD! HOW DO YOU EXPECT TO PITCH THE CHAMPIONSHIP GAME WITHOUT A GLOVE?
HAPPINESS IS AN ANNUAL OUTING
BUS

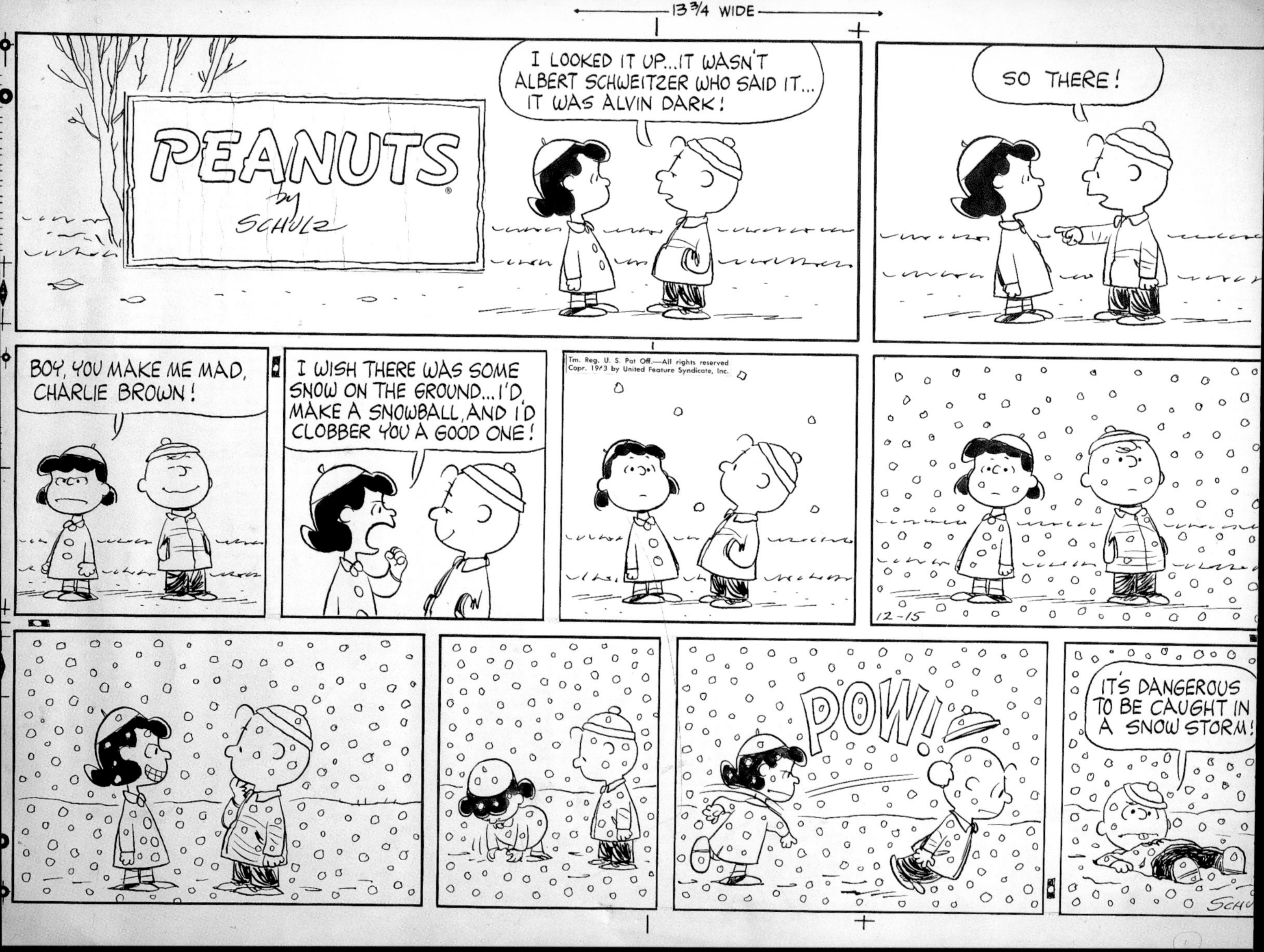
13 3/4 WIDE
PEANUTS
by SCHULZ
I LOOKED IT UP...IT WASN'T ALBERT SCHWEITZER WHO SAID IT... IT WAS ALVIN DARK!
SO THERE!
BOY, YOU MAKE ME MAD, CHARLIE BROWN!
I WISH THERE WAS SOME SNOW ON THE GROUND...I'D MAKE A SNOWBALL, AND I'D CLOBBER YOU A GOOD ONE!
Tm. Reg. U. S. Pat Off.—All rights reserved
12-15
POW!
IT'S DANGEROUS TO BE CAUGHT IN A SNOW STORM!

Opposite, top: Schulz takes a joke one step further than expected and exploits Snoopy's combination of hopeless romanticism and cheeky mischief. Of *course* he'd eat the carrot.

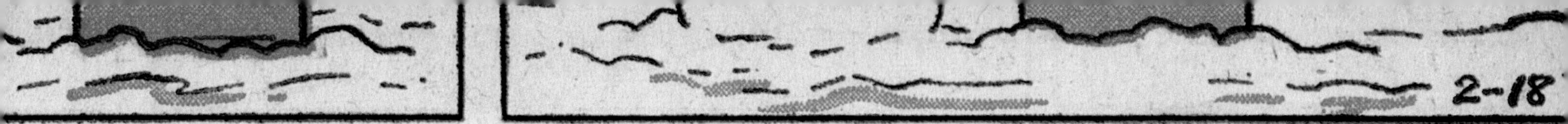
2-18

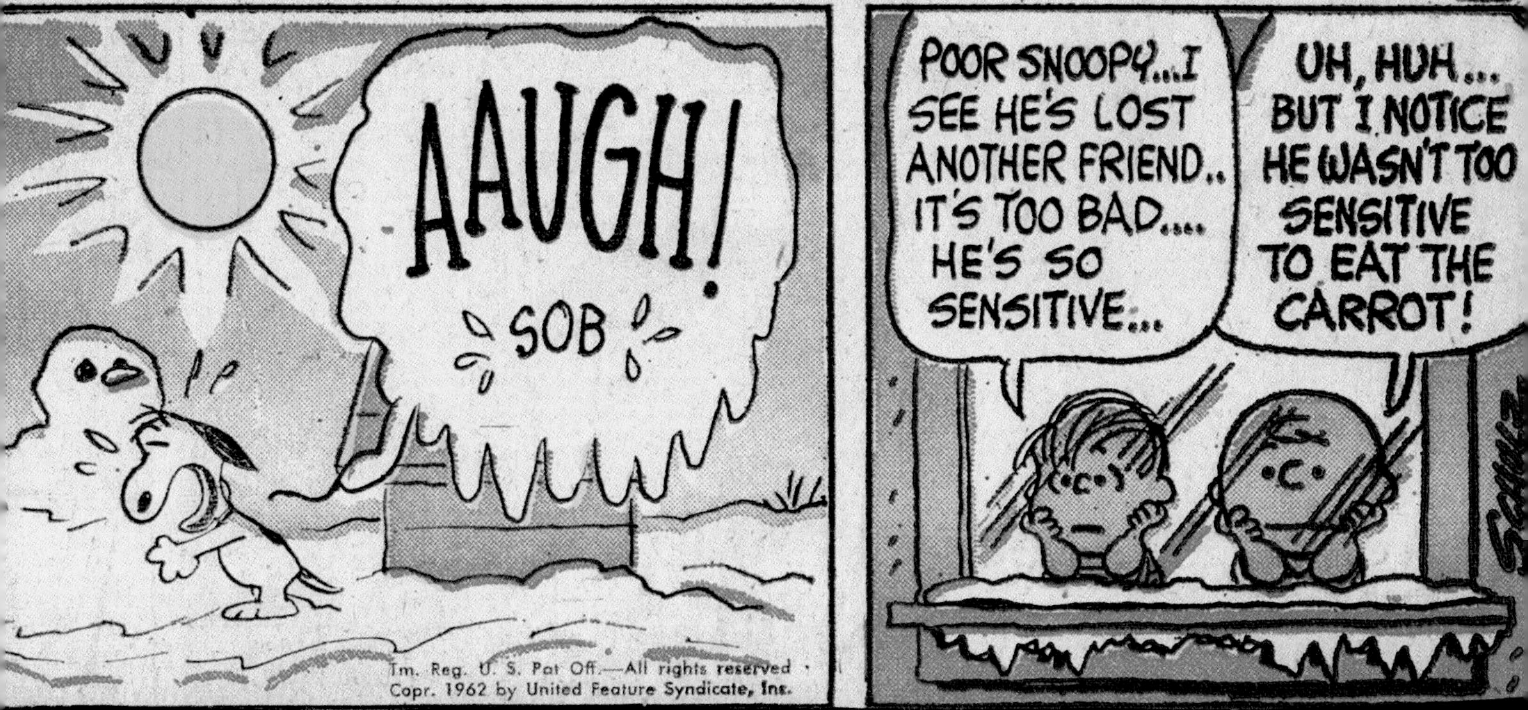
AAUGH!
SOB
POOR SNOOPY...I SEE HE'S LOST ANOTHER FRIEND.. IT'S TOO BAD.... HE'S SO SENSITIVE...
UH, HUH... BUT I NOTICE HE WASN'T TOO SENSITIVE TO EAT THE CARROT!
Tm. Reg. U. S. Pat Off.—All rights reserved
Copr. 1962 by United Feature Syndicate, Inc.
SCHULZ

To Jerry + Nora with friendship – Charles Schulz

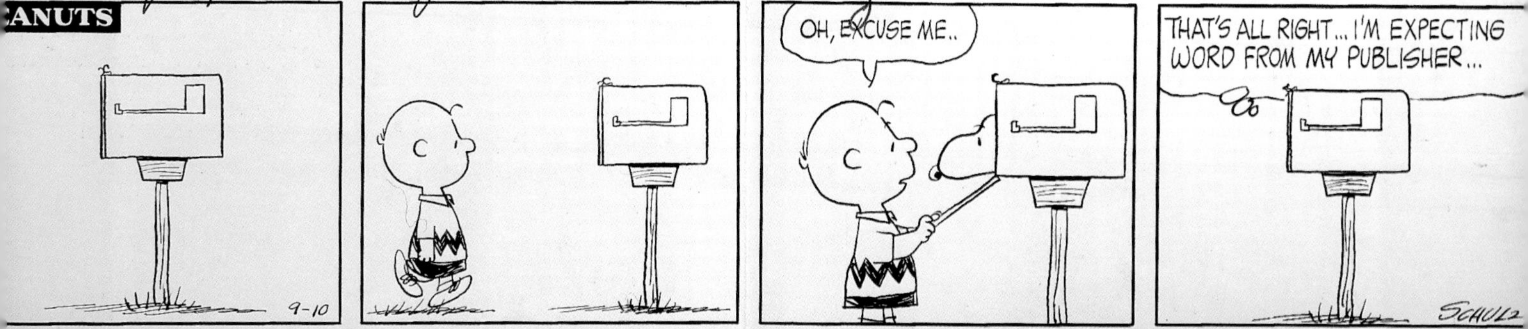
ANUTS
9-10
OH, EXCUSE ME..
THAT'S ALL RIGHT... I'M EXPECTING WORD FROM MY PUBLISHER...
SCHULZ

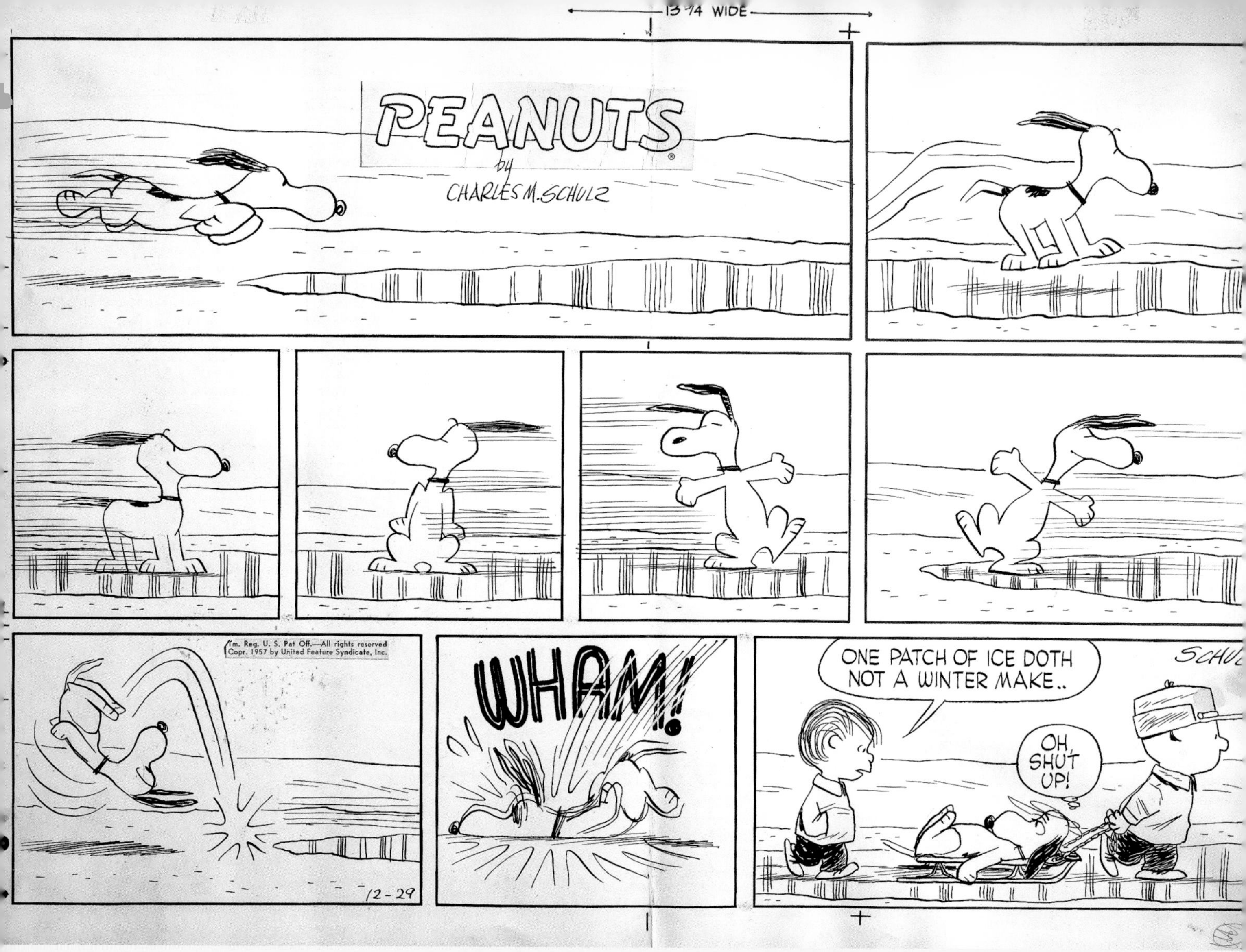
13 1/4 WIDE
PEANUTS
by
CHARLES M. SCHULZ
Tm. Reg. U. S. Pat Off.—All rights reserved
Copr. 1957 by United Feature Syndicate, Inc.
12-29
WHAM!
ONE PATCH OF ICE DOTH NOT A WINTER MAKE..
OH, SHUT UP!
SCHULZ

Once Snoopy rose up on two feet, there was no going back. "He began to do more and more things that were more and more fantastic," Schulz said in 1977, "it just seemed funnier at times to get him up. Some things demanded that he walk on his two hind legs. In a lot of instances, once you commit yourself that way you can't back up. It would be too late to put him back on four feet now. It would just destroy him."

SNOOPY

® SNOOPY TRADE MARK

A DOG-ON FUNNY GAME

AGES 6 TO 12

A COMPANION GAME TO THE "PEANUTS" GAME

MANUFACTURED BY Selchow & Righter Co., NEW YORK 7, MADE IN U.S.A.

SEL RIGHT

CHARACTER CREATED By Charles M. Schulz
UNITED FEATURE SYNDICATE, INC.

The Hungerford Plastics Snoopy doll, 1958.

Right: The first Snoopy game, Selchow and Richtor Co., 1967.

Charlie Brown often found himself in the frustrating position of being constantly ridiculed by Snoopy even as he did his best to take care of him—something any parent could identify with.

The idea that Snoopy rarely referred to Charlie Brown by name, but almost always as “That round-headed kid,” only added insult to injury.

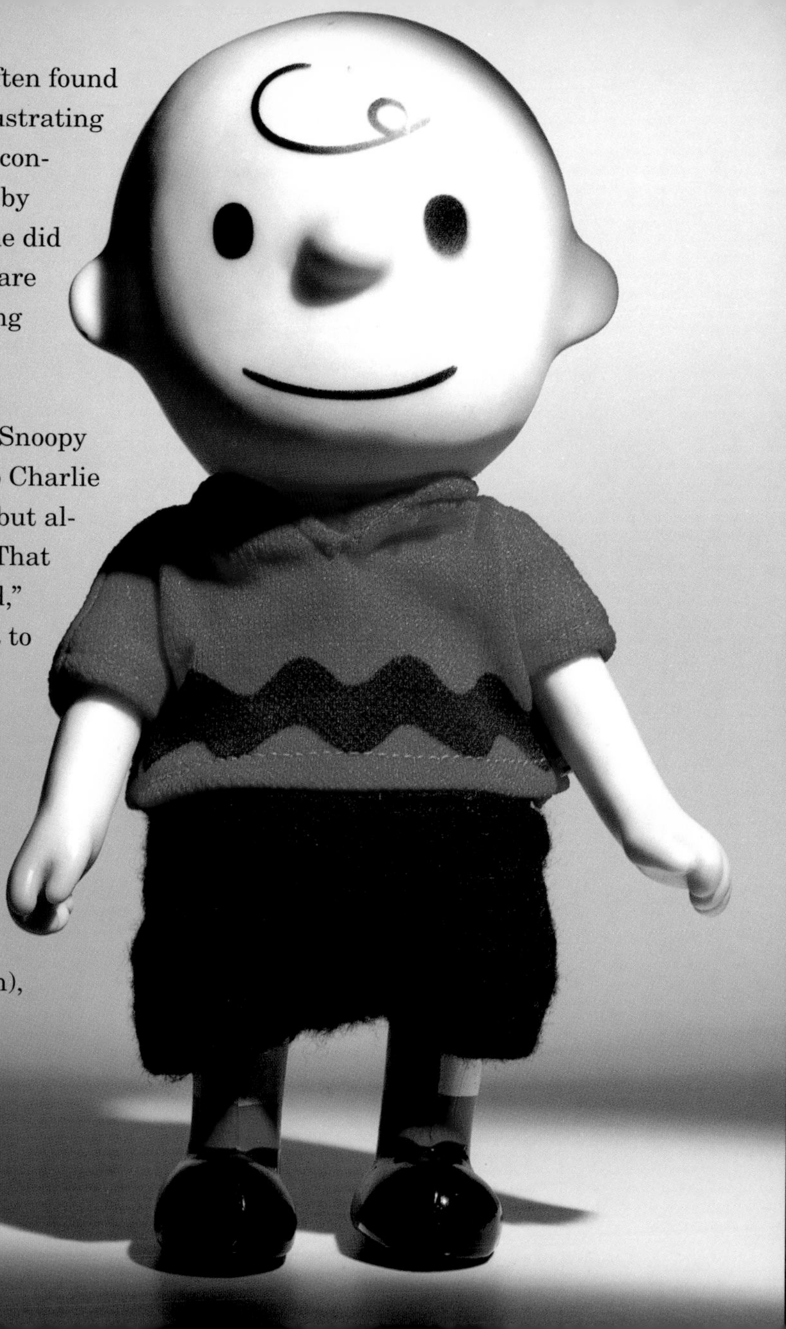

Right: A Charlie Brown “Pocket Doll,” from 1968. H. Boucher and Company also produced Snoopy (as the Red Baron), Lucy, Linus and Schroeder.

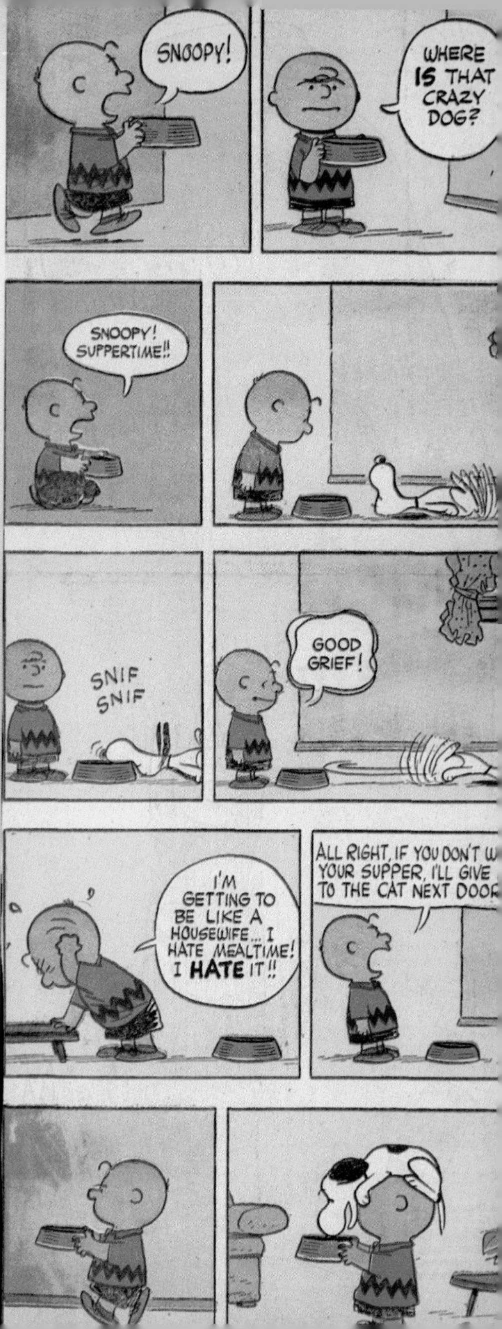
SNOOPY!
WHERE IS THAT CRAZY DOG?
SNOOPY! SUPPERTIME!!
SNIF SNIF
GOOD GRIEF!
I'M GETTING TO BE LIKE A HOUSEWIFE... I HATE MEALTIME! I HATE IT!!
ALL RIGHT, IF YOU DON'T W
YOUR SUPPER, I'LL GIVE
TO THE CAT NEXT DOOR

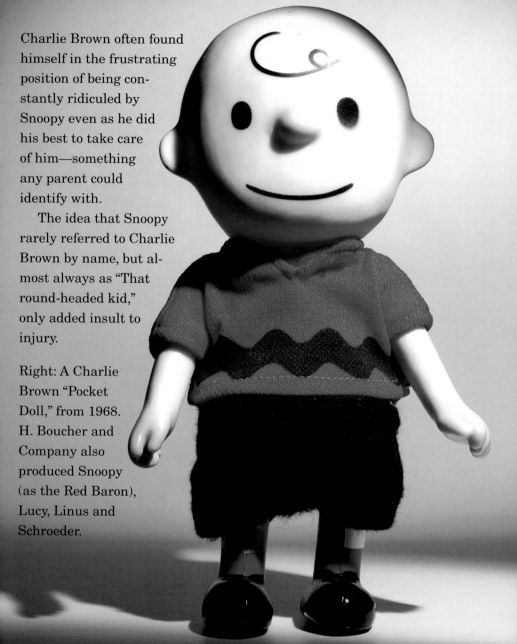

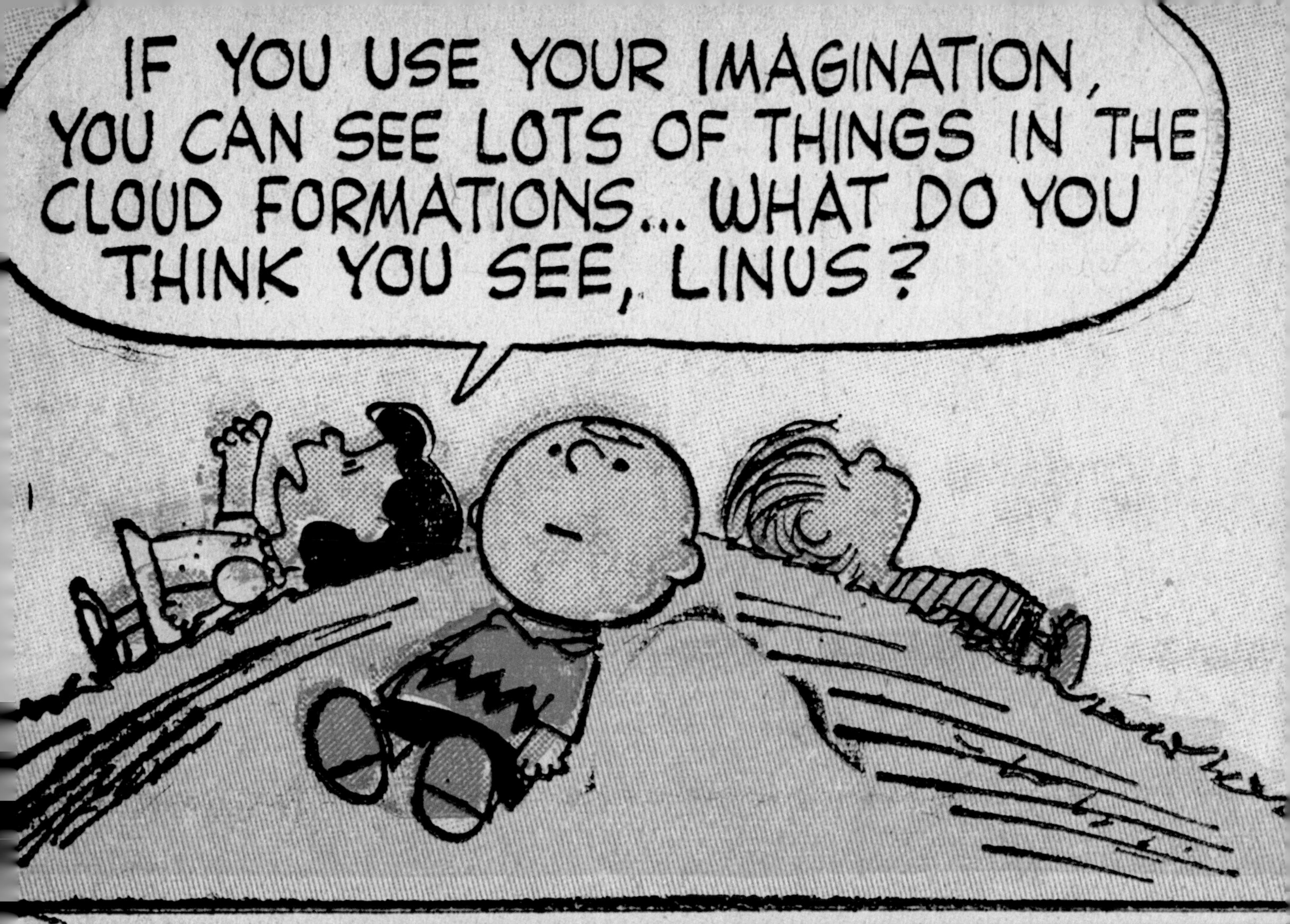
IF YOU USE YOUR IMAGINATION, YOU CAN SEE LOTS OF THINGS IN THE CLOUD FORMATIONS... WHAT DO YOU THINK YOU SEE, LINUS?

When asked which of all the strips was the most popular, Schulz answered that this one, from 1960, was "The one I got the most mail on." The pacing is as leisurely as lying in the grass on a summer afternoon, with the only "action" Charlie Brown's gently increasing alarm. Linus's references are priceless, and no doubt gave a nation of grade-schoolers a vicarious introduction to Thomas Eakins (whose style Schulz admired). This sequence also became an integral part of the musical *You're a Good Man Charlie Brown*

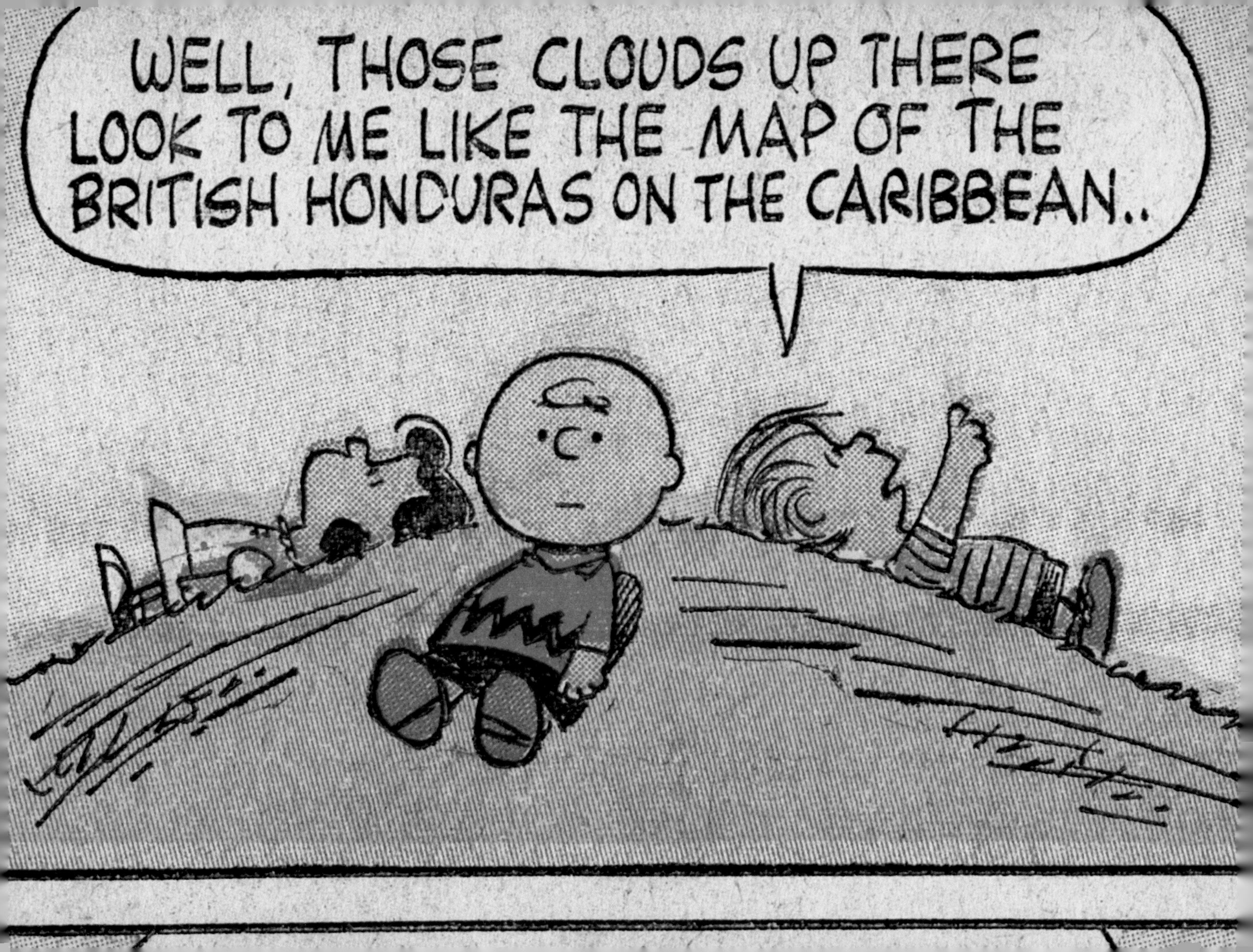
WELL, THOSE CLOUDS UP THERE LOOK TO ME LIKE THE MAP OF THE BRITISH HONDURAS ON THE CARIBBEAN..

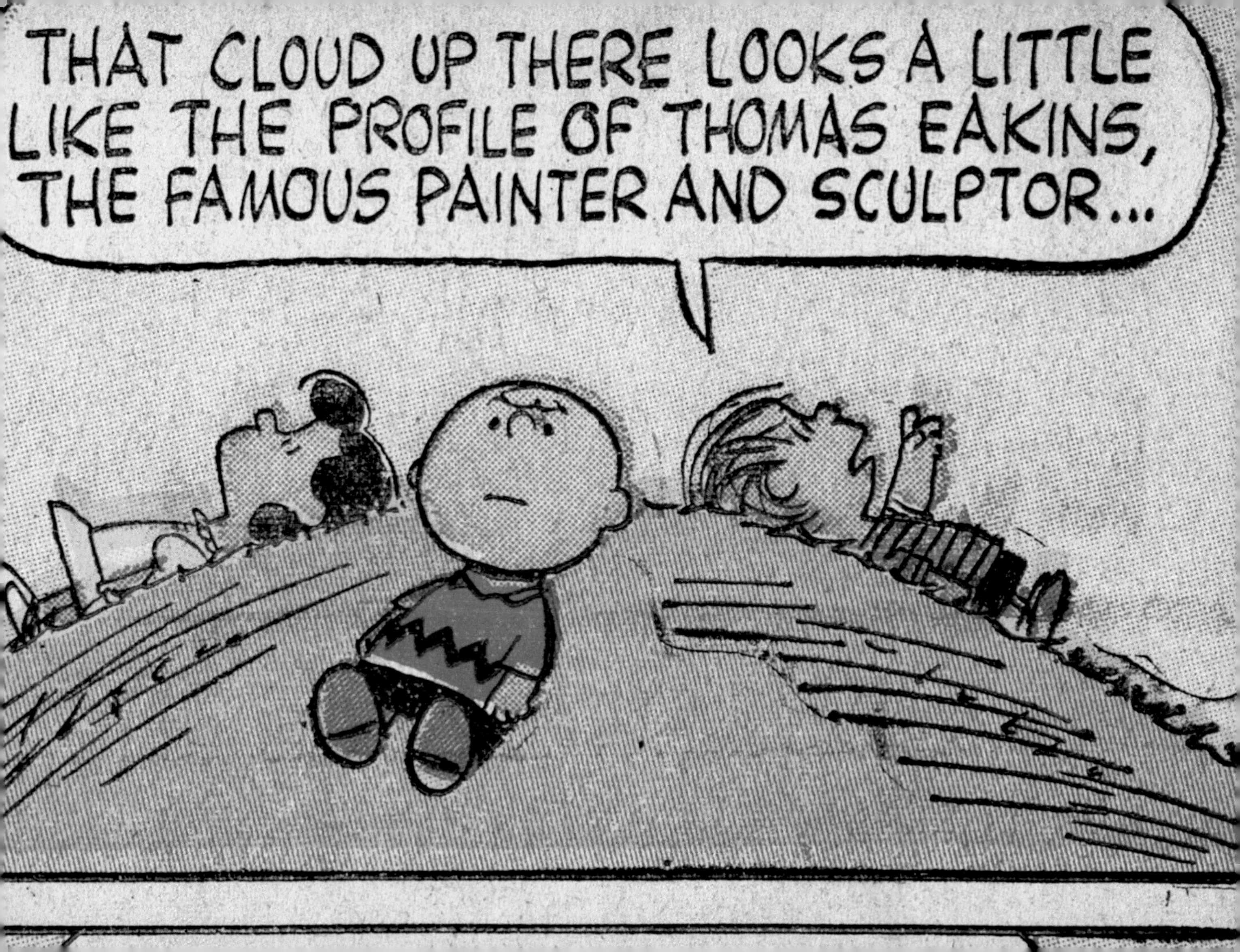
THAT CLOUD UP THERE LOOKS A LITTLE LIKE THE PROFILE OF THOMAS EAKINS, THE FAMOUS PAINTER AND SCULPTOR...

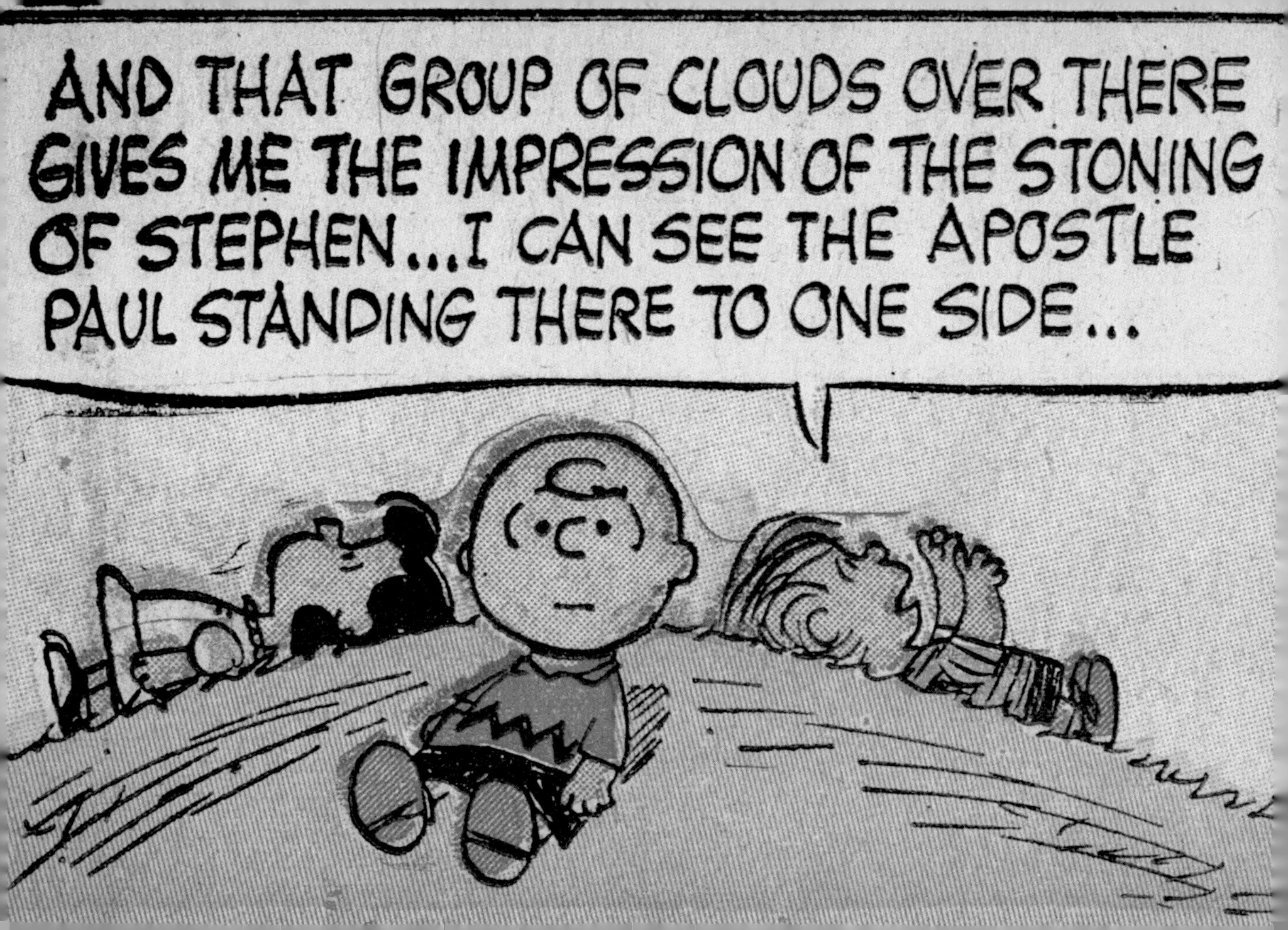
AND THAT GROUP OF CLOUDS OVER THERE GIVES ME THE IMPRESSION OF THE STONING OF STEPHEN...I CAN SEE THE APOSTLE PAUL STANDING THERE TO ONE SIDE...

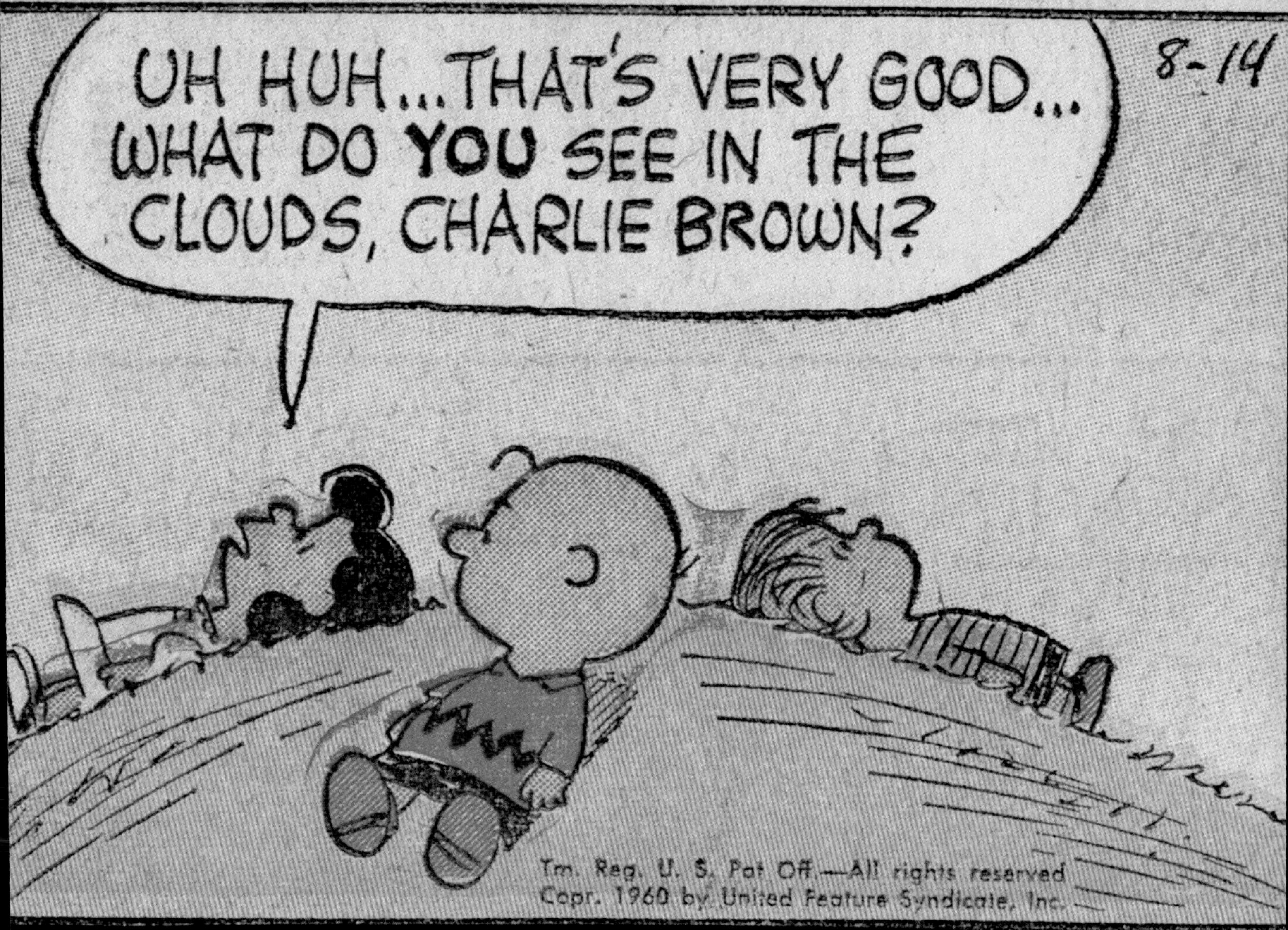
UH HUH...THAT'S VERY GOOD... WHAT DO **YOU** SEE IN THE CLOUDS, CHARLIE BROWN?
8-14
Tm. Reg. U. S. Pat Off.—All rights reserved
Copr. 1960 by United Feature Syndicate, Inc.

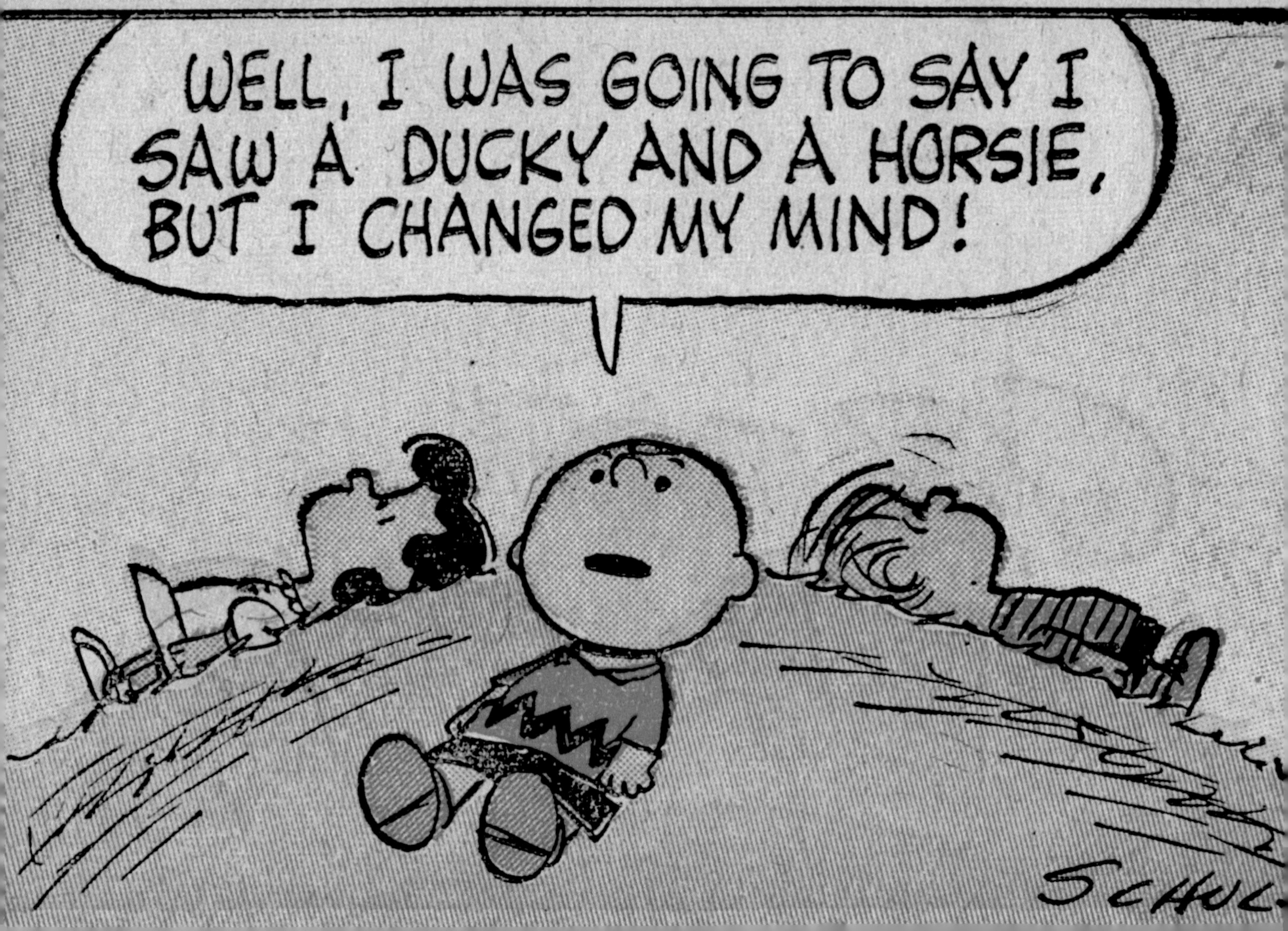
WELL, I WAS GOING TO SAY I SAW A DUCKY AND A HORSIE, BUT I CHANGED MY MIND!
SCHULZ

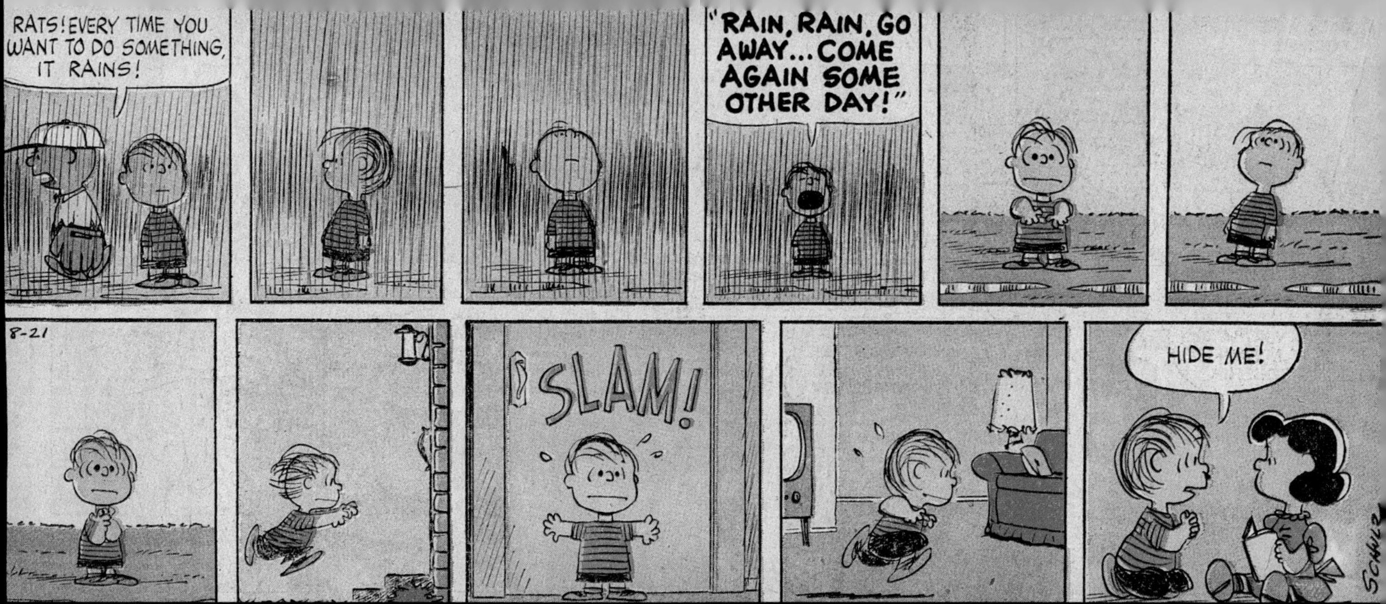
RATS! EVERY TIME YOU WANT TO DO SOMETHING, IT RAINS!
"RAIN, RAIN, GO AWAY... COME AGAIN SOME OTHER DAY!"
8-21
SLAM!
HIDE ME!
SCHULZ

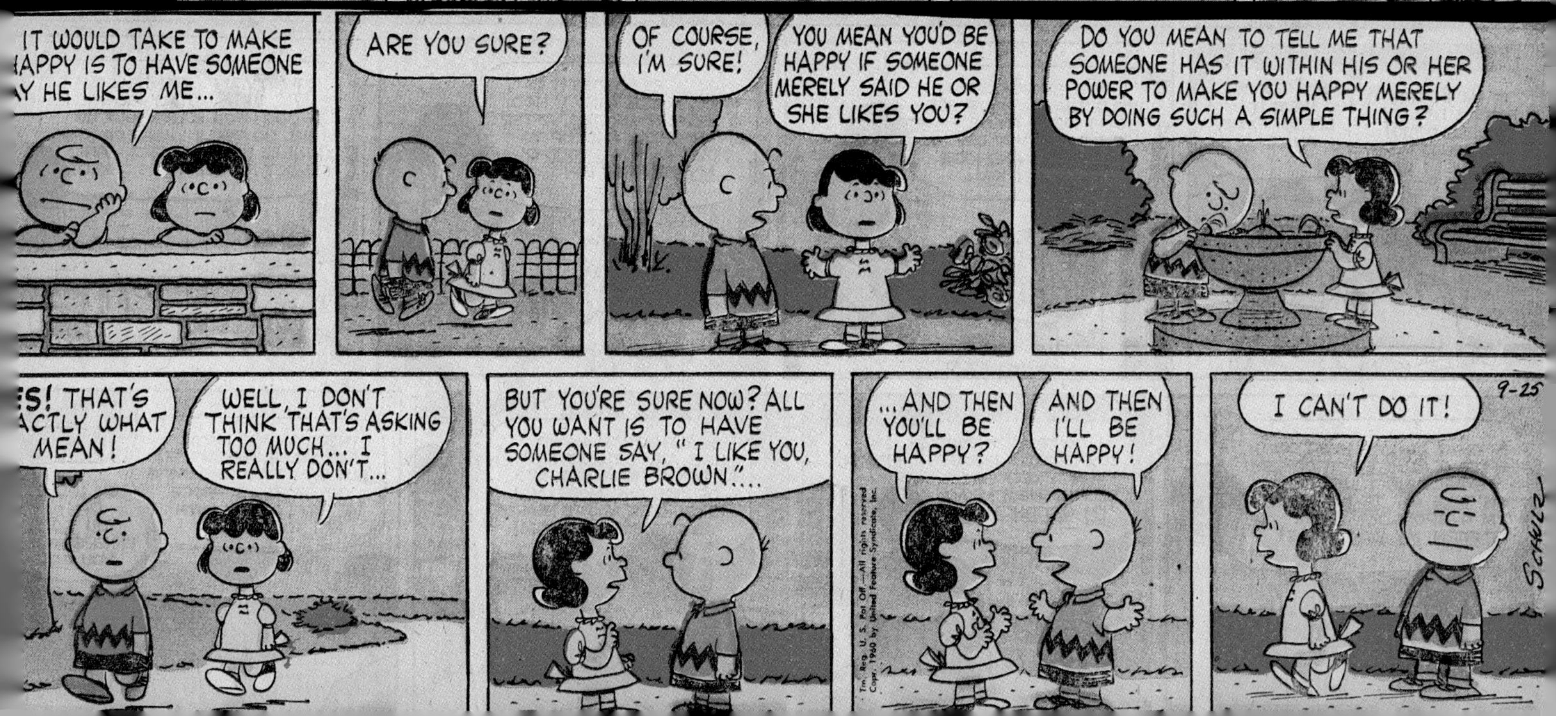
IT WOULD TAKE TO MAKE
APPY IS TO HAVE SOMEONE
Y HE LIKES ME...
ARE YOU SURE?
OF COURSE, I'M SURE!
YOU MEAN YOU'D BE HAPPY IF SOMEONE MERELY SAID HE OR SHE LIKES YOU?
DO YOU MEAN TO TELL ME THAT SOMEONE HAS IT WITHIN HIS OR HER POWER TO MAKE YOU HAPPY MERELY BY DOING SUCH A SIMPLE THING?
S! THAT'S
CTLY WHAT
MEAN!
WELL, I DON'T THINK THAT'S ASKING TOO MUCH... I REALLY DON'T...
BUT YOU'RE SURE NOW? ALL YOU WANT IS TO HAVE SOMEONE SAY, "I LIKE YOU, CHARLIE BROWN."...
Tm. Reg. U. S. Pat. Off.—All rights reserved
Copr. 1960 by United Feature Syndicate, Inc.
...AND THEN YOU'LL BE HAPPY?
AND THEN I'LL BE HAPPY!
9-25
I CAN'T DO IT!
SCHULZ

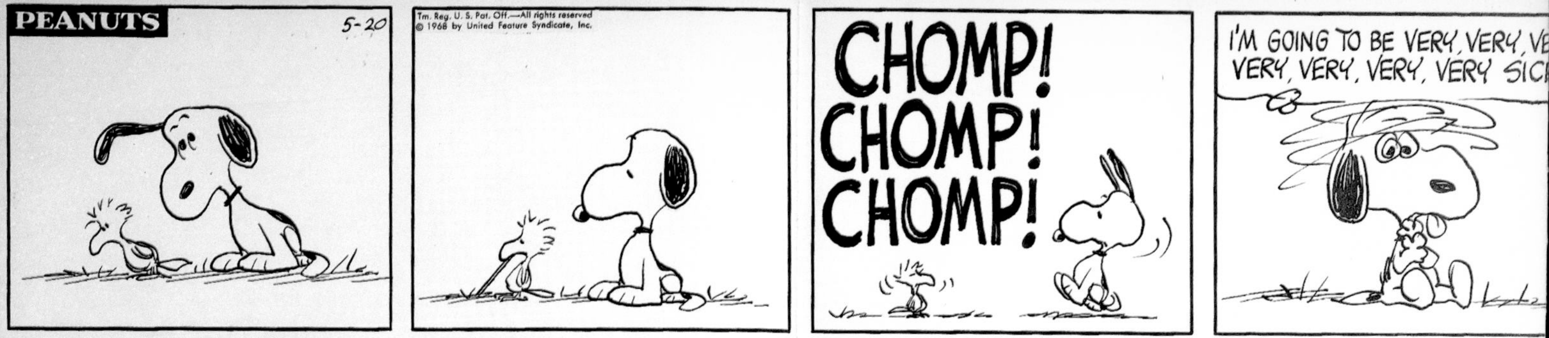
PEANUTS
5-20
Tm. Reg. U. S. Pat. Off.—All rights reserved
© 1968 by United Feature Syndicate, Inc.
CHOMP! CHOMP! CHOMP!
I'M GOING TO BE VERY, VERY, VERY, VERY, VERY, VERY

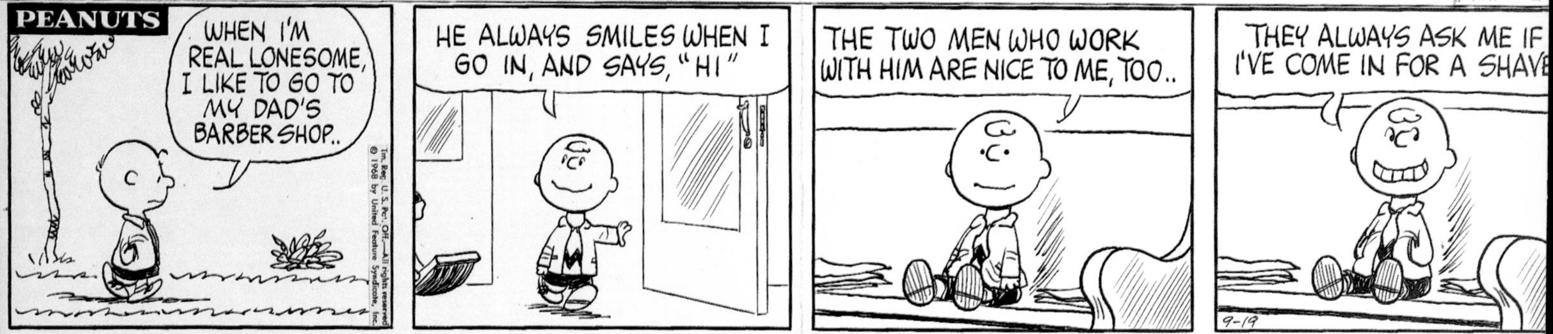
PEANUTS
WHEN I'M REAL LONESOME, I LIKE TO GO TO MY DAD'S BARBER SHOP..
Tm. Reg. U. S. Pat. Off.—All rights reserved
© 1968 by United Feature Syndicate, Inc.
HE ALWAYS SMILES WHEN I GO IN, AND SAYS, "HI"
THE TWO MEN WHO WORK WITH HIM ARE NICE TO ME, TOO..
THEY ALWAYS ASK ME IF I'VE COME IN FOR A SHAVE
9-19

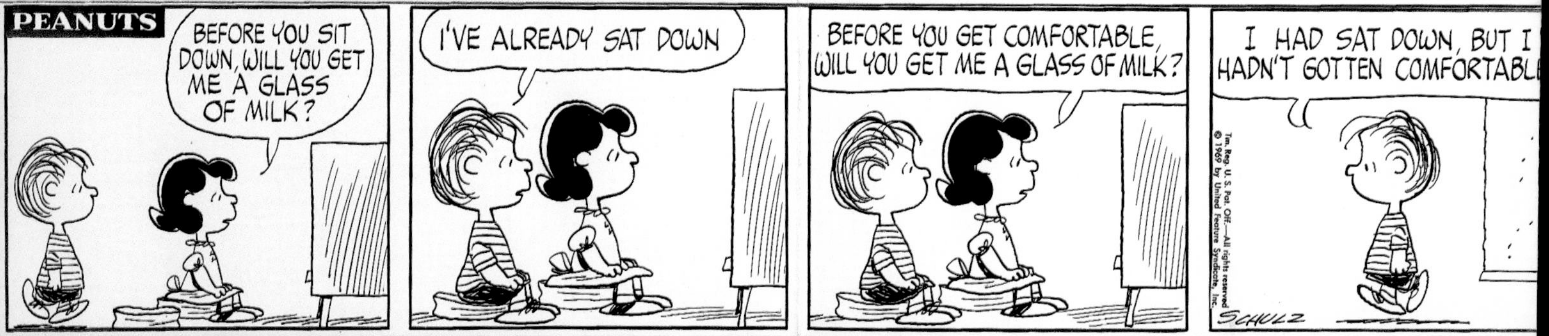
PEANUTS
BEFORE YOU SIT DOWN, WILL YOU GET ME A GLASS OF MILK?
I'VE ALREADY SAT DOWN
BEFORE YOU GET COMFORTABLE, WILL YOU GET ME A GLASS OF MILK?
I HAD SAT DOWN, BUT I HADN'T GOTTEN COMFORTABLE
Tm. Reg. U. S. Pat. Off.—All rights reserved
© 1969 by United Feature Syndicate, Inc.
SCHULZ

Schulz was a voracious reader. Among his favorite authors were Leo Tolstoy, Fyodor Dostoevsky, F. Scott Fitzgerald, Thomas Wolfe, Flannery O'Connor, Carson McCullers, Anne Tyler, and Joan Didion, just to name a few. *War and Peace* was his favorite novel, and his characters read and discussed it in dozens of strips. The reference to Edgar Allan Poe (opposite, top) is typical of the strip's many literary allusions.

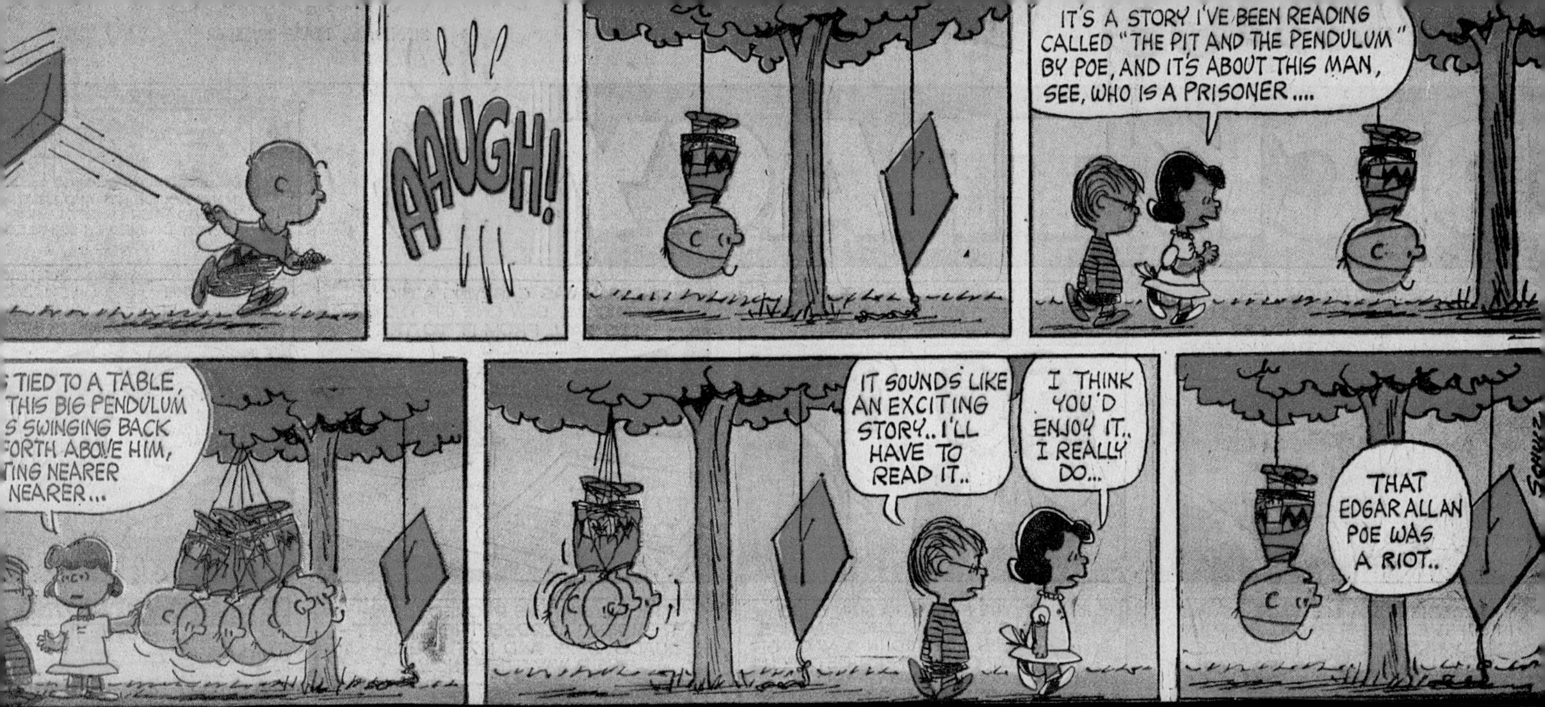
AAUGH!
IT'S A STORY I'VE BEEN READING CALLED "THE PIT AND THE PENDULUM" BY POE, AND IT'S ABOUT THIS MAN, SEE, WHO IS A PRISONER....
TIED TO A TABLE, THIS BIG PENDULUM S SWINGING BACK FORTH ABOVE HIM, TING NEARER NEARER...
IT SOUNDS LIKE AN EXCITING STORY.. I'LL HAVE TO READ IT..
I THINK YOU'D ENJOY IT.. I REALLY DO...
THAT EDGAR ALLAN POE WAS A RIOT..
SCHULZ

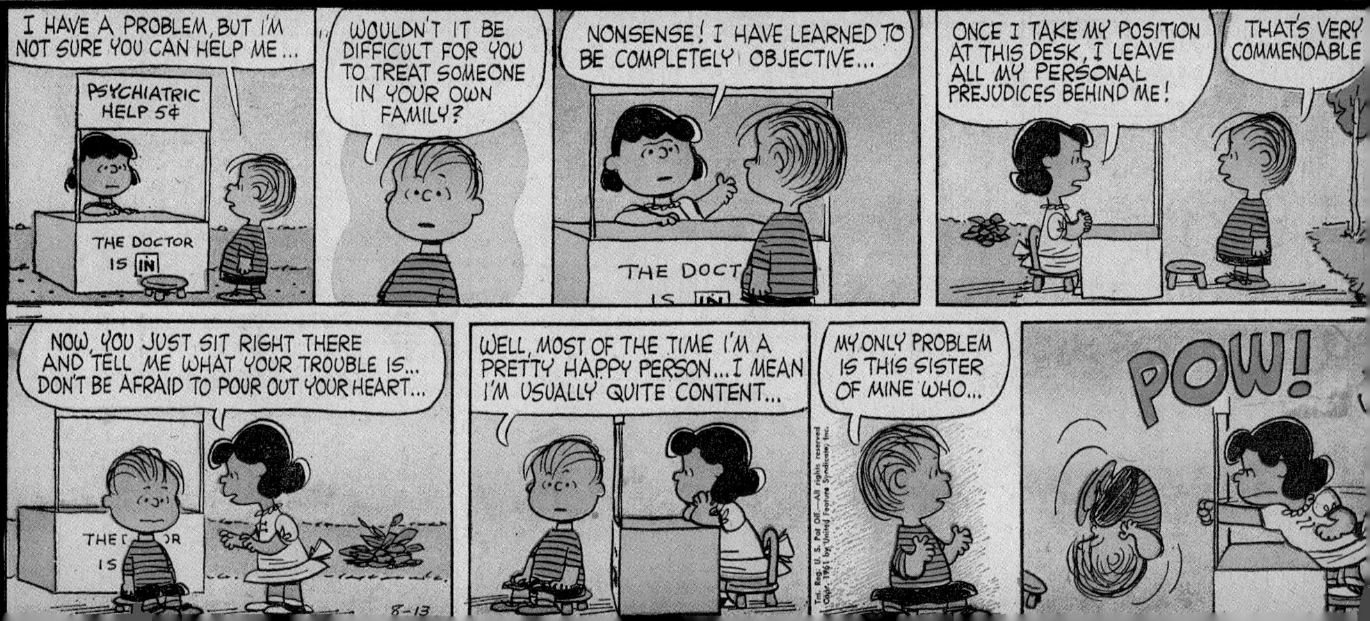
I HAVE A PROBLEM, BUT I'M NOT SURE YOU CAN HELP ME...
PSYCHIATRIC HELP 5¢
THE DOCTOR IS IN
WOULDN'T IT BE DIFFICULT FOR YOU TO TREAT SOMEONE IN YOUR OWN FAMILY?
NONSENSE! I HAVE LEARNED TO BE COMPLETELY OBJECTIVE...
ONCE I TAKE MY POSITION AT THIS DESK, I LEAVE ALL MY PERSONAL PREJUDICES BEHIND ME!
THAT'S VERY COMMENDABLE
NOW, YOU JUST SIT RIGHT THERE AND TELL ME WHAT YOUR TROUBLE IS... DON'T BE AFRAID TO POUR OUT YOUR HEART...
8-13
WELL, MOST OF THE TIME I'M A PRETTY HAPPY PERSON... I MEAN I'M USUALLY QUITE CONTENT...
MY ONLY PROBLEM IS THIS SISTER OF MINE WHO...
POW!

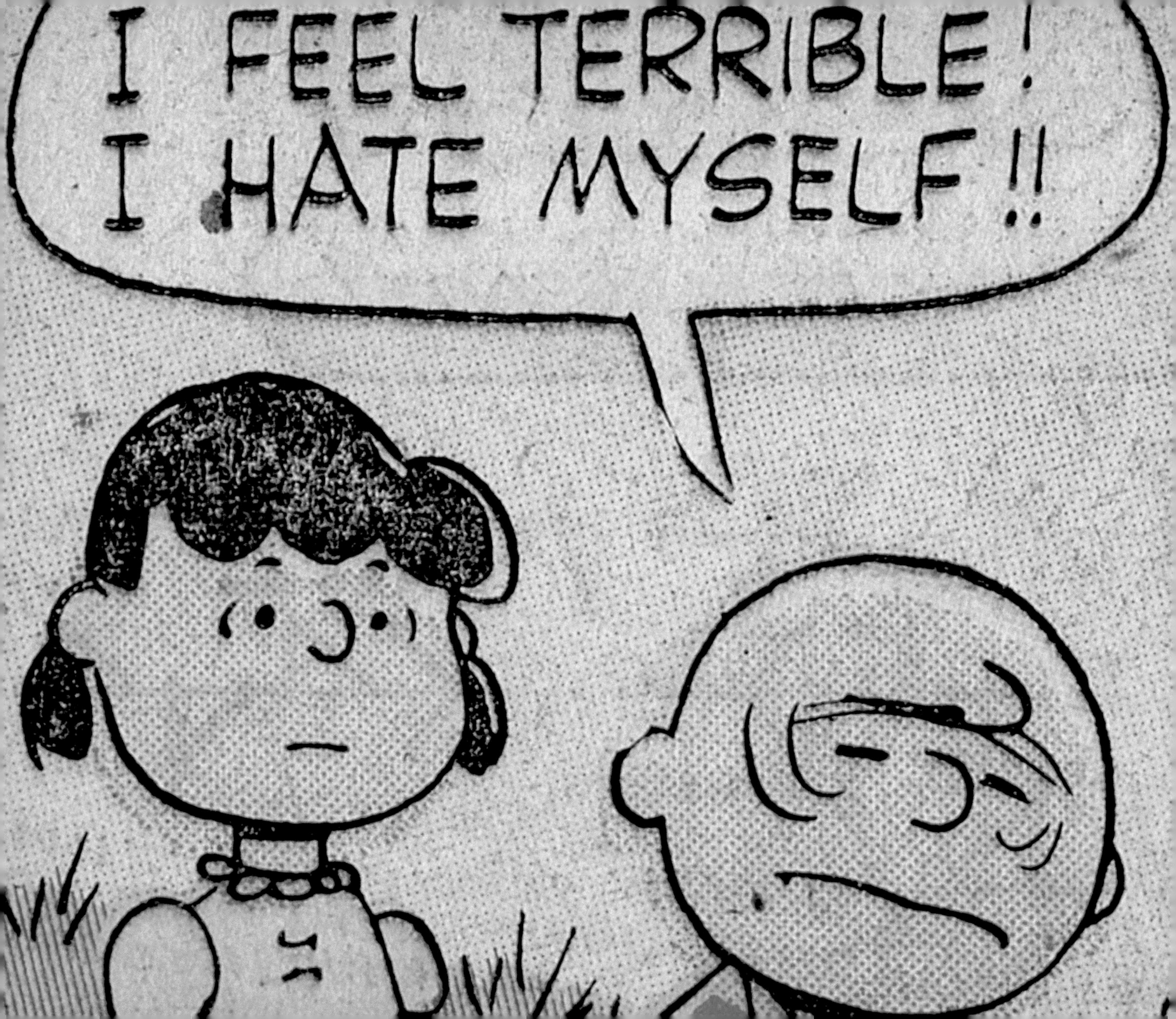
I FEEL TERRIBLE! I HATE MYSELF!!

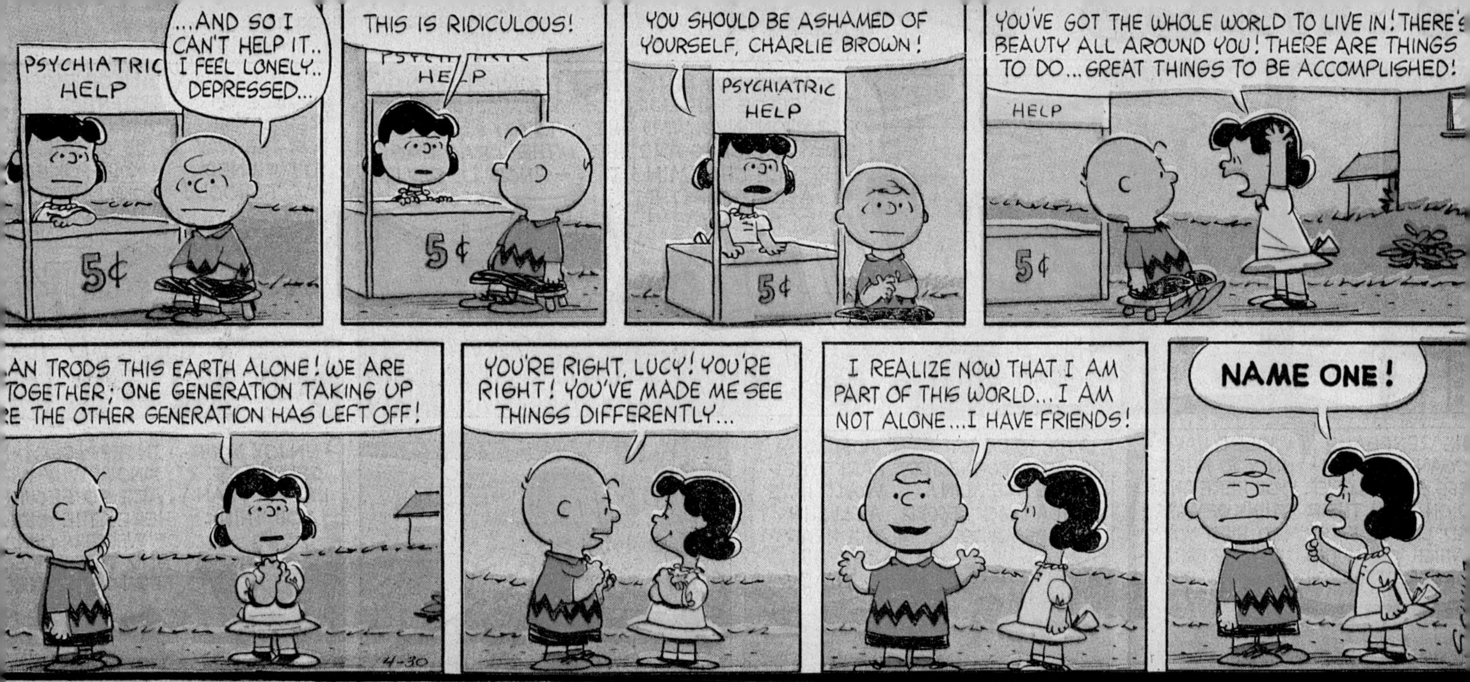
PSYCHIATRIC HELP
...AND SO I CAN'T HELP IT.. I FEEL LONELY.. DEPRESSED...
5¢
THIS IS RIDICULOUS!
YOU SHOULD BE ASHAMED OF YOURSELF, CHARLIE BROWN!
PSYCHIATRIC HELP
YOU'VE GOT THE WHOLE WORLD TO LIVE IN! THERE'S BEAUTY ALL AROUND YOU! THERE ARE THINGS TO DO...GREAT THINGS TO BE ACCOMPLISHED!
AN TRODS THIS EARTH ALONE! WE ARE TOGETHER; ONE GENERATION TAKING UP E THE OTHER GENERATION HAS LEFT OFF!
4-30
YOU'RE RIGHT, LUCY! YOU'RE RIGHT! YOU'VE MADE ME SEE THINGS DIFFERENTLY...
I REALIZE NOW THAT I AM PART OF THIS WORLD... I AM NOT ALONE...I HAVE FRIENDS!
NAME ONE!

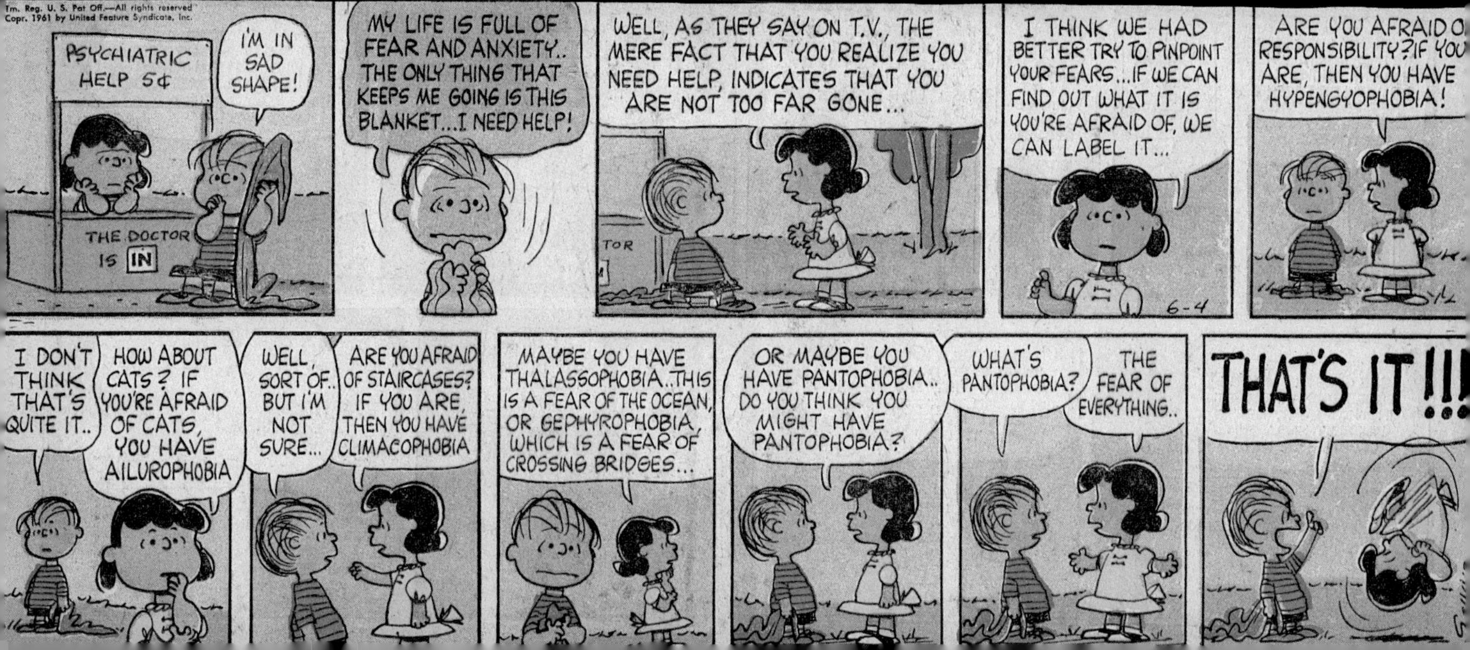
Tm. Reg. U. S. Pat. Off.—All rights reserved
Copr. 1961 by United Feature Syndicate, Inc.
PSYCHIATRIC HELP 5¢
I'M IN SAD SHAPE!
THE DOCTOR IS IN
MY LIFE IS FULL OF FEAR AND ANXIETY.. THE ONLY THING THAT KEEPS ME GOING IS THIS BLANKET...I NEED HELP!
WELL, AS THEY SAY ON T.V., THE MERE FACT THAT YOU REALIZE YOU NEED HELP, INDICATES THAT YOU ARE NOT TOO FAR GONE...
I THINK WE HAD BETTER TRY TO PINPOINT YOUR FEARS...IF WE CAN FIND OUT WHAT IT IS YOU'RE AFRAID OF, WE CAN LABEL IT...
6-4
ARE YOU AFRAID OF RESPONSIBILITY? IF YOU ARE, THEN YOU HAVE HYPENGYOPHOBIA!
I DON'T THINK THAT'S QUITE IT..
HOW ABOUT CATS? IF YOU'RE AFRAID OF CATS, YOU HAVE AILUROPHOBIA
WELL, SORT OF.. BUT I'M NOT SURE...
ARE YOU AFRAID OF STAIRCASES? IF YOU ARE, THEN YOU HAVE CLIMACOPHOBIA
MAYBE YOU HAVE THALASSOPHOBIA..THIS IS A FEAR OF THE OCEAN, OR GEPHYROPHOBIA, WHICH IS A FEAR OF CROSSING BRIDGES...
OR MAYBE YOU HAVE PANTOPHOBIA.. DO YOU THINK YOU MIGHT HAVE PANTOPHOBIA?
WHAT'S PANTOPHOBIA?
THE FEAR OF EVERYTHING..
THAT'S IT!!!

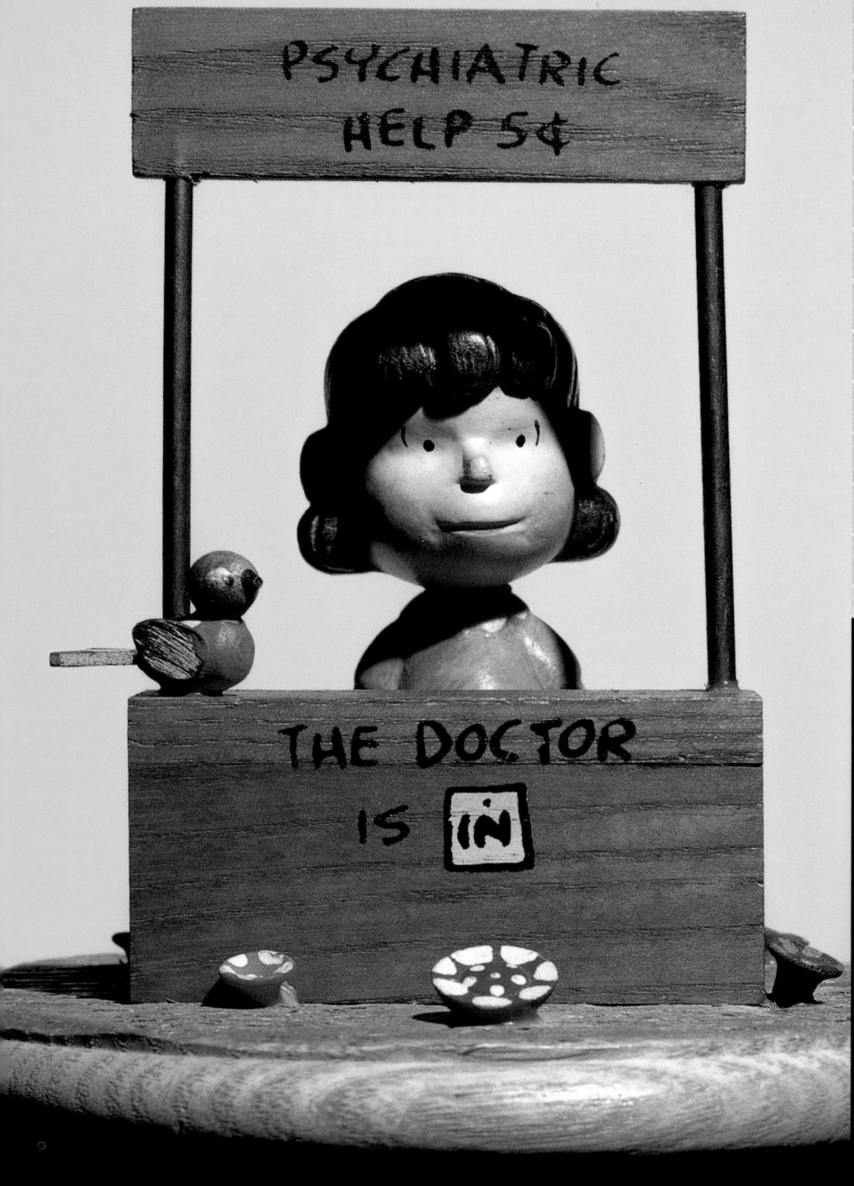
PSYCHIATRIC
HELP 5¢
THE DOCTOR
IS IN

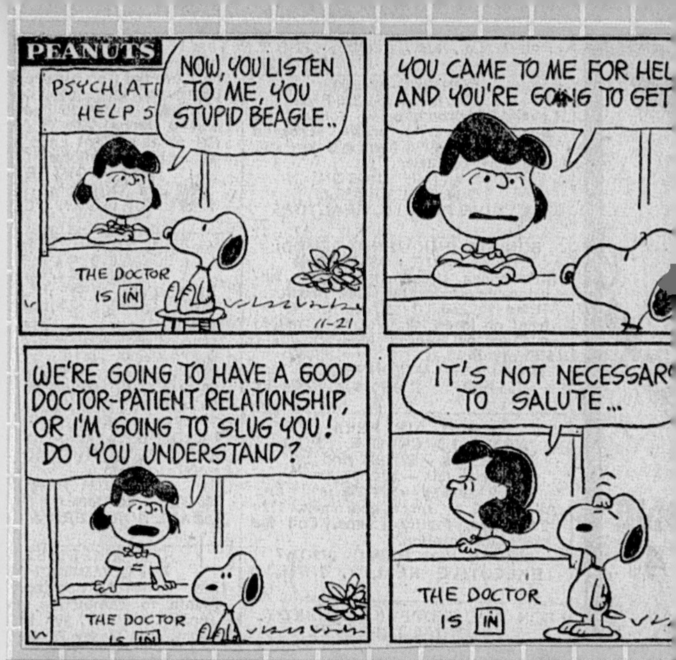
PEANUTS
NOW, YOU LISTEN TO ME, YOU STUPID BEAGLE..
THE DOCTOR IS IN
11-21
WE'RE GOING TO HAVE A GOOD DOCTOR-PATIENT RELATIONSHIP, OR I'M GOING TO SLUG YOU! DO YOU UNDERSTAND?
THE DOCTOR

Lucy's psychiatric booth is one of Schulz's most brilliantly conceived creations. For someone who never actually went to a psychiatrist, his insight into their thought processes and methods was uncanny. Lucy's attitude about the entire enterprise could probably be best summed up by this exchange with Franklin from 1968, as he encountered her for the first time:

Franklin: "How's the lemonade business?"

Lucy: "This isn't a lemonade stand . . . this is a psychiatric booth."

Franklin: "Are you a real doctor?"

Lucy: "Was the lemonade ever any good?"

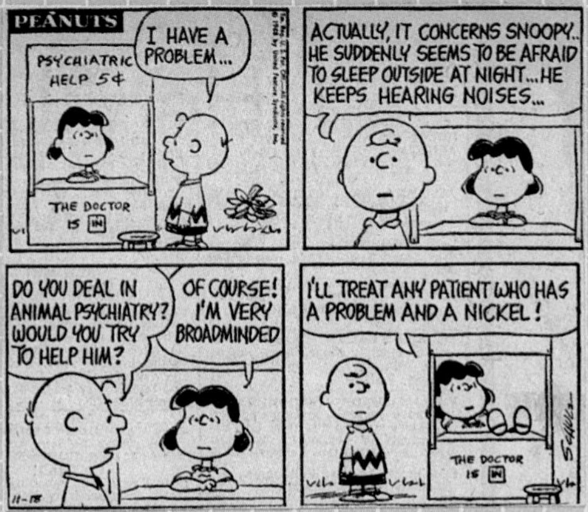
PEANUTS
PSYCHIATRIC HELP 5¢
I HAVE A PROBLEM...
THE DOCTOR IS IN
ACTUALLY, IT CONCERNS SNOOPY.. HE SUDDENLY SEEMS TO BE AFRAID TO SLEEP OUTSIDE AT NIGHT...HE KEEPS HEARING NOISES...
DO YOU DEAL IN ANIMAL PSYCHIATRY? WOULD YOU TRY TO HELP HIM?
OF COURSE! I'M VERY BROADMINDED
11-18
I'LL TREAT ANY PATIENT WHO HAS A PROBLEM AND A NICKEL!
THE DOCTOR IS IN
SCHULZ

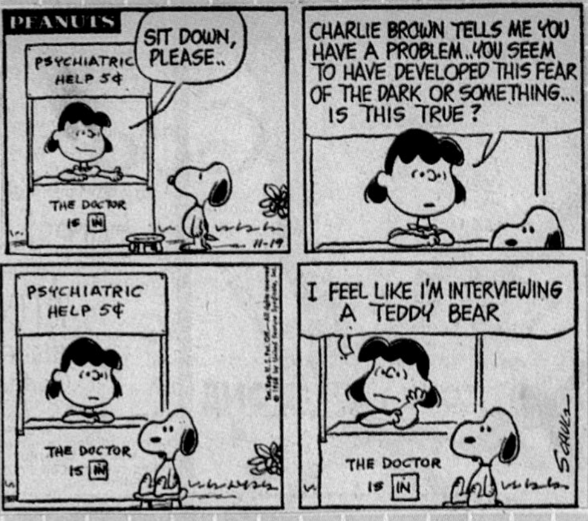
PEANUTS
PSYCHIATRIC HELP 5¢
SIT DOWN, PLEASE..
THE DOCTOR IS IN
11-19
CHARLIE BROWN TELLS ME YOU HAVE A PROBLEM..YOU SEEM TO HAVE DEVELOPED THIS FEAR OF THE DARK OR SOMETHING... IS THIS TRUE?
PSYCHIATRIC HELP 5¢
THE DOCTOR IS IN
I FEEL LIKE I'M INTERVIEWING A TEDDY BEAR
THE DOCTOR IS IN
SCHULZ

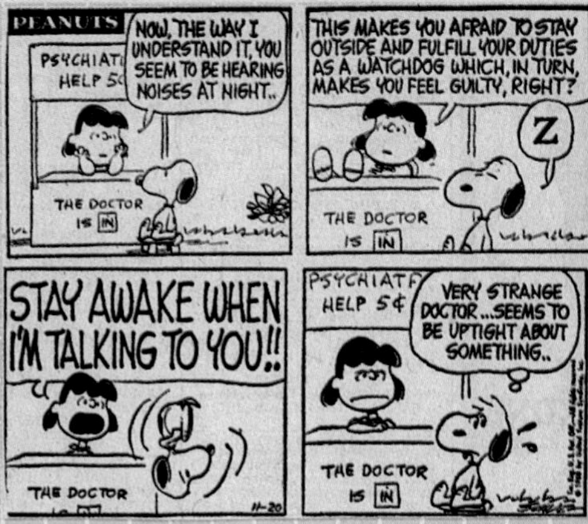
PEANUTS
PSYCHIATRIC HELP 5¢
NOW, THE WAY I UNDERSTAND IT, YOU SEEM TO BE HEARING NOISES AT NIGHT..
THE DOCTOR IS IN
THIS MAKES YOU AFRAID TO STAY OUTSIDE AND FULFILL YOUR DUTIES AS A WATCHDOG WHICH, IN TURN, MAKES YOU FEEL GUILTY, RIGHT?
Z
THE DOCTOR IS IN
STAY AWAKE WHEN I'M TALKING TO YOU!!
THE DOCTOR
11-20
PSYCHIATR HELP 5¢
VERY STRANGE DOCTOR...SEEMS TO BE UPTIGHT ABOUT SOMETHING..
THE DOCTOR IS IN
SCHULZ

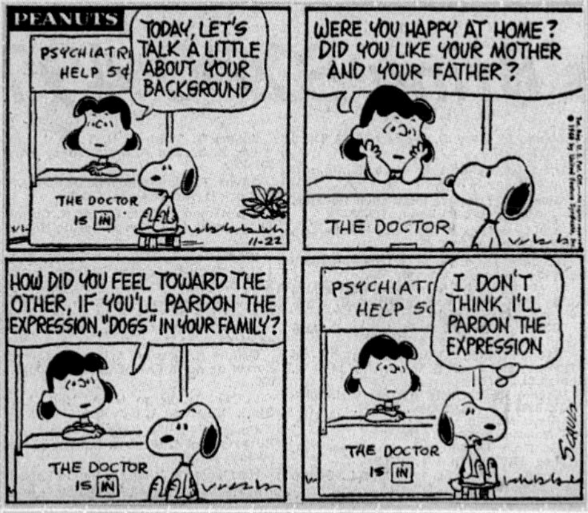
PEANUTS
PSYCHIATRI HELP 5¢
TODAY, LET'S TALK A LITTLE ABOUT YOUR BACKGROUND
THE DOCTOR IS IN
11-22
WERE YOU HAPPY AT HOME? DID YOU LIKE YOUR MOTHER AND YOUR FATHER?
THE DOCTOR
HOW DID YOU FEEL TOWARD THE OTHER, IF YOU'LL PARDON THE EXPRESSION, "DOGS" IN YOUR FAMILY?
THE DOCTOR IS IN
PSYCHIATI HELP 5¢
I DON'T THINK I'LL PARDON THE EXPRESSION
THE DOCTOR IS IN
SCHULZ

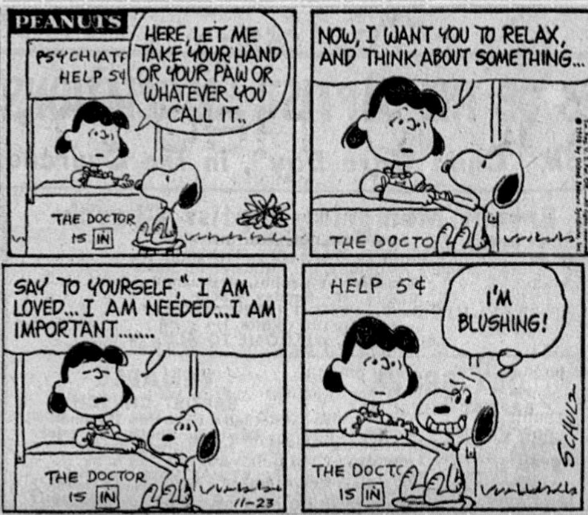
PEANUTS
PSYCHIATR HELP 5¢
HERE, LET ME TAKE YOUR HAND OR YOUR PAW OR WHATEVER YOU CALL IT..
THE DOCTOR IS IN
NOW, I WANT YOU TO RELAX, AND THINK ABOUT SOMETHING...
THE DOCTO
SAY TO YOURSELF," I AM LOVED... I AM NEEDED...I AM IMPORTANT.......
THE DOCTOR IS IN
11-23
HELP 5¢
I'M BLUSHING!
THE DOCTC IS IN
SCHULZ

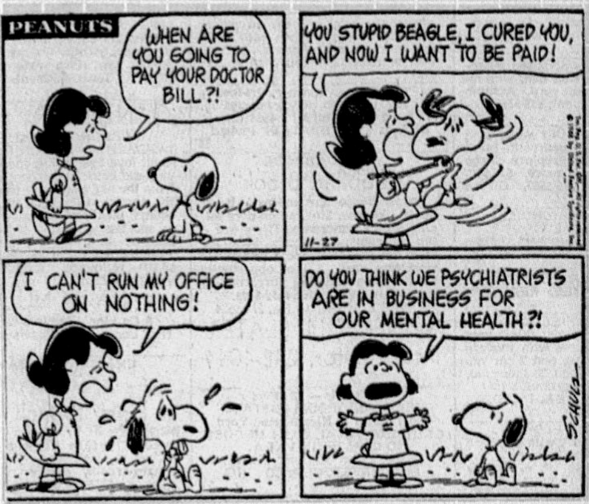
PEANUTS
WHEN ARE YOU GOING TO PAY YOUR DOCTOR BILL ?!
YOU STUPID BEAGLE, I CURED YOU, AND NOW I WANT TO BE PAID!
11-27
I CAN'T RUN MY OFFICE ON NOTHING!
DO YOU THINK WE PSYCHIATRISTS ARE IN BUSINESS FOR OUR MENTAL HEALTH ?!
SCHULZ

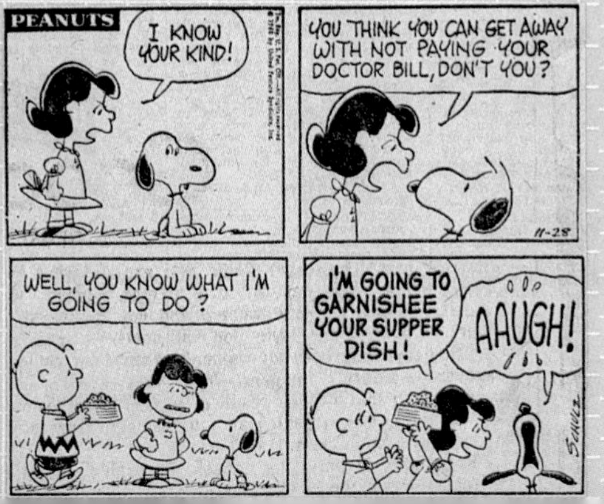
PEANUTS
I KNOW YOUR KIND!
YOU THINK YOU CAN GET AWAY WITH NOT PAYING YOUR DOCTOR BILL, DON'T YOU?
11-28
WELL, YOU KNOW WHAT I'M GOING TO DO?
I'M GOING TO GARNISHEE YOUR SUPPER DISH!
AAUGH!
SCHULZ

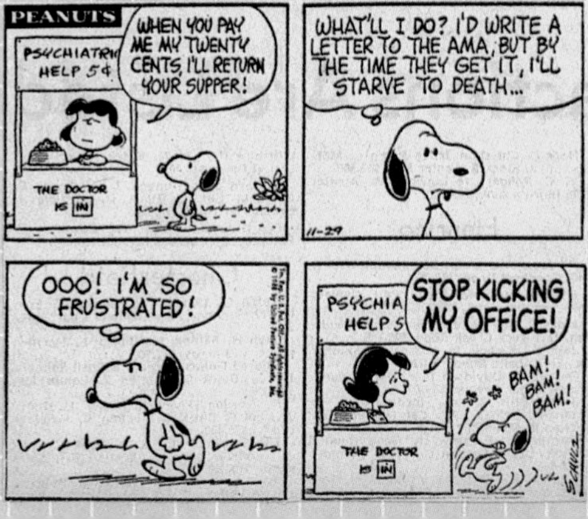
PEANUTS
PSYCHIATRIC HELP 5¢
WHEN YOU PAY ME MY TWENTY CENTS, I'LL RETURN YOUR SUPPER!
THE DOCTOR IS IN
11-29
WHAT'LL I DO? I'D WRITE A LETTER TO THE AMA, BUT BY THE TIME THEY GET IT, I'LL STARVE TO DEATH...
OOO! I'M SO FRUSTRATED!
PSYCHIA HELP 5
STOP KICKING MY OFFICE!
BAM! BAM! BAM!
THE DOCTOR IS IN
SCHULZ

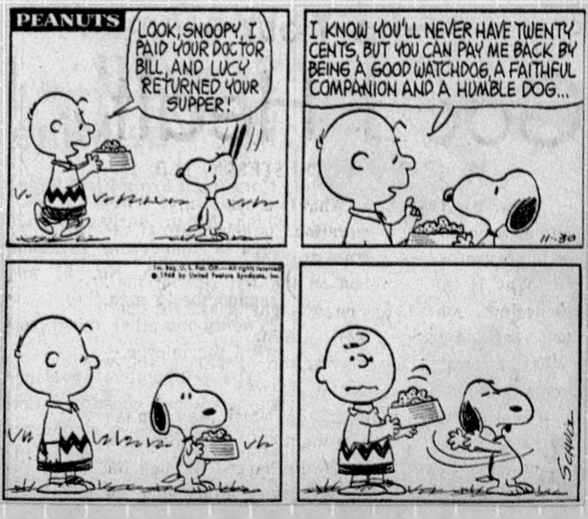
PEANUTS
LOOK, SNOOPY, I PAID YOUR DOCTOR BILL, AND LUCY RETURNED YOUR SUPPER!
I KNOW YOU'LL NEVER HAVE TWENTY CENTS, BUT YOU CAN PAY ME BACK BY BEING A GOOD WATCHDOG, A FAITHFUL COMPANION AND A HUMBLE DOG...
11-30
SCHULZ

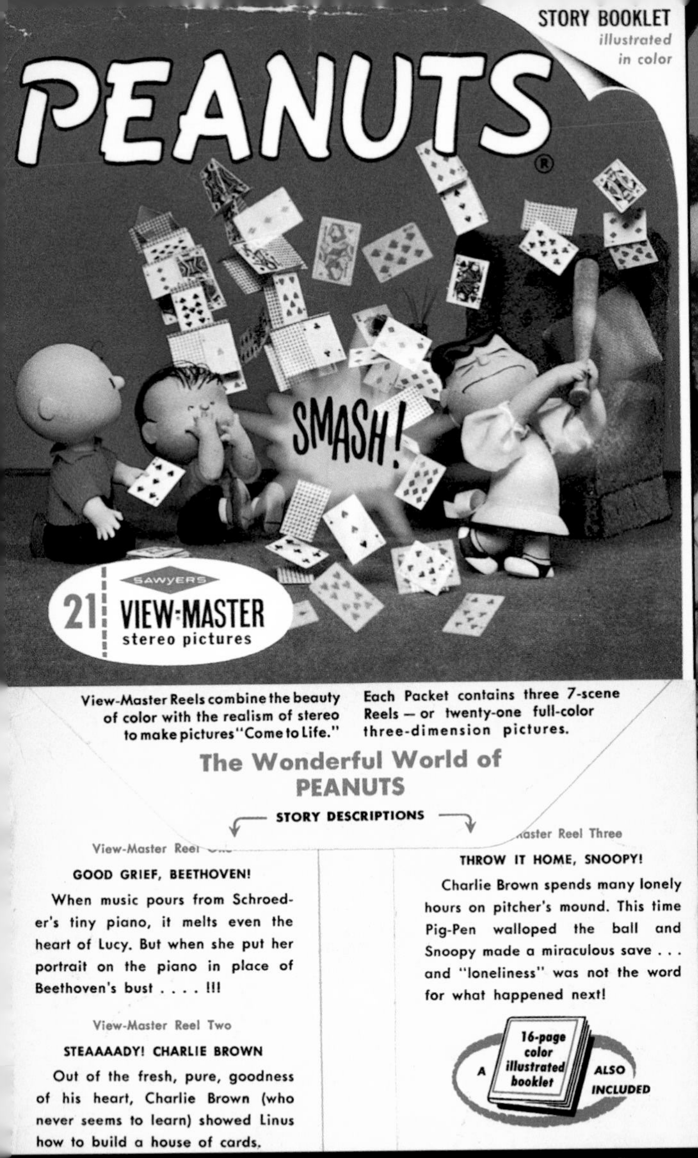
STORY BOOKLET
illustrated in color
PEANUTS®
SMASH!
SAWYER'S
21 VIEW-MASTER stereo pictures
View-Master Reels combine the beauty of color with the realism of stereo to make pictures "Come to Life."
Each Packet contains three 7-scene Reels — or twenty-one full-color three-dimension pictures.
The Wonderful World of PEANUTS
STORY DESCRIPTIONS
View-Master Reel
GOOD GRIEF, BEETHOVEN!
When music pours from Schroeder's tiny piano, it melts even the heart of Lucy. But when she put her portrait on the piano in place of Beethoven's bust . . . . !!!
View-Master Reel Two
STEAAAADY! CHARLIE BROWN
Out of the fresh, pure, goodness of his heart, Charlie Brown (who never seems to learn) showed Linus how to build a house of cards.
aster Reel Three
THROW IT HOME, SNOOPY!
Charlie Brown spends many lonely hours on pitcher's mound. This time Pig-Pen walloped the ball and Snoopy made a miraculous save . . . and "loneliness" was not the word for what happened next!
A 16-page color illustrated booklet ALSO INCLUDED

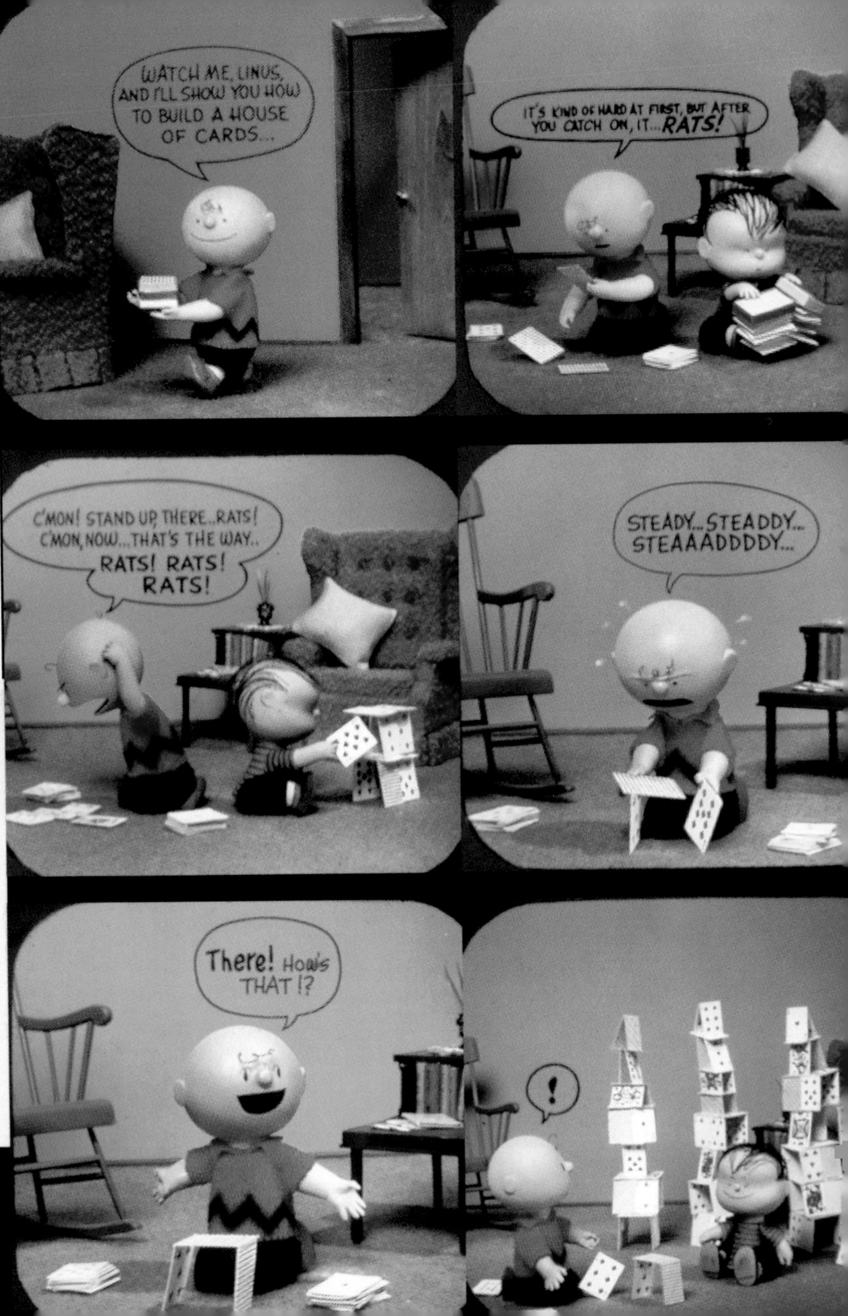
WATCH ME, LINUS, AND I'LL SHOW YOU HOW TO BUILD A HOUSE OF CARDS...
IT'S KIND OF HARD AT FIRST, BUT AFTER YOU CATCH ON, IT...RATS!
C'MON! STAND UP, THERE...RATS! C'MON, NOW...THAT'S THE WAY.. RATS! RATS! RATS!
STEADY...STEADDY... STEAAADDDDY...
There! How's THAT !?
!

In 1966 View-Master created a series of tableaux based on *Peanuts* strips, to be seen through one of their trademark stereoptic viewers. Translating Schulz's drawings into three dimensions is no easy task, but these offer a charming take on what the characters could look like in the "real world."

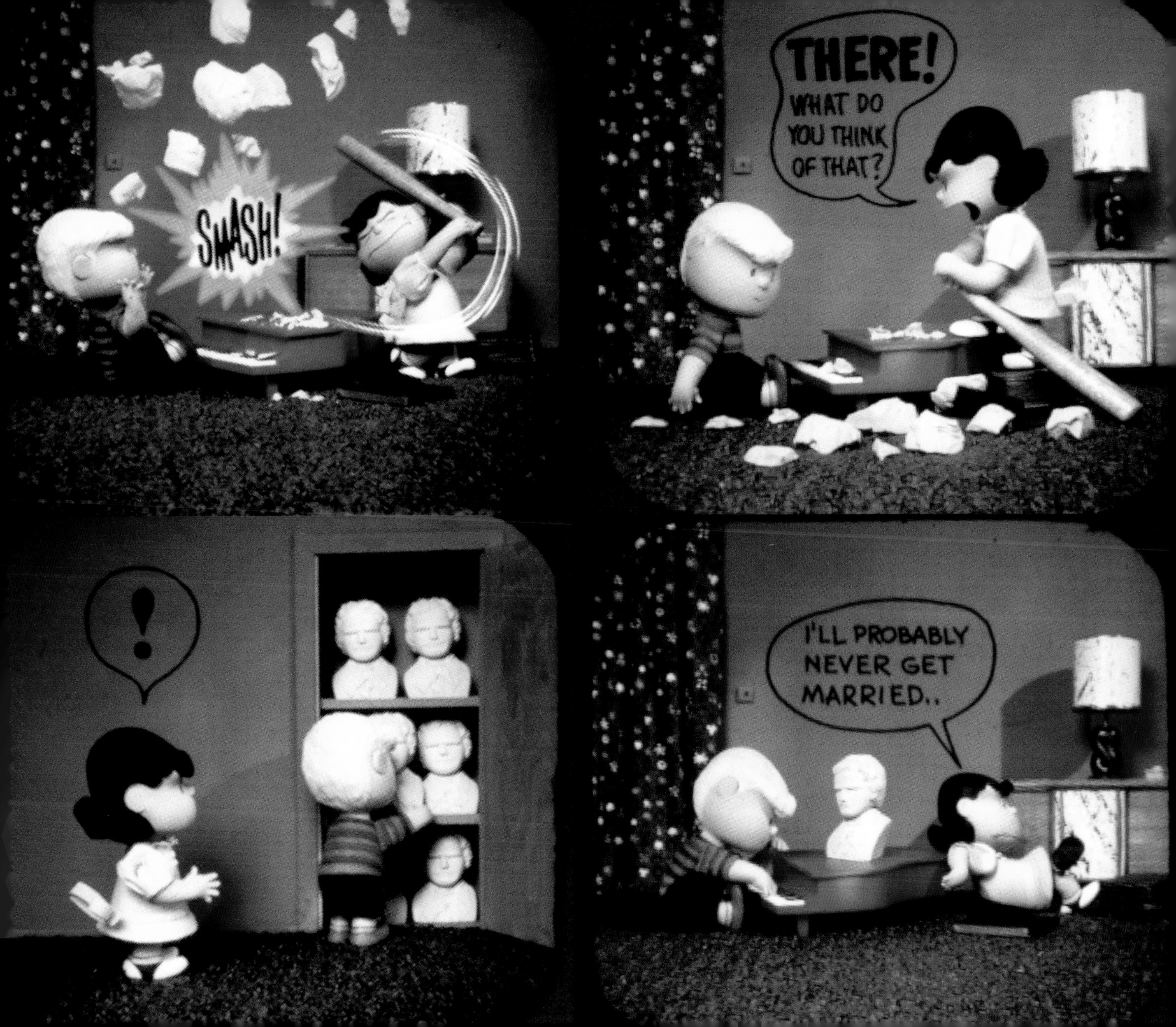
SMASH!
THERE! WHAT DO YOU THINK OF THAT?
!
I'LL PROBABLY NEVER GET MARRIED..

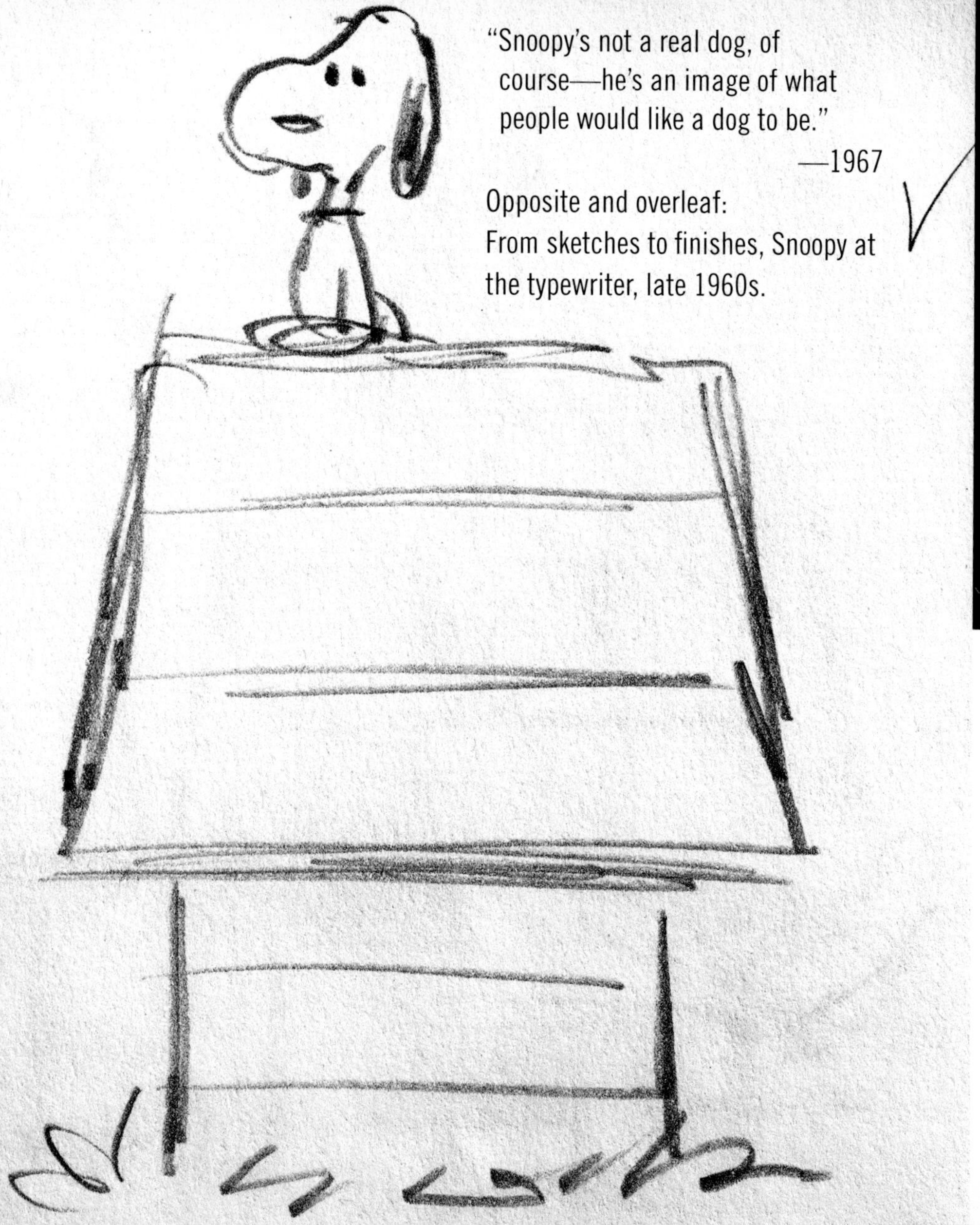

"Snoopy's not a real dog, of course—he's an image of what people would like a dog to be."

—1967

Opposite and overleaf:
From sketches to finishes, Snoopy at the typewriter, late 1960s.

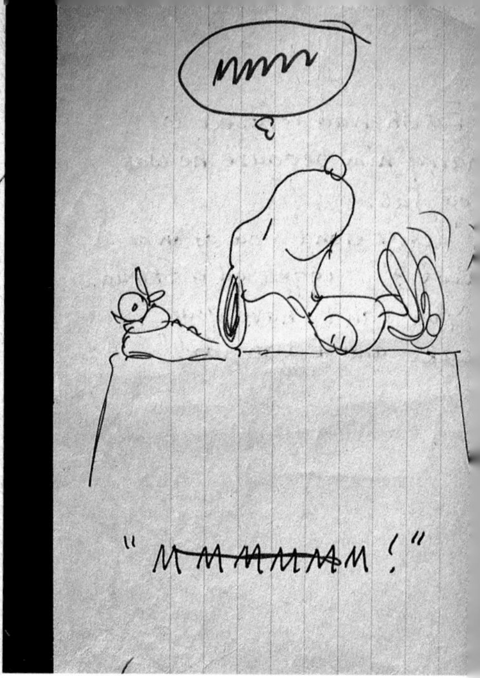

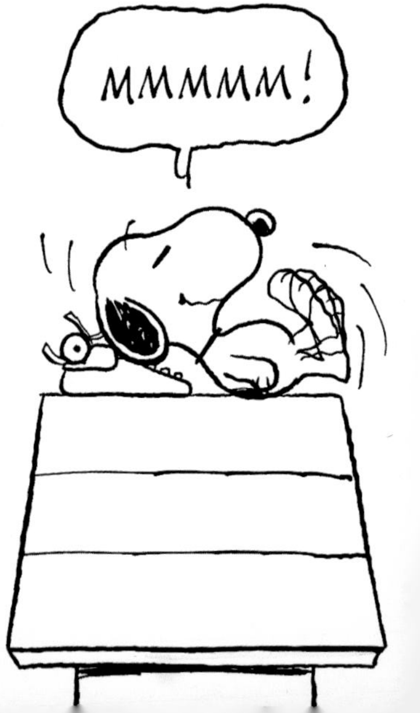
MMMMM!

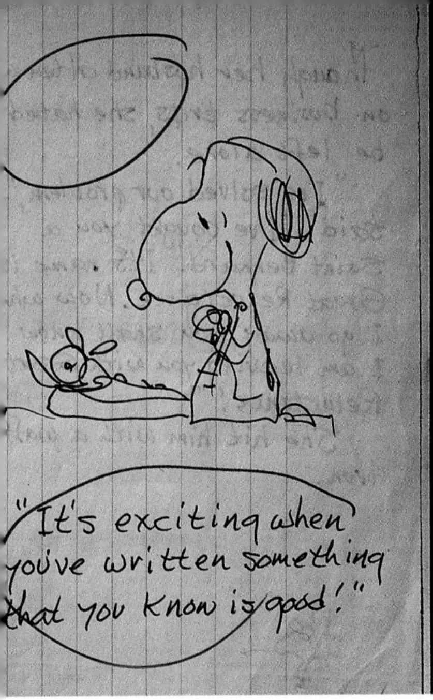
"It's exciting when you've written something that you know is good!"

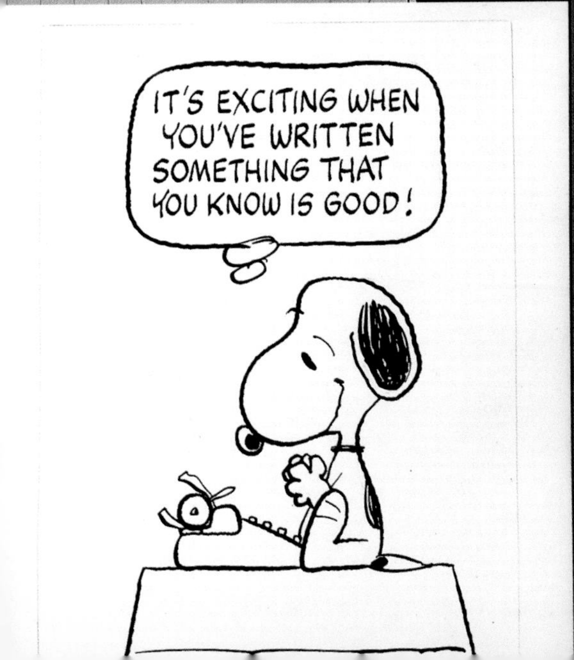
IT'S EXCITING WHEN YOU'VE WRITTEN SOMETHING THAT YOU KNOW IS GOOD!

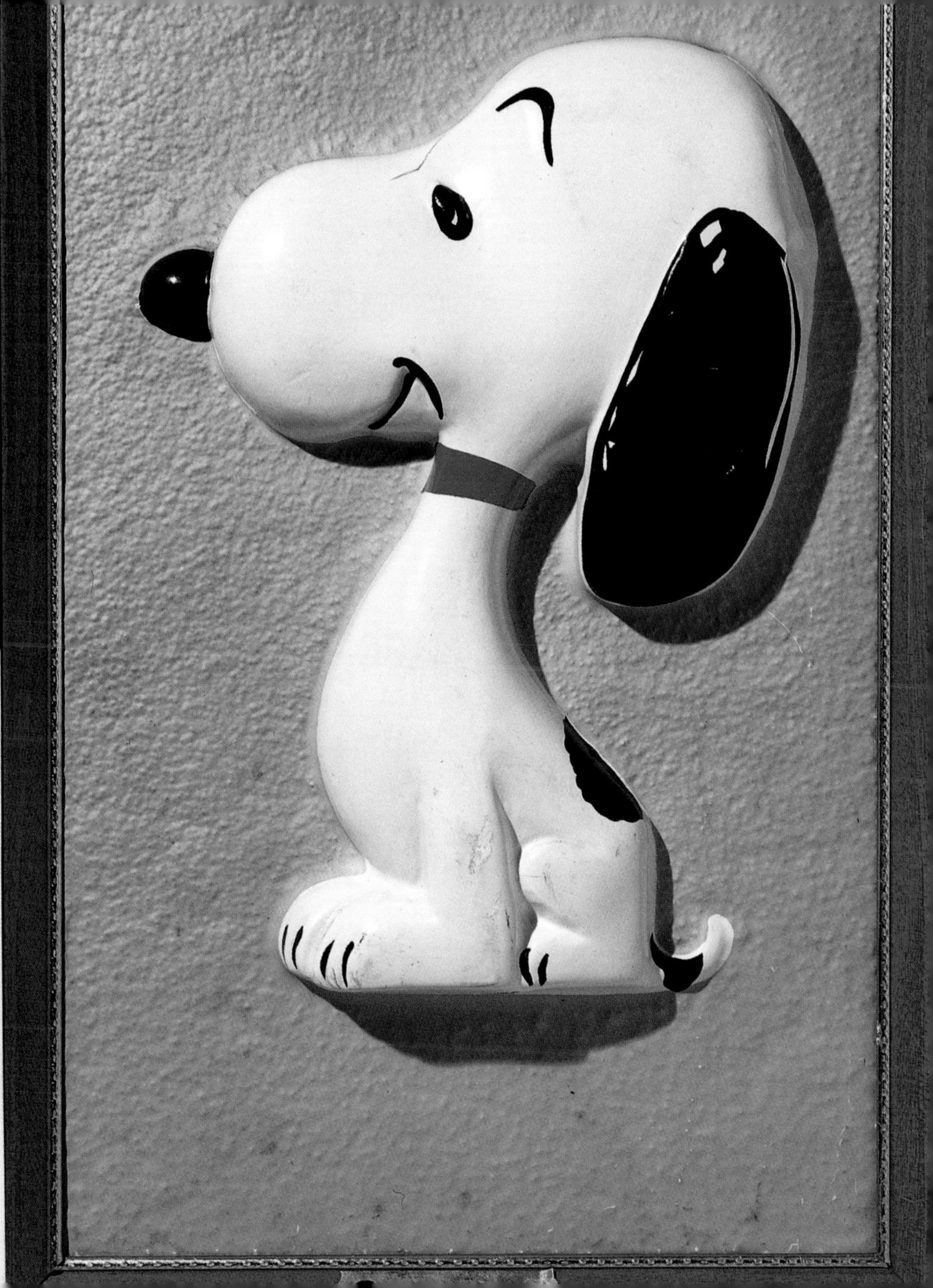

Joe Anthro was an authority on Egyptian and Babylonian culture. His greatest accomplishment, however, was his famous work on the Throat culture.

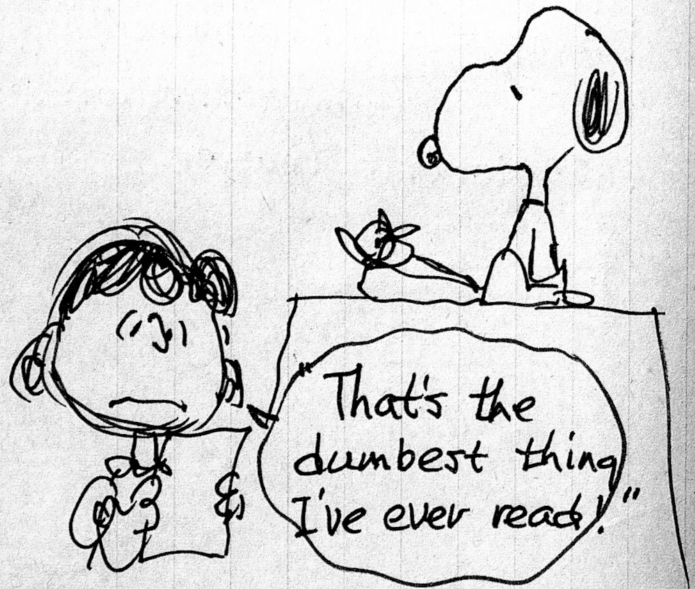
"That's the dumbest thing I've ever read!"

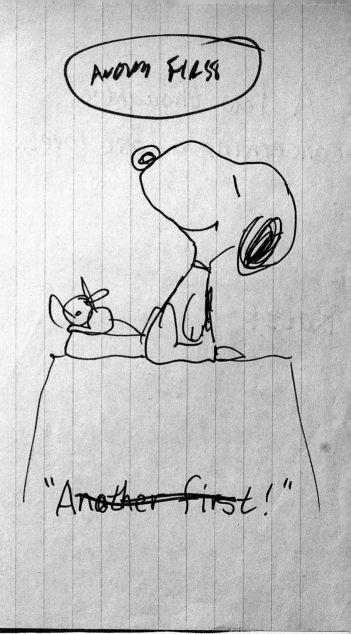

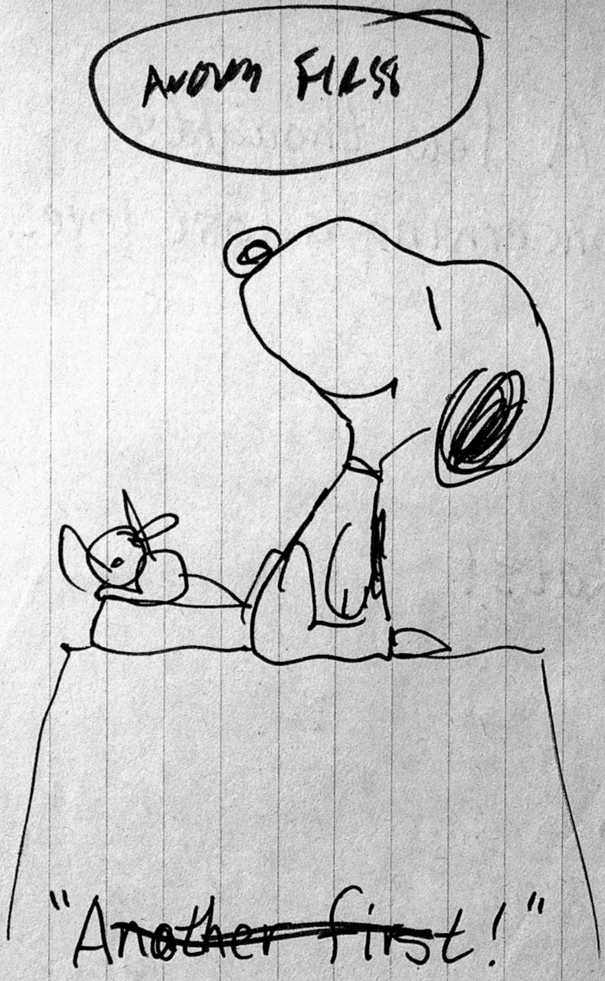
"Another first!"

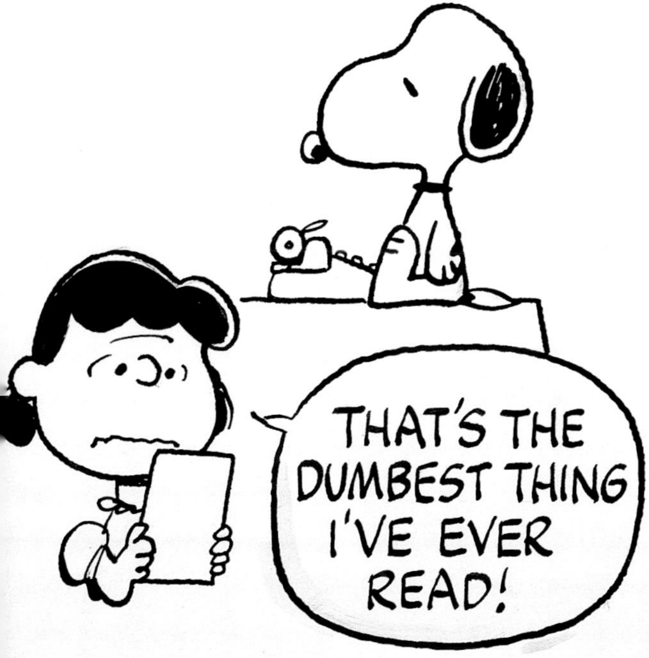
THAT'S THE DUMBEST THING I'VE EVER READ!

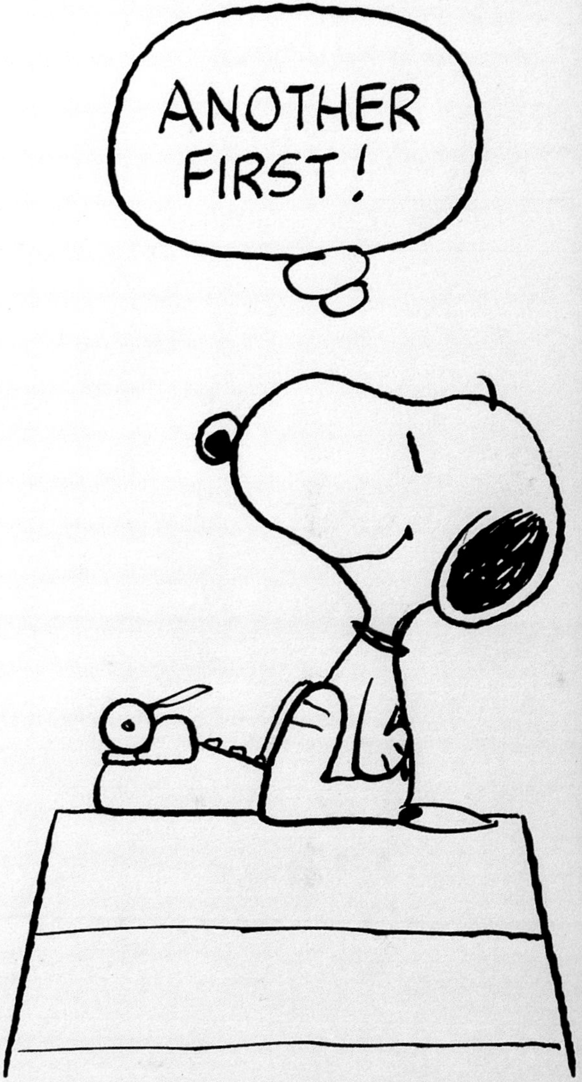
ANOTHER FIRST!

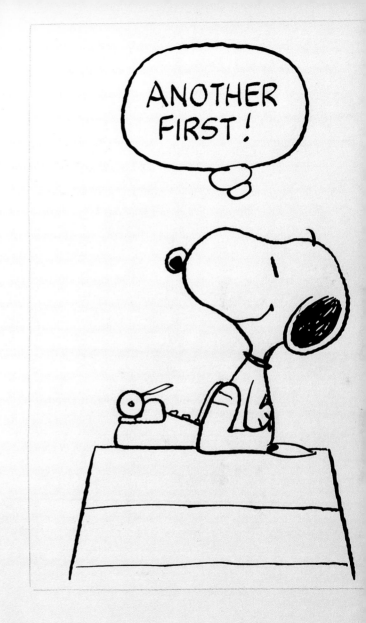

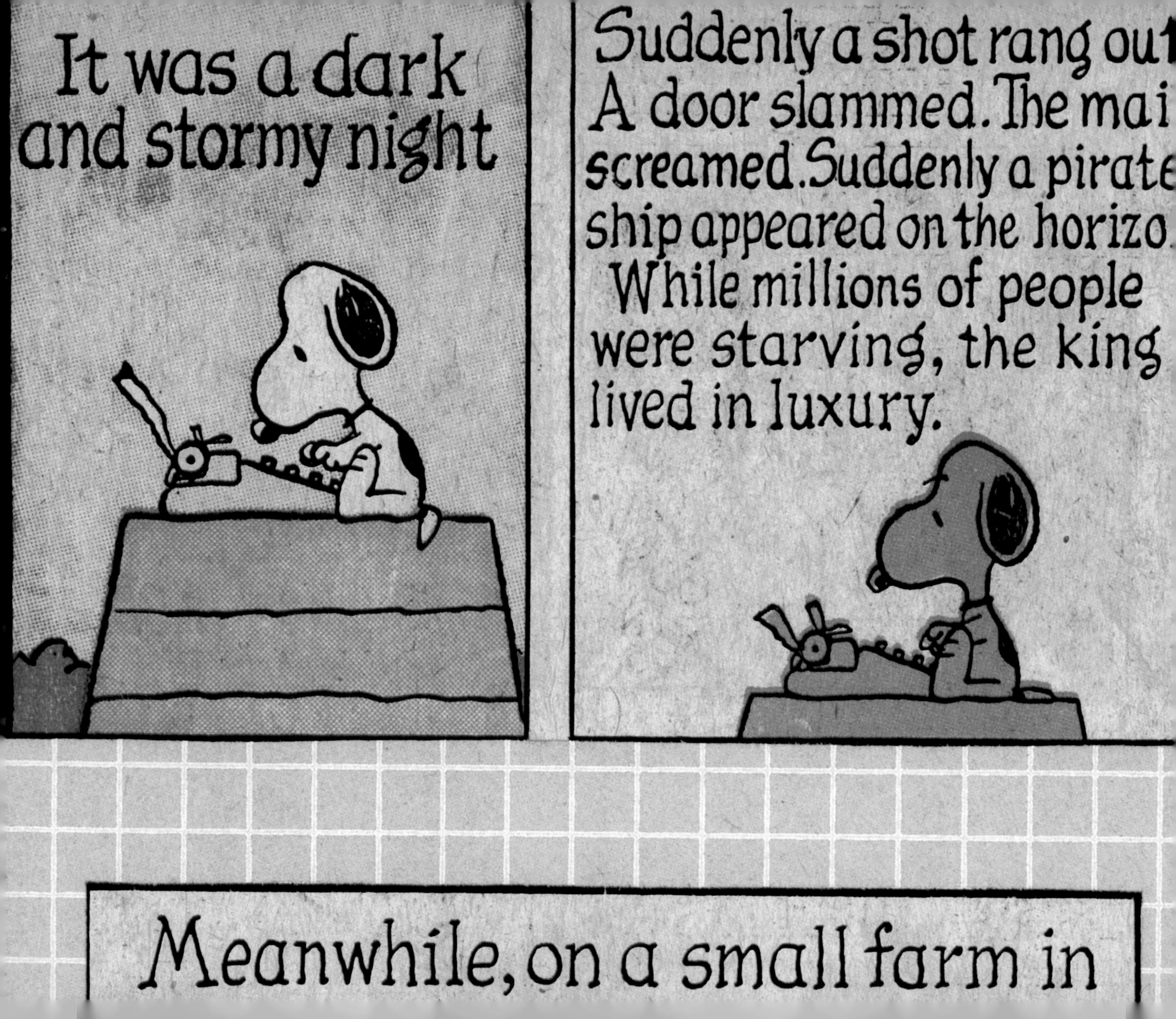
It was a dark and stormy night
Suddenly a shot rang ou
A door slammed. The mai
screamed. Suddenly a pirat
ship appeared on the horizo
While millions of people were starving, the king lived in luxury.
Meanwhile, on a small farm in

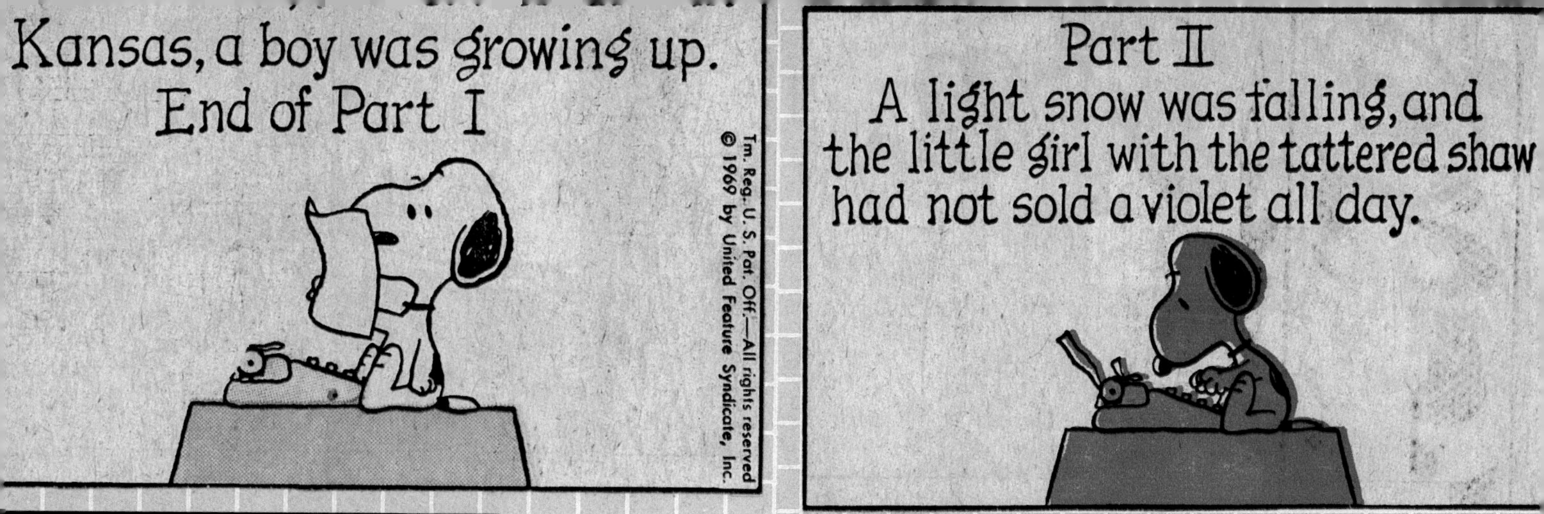
Kansas, a boy was growing up.
End of Part I
Tm. Reg. U. S. Pat. Off.—All rights reserved
© 1969 by United Feature Syndicate, Inc.
Part II
A light snow was falling, and the little girl with the tattered shaw had not sold a violet all day.

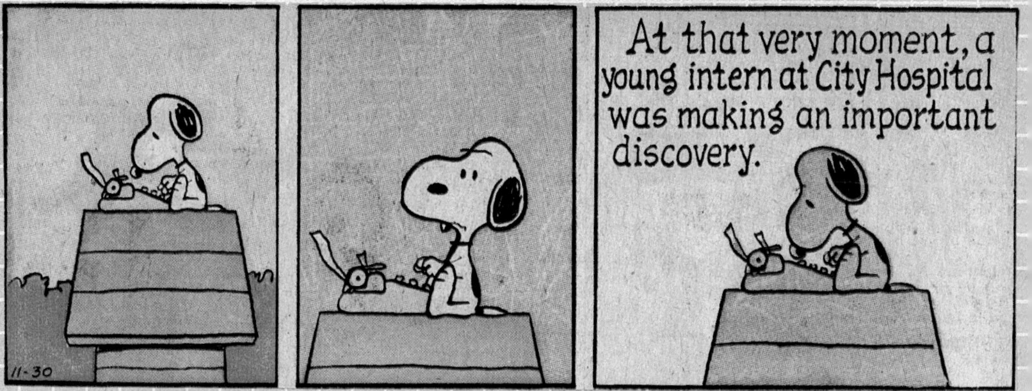
11-30
At that very moment, a young intern at City Hospital was making an important discovery.

From *Newsday*, 1977:

Interviewer: "Snoopy writing at the typewriter, how did that start?"

Schulz: "It probably began with the dark and stormy night sequence. It might have been that I thought of that first and simply applied it to the dog writing at the typewriter. But since then I have done a lot of things with it and I have enjoyed it. Again, each theme that you think of seems to serve its purpose by giving you an outlet for all the ideas that come to you. Now some of the ideas for puns that Snoopy writes could never be used in the strip itself; they are simply too corny. But when Snoopy writes them, and writes them with all sincerity, then they are funny. You don't think that Snoopy is being stupid or anything like that. You like him for his naiveté because he innocently thinks he has done something great, and that makes it acceptable."

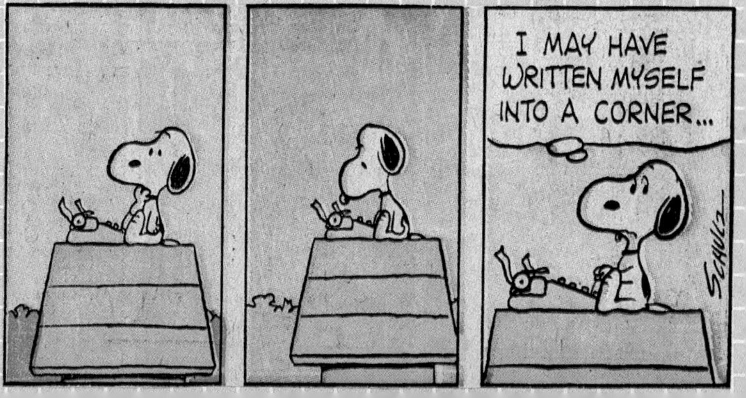
I MAY HAVE WRITTEN MYSELF INTO A CORNER...
SCHULZ

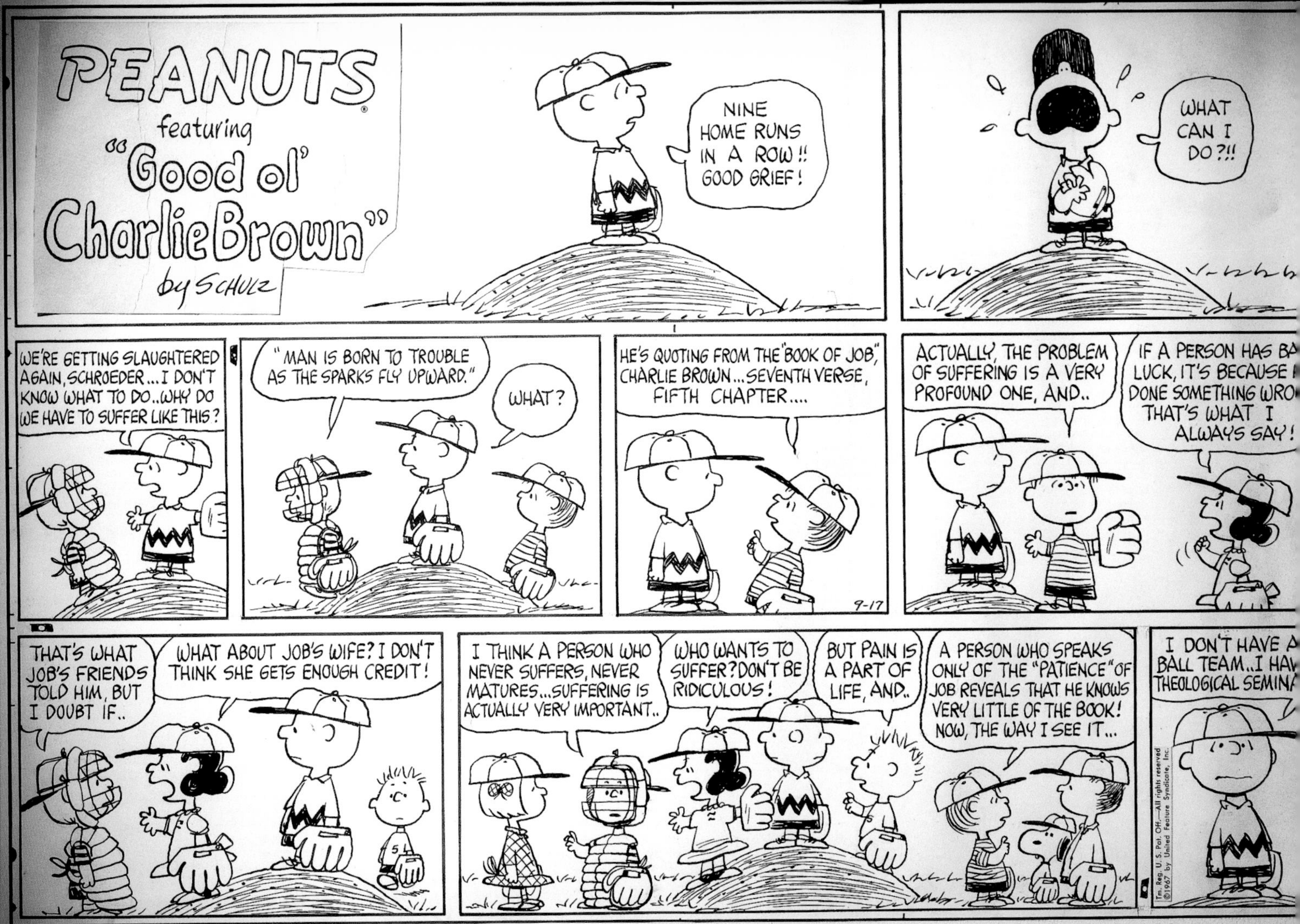
PEANUTS
featuring "Good ol' Charlie Brown"
by SCHULZ
NINE HOME RUNS IN A ROW!! GOOD GRIEF!
WHAT CAN I DO?!!
WE'RE GETTING SLAUGHTERED AGAIN, SCHROEDER... I DON'T KNOW WHAT TO DO.. WHY DO WE HAVE TO SUFFER LIKE THIS?
"MAN IS BORN TO TROUBLE AS THE SPARKS FLY UPWARD."
WHAT?
HE'S QUOTING FROM THE "BOOK OF JOB," CHARLIE BROWN... SEVENTH VERSE, FIFTH CHAPTER....
9-17
ACTUALLY, THE PROBLEM OF SUFFERING IS A VERY PROFOUND ONE, AND..
IF A PERSON HAS BA
LUCK, IT'S BECAUSE
DONE SOMETHING WRO
THAT'S WHAT I ALWAYS SAY!
THAT'S WHAT JOB'S FRIENDS TOLD HIM, BUT I DOUBT IF..
WHAT ABOUT JOB'S WIFE? I DON'T THINK SHE GETS ENOUGH CREDIT!
I THINK A PERSON WHO NEVER SUFFERS, NEVER MATURES... SUFFERING IS ACTUALLY VERY IMPORTANT..
WHO WANTS TO SUFFER? DON'T BE RIDICULOUS!
BUT PAIN IS A PART OF LIFE, AND..
A PERSON WHO SPEAKS ONLY OF THE "PATIENCE" OF JOB REVEALS THAT HE KNOWS VERY LITTLE OF THE BOOK! NOW, THE WAY I SEE IT...
I DON'T HAVE A
BALL TEAM..I HAV
THEOLOGICAL SEMINA
Tm. Reg. U.S. Pat. Off.—All rights reserved ©1967 by United Feature Syndicate, Inc.

This unusual exchange took place in the *Los Angeles Times* in 1973:

Schulz: "Apparently Linus is a good [baseball] player and Schroeder is a good catcher. I think Charlie Brown's outfield is no good. He has the three girls out there. Lucy is obviously a bad player. But we've never found out, really, why they lose all those games. Charlie Brown looks as though he's pitching pretty well."

Interviewer: "You talk as if you're puzzled yourself."
Schulz: "Yeah. I really don't know why it is."
Interviewer: "Well, if you don't know, we're in trouble."
Schulz: "Yes, I suppose. You know, we don't even know who they're playing.

Whether or not Schulz is just having a little fun here is unclear, but he ofte spoke of the characters as if he had little or no control over them.

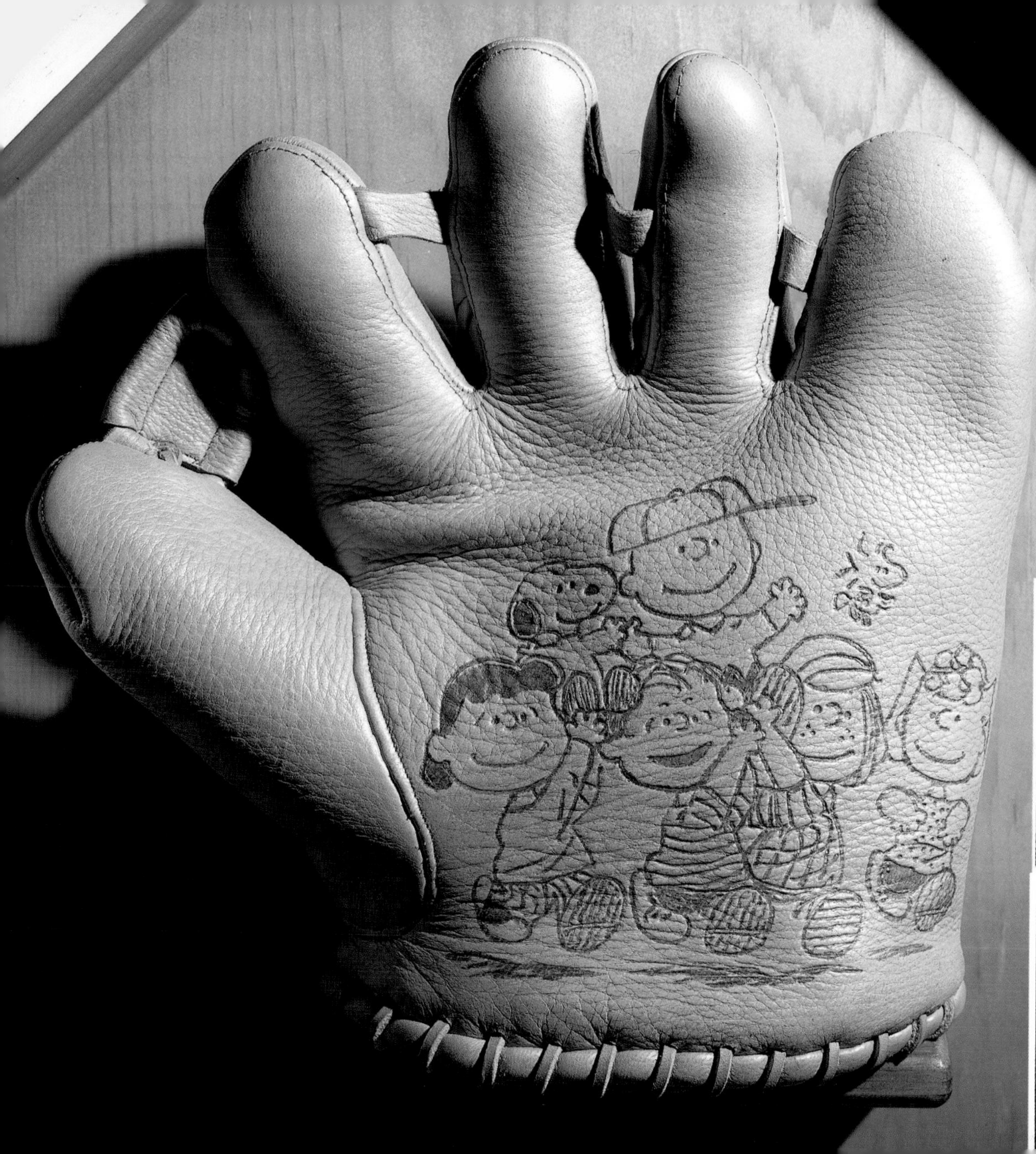

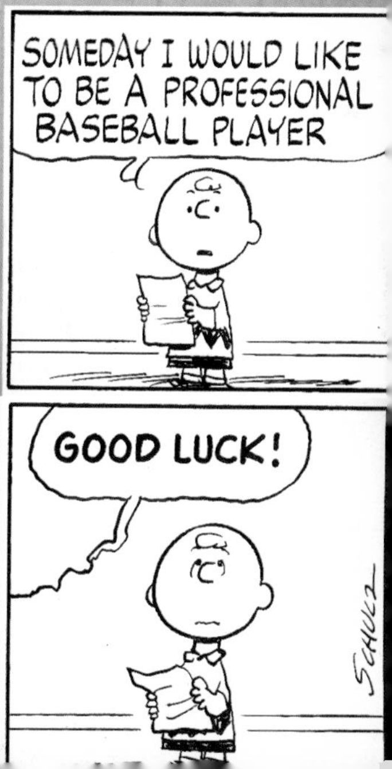
SOMEDAY I WOULD LIKE TO BE A PROFESSIONAL BASEBALL PLAYER
GOOD LUCK!
SCHULZ

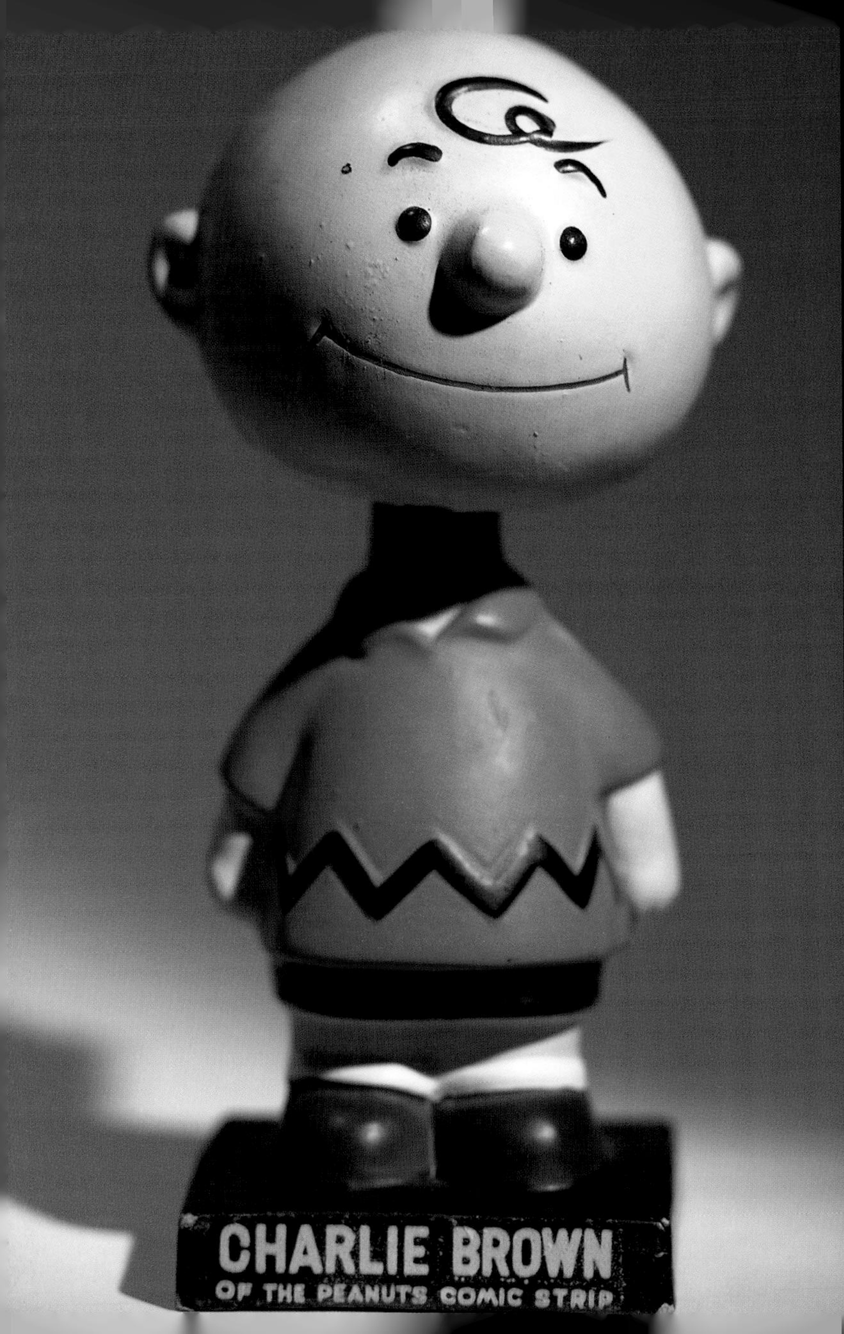
CHARLIE BROWN
OF THE PEANUTS COMIC STRIP

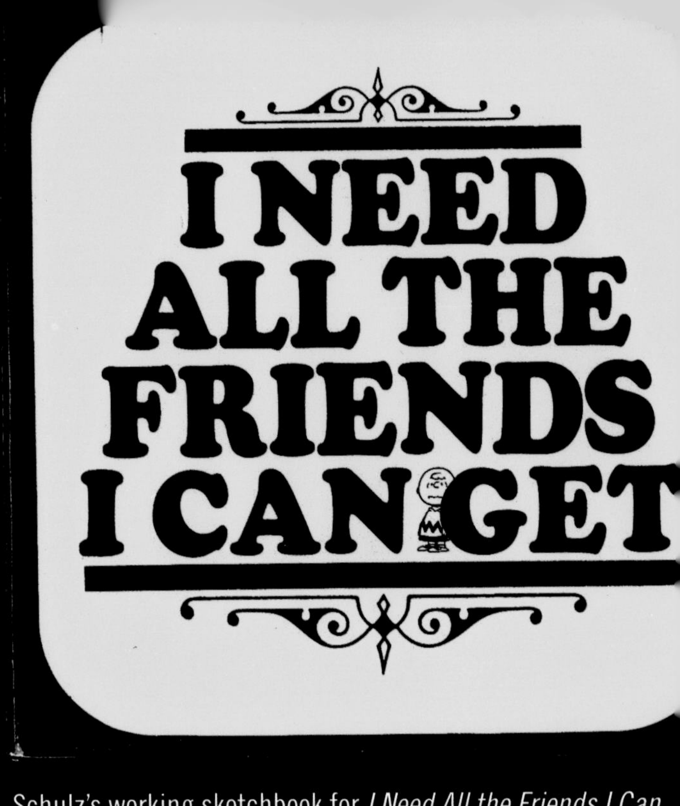
I NEED
ALL THE
FRIENDS
I CAN GET

Schulz's working sketchbook for *I Need All the Friends I Can Get* affords a rare look at his thought process from initial drawings and text to the final form (above, and subsequent yellow pages). *Friends* is the 1964 follow-up title to the immensely popular *Happiness is a Warm Puppy* and *Security is a Thumb and a Blanket*, in which a single theme is explored—this time, Friendship.

What started out as a horizontal format ended up square, which when opened then became the extended rectangle. We present here the entire sketchbook, which contains material that didn't make the cut. Likewise, passages that are found in the printed book were not part of his initial ideas.

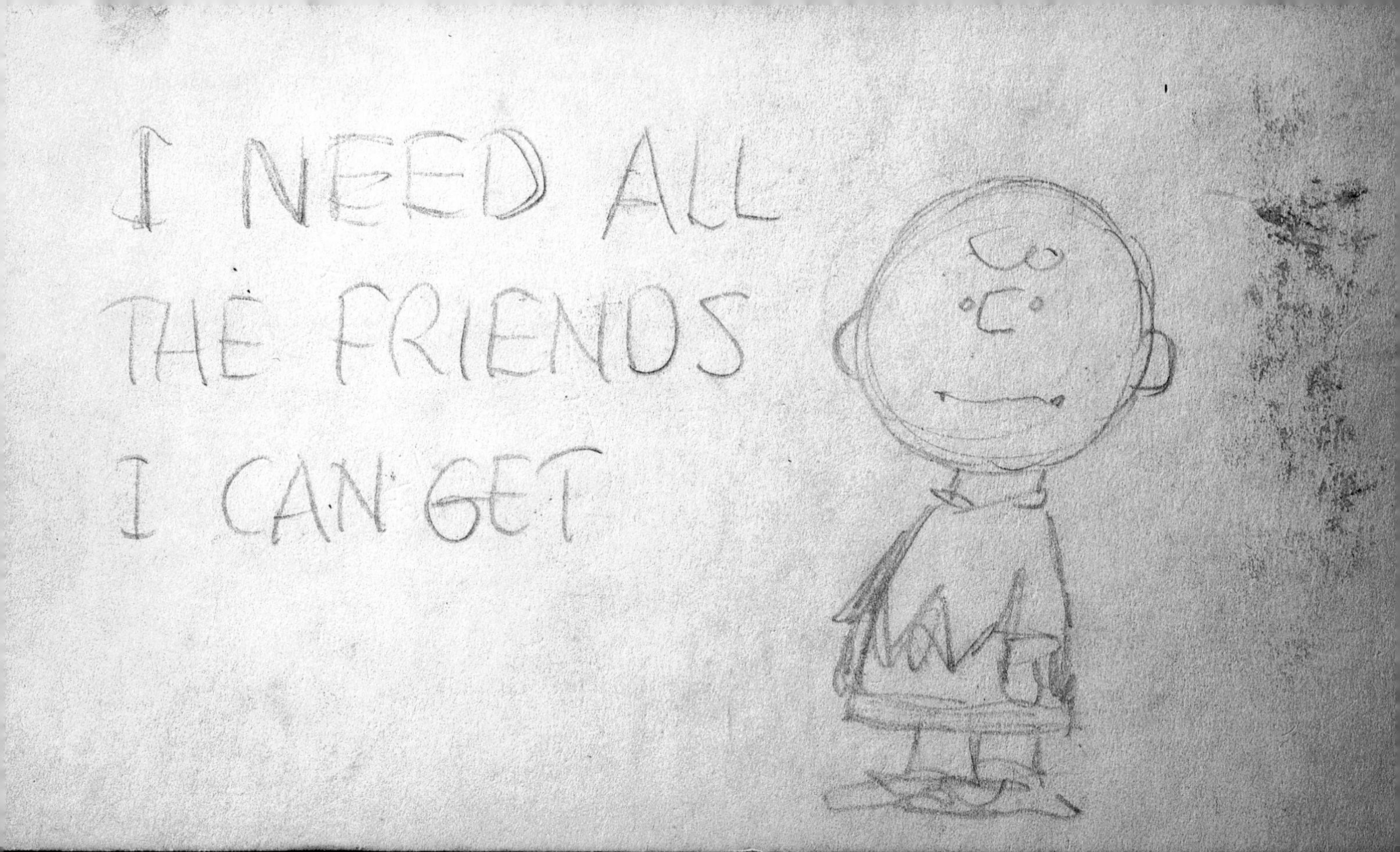
I NEED ALL
THE FRIENDS
I CAN GET

This sketchbook is from the private collection of Schulz's son Craig, who found it after the fire in 1966 that burned Schulz's Sebastopol (Ca.) studio to the ground. Schulz gave the book to a friend of Craig's named Dan Northern, who kept it for 25 years. When Northern came across it in the 1990s, he returned it to Craig. This is its first publication.

I NEED ALL THE FRIENDS I CAN GET

I NEED ALL THE FRIENDS I CAN GET 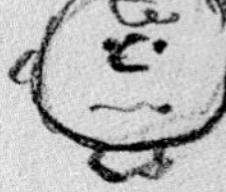

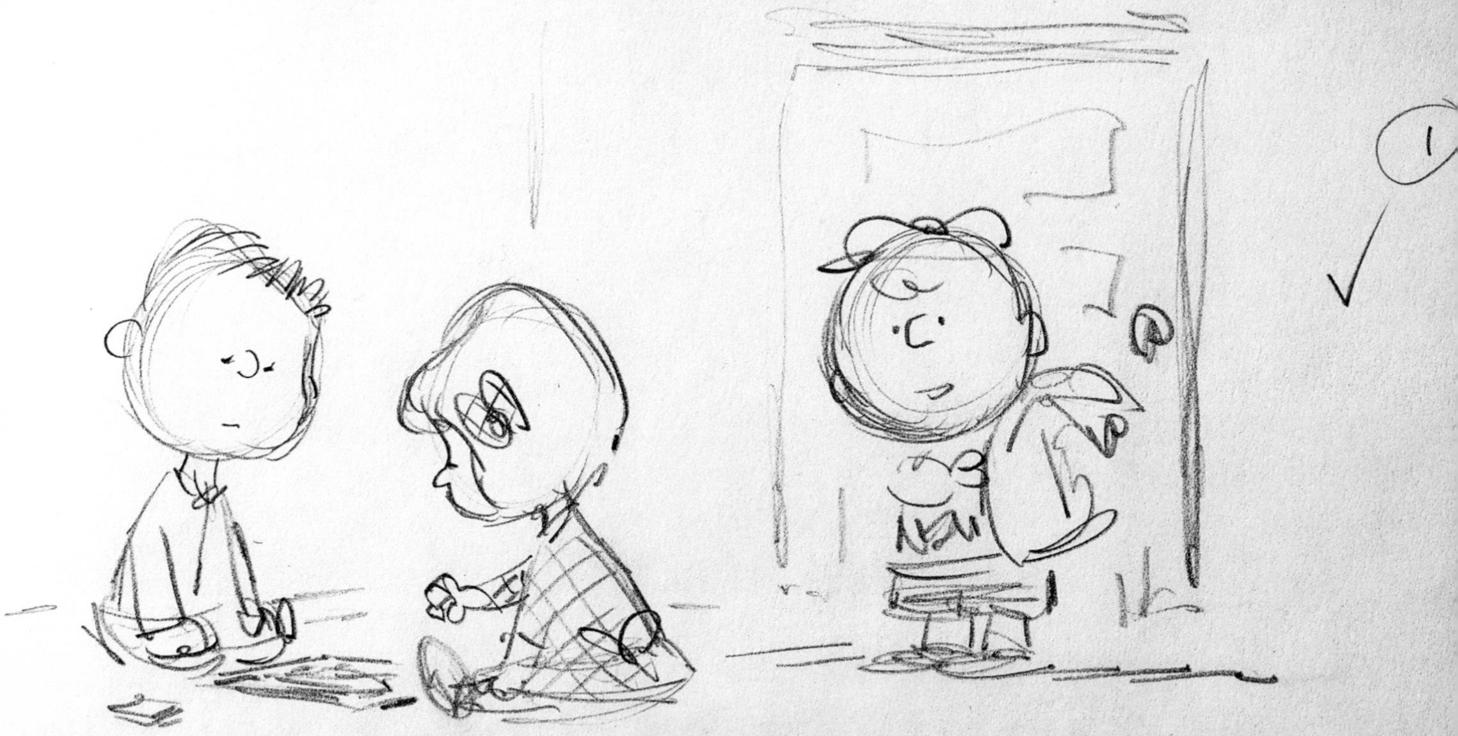

"WELL, I HATE TO SPOIL ALL THE FUN, BUT I HAVE TO BE GOING."

"Well,
I hate
to spoil all
the fun, but I
have to be
going."

" I SAID I HATE TO SPOIL ALL THE FUN, BUT I
HAVE TO BE GOING... "

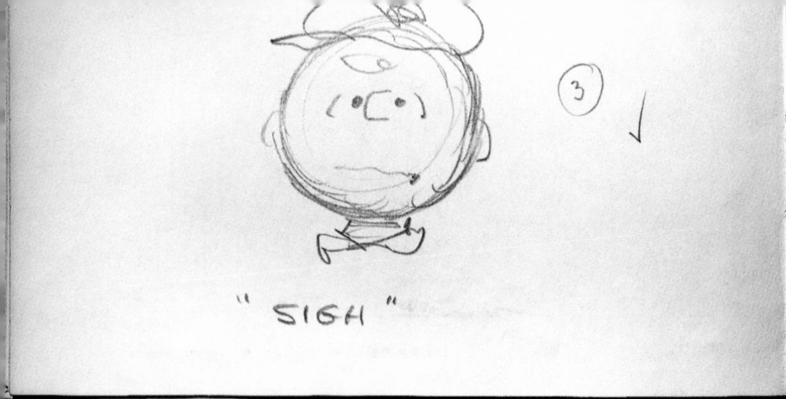

3
" SIGH "

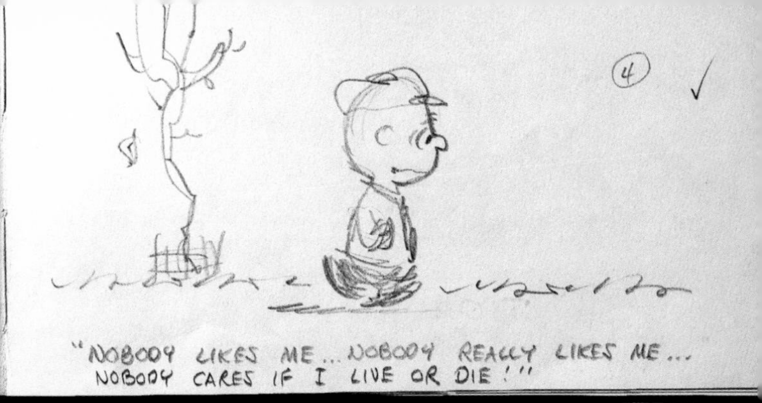

4
"NOBODY LIKES ME... NOBODY REALLY LIKES ME... NOBODY CARES IF I LIVE OR DIE!"

"Nobody likes me . . . Nobody cares if I live or die!"

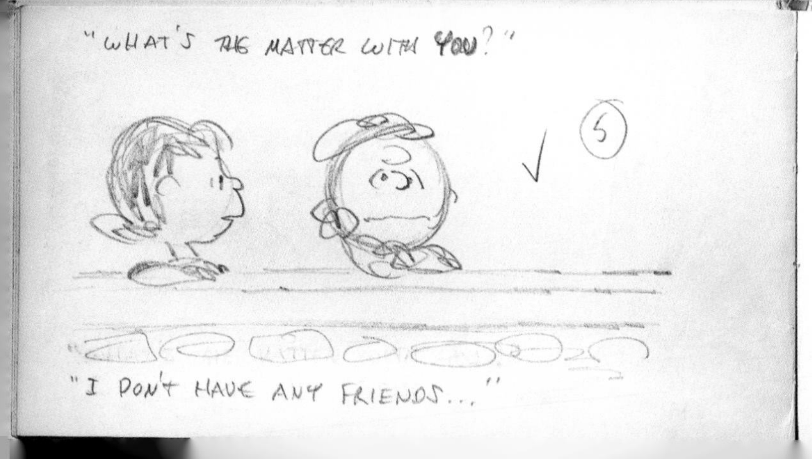

"WHAT'S THE MATTER WITH YOU?"
5
"I DON'T HAVE ANY FRIENDS..."

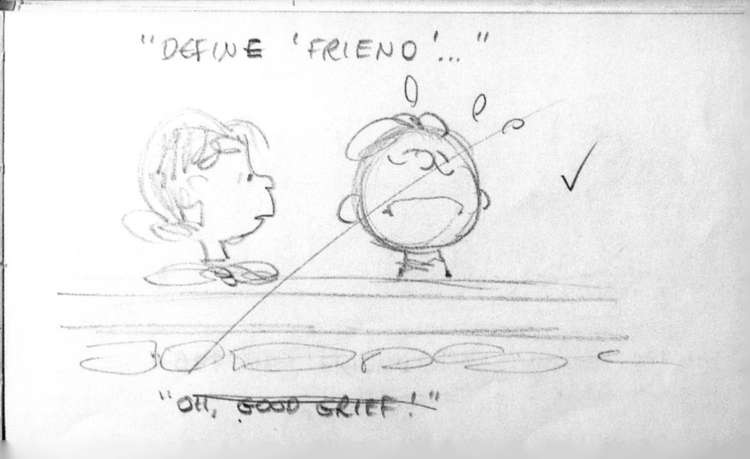

"DEFINE 'FRIEND'..."
"OH, GOOD GRIEF!"

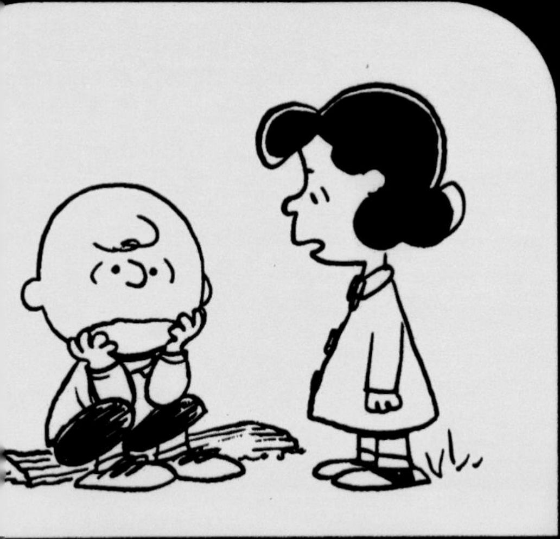

hat's the matter with you?"

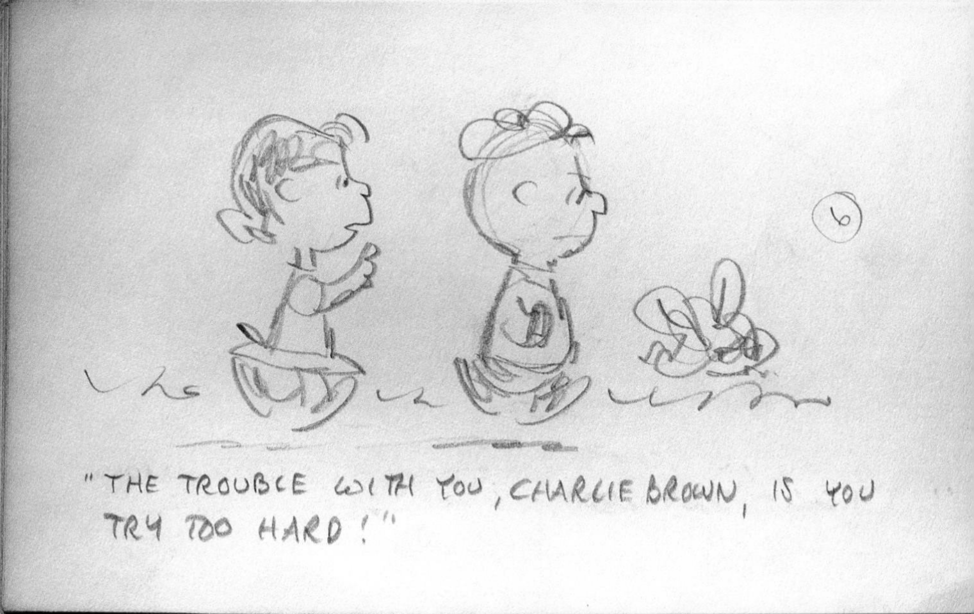

6
"THE TROUBLE WITH YOU, CHARLIE BROWN, IS YOU TRY TOO HARD!"

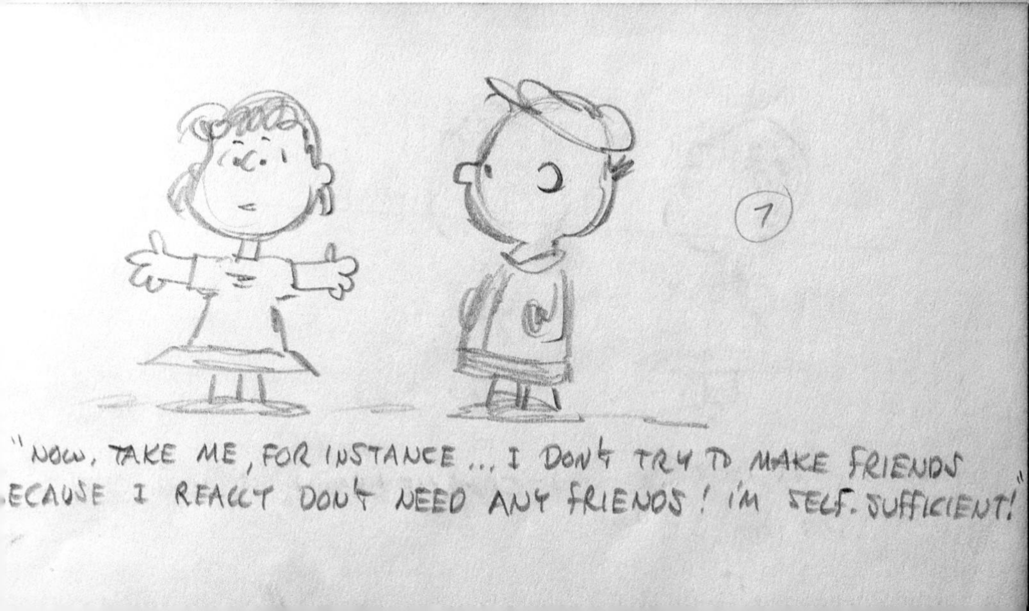

7
"NOW, TAKE ME, FOR INSTANCE ... I DON'T TRY TO MAKE FRIENDS
ECAUSE I REALLY DON'T NEED ANY FRIENDS! I'M SELF-SUFFICIENT!"

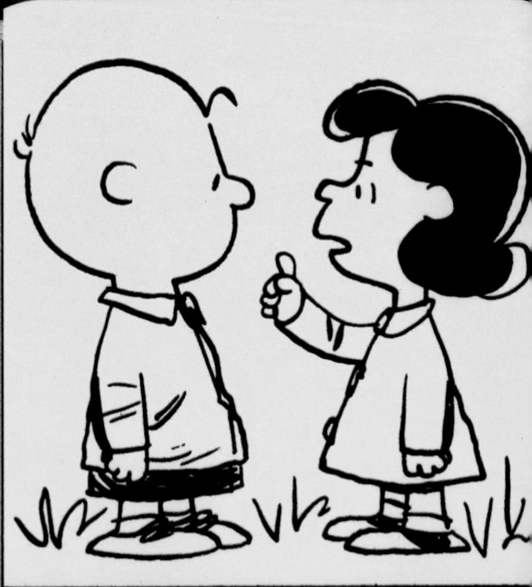

"Define 'Friend'!"

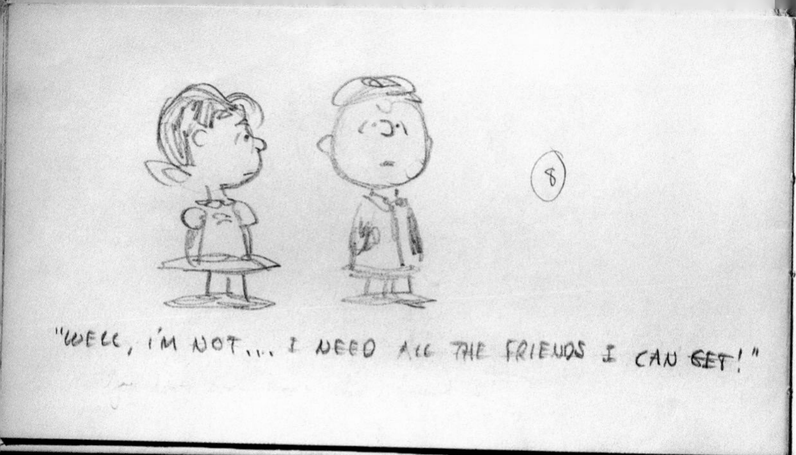
8
"WELL, I'M NOT... I NEED ALL THE FRIENDS I CAN GET!"

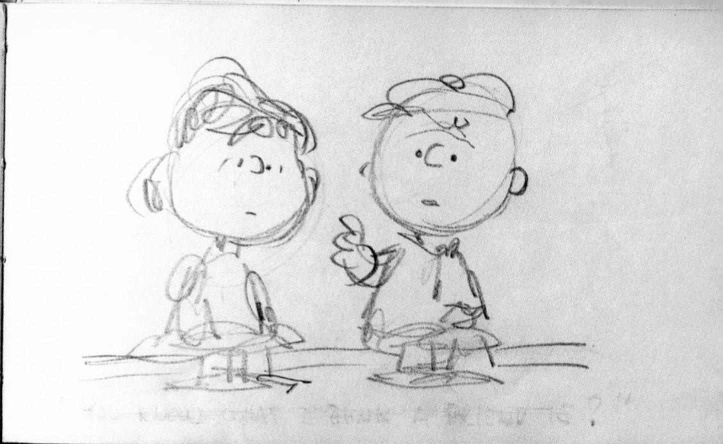

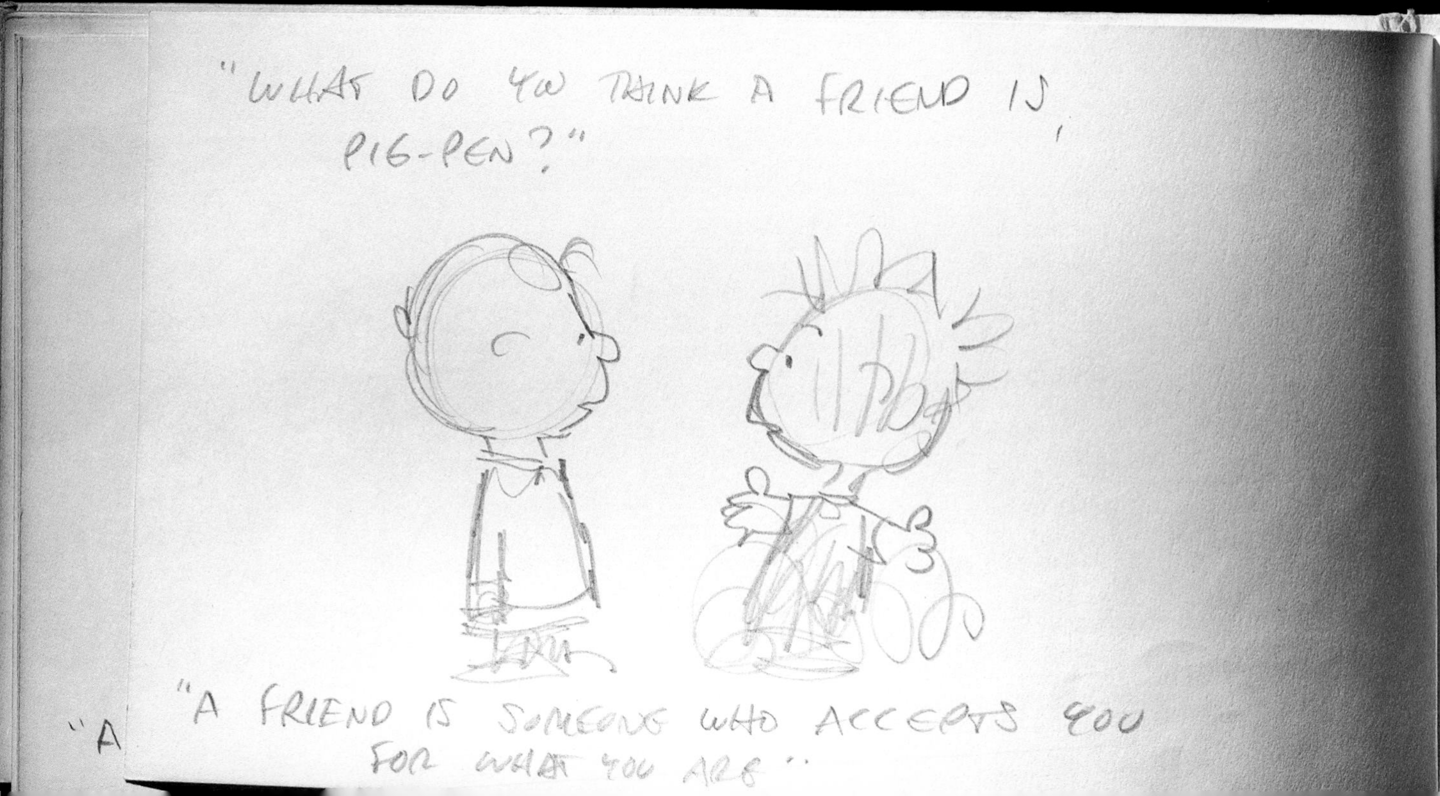
"WHAT DO YOU THINK A FRIEND IS, PIG-PEN?"
"A FRIEND IS SOMEONE WHO ACCEPTS YOU FOR WHAT YOU ARE."

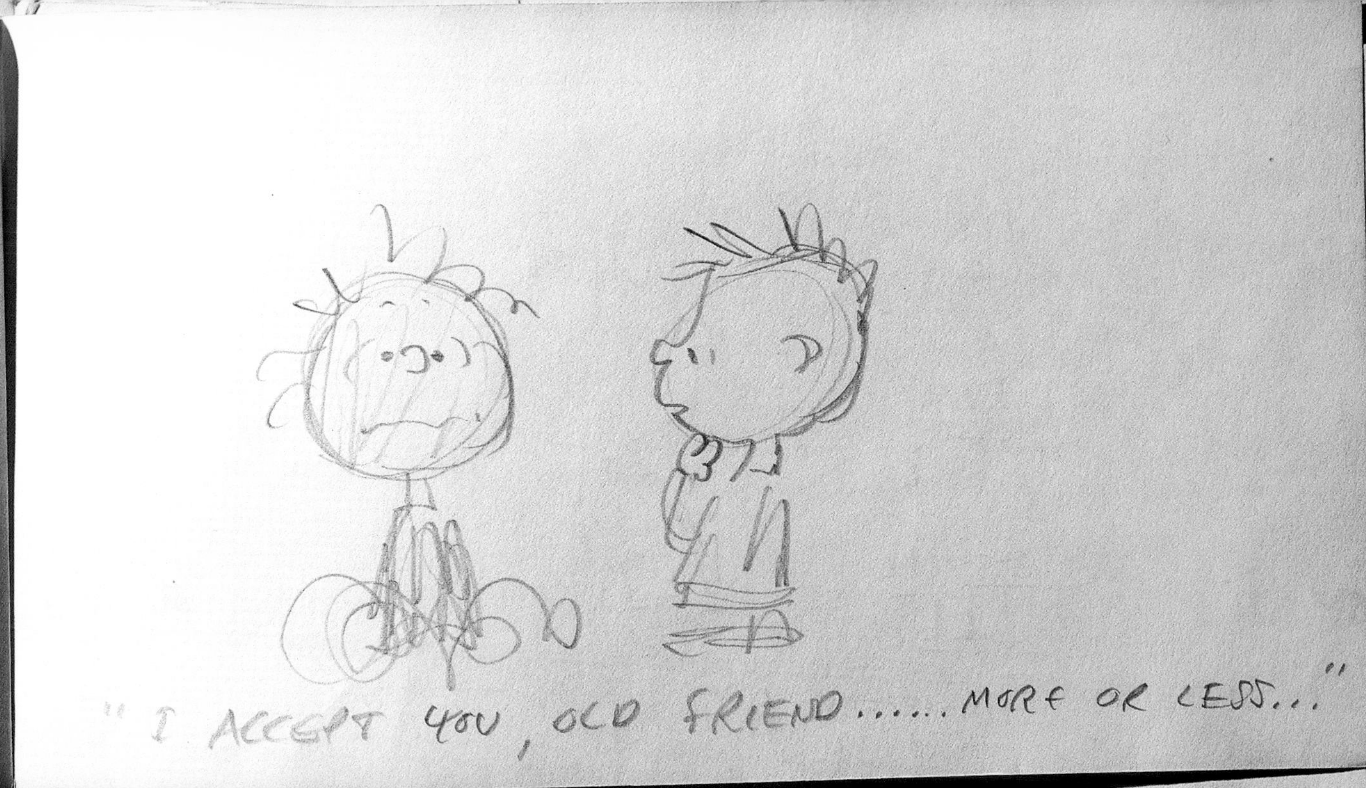
"I ACCEPT YOU, OLD FRIEND...... MORE OR LESS..."

"A friend is someone who accepts you for what you are."

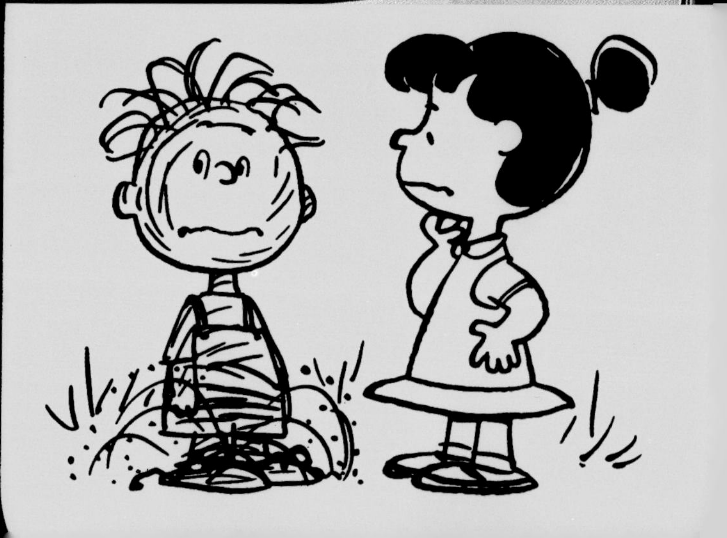

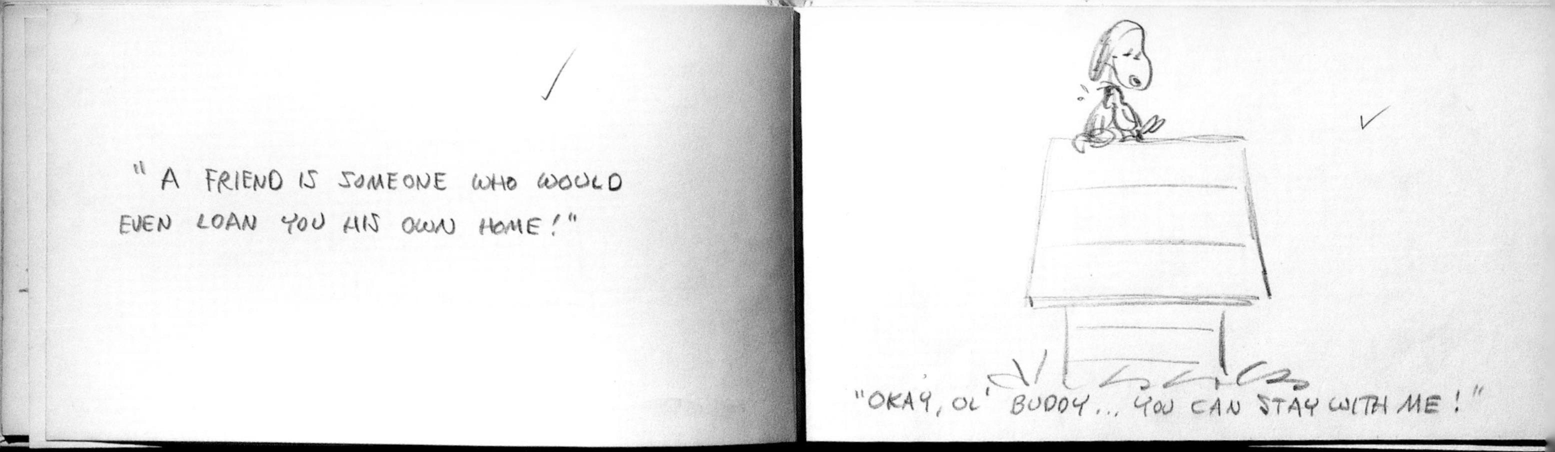
"A FRIEND IS SOMEONE WHO WOULD EVEN LOAN YOU HIS OWN HOME!"
"OKAY, OL' BUDDY... YOU CAN STAY WITH ME!"

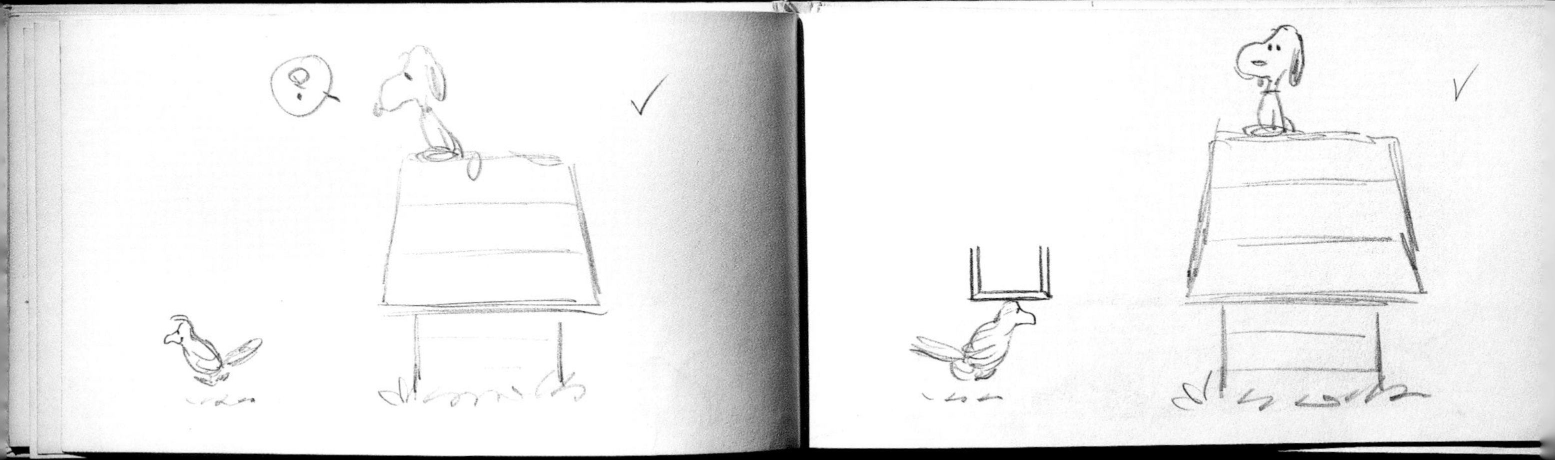

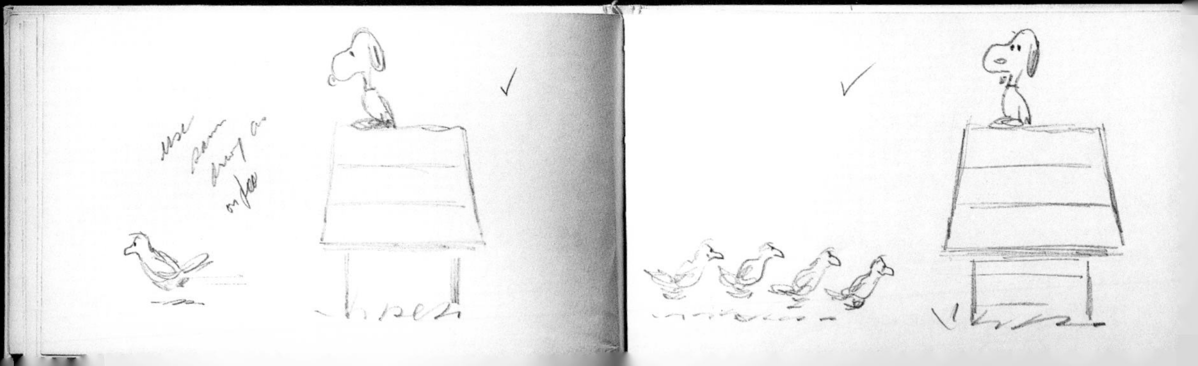

This extended sequence with Snoopy and the birds was eventually cut, because it didn't fit the single panel format.

But it did appear in the regular daily strip, and Snoopy's little feathered pals would eventually evolve into Woodstock.

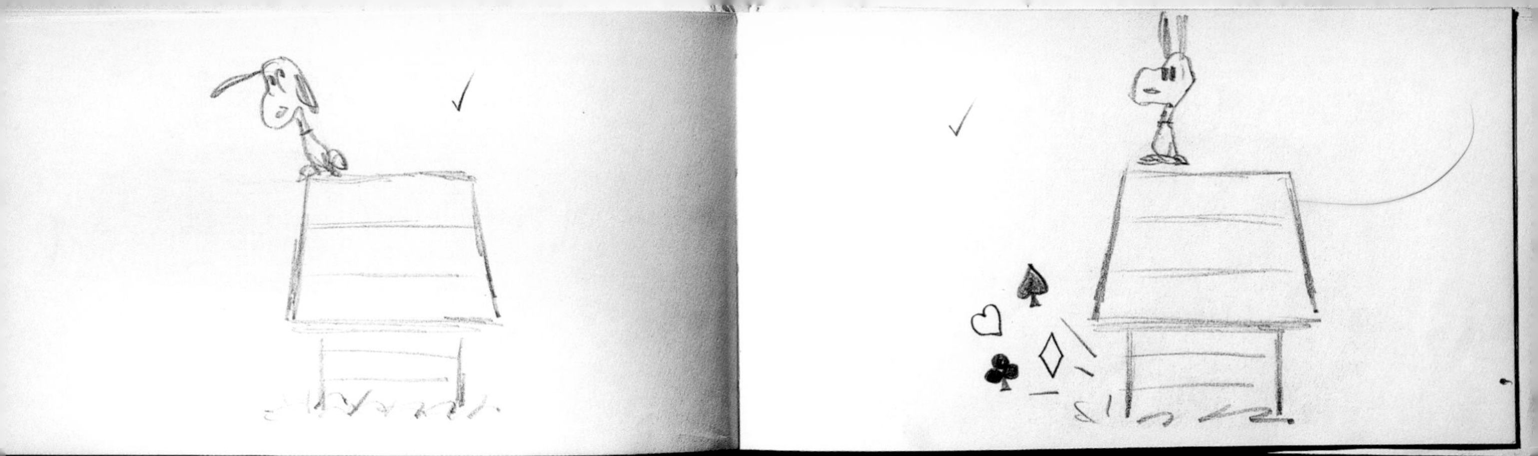

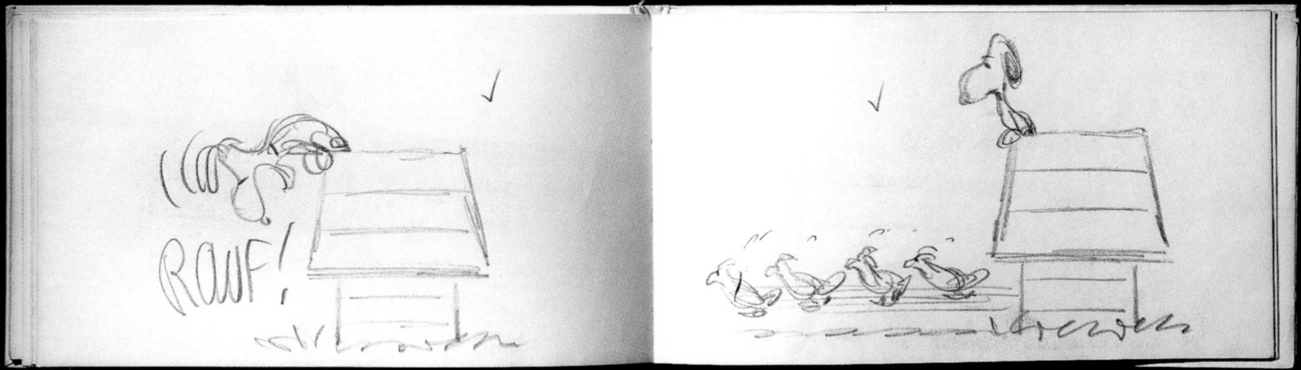
ROUF!

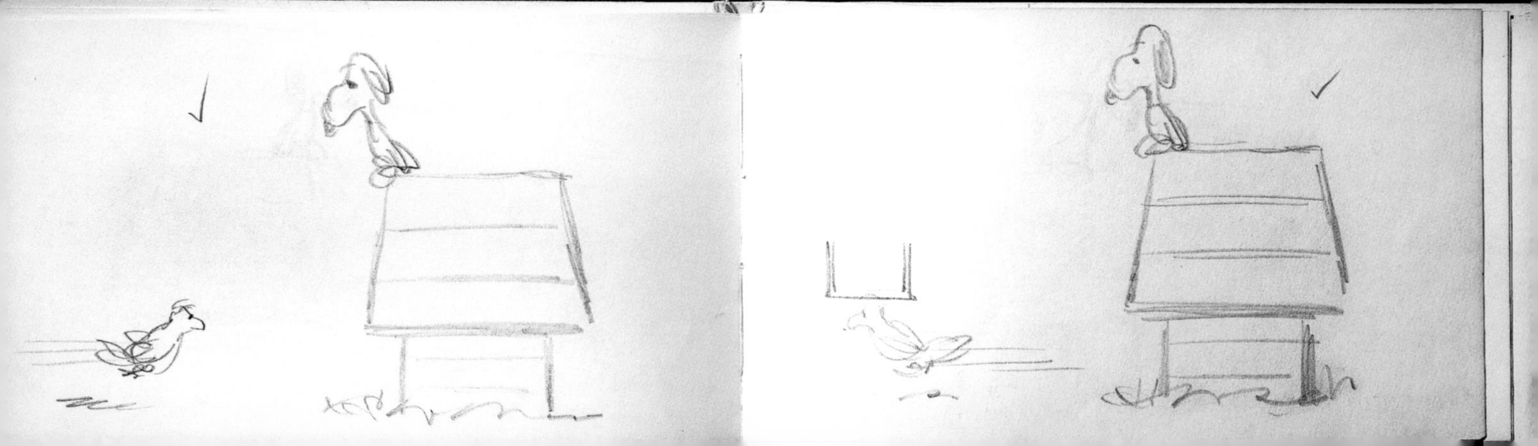

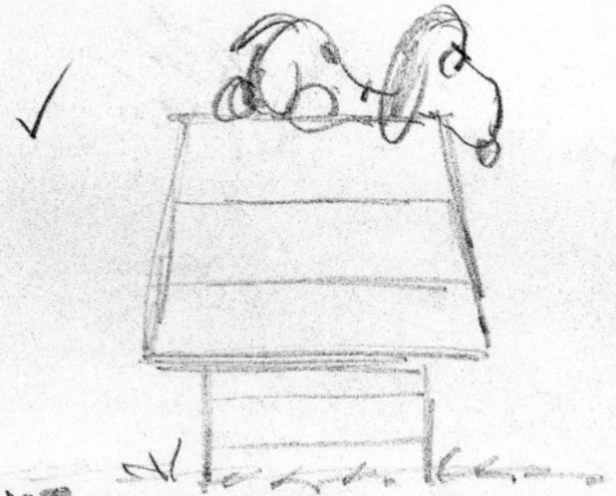

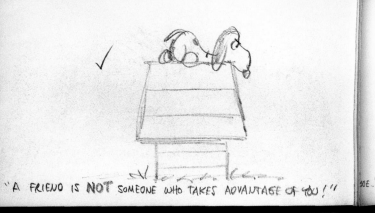

"A FRIEND IS **NOT** SOMEONE WHO TAKES ADVANTAGE OF YOU!"

OE."

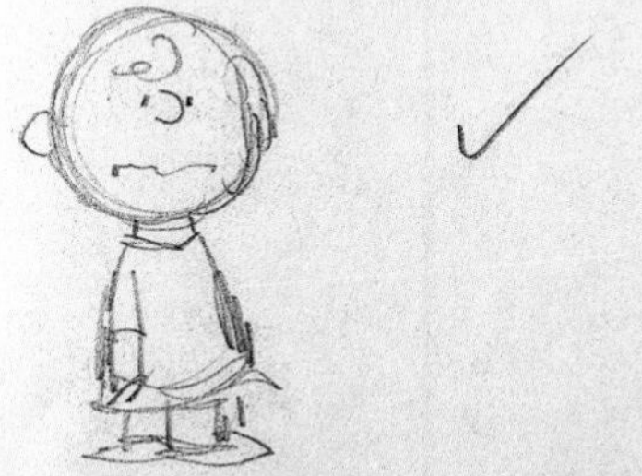

I ~~DON'T KNOW..~~ I THINK I'D SETTLE FOR EVEN A 'FAIR-WEATHER FRIEND.'"

"A friend is someone who's willing to watch the program you want to watch!"

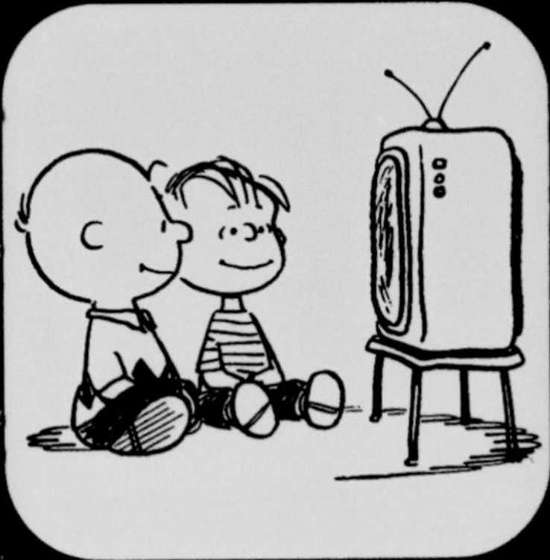

"A friend is someone who likes you even when the other guys are around."

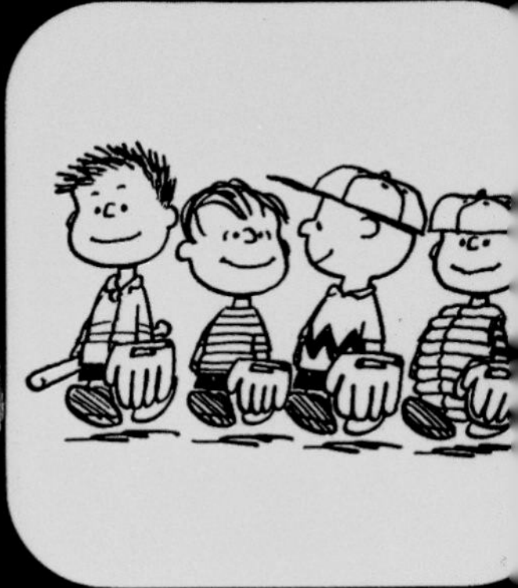

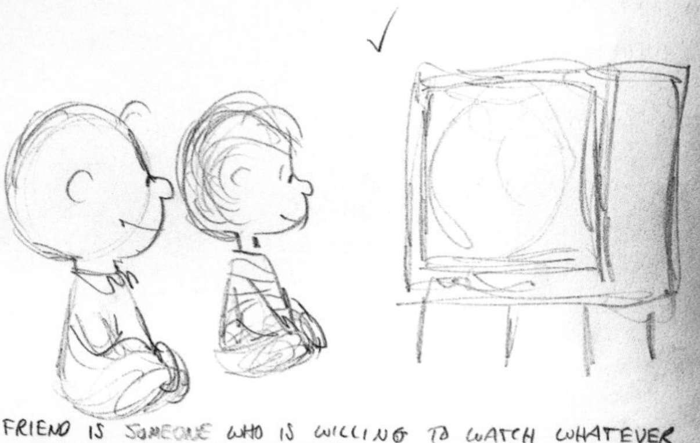

"A FRIEND IS SOMEONE WHO IS WILLING TO WATCH WHATEVER YOU WANT TO WATCH"

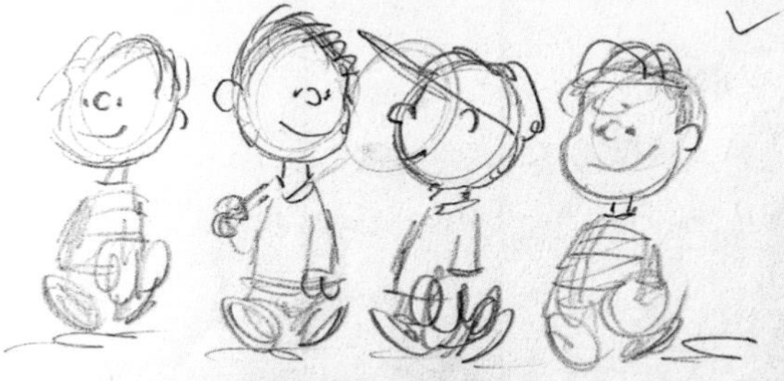

"A FRIEND IS SOMEONE WHO LIKES YOU EVEN WHEN THE OTHER GUYS ARE AROUND"

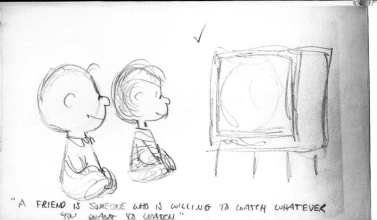

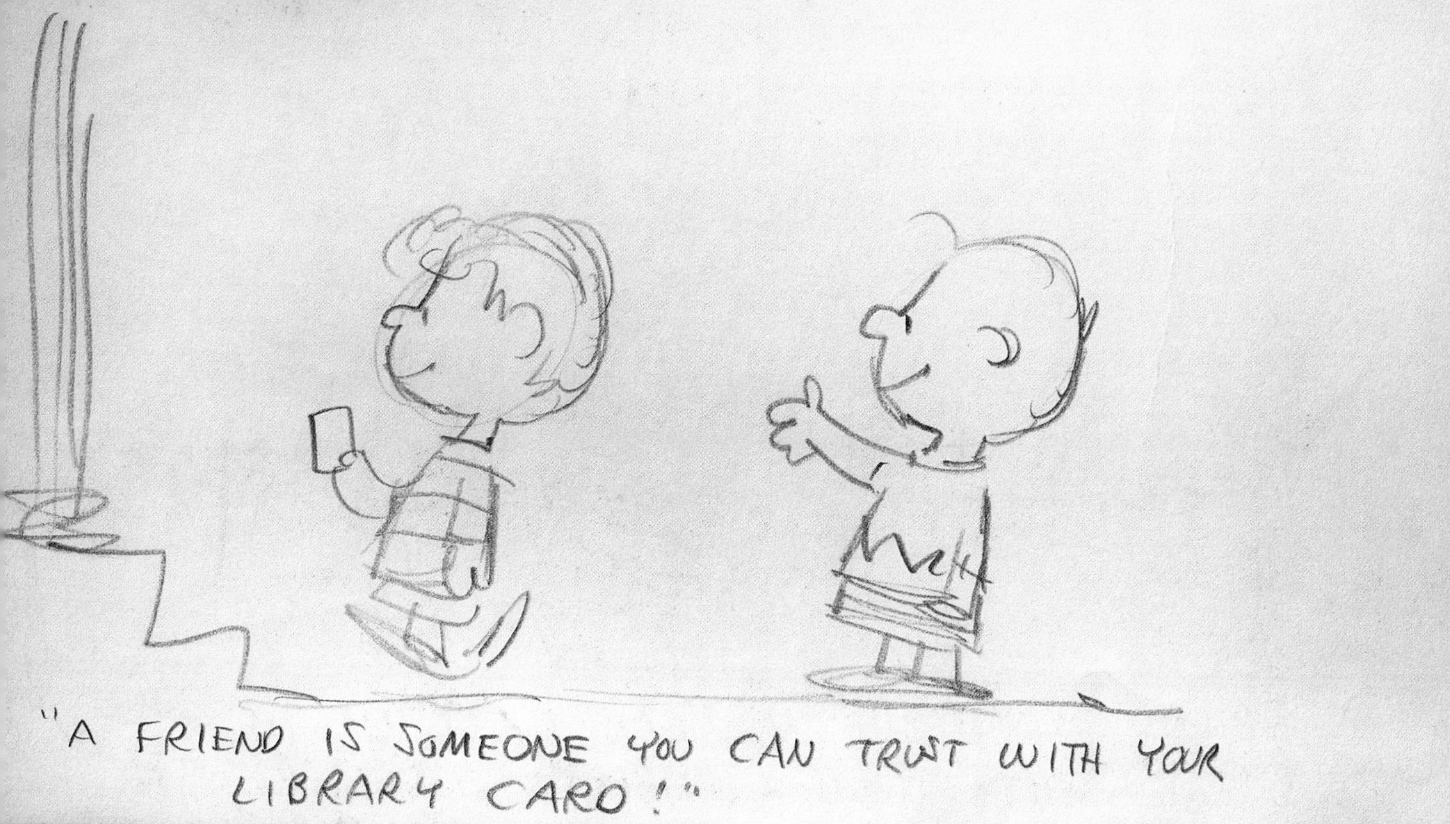
"A FRIEND IS SOMEONE YOU CAN TRUST WITH YOUR
LIBRARY CARD!"

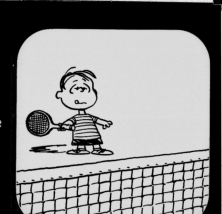

'A friend is
omeone who
l take the side
vith the sun
n his eyes."

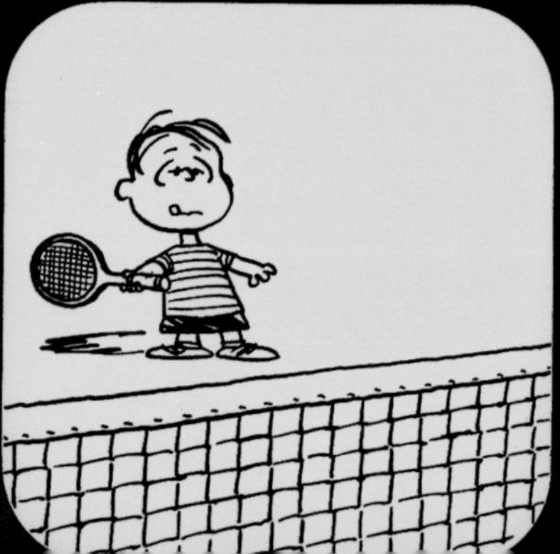

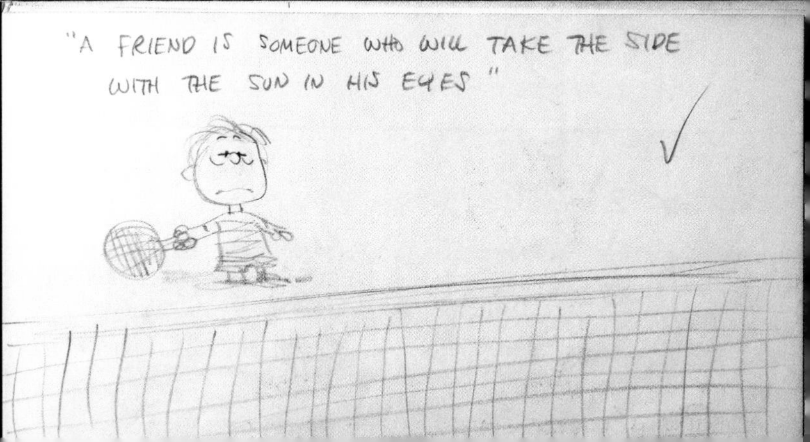
"A FRIEND IS SOMEONE WHO WILL TAKE THE SIDE
WITH THE SUN IN HIS EYES"

"A FRIEND IS SOMEONE YOU CAN SOCK ON THE ~~SHOULDER~~ arm"

"A FRIEND IS SOMEONE YOU CAN CALL UP IN THE MIDDLE OF THE NIGHT"

"A FRIEND IS SOMEONE WHO LIKES YOU IN SPITE OF YOUR FAULTS"

"WELL, WHAT I MEAN IS, IF TWO PEOPLE, A BOY AND A GIRL, THAT IS... ARE FRIENDS, CAN'T THAT FRIENDSHIP GROW TO BE... WELL, YOU KNOW WHAT I MEAN..."

"NO, I DON'T KNOW WHAT YOU MEAN"

"A friend
is someone
you have things
in common with,
Charlie Brown."

"A friend
is someone
who doesn't think
it's crazy to collect
old Henry Busse
records!"

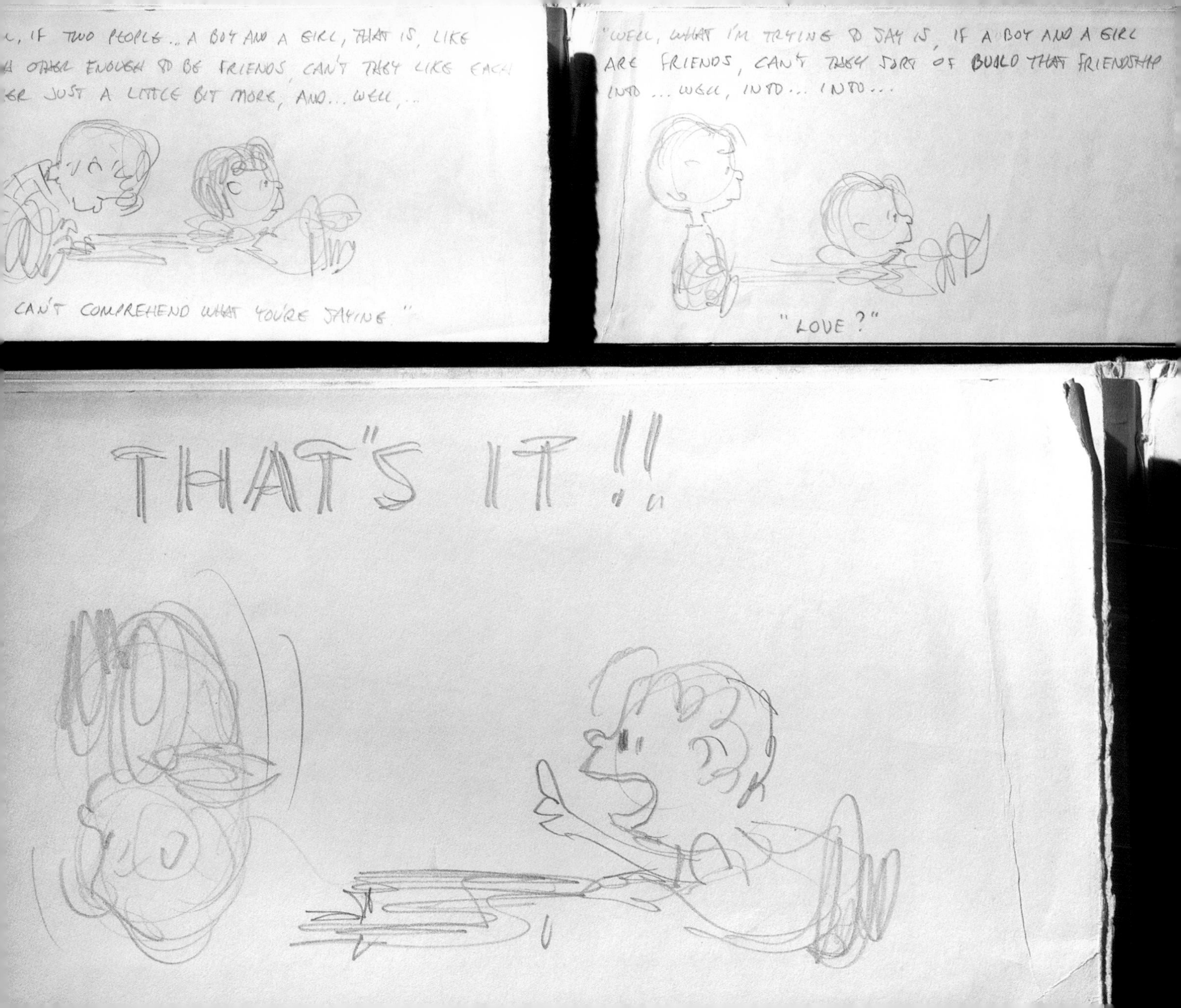
L, IF TWO PEOPLE.. A BOY AND A GIRL, THAT IS, LIKE
H OTHER ENOUGH TO BE FRIENDS, CAN'T THEY LIKE EACH
ER JUST A LITTLE BIT MORE, AND... WELL,..
CAN'T COMPREHEND WHAT YOU'RE SAYING."
"WELL, WHAT I'M TRYING TO SAY IS, IF A BOY AND A GIRL ARE FRIENDS, CAN'T THEY SORT OF BUILD THAT FRIENDSHIP INTO... WELL, INTO... INTO...
"LOVE?"
THAT'S IT!!

The sketchbook and the final version end very differently. In the former, Lucy grudgingly consoles Charlie Brown (even though he is a blockhead). In the latter, Linus offers his allegiance, with genuine feeling (below). The Gentle wins out over the Crabby yet again.

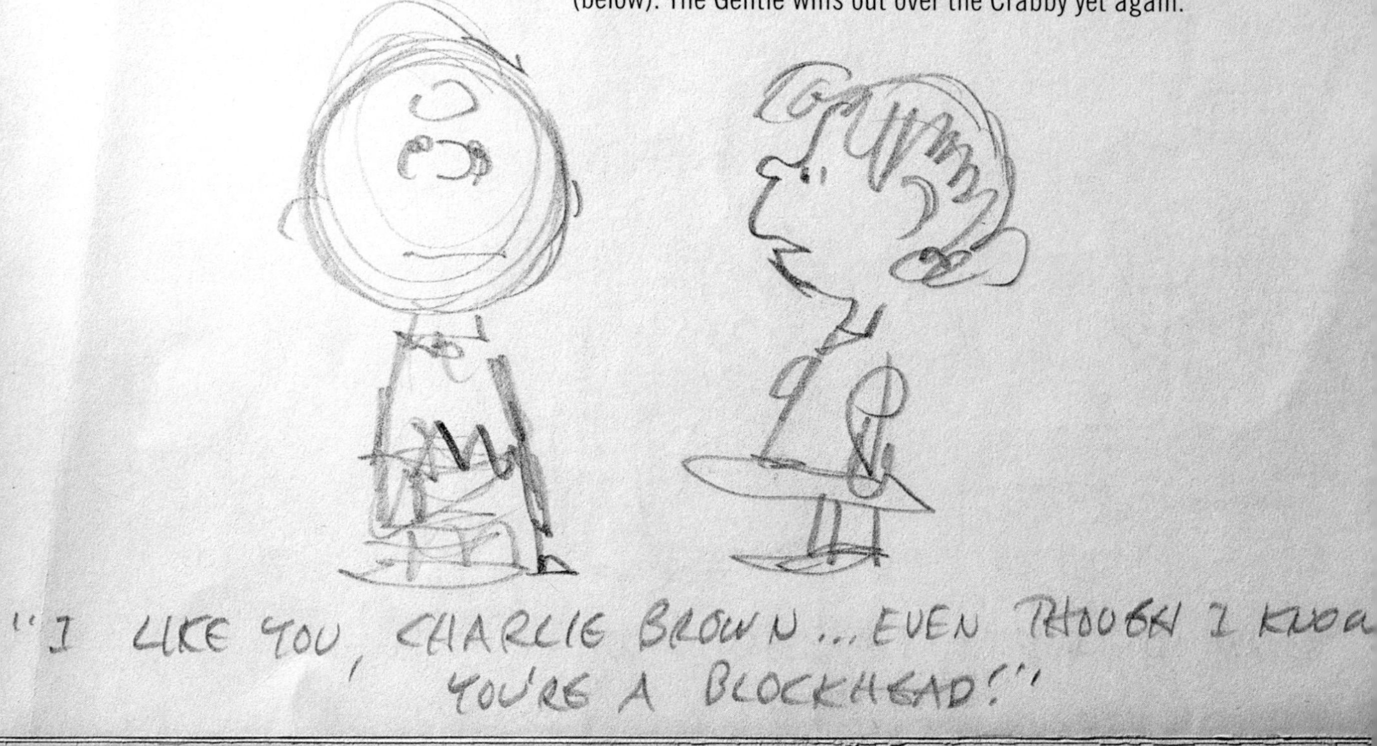
"I LIKE YOU, CHARLIE BROWN... EVEN THOUGH I KNOW YOU'RE A BLOCKHEAD!"

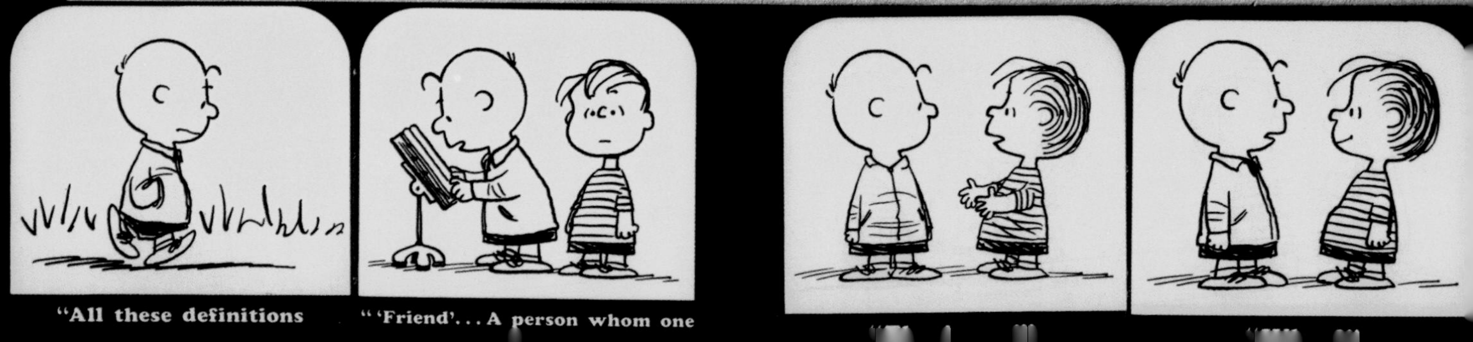
"All these definitions
" 'Friend'... A person whom one

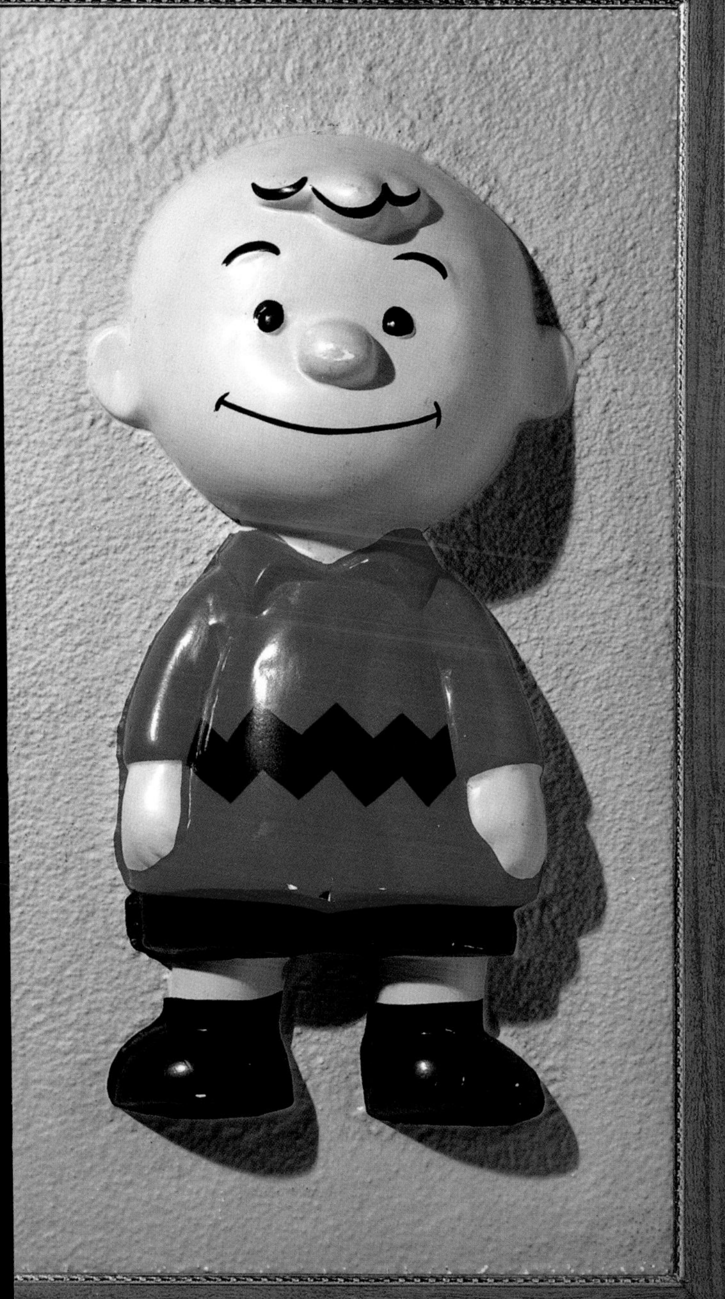

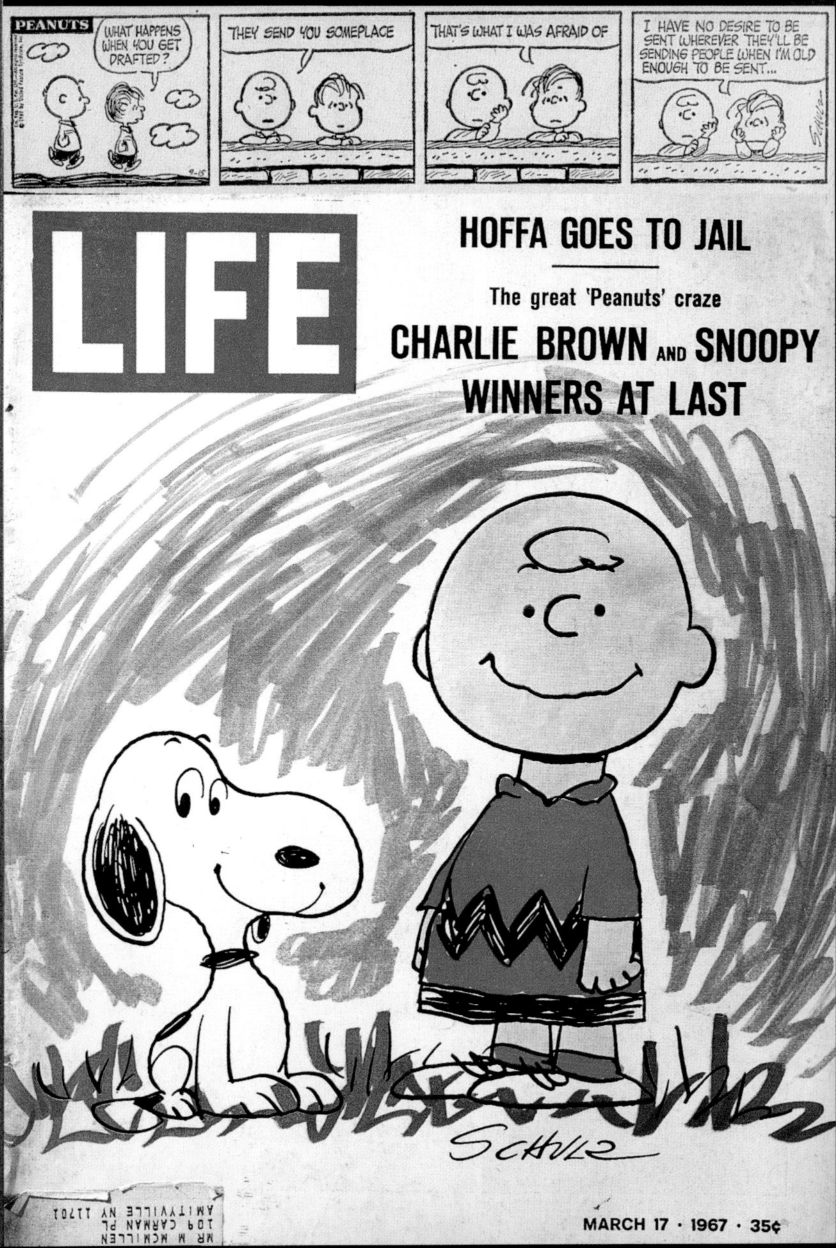
PEANUTS
WHAT HAPPENS WHEN YOU GET DRAFTED?
THEY SEND YOU SOMEPLACE
THAT'S WHAT I WAS AFRAID OF
I HAVE NO DESIRE TO BE SENT WHEREVER THEY'LL BE SENDING PEOPLE WHEN I'M OLD ENOUGH TO BE SENT...
LIFE
HOFFA GOES TO JAIL
The great 'Peanuts' craze
CHARLIE BROWN AND SNOOPY
WINNERS AT LAST
SCHULZ
MARCH 17 · 1967 · 35¢

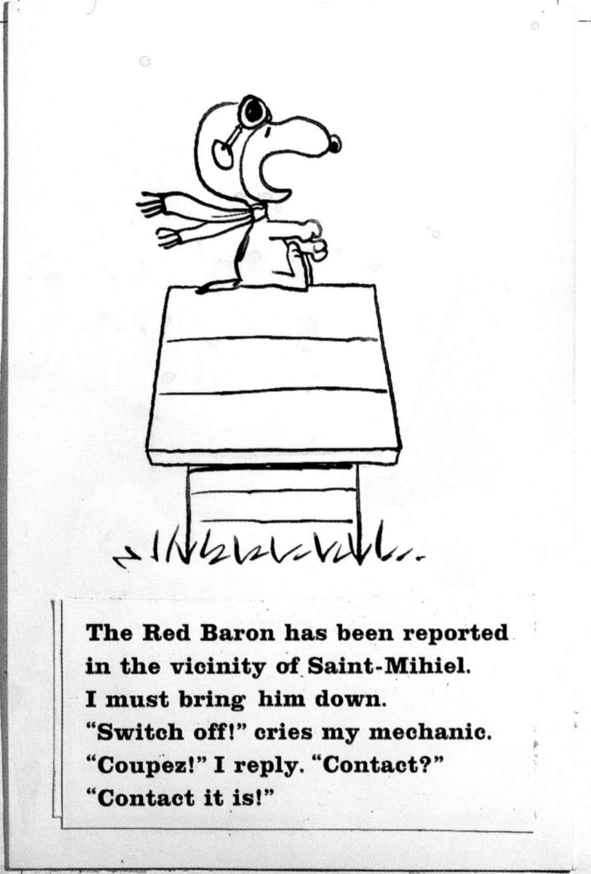
The Red Baron has been reported
in the vicinity of Saint-Mihiel.
I must bring him down.
"Switch off!" cries my mechanic.
"Coupez!" I reply. "Contact?"
"Contact it is!"

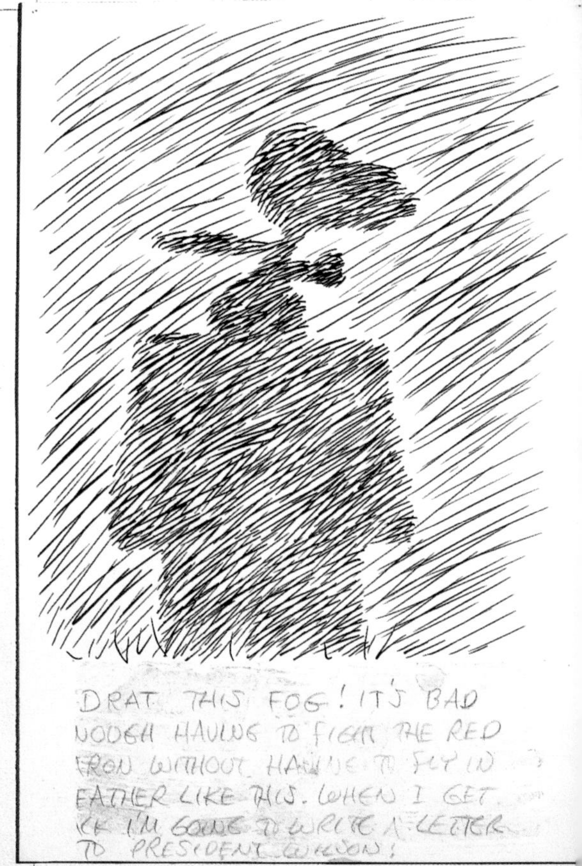
DRAT THIS FOG! IT'S BAD
NOUGH HAVING TO FIGHT THE RED
RON WITHOUT HAVING TO FLY IN
EATHER LIKE THIS. WHEN I GET
K I'M GOING TO WRITE A LETTER
TO PRESIDENT WILSON!

Snoopy's busy fantasy life emerged in the mid-1960s, as he assumed the mantle of a World War I flying ace, battling it out with his nemesis, the Red Baron. This surreal turn of events brought the strip into new, and newly delightful, territory by achieving a level of absurdity that seemed somehow perfectly normal. To Snoopy at least. "He has to retreat into his fanciful world in order to survive," said Schulz in 1997. "Otherwise, he leads kind of a dull, miserable life. I don't envy dogs the way they have to live."

SECTION

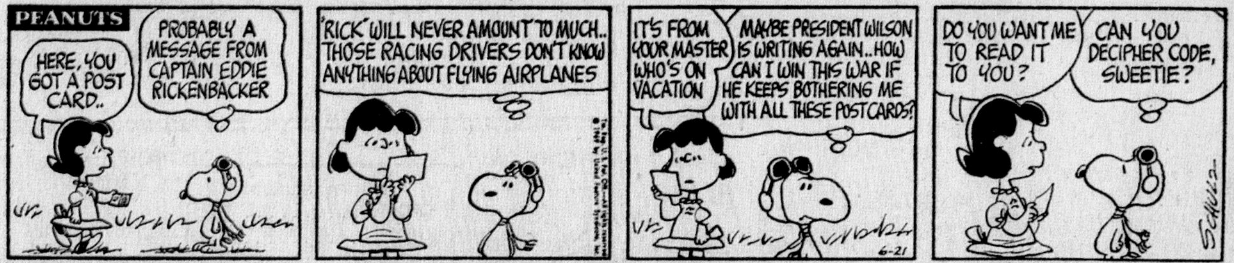
PEANUTS
HERE, YOU GOT A POST CARD..
PROBABLY A MESSAGE FROM CAPTAIN EDDIE RICKENBACKER
"RICK" WILL NEVER AMOUNT TO MUCH.. THOSE RACING DRIVERS DON'T KNOW ANYTHING ABOUT FLYING AIRPLANES
IT'S FROM YOUR MASTER WHO'S ON VACATION
MAYBE PRESIDENT WILSON IS WRITING AGAIN..HOW CAN I WIN THIS WAR IF HE KEEPS BOTHERING ME WITH ALL THESE POSTCARDS?
6-21
DO YOU WANT ME TO READ IT TO YOU?
CAN YOU DECIPHER CODE, SWEETIE?
SCHULZ

THIRD SECTION **San Francisco Chronicle** ☆☆ Mon., June 23, 196

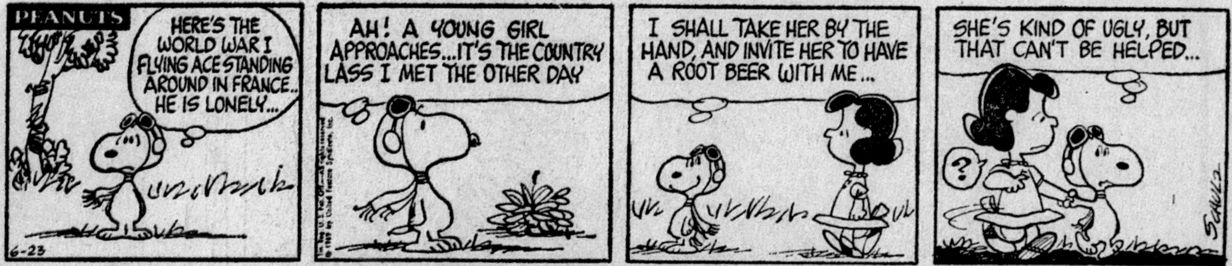
PEANUTS
HERE'S THE WORLD WAR I FLYING ACE STANDING AROUND IN FRANCE.. HE IS LONELY...
6-23
AH! A YOUNG GIRL APPROACHES...IT'S THE COUNTRY LASS I MET THE OTHER DAY
I SHALL TAKE HER BY THE HAND, AND INVITE HER TO HAVE A ROOT BEER WITH ME...
SHE'S KIND OF UGLY, BUT THAT CAN'T BE HELPED...
?
SCHULZ

THIRD SECTION **San Francisco Chronicle** Mon., May 25, 197

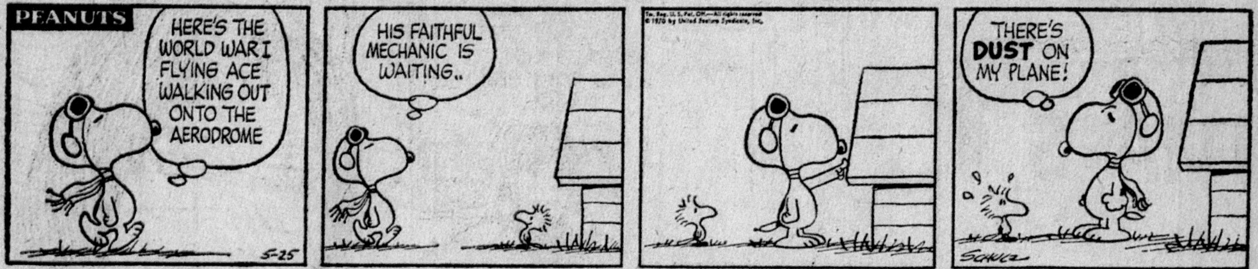
PEANUTS
HERE'S THE WORLD WAR I FLYING ACE WALKING OUT ONTO THE AERODROME
5-25
HIS FAITHFUL MECHANIC IS WAITING..
THERE'S **DUST** ON MY PLANE!
SCHULZ

SECTION

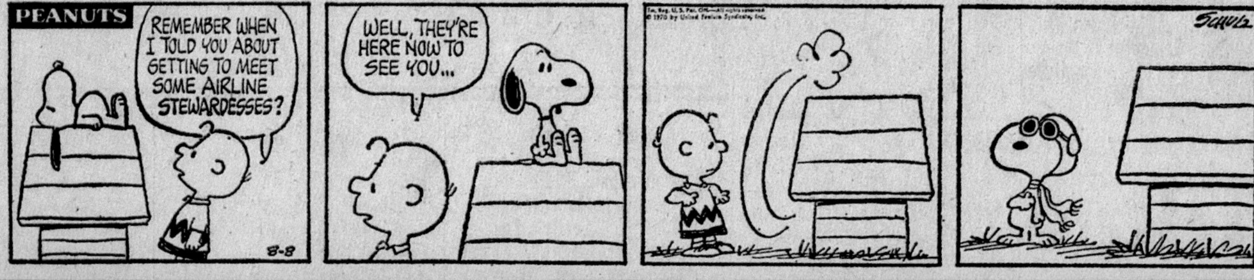
PEANUTS
REMEMBER WHEN I TOLD YOU ABOUT GETTING TO MEET SOME AIRLINE STEWARDESSES?
8-8
WELL, THEY'RE HERE NOW TO SEE YOU...
SCHULZ

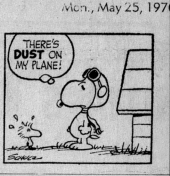

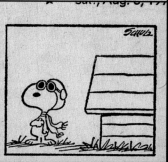

SNOOPY
ASTRONAUT
A "PEANUTS® POCKET Ⓣ DOLL"
FROM AMERICA'S FAVORITE
COMIC STRIP "PEANUTS" BY
CHARLES M. SCHULZ
© UNITED FEATURE SYNDICATE, INC., 1969
PRODUCED AND DISTRIBUTED BY
DETERMINED PRODUCTIONS, INC.
BOX 2150, SAN FRANCISCO, CALIF.

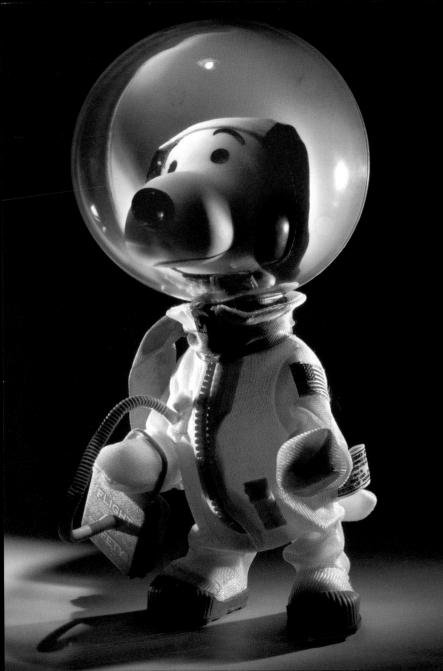

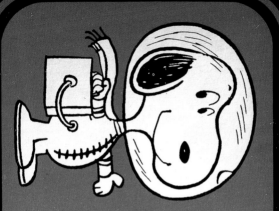

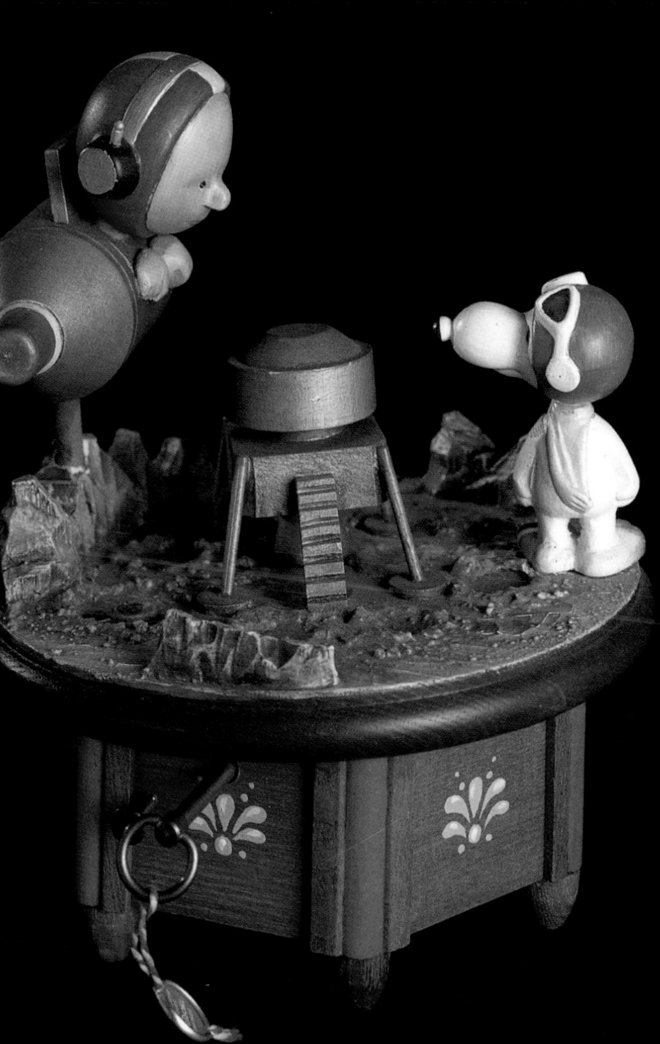

In 1969 the Apollo X space mission named their command module "Charlie Brown," and their lunar module "Snoopy." They didn't actually land on the moon, but the "real" Snoopy did.

Above: This 1969 Anri music box from Italy commemorating the event is extremely rare and plays the song "The Battle Hymn of the Republic."

Opposite: Determined Production's Snoopy Astronaut doll, 1969.

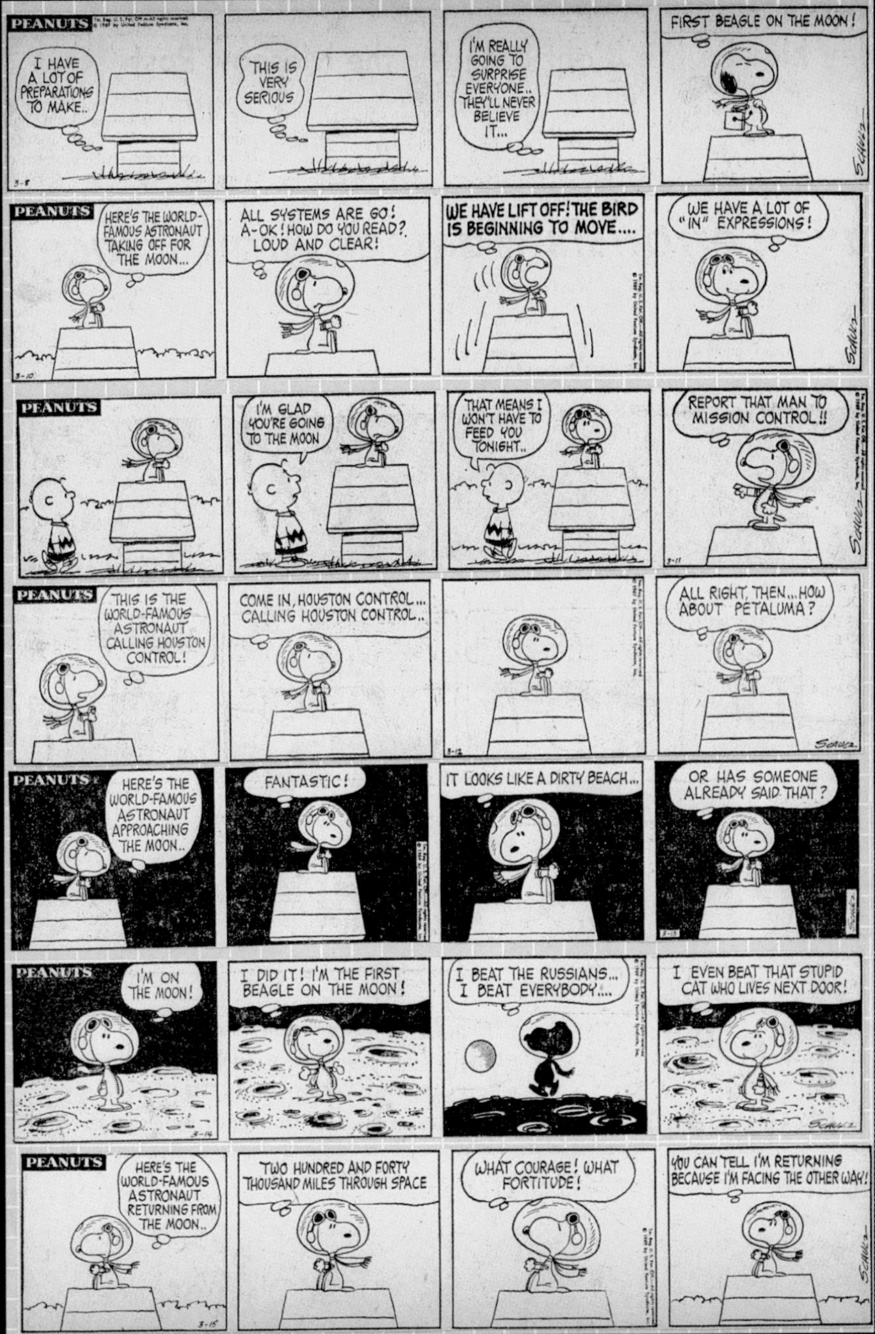
PEANUTS
I HAVE A LOT OF PREPARATIONS TO MAKE..
THIS IS VERY SERIOUS
I'M REALLY GOING TO SURPRISE EVERYONE.. THEY'LL NEVER BELIEVE IT...
FIRST BEAGLE ON THE MOON!
PEANUTS
HERE'S THE WORLD-FAMOUS ASTRONAUT TAKING OFF FOR THE MOON...
ALL SYSTEMS ARE GO! A-OK! HOW DO YOU READ? LOUD AND CLEAR!
WE HAVE LIFT OFF! THE BIRD IS BEGINNING TO MOVE....
WE HAVE A LOT OF "IN" EXPRESSIONS!
PEANUTS
I'M GLAD YOU'RE GOING TO THE MOON
THAT MEANS I WON'T HAVE TO FEED YOU TONIGHT..
REPORT THAT MAN TO MISSION CONTROL!!
PEANUTS
THIS IS THE WORLD-FAMOUS ASTRONAUT CALLING HOUSTON CONTROL!
COME IN, HOUSTON CONTROL... CALLING HOUSTON CONTROL..
ALL RIGHT, THEN... HOW ABOUT PETALUMA?
PEANUTS
HERE'S THE WORLD-FAMOUS ASTRONAUT APPROACHING THE MOON..
FANTASTIC!
IT LOOKS LIKE A DIRTY BEACH...
OR HAS SOMEONE ALREADY SAID THAT?
PEANUTS
I'M ON THE MOON!
I DID IT! I'M THE FIRST BEAGLE ON THE MOON!
I BEAT THE RUSSIANS... I BEAT EVERYBODY....
I EVEN BEAT THAT STUPID CAT WHO LIVES NEXT DOOR!
PEANUTS
HERE'S THE WORLD-FAMOUS ASTRONAUT RETURNING FROM THE MOON..
TWO HUNDRED AND FORTY THOUSAND MILES THROUGH SPACE
WHAT COURAGE! WHAT FORTITUDE!
YOU CAN TELL I'M RETURNING BECAUSE I'M FACING THE OTHER WAY!

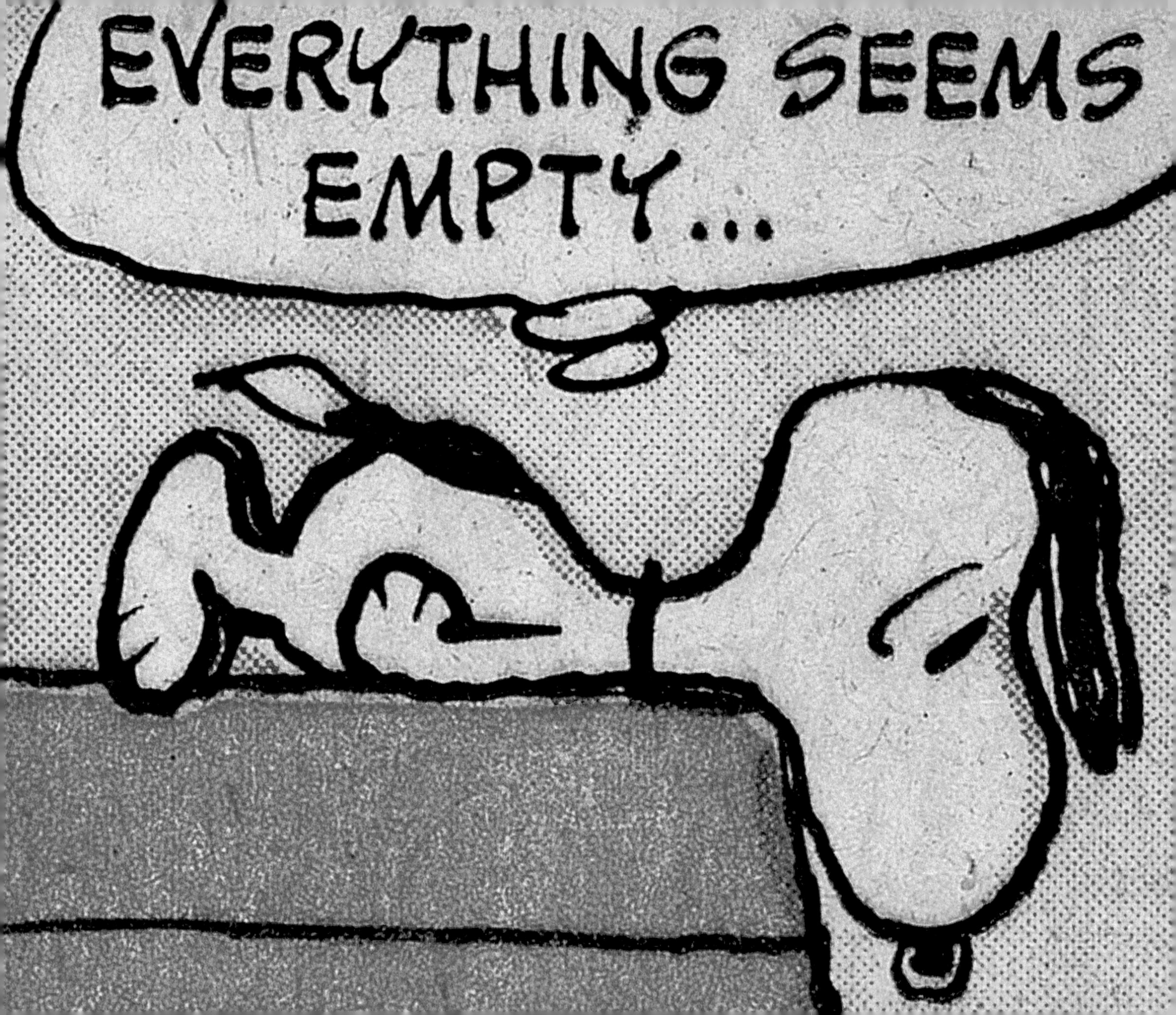
EVERYTHING SEEMS EMPTY...

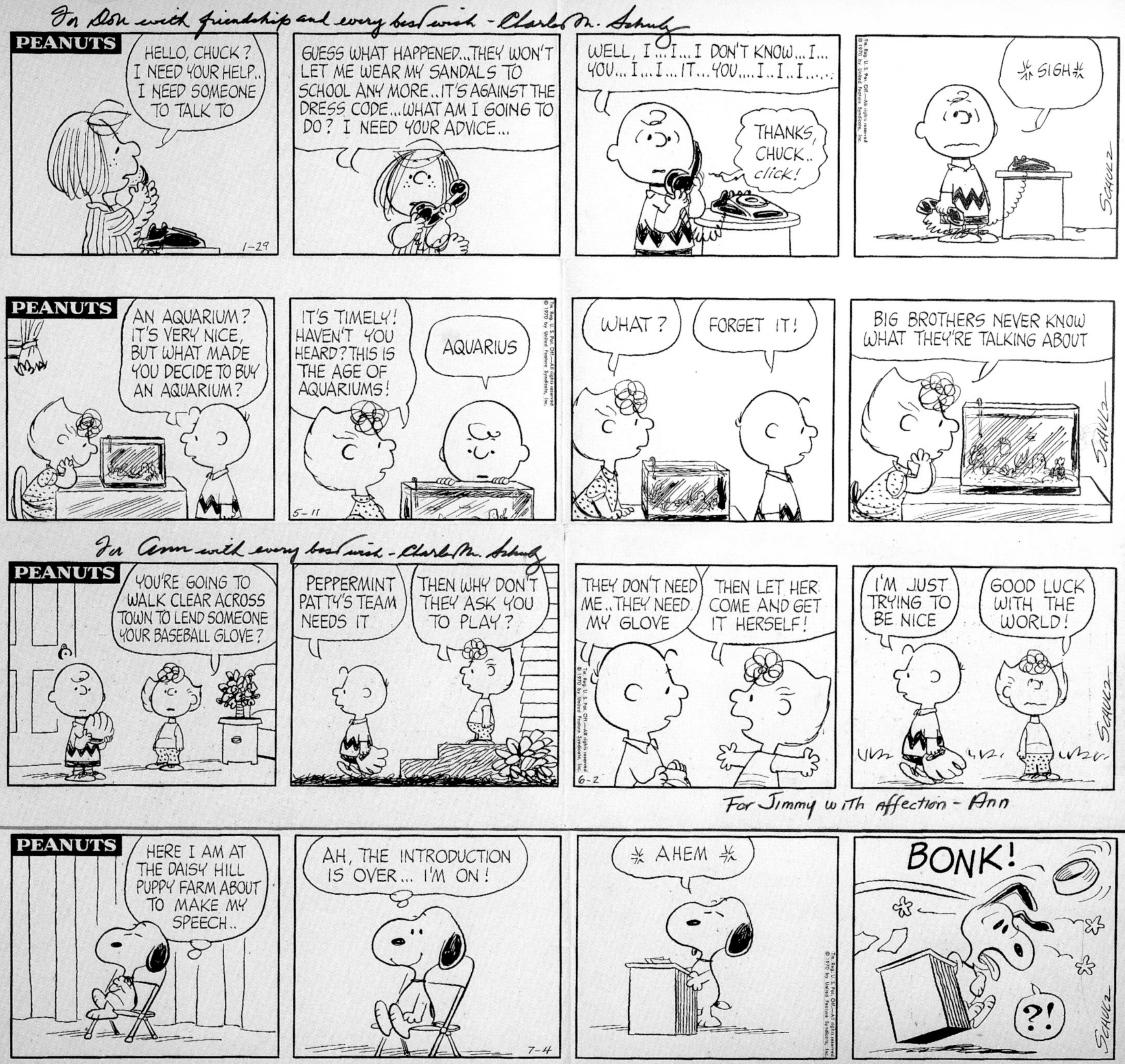
For Don with friendship and every best wish - Charles M. Schulz
PEANUTS
HELLO, CHUCK? I NEED YOUR HELP.. I NEED SOMEONE TO TALK TO
1-29
GUESS WHAT HAPPENED...THEY WON'T LET ME WEAR MY SANDALS TO SCHOOL ANY MORE..IT'S AGAINST THE DRESS CODE...WHAT AM I GOING TO DO? I NEED YOUR ADVICE...
WELL, I...I...I DON'T KNOW...I... YOU...I...I...IT...YOU....I..I..I.......
THANKS, CHUCK.. click!
Tm. Reg. U.S. Pat. Off.—All rights reserved © 1970 by United Feature Syndicate, Inc.
SIGH
SCHULZ
PEANUTS
AN AQUARIUM? IT'S VERY NICE, BUT WHAT MADE YOU DECIDE TO BUY AN AQUARIUM?
IT'S TIMELY! HAVEN'T YOU HEARD? THIS IS THE AGE OF AQUARIUMS!
AQUARIUS
5-11
Tm. Reg. U.S. Pat. Off.—All rights reserved © 1970 by United Feature Syndicate, Inc.
WHAT?
FORGET IT!
BIG BROTHERS NEVER KNOW WHAT THEY'RE TALKING ABOUT
SCHULZ
For Ann with every best wish - Charles M. Schulz
PEANUTS
YOU'RE GOING TO WALK CLEAR ACROSS TOWN TO LEND SOMEONE YOUR BASEBALL GLOVE?
PEPPERMINT PATTY'S TEAM NEEDS IT
THEN WHY DON'T THEY ASK YOU TO PLAY?
THEY DON'T NEED ME..THEY NEED MY GLOVE
THEN LET HER COME AND GET IT HERSELF!
Tm. Reg. U.S. Pat. Off.—All rights reserved © 1970 by United Feature Syndicate, Inc.
6-2
I'M JUST TRYING TO BE NICE
GOOD LUCK WITH THE WORLD!
SCHULZ
For Jimmy with affection - Ann
PEANUTS
HERE I AM AT THE DAISY HILL PUPPY FARM ABOUT TO MAKE MY SPEECH..
AH, THE INTRODUCTION IS OVER... I'M ON!
7-4
AHEM
Tm. Reg. U.S. Pat. Off.—All rights reserved © 1970 by United Feature Syndicate, Inc.
BONK!
?!
SCHULZ

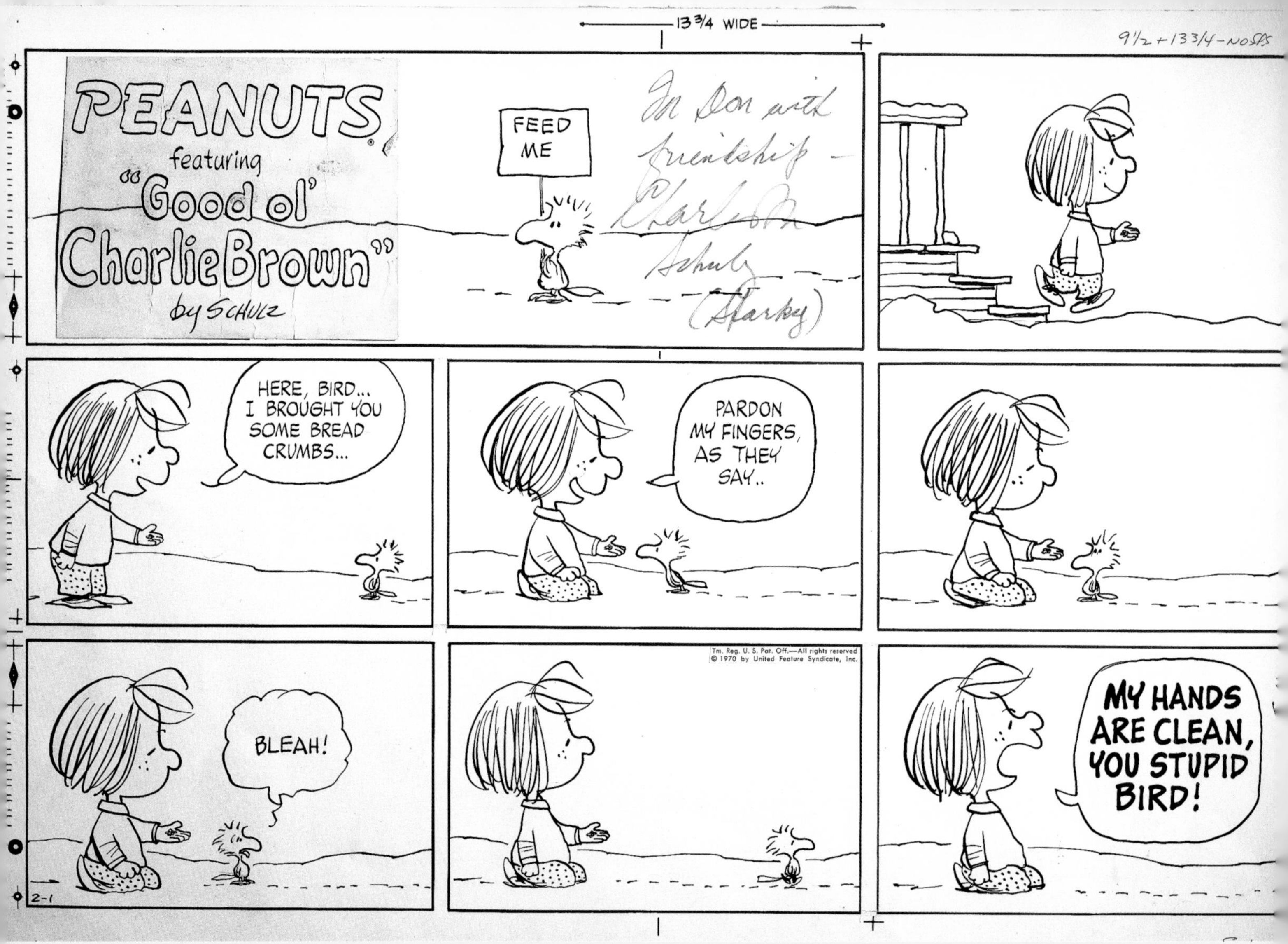
13 3/4 WIDE
PEANUTS
featuring "Good ol' Charlie Brown"
by SCHULZ
FEED ME
HERE, BIRD... I BROUGHT YOU SOME BREAD CRUMBS...
PARDON MY FINGERS, AS THEY SAY..
BLEAH!
Tm. Reg. U. S. Pat. Off.—All rights reserved © 1970 by United Feature Syndicate, Inc.
MY HANDS ARE CLEAN, YOU STUPID BIRD!

"I developed the character Peppermint Patty because I happened to be walking through our living room. I saw a dish of Peppermint Patties and I thought that would make a good name for a character, so I drew the face to match the name. One day I sent her to camp, and a little girl came into her tent one night and said, 'Sir, my stomach hurts.' That was Marcie."

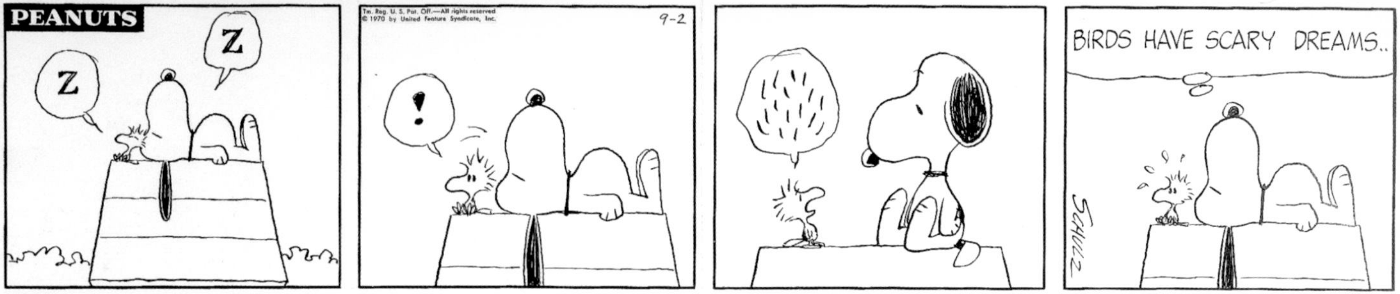
PEANUTS
Z
Z
Tm. Reg. U. S. Pat. Off.—All rights reserved © 1970 by United Feature Syndicate, Inc.
9-2
!
BIRDS HAVE SCARY DREAMS..
SCHULZ

7½ + 9½ NO SPS

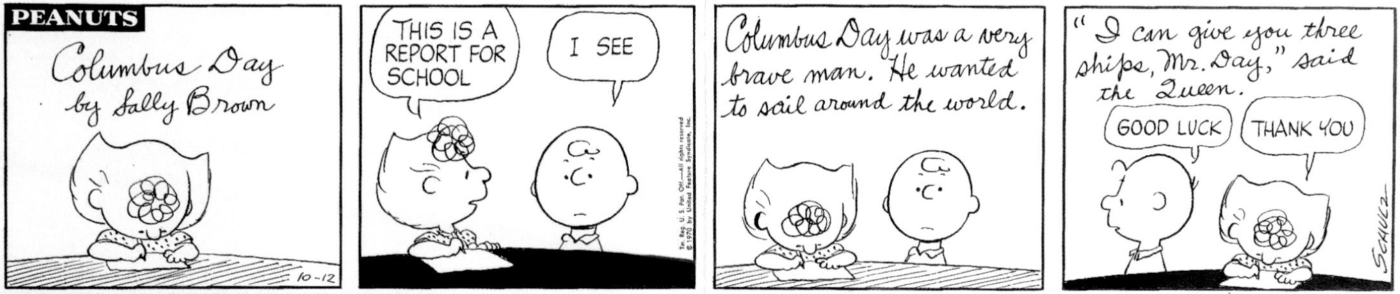
PEANUTS
Columbus Day
by Sally Brown
10-12
THIS IS A REPORT FOR SCHOOL
I SEE
Tm. Reg. U. S. Pat. Off.—All rights reserved © 1970 by United Feature Syndicate, Inc.
Columbus Day was a very brave man. He wanted to sail around the world.
"I can give you three ships, Mr. Day," said the Queen.
GOOD LUCK
THANK YOU
SCHULZ

7½ – 9½

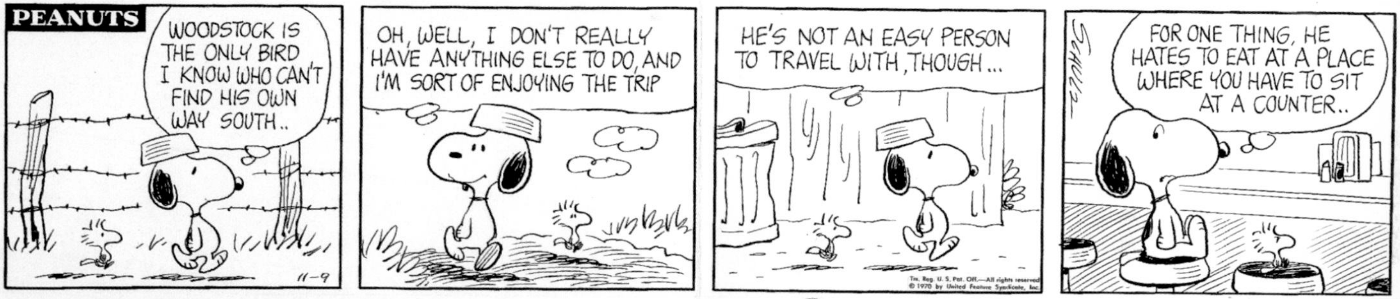
PEANUTS
WOODSTOCK IS THE ONLY BIRD I KNOW WHO CAN'T FIND HIS OWN WAY SOUTH..
11-9
OH, WELL, I DON'T REALLY HAVE ANYTHING ELSE TO DO, AND I'M SORT OF ENJOYING THE TRIP
HE'S NOT AN EASY PERSON TO TRAVEL WITH, THOUGH...
Tm. Reg. U. S. Pat. Off.—All rights reserved © 1970 by United Feature Syndicate, Inc.
SCHULZ
FOR ONE THING, HE HATES TO EAT AT A PLACE WHERE YOU HAVE TO SIT AT A COUNTER..

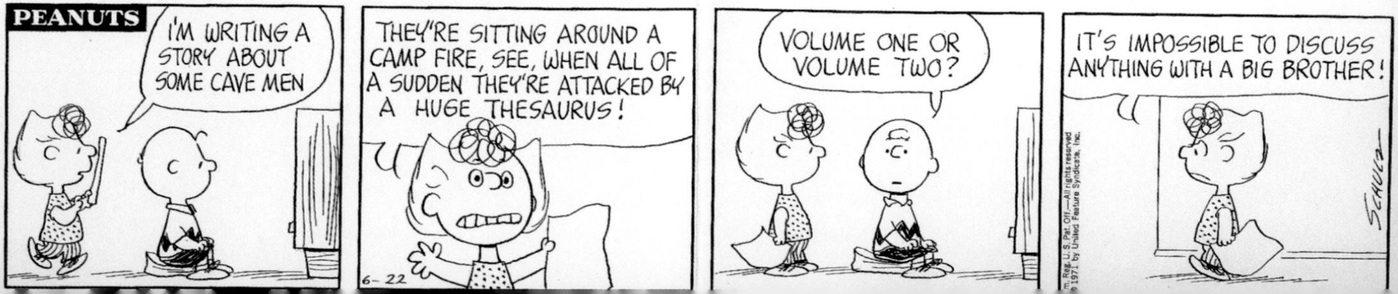
PEANUTS
I'M WRITING A STORY ABOUT SOME CAVE MEN
THEY'RE SITTING AROUND A CAMP FIRE, SEE, WHEN ALL OF A SUDDEN THEY'RE ATTACKED BY A HUGE THESAURUS!
6-22
VOLUME ONE OR VOLUME TWO?
IT'S IMPOSSIBLE TO DISCUSS ANYTHING WITH A BIG BROTHER!
Tm. Reg. U. S. Pat. Off.—All rights reserved © 1971 by United Feature Syndicate, Inc.
SCHULZ

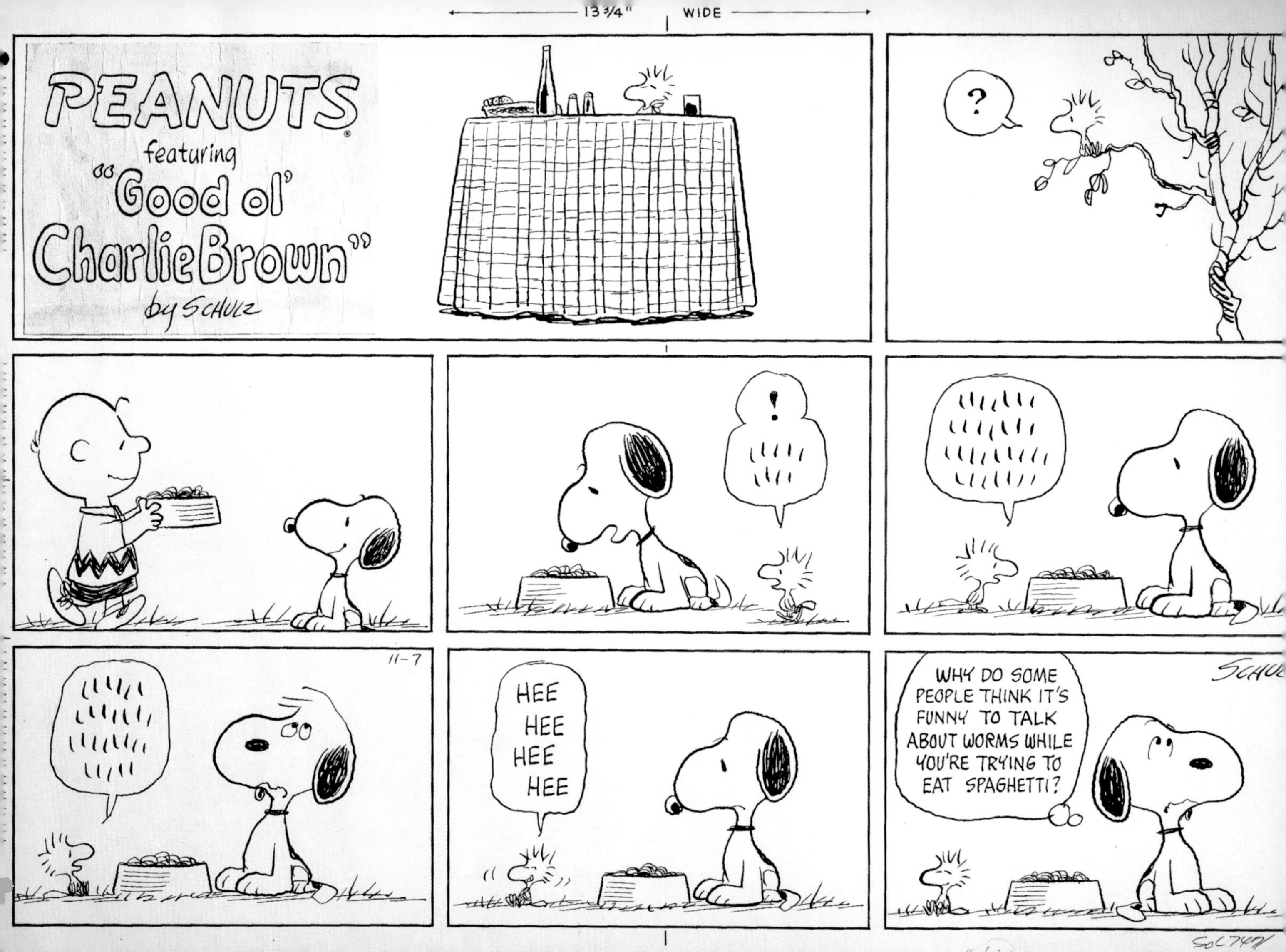
13 3/4" WIDE
PEANUTS
featuring
"Good ol' Charlie Brown"
by SCHULZ
?
!
11-7
HEE
HEE
HEE
HEE
WHY DO SOME PEOPLE THINK IT'S FUNNY TO TALK ABOUT WORMS WHILE YOU'RE TRYING TO EAT SPAGHETTI?
SCHULZ

"Cartooning really is just designing," Schulz said in 1997. "It's a lot like Picasso on paintings. Take the shape of Charlie Brown's head . . . If a cartooning style is too extreme, the artist can never do or say anything that is at all sensitive. If you look back upon all of the great comic strips down through the years, every one of them was drawn in a style that was relatively quiet." By way of example, some of Schulz's favorite strips were *Krazy Kat*, *Skippy*, and *Gasoline Alley*.

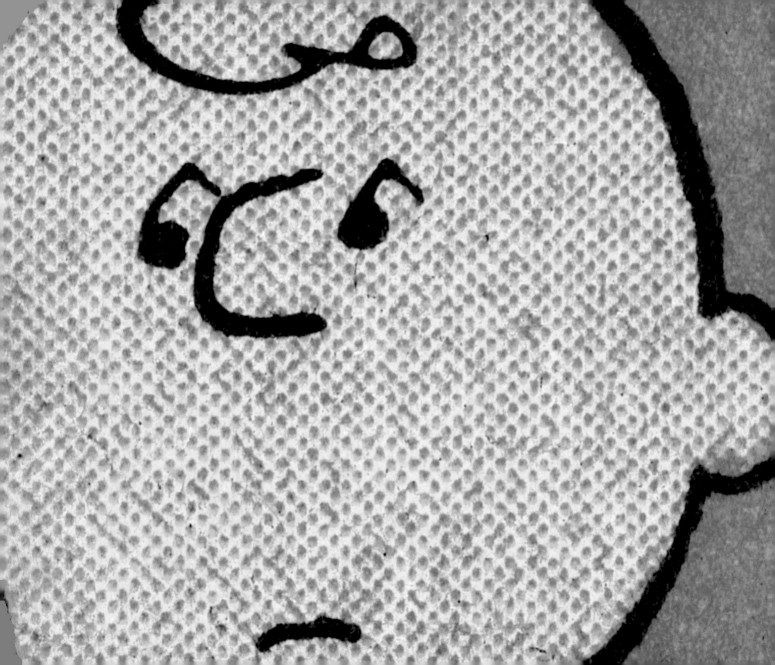

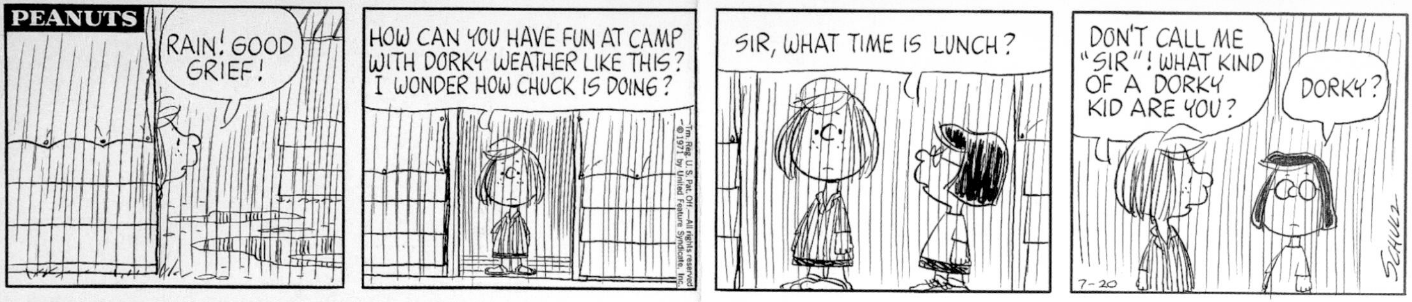
PEANUTS
RAIN! GOOD GRIEF!
HOW CAN YOU HAVE FUN AT CAMP WITH DORKY WEATHER LIKE THIS? I WONDER HOW CHUCK IS DOING?
Tm. Reg. U.S. Pat. Off.—All rights reserved © 1971 by United Feature Syndicate, Inc.
SIR, WHAT TIME IS LUNCH?
DON'T CALL ME "SIR"! WHAT KIND OF A DORKY KID ARE YOU?
DORKY?
7-20
SCHULZ

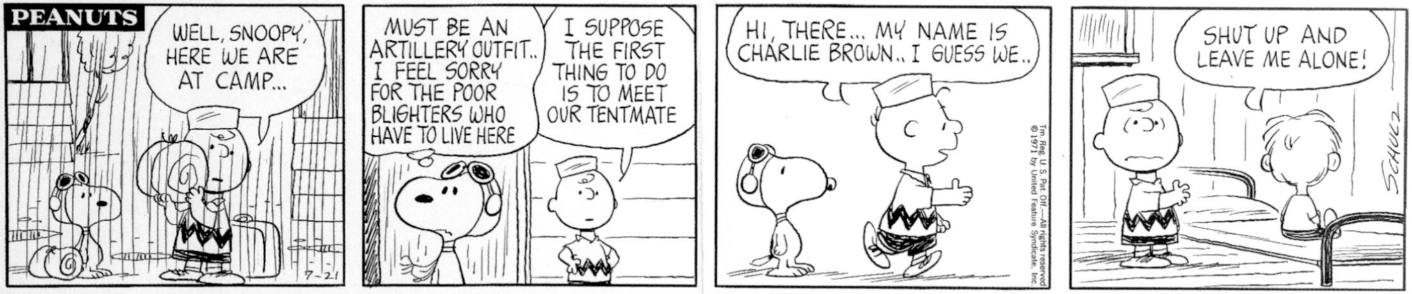
PEANUTS
WELL, SNOOPY, HERE WE ARE AT CAMP...
7-21
MUST BE AN ARTILLERY OUTFIT.. I FEEL SORRY FOR THE POOR BLIGHTERS WHO HAVE TO LIVE HERE
I SUPPOSE THE FIRST THING TO DO IS TO MEET OUR TENTMATE
HI, THERE... MY NAME IS CHARLIE BROWN.. I GUESS WE..
Tm. Reg. U.S. Pat. Off.—All rights reserved © 1971 by United Feature Syndicate, Inc.
SHUT UP AND LEAVE ME ALONE!
SCHULZ

7½+9½

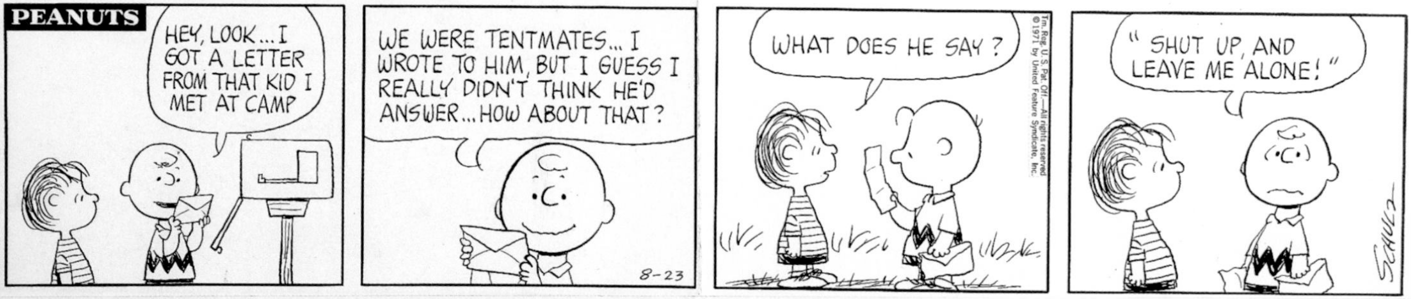
PEANUTS
HEY, LOOK... I GOT A LETTER FROM THAT KID I MET AT CAMP
WE WERE TENTMATES... I WROTE TO HIM, BUT I GUESS I REALLY DIDN'T THINK HE'D ANSWER... HOW ABOUT THAT?
8-23
Tm. Reg. U.S. Pat. Off.—All rights reserved © 1971 by United Feature Syndicate, Inc.
WHAT DOES HE SAY?
"SHUT UP, AND LEAVE ME ALONE!"
SCHULZ

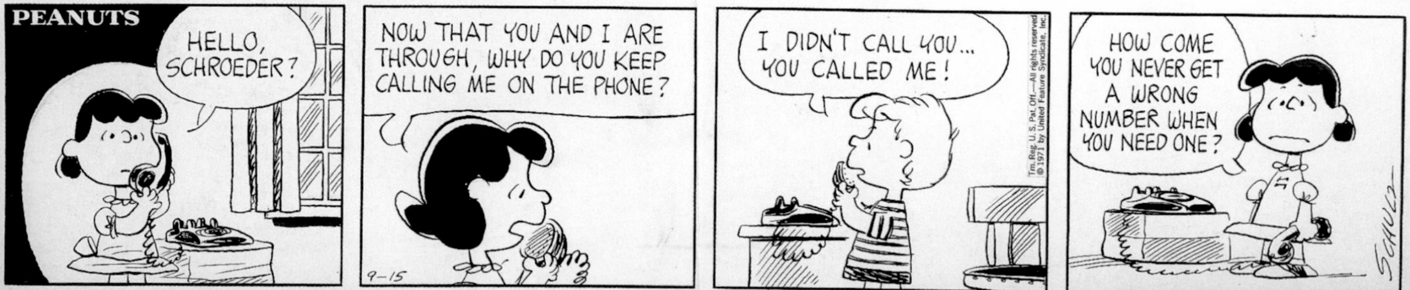
PEANUTS
HELLO, SCHROEDER?
NOW THAT YOU AND I ARE THROUGH, WHY DO YOU KEEP CALLING ME ON THE PHONE?
9-15
Tm. Reg. U.S. Pat. Off.—All rights reserved © 1971 by United Feature Syndicate, Inc.
I DIDN'T CALL YOU... YOU CALLED ME!
HOW COME YOU NEVER GET A WRONG NUMBER WHEN YOU NEED ONE?
SCHULZ

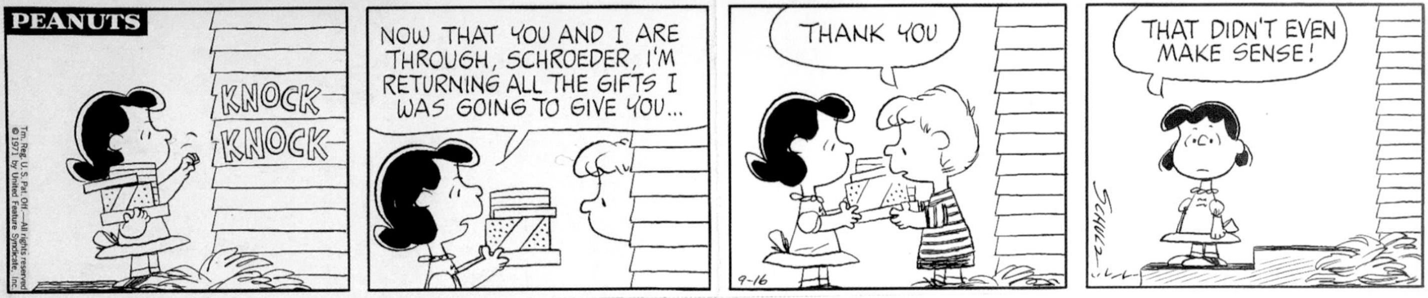
PEANUTS
KNOCK
KNOCK
Tm. Reg. U.S. Pat. Off.—All rights reserved © 1971 by United Feature Syndicate, Inc.
NOW THAT YOU AND I ARE THROUGH, SCHROEDER, I'M RETURNING ALL THE GIFTS I WAS GOING TO GIVE YOU...
THANK YOU
9-16
THAT DIDN'T EVEN MAKE SENSE!
SCHULZ

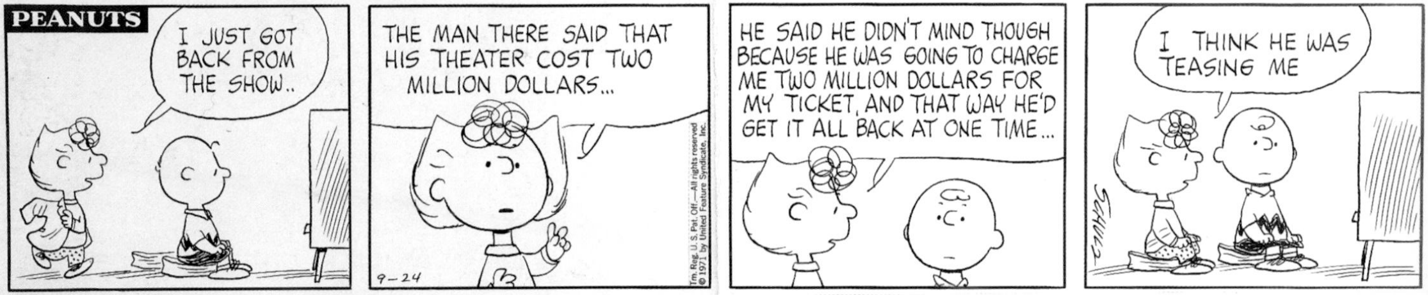
PEANUTS
I JUST GOT BACK FROM THE SHOW..
THE MAN THERE SAID THAT HIS THEATER COST TWO MILLION DOLLARS...
9-24
Tm. Reg. U.S. Pat. Off.—All rights reserved © 1971 by United Feature Syndicate, Inc.
HE SAID HE DIDN'T MIND THOUGH BECAUSE HE WAS GOING TO CHARGE ME TWO MILLION DOLLARS FOR MY TICKET, AND THAT WAY HE'D GET IT ALL BACK AT ONE TIME...
I THINK HE WAS TEASING ME
SCHULZ

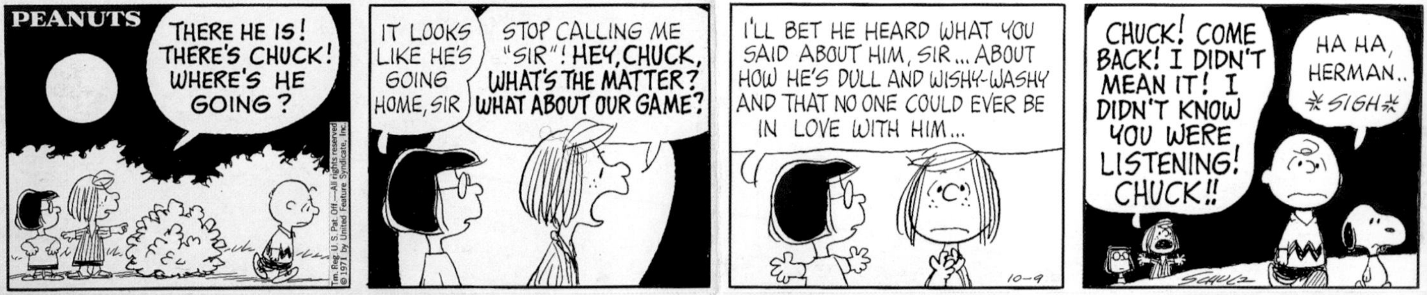
PEANUTS
THERE HE IS! THERE'S CHUCK! WHERE'S HE GOING?
Tm. Reg. U.S. Pat. Off.—All rights reserved © 1971 by United Feature Syndicate, Inc.
IT LOOKS LIKE HE'S GOING HOME, SIR
STOP CALLING ME "SIR"! HEY, CHUCK, WHAT'S THE MATTER? WHAT ABOUT OUR GAME?
I'LL BET HE HEARD WHAT YOU SAID ABOUT HIM, SIR... ABOUT HOW HE'S DULL AND WISHY-WASHY AND THAT NO ONE COULD EVER BE IN LOVE WITH HIM...
10-9
CHUCK! COME BACK! I DIDN'T MEAN IT! I DIDN'T KNOW YOU WERE LISTENING! CHUCK!!
HA HA, HERMAN.. *SIGH*
SCHULZ

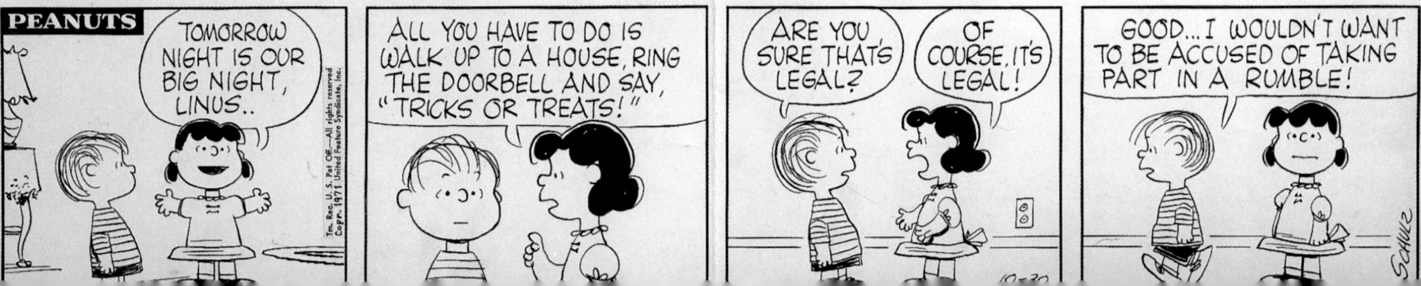
PEANUTS
TOMORROW NIGHT IS OUR BIG NIGHT, LINUS..
Tm. Reg. U.S. Pat. Off.—All rights reserved Copr. 1971 United Feature Syndicate, Inc.
ALL YOU HAVE TO DO IS WALK UP TO A HOUSE, RING THE DOORBELL AND SAY, "TRICKS OR TREATS!"
ARE YOU SURE THAT'S LEGAL?
OF COURSE, IT'S LEGAL!
GOOD... I WOULDN'T WANT TO BE ACCUSED OF TAKING PART IN A RUMBLE!
SCHULZ

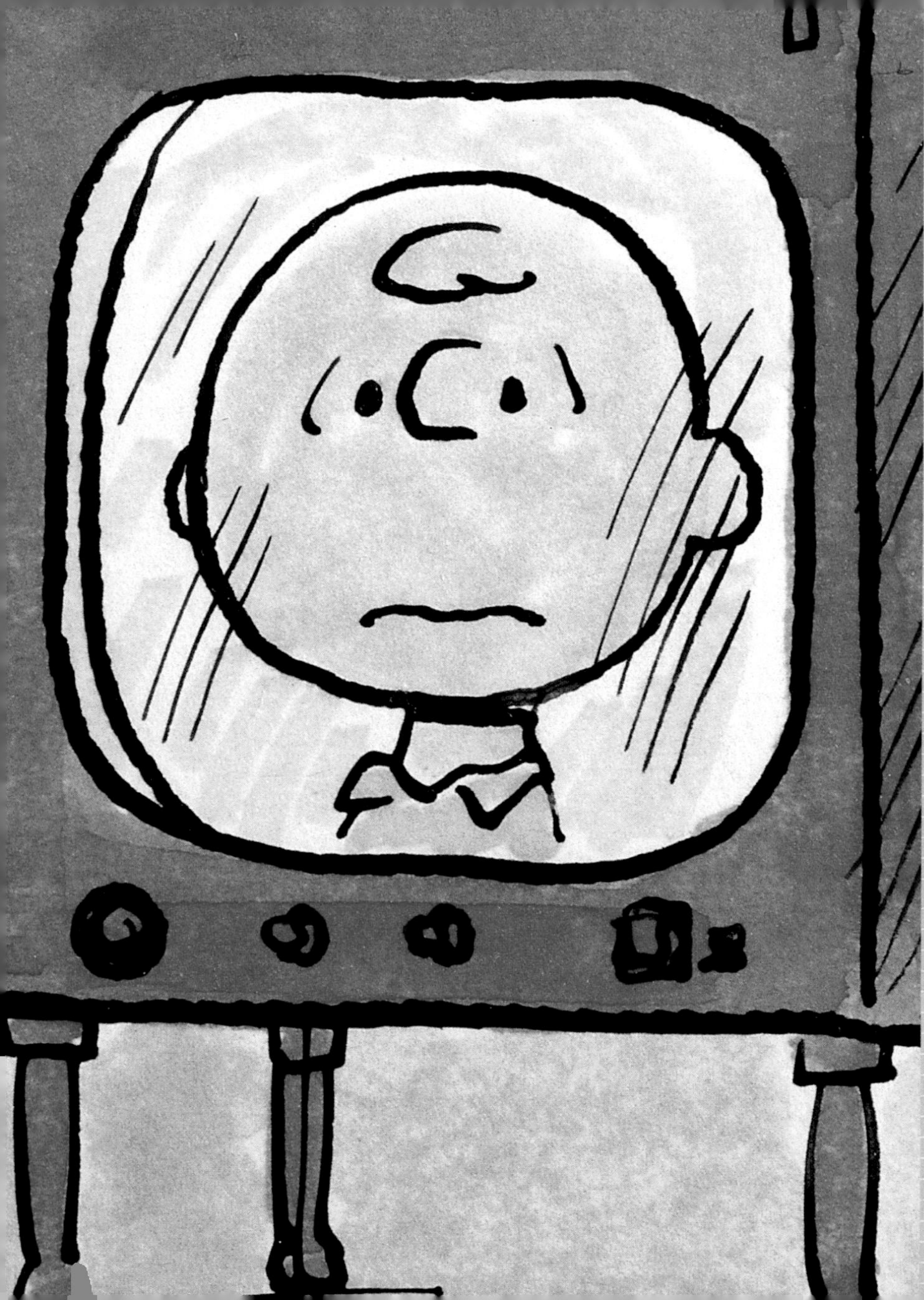

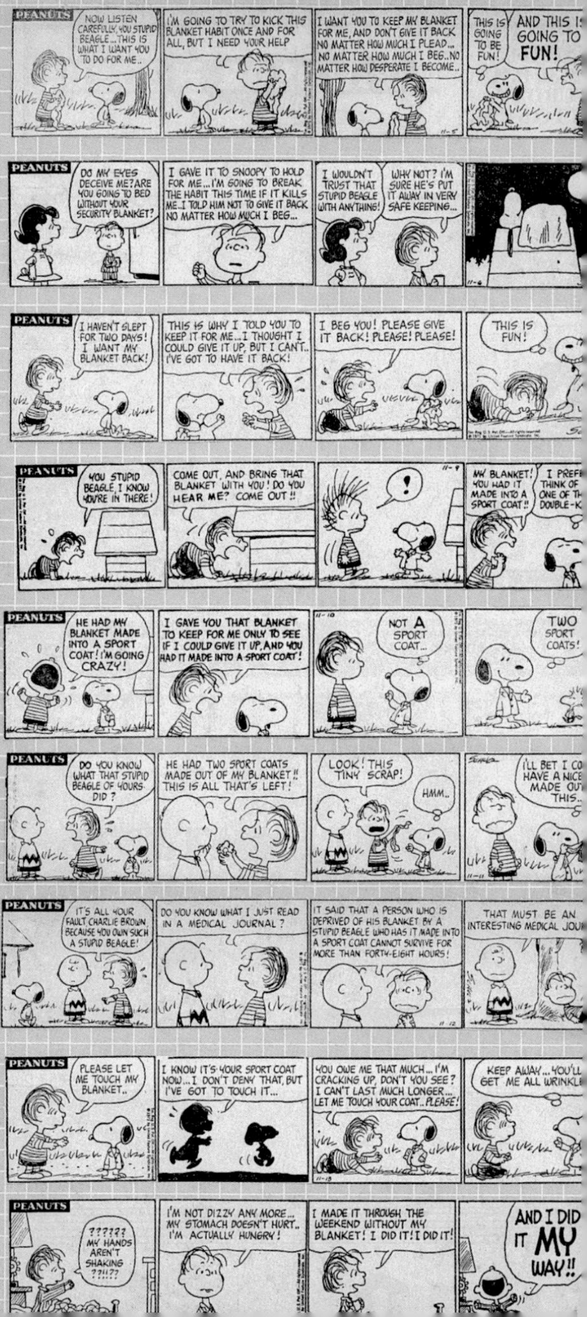
PEANUTS
NOW LISTEN CAREFULLY, YOU STUPID BEAGLE...THIS IS WHAT I WANT YOU TO DO FOR ME..
I'M GOING TO TRY TO KICK THIS BLANKET HABIT ONCE AND FOR ALL, BUT I NEED YOUR HELP
I WANT YOU TO KEEP MY BLANKET FOR ME, AND DON'T GIVE IT BACK NO MATTER HOW MUCH I PLEAD... NO MATTER HOW MUCH I BEG..NO MATTER HOW DESPERATE I BECOME..
THIS IS GOING TO BE FUN!
AND THIS I GOING TO FUN!
PEANUTS
DO MY EYES DECEIVE ME? ARE YOU GOING TO BED WITHOUT YOUR SECURITY BLANKET?
I GAVE IT TO SNOOPY TO HOLD FOR ME...I'M GOING TO BREAK THE HABIT THIS TIME IF IT KILLS ME..I TOLD HIM NOT TO GIVE IT BACK NO MATTER HOW MUCH I BEG...
I WOULDN'T TRUST THAT STUPID BEAGLE WITH ANYTHING!
WHY NOT? I'M SURE HE'S PUT IT AWAY IN VERY SAFE KEEPING...
PEANUTS
I HAVEN'T SLEPT FOR TWO DAYS! I WANT MY BLANKET BACK!
THIS IS WHY I TOLD YOU TO KEEP IT FOR ME...I THOUGHT I COULD GIVE IT UP, BUT I CAN'T.. I'VE GOT TO HAVE IT BACK!
I BEG YOU! PLEASE GIVE IT BACK! PLEASE! PLEASE!
THIS IS FUN!
PEANUTS
YOU STUPID BEAGLE, I KNOW YOU'RE IN THERE!
COME OUT, AND BRING THAT BLANKET WITH YOU! DO YOU HEAR ME? COME OUT!!
!
MY BLANKET! YOU HAD IT MADE INTO A SPORT COAT!!
PEANUTS
HE HAD MY BLANKET MADE INTO A SPORT COAT! I'M GOING CRAZY!
I GAVE YOU THAT BLANKET TO KEEP FOR ME ONLY TO SEE IF I COULD GIVE IT UP, AND YOU HAD IT MADE INTO A SPORT COAT!
NOT A SPORT COAT...
TWO SPORT COATS!
PEANUTS
DO YOU KNOW WHAT THAT STUPID BEAGLE OF YOURS DID?
HE HAD TWO SPORT COATS MADE OUT OF MY BLANKET!! THIS IS ALL THAT'S LEFT!
LOOK! THIS TINY SCRAP!
HMM..
PEANUTS
IT'S ALL YOUR FAULT, CHARLIE BROWN, BECAUSE YOU OWN SUCH A STUPID BEAGLE!
DO YOU KNOW WHAT I JUST READ IN A MEDICAL JOURNAL?
IT SAID THAT A PERSON WHO IS DEPRIVED OF HIS BLANKET BY A STUPID BEAGLE WHO HAS IT MADE INTO A SPORT COAT CANNOT SURVIVE FOR MORE THAN FORTY-EIGHT HOURS!
THAT MUST BE AN INTERESTING MEDICAL JOU
PEANUTS
PLEASE LET ME TOUCH MY BLANKET..
I KNOW IT'S YOUR SPORT COAT NOW...I DON'T DENY THAT, BUT I'VE GOT TO TOUCH IT...
YOU OWE ME THAT MUCH...I'M CRACKING UP, DON'T YOU SEE? I CAN'T LAST MUCH LONGER... LET ME TOUCH YOUR COAT..PLEASE!
PEANUTS
?????? MY HANDS AREN'T SHAKING ??!!??
I'M NOT DIZZY ANY MORE... MY STOMACH DOESN'T HURT.. I'M ACTUALLY HUNGRY!
I MADE IT THROUGH THE WEEKEND WITHOUT MY BLANKET! I DID IT! I DID IT!
AND I DID IT MY WAY!!

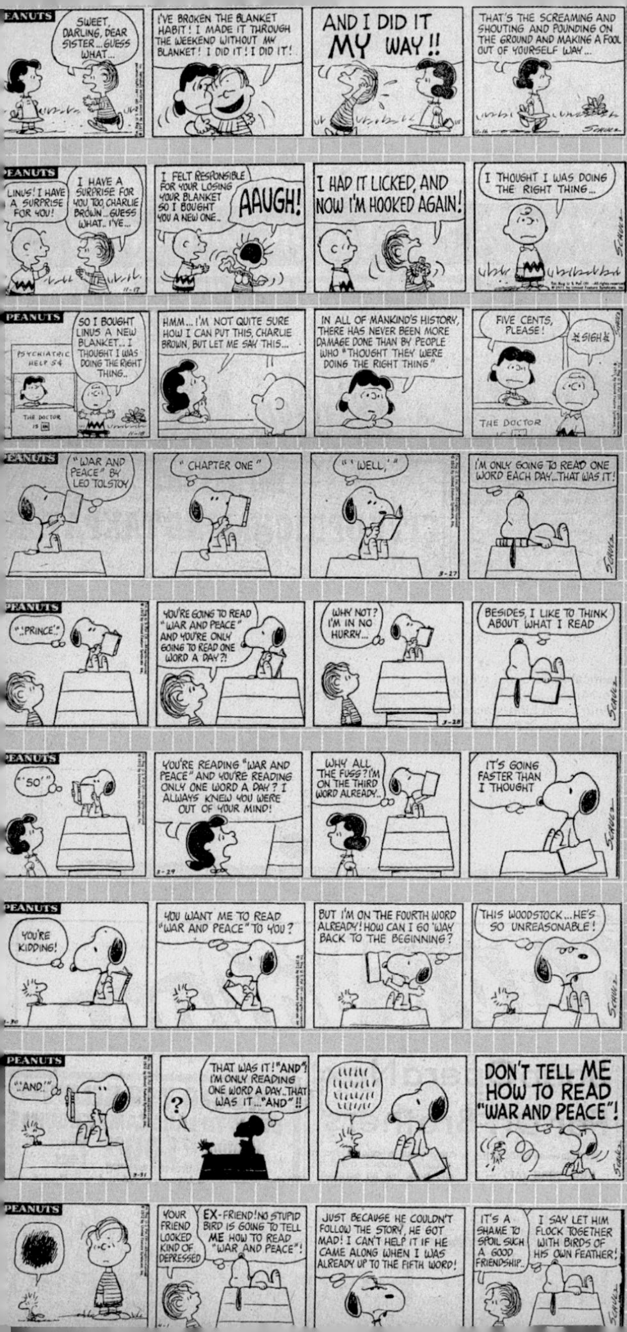
PEANUTS
SWEET, DARLING, DEAR SISTER...GUESS WHAT...
I'VE BROKEN THE BLANKET HABIT! I MADE IT THROUGH THE WEEKEND WITHOUT MY BLANKET! I DID IT! I DID IT!
AND I DID IT MY WAY!!
THAT'S THE SCREAMING AND SHOUTING AND POUNDING ON THE GROUND AND MAKING A FOOL OUT OF YOURSELF WAY...
PEANUTS
LINUS! I HAVE A SURPRISE FOR YOU!
I HAVE A SURPRISE FOR YOU, TOO, CHARLIE BROWN...GUESS WHAT...I'VE...
I FELT RESPONSIBLE FOR YOUR LOSING YOUR BLANKET SO I BOUGHT YOU A NEW ONE...
AAUGH!
I HAD IT LICKED, AND NOW I'M HOOKED AGAIN!
I THOUGHT I WAS DOING THE RIGHT THING...
PEANUTS
PSYCHIATRIC HELP 5¢
SO I BOUGHT LINUS A NEW BLANKET...I THOUGHT I WAS DOING THE RIGHT THING..
THE DOCTOR IS IN
HMM...I'M NOT QUITE SURE HOW I CAN PUT THIS, CHARLIE BROWN, BUT LET ME SAY THIS...
IN ALL OF MANKIND'S HISTORY, THERE HAS NEVER BEEN MORE DAMAGE DONE THAN BY PEOPLE WHO "THOUGHT THEY WERE DOING THE RIGHT THING"
FIVE CENTS, PLEASE!
SIGH
THE DOCTOR
PEANUTS
"WAR AND PEACE" BY LEO TOLSTOY
" CHAPTER ONE "
" 'WELL,' "
I'M ONLY GOING TO READ ONE WORD EACH DAY...THAT WAS IT!
PEANUTS
" 'PRINCE' "
YOU'RE GOING TO READ "WAR AND PEACE" AND YOU'RE ONLY GOING TO READ ONE WORD A DAY?!
WHY NOT? I'M IN NO HURRY...
BESIDES, I LIKE TO THINK ABOUT WHAT I READ
PEANUTS
" 'SO' "
YOU'RE READING "WAR AND PEACE" AND YOU'RE READING ONLY ONE WORD A DAY? I ALWAYS KNEW YOU WERE OUT OF YOUR MIND!
WHY ALL THE FUSS? I'M ON THE THIRD WORD ALREADY...
IT'S GOING FASTER THAN I THOUGHT
PEANUTS
YOU'RE KIDDING!
YOU WANT ME TO READ "WAR AND PEACE" TO YOU?
BUT I'M ON THE FOURTH WORD ALREADY! HOW CAN I GO 'WAY BACK TO THE BEGINNING?
THIS WOODSTOCK...HE'S SO UNREASONABLE!
PEANUTS
" 'AND' "
?
THAT WAS IT! "AND"! I'M ONLY READING ONE WORD A DAY..THAT WAS IT..."AND"!!
DON'T TELL ME HOW TO READ "WAR AND PEACE"!
PEANUTS
YOUR FRIEND LOOKED KIND OF DEPRESSED
EX-FRIEND! NO STUPID BIRD IS GOING TO TELL ME HOW TO READ "WAR AND PEACE"!
JUST BECAUSE HE COULDN'T FOLLOW THE STORY, HE GOT MAD! I CAN'T HELP IT IF HE CAME ALONG WHEN I WAS ALREADY UP TO THE FIFTH WORD!
IT'S A SHAME TO SPOIL SUCH A GOOD FRIENDSHIP..
I SAY LET HIM FLOCK TOGETHER WITH BIRDS OF HIS OWN FEATHER!

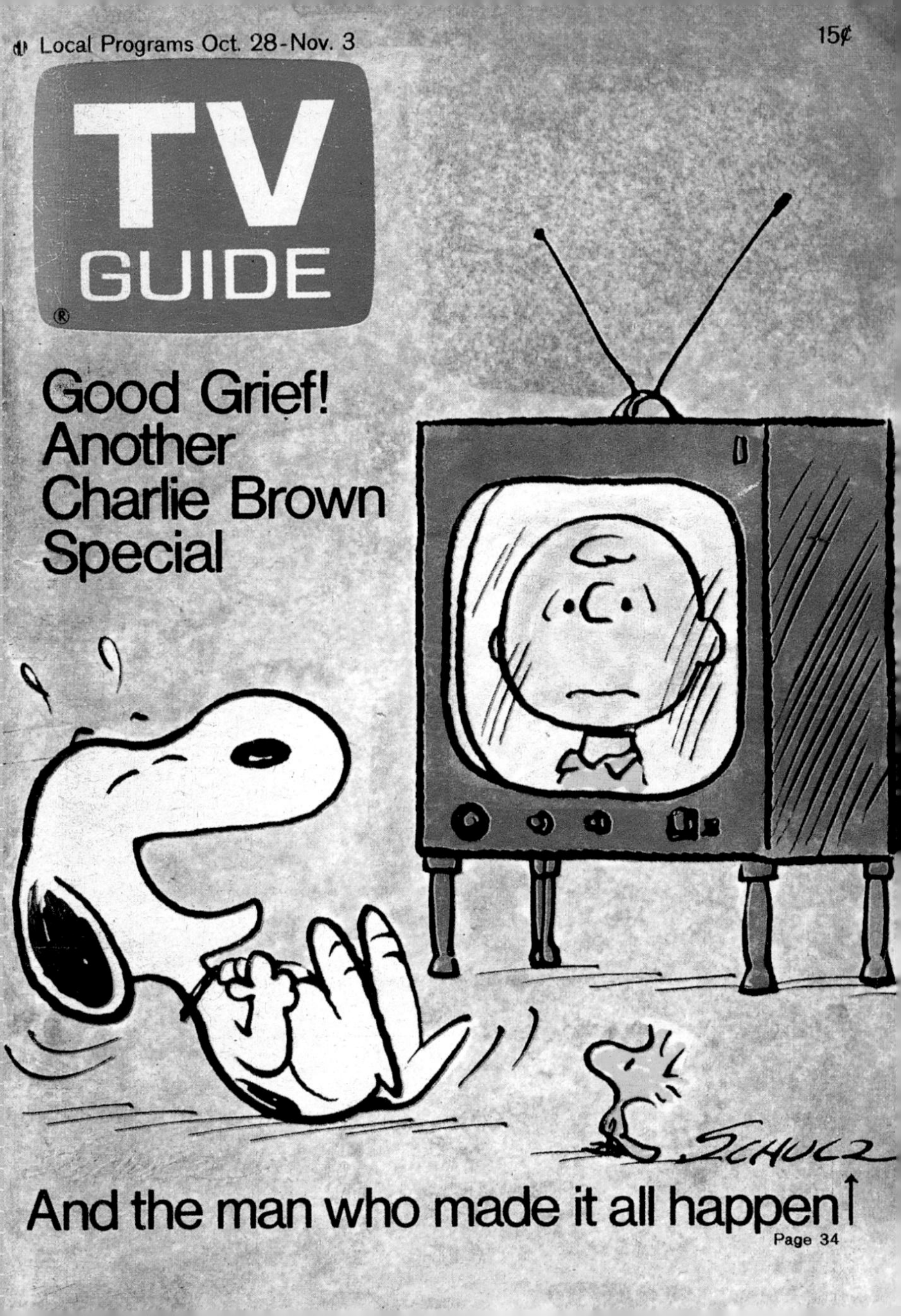
Local Programs Oct. 28-Nov. 3
15¢
TV GUIDE
Good Grief! Another Charlie Brown Special
SCHULZ
And the man who made it all happen
Page 34

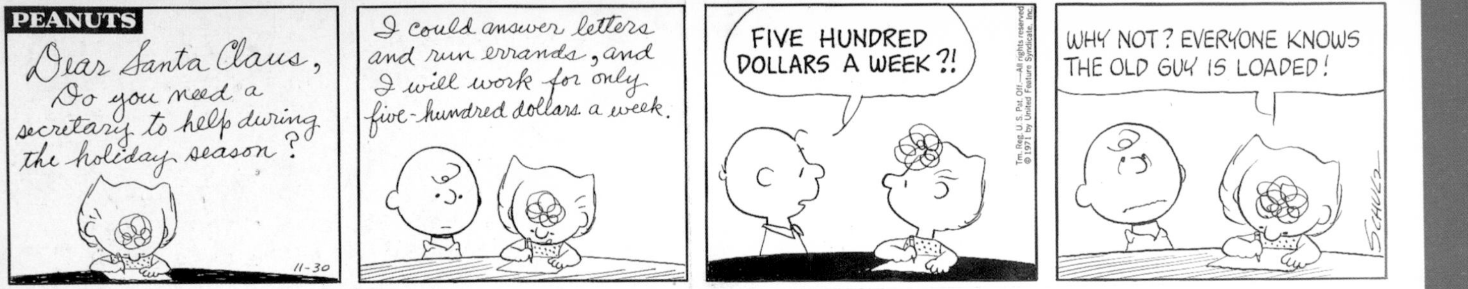
PEANUTS
Dear Santa Claus, Do you need a secretary to help during the holiday season?
11-30
I could answer letters and run errands, and I will work for only five-hundred dollars a week.
FIVE HUNDRED DOLLARS A WEEK?!
Tm. Reg. U.S. Pat. Off.—All rights reserved © 1971 by United Feature Syndicate, Inc.
WHY NOT? EVERYONE KNOWS THE OLD GUY IS LOADED!
SCHULZ

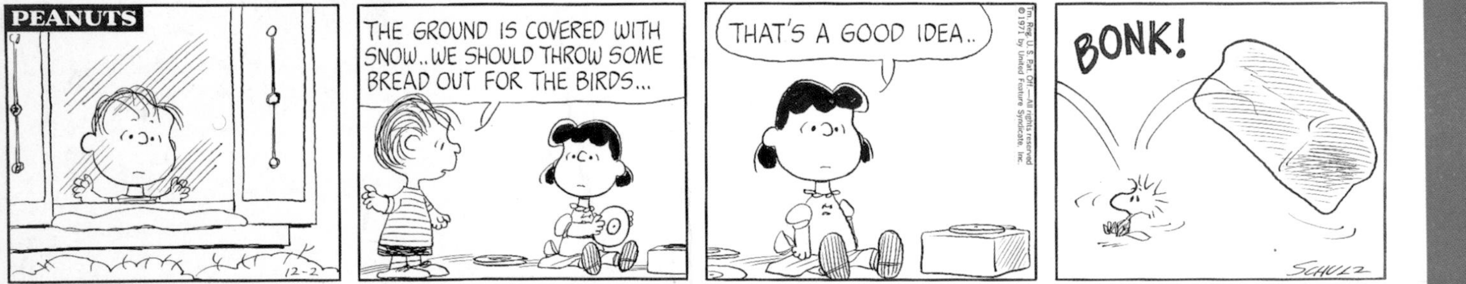
PEANUTS
12-2
THE GROUND IS COVERED WITH SNOW.. WE SHOULD THROW SOME BREAD OUT FOR THE BIRDS...
THAT'S A GOOD IDEA..
Tm. Reg. U.S. Pat. Off.—All rights reserved © 1971 by United Feature Syndicate, Inc.
BONK!
SCHULZ

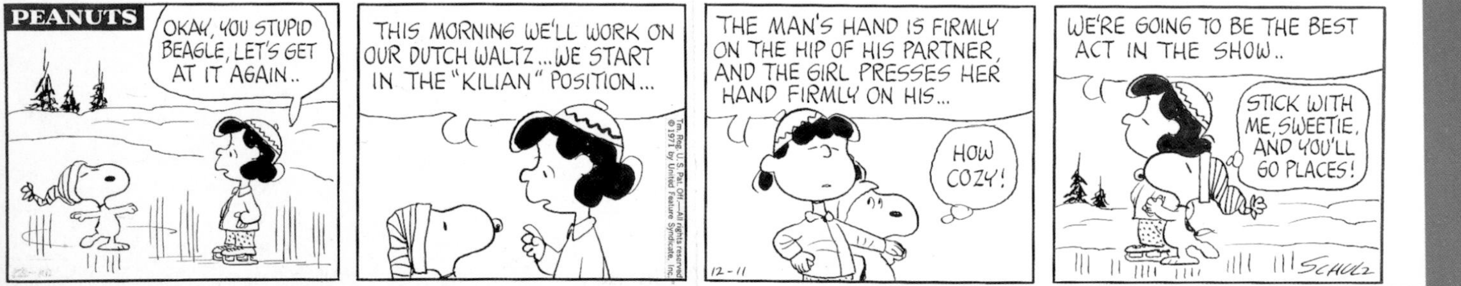
PEANUTS
OKAY, YOU STUPID BEAGLE, LET'S GET AT IT AGAIN..
THIS MORNING WE'LL WORK ON OUR DUTCH WALTZ ... WE START IN THE "KILIAN" POSITION...
Tm. Reg. U.S. Pat. Off.—All rights reserved © 1971 by United Feature Syndicate, Inc.
THE MAN'S HAND IS FIRMLY ON THE HIP OF HIS PARTNER, AND THE GIRL PRESSES HER HAND FIRMLY ON HIS...
HOW COZY!
12-11
WE'RE GOING TO BE THE BEST ACT IN THE SHOW..
STICK WITH ME, SWEETIE, AND YOU'LL GO PLACES!
SCHULZ

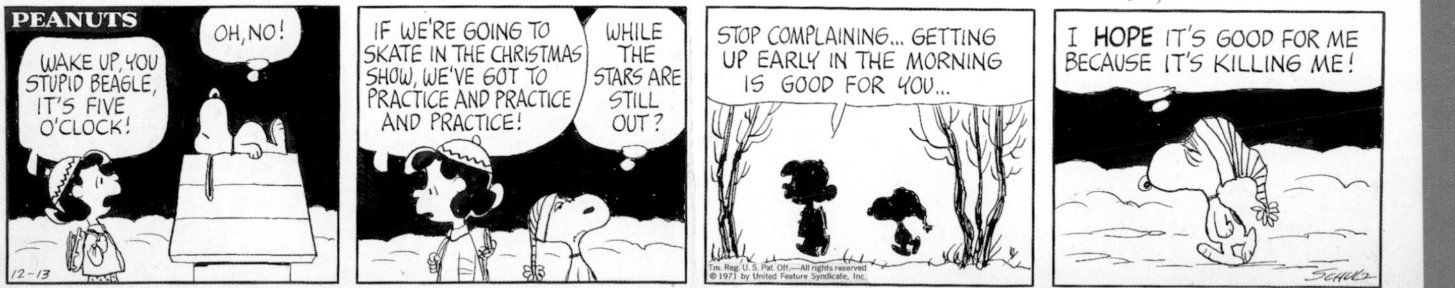
PEANUTS
WAKE UP, YOU STUPID BEAGLE, IT'S FIVE O'CLOCK!
OH, NO!
12-13
IF WE'RE GOING TO SKATE IN THE CHRISTMAS SHOW, WE'VE GOT TO PRACTICE AND PRACTICE AND PRACTICE!
WHILE THE STARS ARE STILL OUT?
STOP COMPLAINING... GETTING UP EARLY IN THE MORNING IS GOOD FOR YOU...
Tm. Reg. U.S. Pat. Off.—All rights reserved © 1971 by United Feature Syndicate, Inc.
I HOPE IT'S GOOD FOR ME BECAUSE IT'S KILLING ME!
SCHULZ

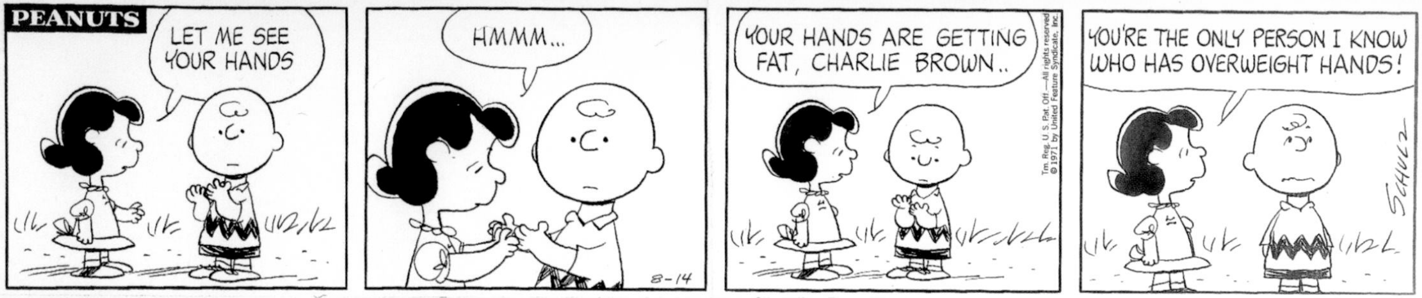
PEANUTS
LET ME SEE YOUR HANDS
HMMM...
8-14
YOUR HANDS ARE GETTING FAT, CHARLIE BROWN..
Tm. Reg. U. S. Pat. Off.—All rights reserved © 1971 by United Feature Syndicate, Inc.
YOU'RE THE ONLY PERSON I KNOW WHO HAS OVERWEIGHT HANDS!
SCHULZ

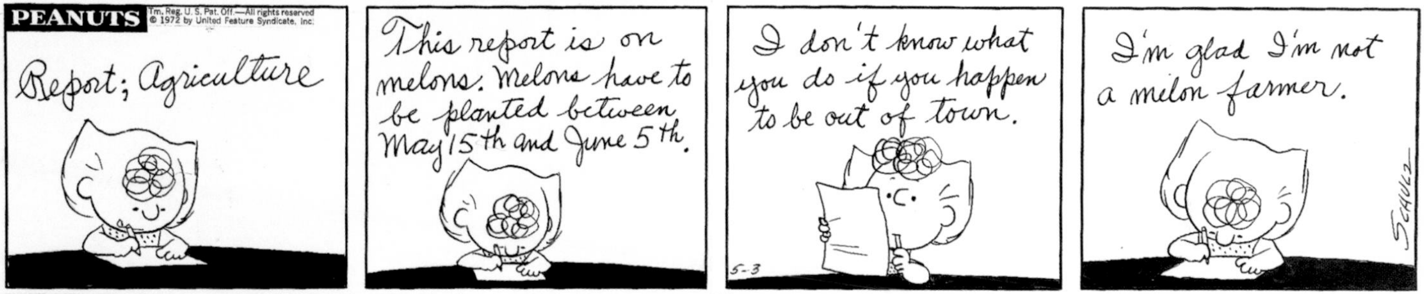
PEANUTS
Tm. Reg. U. S. Pat. Off.—All rights reserved © 1972 by United Feature Syndicate, Inc.
Report; Agriculture
This report is on melons. Melons have to be planted between May 15th and June 5th.
I don't know what you do if you happen to be out of town.
5-3
I'm glad I'm not a melon farmer.
SCHULZ

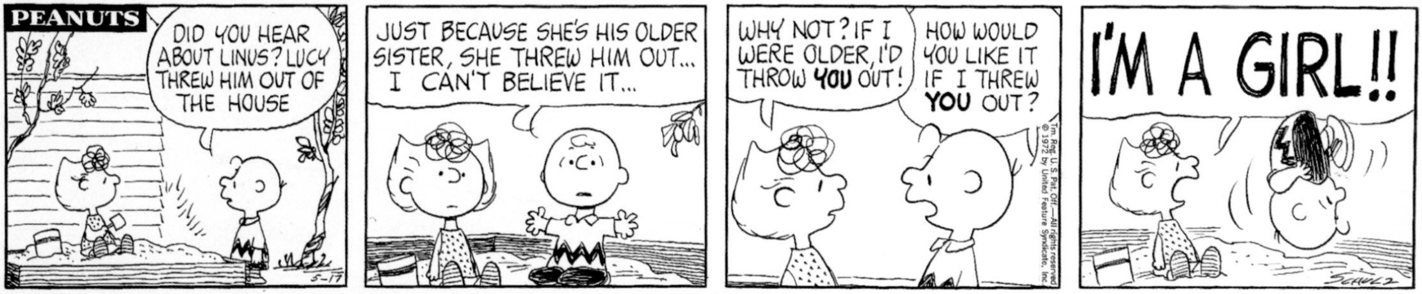
PEANUTS
DID YOU HEAR ABOUT LINUS? LUCY THREW HIM OUT OF THE HOUSE
5-17
JUST BECAUSE SHE'S HIS OLDER SISTER, SHE THREW HIM OUT... I CAN'T BELIEVE IT...
WHY NOT? IF I WERE OLDER, I'D THROW YOU OUT!
HOW WOULD YOU LIKE IT IF I THREW YOU OUT?
Tm. Reg. U. S. Pat. Off.—All rights reserved © 1972 by United Feature Syndicate, Inc.
I'M A GIRL!!
SCHULZ

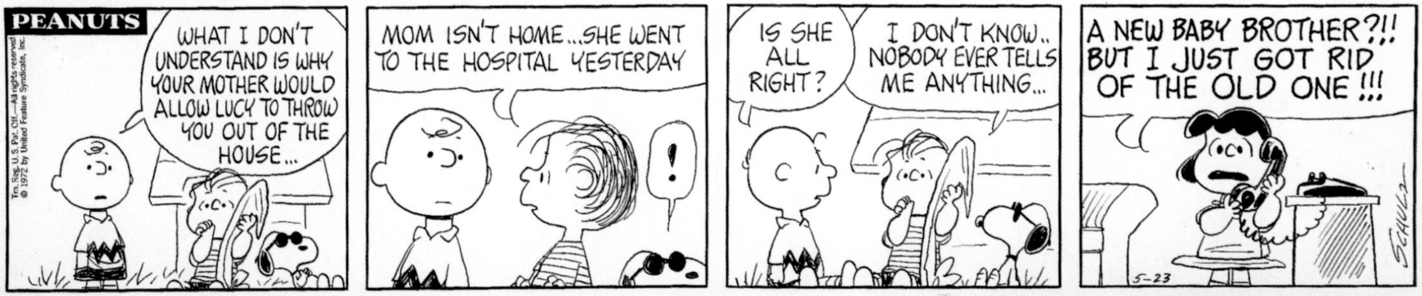
PEANUTS
Tm. Reg. U. S. Pat. Off.—All rights reserved © 1972 by United Feature Syndicate, Inc.
WHAT I DON'T UNDERSTAND IS WHY YOUR MOTHER WOULD ALLOW LUCY TO THROW YOU OUT OF THE HOUSE...
MOM ISN'T HOME...SHE WENT TO THE HOSPITAL YESTERDAY
!
IS SHE ALL RIGHT?
I DON'T KNOW.. NOBODY EVER TELLS ME ANYTHING...
A NEW BABY BROTHER?!! BUT I JUST GOT RID OF THE OLD ONE!!!
5-23
SCHULZ

"I think the Little League setup is deplorable," said Schulz in 1973. "First, the players are judged by age. Age has almost nothing to do with evaluating or placing players. If there's a 12-year-old kid who stands 6 feet and can throw the ball so fast the other kids can't see it, he shouldn't be allowed to dominate the game. He should be pushed up to a higher league, where he fits in."

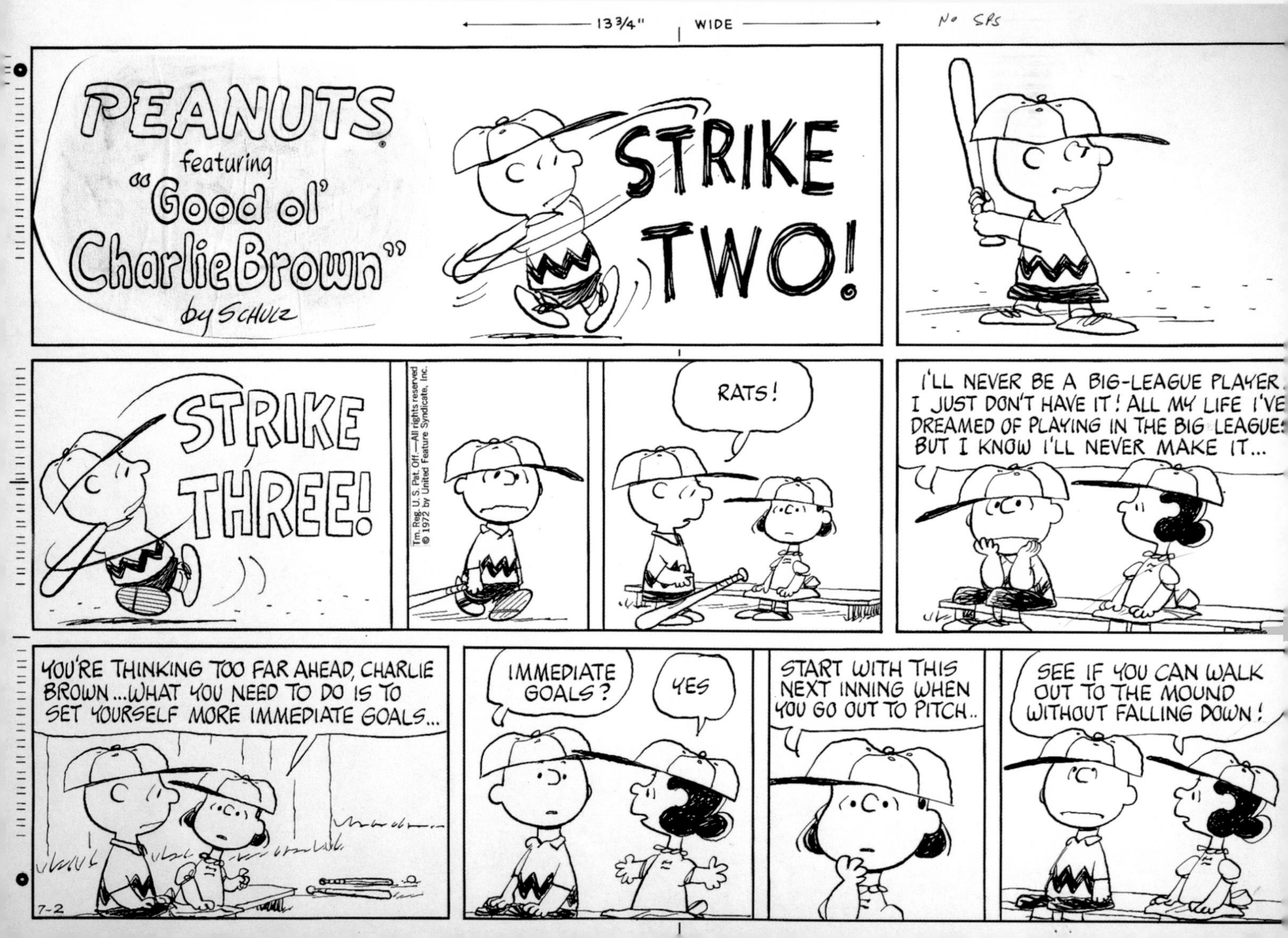
13 3/4" WIDE
No SPS
PEANUTS featuring "Good ol' Charlie Brown" by SCHULZ
STRIKE TWO!
STRIKE THREE!
Tm. Reg. U.S. Pat. Off.—All rights reserved © 1972 by United Feature Syndicate, Inc.
RATS!
I'LL NEVER BE A BIG-LEAGUE PLAYER. I JUST DON'T HAVE IT! ALL MY LIFE I'VE DREAMED OF PLAYING IN THE BIG LEAGUES BUT I KNOW I'LL NEVER MAKE IT...
YOU'RE THINKING TOO FAR AHEAD, CHARLIE BROWN...WHAT YOU NEED TO DO IS TO SET YOURSELF MORE IMMEDIATE GOALS...
IMMEDIATE GOALS?
YES
START WITH THIS NEXT INNING WHEN YOU GO OUT TO PITCH..
SEE IF YOU CAN WALK OUT TO THE MOUND WITHOUT FALLING DOWN!
7-2

Nor did he share the American obsession with winning. "No sooner does the season start than we begin to record how far a team is out of first place. A game between two teams in 7th and 10th place can be just as exciting as any game. But all we're worrying about is who wins. It should be the plays, great goals being scored, great baskets being made, great overhand shots hit. These are the things that count in sports."

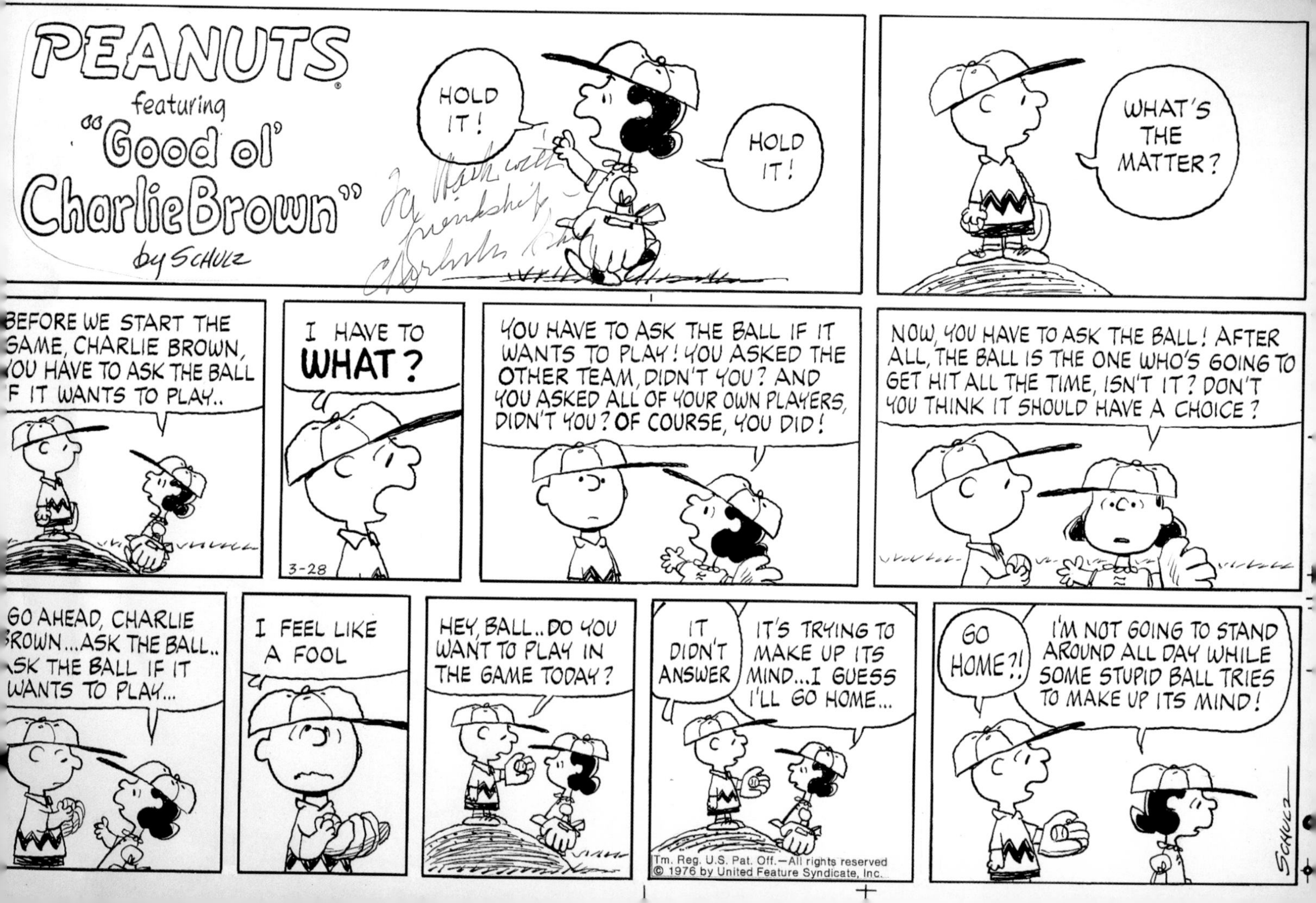
PEANUTS
featuring "Good ol' Charlie Brown"
by SCHULZ
HOLD IT!
HOLD IT!
WHAT'S THE MATTER?
BEFORE WE START THE GAME, CHARLIE BROWN, YOU HAVE TO ASK THE BALL IF IT WANTS TO PLAY..
I HAVE TO WHAT?
3-28
YOU HAVE TO ASK THE BALL IF IT WANTS TO PLAY! YOU ASKED THE OTHER TEAM, DIDN'T YOU? AND YOU ASKED ALL OF YOUR OWN PLAYERS, DIDN'T YOU? OF COURSE, YOU DID!
NOW, YOU HAVE TO ASK THE BALL! AFTER ALL, THE BALL IS THE ONE WHO'S GOING TO GET HIT ALL THE TIME, ISN'T IT? DON'T YOU THINK IT SHOULD HAVE A CHOICE?
GO AHEAD, CHARLIE BROWN...ASK THE BALL.. ASK THE BALL IF IT WANTS TO PLAY...
I FEEL LIKE A FOOL
HEY, BALL..DO YOU WANT TO PLAY IN THE GAME TODAY?
IT DIDN'T ANSWER
IT'S TRYING TO MAKE UP ITS MIND...I GUESS I'LL GO HOME...
GO HOME?!
I'M NOT GOING TO STAND AROUND ALL DAY WHILE SOME STUPID BALL TRIES TO MAKE UP ITS MIND!
SCHULZ
Tm. Reg. U.S. Pat. Off.—All rights reserved
© 1976 by United Feature Syndicate, Inc.

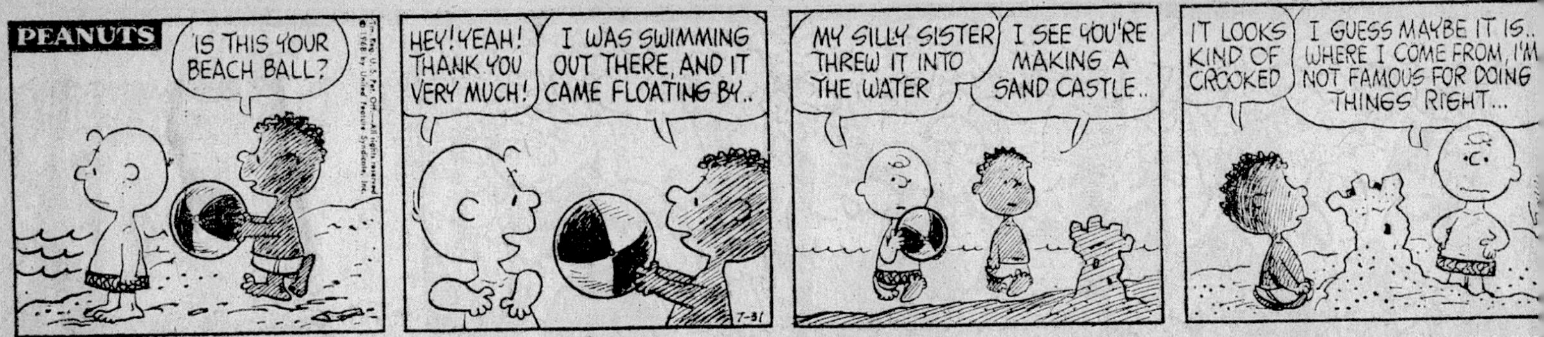
PEANUTS
IS THIS YOUR BEACH BALL?
HEY! YEAH! THANK YOU VERY MUCH!
I WAS SWIMMING OUT THERE, AND IT CAME FLOATING BY..
MY SILLY SISTER THREW IT INTO THE WATER
I SEE YOU'RE MAKING A SAND CASTLE..
IT LOOKS KIND OF CROOKED
I GUESS MAYBE IT IS.. WHERE I COME FROM, I'M NOT FAMOUS FOR DOING THINGS RIGHT...

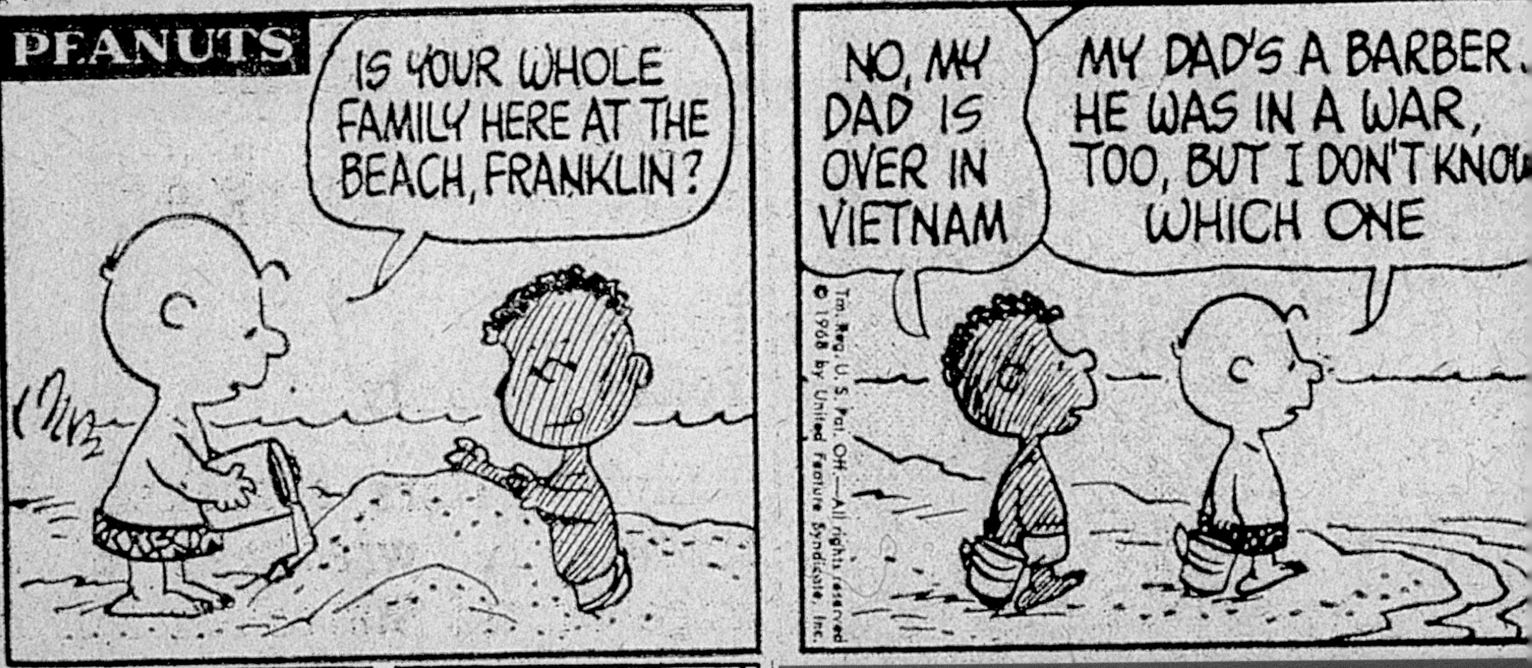
PEANUTS
IS YOUR WHOLE FAMILY HERE AT THE BEACH, FRANKLIN?
NO, MY DAD IS OVER IN VIETNAM
MY DAD'S A BARBER. HE WAS IN A WAR, TOO, BUT I DON'T KNOW WHICH ONE
Tm. Reg. U. S. Pat. Off.—All rights reserved © 1968 by United Feature Syndicate, Inc.

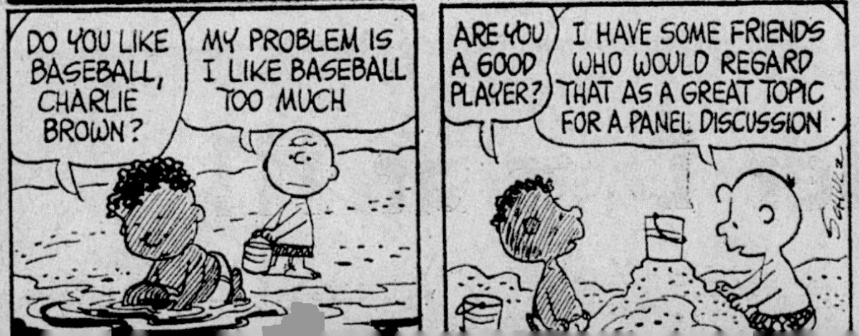
DO YOU LIKE BASEBALL, CHARLIE BROWN?
MY PROBLEM IS I LIKE BASEBALL TOO MUCH
ARE YOU A GOOD PLAYER?
I HAVE SOME FRIENDS WHO WOULD REGARD THAT AS A GREAT TOPIC FOR A PANEL DISCUSSION
SCHULZ

Franklin, the strip's first African-American, debuted in 1968. Not meant as a comment on any specific facet of urban culture, he was just a *Peanuts* character who happened to be black. Even at that time, it was a problem for some. "I got a letter from one southern editor," Schulz remembered in 1997, "who said something about 'I don't mind you having a black character, but please don't show them in school together.' Because I had shown Franklin sitting in front of Peppermint Patty. I didn't even answer him."

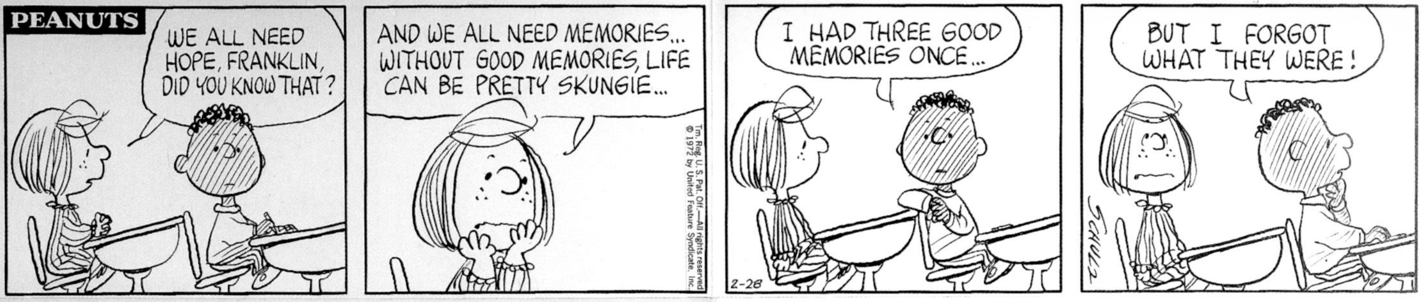
PEANUTS
WE ALL NEED HOPE, FRANKLIN, DID YOU KNOW THAT?
AND WE ALL NEED MEMORIES... WITHOUT GOOD MEMORIES, LIFE CAN BE PRETTY SKUNGIE...
Tm. Reg. U.S. Pat. Off.—All rights reserved © 1972 by United Feature Syndicate, Inc.
I HAD THREE GOOD MEMORIES ONCE...
2-28
BUT I FORGOT WHAT THEY WERE!
SCHULZ

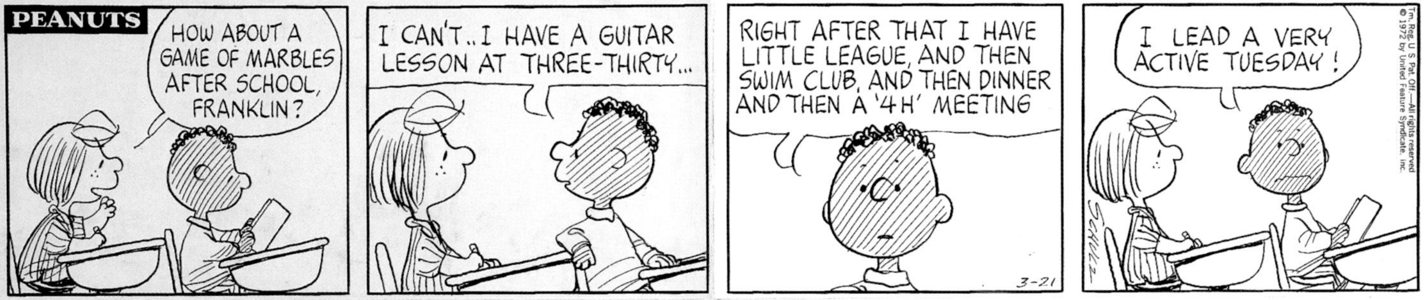
PEANUTS
HOW ABOUT A GAME OF MARBLES AFTER SCHOOL, FRANKLIN?
I CAN'T..I HAVE A GUITAR LESSON AT THREE-THIRTY...
RIGHT AFTER THAT I HAVE LITTLE LEAGUE, AND THEN SWIM CLUB, AND THEN DINNER AND THEN A '4 H' MEETING
3-21
I LEAD A VERY ACTIVE TUESDAY!
SCHULZ
Tm. Reg. U S Pat. Off.—All rights reserved © 1972 by United Feature Syndicate, Inc.

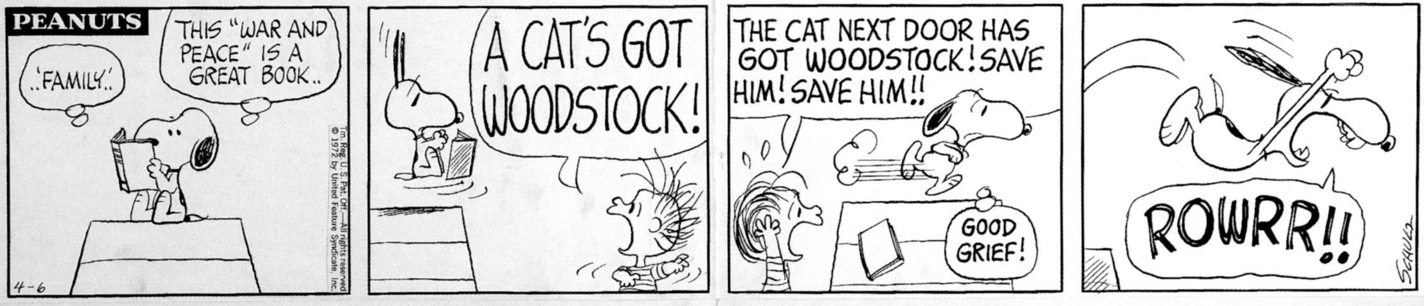
PEANUTS
THIS "WAR AND PEACE" IS A GREAT BOOK..
..'FAMILY.'..
4-6
Tm. Reg. U. S. Pat. Off.—All rights reserved © 1972 by United Feature Syndicate, Inc.
A CAT'S GOT WOODSTOCK!
THE CAT NEXT DOOR HAS GOT WOODSTOCK! SAVE HIM! SAVE HIM!!
GOOD GRIEF!
ROWRR!!
SCHULZ

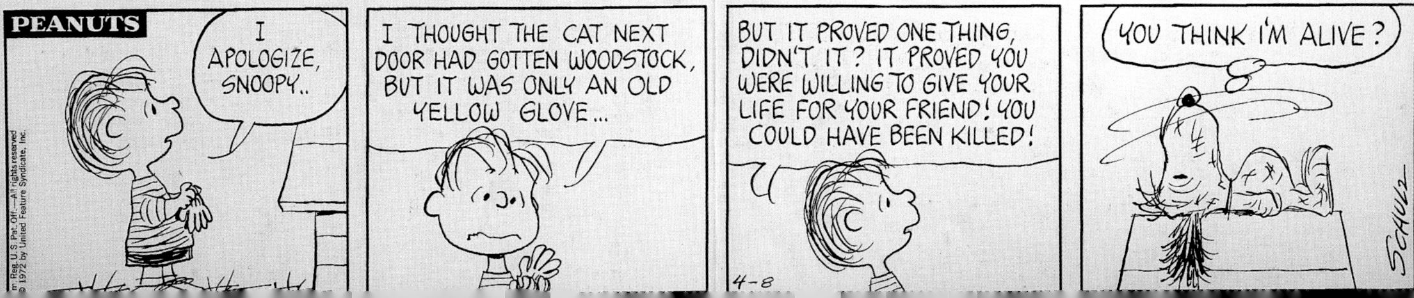
PEANUTS
I APOLOGIZE, SNOOPY..
Tm. Reg. U.S. Pat. Off.—All rights reserved © 1972 by United Feature Syndicate, Inc.
I THOUGHT THE CAT NEXT DOOR HAD GOTTEN WOODSTOCK, BUT IT WAS ONLY AN OLD YELLOW GLOVE...
BUT IT PROVED ONE THING, DIDN'T IT? IT PROVED YOU WERE WILLING TO GIVE YOUR LIFE FOR YOUR FRIEND! YOU COULD HAVE BEEN KILLED!
4-8
YOU THINK I'M ALIVE?
SCHULZ

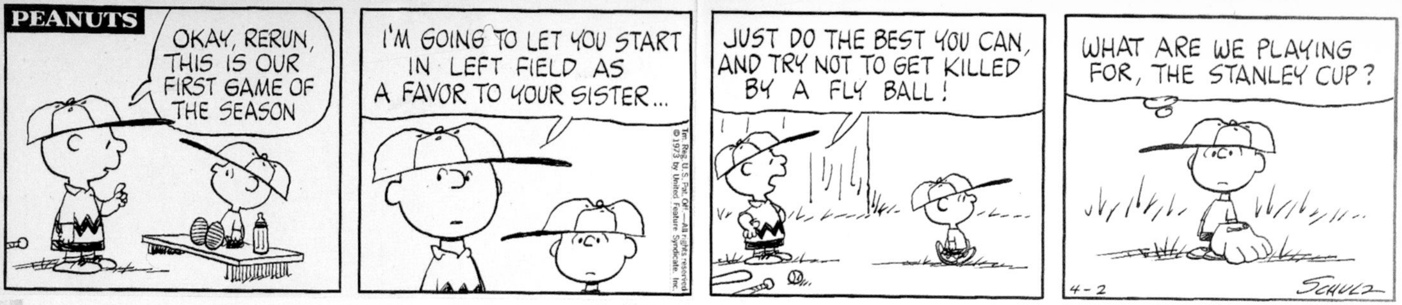
PEANUTS
OKAY, RERUN, THIS IS OUR FIRST GAME OF THE SEASON
I'M GOING TO LET YOU START IN LEFT FIELD AS A FAVOR TO YOUR SISTER...
Tm. Reg. U.S. Pat. Off.—All rights reserved ©1973 by United Feature Syndicate, Inc.
JUST DO THE BEST YOU CAN, AND TRY NOT TO GET KILLED BY A FLY BALL!
WHAT ARE WE PLAYING FOR, THE STANLEY CUP?
4-2
SCHULZ

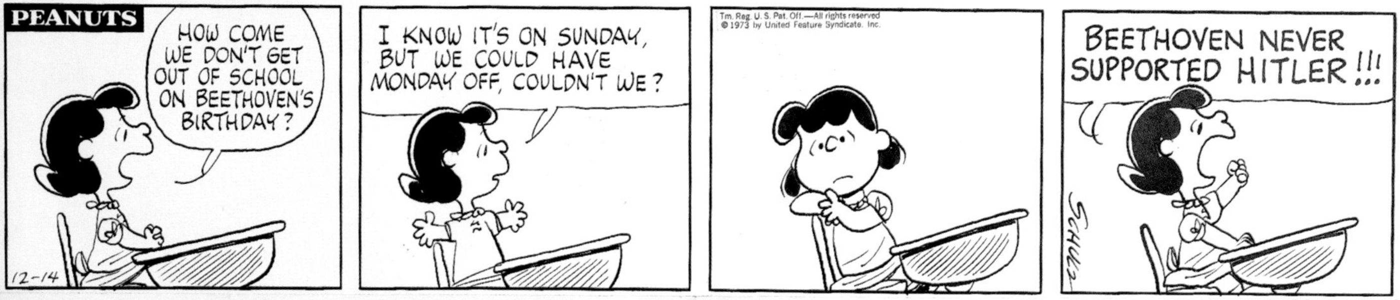
PEANUTS
HOW COME WE DON'T GET OUT OF SCHOOL ON BEETHOVEN'S BIRTHDAY?
12-14
I KNOW IT'S ON SUNDAY, BUT WE COULD HAVE MONDAY OFF, COULDN'T WE?
Tm. Reg. U.S. Pat. Off.—All rights reserved ©1973 by United Feature Syndicate, Inc.
BEETHOVEN NEVER SUPPORTED HITLER!!!
SCHULZ

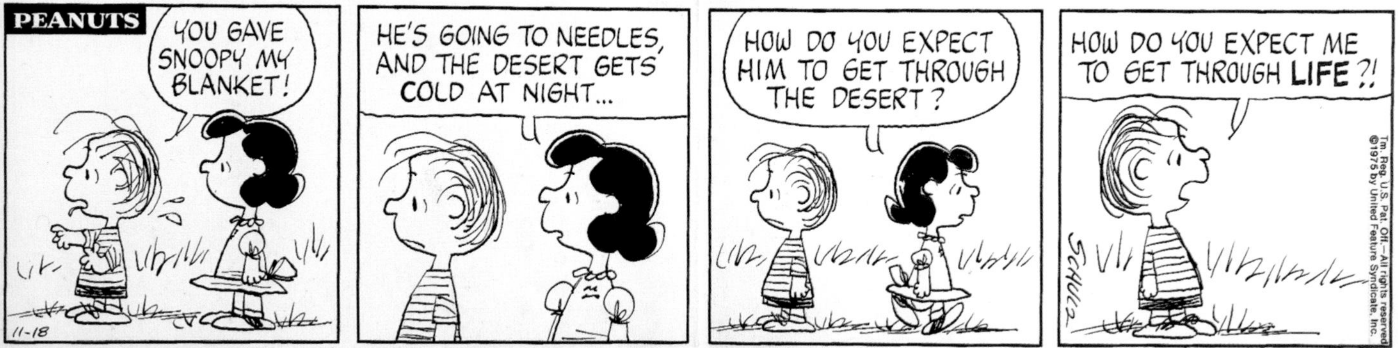
PEANUTS
YOU GAVE SNOOPY MY BLANKET!
11-18
HE'S GOING TO NEEDLES, AND THE DESERT GETS COLD AT NIGHT...
HOW DO YOU EXPECT HIM TO GET THROUGH THE DESERT?
HOW DO YOU EXPECT ME TO GET THROUGH LIFE?!
SCHULZ
Tm. Reg. U.S. Pat. Off.—All rights reserved ©1975 by United Feature Syndicate, Inc.

To John with every best wish - Charles M. Schulz

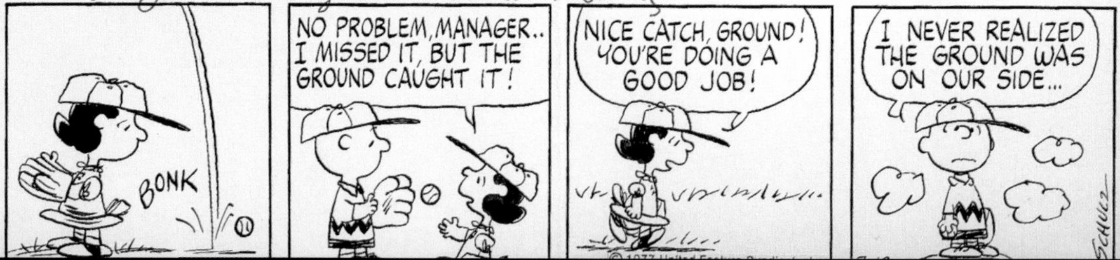
BONK
NO PROBLEM, MANAGER.. I MISSED IT, BUT THE GROUND CAUGHT IT!
NICE CATCH, GROUND! YOU'RE DOING A GOOD JOB!
I NEVER REALIZED THE GROUND WAS ON OUR SIDE...
SCHULZ

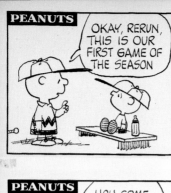

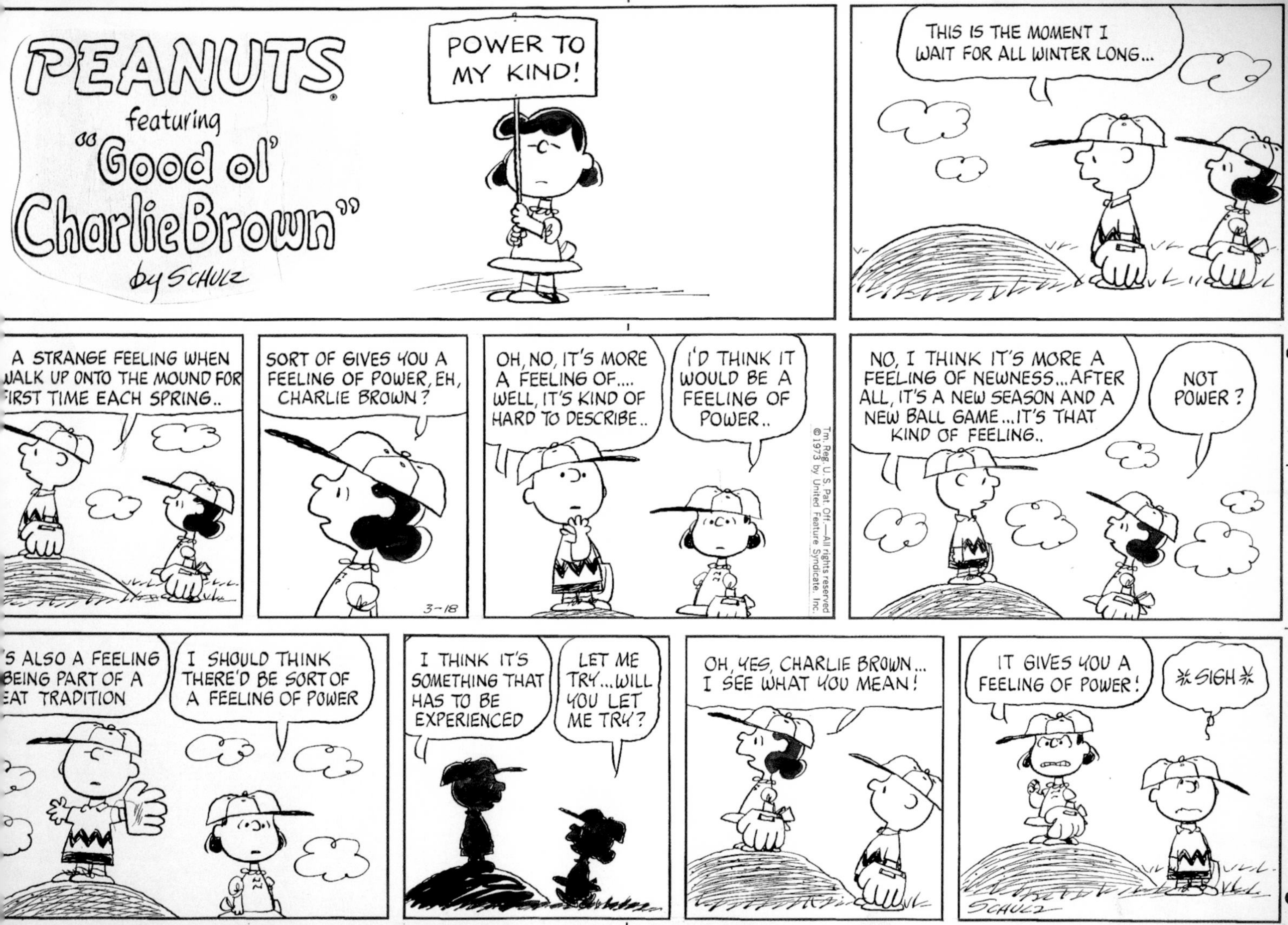
PEANUTS
featuring "Good ol' Charlie Brown"
by SCHULZ
POWER TO MY KIND!
THIS IS THE MOMENT I WAIT FOR ALL WINTER LONG...
A STRANGE FEELING WHEN
WALK UP ONTO THE MOUND FOR
FIRST TIME EACH SPRING..
SORT OF GIVES YOU A FEELING OF POWER, EH, CHARLIE BROWN?
3-18
OH, NO, IT'S MORE A FEELING OF.... WELL, IT'S KIND OF HARD TO DESCRIBE..
I'D THINK IT WOULD BE A FEELING OF POWER..
Tm. Reg. U.S. Pat. Off.—All rights reserved © 1973 by United Feature Syndicate, Inc.
NO, I THINK IT'S MORE A FEELING OF NEWNESS...AFTER ALL, IT'S A NEW SEASON AND A NEW BALL GAME...IT'S THAT KIND OF FEELING..
NOT POWER?
'S ALSO A FEELING
BEING PART OF A
EAT TRADITION
I SHOULD THINK THERE'D BE SORT OF A FEELING OF POWER
I THINK IT'S SOMETHING THAT HAS TO BE EXPERIENCED
LET ME TRY...WILL YOU LET ME TRY?
OH, YES, CHARLIE BROWN... I SEE WHAT YOU MEAN!
IT GIVES YOU A FEELING OF POWER!
SIGH
SCHULZ

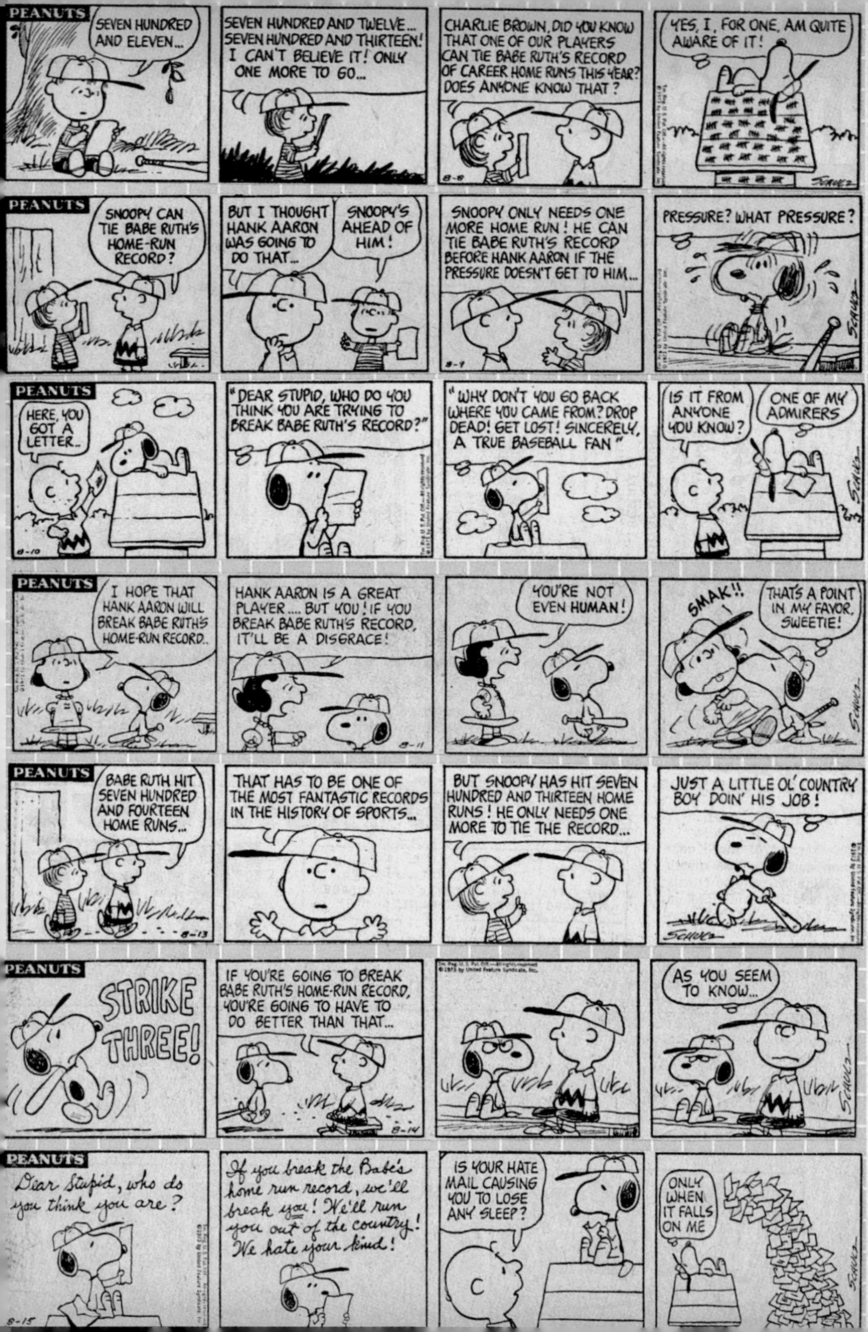
PEANUTS
SEVEN HUNDRED AND ELEVEN...
SEVEN HUNDRED AND TWELVE... SEVEN HUNDRED AND THIRTEEN! I CAN'T BELIEVE IT! ONLY ONE MORE TO GO...
CHARLIE BROWN, DID YOU KNOW THAT ONE OF OUR PLAYERS CAN TIE BABE RUTH'S RECORD OF CAREER HOME RUNS THIS YEAR? DOES ANYONE KNOW THAT?
YES, I, FOR ONE, AM QUITE AWARE OF IT!
SNOOPY CAN TIE BABE RUTH'S HOME-RUN RECORD?
BUT I THOUGHT HANK AARON WAS GOING TO DO THAT...
SNOOPY'S AHEAD OF HIM!
SNOOPY ONLY NEEDS ONE MORE HOME RUN! HE CAN TIE BABE RUTH'S RECORD BEFORE HANK AARON IF THE PRESSURE DOESN'T GET TO HIM...
PRESSURE? WHAT PRESSURE?
HERE, YOU GOT A LETTER..
"DEAR STUPID, WHO DO YOU THINK YOU ARE TRYING TO BREAK BABE RUTH'S RECORD?"
"WHY DON'T YOU GO BACK WHERE YOU CAME FROM? DROP DEAD! GET LOST! SINCERELY, A TRUE BASEBALL FAN"
IS IT FROM ANYONE YOU KNOW?
ONE OF MY ADMIRERS
I HOPE THAT HANK AARON WILL BREAK BABE RUTH'S HOME-RUN RECORD..
HANK AARON IS A GREAT PLAYER.... BUT YOU! IF YOU BREAK BABE RUTH'S RECORD, IT'LL BE A DISGRACE!
YOU'RE NOT EVEN HUMAN!
SMAK!!
THAT'S A POINT IN MY FAVOR, SWEETIE!
BABE RUTH HIT SEVEN HUNDRED AND FOURTEEN HOME RUNS...
THAT HAS TO BE ONE OF THE MOST FANTASTIC RECORDS IN THE HISTORY OF SPORTS...
BUT SNOOPY HAS HIT SEVEN HUNDRED AND THIRTEEN HOME RUNS! HE ONLY NEEDS ONE MORE TO TIE THE RECORD...
JUST A LITTLE OL' COUNTRY BOY DOIN' HIS JOB!
STRIKE THREE!
IF YOU'RE GOING TO BREAK BABE RUTH'S HOME-RUN RECORD, YOU'RE GOING TO HAVE TO DO BETTER THAN THAT...
AS YOU SEEM TO KNOW...
Dear Stupid, who do you think you are?
If you break the Babe's home run record, we'll break you! We'll run you out of the country! We hate your kind!
IS YOUR HATE MAIL CAUSING YOU TO LOSE ANY SLEEP?
ONLY WHEN IT FALLS ON ME

Peanuts team rosters, over the years:
Pitcher/Manager: Charlie Brown, Catcher: Schroeder, First Base: Shermy, Second Base: Linus (and Pig-Pen, at least once), Third base: Pig-Pen (and Violet, at least once), Shortstop: Snoopy (also a sometime outfielder), Left Field: Patty (and Rerun, once), Center Field: Frieda (and Violet or Lucy, on occasion), Right Field: Lucy.

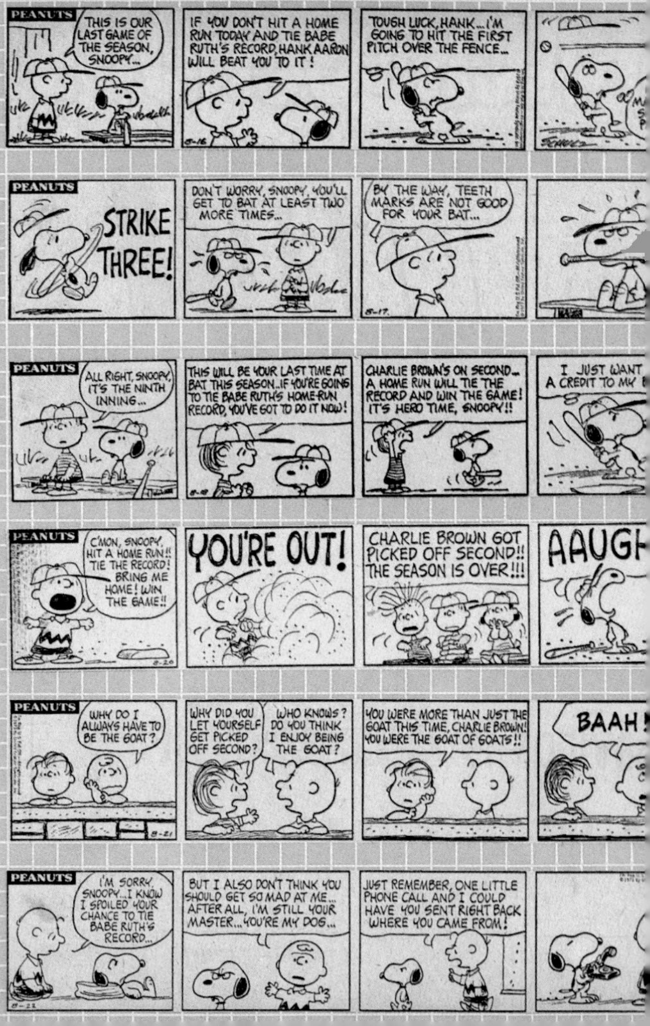
THIS IS OUR LAST GAME OF THE SEASON, SNOOPY...
IF YOU DON'T HIT A HOME RUN TODAY AND TIE BABE RUTH'S RECORD, HANK AARON WILL BEAT YOU TO IT!
TOUGH LUCK, HANK... I'M GOING TO HIT THE FIRST PITCH OVER THE FENCE...
STRIKE THREE!
DON'T WORRY, SNOOPY, YOU'LL GET TO BAT AT LEAST TWO MORE TIMES...
BY THE WAY, TEETH MARKS ARE NOT GOOD FOR YOUR BAT...
ALL RIGHT, SNOOPY, IT'S THE NINTH INNING...
THIS WILL BE YOUR LAST TIME AT BAT THIS SEASON..IF YOU'RE GOING TO TIE BABE RUTH'S HOME-RUN RECORD, YOU'VE GOT TO DO IT NOW!
CHARLIE BROWN'S ON SECOND... A HOME RUN WILL TIE THE RECORD AND WIN THE GAME! IT'S HERO TIME, SNOOPY!!
I JUST WANT A CREDIT TO MY
C'MON, SNOOPY, HIT A HOME RUN!! TIE THE RECORD! BRING ME HOME! WIN THE GAME!!
YOU'RE OUT!
CHARLIE BROWN GOT PICKED OFF SECOND!! THE SEASON IS OVER!!!
WHY DO I ALWAYS HAVE TO BE THE GOAT?
WHY DID YOU LET YOURSELF GET PICKED OFF SECOND?
WHO KNOWS? DO YOU THINK I ENJOY BEING THE GOAT?
YOU WERE MORE THAN JUST THE GOAT THIS TIME, CHARLIE BROWN! YOU WERE THE GOAT OF GOATS!!
BAAH!
I'M SORRY, SNOOPY...I KNOW I SPOILED YOUR CHANCE TO TIE BABE RUTH'S RECORD...
BUT I ALSO DON'T THINK YOU SHOULD GET SO MAD AT ME... AFTER ALL, I'M STILL YOUR MASTER... YOU'RE MY DOG...
JUST REMEMBER, ONE LITTLE PHONE CALL AND I COULD HAVE YOU SENT RIGHT BACK WHERE YOU CAME FROM!

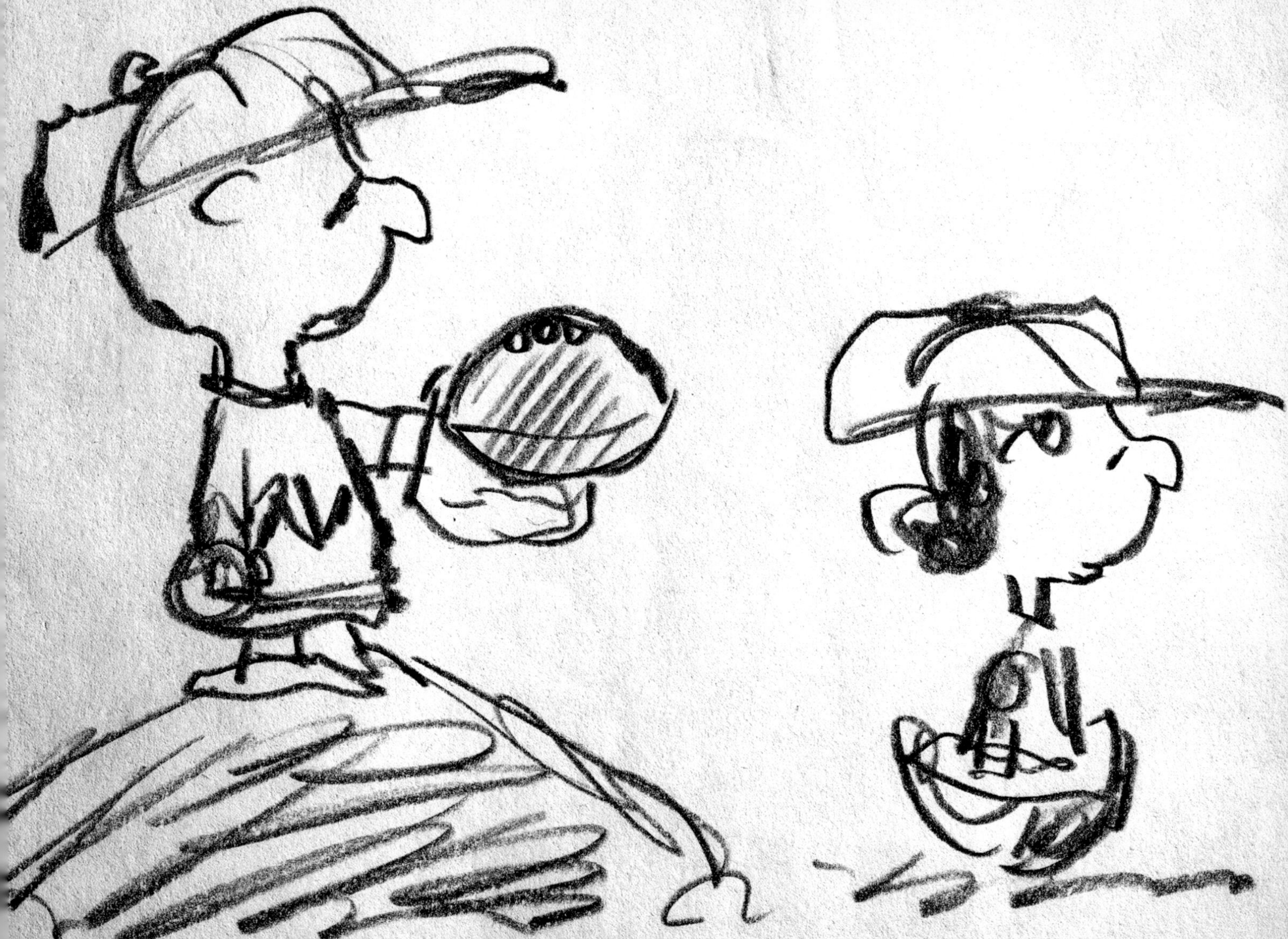

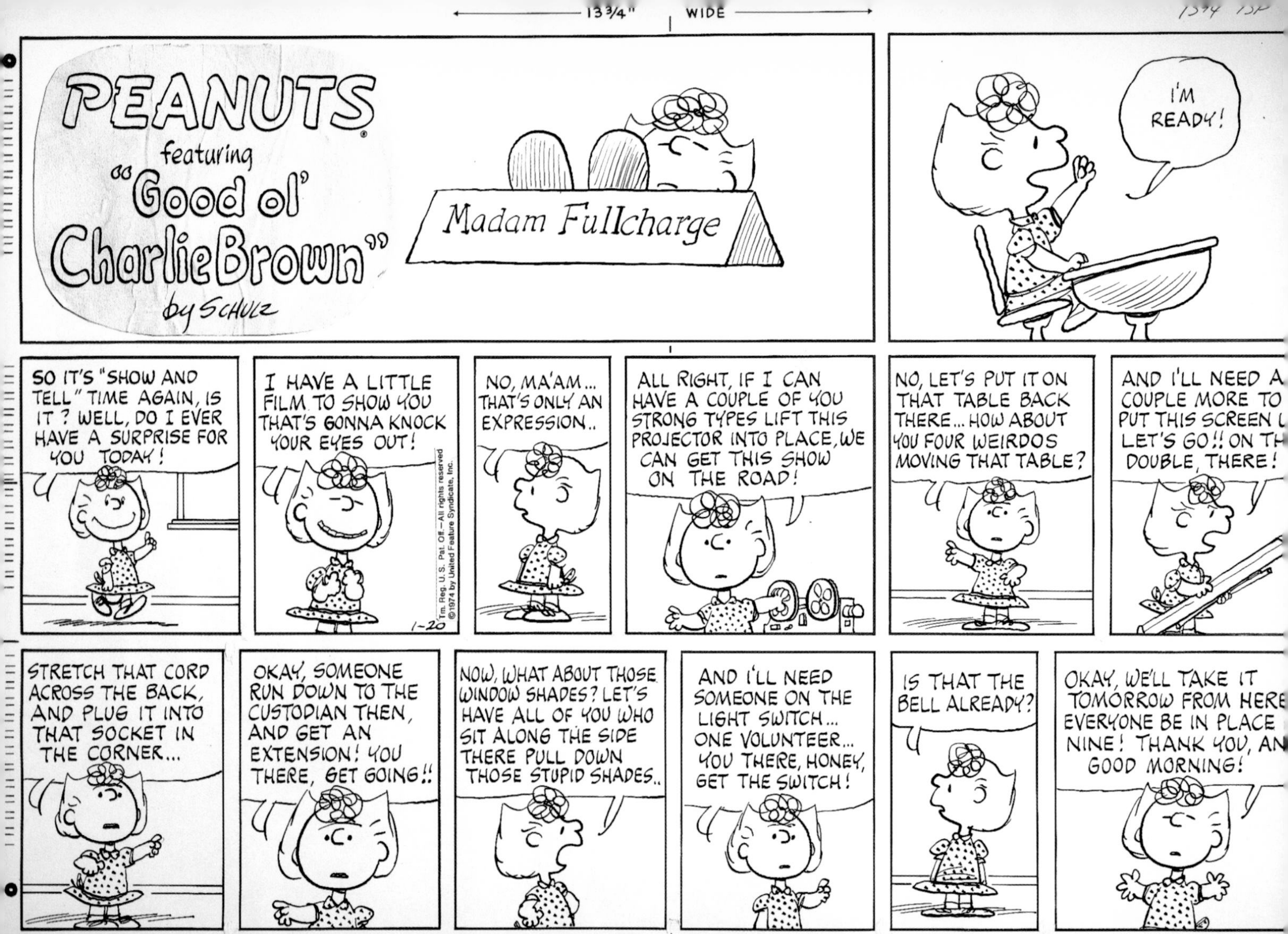
PEANUTS
featuring "Good ol' Charlie Brown"
by SCHULZ
Madam Fullcharge
I'M READY!
SO IT'S "SHOW AND TELL" TIME AGAIN, IS IT? WELL, DO I EVER HAVE A SURPRISE FOR YOU TODAY!
I HAVE A LITTLE FILM TO SHOW YOU THAT'S GONNA KNOCK YOUR EYES OUT!
Tm. Reg. U. S. Pat. Off.—All rights reserved
© 1974 by United Feature Syndicate, Inc.
1-20
NO, MA'AM... THAT'S ONLY AN EXPRESSION..
ALL RIGHT, IF I CAN HAVE A COUPLE OF YOU STRONG TYPES LIFT THIS PROJECTOR INTO PLACE, WE CAN GET THIS SHOW ON THE ROAD!
NO, LET'S PUT IT ON THAT TABLE BACK THERE... HOW ABOUT YOU FOUR WEIRDOS MOVING THAT TABLE?
STRETCH THAT CORD ACROSS THE BACK, AND PLUG IT INTO THAT SOCKET IN THE CORNER...
OKAY, SOMEONE RUN DOWN TO THE CUSTODIAN THEN, AND GET AN EXTENSION! YOU THERE, GET GOING!!
NOW, WHAT ABOUT THOSE WINDOW SHADES? LET'S HAVE ALL OF YOU WHO SIT ALONG THE SIDE THERE PULL DOWN THOSE STUPID SHADES..
AND I'LL NEED SOMEONE ON THE LIGHT SWITCH... ONE VOLUNTEER... YOU THERE, HONEY, GET THE SWITCH!
IS THAT THE BELL ALREADY?

Sally's travails at school provided hilarious material, and her presentations to the class became a *Peanuts* staple, starting in 1970. A few excerpts from her "reports," delivered with the utmost authority: "Abraham Lincoln was our sixteenth king, and the father of Lot's wife." (2/12/70); "The largest dinosaur that ever lived was the Bronchitis. It soon became extinct . . . it coughed a lot." (12/11/72); "Butterflies are free. What does this mean? It means you can have all of them you want." (5/4/73); "This is my report on rain. Rain is water which does not come out of faucets . . . after a storm, the rain goes down the drain, which is where I sometimes feel my education is also going." (11/7/73); "Light travels at a speed of 186,000 miles per second . . . so why are afternoons so long?" (6/1/76)

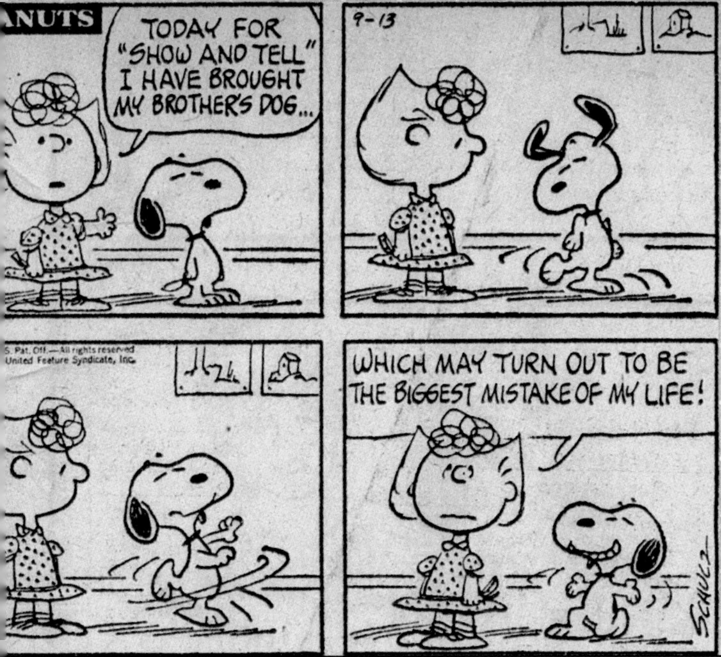
PEANUTS
TODAY FOR "SHOW AND TELL" I HAVE BROUGHT MY BROTHER'S DOG...
9-13
WHICH MAY TURN OUT TO BE THE BIGGEST MISTAKE OF MY LIFE!
SCHULZ

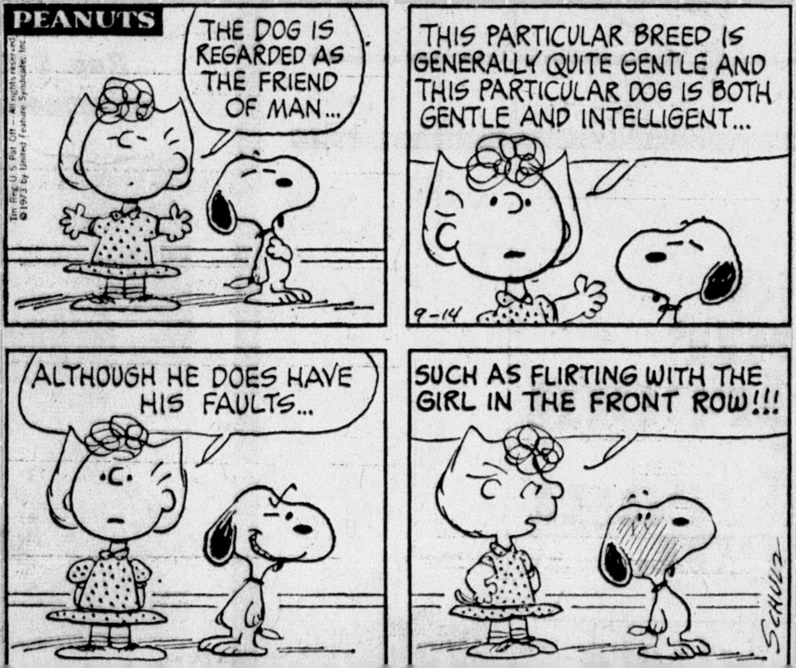
PEANUTS
THE DOG IS REGARDED AS THE FRIEND OF MAN...
THIS PARTICULAR BREED IS GENERALLY QUITE GENTLE AND THIS PARTICULAR DOG IS BOTH GENTLE AND INTELLIGENT...
9-14
ALTHOUGH HE DOES HAVE HIS FAULTS...
SUCH AS FLIRTING WITH THE GIRL IN THE FRONT ROW!!!
SCHULZ

In 1973 Sally brought Snoopy in for Show and Tell and lived to regret it.

This is yet another example at how good Schulz was when it came to the characters "acting."

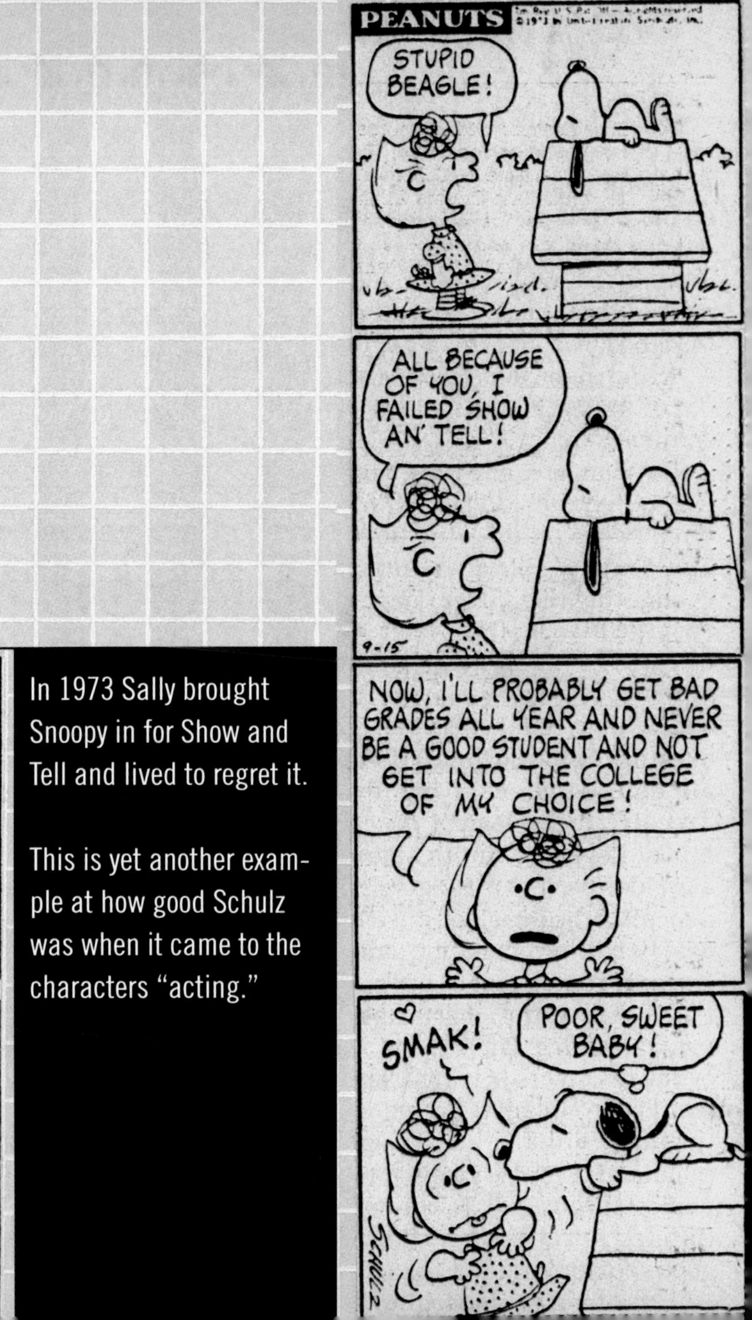
PEANUTS
STUPID BEAGLE!
ALL BECAUSE OF YOU, I FAILED SHOW AN' TELL!
9-15
NOW, I'LL PROBABLY GET BAD GRADES ALL YEAR AND NEVER BE A GOOD STUDENT AND NOT GET INTO THE COLLEGE OF MY CHOICE!
SMAK!
POOR, SWEET BABY!
SCHULZ

13 1/4 WIDE

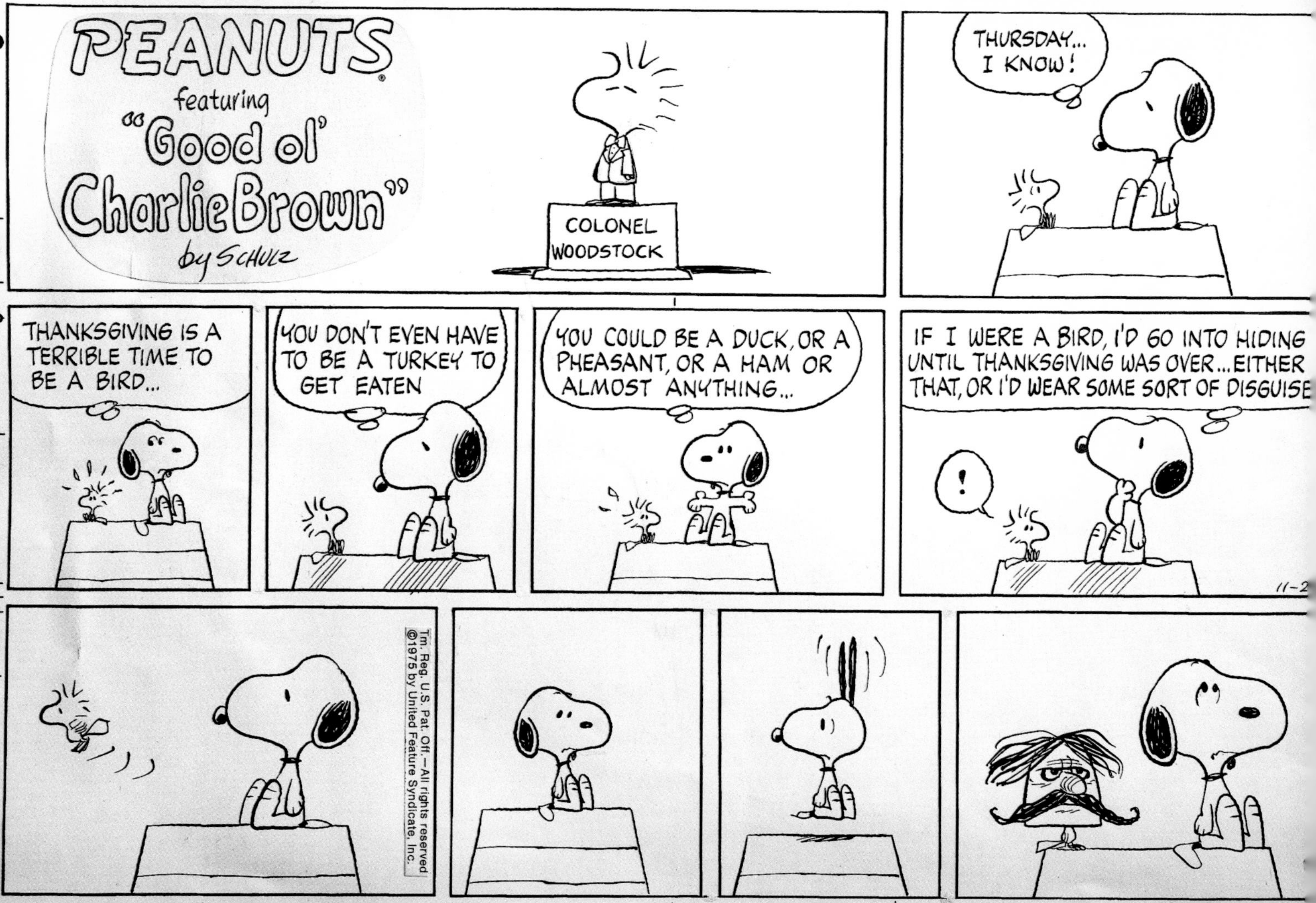
PEANUTS®
featuring
"Good ol' CharlieBrown"
by SCHULZ
COLONEL WOODSTOCK
THURSDAY... I KNOW!
THANKSGIVING IS A TERRIBLE TIME TO BE A BIRD...
YOU DON'T EVEN HAVE TO BE A TURKEY TO GET EATEN
YOU COULD BE A DUCK, OR A PHEASANT, OR A HAM OR ALMOST ANYTHING...
IF I WERE A BIRD, I'D GO INTO HIDING UNTIL THANKSGIVING WAS OVER...EITHER THAT, OR I'D WEAR SOME SORT OF DISGUISE
!
11-2
Tm. Reg. U.S. Pat. Off.—All rights reserved
©1975 by United Feature Syndicate, Inc.

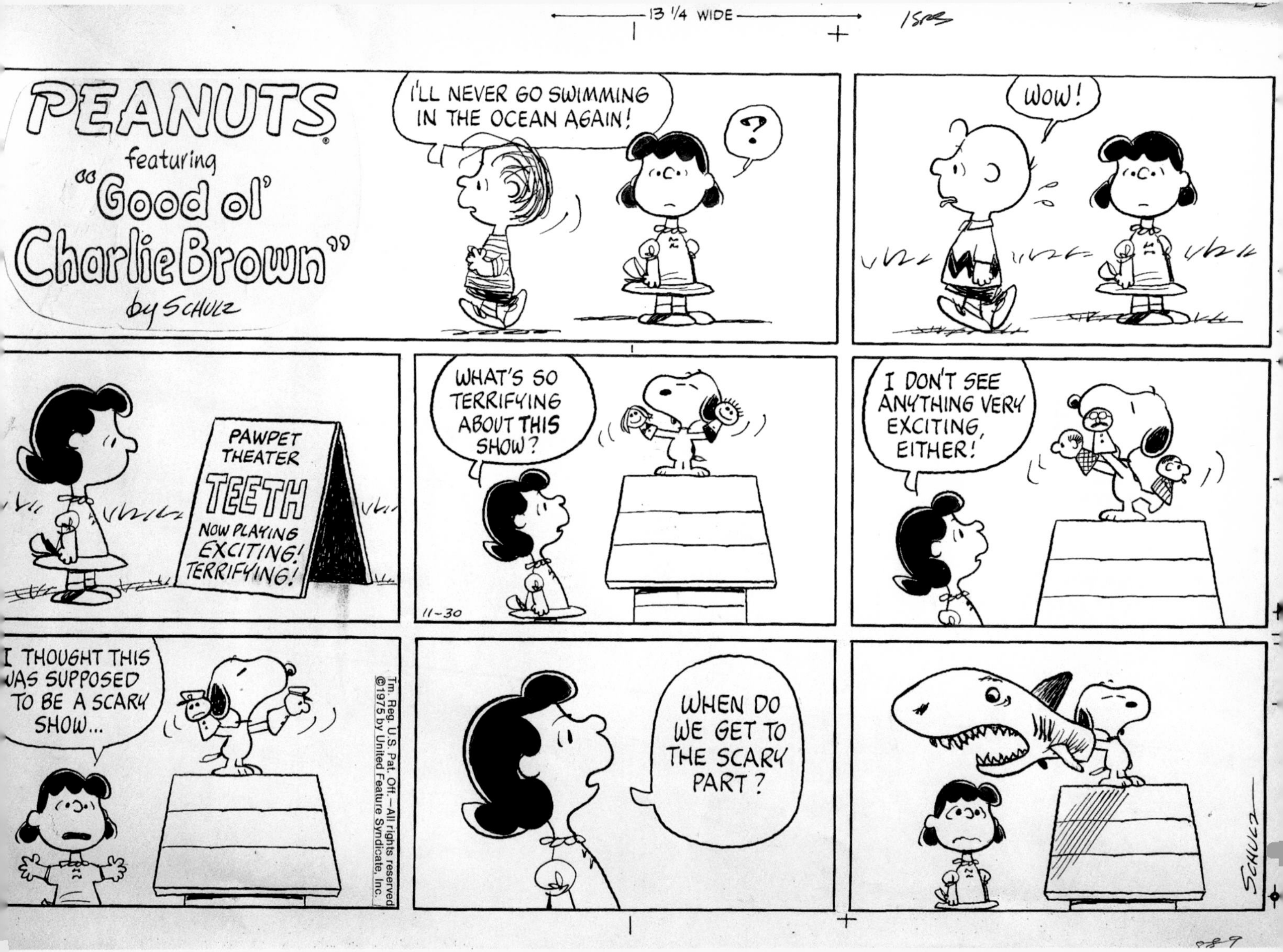
13 1/4 WIDE
PEANUTS® featuring "Good ol' Charlie Brown" by SCHULZ
I'LL NEVER GO SWIMMING IN THE OCEAN AGAIN!
?
WOW!
PAWPET THEATER
TEETH
NOW PLAYING
EXCITING!
TERRIFYING!
WHAT'S SO TERRIFYING ABOUT THIS SHOW?
11-30
I DON'T SEE ANYTHING VERY EXCITING, EITHER!
I THOUGHT THIS WAS SUPPOSED TO BE A SCARY SHOW...
Tm. Reg. U.S. Pat. Off.—All rights reserved
©1975 by United Feature Syndicate, Inc.
WHEN DO WE GET TO THE SCARY PART?
SCHULZ

For John Martone with every best wish – Charles M. Schulz

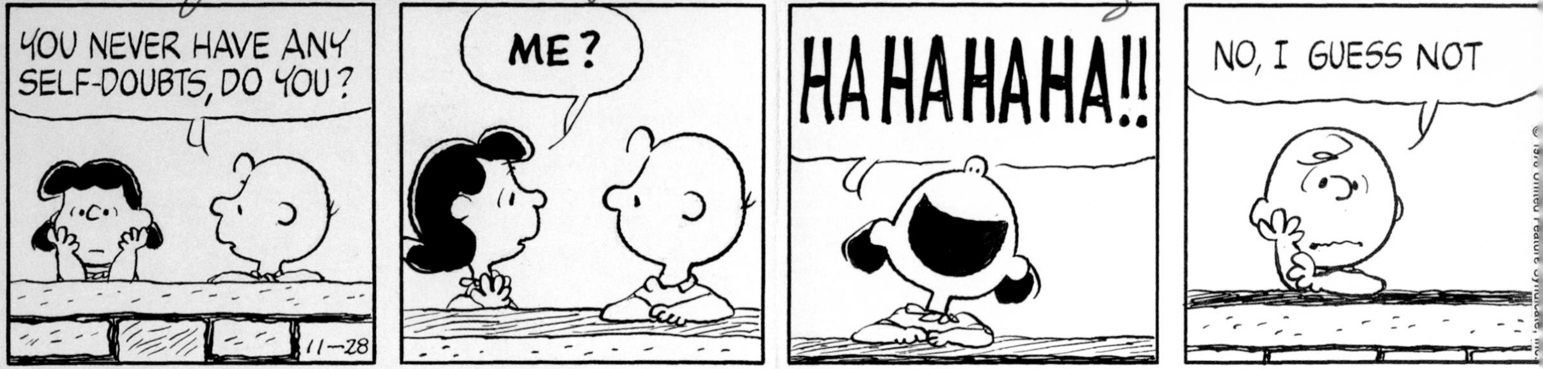

YOU NEVER HAVE ANY SELF-DOUBTS, DO YOU?
11-28
ME?
HAHAHAHA!!
NO, I GUESS NOT
© 1978 United Feature Syndicate, Inc.

For James Heineman – Best wishes – Charles M. Schulz

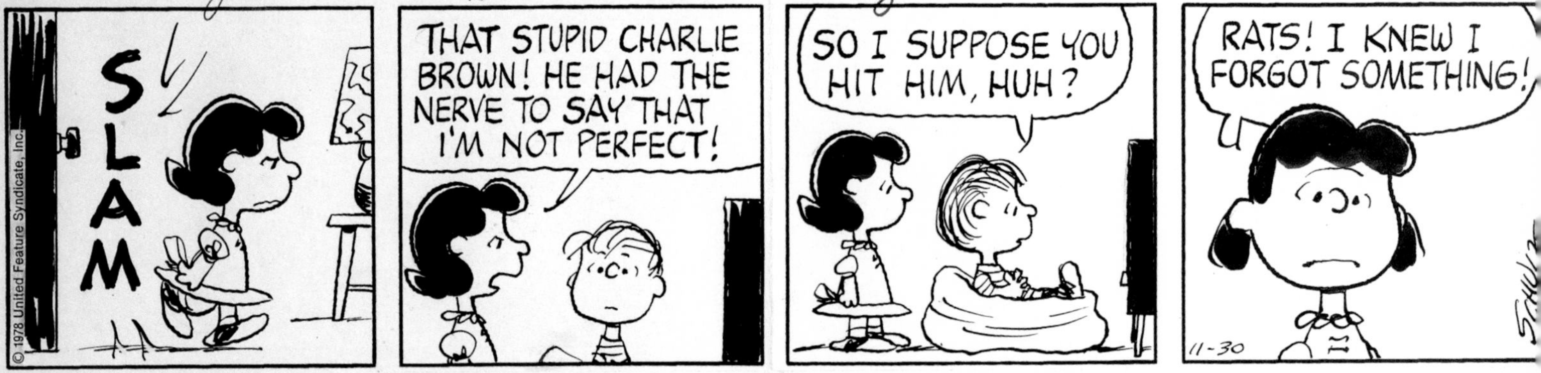

SLAM
© 1978 United Feature Syndicate, Inc.
THAT STUPID CHARLIE BROWN! HE HAD THE NERVE TO SAY THAT I'M NOT PERFECT!
SO I SUPPOSE YOU HIT HIM, HUH?
RATS! I KNEW I FORGOT SOMETHING!
11-30
SCHULZ

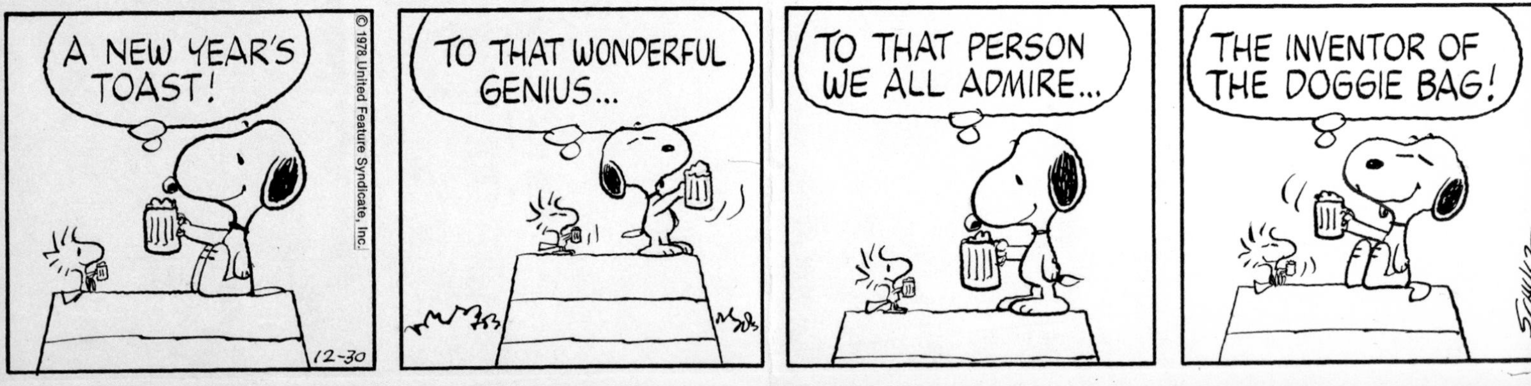

A NEW YEAR'S TOAST!
12-30
© 1978 United Feature Syndicate, Inc.
TO THAT WONDERFUL GENIUS...
TO THAT PERSON WE ALL ADMIRE...
THE INVENTOR OF THE DOGGIE BAG!
SCHULZ

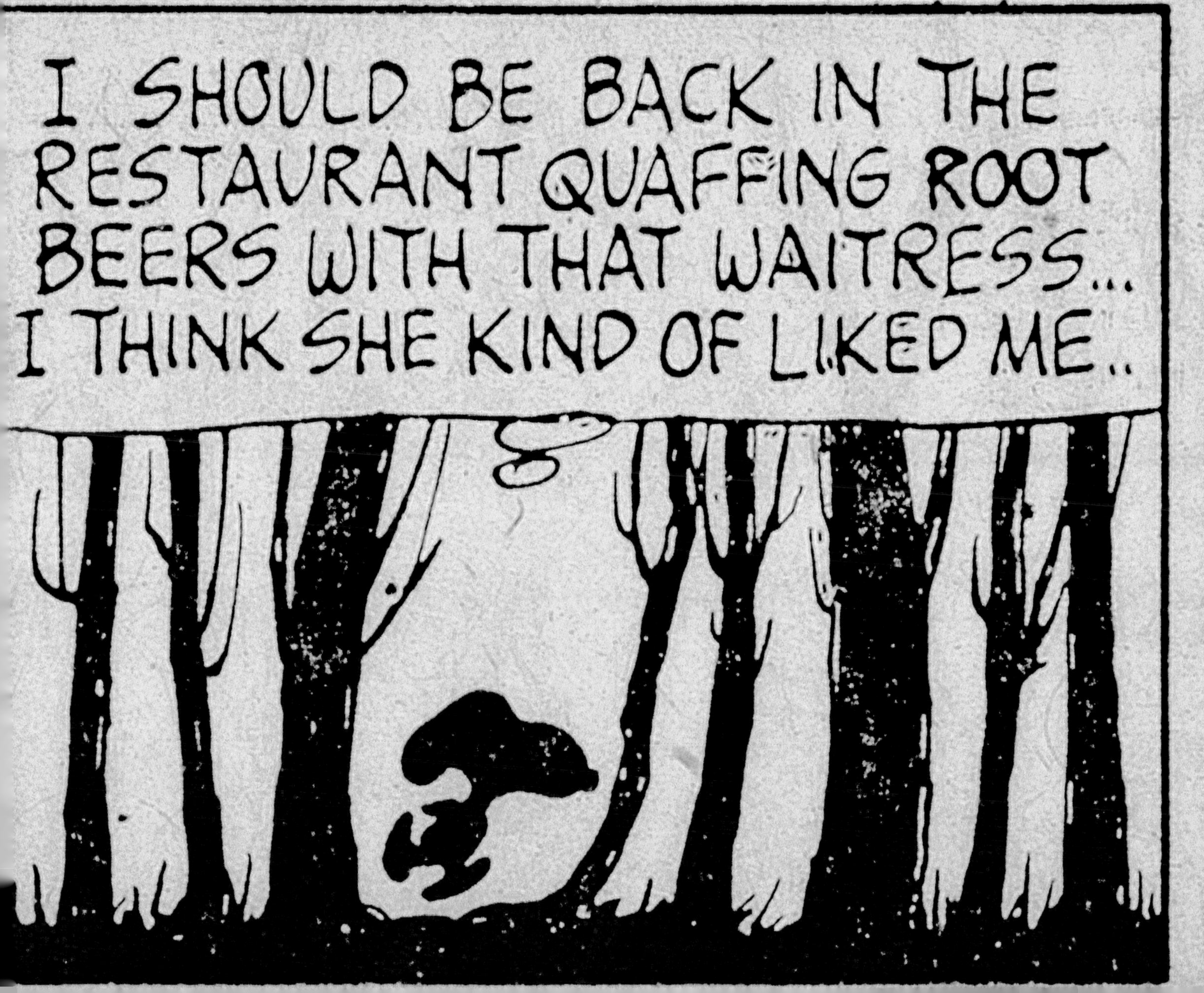
I SHOULD BE BACK IN THE RESTAURANT QUAFFING ROOT BEERS WITH THAT WAITRESS... I THINK SHE KIND OF LIKED ME..

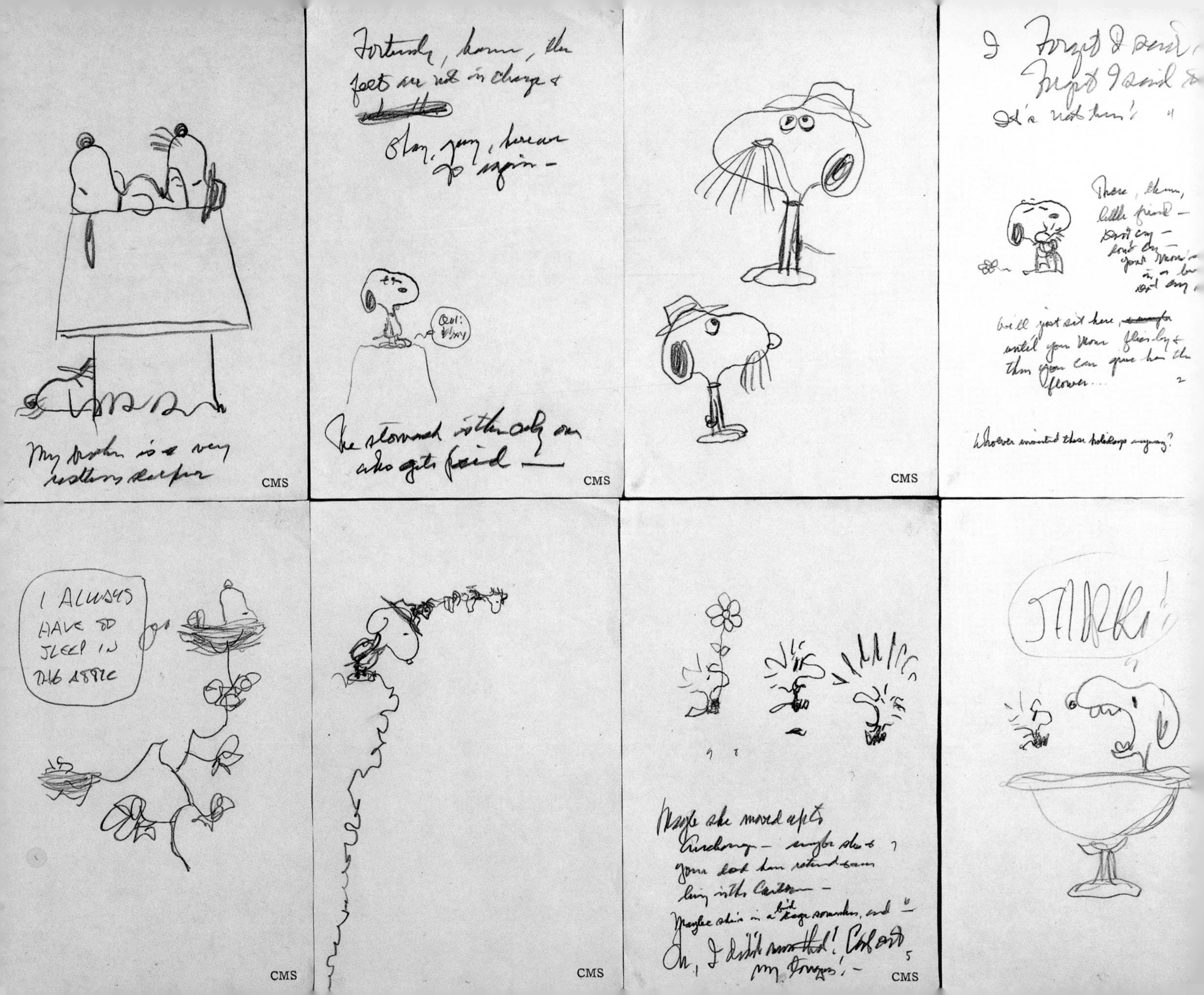
My brother is a very restless sleeper
CMS
The stomach is the only one who gets fed —
CMS
CMS
Whoever invented these holidays anyway?
I ALWAYS HAVE TO SLEEP IN THE ATTIC
CMS
CMS
CMS

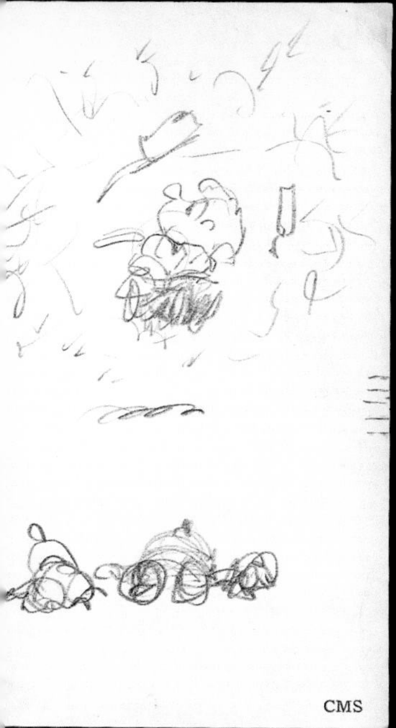
CMS

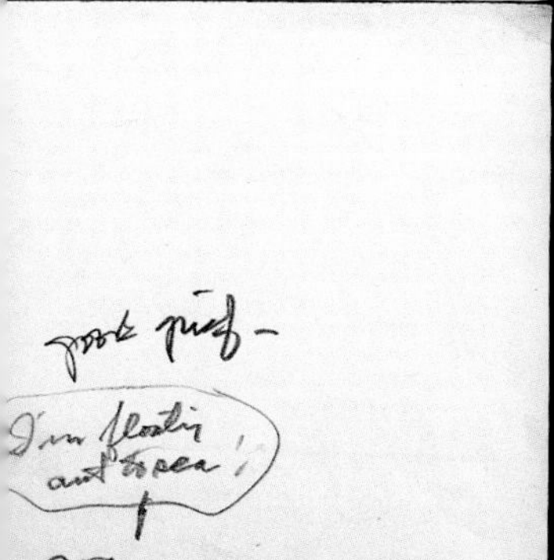
CMS

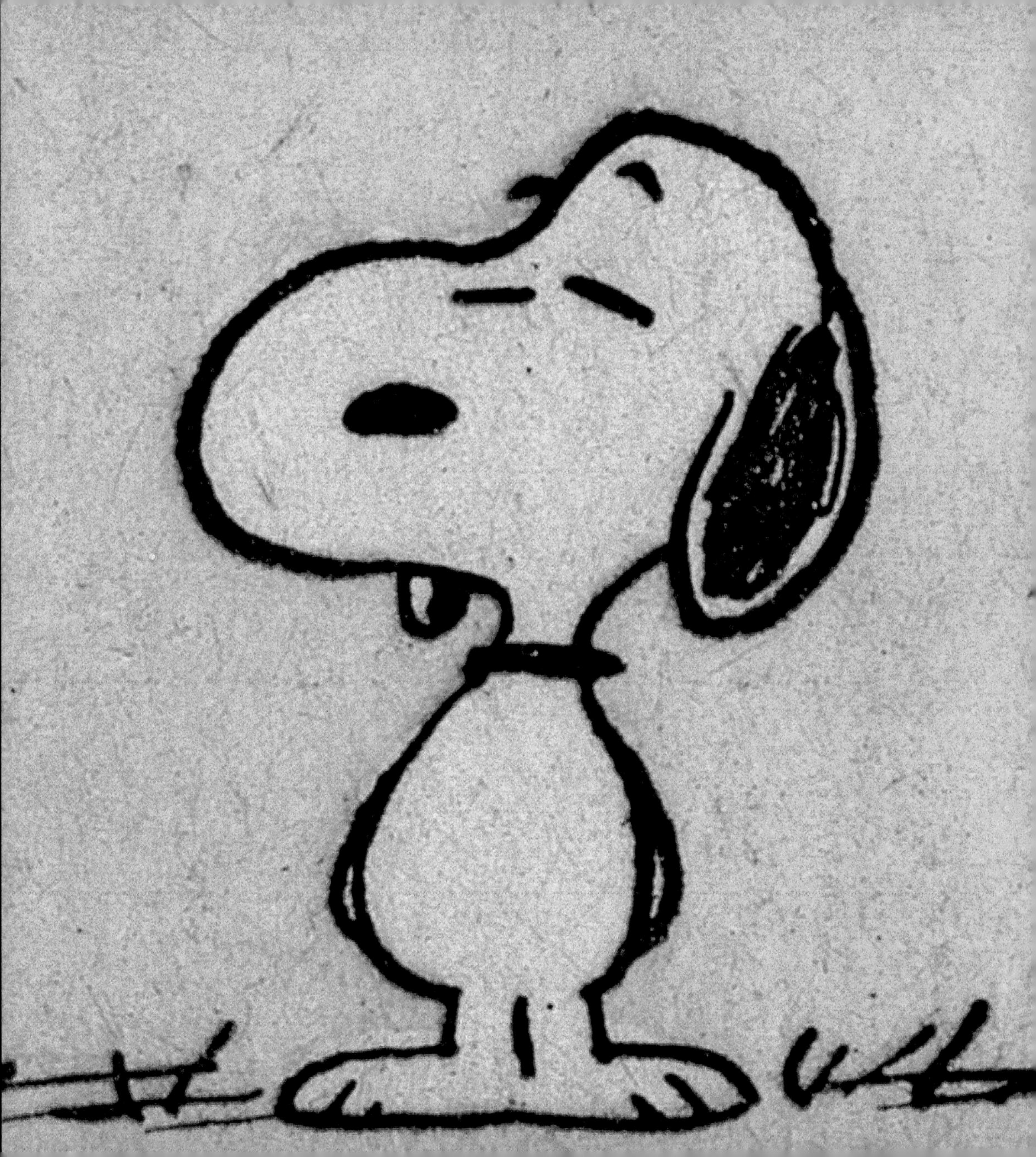

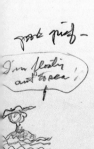

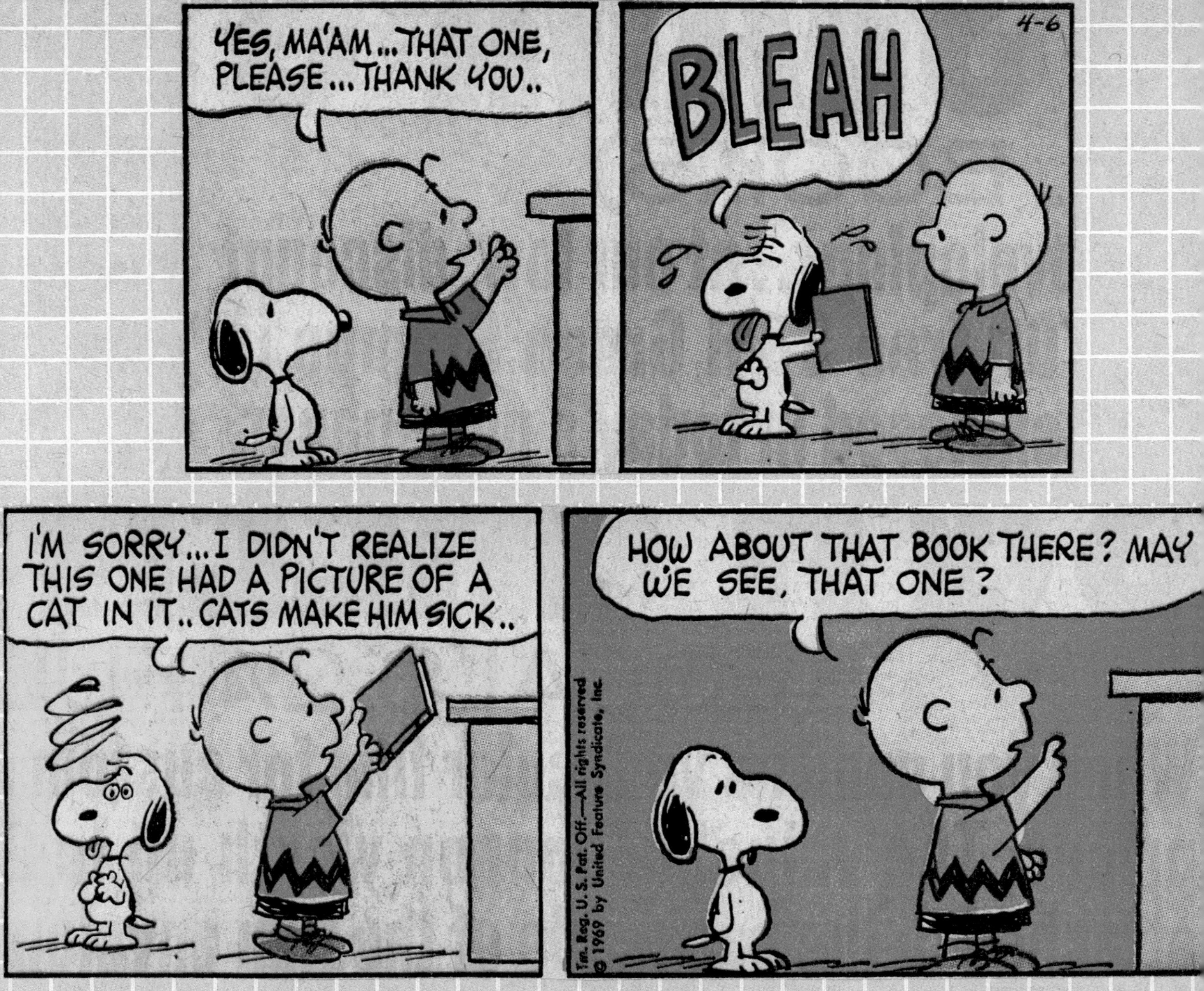
YES, MA'AM...THAT ONE, PLEASE...THANK YOU..
4-6
BLEAH
I'M SORRY...I DIDN'T REALIZE THIS ONE HAD A PICTURE OF A CAT IN IT.. CATS MAKE HIM SICK..
HOW ABOUT THAT BOOK THERE? MAY WE SEE, THAT ONE?
Tm. Reg. U. S. Pat. Off.—All rights reserved
© 1969 by United Feature Syndicate, Inc.

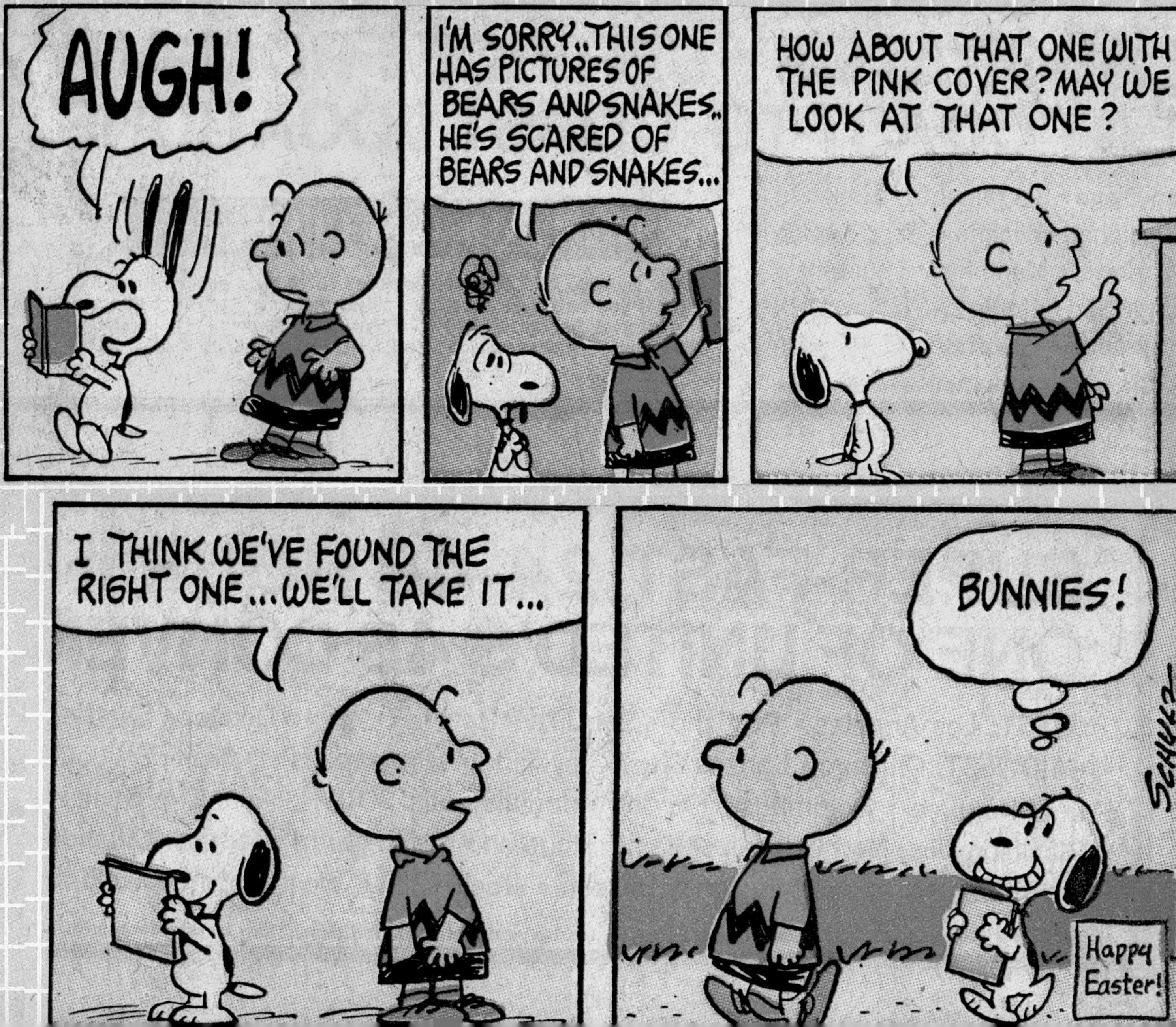

AUGH!
I'M SORRY.. THIS ONE HAS PICTURES OF BEARS AND SNAKES.. HE'S SCARED OF BEARS AND SNAKES...
HOW ABOUT THAT ONE WITH THE PINK COVER? MAY WE LOOK AT THAT ONE?
I THINK WE'VE FOUND THE RIGHT ONE... WE'LL TAKE IT...
BUNNIES!
SCHULZ
Happy Easter!

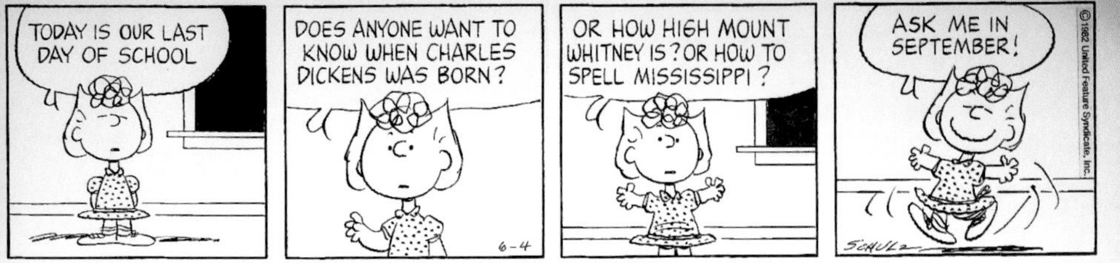
TODAY IS OUR LAST DAY OF SCHOOL
DOES ANYONE WANT TO KNOW WHEN CHARLES DICKENS WAS BORN?
6-4
OR HOW HIGH MOUNT WHITNEY IS? OR HOW TO SPELL MISSISSIPPI?
ASK ME IN SEPTEMBER!
© 1982 United Feature Syndicate, Inc.
SCHULZ

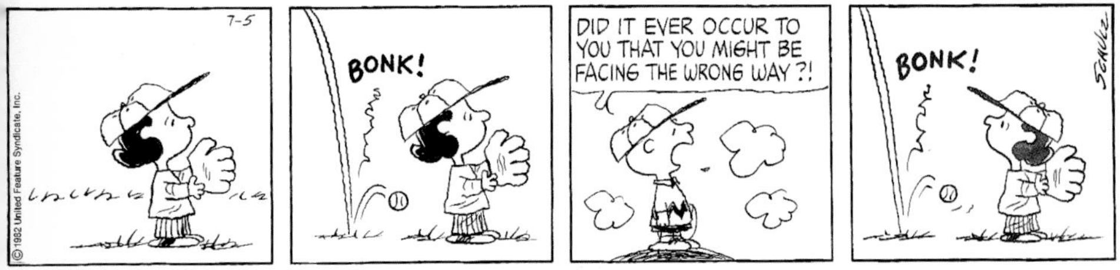
7-5
© 1982 United Feature Syndicate, Inc.
BONK!
DID IT EVER OCCUR TO YOU THAT YOU MIGHT BE FACING THE WRONG WAY?!
BONK!
SCHULZ

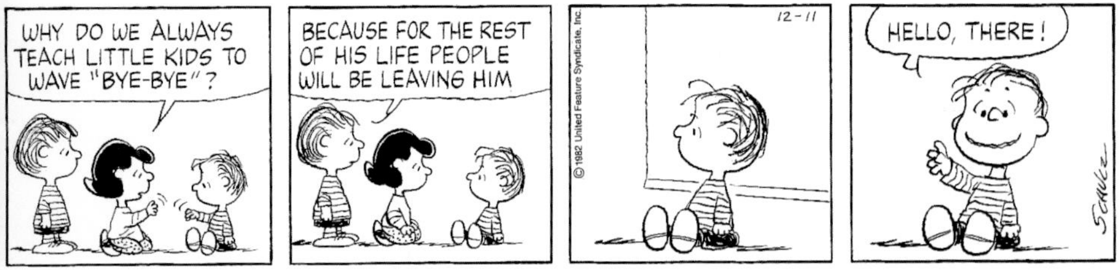
WHY DO WE ALWAYS TEACH LITTLE KIDS TO WAVE "BYE-BYE"?
BECAUSE FOR THE REST OF HIS LIFE PEOPLE WILL BE LEAVING HIM
© 1982 United Feature Syndicate, Inc.
12-11
HELLO, THERE!
SCHULZ

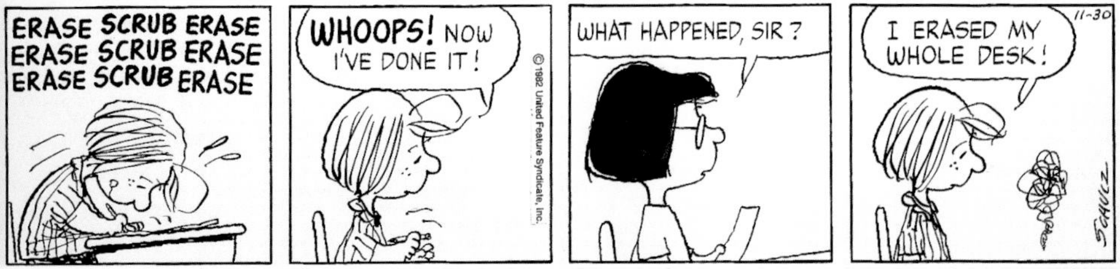
ERASE SCRUB ERASE
ERASE SCRUB ERASE
ERASE SCRUB ERASE
WHOOPS! NOW I'VE DONE IT!
© 1982 United Feature Syndicate, Inc.
WHAT HAPPENED, SIR?
11-30
I ERASED MY WHOLE DESK!
SCHULZ

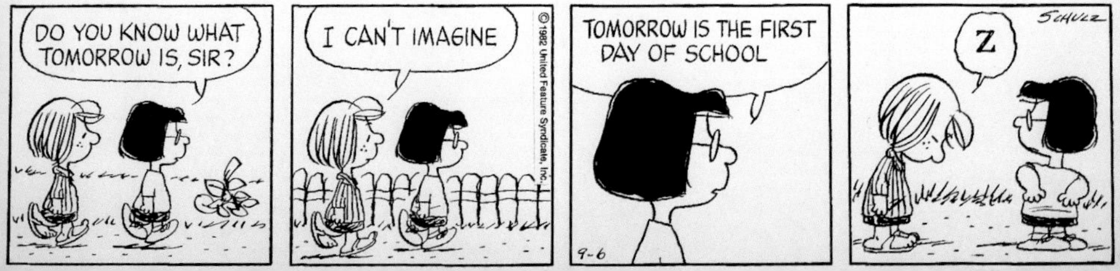
DO YOU KNOW WHAT TOMORROW IS, SIR?
I CAN'T IMAGINE
© 1982 United Feature Syndicate, Inc.
TOMORROW IS THE FIRST DAY OF SCHOOL
9-6
SCHULZ
Z

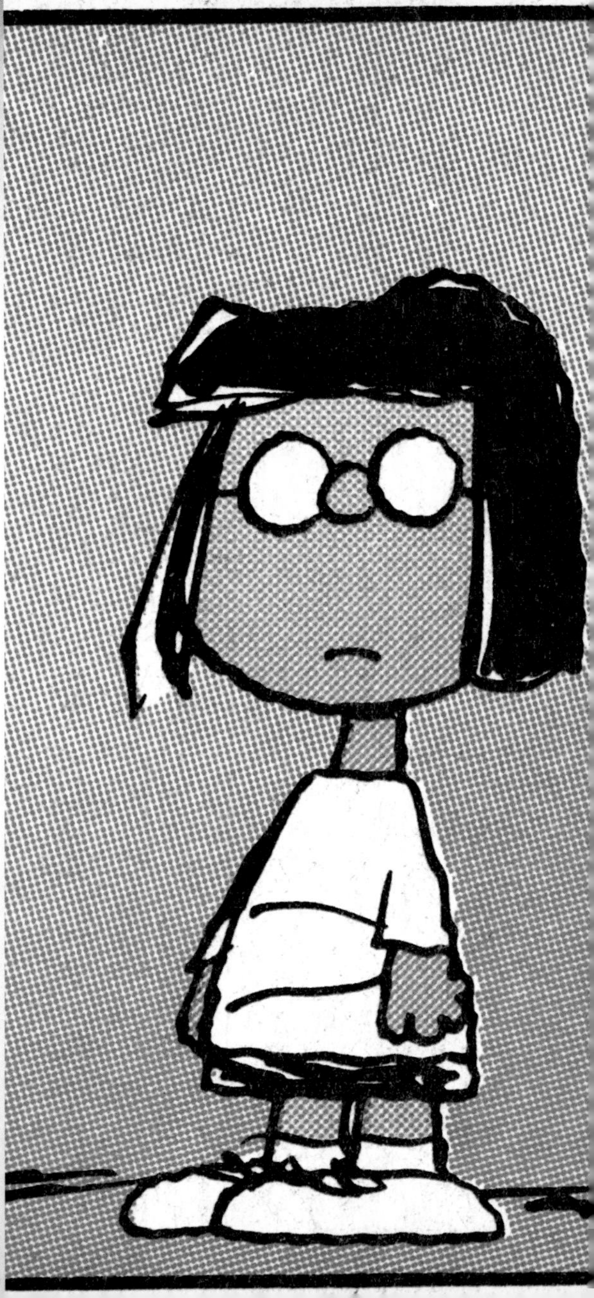

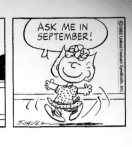

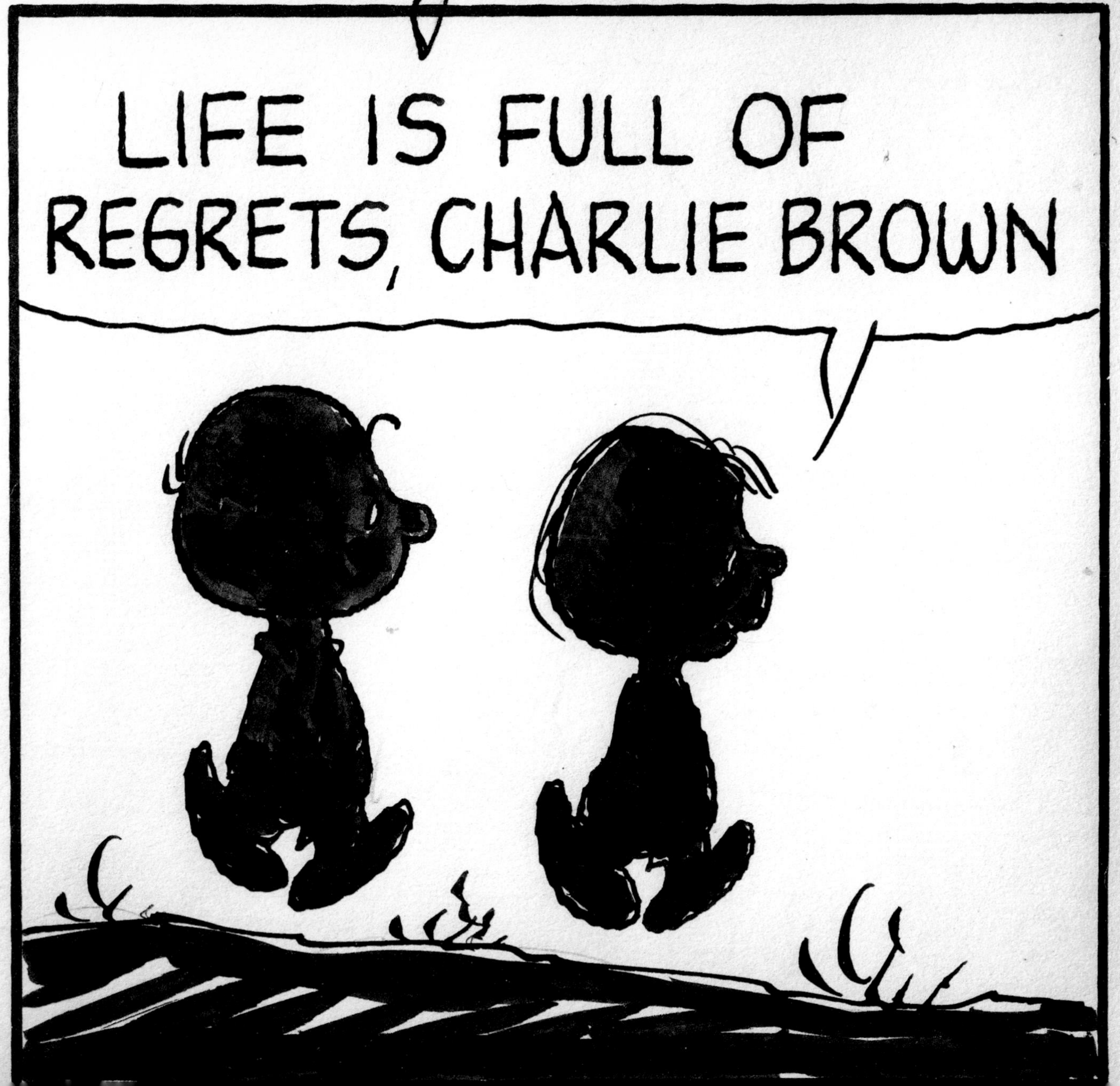
LIFE IS FULL OF REGRETS, CHARLIE BROWN

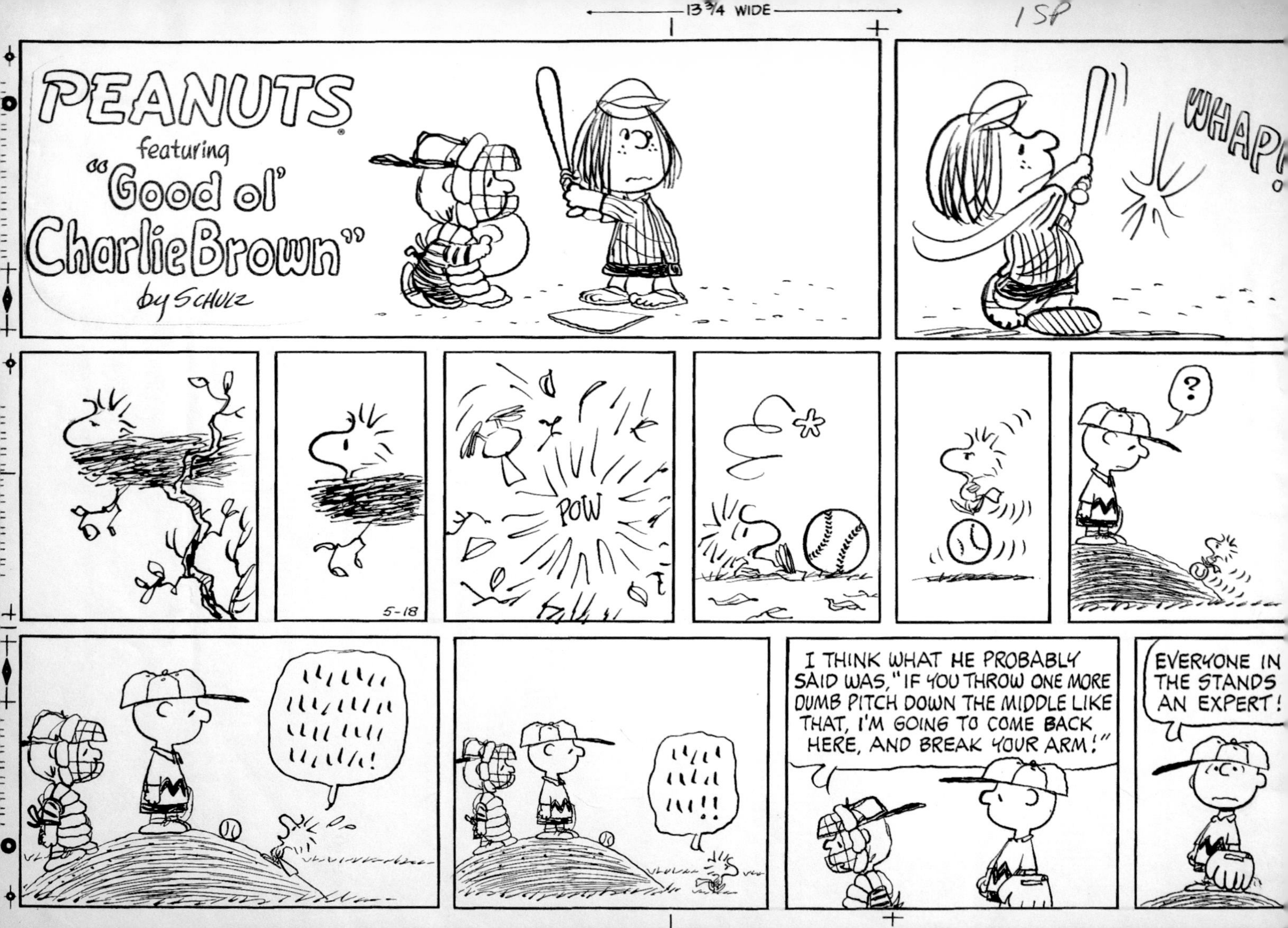
13 3/4 WIDE
1SP
PEANUTS
featuring
"Good ol' Charlie Brown"
by SCHULZ
WHAP!
5-18
POW
?
I THINK WHAT HE PROBABLY SAID WAS, "IF YOU THROW ONE MORE DUMB PITCH DOWN THE MIDDLE LIKE THAT, I'M GOING TO COME BACK HERE, AND BREAK YOUR ARM!"
EVERYONE IN THE STANDS AN EXPERT!

"How can we lose when we're so sincere?"

—Charlie Brown, 1963

PEANUTS
featuring
"Good ol'
Charlie Brown"
by SCHULZ

:YAWN:

© 1986 United Feature Syndicate, Inc.

BONK!

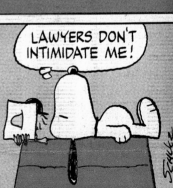

LAWYERS DON'T INTIMIDATE ME!

"I did a strip once where Charlie Brown was wondering out loud," Schulz said in 1997. "He was sitting on a bench with Linus. [They were discussing] *War and Peace*, or Beethoven's Ninth, or something like that. Then he gets up and strikes out. I think he sits down and says something like 'And I'll probably never write *War and Peace*, either.'

"I always think about things like that. What is of importance? I suppose the most important thing is just to do what you do best. You have no other choice, do you?"

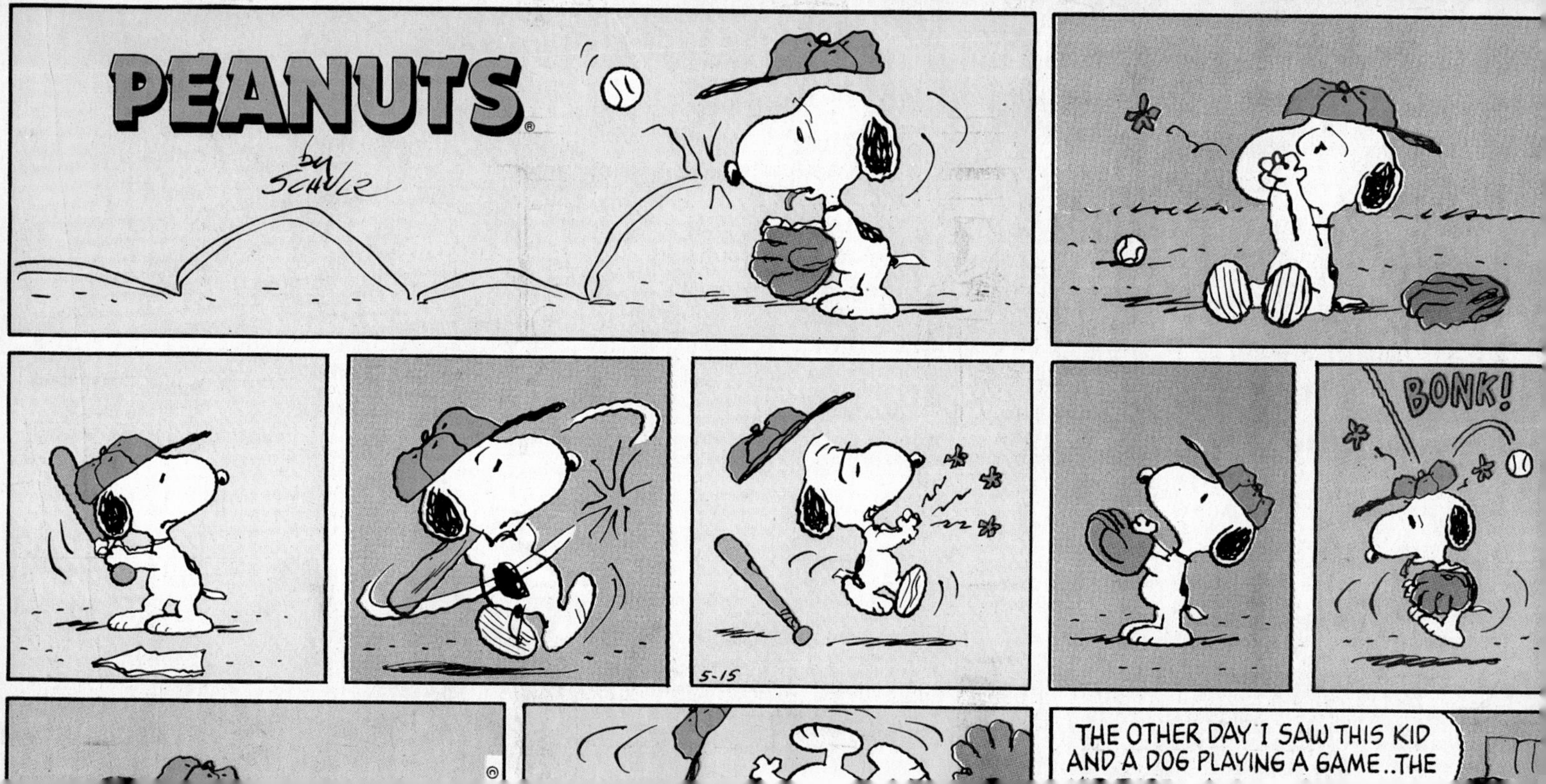
PEANUTS®
by SCHULZ
BONK!
5-15
THE OTHER DAY I SAW THIS KID
AND A DOG PLAYING A GAME..THE

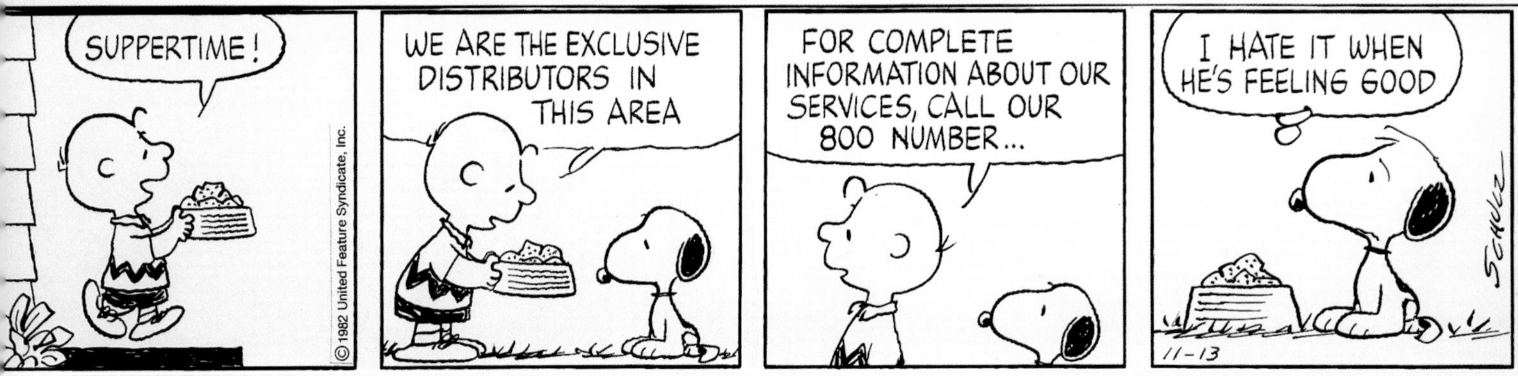
SUPPERTIME!
© 1982 United Feature Syndicate, Inc.
WE ARE THE EXCLUSIVE DISTRIBUTORS IN THIS AREA
FOR COMPLETE INFORMATION ABOUT OUR SERVICES, CALL OUR 800 NUMBER...
I HATE IT WHEN HE'S FEELING GOOD
SCHULZ
11-13

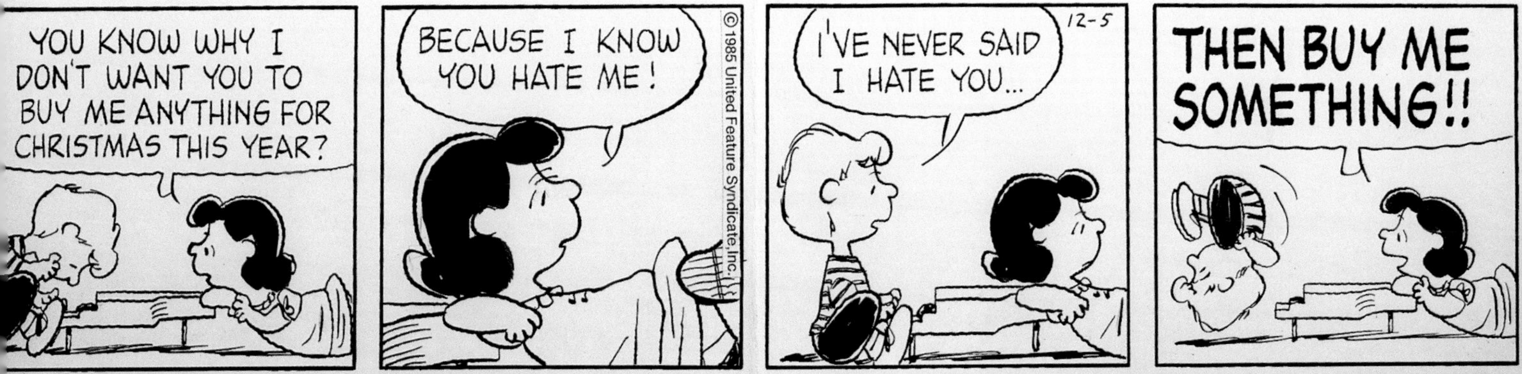
YOU KNOW WHY I DON'T WANT YOU TO BUY ME ANYTHING FOR CHRISTMAS THIS YEAR?
BECAUSE I KNOW YOU HATE ME!
© 1985 United Feature Syndicate, Inc.
12-5
I'VE NEVER SAID I HATE YOU...
THEN BUY ME SOMETHING!!

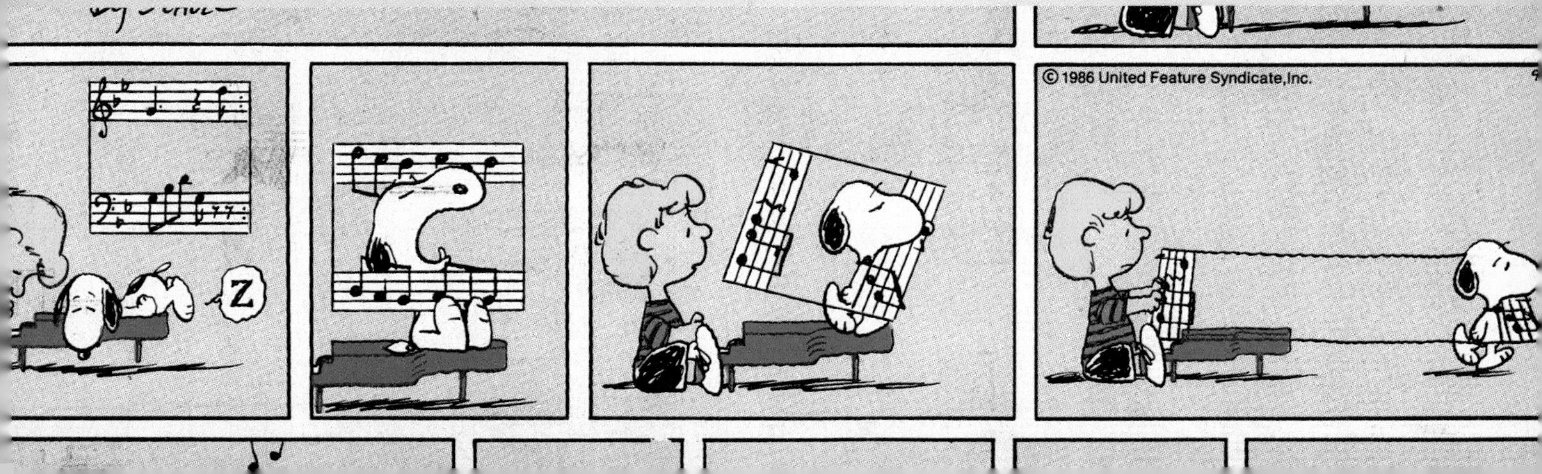
Z
© 1986 United Feature Syndicate, Inc.

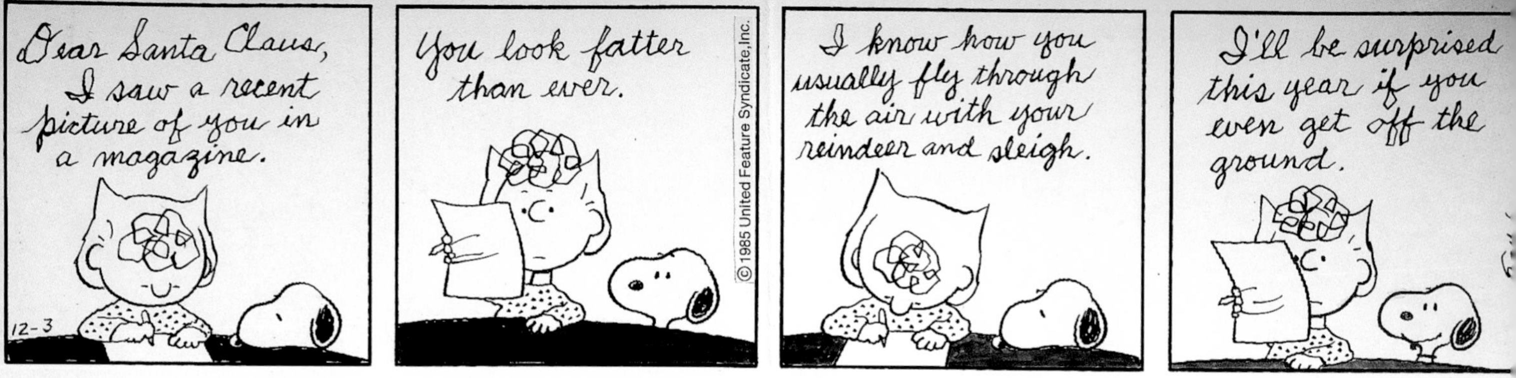
Dear Santa Claus,
I saw a recent picture of you in a magazine.
12-3
You look fatter than ever.
© 1985 United Feature Syndicate, Inc.
I know how you usually fly through the air with your reindeer and sleigh.
I'll be surprised this year if you even get off the ground.

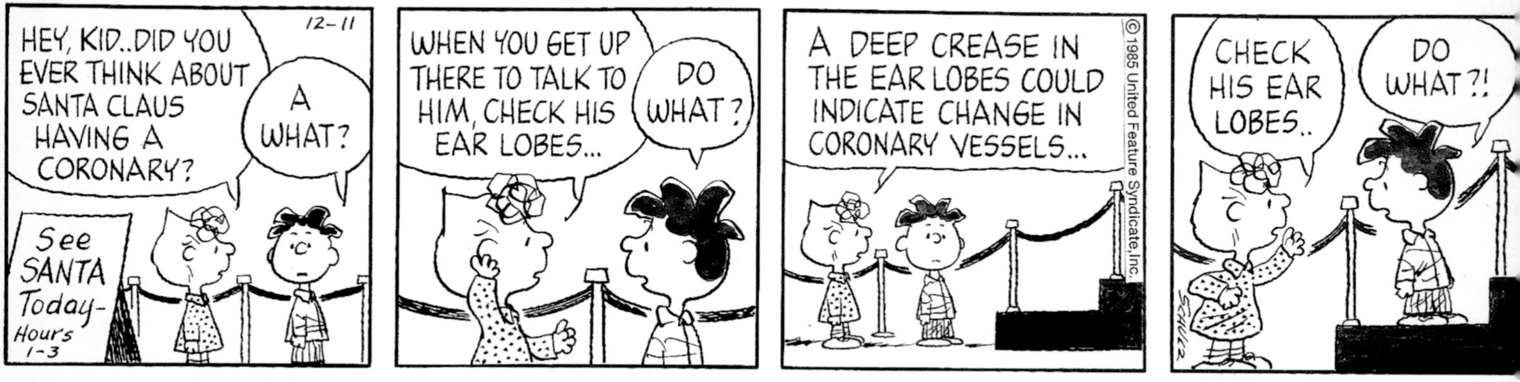
12-11
HEY, KID..DID YOU EVER THINK ABOUT SANTA CLAUS HAVING A CORONARY?
A WHAT?
See SANTA Today-
Hours 1-3
WHEN YOU GET UP THERE TO TALK TO HIM, CHECK HIS EAR LOBES...
DO WHAT?
A DEEP CREASE IN THE EAR LOBES COULD INDICATE CHANGE IN CORONARY VESSELS...
© 1985 United Feature Syndicate, Inc.
CHECK HIS EAR LOBES..
DO WHAT?!

In 1987, the Peanuts logo changed, from the original hand lettering to this new machine font.

PEANUTS®

by

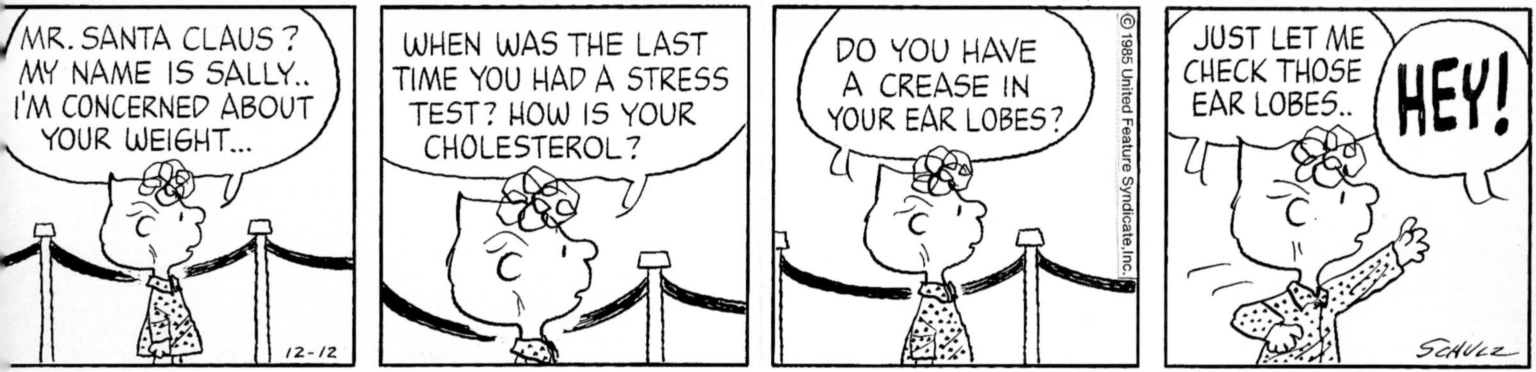
MR. SANTA CLAUS? MY NAME IS SALLY.. I'M CONCERNED ABOUT YOUR WEIGHT...
12-12
WHEN WAS THE LAST TIME YOU HAD A STRESS TEST? HOW IS YOUR CHOLESTEROL?
© 1985 United Feature Syndicate, Inc.
DO YOU HAVE A CREASE IN YOUR EAR LOBES?
JUST LET ME CHECK THOSE EAR LOBES..
HEY!
SCHULZ

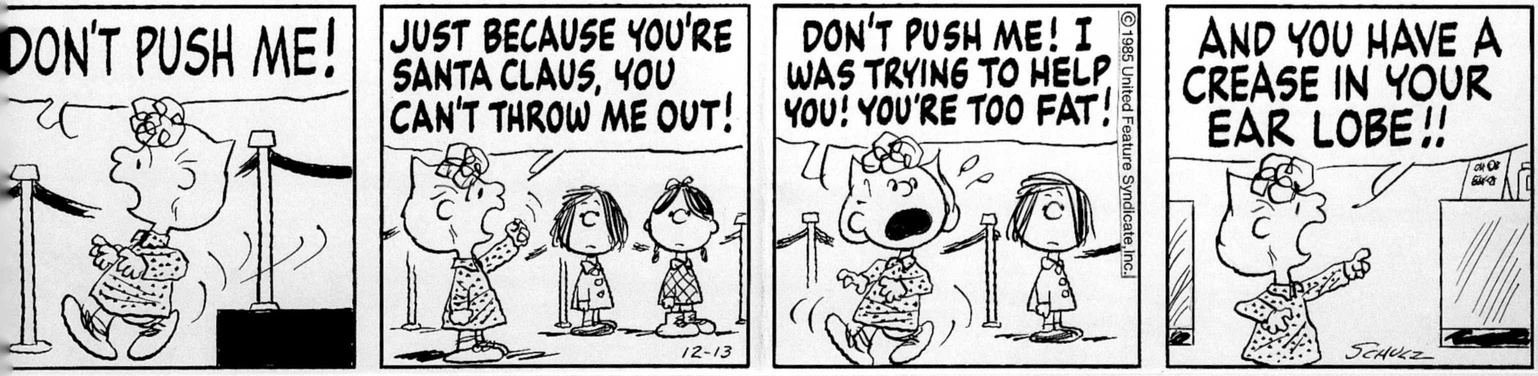
DON'T PUSH ME!
JUST BECAUSE YOU'RE SANTA CLAUS, YOU CAN'T THROW ME OUT!
12-13
© 1985 United Feature Syndicate, Inc.
DON'T PUSH ME! I WAS TRYING TO HELP YOU! YOU'RE TOO FAT!
AND YOU HAVE A CREASE IN YOUR EAR LOBE!!
SCHULZ

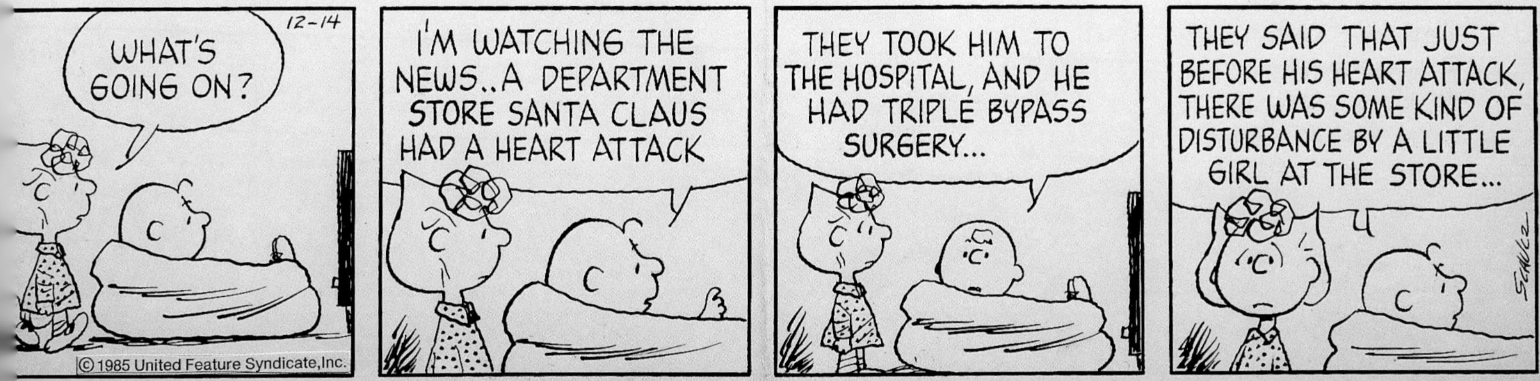
12-14
WHAT'S GOING ON?
© 1985 United Feature Syndicate, Inc.
I'M WATCHING THE NEWS..A DEPARTMENT STORE SANTA CLAUS HAD A HEART ATTACK
THEY TOOK HIM TO THE HOSPITAL, AND HE HAD TRIPLE BYPASS SURGERY...
THEY SAID THAT JUST BEFORE HIS HEART ATTACK, THERE WAS SOME KIND OF DISTURBANCE BY A LITTLE GIRL AT THE STORE...
SCHULZ

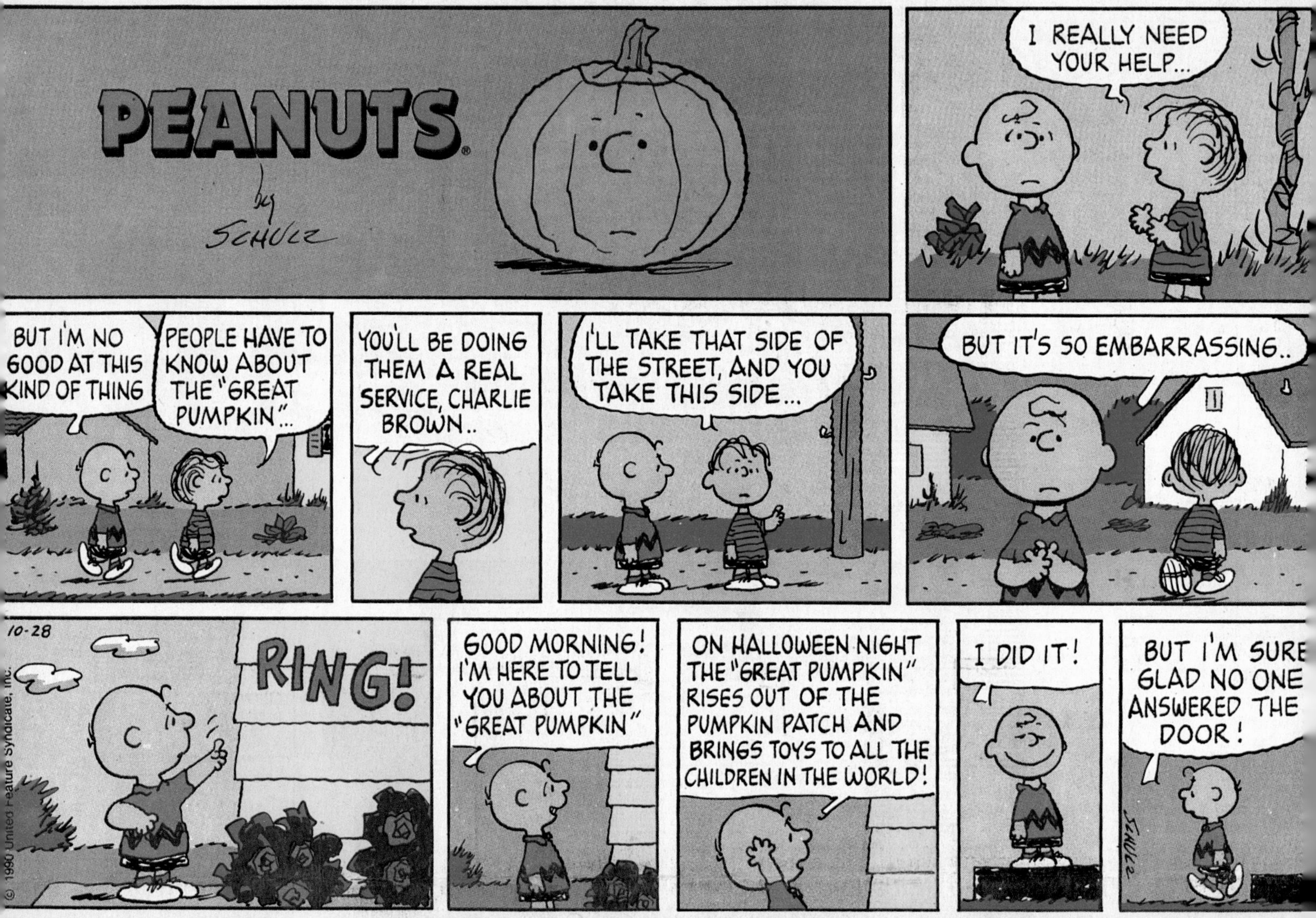
PEANUTS
by SCHULZ
I REALLY NEED YOUR HELP...
BUT I'M NO GOOD AT THIS KIND OF THING
PEOPLE HAVE TO KNOW ABOUT THE "GREAT PUMPKIN"...
YOU'LL BE DOING THEM A REAL SERVICE, CHARLIE BROWN..
I'LL TAKE THAT SIDE OF THE STREET, AND YOU TAKE THIS SIDE...
BUT IT'S SO EMBARRASSING..
10-28
RING!
GOOD MORNING! I'M HERE TO TELL YOU ABOUT THE "GREAT PUMPKIN"
ON HALLOWEEN NIGHT THE "GREAT PUMPKIN" RISES OUT OF THE PUMPKIN PATCH AND BRINGS TOYS TO ALL THE CHILDREN IN THE WORLD!
I DID IT!
BUT I'M SURE GLAD NO ONE ANSWERED THE DOOR!
SCHULZ

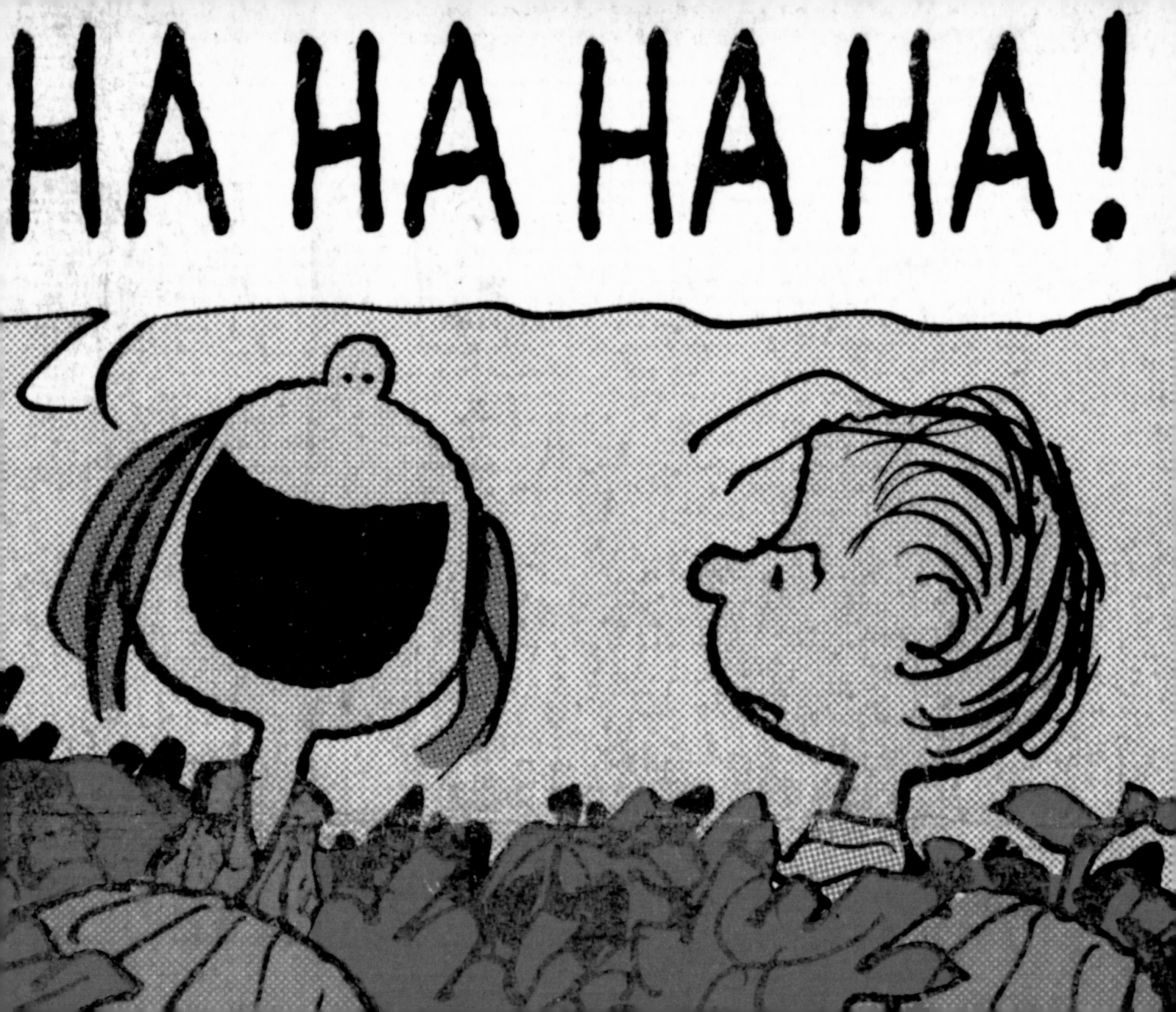
HA HA HA HA!

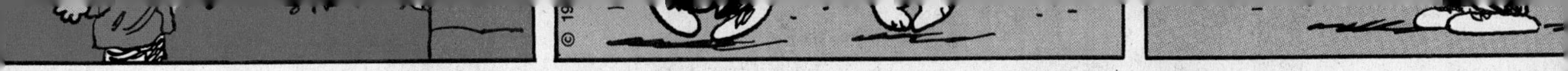

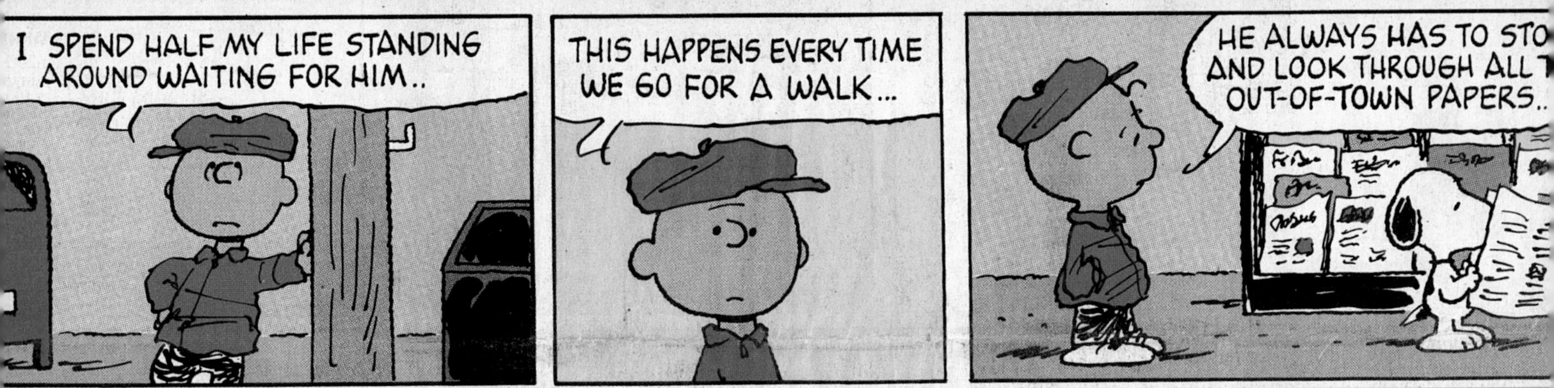
I SPEND HALF MY LIFE STANDING AROUND WAITING FOR HIM..
THIS HAPPENS EVERY TIME WE GO FOR A WALK...
HE ALWAYS HAS TO STO
AND LOOK THROUGH ALL T
OUT-OF-TOWN PAPERS..

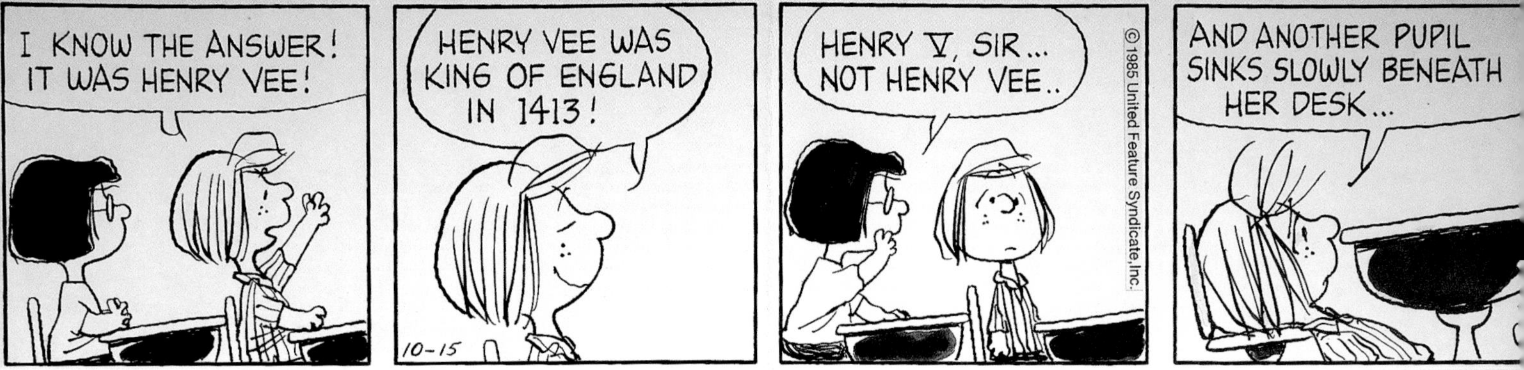
I KNOW THE ANSWER! IT WAS HENRY VEE!
HENRY VEE WAS KING OF ENGLAND IN 1413!
10-15
HENRY V, SIR... NOT HENRY VEE..
© 1985 United Feature Syndicate, Inc.
AND ANOTHER PUPIL SINKS SLOWLY BENEATH HER DESK...

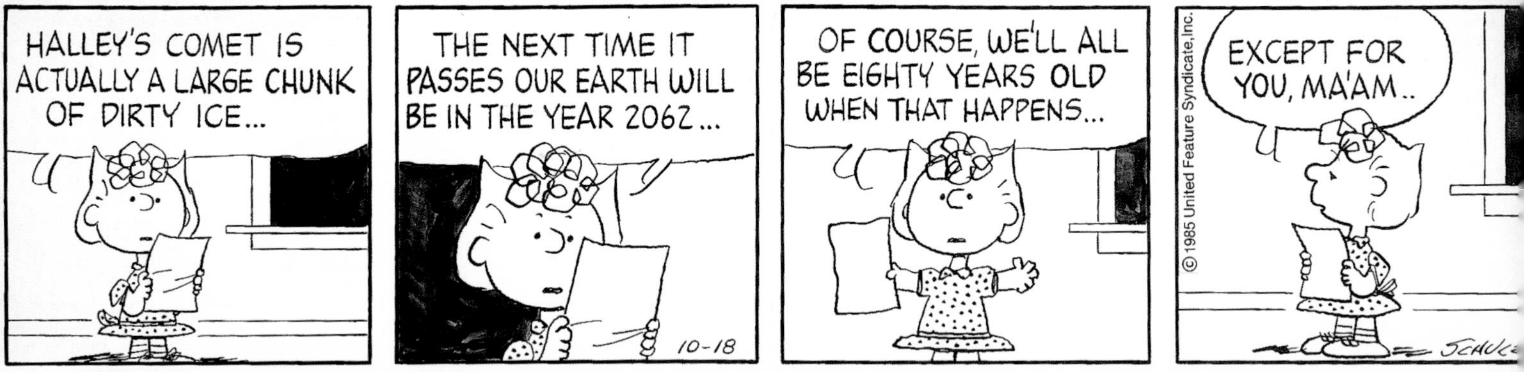
HALLEY'S COMET IS ACTUALLY A LARGE CHUNK OF DIRTY ICE...
THE NEXT TIME IT PASSES OUR EARTH WILL BE IN THE YEAR 2062...
10-18
OF COURSE, WE'LL ALL BE EIGHTY YEARS OLD WHEN THAT HAPPENS...
© 1985 United Feature Syndicate, Inc.
EXCEPT FOR YOU, MA'AM..

The highlight of our lives [as children] was, of course, Saturday afternoons, going to the local theater," Schulz remembered, in 1997. "My favorite movie, I still remember, was *Lost Patrol*, with Victor McLagen. I love those desert movies, which is why I like drawing Snoopy as the foreign legionnaire."

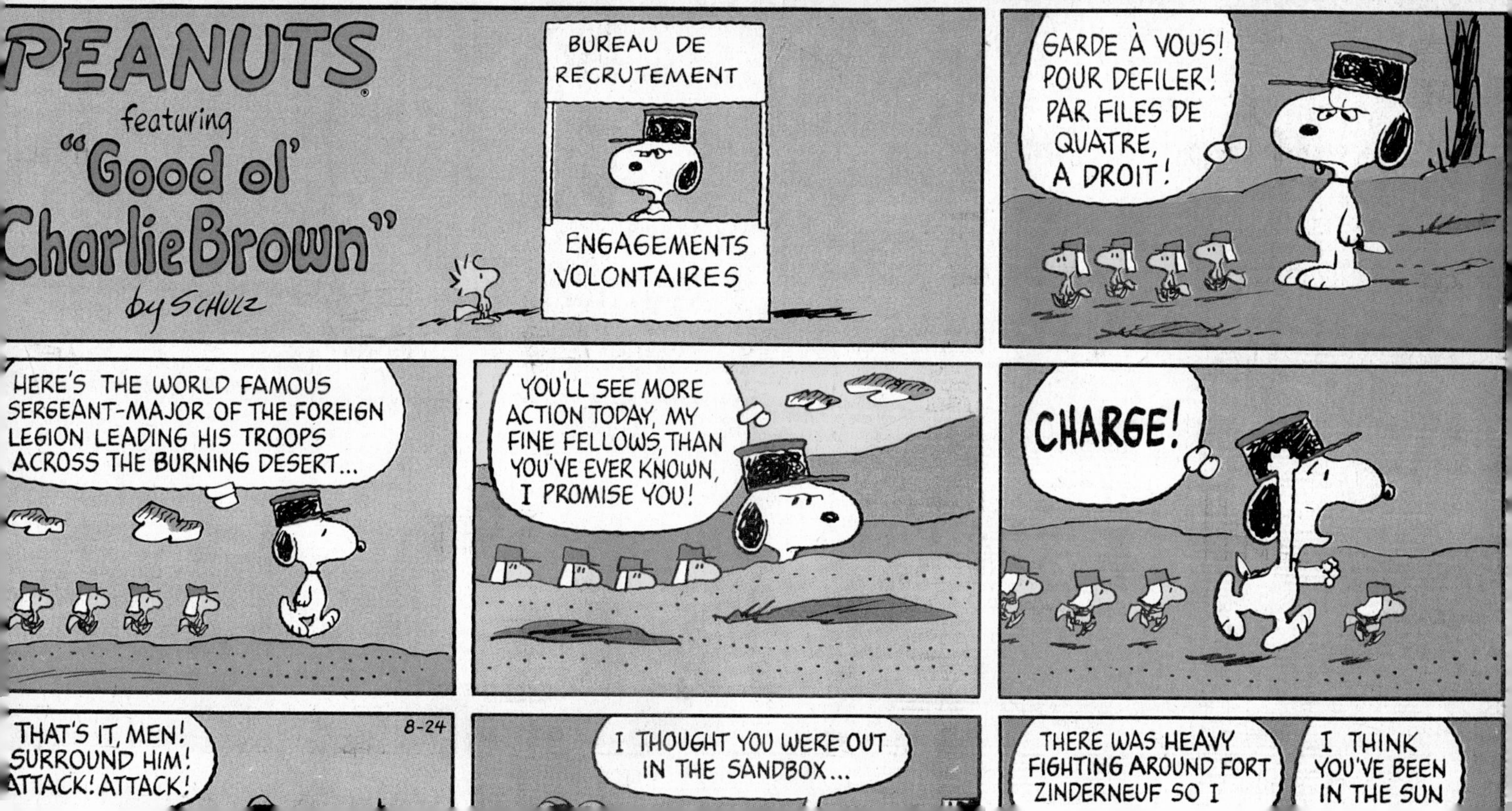

PEANUTS®
featuring "Good ol' Charlie Brown"
by SCHULZ
BUREAU DE RECRUTEMENT
ENGAGEMENTS VOLONTAIRES
GARDE À VOUS! POUR DEFILER! PAR FILES DE QUATRE, A DROIT!
HERE'S THE WORLD FAMOUS SERGEANT-MAJOR OF THE FOREIGN LEGION LEADING HIS TROOPS ACROSS THE BURNING DESERT...
YOU'LL SEE MORE ACTION TODAY, MY FINE FELLOWS, THAN YOU'VE EVER KNOWN, I PROMISE YOU!
CHARGE!
THAT'S IT, MEN! SURROUND HIM! ATTACK! ATTACK!
8-24
I THOUGHT YOU WERE OUT IN THE SANDBOX...
THERE WAS HEAVY FIGHTING AROUND FORT ZINDERNEUF SO I
I THINK YOU'VE BEEN IN THE SUN

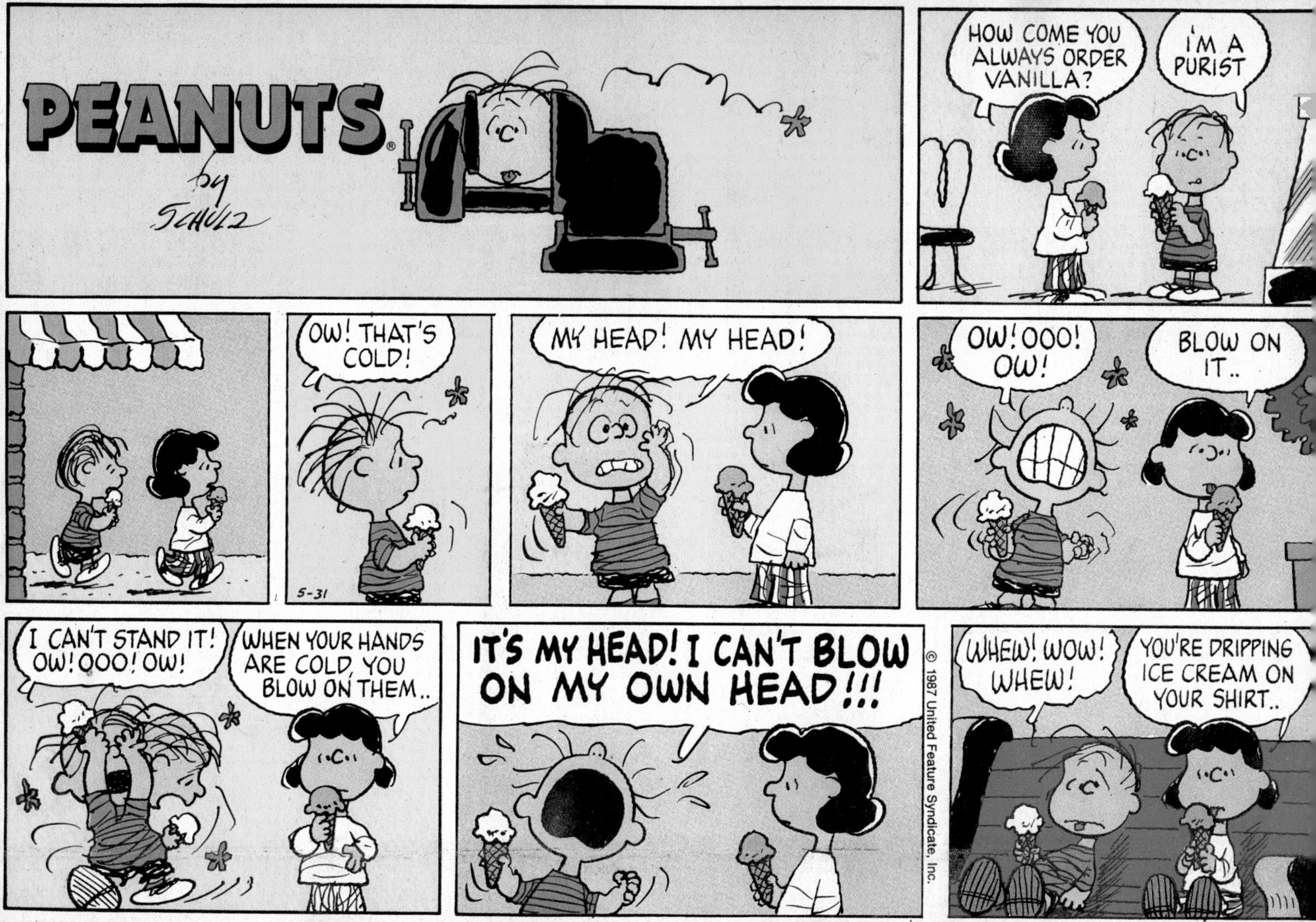
PEANUTS®
by SCHULZ
HOW COME YOU ALWAYS ORDER VANILLA?
I'M A PURIST
OW! THAT'S COLD!
5-31
MY HEAD! MY HEAD!
OW! OOO! OW!
BLOW ON IT..
I CAN'T STAND IT! OW! OOO! OW!
WHEN YOUR HANDS ARE COLD, YOU BLOW ON THEM..
IT'S MY HEAD! I CAN'T BLOW ON MY OWN HEAD!!!
© 1987 United Feature Syndicate, Inc.
WHEW! WOW! WHEW!
YOU'RE DRIPPING ICE CREAM ON YOUR SHIRT..

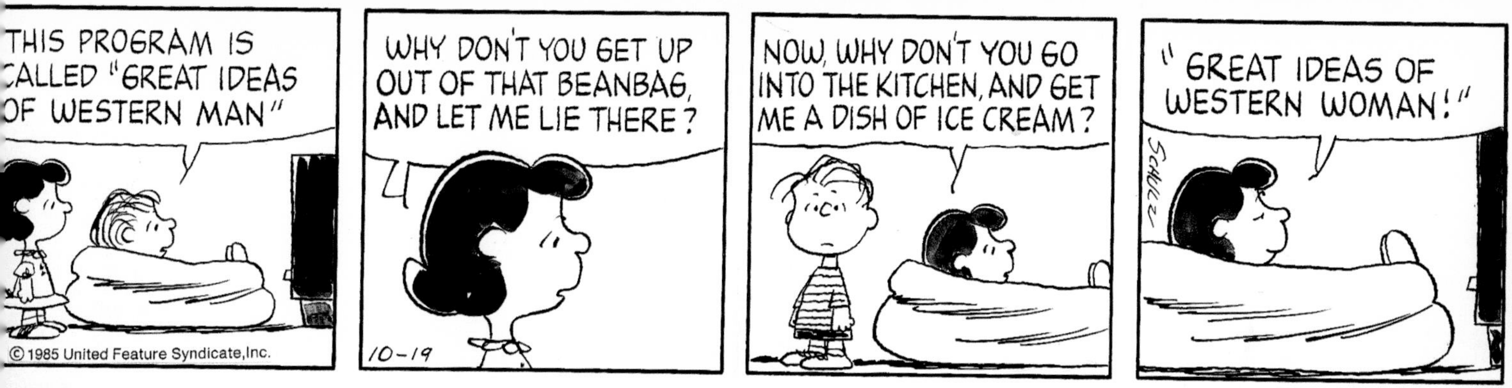
THIS PROGRAM IS
:ALLED "GREAT IDEAS
OF WESTERN MAN"
© 1985 United Feature Syndicate,Inc.
WHY DON'T YOU GET UP OUT OF THAT BEANBAG, AND LET ME LIE THERE?
10-19
NOW, WHY DON'T YOU GO INTO THE KITCHEN, AND GET ME A DISH OF ICE CREAM?
"GREAT IDEAS OF WESTERN WOMAN!"
SCHULZ

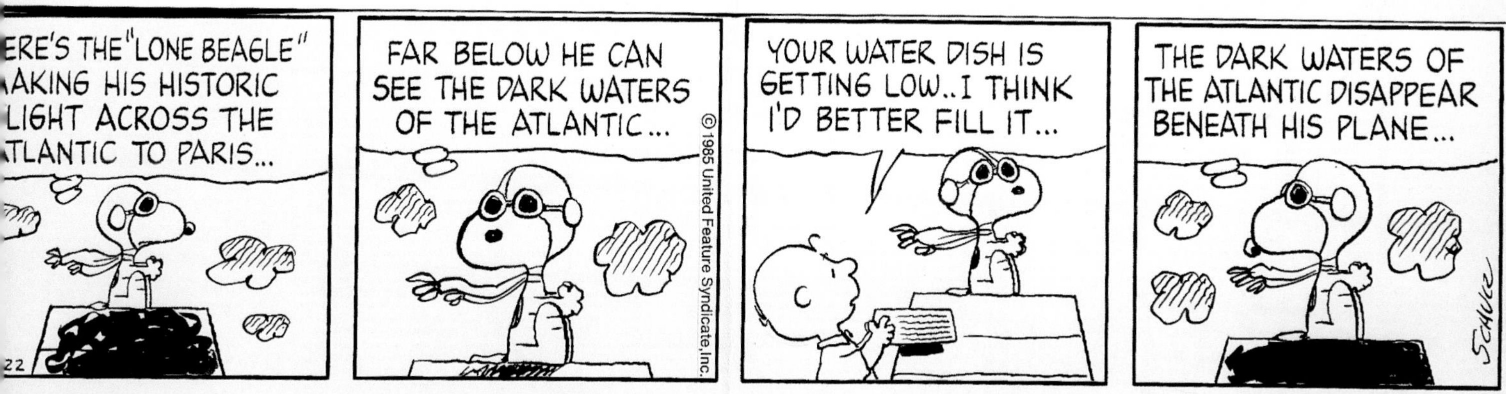
ERE'S THE "LONE BEAGLE"
AKING HIS HISTORIC
LIGHT ACROSS THE
TLANTIC TO PARIS...
22
FAR BELOW HE CAN SEE THE DARK WATERS OF THE ATLANTIC...
© 1985 United Feature Syndicate,Inc.
YOUR WATER DISH IS GETTING LOW..I THINK I'D BETTER FILL IT...
THE DARK WATERS OF THE ATLANTIC DISAPPEAR BENEATH HIS PLANE...
SCHULZ

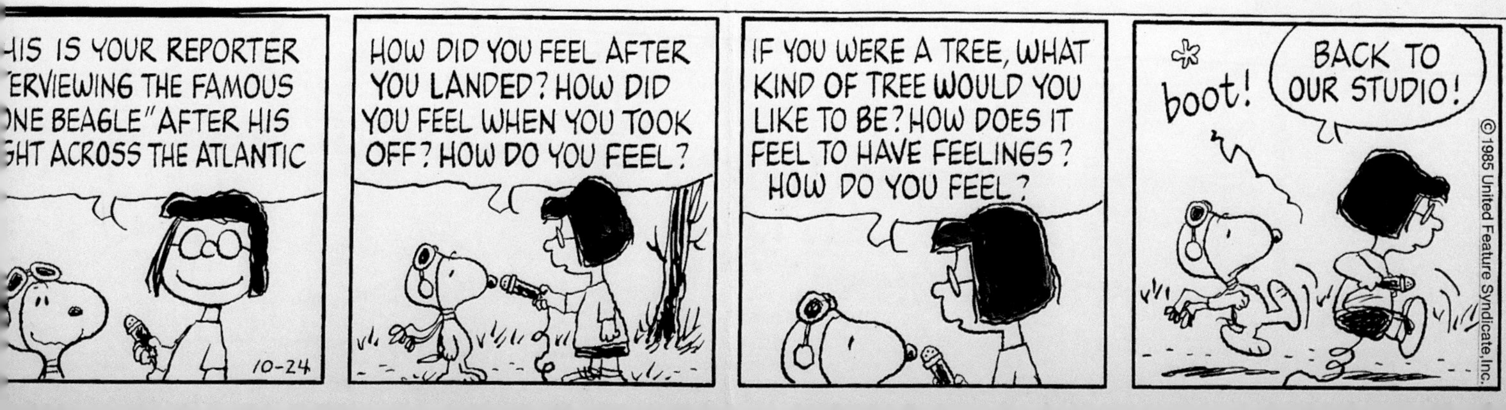
HIS IS YOUR REPORTER
TERVIEWING THE FAMOUS
ONE BEAGLE" AFTER HIS
GHT ACROSS THE ATLANTIC
10-24
HOW DID YOU FEEL AFTER YOU LANDED? HOW DID YOU FEEL WHEN YOU TOOK OFF? HOW DO YOU FEEL?
IF YOU WERE A TREE, WHAT KIND OF TREE WOULD YOU LIKE TO BE? HOW DOES IT FEEL TO HAVE FEELINGS? HOW DO YOU FEEL?
boot!
BACK TO OUR STUDIO!
© 1985 United Feature Syndicate,Inc.

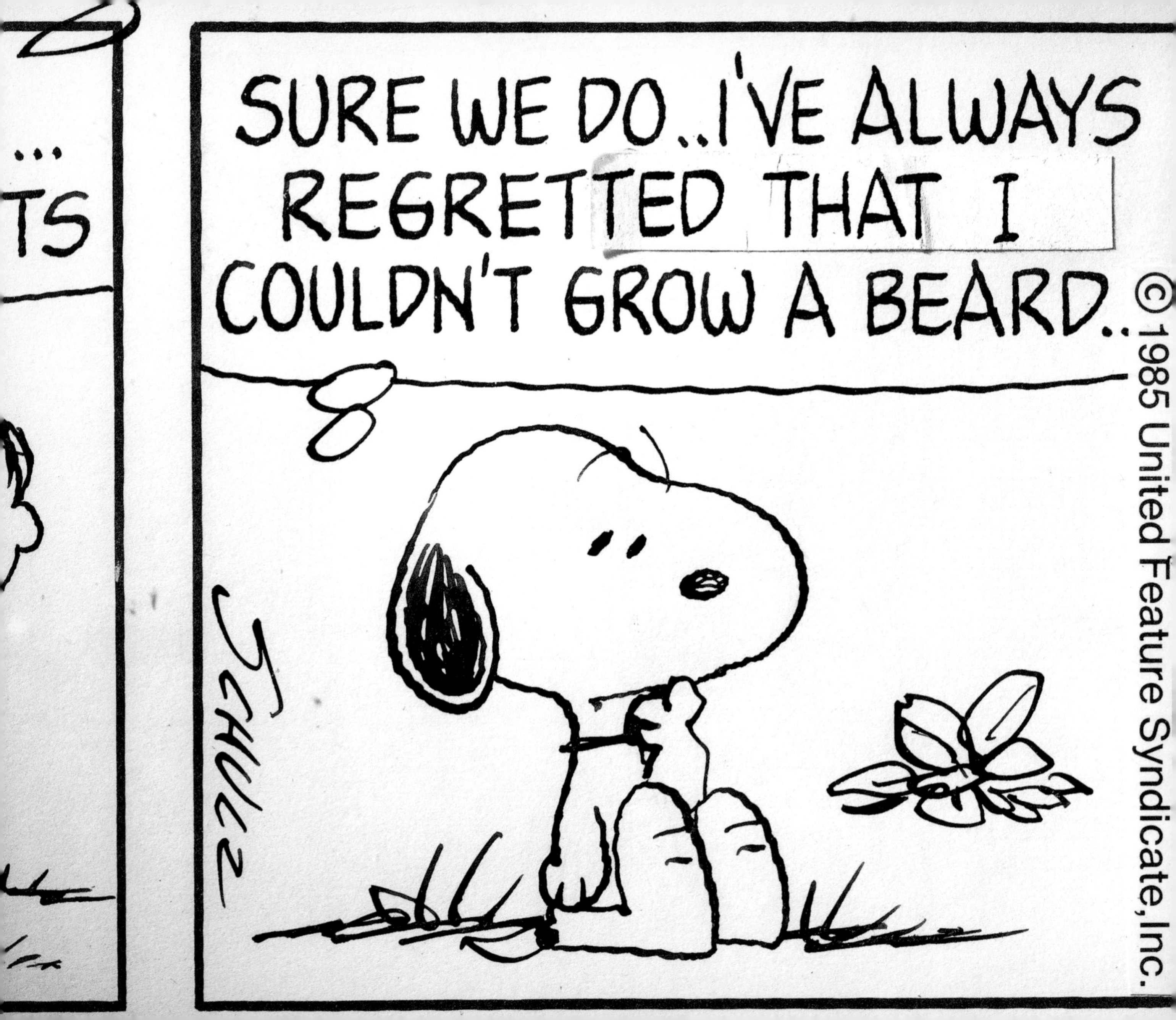

SURE WE DO..I'VE ALWAYS REGRETTED THAT I COULDN'T GROW A BEARD..
SCHULZ
© 1985 United Feature Syndicate, Inc.

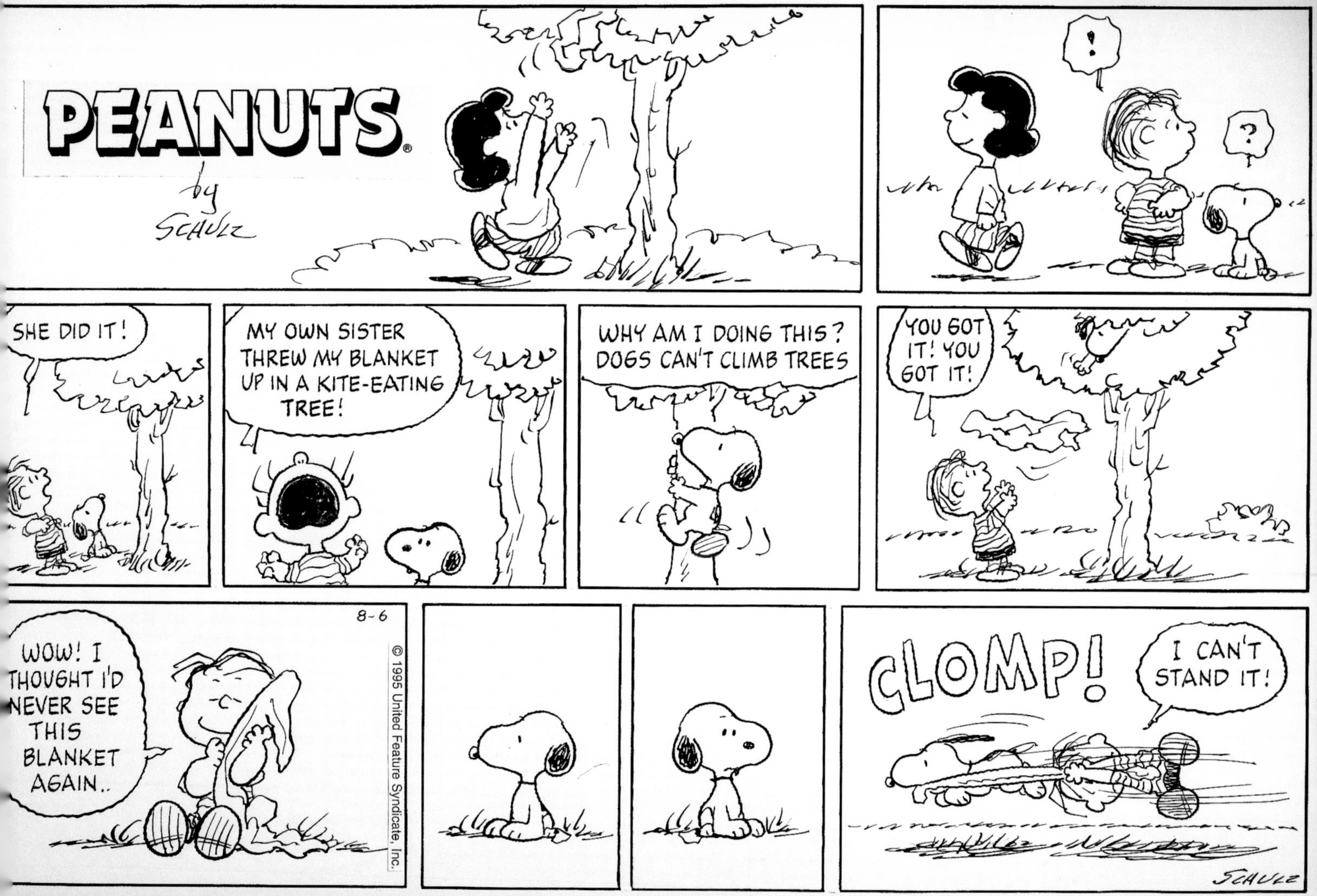
PEANUTS
by SCHULZ
!
?
SHE DID IT!
MY OWN SISTER THREW MY BLANKET UP IN A KITE-EATING TREE!
WHY AM I DOING THIS? DOGS CAN'T CLIMB TREES
YOU GOT IT! YOU GOT IT!
8-6
© 1995 United Feature Syndicate, Inc.
WOW! I THOUGHT I'D NEVER SEE THIS BLANKET AGAIN..
CLOMP!
I CAN'T STAND IT!
SCHULZ

From Schulz's keynote speech to the National Cartoonists' Society convention, 1994:

"I am still searching for that wonderful pen line that comes down when you are drawing Linus standing there, and you start with the pen up near the back of his neck, and you bring it down and bring it out, and the pen point fans a little bit, and you come down here and draw the lines this way for the marks on his sweater. This is what it's all about—to get feelings of depth and roundness, and the pen line is the best pen line you can make. That's what it's all about."

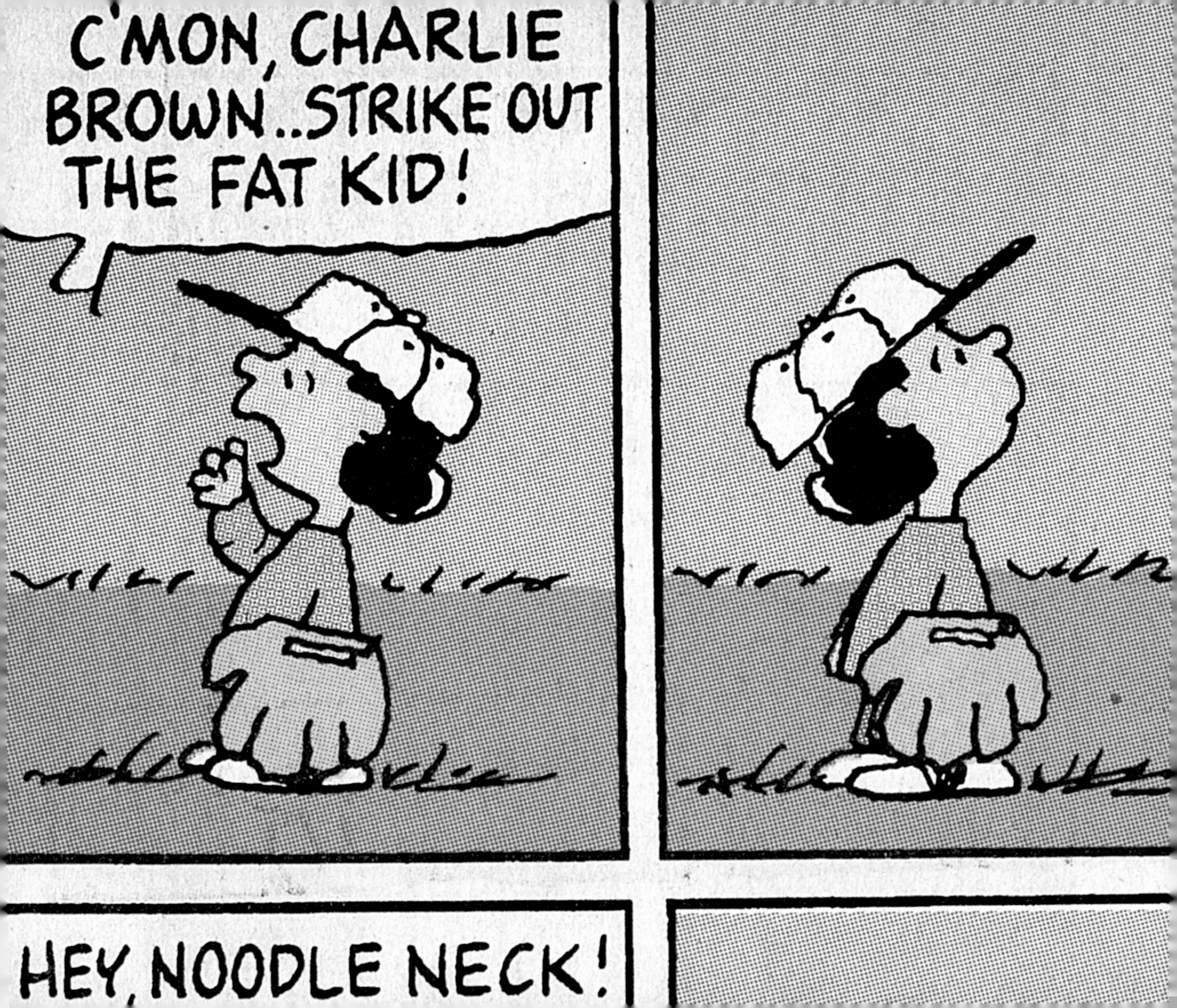
C'MON, CHARLIE BROWN..STRIKE OUT THE FAT KID!
HEY, NOODLE NECK!

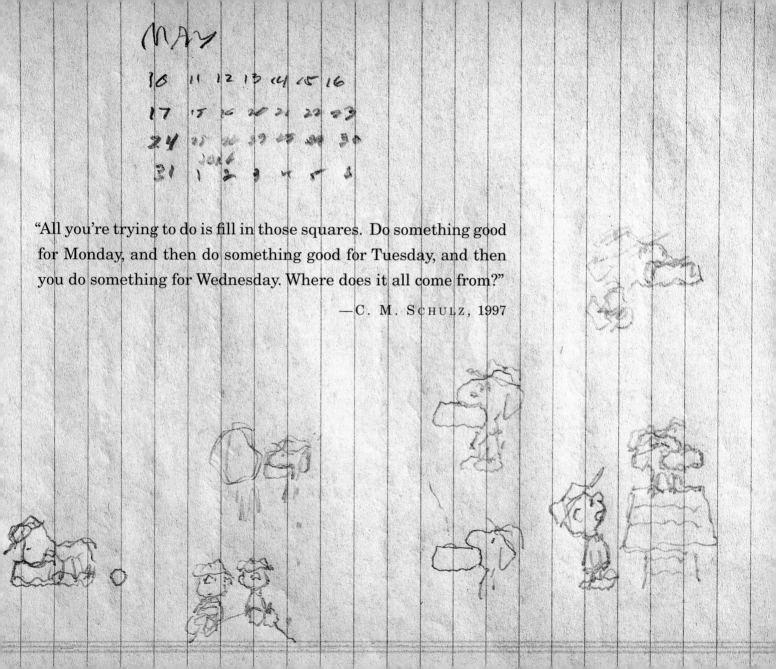

MAY

10 11 12 13 14 15 16
17 18 19 20 21 22 23
24 25 26 27 28 29 30
31 | JUNE 1 2 3 4 5 6

"All you're trying to do is fill in those squares. Do something good
for Monday, and then do something good for Tuesday, and then
you do something for Wednesday. Where does it all come from?"

—C. M. SCHULZ, 1997

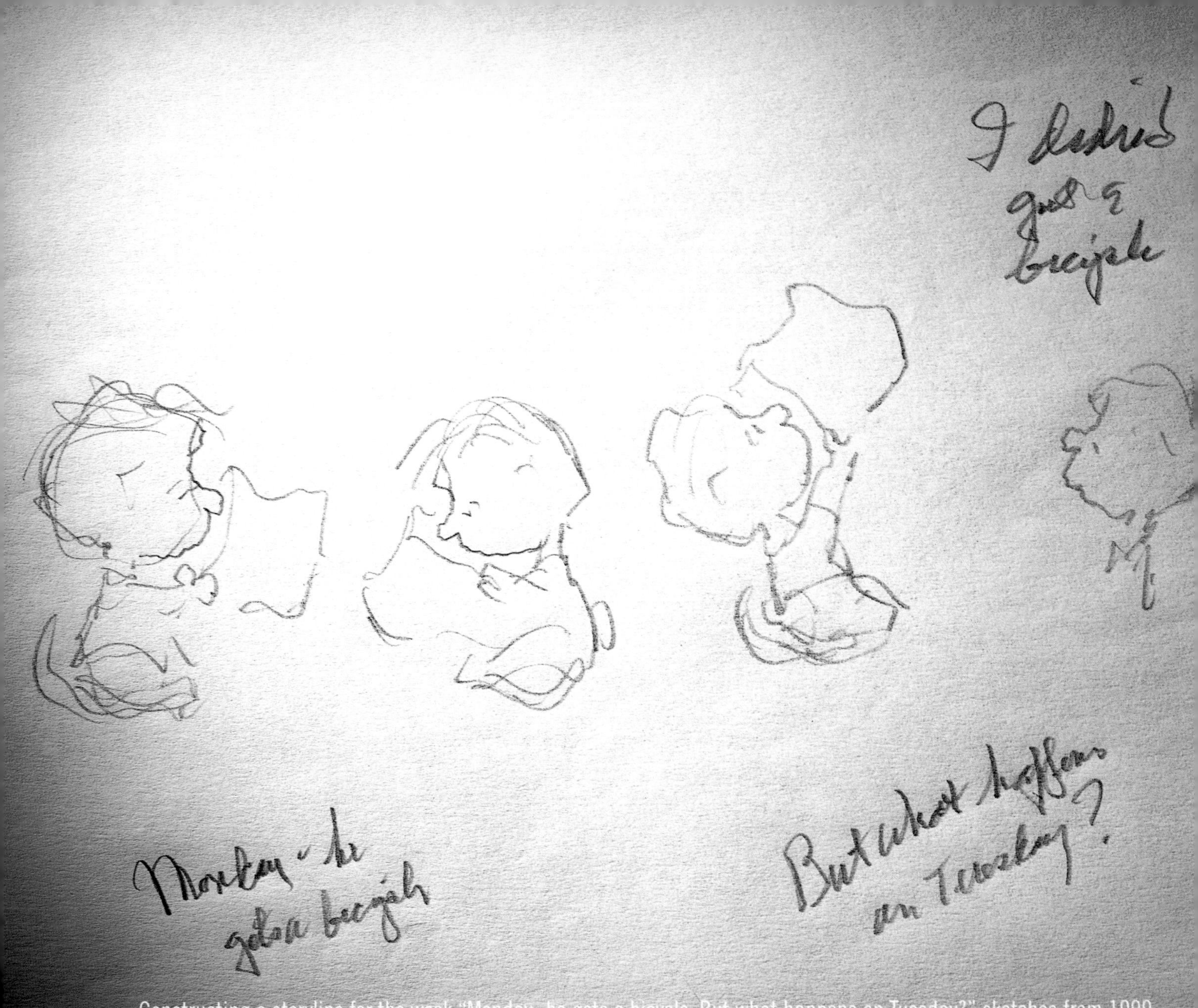
Monday - he gets a bicycle
But what happens on Tuesday?

Constructing a storyline for the week: "Monday- he gets a bicycle. But what happens on Tuesday?" sketches from 1999.

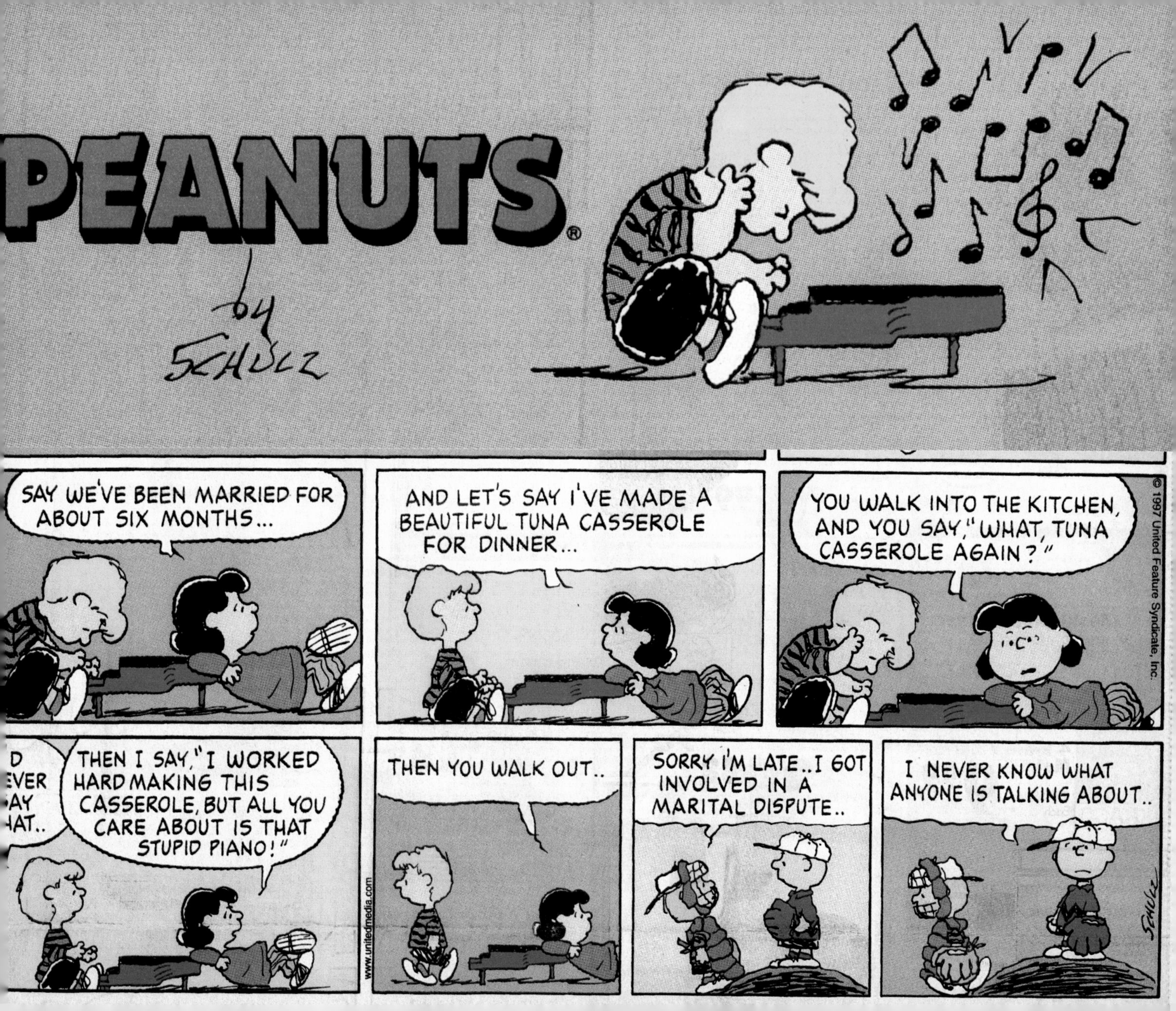
PEANUTS®
by SCHULZ
SAY WE'VE BEEN MARRIED FOR ABOUT SIX MONTHS...
AND LET'S SAY I'VE MADE A BEAUTIFUL TUNA CASSEROLE FOR DINNER...
YOU WALK INTO THE KITCHEN, AND YOU SAY, "WHAT, TUNA CASSEROLE AGAIN?"
© 1997 United Feature Syndicate, Inc.
THEN I SAY, "I WORKED HARD MAKING THIS CASSEROLE, BUT ALL YOU CARE ABOUT IS THAT STUPID PIANO!"
www.unitedmedia.com
THEN YOU WALK OUT..
SORRY I'M LATE..I GOT INVOLVED IN A MARITAL DISPUTE..
I NEVER KNOW WHAT ANYONE IS TALKING ABOUT..
SCHULZ

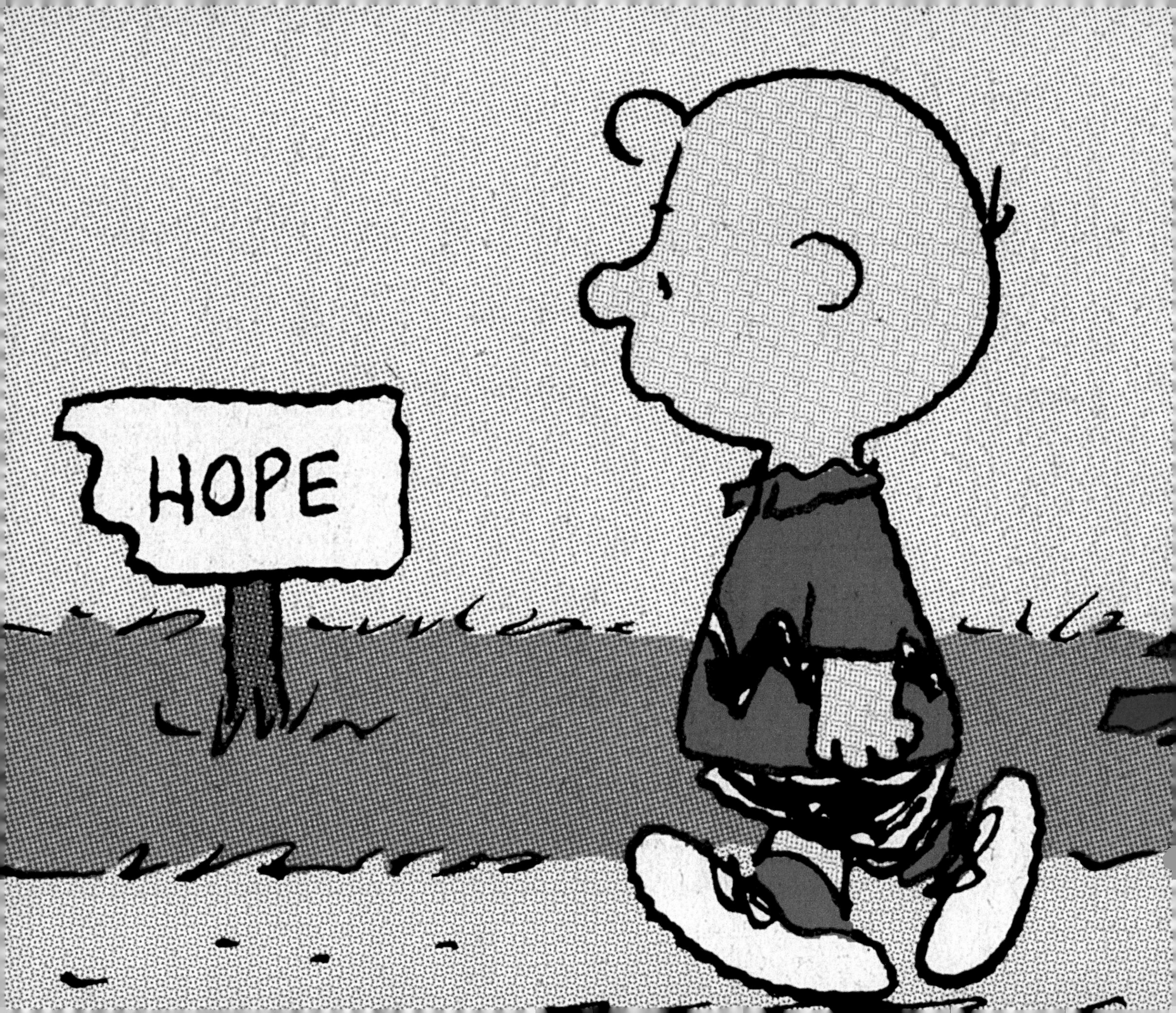
HOPE

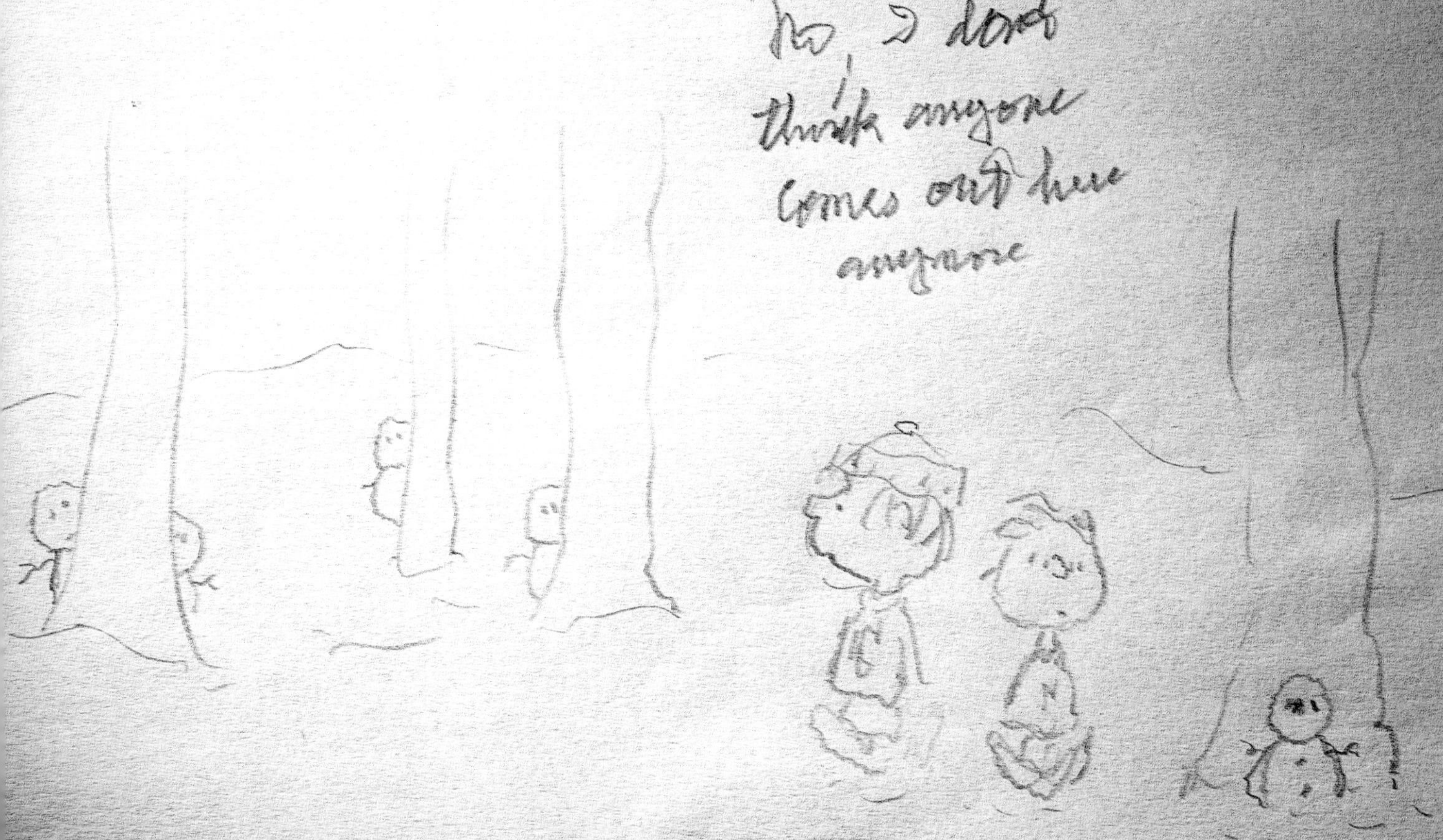
No, I don't
think anyone
comes out here
anymore

Oct. 30, 1998

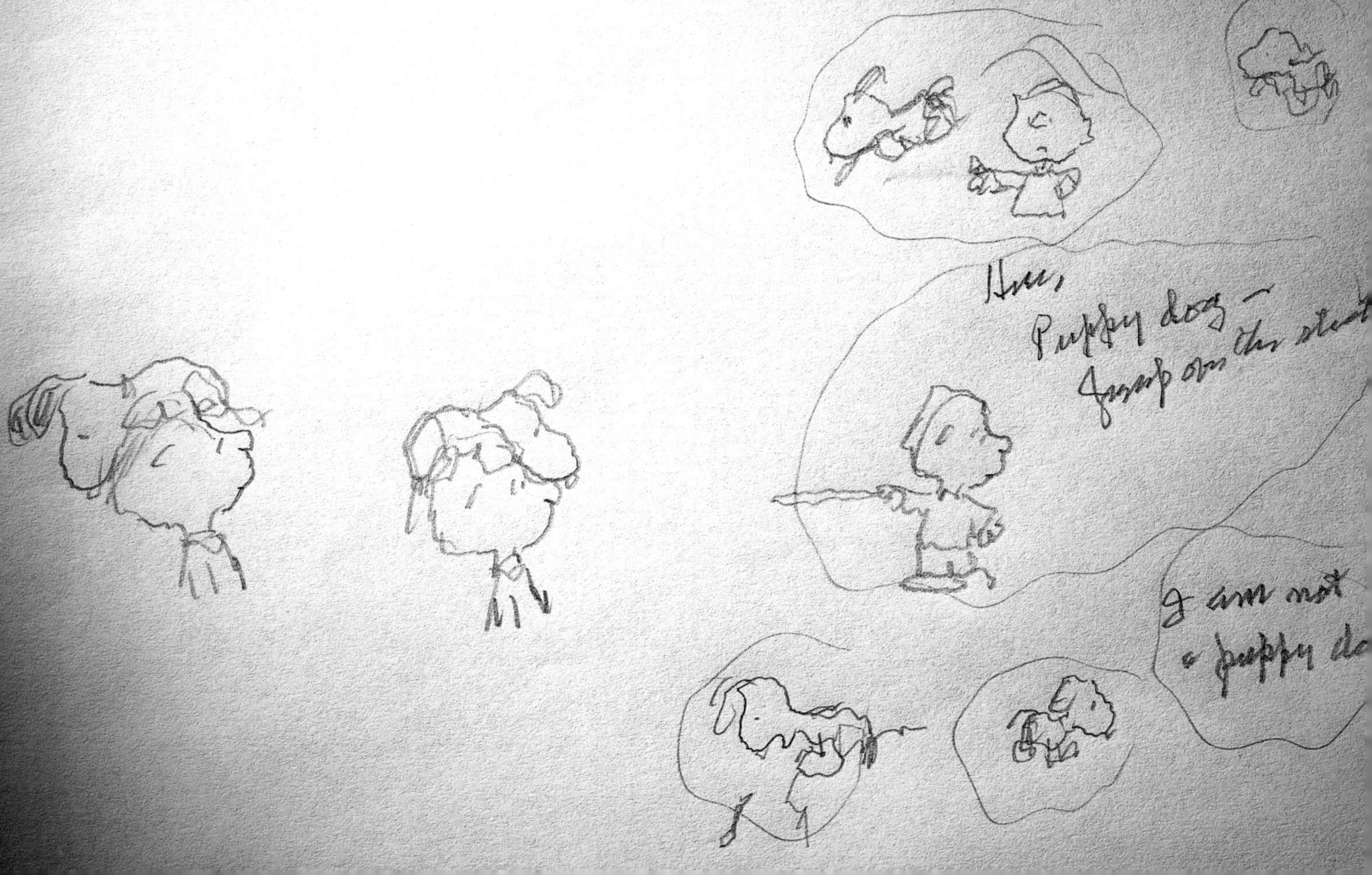
Hmm,
Puppy dog —
Jump over the
I am not
a puppy

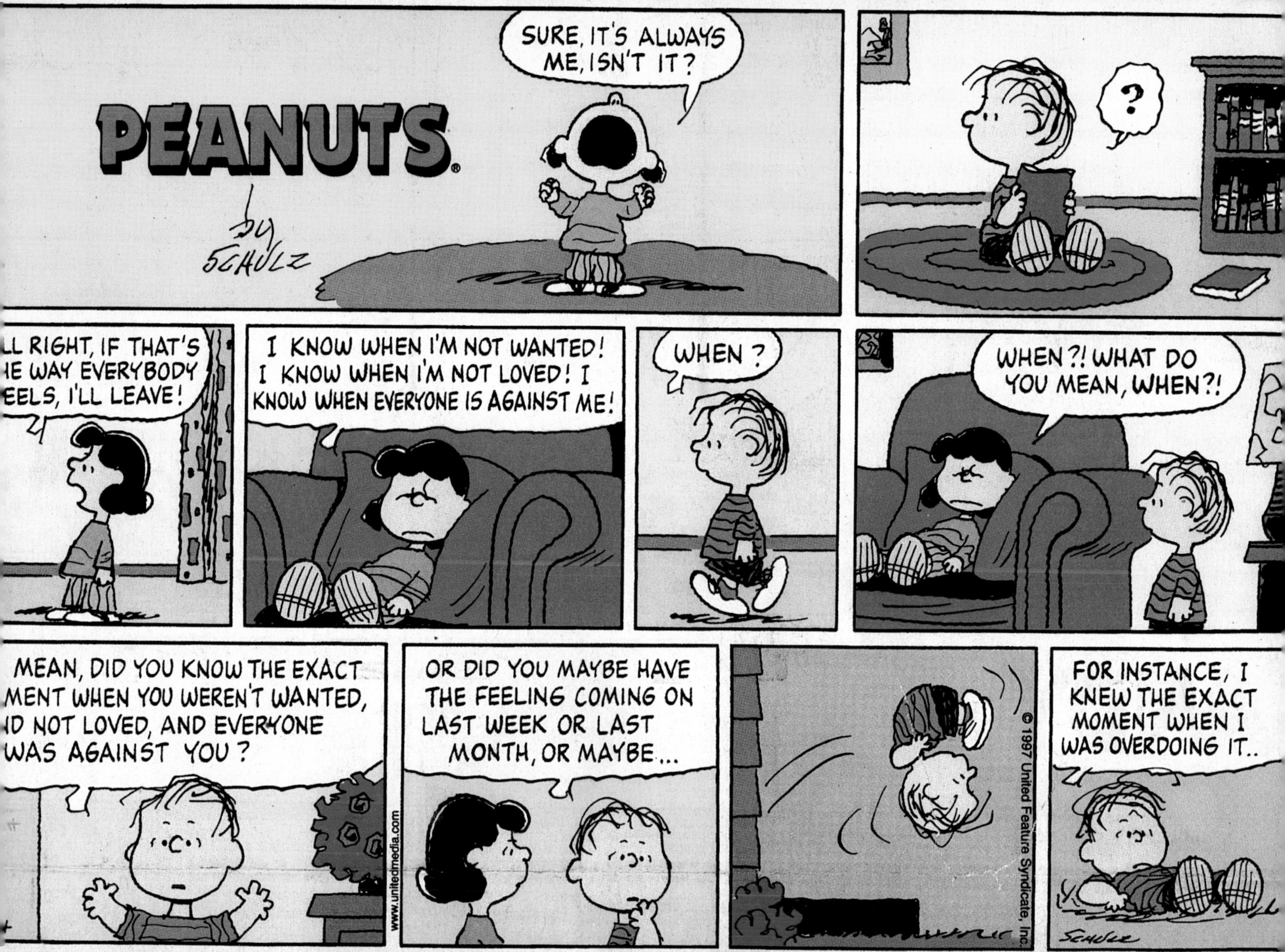
PEANUTS
by SCHULZ
SURE, IT'S ALWAYS ME, ISN'T IT?
?
LL RIGHT, IF THAT'S
IE WAY EVERYBODY
EELS, I'LL LEAVE!
I KNOW WHEN I'M NOT WANTED! I KNOW WHEN I'M NOT LOVED! I KNOW WHEN EVERYONE IS AGAINST ME!
WHEN ?
WHEN ?! WHAT DO YOU MEAN, WHEN ?!
MEAN, DID YOU KNOW THE EXACT
MENT WHEN YOU WEREN'T WANTED,
ID NOT LOVED, AND EVERYONE
WAS AGAINST YOU ?
www.unitedmedia.com
OR DID YOU MAYBE HAVE THE FEELING COMING ON LAST WEEK OR LAST MONTH, OR MAYBE...
© 1997 United Feature Syndicate, Inc.
FOR INSTANCE, I KNEW THE EXACT MOMENT WHEN I WAS OVERDOING IT..
SCHULZ

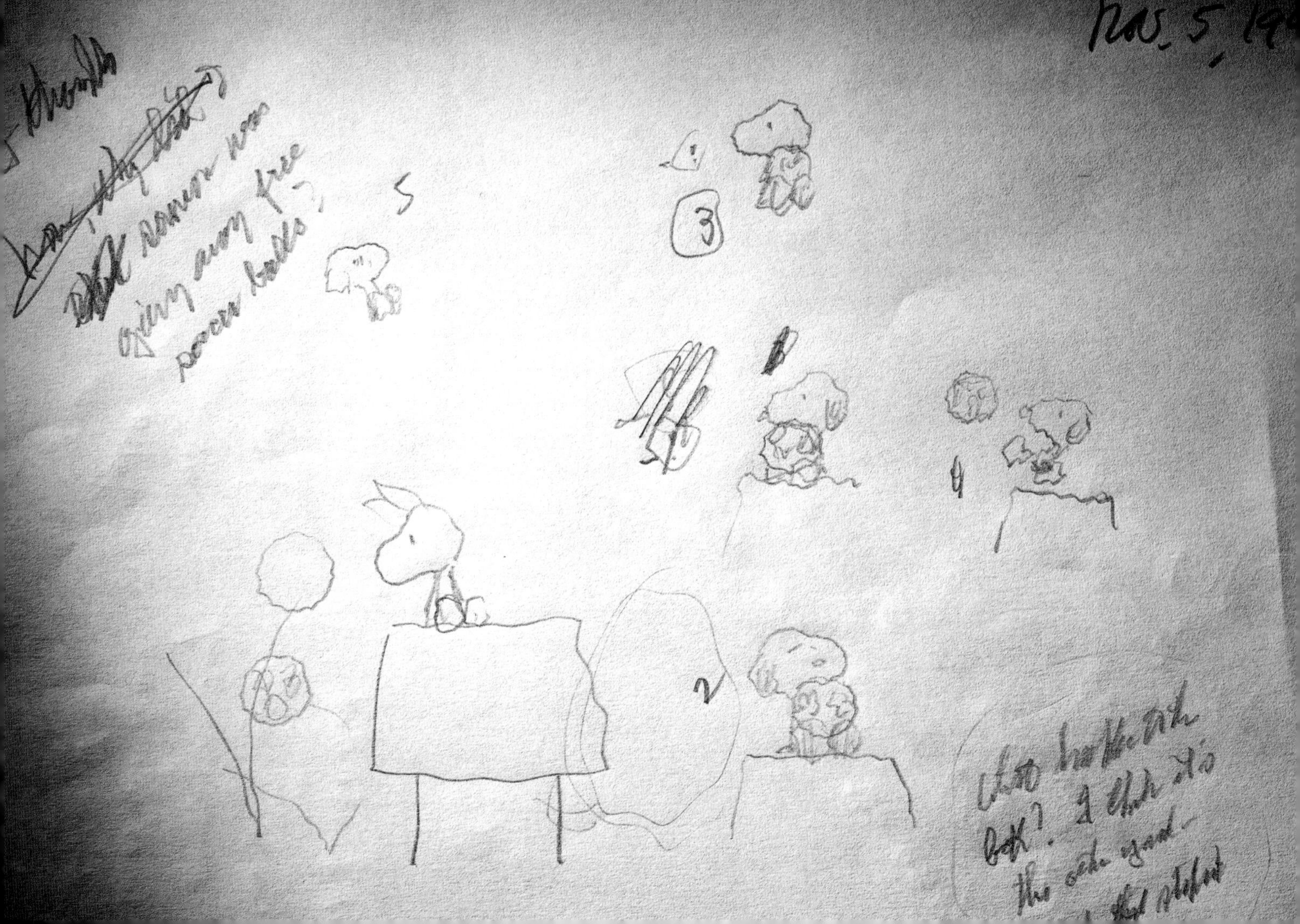

Nov. 5, 19
giving away free
5
3
4
2
I think it's

"I have been thinking of you and your very remarkable quality of expressing in simple, direct statements the American way of life. It has brought pleasure to so many of us. Bless you always."

—ANDREW WYETH,

in a letter to Charles Schulz,

DECEMBER 30, 1999

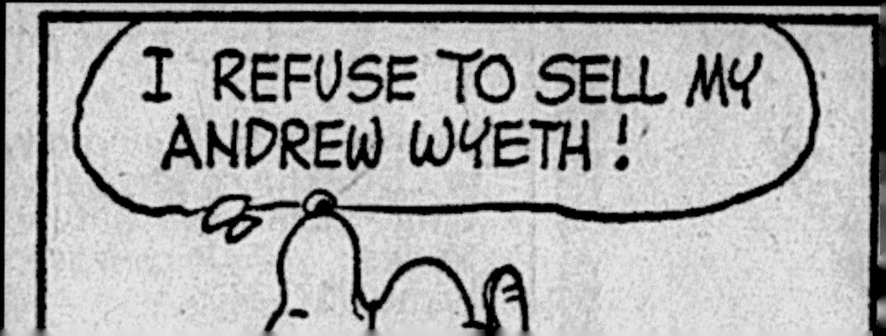
I REFUSE TO SELL MY ANDREW WYETH !

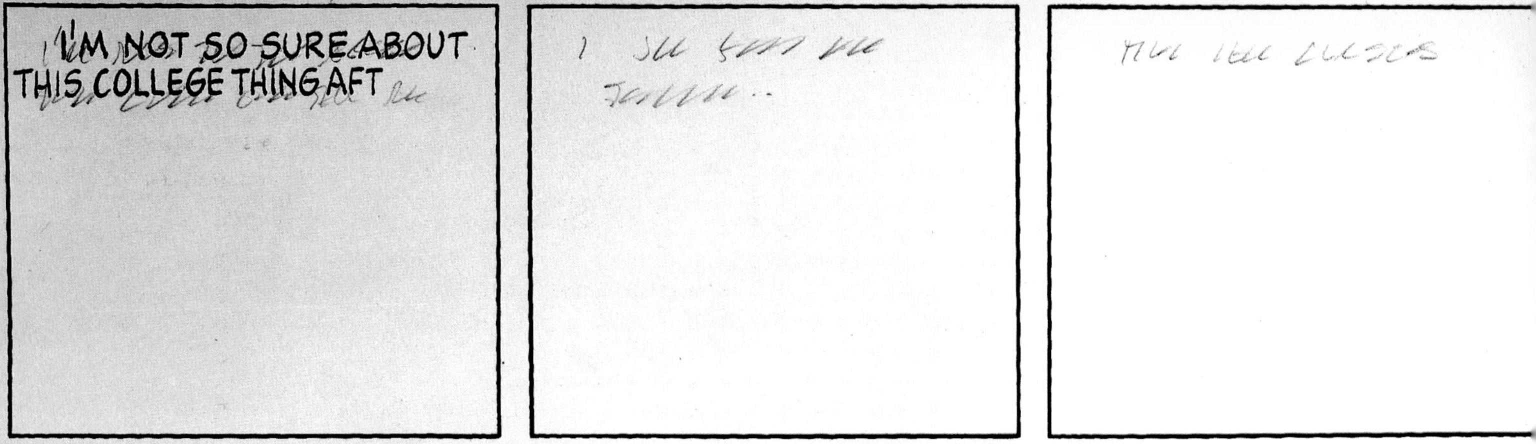
I'M NOT SO SURE ABOUT
THIS COLLEGE THING AFT

THANK YOU

First and foremost, heartfelt thanks to Jean Schulz for her generous support for this project. It would not have been possible without her. Likewise Paige Braddock and all the staff at Creative Associates in Santa Rosa, Ca. Monte and Craig Schulz graciously allowed us into their homes to photograph memorabilia and artwork, which was invaluable.

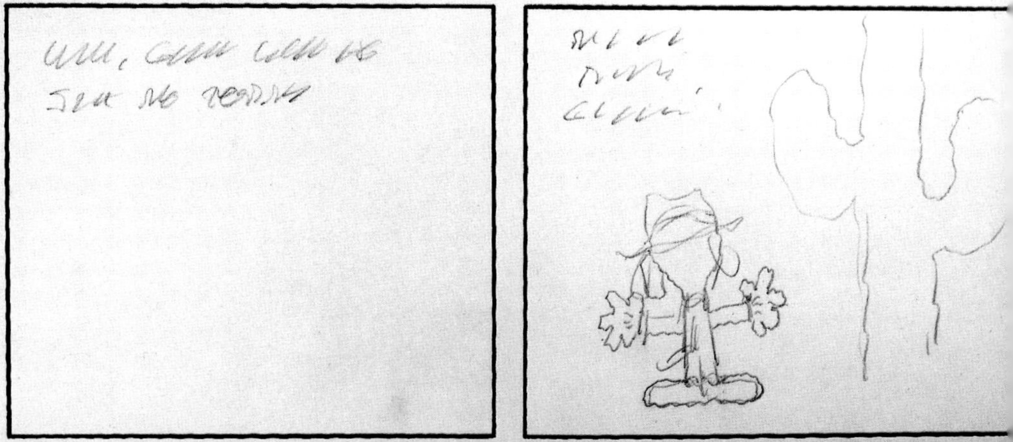

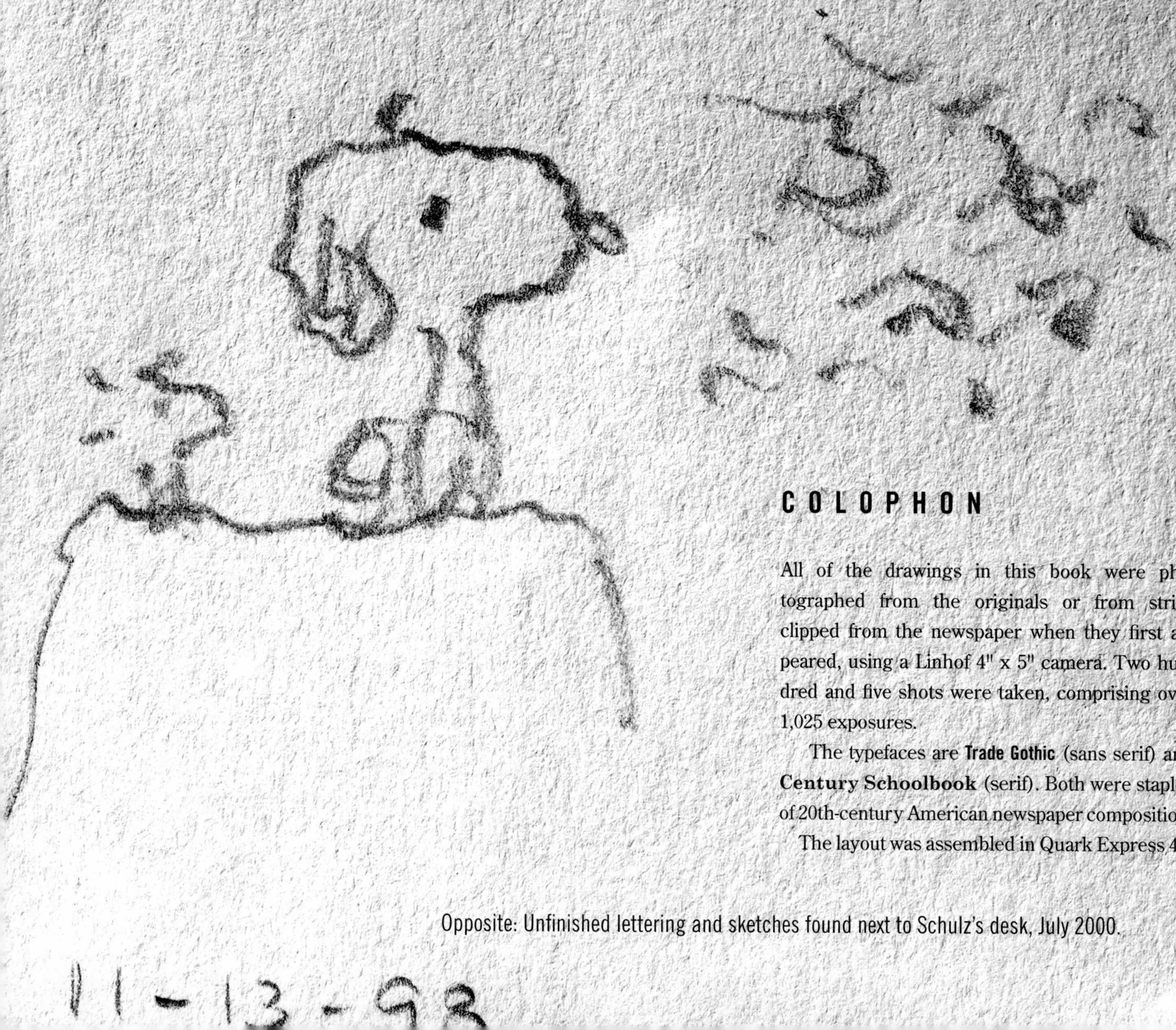
11-13-98

COLOPHON

All of the drawings in this book were photographed from the originals or from strips clipped from the newspaper when they first appeared, using a Linhof 4" x 5" camera. Two hundred and five shots were taken, comprising over 1,025 exposures.

The typefaces are **Trade Gothic** (sans serif) and **Century Schoolbook** (serif). Both were staples of 20th-century American newspaper composition.

The layout was assembled in Quark Express 4.1

Opposite: Unfinished lettering and sketches found next to Schulz's desk, July 2000.

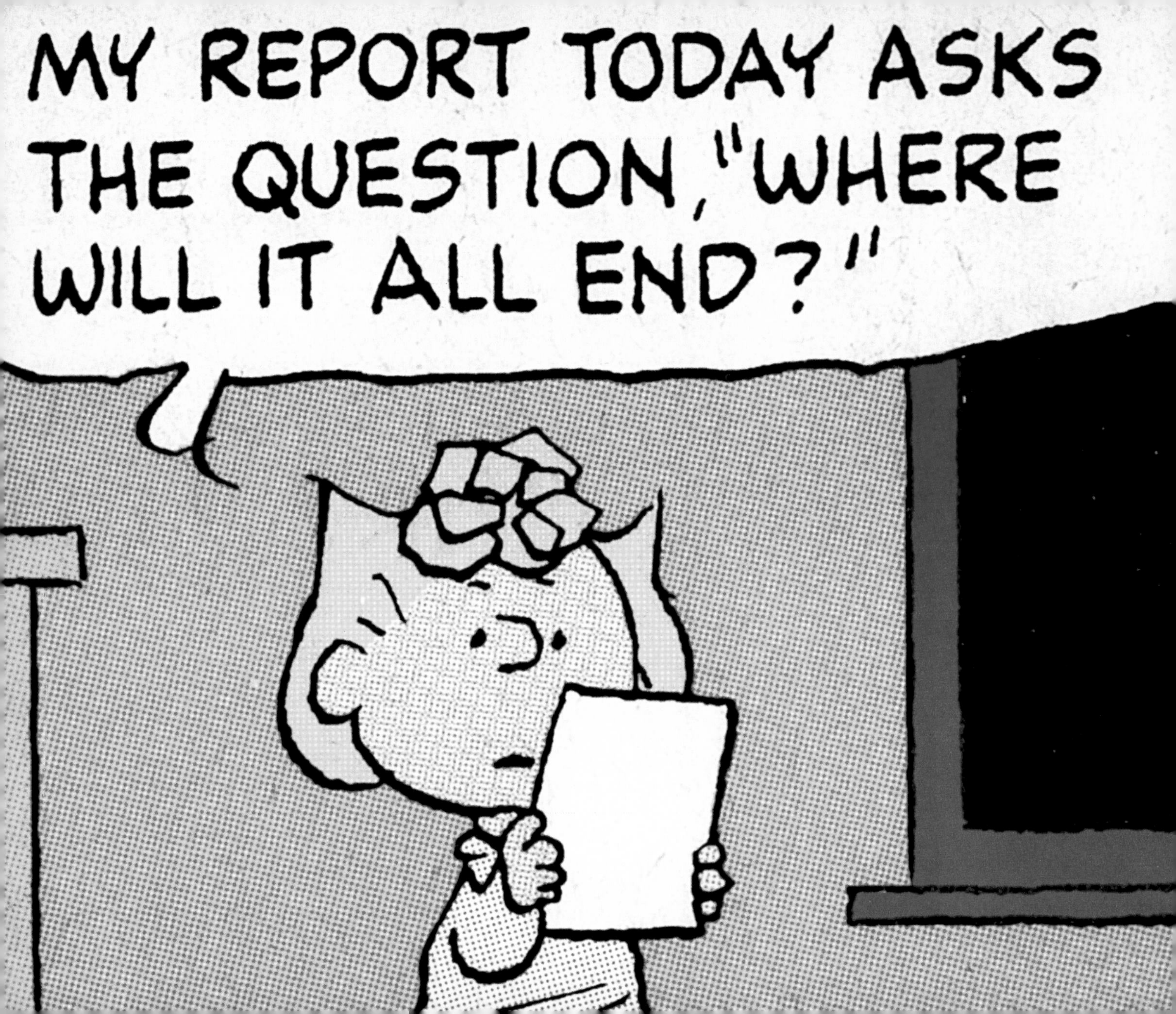
MY REPORT TODAY ASKS THE QUESTION, "WHERE WILL IT ALL END?"

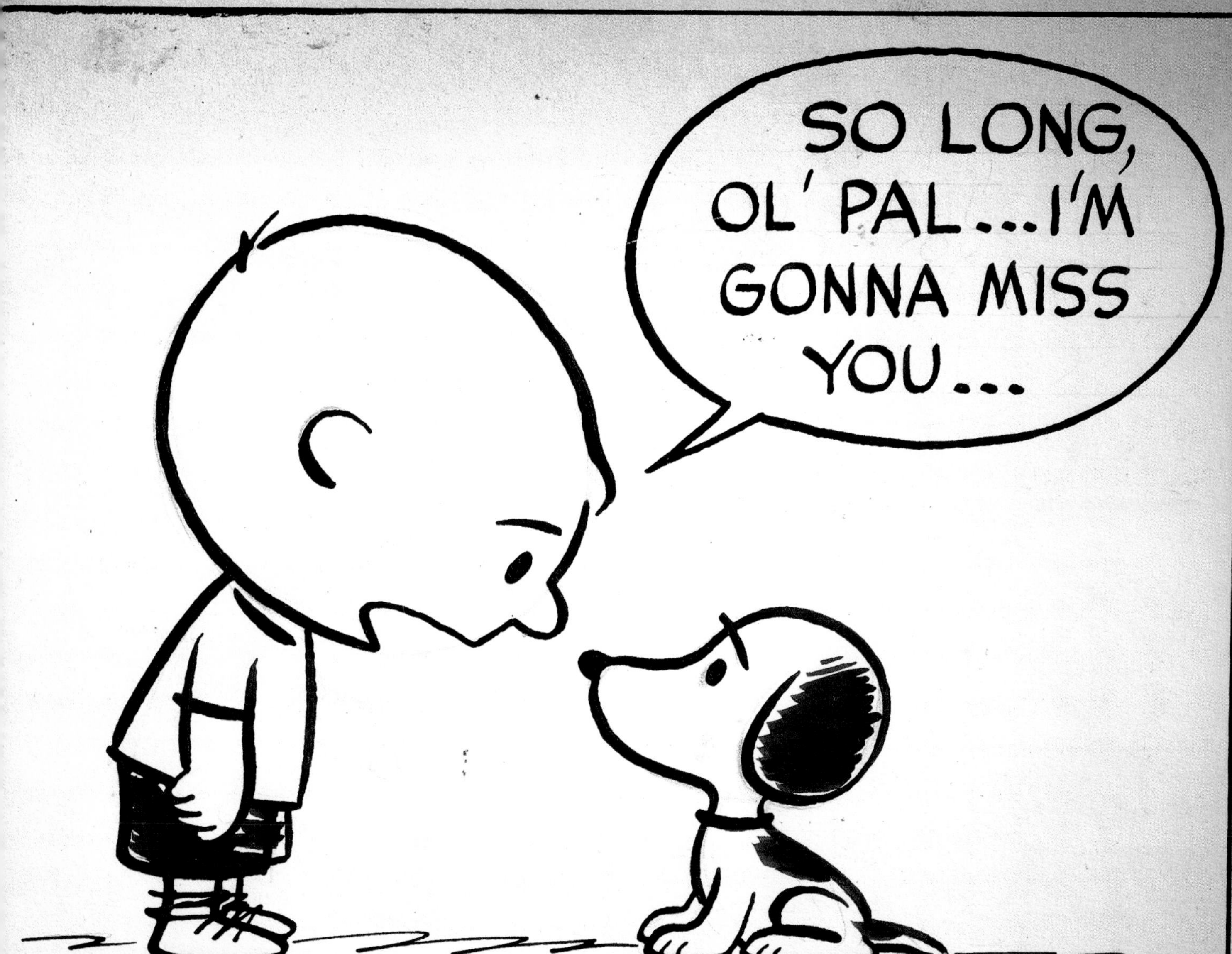
SO LONG, OL' PAL...I'M GONNA MISS YOU...

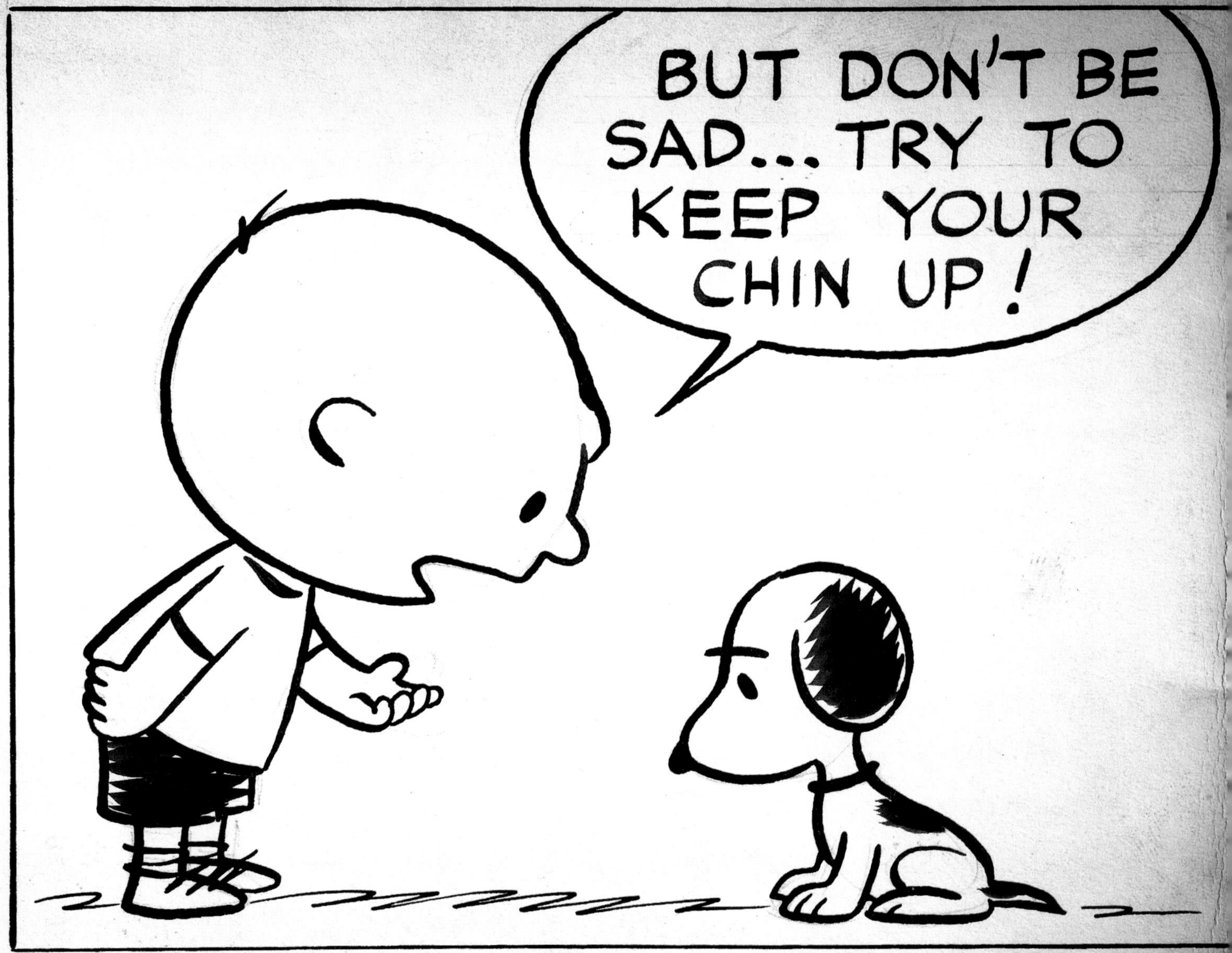
BUT DON'T BE SAD... TRY TO KEEP YOUR CHIN UP!

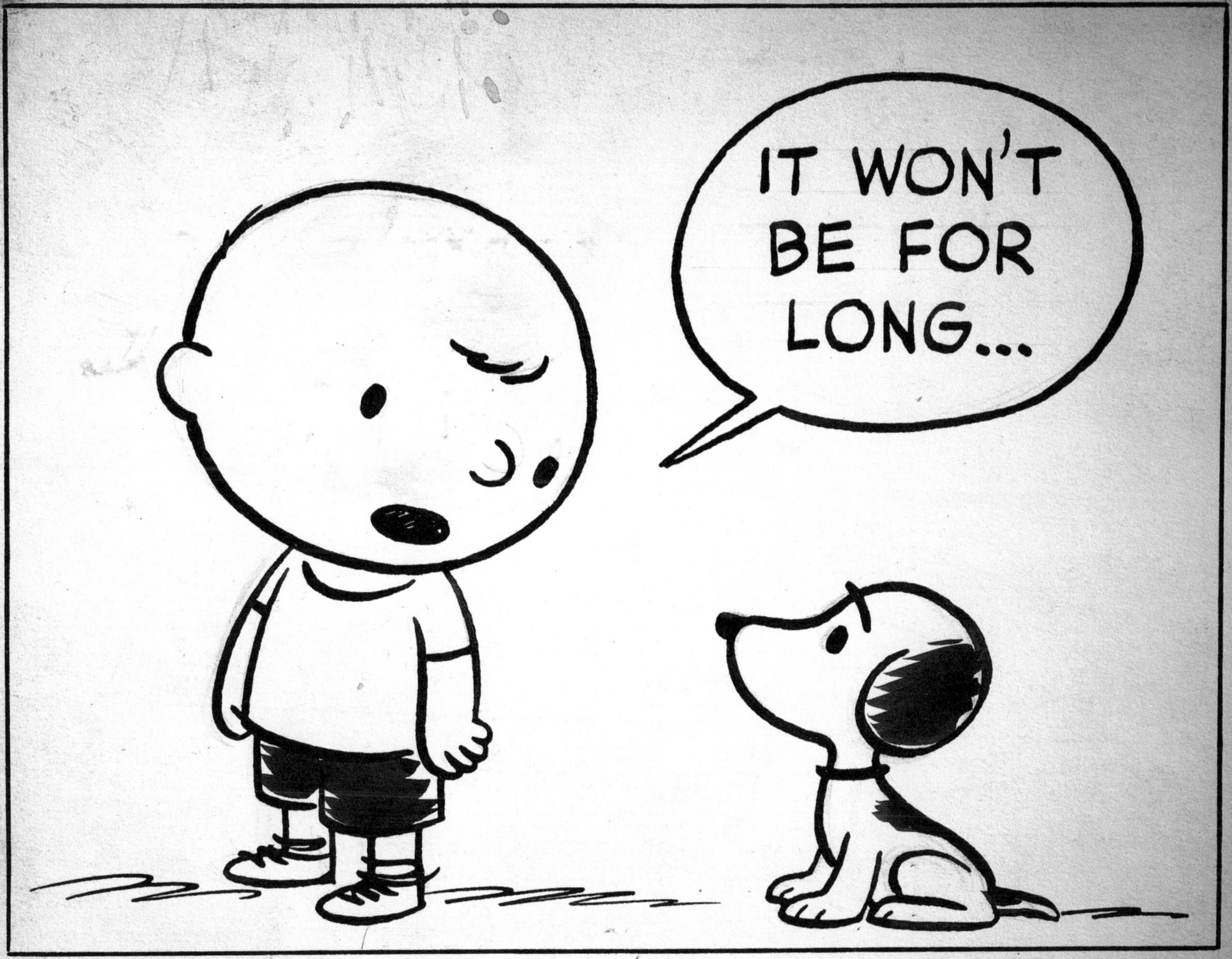
IT WON'T BE FOR LONG...

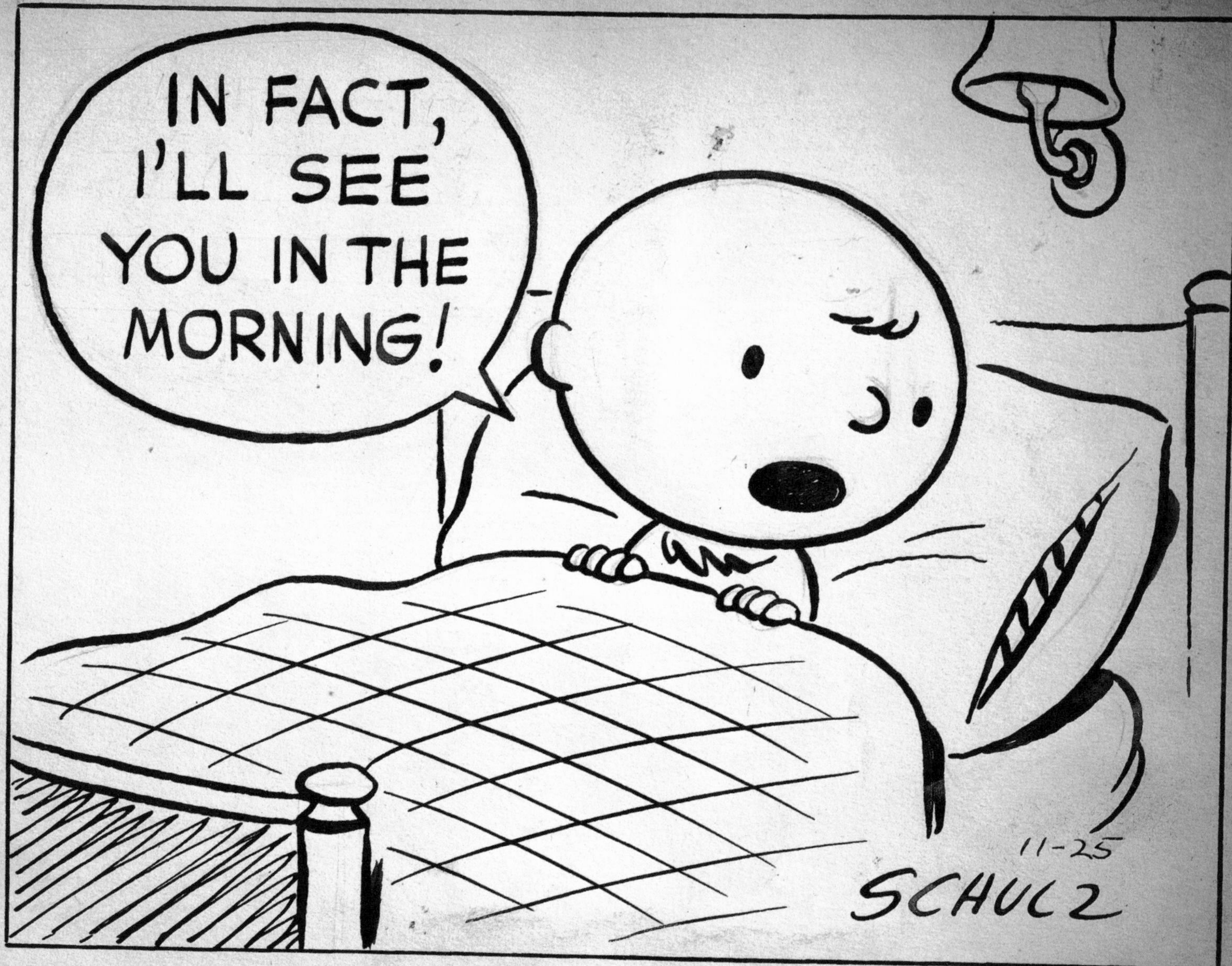
IN FACT, I'LL SEE YOU IN THE MORNING!
11-25
SCHULZ